SAINT
VINCENT DE PAUL

CORRESPONDENCE

CONFERENCES, DOCUMENTS

CORRESPONDENCE

VOLUME VIII **(July 1659 - September 1660)**

NEWLY TRANSLATED, EDITED, AND ANNOTATED

FROM THE 1923 EDITION

OF

PIERRE COSTE, C.M.

Edited by:

SR. MARIE POOLE, D.C., *Editor-in-Chief*
SR. JULIA DENTON, D.C.
SR. ELINOR HARTMAN, D.C.

Translated by:

SR. MARIE POOLE, D.C.
REV. FRANCIS GERMOVNIK, C.M. (Latin)

Annotated by:

REV. JOHN W. CARVEN, C.M.

NIHIL OBSTAT
Very Rev. George J. Weber, C.M.
Censor Deputatus

IMPRIMATUR
Right Rev. Msgr. W. Francis Malooly
Vicar General, Archdiocese of Baltimore

January 8, 1999

This final volume of the Correspondence

of

Saint Vincent de Paul

is dedicated

to

SISTER MARIE-GENEVIÈVE ROUX, D.C.

for her tireless commitment to deepening the love and knowledge

of

Saint Vincent and Saint Louise

through the promotion of Vincentian values and heritage

Published in the United States by New City Press
202 Cardinal Rd., Hyde Park, NY 12538

Printed in the United States of America

Library of Congress Cataloging-in-Publication Data:

Vincent de Paul, Saint, 1581-1660.
Correspondence, conferences, documents.

Translation of: Correspondance, entretiens, documents.
Includes bibliographical references and index.
Contents: I. Correspondence. v. 1. 1607-1639. —
v. 7. December 1657-June 1659.
1. Vincent de Paul, Saint, 1581-1660—Correspondence.
2. Christian saints—France—Correspondence. I. Coste, Pierre, 1873-1935. II. Title.
BX4700.V6A4 1985 271'.77'024 [B] 83-63559
ISBN 0-911782-50-8 (v. 1)
ISBN 1-56548-125-9 (v. 8)

TABLE OF CONTENTS

APPENDIX

INTRODUCTION

The correspondence of Saint Vincent de Paul contains a wealth of information about the man, the Saint, and his milieu. To facilitate the informed reading of this volume, the editors felt it would be useful to preface the work with some explanatory remarks regarding language, style, and placement. In this way, a fuller image of the multifaceted personality and influence of the Saint will emerge from these pages, giving the reader a broader understanding of his life and the world in which he lived and worked.

In placing new letters within the volume or changing the placement of letters we have relied on Coste's corrections given in volumes VIII and XIII, the listings found in the *Annales*,[1] the dates on recently discovered letters or, in the absence of a date, on internal evidence. To facilitate research in Coste's work, we have chosen to keep the letter numbers of the original volumes and to indicate material newly added or relocated within each volume by adding a, b, c, etc., to the number of the preceding item. We have also decided to adhere to the span of years assigned by Coste for each volume.

In some cases, the finding of an original has enabled us to join fragments formerly considered separate letters. Such combined letters have been assigned a single number followed by a letter to differentiate the whole from the segments as published in the original Coste volume. Where variations of a single letter exist, only the most correct version has been included in the volume. Likewise, although Coste chose to publish letters originally written in Latin both in that language and in French, the present edition sometimes bears only the English translation of the original Latin.

---

[1]*Annales de la Congregation de la Mission* (1937), pp. 234-237.

Three different types of letters are presented in these volumes: letters *from* Saint Vincent, letters *to* Saint Vincent and, at times, mere summaries of letters where the existence of a letter is known but no text is available. The letters written by Saint Vincent appear in regular type, while those addressed to him are printed in italics. Smaller type has been used to differentiate the summaries.

As Coste states in his introduction, almost all the letters we now possess are either in Saint Vincent's handwriting or in that of one of his secretaries. The term *original autograph* found in the citation of a letter indicates that the manuscript was written entirely in the Saint's hand. If the citation uses the term *signed letter,* the manuscript was written by a secretary and signed by the Saint. For some letters only a facsimile, a handwritten copy, a photocopy, or a photograph is known. Such indications are given in the citation of the letters for which this information is available.

The citations usually state as well the actual location of the manuscript or copy used for the present edition. Great care has been taken to verify these locations where possible. Letters drawn from other publications and those belonging to special collections, private or museum, have not been checked due to the near impossibility of such a task. However, an attempt has been made to verify all letters belonging to private houses of the Daughters of Charity, the Priests of the Mission, other religious houses, churches, and various religious institutions. In checking these locations and in the search for unpublished letters, we have at times been fortunate enough to locate the originals of letters for which only copies were known formerly. In these instances as well no mention has been made of the correction—the citation simply states that the manuscript is an original.

We have updated as well the department names given in the footnotes. Several departments have had name changes since the time of Coste, while two others have been subdivided.[2]

Although the project has undergone many delays, each has contributed in some way to the overall quality of the work. The appearance, in 1983, of the revised edition of Saint Louise de Marillac's writings[3] has permitted us to check her letters to Saint Vincent and her spiritual writings for any corrections which may have come to light. We have also adjusted all the footnote references to the appropriate indication as given in the new edition.

In any work of translation the question of style invariably arises, so it was not strange that we should be faced with the problem. Should we smooth out clumsy or elliptical phrasing in the interest of producing a more "readable" translation or should we preserve the roughness and unpolished style of the original in order to reflect the flavor and spontaneous quality of Saint Vincent's expression, supplying explanations where needed to make the sense clear? As our response to this question, we have attempted to make our translation as "readable" as possible while adhering closely to the style of each correspondent. For that purpose we have made an effort to give as literal a meaning as we could to the expressions used, while still adapting them to modern terminology. We have tried to reproduce even the grammatical constructions used by each correspondent unless the true meaning of the sentence would suffer thereby. Very long sentences have been shortened and short phrases joined together to render thoughts more readily intelligible, though still

---

[2]*Department* is the term used to designate each of the principal divisions of French territory. It denotes a geographical area similar to that of the American *state*. In the names of several departments, the word *maritime*, indicating *near the sea*, has replaced the word *inférieure* of the same meaning: Charente-Maritime, Seine-Maritime, Alpes-Maritime. In 1964, the Department of Seine was subdivided into Hauts-de-Seine, Paris, Seine-Saint-Denis, and Val-de-Marne; Seine-et-Oise became Essonne, Val-d'Oise, and Yvelines.

[3][Sr. Elisabeth Charpy, D.C., ed.] *Sainte Louise de Marillac. Ecrits Spirituels* (Tours: Mame, 1983), trans. Sr. Louise Sullivan, D.C., *Spiritual Writings of Louise de Marillac, Correspondence and Thoughts* (New York: New City Press, 1991).

preserving the sense of the original. The vocabulary and expression have deliberately been kept simple. Saint Vincent's love for and practice of simplicity are no secret to anyone familiar with his life; therefore, it was judged fitting to follow his own simplicity in the choice of words and style unless he himself opted for more elegant forms.

To retain the French atmosphere of the work we have left certain terms and expressions in the original French. General terms of greeting such as *Monsieur, Madame, etc.,* have not been translated, nor have we attempted an English version for expressions such as *O mon Dieu!, O Jésus!* Land-holding titles which often form part of a proper name—*Comte, Duc, Marquis*—have also been left in French. Other titles have been translated by the closest English equivalent possible. Proper names are given in the original language unless there is a familiar English form. This holds true for both people and places. Therefore, *Sainte Jeanne-Françoise Frémiot de Chantal* has been rendered as *Saint Jane Frances* Frémiot de Chantal, whereas *Pierre Séguier* remains in French. For places, *Brittany* is used instead of *Bretagne,* while *Granada, Villeneuve,* and similar names remain in the original language. Proper foreign names within the text of the manuscripts have been left as written by the correspondents. However, the footnotes and index present the name in its original language form—*Alessandro* Bichi for *Alexandre* Bichi; *Patrick Walsh* for *Patrice Valois.*

An attempt has been made to standardize name variations appearing in the original manuscripts: *Gondi* is always used in this edition although the form *Gondy* is often seen in the manuscripts. We have, however, left the variations *Pollalion* and *Poulaillon.* Although the correct spelling is the former, Saint Vincent always wrote the latter.

We have also standardized the various forms of the phrase used by Saint Vincent after his signature: *unworthy priest of the Congregation of the Mission.* Throughout this edition the abbreviation *i.s.C.M. (indignus sacerdos Congregationis Missionis)* has been used.

The word *fille,* meaning girl, daughter, young woman, appears in many of the manuscripts. In the seventeenth century, this word also denoted a woman religious or nun. We have tried to adjust the meaning of *fille* to the context of the various letters and have sometimes rendered the word as *Sister* rather than *Daughter* when referring to a member of Saint Louise's nascent community.

Monetary terms—*livre, écu,* etc.—have not been translated for it would be difficult to assign them an equivalent value in modern currency. Several other words and phrases have likewise been left in French—*Parlement, Chambre des Comptes, collège*—since English has no corresponding institution. These terms have been explained in footnotes. For other words of foreign origin used in English and found in English dictionaries no explanation has been given, for example, *faubourg.*

Saint Vincent often makes use of scriptural references which, however, are not always direct quotes. Where he has done so, the translation has been adjusted to flow with the meaning of the sentence. The scriptural quotations given in the footnotes are usually taken from the *New American Bible,* unless a passage cannot be found in that edition or a more suitable rendering of the phrase is found elsewhere. In such instances, the *Douay-Rheims Bible* has been used. In the case of the psalms, both versions have been cited because of the variations.

Coste almost always refers to Vincent de Paul as Saint Vincent or the Saint. In the present edition we have added this title to the names of Louise de Marillac and any other individual who has been canonized since Coste's time.

Generally speaking, in the titles of the letters, Coste gave the location of the addressee only when he was sure of it and when the locality was outside the then city of Paris. We have continued this practice and have attempted to make it more consistent. We have also followed Coste's custom of placing within brackets dates that are uncertain or conjectural. Brackets have also been used to indicate words either missing from the manuscript or inserted by the editors.

The capitalization forms of the original manuscripts have been adjusted to American usage as has the punctuation. Number forms—words versus figures—follow common American practice as well.

In addition to our goal of producing a smooth English translation which is faithful insofar as possible to the meaning and style of the original French, we have also purposed to present a work which is interesting and informative with regard to Saint Vincent, his correspondents, and his times. Both the scholar who may wish to use this work as a research tool and the ordinary reader unfamiliar with the Vincentian Family and with the religio-political history of the period have been kept in mind. A great effort has been made to update, correct, and amplify Coste's footnote material. Irrelevant notes have been eliminated and new annotation added whenever this has been deemed necessary or helpful. In the case of new matter, no indication has been given to distinguish Coste's footnotes from the annotation added by our editor.

A biographical sketch of each personage has been supplied throughout the work the first time that he or she appears in a volume. To facilitate reference to this data and also to the explanations of terms and places given throughout the text an index has been added to each book. The index indicates the number of the letter to which the reader should refer for the information sought. A general index will also be provided as an appendix to the entire work.

All references in the indices and the footnotes have been given by citing the volume and the number of the item rather than the page. Since Coste's volume span and his numbering of items have been retained, this practice should facilitate research in both his edition and the present translation.

In order to enjoy these volumes more thoroughly, the reader would do well to keep in mind that, as now, so then, one correspondent did not spell out to the other details that were already known and understood by both. Reading these letters at a distance of some three hundred years will often arouse a curiosity which in many cases must remain unsatisfied. The allusions made will not always be clear, nor can they be. However, a familiarity beforehand with the life of Saint Vincent will greatly aid one's knowledge and understanding of the situations mentioned and the people involved. The three-volume definitive biography written by Coste[4] provides extensive information, but many shorter versions of the Saint's life can be found. Placed against such a background, these writings take on still more a life of their own and make the Saint vividly present once again. The twinkle in his eyes and the smile or tenderness in his voice seep through the words and we meet the delightful, charming man known to his contemporaries. The severe, ascetic Saint takes on a new personality and somehow becomes more human.

Let us not fail to seek the man beyond these words, the man of compassion, warmth, humor, savoir faire, authority, and, most of all, the mystic whose sanctity was carved amid the bustle and involvement of very human situations. He will give us hope that we, too, can find holiness in an ordinary, busy life. May this personal acquaintance with the real Vincent de Paul lead us to encounter the dynamic force behind his life, Jesus Christ, who, for him, was all things.

NOTE TO THE READER

The editors felt that it was not necessary to reproduce in each volume the lengthy "Introduction to the French Edition" and the entire "Introduction to the English Edition," which appear at the beginning of Volume I. They would like to remind the reader, however, that these introductions contain valuable information regarding the background and major sources of the letters and facilitate an informed reading of the correspondence.

---

[4]Pierre Coste, C.M., *The Life and Works of Saint Vincent de Paul,* trans. Joseph Leonard, C.M., 3 vols. (Westminster, Maryland: Newman Press, 1952; repr., New York: New City Press, 1987).

ACKNOWLEDGEMENTS

Special thanks should be given to Vincentian Fathers Thomas Davitt, Ignatius M. Melito, and John E. Rybolt for their dedication in reading the manuscript of this volume and of the preceding ones. Their expertise in history, theology, Sacred Scripture, and/or English, and their knowledge of Vincentian history and spirituality have allowed us to correct errors, clarify the text, and make stylistic changes which render it more readable. By the invaluable contribution each has made to this translation of Saint Vincent's correspondence, they have merited the gratitude, not only of the editorial staff, but of all who will be enriched by reflective reading of the Saint's own words.

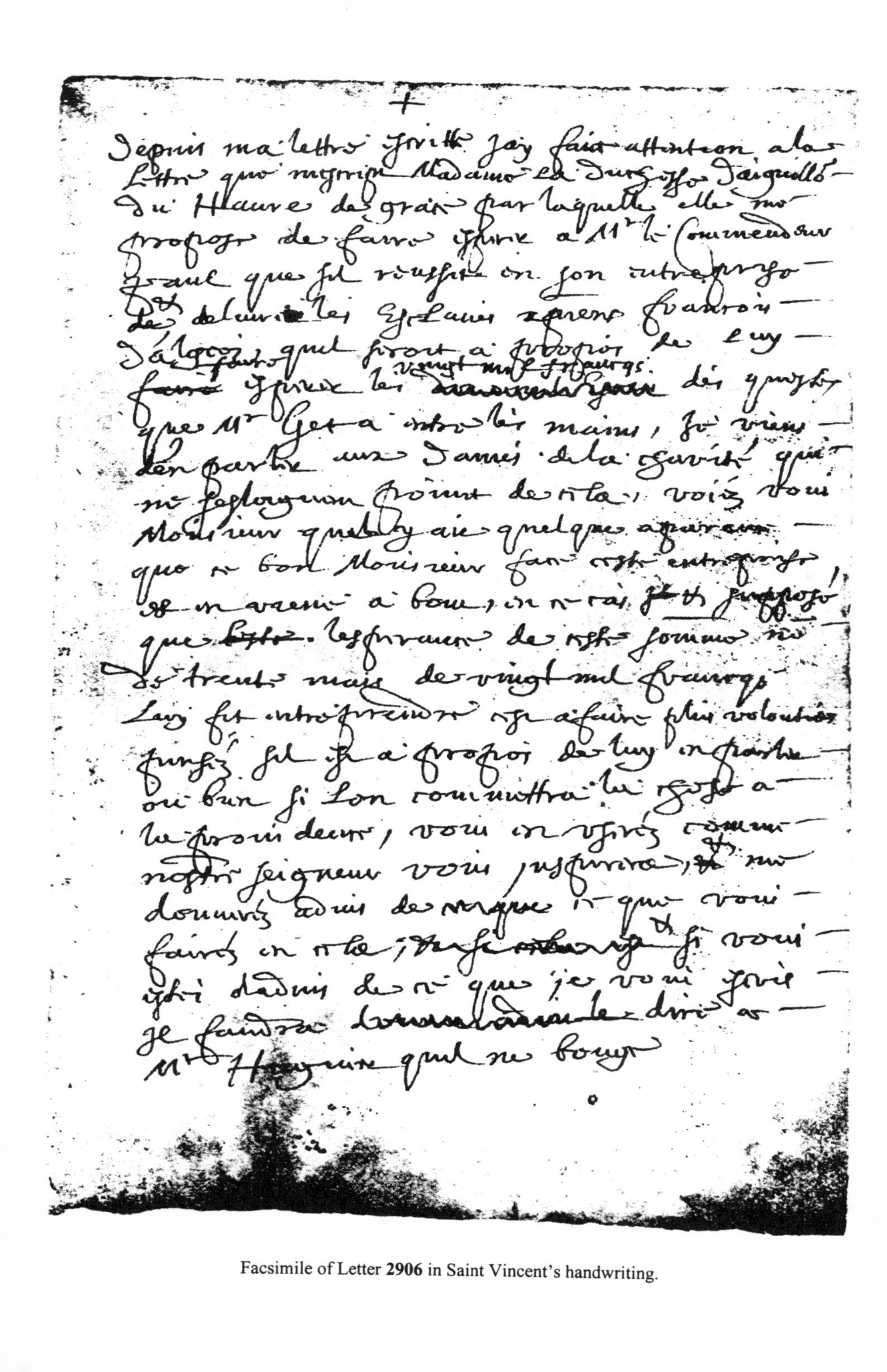

Facsimile of Letter **2906** in Saint Vincent's handwriting.

SAINT VINCENT DE PAUL

CORRESPONDENCE

2888. - TO FRANÇOIS FOURNIER,[1] IN CAHORS

[July 2, 1659] [2]

[Monsieur,]

The g[race of O[ur] L[ord] be with you for]ever!

[I am very disappointed] to have to tell you [that I cannot] ans[wer your letter] today because, although I would like to do so [immediately], I am prevented by an in[flammation] of the eyes, which obliges me to keep a bandage over them.

Thank you for the encouragement you are giving Brother Guillaume[3] and for the good order you desire and are procuring in every respect.

Letter 2888. - Archives of the Mission, 95 rue de Sèvres, Paris, original signed letter.

[1]François Fournier, born in Laval (Mayenne) on February 2, 1625, entered the Congregation of the Mission on August 12, 1644, took his vows on September 24, 1646, and was ordained a priest on September 25, 1650. He was professor of theology at the Agen Seminary (1649-58) and in Cahors (1658-63), Secretary General of the Congregation (1663-77), and Assistant General from 1667 to April 4, 1677, the day he died. The life of Saint Vincent, commonly and correctly attributed to Abelly, was erroneously thought to have been written by Fournier. It is quite possible and even probable that, as Secretary General, he helped prepare the material, but that is the extent of his role. Brother Ducournau may well have contributed much more than he. (Cf. *Notices sur les prêtres, clercs, et frères défunts de la Congrégation de la Mission* [1st series, 5 vols., Paris: Dumoulin, 1881-1911], vol. I, pp. 247-67.)

[2]In a letter to Denis Laudin on June 28, 1659 (cf. vol. VII, no. 2887), the Saint refers to an ailment, which Coste notes is an inflammation of the eye. Saint Vincent himself speaks of an inflamed eye he has had for "five or six weeks" (cf. no. 2905 to Louis Rivet, dated July 13, 1659). His mention here of this same trouble enables us to fix the year for this letter.

[3]Guillaume Vagré, born in Annay (Pas-de-Calais), entered the Congregation of the Mission as a coadjutor Brother on March 7, 1656, and took his vows in Cahors on November 30, 1658, in the presence of M. Cuissot.

You know it is very difficult to send a Sister alone from here to Cahors; and even if it were easy, we could not do so if the Bishop[4] is not asking for her. We will see if it is advisable for the Sisters to accept among them young women from the area who would like to go there. Meanwhile, I am, in the love of O[ur] L[ord], Monsieur, your most humble servant.

VINCENT DEPAUL,
i.s.C.M.[5]

Today is July 2. I received another letter from you[6] but have not yet opened it because of the trouble with my eyes. They are beginning to get better.

Addressed: Monsieur Fournier, Priest of the Mission, in Cahors

---

[4]Alain de Solminihac was born in the Château de Belet in Périgord on November 25, 1593. He was only twenty-two when one of his uncles resigned in his favor Chancelade Abbey (Dordogne), which depended on the Order of Canons Regular of Saint Augustine. He replaced the old buildings and had discipline restored. On January 21, 1630, Cardinal de la Rochefoucauld sent him full powers to make visitations of the houses belonging to the Canons of Saint Augustine in the dioceses of Périgueux, Limoges, Saintes, Angoulême, and Maillezais. Solminihac was sought after in many places to establish the reform. Appointed to the Cahors diocese on June 17, 1636, he devoted himself body and soul to the Church of which he was the shepherd. He procured for his people the benefit of missions, visited the parishes of his diocese regularly, created a seminary for the formation of his clergy, and entrusted its direction to the sons of Saint Vincent. By the time he died on December 21, 1659, the Cahors diocese was completely renewed. Since God had manifested his sanctity by several miracles, his cause was introduced in Rome at the request of the clergy of France. (Cf. Léonard Chastenet, *La vie de Mgr Alain de Solminihac* [new ed., Saint-Brieuc: Prud'homme, 1817]; Abel de Valon, *Histoire d'Alain de Solminihac, évêque de Cahors* [Cahors: Delsaud, 1900].) He was beatified by Pope John Paul II on October 4, 1981.

[5]Saint Vincent subscribed the initials *i.p.d.l.M.* (*indigne prêtre de la Mission*) [unworthy priest of the Mission] to his signature. It has been traditional in the Congregation of the Mission to append to one's name the Latin of this phrase, *indignus sacerdos Congregationis Missionis* or the initials *i.s.C.M.* The editors have adopted this traditional practice, substituting the initials of the Latin phrase for the French used by Saint Vincent.

[6]It is evident from innumerable references in the Saint's correspondence that a great many letters written to him are no longer extant. Much of this loss can be attributed to those who pillaged Saint-Lazare during the French Revolution.

2889. - TO THE KING'S ATTORNEY IN PARIS

[1659] [1]

Vincent de Paul supports the petition of the Daughters of Charity, who request ". . . permission to lay some pipelines to draw water from the conduit opposite Saint-Lazare for their house, which is nearby."

2890. - TO FIRMIN GET,[1] IN MONTPELLIER

Paris, July 4, 1659

Monsieur,

The grace of O[ur] L[ord] be with you forever!

Although your letter does not require an answer, I still cannot refrain from writing to you, and I do so today to thank God that you foresee a favorable continuation of the work that has begun. We must hope that God will bless it. I ask Him to give you His Spirit in abundance so that you may impart it to the clergy; for, indeed, if the priests are good, the people will also be good, and heretics will return to the Church. What I recommend to you in the name of O[ur] L[ord] is to incline your boarders to the interior life. They will not lack knowledge if they have virtue, nor lack virtue if they devote themselves to mental prayer which, if it is made well and exactly, will lead them infallibly to the practice of mortification, detachment from possessions, love of obedience, zeal for souls, and all their other obligations.

Letter 2889. - The few lines of this excerpt were taken from the catalogue of M. Charavay, a merchant in historical documents and autograph letters in Paris, who at various times put on sale a number of Saint Vincent's letters. The catalogue seems to give the actual terms of the Saint's request.

[1]The text of the Sisters' petition and that of the concession granted on August 19, 1659, are preserved in the Archives Nationales Q[1] 1200.

Letter 2890. - Archives of the Mission, Paris, Sister Hains collection, original signed letter.

[1]Firmin Get, born in Chépy (Somme) on January 19, 1621, entered the Congregation of the Mission on January 6, 1641, and took his vows in January 1643. In 1648 he was placed in

I have asked you to make a trip to Marseilles when M. Le Vacher[2] tells you it is time to send to Algiers, not the money from the collections, but what we have received for certain specific captives, because people do not think that the other should be risked too soon. They want the Bastion[3] to be reestablished first and for M. Constans[4] to be out of Algiers, even before M. Le Vacher returns there; or at least, if he does return, for him to take back very little money.

If, in your absence, M. Durand[5] has to take your place in

Marseilles, where he was Superior (1654-62), except for a very short time spent in Montpellier (1659-60) to open a seminary, which lasted only a few months. Later he became Superior in Sedan (1663-66, 1673-81) and in Le Mans (1670-73), and Visitor of the Province of Poitou, an office he held until April 4, 1682.

[2]Philippe Le Vacher, born in Écouen (Val-d'Oise) on March 23, 1622, entered the Congregation of the Mission on October 5, 1643, and took his vows on August 5, 1646. He was part of the first group sent to Ireland in 1646. Recalled to France in 1649, he was sent to Marseilles, where he was ordained a priest on April 2, 1650, and sailed for Algiers as Vicar Apostolic and Vicar-General of Carthage. He returned to France in 1657 to collect alms for the captives. His absence, which was supposed to last only a few months, was prolonged for two years. He set out again in September 1659, reached Barbary, and in 1661 accompanied Brother Jean Dubourdieu to Algiers, where the latter was destined to replace Jean Barreau, French Consul in that city. Le Vacher paid Barreau's debts, settled a number of business matters, and finally left Barbary in 1662, accompanied by seventy captives whom he had ransomed. He was sent to Fontainebleau, where he led a most exemplary life until August 5, 1679, the day of his death. (Cf. *Notices,* vol. III, pp. 595-606.)

[3]To protect their coral fishing grounds, merchants from Marseilles established around 1650 a fort on the North African coast, near El Kalá. This fort, known as the Bastion of France, became an important commercial center. The Turks sacked it repeatedly during the seventeenth century. In 1692 the Sultan Achmet recognized it officially as a French possession, along with the other African concessions, when the French promised an annual payment of seventeen thousand francs. Later, the demands of the Dey, who wanted an increase in this tax and who had insulted the French Consul in Algiers in 1827, were among the causes of the incursion of a French expeditionary force in 1830 to depose the Dey. The Bastion was abandoned in 1827; its ruins can be seen at Mers-el-Kerraz.

[4]François Constans, secretary of Jean Barreau, Consul in Algiers.

[5]Antoine Durand was a chosen soul. Born in Beaumont-sur-Oise (Val-d'Oise) in April 1629, he entered the Congregation of the Mission on September 15, 1647, took his vows in 1651, and was ordained a priest in September 1654, a few days after his arrival in Poland. He returned to France in 1655, was assigned to Agde, and became Superior there the following year. The Savoy Province sent him as delegate to the General Assembly in 1661. In 1662 he was put in charge of the house and parish in Fontainebleau, a very important and delicate position because of the dealings the Pastor was obliged to have with the Court. In his interesting memoirs, published by Abbé Octave Estournet (*Journal de Antoine Durand, prêtre de la Mission, premier curé de Fontainebleau (1661-67)* [Fontainebleau: Libr. cathol., 1900]), he retraces the events in which he was involved during his stay in Fontainebleau. From there Durand went to Agde (1679-81),

Montpellier, I am writing to ask him to do you this good turn. M. Durand tells me that the Archbishop[6] has instructed him to go to Narbonne when he returns from Toulouse. I am afraid this may interfere with your journey to Marseilles and with his replacing you in Montpellier. May God in His infinite goodness continue to give and increase His graces to you! I am, in His love, Monsieur, your most humble servant.

VINCENT DEPAUL,
i.s.C.M.

Addressed: Monsieur Get, Superior of the Priests of the Mission of Marseilles, at the Montpellier Seminary, in Montpellier

---

then to Dijon (1681-83), Sedan (1683-90), Saint-Cyr (1691-92), and the Arras Seminary (1692-95); in all these places he was Superior. Despite his advanced age, he was given the duty of Secretary General, which he performed until 1707. For two years he was also Director of the Daughters of Charity. Besides his memoirs, he wrote three books, still in manuscript form: *Vie de Julienne Loret, Fille de la Charité; Livre contenant les marques d'un homme juste* (Bibl. Maz., Ms. 1250); and *Réflexions sur les masques, le bal et les danses,* Ms. 1679. The exact date of his death is not known. His biography is in *Notices,* vol. II, pp. 389-424.

[6]François Fouquet was the son of another François Fouquet, Comte de Vaux, and Marie de Maupeou, a Lady of Charity most admirable for her zeal and her devotion to Saint Vincent. Fouquet's brothers were Nicolas Fouquet, Superintendent of Finances, and Louis, Bishop of Agde. His sister, Louise-Agnès, was a nun in the First Monastery of the Visitation. François, named Bishop of Bayonne in 1636, was not consecrated until March 15, 1639. He was transferred to the Agde diocese in 1643, appointed Coadjutor of Narbonne on December 18, 1656, and Archbishop of that diocese in 1659. Relegated to Alençon in 1661, he died in exile on October 19, 1673. He brought the Priests of the Mission to Agde and Narbonne and established the Daughters of Charity in the latter town. A very zealous Prelate--too zealous perhaps--he found Saint Vincent's slowness hard to understand, but greatly admired his virtue. The Saint's death affected him deeply; as soon as he received news of it, he wrote to the priests of Saint-Lazare: "However prepared I may have been for M. Vincent's death, since he was advanced in age, I assure you that I did not hear the news of his passing without surprise and without being moved by great sorrow, humanly speaking, at seeing the Church deprived of a most worthy subject, the Congregation of its very dear Father, and myself of a very charitable friend to whom I am so deeply indebted. I think that, of all those whom his charity caused him to embrace as his children, there is no one to whom he showed greater affection and gave more signs of friendship than to me."

2891. - TO JEAN MONVOISIN,[1] IN MONTMIRAIL [2]

Paris, July 4, 1659

Monsieur,

The grace of O[ur] L[ord] be with you forever!

I am answering in haste your letter of June 29. I praise God for your continued strength and hard work and for the good God is pleased to draw from them. I ask Him to invigorate you more and more with His own strength.

To arrange matters with the widow Moreau, I consent to your taking the meadow she is offering you in payment for what she owes, on condition of your giving her the surplus, if it is worth more. I have nothing to say about the price; it is up to you to decide.

We have no news here; everything is going along as usual.

I am, in O[ur] L[ord], Monsieur, your most humble servant.

VINCENT DEPAUL,
i.s.C.M.

Letter 2891. - Archives of the Mission, Paris, original signed letter.

[1]Jean Monvoisin, born in Arras on October 16, 1616, was ordained a priest in December 1640 and entered the Congregation of the Mission in Paris on July 13, 1641. Although the recipient of the letter is not indicated on the original, there is little doubt as to his identity.

[2]Reference to the widow Moreau indicates that Montmirail was the house in question (cf. vol. VI, no. 2258, where she was seeking some adjustment to her obligations); Jean Monvoisin was Superior in this house in 1659.

2892. - TO EDME JOLLY,[1] SUPERIOR, IN ROME

Paris, July 4, 1659

Monsieur,

The grace of O[ur] L[ord] be with you forever!

We will await the *extra tempora*[2] you lead us to expect and the time when Brother de Marthe[3] will be old enough to have a similar one and to make use of it. Thank you for the trouble you have taken in this matter and in all the others I entrust to you. God grant that your health will allow you to continue them for His glory and the good of the Company!

I had an excerpt taken from your letter regarding the money received by Abbé Tinti[4] and the chaplain you are sending to Loreto,

---

Letter 2892. - Archives of the Mission, Paris, original signed letter.

[1]Edme Jolly, born in Doué (Seine-et-Marne) on October 24, 1622, was acquainted in his youth with the Marquis de Fontenay-Mareuil, the French Ambassador in Rome, who took him to that city. He even entrusted Jolly with a delicate mission in the service of the King, which the young man handled most successfully. Before being admitted to Saint-Lazare on November 13, 1646, he had a post in the Apostolic Datary. This office of the Roman Curia, formed in the fourteenth century, was in charge of examining the fitness of candidates for Papal benefices and of handling the claims of those with rights to pensions. After his seminary, he returned to Rome, reviewed philosophy, theology, and Canon Law, and was ordained a priest on May 1, 1649. In May 1654 he became Director of the Saint-Lazare Seminary, and in 1655 he was appointed Superior of the house in Rome, from where Thomas Berthe had just been recalled by order of the King. Jolly rendered immense service to his Congregation because of the concessions he obtained from the Holy See. After the Saint's death he became Assistant to the Superior General and Assistant of the Motherhouse. The General Assembly of 1673 elected him successor to René Alméras as Superior General. His generalate was one of the most fruitful the Company has ever known. Jolly died in Paris on March 26, 1697. His biography, written by a contemporary, was published with some alterations in vol. III of *Notices,* pp. 387-512.

[2]An *extra tempora* was an indult from the Holy See granting religious Institutes the privilege of conferring Sacred Orders outside the times prescribed by Church law.

[3]Ignace-Joseph de Marthe, born in Arras on March 19, 1637, entered the seminary of the Congregation of the Mission in Paris on July 7, 1654, and took his vows on October 14, 1656, in the presence of M. Berthe. He was Superior in Noyon (1668-74) and Toul (1678-83). Saint Vincent had asked Edme Jolly to seek from the Holy See a dispensation for Marthe to receive ordination before the age required for Sacred Orders. He also wanted a dispensation to have him receive Orders outside the stipulated time so that he could be sent to Madagascar (cf. vol. VII, no. 2843).

[4]By a decree of December 15, 1651, the King had appointed Tinti "deputy and general commission-agent of his Majesty at the Court of Rome to follow up all Bulls and appointments of the Pope."

so as to inform the Duchesse d'Aguillon.[5] She will be surprised by the one and consoled by the other.

I am writing to you briefly this time.

I am, in O[ur] L[ord], Monsieur, your most humble servant.

VINCENT DEPAUL,
i.s.C.M.

---

[5]Marie de Vignerod de Pontcourlay, Duchesse d'Aiguillon, was born in the Château de Glenay near Bressuire in 1604, of René de Vignerod and Françoise de Richelieu, eldest sister of the great Cardinal. She married the nephew of the Duc de Luynes, Antoine de Beauvoir de Grimoard de Roure, chevalier, Seigneur de Combalet, whom she had never seen and did not love. During the two years this union lasted, the couple lived together only six months. The Marquis de Combalet, kept away from home by the war, died at the siege of Montpellier on September 3, 1622. His wife, widowed at the age of eighteen, left the Court and entered the Carmelite convent in Paris. After a year of novitiate, she received the habit from the hands of Father de Bérulle and took her first vows. Richelieu, who loved her dearly, did his utmost to bring her back to the Court. At his request the Pope forbade her to remain in the cloister, Marie de Médicis chose her as lady of the bedchamber on January 1, 1625, and the King elevated her estate of Aiguillon to a duchy-peerage on January 1, 1638.

The Cardinal gave her a small mansion on rue de Vaugirard, one of the dependencies of the Petit Luxembourg Palace where he lived. The Duchess made noble use of her immense wealth and great influence. She frequented and protected men of letters and took charge of all works of charity. She established the Priests of the Mission in Notre-Dame de La Rose and in Marseilles, entrusting them in the last-named place with the direction of a hospital she had built for sick galley convicts. The Richelieu and Rome houses subsisted on her generosity. She had the consulates of Algiers and Tunis given to the Congregation of the Mission. She contributed to the foundation of the General Hospital and of the Society of the Foreign Missions, took under her protection the Daughters of the Cross and the Daughters of Providence, and was a great benefactress of Carmel. She was President of the Confraternity of Charity at Saint-Sulpice, and replaced Madame de Lamoignon as President of the Ladies of Charity of the Hôtel-Dieu. The Duchesse d'Aiguillon must be placed, along with Saint Louise de Marillac, Madame de Gondi, and Madame Goussault, in the first rank of Saint Vincent's collaborators. No one perhaps gave him more; few were as attached to him. She watched over his health with maternal solicitude; the carriage and horses the Saint used in his old age came from her stables. Saint Vincent's death grieved her deeply. She had a silver-gilt reliquary made in the shape of a heart, surmounted by a flame, to enclose his heart. The Duchess died on April 17, 1675, at the age of seventy-one and was buried in the Carmelite habit. Bishops Bresacier and Fléchier preached her funeral oration. (Cf. Comte de Bonneau-Avenant, *La duchesse d'Aiguillon* [2nd ed., Paris: Didier, 1882].) Le Long mentions in his *Bibliothèque historique de la France* (Fontette ed., 5 vols., Paris: Hérissant, 1768-78), vol. III, no. 30.854, a manuscript collection of her letters, which has since been lost. Any further mention in the text of "the Duchess" refers to her, unless a footnote indicates otherwise.

One of our students, named Ignace Boucher,[6] a seminarian of the Arras diocese who was in the war for some time, was involved in an incident in which some persons were killed or wounded—though not by him, since he did not fire a shot. On another occasion he fired over the wall of a besieged city against its attackers, without knowing whether he killed or wounded anyone. Just in case, see if it will be a good idea to obtain a dispensation for him to receive Holy Orders.

Addressed: Monsieur Jolly, Superior of the Priests of the Mission of Rome, in Rome.

2893. - TO JÉRÔME LEJUGE,[1] IN GENOA

Paris, July 4, 1659

Monsieur,

The grace of O[ur] L[ord] be with you forever!

For the reasons you give me, I am glad you did not leave for

---

[6]Philippe-Ignace Boucher, born in Arras on January 29, 1631, entered the Congregation of the Mission on June 20, 1654, took his vows on January 1, 1657, in the presence of M. Berthe, and left in 1660, shortly after his ordination. During the repetition of prayer of March 12, 1656 (cf. vol. XI, no. 147), Saint Vincent reproved him for his fault and imposed a penance on him. In a letter to Guillaume Delville (cf. no. 2130, dated August 28, 1656) the Saint mentions that he was still in the Internal Seminary.

In the Congregation of the Mission, those in the years of formation went through the Internal Seminary, which corresponded to the novitiate in religious Orders. All new applicants were received there to be formed to the practice of the virtues of their state and to be prepared for the lifestyle and duties of the Missionaries.

Letter 2893. - Archives of the Mission, Paris, unsigned rough draft in the secretary's handwriting.

[1]Girolamo Giudice (Jérôme Lejuge), born in Diano, Albenga diocese (Italy), on September 30, 1611, was ordained a priest on December 22, 1635, entered the Congregation of the Mission on March 25, 1650, and took his vows on September 30, 1652. The terrible epidemic of 1657 that killed almost all the men in the Genoa house brought him to death's door (cf. *Notices,* vol. III, pp. 82-87). His self-sacrifice was admirable, but his character was difficult. He died on October 16, 1665.

Rome. When I asked you to go there, I did not pay attention to the fact that it was well into the season, and I would have been very sorry to have exposed you to the bad air. God be praised, Monsieur, that you are ready to do His most holy Will everywhere and to live and die wherever His Will chooses to call you! That is the disposition of His good servants and of apostolic men who are not attached to anything. It is the sign of the true children of God, always at liberty to respond to the designs of so worthy a Father.[2] I thank Him for it on your behalf, Monsieur, with a great sentiment of tenderness and gratitude, being sure that your heart, prepared in this way, will receive graces in abundance from heaven to do much good in this world, which I ask of His Divine Goodness.

So then, Monsieur, please be ready to depart for Rome once the hot weather is over. Meanwhile, put the affairs of your family in order, as you desire, and please familiarize M. Sappia[3] with the income of our family[4] and those matters that concern your office as bursar, so he can look after them in your absence, according to the information you give him and in line with the orders of his Superior.[5]

I recommend myself to your prayers and assure you of mine and of the affection of my heart, which deeply cherishes yours in that of Our Lord, who, by His grace has made me, in His love, Monsieur, your most humble servant.

---

[2]Cf. Rom 8:21. (NAB)

[3]Giacomo Sappia, born in San Remo, Albenga diocese (Italy), on October 8, 1633, entered the Congregation of the Mission in Genoa on May 30, 1655, and took his vows on June 3, 1657, in the presence of M. Duport. He was Superior in Genoa (1692-95).

[4]Saint Vincent often uses the term "family" to refer to the local Community, as in "the income of our family" mentioned here, but "the affairs of your family," in the first part of the sentence are those of Giudice's natural family.

[5]First redaction: "of his Superior, who is responsible for every duty." The last phrase was crossed out.

2894. - TO MONSIEUR FAVIER, LIEUTENANT-GENERAL OF THE TRIBUNAL OF TOUL

July 5, 1659

I would need your mind and your writing skill to express the respect with which I received your letter and the perfect gratitude God has given me for your superabundant charity. I ask Our Lord, who sees my sentiments, to be pleased to reveal them to you. Meanwhile, I thank you with all the affection of my heart for the many favors you shower upon us. God must have given you a great share in His goodness for you to be constantly so good to a poor, wretched Company like ours. He Himself will also be your reward, since He is the end of all your actions.

In particular, Monsieur, I thank you a thousand times for the overtures you made to M. Dulys [1] to get him to establish us at Notre-Dame des Trois-Épis, and for your willingness to come here to settle the business, if there is any need.

Mon Dieu! Monsieur, what benefits you confer on us! We were no longer considering the proposal formerly made to us about the above, when you took the trouble of writing to M. Demonchy,[2]

Letter 2894. - Reg. 2, p. 60.

[1]Pierre Dulys, Canon of Saint-Dié (Vosges) and Director of the Shrine of the Trois-Épis in Ammerschwihr, near Colmar. He was a very zealous priest, but of a "restless, agitated, interfering, and inconstant" disposition (cf. J. Beuchot, *Notre-Dame des Trois-Épis dans la Haute-Alsace* [Rixheim: A. Sutter, 1891], p. 48). The shrine, which is said to date from the fifteenth century, owes its name to a lovely legend: a consecrated host, thrown away by an unworthy profaner, fell on three ears of wheat growing from the same stem; immediately some bees gathered there and built an elegant wax monstrance around it. After the destruction of the chapel by the Swedes in 1636, pilgrims no longer went there. Canon Dulys restored the shrine, which he entrusted in 1652 to the Canons Regular of Saint Peter Fourier. He dismissed them in 1655 and replaced them with the monks of the Benedictine Abbey of Paris, who by 1657 no longer satisfied him. That was when he turned to Saint Vincent. The suggestions of the latter did not satisfy the Canon, and on July 31, 1659, he began negotiations with the Canons Regular of Saint Anthony of Egypt (Antonines). That very day two Antonines of Isenheim came to be installed in the Priory.

[2]Nicolas Demonchy, born in Eu (Seine-Maritime), on March 21, 1626, entered the Congregation of the Mission on August 19, 1646, and took his vows on March 6, 1649. He was ordained a priest on March 4, 1651, and was Superior in Toul (1653-55, 1657-58, 1669-74), Metz (1661-69), Tréguier (1680-84), and La Rose (1689-92).

thinking that M. Dulys had turned his thoughts elsewhere, and I still do not know if that is the case. Until now we have not seen anyone on his part and, if his nephew[3] was asked to discuss the matter with us, he has not yet informed us of it. In addition, we have been careful not to appeal to him regarding it, since it is a maxim of ours never to act except in a passive way and to do nothing to establish ourselves in a place because we want to depend entirely on the Will of God, to whom it belongs to call us. It will be quite enough if He grants us the grace to respond to the call, without our taking the initiative.

If His good pleasure wants us in that holy place, He will make this known to us by those who have the authority to summon us there. We will await their action, as I, by God's mercy, await opportunities of obeying you. I assure you that for the whole of my life, I am, as I am bound to be, in the love of Our Lord. . . .[4]

2895. - TO MONSIEUR DE SÉRAUCOURT

Paris, July 5, 1659

Monsieur,

The grace of O[ur] L[ord] be with you forever!

Our priests in Sedan have received more honor from your presence and kindness than they have rendered you service; and, as long as we live, we have a greater obligation to respect your dear person and to acknowledge the effects of your great charity than

---

[3]Two of Pierre Dulys' nephews became priests: Charles Dulys, Abbot of Lunéville, Dean of the church in Brisach, and Canon of Saint-Dié, died in 1725; and François Dulys, who later became Canon of Saint-Thiébaud de Thann.

[4]As indicated in n. 1 above, Canon Dulys withdrew his proposal.

Letter 2895. - Archives of the Mission, Paris, unsigned rough draft in the secretary's handwriting.

we will ever have the grace to do. Our Lord, however, will make up for us, if He so pleases.

I have informed the Ladies [1] of the idea you have had, Monsieur, of helping the late Mademoiselle de Neufville's niece[2] to teach little girls in Sedan and to receive some as paying boarders, using the Daughters of Sainte-Marthe[3] for that purpose and providing from here what may be lacking for their maintenance. We discussed this good work, and I really wanted the Company to take it on, but they feared the expense, since they do not see any available funds or anyone willing or able to contribute to this. So, the question has remained undecided. I do not intend to leave matters at that, Monsieur, for when I see a favorable opportunity, I will try again to see if your proposal can be put into effect.

Meanwhile, Monsieur, I praise God for the zeal He gives you for the advancement of His glory and the public good. I ask Him to preserve you for this purpose. I am, in Him, Monsieur, your most humble and very obedient servant.

2896. - TO THOMAS BERTHE,[1] IN TOUL

Paris, July 5, 1659

Monsieur,

The grace of O[ur] L[ord] be with you forever!

Your dear letter of June 21 states that you will be in Toul for

---

[1]Ladies of Charity.

[2]To dissuade poor Catholic families in Sedan from sending their daughters to Protestant schools, Louise de Malval, Mademoiselle de Neufville, had established a free school and a boarding school in that town, where young girls learned to read and write, to do handwork, and, above all, to learn good habits; it was also a place where women wanting to abjure heresy found shelter.

[3]The Hospital Sisters of Sainte-Marthe, who served during the Ancien Régime (France before 1789) in a large number of hospitals in Burgundy and Champagne.

Letter 2896. - Archives of the Mission, Paris, original signed letter. The postscript is in the Saint's handwriting.

[1]Thomas Berthe, born in Donchery (Ardennes), entered the Congregation of the Mission on

another two weeks. If this letter reaches you there, I ask you to renew once again our most humble submission and gratitude to the Bishop,[2] and in particular the offer of my perpetual obedience. I often think of his sacred person and of the fatherly kindness with which he honors us, and it is always with sentiments of respect and reverence that only God alone can make known to him.

I thank God, Monsieur, for your fine leadership there; it gives me renewed consolations everywhere, and I hope it will do so all my life.

You lead me to hope that you will pass through Metz, and perhaps this letter will find you there. Please share with President Frémyn[3] alone the resolution a certain person[4] has made to establish us there, so that he may see fit to look around the town and suburbs to find us a house for sale that is suitable for this establishment and

---

December 26, 1640, at the age of eighteen, and took his vows on December 8, 1645. After ordination in 1646, he was assigned to Sedan. Convinced that he had been sent there as Superior, he felt humiliated to see less important work entrusted to him, and he returned to his family. A short time later he came to his senses, and Saint Vincent, who recognized his virtues and appreciated his talents, joyfully took him back. He subsequently served the Community as Superior in Picardy and Champagne and in other important positions: Superior at the Bons-Enfants Seminary (1649-50) and in Rome (1653-55), Secretary of the Congregation (1660), Assistant to the Superior General (1661-67), Superior in Lyons (1668-71), at Saint-Charles Seminary (1673-82, 1687-89), and Richelieu (1682-85). In October 1659 Saint Vincent decided that among his Missionaries none was more suitable to succeed him as head of the Congregation than René Alméras or Thomas Berthe. He proposed the two names in advance, in writing, to the General Assembly that was to choose his successor. (René Alméras was elected.) There were some clashes between Berthe and Edme Jolly, Superior General, which clouded his last years. Berthe died in 1697. (Cf. *Notices,* vol. II, pp. 247-313.)

[2]André du Saussay, Bishop of Toul. Born in Paris around 1589, he was a Doctor in both civil and canon law, a talented controversialist, renowned orator, prolific writer, and the Pastor of Saint-Leu and Saint-Gilles (1624-56). He found favor with the King, who made him his counselor and preacher and became Ecclesiastical Judge and Vicar-General of Paris (1643-55). Proposed by the Queen Regent for the office of Bishop in 1649, he was not approved by the Pope until 1656. The Bishop governed his diocese wisely and died on September 9, 1675, after meriting the praise engraved on his tomb: *vir clero et populo amabilis* [a man beloved by the clergy and the people]. (Cf. Eugène Martin, *Histoire des diocèses de Toul, de Nancy et de Saint-Dié* [3 vols., Nancy: A. Crépin-Leblond, 1900-03].)

[3]Presiding Judge of the Parlement of Metz.

[4]Anne of Austria, Queen Regent of France, who provided the funds for the establishment of the Congregation of the Mission in Metz. Out of gratitude, the seminary was named after her.

to let us know the price. We will have the money to pay for it by tomorrow or the day after.

We want to keep the matter confidential, not only with regard to the person who is the foundress, but also with regard to the plan. If I did not know that the President's kindness for us is incomparable, I would not venture to be so confident in turning to him in this way. Please assure him of my obedience.

You will find in Sedan the money you left in Troyes; we have already paid it here on the bill of exchange of M. Cabel,[5] who is awaiting you.

I have been told that the army of Maréchal de la Ferté is spread over the environs of Stenay and Montmédy. Find out if that is so, and take precautions to avoid any misadventure. I ask O[ur] L[ord] to be your guide and protector. As for myself, I am, in His love, Monsieur, your most humble servant.

VINCENT DEPAUL,
i.s.C.M.

The question of the house demands the utmost secrecy in regard to the person who desires to do that good work and to ourselves.

Addressed: Monsieur Berthe, Priest of the Mission, in Toul

---

[5]Pierre Cabel, born in Chézery (Ain), was ordained a priest on March 13, 1642, and entered the Congregation of the Mission in Annecy in January 1643, at twenty-six years of age. He arrived in Paris on February 24, 1644, and was sent to Sedan, where he took his vows on August 9, 1645, and was Superior (1657-63). He was also Superior in Saint-Méen (1670-71), Visitor for the Province of Champagne, and a member of the General Assembly that elected René Alméras Superior General. Cabel died at Saint-Lazare on September 26, 1688, leaving the reputation of an exemplary priest. His biography, written by one of his contemporaries, was published in *Notices,* vol. II, pp. 315-37.

2897. - TO THOMAS BERTHE, IN TOUL

Paris, July 9, 1659

Monsieur,

The grace of O[ur] L[ord] be with you forever!

If you are receiving now the letter I wrote you on Saturday, you will receive this one as well because the former was sent to the mail too late and remained there until today; I think, however, that both will arrive too late. Whatever the case, I asked you to confide to President Frémyn a certain person's [1] plan to establish us in Metz, so that he might see fit to look for a house there that might be suitable for a seminary. Since then, however, I have thought that it is better not to mention this to him; for the matter must be kept so confidential that I fear it may not be secret enough.

So, I ask you, Monsieur, to be content with seeing personally—without seeming to do so—if you can locate an appropriate place for sale and find out its price, telling no one whomsoever your reason. That is the object of this letter. May God preserve you by His grace! I am, in His love, Monsieur, your most humble servant.

VINCENT DEPAUL,
i.s.C.M.

Someone mentioned to me the Hôtel de Montgommery, built in the old way. If you can take a look at it or any other, fine; if not, I

Letter 2897. - Archives of the Mission, Paris, original signed letter. The postscript is in the Saint's handwriting.

[1]Anne of Austria (cf. no. 2896, n. 4).

think Sister Raportebled[2] is tactful and discreet enough to do so and to write to me about it, without anyone taking notice.[3]

At the bottom of the first page: M. Berthe

2898. - TO EDME MENESTRIER,[1] SUPERIOR, IN AGEN

Paris, July 9, 1659

Monsieur,

The grace of O[ur] L[ord] be with you forever!

I received your letter of June 27 yesterday. I have not heard that the Duchesse d'Aiguillon is supposed to be going to her duchy. If she were to go, it would be well to pay her a visit, but in a simple manner, for she herself does not stand on ceremony and does not wish it from others.

As for the Court, that is another matter—or rather, it is one in which you do not have anything to do or any visit to pay. Just leave things as they are.

I share your anxiety to be paid, and I ask O[ur] L[ord] to inspire your debtors to give you the means of sustaining and expanding God's work. I am, in Him, Monsieur, your most humble servant.

VINCENT DEPAUL,
i.s.C.M.

---

[2]Madeleine Raportebled was at Saint-Sulpice in 1652. Named for Poland, she was unable to go because of the political situation and was sent instead to Saint-Denis. The Council of February 1656 assigned her to Nantes.

[3]This townhouse, the property of the Carmelites, who rented rooms there, was situated on rue du Neufbourg, today rue de la Fontaine, almost directly across from Saint-Nicolas Hospital. There were five separate pavilions, with courtyards and gardens surrounded by walls. Negotiations ended in 1661, thanks in great part to Bossuet, Archdeacon of Metz, and to his father. The deed is in the National Archives, S 6707.

Letter 2898. - Archives of the Mission, Paris, original signed letter.

[1]Edme Menestrier, born in Rugney (Vosges) on June 18, 1618, entered the Congregation of

2899. - TO FIRMIN GET, SUPERIOR, IN MONTPELLIER

Saint-Lazare-lez-Paris, July 11, 1659

Monsieur,

The grace of O[ur] L[ord] be with you forever!

In your letter of the first, you tell me you are leaving for Marseilles and were waiting for M. Durand to replace you in Montpellier. Let me tell you that I did not intend that you should go there so soon but that M. Le Vacher [1] should wait to summon you there until we had sent someone to be in charge, to whom you could hand over the key of the strongbox. Meanwhile, it is advisable for you to keep it. In fact, if you have not left Montpellier when this letter arrives, please do not budge from there until the Superior we assigned for Marseilles arrives. Then you may go there to hand over to him the key and the money from the strongbox and inform him of the order he should observe for the affairs of Barbary.

If you are already in Marseilles, please hand over to M. Le Vacher the money for the captives, which we received from their relatives and which does not come from the collections, plus four or five thousand livres [2] which you will deduct from the thirty thousand, so that M. Le Vacher can take them when he leaves for Algiers. That will be when we have sent priests to Marseilles and no sooner, as it is not advisable for him to leave the house unattended—or almost unattended—nor for you to stay there for more than two days, since M. Durand is needed in Agde.

---

the Mission on September 10, 1640, took his vows in October 1646, and was ordained a priest in 1648. He spent the rest of his Community life at the Agen Seminary, where he was Superior (1651-65, 1672-85) and Procurator (1665-72). Saint Vincent always called him by his first name only.

Letter 2899. - Archives of the Mission, Paris, original signed letter.

[1] Philippe Le Vacher.

[2] Throughout this edition the various denominations of French money have been left in French, since no adequate, unchanging value in American dollars can be assigned. One écu equaled three livres; one thousand livres could support two priests and a Brother for one year on the missions (cf. vol. V, no. 1972).

Moreover, it is inadvisable for M. Le Vacher to carry a larger sum of money with him, for fear lest the Turks be tempted to seize it. The rest will be forwarded to him gradually or in two or three installments, when we see that it is safe to do so.

I am writing to tell M. Durand to divert M. Brisjonc,[3] if possible, from his desire to return to Marseilles because he would not get along with the person we plan to send there.

I am worried about M. Parisy's[4] indisposition. I ask O[ur] L[ord] to restore and preserve his health, and yours as well, for the accomplishment of God's plans.

I am taking the honor of writing to the Bishop of Montpellier,[5] in accordance with your wishes.

I am sending this letter both to Montpellier and Marseilles.

I am, in the love of O[ur] L[ord], Monsieur, your most humble servant.

VINCENT DEPAUL,
i.s.C.M.

Addressed: Monsieur Get

---

[3]François Brisjonc, born in Tréfumel (Côtes-du-Nord) on April 13, . . . entered the Congregation of the Mission on August 7, 1654, in Richelieu, where he had been ordained on June 7, 1653. He took his vows there in the presence of M. Thieulin. Brisjonc left the Company of his own accord in 1659 but was readmitted on May 17, 1664.

[4]Antoine Parisy, born in Mesnil-Réaume (Seine-Maritime) on December 7, 1632, entered the Congregation of the Mission on November 18, 1651, took his vows in 1653, and was ordained a priest in 1657. In 1659 he was sent from Marseilles to Montpellier, returning to Marseilles in 1660. He was Superior there (1672-75), then in Metz (1676-85) and Saint-Méen (1689-1701).

[5]François de Bosquet, Administrator for Justice in Languedoc, who later became Bishop of Lodève (1648-57), then of Montpellier (1657-76). He died on June 24, 1676. (Cf. Abbé Paul-Émile-Marie-Joseph Henry, *François Bosquet* [Paris: Ernest Thorin, 1889].)

2900. - TO EDME JOLLY, SUPERIOR, IN ROME

Paris, July 11, 1659

Monsieur,

The grace of O[ur] L[ord] be with you forever!

When I received your letter of June 16, I believed you were outside of Rome and was greatly consoled by the thought that you were therefore somewhat sheltered from the great heat. But, from what I see, Monsieur, you prefer the interests of our Company to the care of your own health. This is very exemplary, and I thank God for it, asking Our Lord to be Himself your strength and your life, as He is of all those whose food is His love.

Nevertheless, Monsieur, do everything in your power to preserve your health. Do not go out except in case of necessity; send someone else into the city to take care of business and to see those who will have to be seen. If there are any urgent, important things that only you can do, hire a carriage to take you there. Please do not fail to do so, Monsieur; continue also to drink *aigre de cèdre,*[1] rest, and take the remedies the doctors will prescribe. You would be acting contrary to the intention of the Company if you were to spare the expense when your health, which is so dear to us, is at stake.

I thank God for the long, effective labors of your workers. God must certainly give special strength to those who serve Him as they do. Despite that, Monsieur, have them take some rest and regain their strength.

Thank you for the dispensation you sent me for Brother Étienne.[2] We will hold on to it, without mentioning it to him, since

---

Letter 2900. - Archives of the Mission, Paris, original signed letter.

[1]Juice made from a lemon, or from a partially ripe, yellow, thick-skinned fruit called a citron, which resembles a lime or lemon but is larger and contains less acid.

[2]The personnel catalogue states: "Nicolas Étienne, born on September 17, 1634, was admitted on August 8, 1653, provided that he remain a seminarian all his life because of the serious deformity of one of his hands. He took his vows on August 8, 1655, and with a dispensation

it is not advisable for him to know about it—at least for the present. We shall see in time.

It is true, Monsieur, that the Cardinal of Genoa[3] is very kind to our little Congregation. What can we do to acknowledge this, except to praise God for having given him this kindness and, while admitting our own unworthiness ever to deserve such a grace, to console ourselves with the thought that Our Lord Himself has merited it for us? Assure His Eminence of our prayers for his preservation, so important to the Church, and of our immense gratitude for his great, innumerable benefits.

I had someone inform the Duchesse d'Aiguillon of what you did for her foundation.[4] She told me she would write to you today; I do not know if she will send me her letter. She was quite surprised to learn that Abbé Tinti had fraudulently carried off the sixteen hundred écus in arrears; she was sure she had never given him power of attorney to receive them.

I will write to Poitou as soon as possible to ascertain if the ministers are baptizing validly.[5] So far, I have heard nothing to the

---

was ordained a priest on August 31, 1659, on condition that he go to Madagascar." (Cf. *Notices,* vol. I, p. 480.) Étienne had already asked to go there as a catechist; as implied in this letter, it was Saint Vincent who sought the dispensation for his ordination. He set off the first time in 1660 but was unable to land and had to return to France. In May 1663 he left again, arriving in Madagascar in September. His apostolate was short-lived: Dian Mananghe, a Malagasy chief who had promised to receive Baptism, invited him to dinner, had him imprisoned, and murdered him, along with Brother Philippe Patte and some indigenous Christians. Coste and *Notices,* vol. V (Supplement), p. 218, give February 27, 1664, as the date of the massacre. *Notices,* vol. III, pp. 350-68, gives a fuller biography of Étienne; on p. 350 it states that he died on March 4, while on p. 367 it says "in the first week of Lent 1664." A short account of Brother Patte is given on pp. 369-71 of the latter volume, which states that he died with M. Étienne on March 4. In both instances, *Mémoires de la Congrégation de la Mission. Madagascar,* vol. IX, is cited; Coste specifies pp. 374-494.

Saint Vincent often refers to clerical students as "Brothers." The context usually determines whether the one referred to is a coadjutor Brother or a student destined for the priesthood.

[3]Stefano Durazzo, Legate in Ferraro, then in Bologna, was created a Cardinal in 1633 and was Archbishop of Genoa (1635-64). He died in Rome on July 22, 1667. Cardinal Durazzo was always most gracious and very devoted to Saint Vincent and his priests.

[4]The foundation of Our Lady of Loreto.

[5]Saint Vincent's letter of inquiry (cf. no. 2905) mentions areas in which validity is questioned.

contrary. I will send you the answer as soon as it is forwarded to me.

M. Levasseur,[6] whom M. Dehorgny [7] took with him to Rome the last time he went there, and who was then only a cleric, is urgently requesting that someone get and send to him the letters of his Major Orders, which he received in . . . in 1653 and 1654 during Lent and at Christmas. If you can obtain them conveniently, please do so.

Some time ago I sent you one of M. Abelly's[8] books entitled *A defense of the Hierarchy of the Church and of the legitimate authority of our Holy Father the Pope and the Bishops against the*

---

[6]Martin Levasseur, born in Eu (Seine-Maritime) on January 5, 1630, entered the Congregation of the Mission on March 7, 1651, took his vows in 1653, and was ordained a priest in Rome on April 4, 1654.

[7]Jean Dehorgny, from Estrées-Saint-Denis (Oise), entered the Congregation of the Mission in August 1627 and was ordained a priest on April 22, 1628. In 1632, when Saint Vincent made the move to Saint-Lazare, Dehorgny took over the direction of the Collège des Bons-Enfants, which he retained until 1635, then took up again (1638-43, 1654-59). He was Assistant to the Superior General (1642-44, 1654-67), Superior of the house in Rome (1644-47, 1651-53), and Director of the Daughters of Charity (1660-67). In 1640, 1641, 1643, 1644, 1659, and 1660, he made the visitation of several houses of the Company, reestablishing good order wherever necessary. His sympathy for Jansenistic ideas merited for us two beautiful letters from Saint Vincent, who had the joy of seeing him return to sounder beliefs. Dehorgny died on July 7, 1667. We still have twenty-three of his conferences to the Daughters of Charity and several letters.

[8]Louis Abelly was born in Paris in 1604. From the earliest years of his priesthood he took part in Saint Vincent's apostolic labors. The Saint spoke so highly of him to François Fouquet, Bishop-elect of Bayonne, that the latter appointed him his Vicar-General. Abelly's stay in Bayonne was short-lived; he accepted a simple village parish near Paris, and shortly afterward (1644) was given charge of Saint-Josse parish in the capital, where he formed an ecclesiastical community. He later became Director of the Sisters of the Cross (1650), chaplain of the General Hospital (1657), and Bishop of Rodez (1664). In 1666 he resigned his diocese for reasons of health and retired to Saint-Lazare, where he spent the last twenty-five years of his life in recollection and study. We have almost thirty of his books on devotion, history, and theology. Abelly is not merely the sponsor of *La vie du Vénérable Serviteur de Dieu Vincent de Paul,* [Paris: F. Lambert, 1664], as has been asserted, but is truly its author. His task was greatly facilitated by Brother Ducournau, one of the Saint's secretaries, who collected and classified the documents. Abelly made a donation to the Saint-Lazare house of some property he owned in Pantin, which became the country house of the students. He died on October 4, 1691, and, according to his wish, was buried in the church of Saint-Lazare, under the Holy Angels chapel. (Cf. Pierre Collet, *La vie de St Vincent de Paul* [2 vols., Nancy: A. Leseure, 1748], vol. I, pp. 5ff.)

pernicious doctrine of an anonymous pamphlet,[9] which was recently burned[10] by a public executioner, by decree of the Supreme Council. I want to send you another two copies of the same book, together with the response the enemies of the truth made to it and M. Abelly's reply. I will have a packet made of them to be sent next Tuesday to M. Delaforcade[11] by the Lyons messenger so he can forward it to you as soon as possible.

I am sending you in advance in the present packet a letter that M. Abelly wrote to me. You will see in it the importance of obtaining official authorization for his book, which contains only sound doctrine. The way to do this would be to have it approved in Rome and to get it translated into Latin for this purpose. Neither the Jesuits nor others will find any fault with it. You could entrust it to the Cardinal Datary [12] so that he may be pleased to appoint someone to examine it, and give a copy to Monsignor Créag, to use it as he thinks best.[13]

I am, in O[ur] L[ord], Monsieur, your most humble servant.

VINCENT DEPAUL,
i.s.C.M.

Addressed: Monsieur Jolly

---

[9]This anonymous work was entitled: *Lettres de l'autheur des Règles très importantes au sieur de Marca, archevesque de Thoulouze.*

[10]On May 21.

[11]A merchant in Lyons who forwarded money, packages, and letters for Saint Vincent and the Missionaries.

[12]Giacomo Cardinal Corradi, a very important member of the Curia and one of the Pope's closest collaborators.

[13]In the original the following sentence has been crossed out: "There is good reason to fear that the General Assembly of the Clergy to be held next year might be persuaded by some of the Bishops, who are calling into question the authority of the Holy See, to establish theirs in its place and to urge it to take some decision in this matter, which would be the cause of schism and a great misfortune. The approval of Rome could remedy this situation."

During the sixteenth, seventeenth, and eighteenth centuries, representatives of the French clergy met every five years in what was known as the Assembly of the Clergy. Each of the thirty ecclesiastical provinces of France sent to it two Bishops and two members of the lower clergy, usually Abbots or Canons. In an era of Gallicanism, Church-State relations were a major consideration, most especially the *don gratuit,* the annual free financial gift or donation to the

2901. - TO JACQUES PESNELLE,[1] SUPERIOR, IN GENOA

Paris, July 11, 1659

Monsieur,

The grace of O[ur] L[ord] be with you forever!

I received your letter of June 24. You have given me the greatest pleasure by sending back to M. Rodolphe-Maria Brignole's father[2] the bond for a life annuity which this good young nobleman gave you, so that he may take from this alms whatever he pleases regarding the time and amount. We must have nothing that has not been given or acquired properly and, if we are truly grateful for the acts of charity that have been done for us, we will always be ready to return willingly the goods our benefactors have given us, if it is in our power.

I already wrote you that I felt that M. Pinon[3] would be suitable to relieve M. Simon[4] in the direction of the Internal Seminary, and

---

King. Additional grants were made on special occasions. The meetings were concerned as much with religious matters as with temporal concerns. The Assemblies thus assigned the French clergy an important role in maintaining the purity of French Catholicism and a voice in determining the extent of secular influence in the Church.

Letter 2901. - Archives of the Mission, Paris, original signed letter.

[1]Jacques Pesnelle, born in Rouen (Seine-Maritime) on June 5, 1624, entered the Congregation of the Mission on September 4, 1646, was ordained a priest in Rome on November 30, 1648, and took his vows there. He was Superior in Genoa (1657-66, 1674-77) and Turin (1667-72, 1677-83). A very gifted man, highly esteemed by Saint Vincent, Pesnelle died in 1683.

[2]Maria Emmanuele Brignole, Marchese di Grappoli (Tuscany), son of Antonio Giulio Brignole, who entered the Jesuits on March 11, 1652.

[3]Pierre Pinon, born in Tours on June 19, 1630, entered the Congregation of the Mission on August 30, 1655, and took his vows in Genoa on October 14, 1657, in the presence of M. Simon.

[4]René Simon, born in Laval (Mayenne) on September 21, 1630, entered the Congregation of the Mission on August 5, 1650. He was a professor at Saint-Charles Seminary, then a Missionary in Poland, where he was ordained a priest in 1654. He returned to France the next year, took his vows on January 25, 1656, and was sent to Genoa. Simon became Superior of the Annecy Seminary in 1663 and of the Turin house (1665-67). He was named Secretary General in 1668 and, after participating in the General Assembly of that year, was appointed Superior in Rome and Visitor of the Province of Italy. In 1677 he was recalled to France; the following year he was made Superior of the Cahors house, where he died in 1682 or shortly thereafter. Simon was very useful to the Congregation, especially because of the favors he obtained for it from the Holy See. His biography was published in *Notices,* vol. II, pp. 447-51.

I see that you are proposing the same thing to me. It will be well, then, for you to give this a try; ask him also to pay attention to the external failings in decorum that are apparent in him so that he may correct them.

To answer the question you ask me about whether to have scholastic theology taught in your seminary, I would have to know the thinking there about this method of teaching, whether it is in use among the Jesuits and other religious and secular houses, and if many students attend. I also think it would be rather hasty to adopt it this coming year and that it would be better to postpone it until next year.

You mention Brother Thiébault[5] in connection with studying scholastic theology. I no longer remember who he is, whether he is French or Italian, nor who is the M. Philippe[6] who, you say, will soon become a good professor of moral theology. Please let me know.

At the first opportunity, I will write to M. Stelle,[7] who has written to me.

I am, in the love of O[ur] L[ord], Monsieur, your most humble servant.

VINCENT DEPAUL,
i.s.C.M.

I thought M. Lej[uge] would raise the objections he is now

---

[5]François Thiébault, born in Moyencourt (Somme) on September 27, 1634, entered the Congregation of the Mission on December 2, 1657, and took his vows in Genoa on December 12, 1659, in the presence of M. Simon.

[6]It is difficult to identify this man with certainty. Perhaps it is Jean Philippe, born in Ploufragan, Saint-Brieuc diocese, on May 3, 1632. He entered the Richelieu Seminary on March 1, 1656, and took his vows there on March 5, 1658, in the presence of M. de Beaumont. The date of his ordination is not recorded.

[7]Gaspard Stelle, born in the Sisteron diocese (Alpes-de-Haute-Provence) on April 5, 1624, entered the Congregation of the Mission as a priest on January 16, 1657, and took his vows in Genoa on January 7, 1659, in the presence of M. Simon. Both Vol. I and vol. V (Supplement) of *Notices* list him as *Estelle*.

raising to have a change of residence; however, wait for the right time to go to Rome, so as to do what can be done to get him to go there and, if he refuses, to see to the remedy.

Addressed: Monsieur Pesnelle, Superior of the Priests of the Mission of Genoa, in Genoa

2902. - TO JEAN PARRE,[1] IN SAINT-QUENTIN

Paris, July 12, 1659

Dear Brother,

The grace of O[ur] L[ord] be with you forever!

I received your letter of the seventh and the pictures of Notre-Dame-de-la-Paix, for which I thank you. I ask both the Son and the Mother, whom you are serving there, to honor you with their protection and to inspire in souls true piety, which implies a good life.

I had someone inform the Bishop of Noyon[2] that you would give ten or twelve days to carrying out what he has instructed you to do.

Madame Fouquet[3] told us that peace has definitely been made

---

Letter 2902. - Archives of the Mission, Paris, original signed letter.

[1]Born in Châtillon-en-Dunois (Eure-et-Loir), Jean Parre entered the Congregation of the Mission on April 16, 1638, at twenty-seven years of age, took his vows in 1643, and died after 1660. He and Brother Mathieu Régnard were two of the most intelligent and active instruments that Divine Providence placed in Saint Vincent's hands. Brother Parre traveled all over Picardy and Champagne assessing and remedying needs. (Cf. *Notices,* vol. II, pp. 223-40.)

[2]Henri de Baradat, Bishop of Noyon (1626-60), had requested that Parre put some order into the ill-regulated devotion manifested at the Shrine of Notre-Dame-de-la-Paix when relief aid was being distributed.

[3]Marie de Maupeou, wife of François Fouquet, Vicomte de Vaux, Master of Requests, and then Councillor of State. Among her eight children were Nicolas, the celebrated Superintendent of Finance; François, Bishop of Narbonne; Louis, Bishop of Agde; and several daughters who entered the Visitation Order, one of whom, Marie-Thérèse, became Superior of the Visitation in Toulouse. Marie de Maupeou was a woman of exceptional piety and immense charity, of whom Saint Vincent said that "if through some mischance the Gospels were lost, their spirit and

and that the King of Spain has signed the conditions.[4] She wanted me to tell you this to console the people of the poor border areas about it.

They want to do something to help the most ruined churches to be restored to such a condition that Mass can be celebrated in them with some propriety. They ask you therefore to find the ones that need this the most but do not require too much, for they cannot give a great deal.

You are also asked to help the poor people to be able to earn their living in this season by supplying them with implements to gather in the harvest.

They say that, of all the ruined churches, the one in Avançon, near Rethel, is the worst, and they recommend it especially to you.

Madame de Labidière has paid three-quarters of the one hundred livres she promised for Masses to be said by poor priests in the border areas. I think you already received twenty-five livres for the first quarter. You can now get twenty-five écus for the remaining three-quarters and draw them on Mademoiselle Viole.[5] Please take care to see that these Masses are said.

---

maxims would be found in the conduct and sentiments of Madame Fouquet." "She makes devotion so attractive," he added, "that she encourages everyone to be devout." (Cf. *Année sainte des religieuses de la Visitation Sainte-Marie* [12 vols., Annecy: Ch. Burdet, 1867-71], vol. I, p. 627.) When she heard that her son, Nicolas, had fallen into disgrace, she exclaimed: "I thank You, O my God. I asked You for the salvation of my son, and this is the way to obtain it." She died in 1681, at the age of ninety-one, mourned by everyone, but especially by the poor, who called her their mother. In the catalogue of the Ladies of Charity, she is listed under the title of Madame Fouquet, the President's wife.

[4]Negotiations for peace, initiated in Lyons and continued in Paris, had resulted in the signing of some preliminary documents on June 4. They continued on the Isle of Pheasants in the Bidassoa River and finally concluded with the Treaty of the Pyrenees (November 7, 1659). This peace marked the end of the Spanish ascendancy in Europe, which now passed to France. Louis XIV married Maria Teresa, daughter of King Philip IV. France received part of Roussillon, Conflans, Cerdagne, and several fortresses in Flanders and Artois on the Belgian border. This alleviated some of the dangers of Brother Jean Parre's ministry.

[5]Mademoiselle Viole, born Madeleine Deffita, was the widow of Jacques Viole, Counselor at the Châtelet in Paris. She was Treasurer of the Ladies of Charity of the Hôtel-Dieu, and her name recurs often in the correspondence of Saint Vincent, who greatly appreciated her charity, intelligence, and activity. Mademoiselle Viole died in Paris on April 4, 1678.

Although I told M. Bourdin, Vicar-General of Noyon, that you would give ten or twelve days to help to build a chapel[6] and to do whatever was needed, you may, however, remain there longer, if necessary. The Ladies leave to your discretion the length of time you think you should spend there, and to leave, when necessary, to go elsewhere to assist the poor and to visit the meetings of the Ladies.[7] After that, you can go back to the chapel, if your presence there is useful.

I am, dear Brother, in O[ur] L[ord], your most affectionate brother and servant.

VINCENT DEPAUL,
i.s.C.M.

Addressed: Brother Jean Parre, of the Mission, in Saint-Quentin

2903. - TO CHARLES DE SAVEUSES [1]

Saint-Lazare, July 12, 1659

Monsieur,

Your most humble servant Vincent here renews the offers of his obedience and presents a most humble request on behalf of the

---

[6]On April 20, 1659, a two hundred-year-old lime tree was felled in Fieulaine, near Saint-Quentin. Workers who were cutting it down unearthed a small statue of the Blessed Virgin, to which rumor attributed some miracles. This was the origin of the pilgrimage to Notre-Dame-de-la-Paix. People flocked to the chapel that was soon built near the site. (Cf. [Charles Bourdin], *Histoire de ce qui s'est passé de plus remarquable à l'occasion d'une image de la sainte Vierge, dite Notre-Dame-de-Paix, nouvellement trouvée au village de Fieulaine* [Saint-Quentin: C. Lequeux, 1662].)

[7]The Ladies of Charity of the Hôtel-Dieu in Paris, who underwrote much of Jean Parre's work.

Letter 2903. - Archives of the Mission, Paris, unsigned rough draft in the secretary's handwriting.

[1]Charles de Saveuses, born in Amiens in 1595, left a military career to enter the Discalced Carmelites on May 5, 1617, notwithstanding the objections of his father who, on August 20, obtained a parlementary decree to force him to leave. He studied theology, was ordained a priest

Ladies of Charity, particularly the Duchesse d'Aiguillon and Madame Fouquet, who have learned that you, Monsieur, are about to go to Reims to visit the churches that depend on your Saint-Nicaise Abbey. They ask you please to give special attention to the needs of the church in Avançon, which is in total ruin. By so doing, you may then persuade the priests of the Sainte-Chapelle to make a contribution to have it restored enough to celebrate Holy Mass and administer the sacraments in it with some propriety, which is impossible in its present state. There is a poor lady here from that locality, who will have the honor of seeing you, Monsieur, about this. It suffices to point out to you some good to be done to see it done, if feasible, because of the great charity God has given you, causing you to embrace effectively every opportunity pleasing to His Divine Goodness and useful to His service.

2904. - *JEAN MARTIN [1] TO SAINT VINCENT*

July 12, 1659

All of us are back from the country now. The mission in Cherasco lasted a little longer than the others because of the huge crowds we had from all the surrounding places. We would have needed about twenty good workers to take care of the people, and they could have found enough work for two months or more.

---

in 1626, and devoted himself to the ministry of rural missions. The assassination of his brother, Jean-Robert, left open the position of Parlementary Councillor, which he assumed in March 1629 and held for forty-one years. The Priory of Saint-Omer-sur-Epte belonged to him; in 1658 he exchanged it for a Canonry of the Sainte-Chapelle. He died on July 1, 1670, and was buried in the church of the Ave Maria nuns on July 3. Saint Vincent greatly esteemed his priestly virtues and his integrity as a magistrate. Speaking of the two, Reverend Jean-Marie de Vernon wrote: "Their union was so perfect that there seemed to be one same soul in the two bodies." (Cf. *Vie de Messire de Saveuses* [Paris: G. Meturas, 1678], p. 155.)

Letter 2904. - Abelly, *op. cit.*, bk. II, chap. I, sect. VI, p. 89.

[1]Jean Martin, born in Paris on May 10, 1620, entered the Congregation of the Mission on October 9, 1638. He was ordained in Rome on April 25, 1645, and that same year was sent to Genoa to found a new house. Saint Vincent probably had no Missionary more gifted in drawing

God was pleased to grant us every blessing to be desired in such circumstances. A large number of quarrels and disputes were settled. Among others, there was a very big town nearby, whose inhabitants were so divided and at odds with one another that four of them were killed on the eve of our arrival. Nevertheless, peace was reestablished in it, by the mercy of God. Still, this was difficult to achieve because it came about only after forty days of preaching and negotiating; however, everything finally ended with great consolation and even edification for all the people, in the presence of the Blessed Sacrament, which had been exposed expressly for this purpose. The main thing is that, after being reconciled, these persons came to the sacrament of Penance with very good dispositions.

2905. - TO LOUIS RIVET,[1] SUPERIOR, IN SAINTES

Paris, July 13, 1659

Monsieur,

The grace of Our Lord be with you forever!

I received your letter of June 29. Thank you for the interest you take in my health. I am not ill otherwise; still, I have not been out for seven or eight months because of the condition of my legs which

---

crowds and converting souls. In 1654 Martin was recalled to France and placed in Sedan as Superior and Pastor; then he was sent to Turin in 1655 for the new establishment founded by the Marchese di Pianezza, Prime Minister of State. There, as in Genoa and Sedan, the zealous Missionary knew how to soften the most hardened hearts. He was given the name "Apostle of Piedmont," and his fellow Missionaries were called "the holy Fathers." In 1665 René Alméras asked him to head the house in Rome. This was a painful sacrifice for Martin, but he resigned himself to it. Subsequently, he was named Superior in Genoa (1670), Turin (1674), Rome (1677), Perugia (1680), and again in Rome in 1681, where he died on February 17, 1694. His obituary, written by one of his contemporaries, is in the Archives of the Mission in Paris. It was published, with some corrections, in vol. I of *Notices,* pp. 269-372.

All the letters in this volume are addressed to this Jean Martin, whom in the index we have called *the elder* to distinguish him from another Jean Martin, referred to as *the younger* (cf. no. 2970).

Letter 2905. - Archives of the Mission, Paris, seventeenth-century copy.

[1]Louis Rivet was born in Houdan (Yvelines) on February 19, 1618. He entered the Congregation of the Mission on June 13, 1640, took his vows on October 16, 1642, and was ordained

has become worse. In addition, one of my eyes has been inflamed for five or six weeks and is no better, even though I have tried several remedies. God be praised for this!

I am more troubled about your stomach ailment and the weakness you are experiencing. These are the results of your hard work, by which you have multiplied merits for your soul at the same time you have worn out your body. Please do all in your power to stay well, Monsieur, and to take better care of yourself than you have done.

What you tell me of the Synod held in Cozes [2] gives me reason to ask you how the Huguenots of Poitou administer Baptism.[3] I had word from Rome that a Prelate said that they do not baptize validly; one, by not pouring the water, another, by not pronouncing the words or failing in some other essential of the form. Please get some information on this, Monsieur, and inform me as soon as possible what you know of it and what you will learn, without however making any noise about it.

I cordially embrace your little family, of which I am—and of you in particular—in the love of Our Lord, Monsieur, the most humble and affectionate servant.

VINCENT DEPAUL,
i.s.C.M.

Please do not tell anyone what I have written you or why you are making enquiries.

---

a priest on September 19, 1643. In 1646 he was placed in Richelieu, then at the Saintes Seminary, which he directed for several years (1648-50, 1656-62, 1665-73). Louis had two brothers in the Congregation: François, who was a priest, and Jacques, a Brother.

[2]Principal town of a canton in Charente-Maritime. This synod was for the Huguenots, the Reformed Church in France, a Protestant sect which espoused the spiritual and political tenets of Jean Calvin.

[3]Saint Vincent had written to Edme Jolly, Superior in Rome, that he should inquire if the "ministers are baptizing validly" (cf. no. 2900).

2906. - TO PHILIPPE LE VACHER, IN MARSEILLES [1]

[Between May and August 1659]

. . . .Since writing my letter, I have given some attention to the one the Duchesse d'Aiguillon wrote me from Le Havre-de-Grâce. In it she proposes to lead Commander Paul[2] to hope that, if he succeeds in his undertaking and rescues the French Christian slaves in Algiers, it would be fitting for him to expect the twenty thousand francs from the collections that are now in M. Get's hands. I have just mentioned this to the Ladies of Charity, who are not opposed to it.

Do you see any likelihood, Monsieur, that the good gentleman will carry out this enterprise and bring it to a successful conclusion? In any case, and supposing that the hope of this sum—not of thirty, but of twenty thousand francs—might induce him to undertake this affair more willingly, consider whether it is more advisable to mention it to him or to entrust the matter to Providence. Act as Our Lord will inspire you and let me know what you are going to do. If you agree with what I am writing you, you will have to tell M. Huguier[3] not to budge.

Letter 2906. - Archives of the Mission, Paris, autograph postscript of one of the Saint's letters.

[1]The name of the addressee is not given on the original. It was intended neither for Firmin Get nor Benjamin Huguier but was sent during an absence of Get and before he had handed over the keys of the strong box that contained the money collected for Barbary, i.e., before the arrival of Gabriel Delespiney. The person who received it was the acting Superior. The general trend of these remarks clearly points to Philippe Le Vacher, who directed the Marseilles house between Get's departure for Montpellier in May 1659 and the arrival of Delespiney in August 1659.

[2]Some historians, rightly or wrongly, claim that Chevalier Paul was the son of a laundress at the Château d'If (a national prison on an islet in the Mediterranean near Marseilles). He became a Knight of Malta, led his desert convoys like all the Knights of the Order, and then joined the French navy, where his bravery soon earned for him the rank of Captain in 1640, Commodore on December 30, 1649, and Lieutenant General in 1654. He died around 1667.

[3]Benjamin-Joseph Huguier, born in Sézanne (Marne) on March 10, 1613, was an attorney at the Châtelet of Paris before his admission into the Congregation of the Mission on September 15, 1647. He served in Tunis (1649-52), returning to France by way of Marseilles in May of 1652, took his vows that same year, and was ordained a priest in February 1655. After ordination, he became chaplain of the galleys in Toulon; however, he felt drawn to Barbary and, on September 19, 1662, was sent to Algiers with the title of Vicar Apostolic. While nursing the plague-stricken there, he contracted the illness and died of it himself in April 1663. (Cf. *Mémoires de la Congrégation of the Mission* [11 vols., Paris, 1863-1899], vol. II, pp. 221-30.)

2907 - TO CARDINAL DE RETZ [1]

Paris, July 15, 1659

Monseigneur,

I am taking the honor of writing this letter, Monseigneur, to renew the offers of perpetual obedience which I owe Your Eminence, with all possible affection and humility, Monseigneur, together with the most humble request that you will be pleased to approve the Rules of your[2] Company of the Mission, which Your Eminence has already been pleased to approve on one occasion, and the late Archbishop[3] on another. We have been obliged to alter some, [both] because of errors that slipped into the written form and because we had made regulations about certain things which experience has shown us to be difficult in practice. Be that as it

---

Letter 2907. - Archives of the Mission, Paris, unsigned rough draft in the secretary's handwriting. The many simple variants of form between the rough draft and the copy in Reg. 2, p. 30, are due to the fact that the copyist could not make out the text. These variants are in the passages that are the most difficult to decipher.

[1]Jean-François-Paul de Gondi, Abbé de Buzay, future Cardinal de Retz, son of Philippe-Emmanuel de Gondi, General of the Galleys, and Françoise-Marguerite de Silly. On June 13, 1643, he was named Coadjutor to his uncle, Jean-François de Gondi, Archbishop of Paris, and was consecrated on January 31, 1644. Although he played an active role in the Fronde, the Queen--no doubt to win him over--obtained the Cardinal's hat for him on February 19, 1652, and he was known subsequently as Cardinal de Retz. Discontented with his influence and plots, Mazarin had him imprisoned in the Château de Vincennes. Becoming Archbishop upon the death of his uncle (1654), and consequently more dangerous to the Prime Minister, Retz was transferred to the Château de Nantes, from which he escaped to Spain and then to Italy. In Rome the Priests of the Mission gave him hospitality, on the orders of Pope Innocent X. Because of this, Mazarin very nearly let all the force of his anger fall upon Saint Vincent and his Congregation. After the accession of Pope Alexander VII (1655), who was less benevolent to him than his predecessor, Cardinal de Retz left Rome on a long journey to Franche-Comté, Germany, Belgium, and Holland. He returned to France in 1662, after Mazarin had died, renounced the archbishopric of Paris, and received in exchange Saint-Denis Abbey. Age and trials had made him wiser; during the last four years of his life, some persons even considered him pious. In this peaceful, studious, simple-mannered man, concerned with paying off his numerous creditors, no one would have recognized the ambitious, flighty, and restless Prelate who had stirred up Paris and made the powerful Mazarin tremble. The Cardinal died on August 24, 1679.

[2]First redaction: "our;" "your" is more tactful. Further on, the Saint says: "your Missionaries," instead of "my Missionaries" with the same intent.

[3]Jean-François de Gondi, first Archbishop of Paris (February 19, 1623-March 21, 1654).

may, Monseigneur, we have made no change in the essence of the Rules nor in any important detail. I assure Your Eminence of this in the sight of God, before whom I must appear to give an account of the actions of my poor, wretched life, since I am now in my seventy-ninth year.

What I am asking Your Eminence, Monseigneur, is not so much the affair of this Little Company as that of Your Eminence, you who are the founder and sole protector of the same Company. I am not appealing to your father[4] for his recommendation, or to any power on earth; it is to your kindness alone that I have recourse. If I knew the whereabouts of Your Eminence,[5] I would have taken the honor of sending one of your Missionaries to present this humble petition in person; but, not knowing it, I make use of this letter, which I place in the hands of God's Providence, begging Him to place it in the hands of Your Eminence,[6] whose blessing I ask, prostrate at your feet.

---

[4]Philippe-Emmanuel de Gondi entered the Oratorian Fathers after becoming a widower (June 23, 1625) and spent the rest of his life in the practice of Christian and religious virtues. He died in Joigny on June 29, 1662. The Congregation of the Mission, the Oratory, and Carmel honor him as one of their greatest benefactors.

[5]Cardinal de Retz was still in exile, and the search by Mazarin's agents obliged him to keep his whereabouts secret.

[6]Following these words the secretary had written the following passage which was scratched out: "What urges me to entreat you to send us your approval is the reason I have to fear that God will not keep me much longer on this earth; and, if I die without an approval, this might be the cause of disastrous consequences in the Company after my death. I have drawn up an act of declaration, which I am sending Your Eminence. In it I have set down more or less what I told Your Eminence that, being obliged to have recourse to you for the approval of these Rules, and not knowing where you are so as to obtain this final approval, I may assure the Company that these are the same Rules that had been approved by you, Monseigneur, and by the late Archbishop, and exhort the members to observe them with exactitude. Whatever the case . . . this will depend on the blessing God will be pleased to give to it. And, if you, Monseigneur, are pleased to grant us the favor I am requesting, there will be no difficulties. I am, in His love. . . ."

2908. - TO ANTOINE DURAND, SUPERIOR, IN AGDE

Paris, July 18, 1659

Monsieur,

The grace of O[ur] L[ord] be with you forever!

Like you, I am deeply grieved, and rightly so, at the conduct of M. Brisjonc and Brother Thierry.[1] May God grant them the grace of opening their eyes to see the danger in which they now are in following the inclinations of rebellious nature in this way, which is never in harmony with the Spirit of Jesus Christ! Oh! how difficult it is, Scripture says, for those who fall, after having been enlightened, to rise again! [2] Surely, they have great reason to fear going dangerously astray, if they leave the path on which God has placed them; for how will they do their duty in the world if they do not do it in their present state of life, aided by all those graces of God and the spiritual and temporal help which they will not have apart from their vocation? Yet, we should not be surprised to see persons who waver and forget themselves; they are to be found in the holiest Companies, and God permits this to show men the wretchedness of man, to give the firmest and most resolute persons reason to fear, to test the good, and to make both practice various virtues.

It is to be desired that that good priest and that poor Brother may feel some remorse for their past faults, resolve to mend their ways, and make reparation for the bad example they have given. I ask O[ur] L[ord] to grant them this grace, and you, Monsieur, to aid them in this. If, then, you see that they are in this disposition and have really left their unruliness behind, send M. Brisjonc to La Rose[3] and the Brother to Cahors. Give them the money they need

---

Letter 2908. - Archives of the Mission, Paris, rough draft in the secretary's handwriting.

[1]Jean Thierry, born in Cahors in 1628, entered the Congregation of the Mission as a coadjutor Brother in Marseilles in 1648.

[2]Cf. Heb 6:4-6. (NAB)

[3]François Brisjonc never went to La Rose; he left the Company in this same month of July. René Alméras readmitted him on May 17, 1664.

to go, and letters for Messieurs Chrétien[4] and Cuissot[5] the Superiors to tell them you have orders from me to send them. I will not fail to inform them of this by the first mail and ask them to receive them.

In speaking of Messieurs Lebas[6] and Dolivet,[7] you tell me that their virtue is a little burdensome to the others, and I believe it; but it is so to those who are less regular, punctual, fervent, and solicitous for their own advancement and that of their confreres. Yes, Monsieur, their zeal and exactness are painful to those who do not have these virtues because their observance is a reproof to their own laxity.

I admit that virtue is accompanied by two vices: excess and default; but excess is praiseworthy in comparison with default, and should be tolerated more. Job complained to God of the severity of His punishments.[8] His friends, who had been witnesses of his righteousness,[9] considered that his complaints did not befit a just

---

[4]Jean Chrétien, born in Oncourt (Vosges) on August 6, 1606, was ordained a priest on April 5, 1631, and entered the Congregation of the Mission on November 26, 1640. He was Superior in Marseilles (1645-53), sub-Assistant at the Motherhouse (1654), and Superior in La Rose (1655-62). On November 26, 1667, he was a member of the Troyes house.

[5]Gilbert Cuissot, born in Moulins (Allier) on November 5, 1607, had been a priest for six years when he entered the Congregation of the Mission on May 14, 1637. After serving as Superior of the Luçon house, he was appointed to the same office in La Rose (1640-44), then at the Collège des Bons-Enfants (1644-46), where he took his vows on November 11, 1644. From there he went to the Le Mans Seminary (1646), then to Saint-Lazare (1646-47). He was Director of the Cahors Seminary (1647-62) and Superior of the Richelieu house (1662-66). Cuissot declared that, at the time of the election of Saint Vincent's successor, he was hesitant about voting for René Alméras, who was in poor health, but the Saint appeared to him and determined his choice. He also said that in 1662, while exorcising a possessed woman, he drew from the demon an acknowledgment of the Founder's holiness and the reward reserved by God for Missionaries faithful to their vocation. Cuissot died in 1666.

[6]Toussaint Lebas, born in Josselin (Morbihan) on November 1, 1625, was ordained a priest on May 25, 1652, eve of the Feast of the Most Holy Trinity, and entered the Congregation of the Mission in Richelieu on January 2, 1653. A short time later he was sent to the Agde house, where he took his vows in 1657, in the presence of Thomas Berthe. He was Superior in Narbonne (1671-73).

[7]Julien Dolivet, born in Cardroc (Ille-et-Vilaine), was ordained a priest on March 30, 1652, entered the Congregation of the Mission in Richelieu on January 2, 1653, and took his vows in Agde in March 1656 in the presence of M. Berthe. He was Superior in Sedan (1668-73) and in Narbonne (1673-82).

[8]Cf. Job 10:1-2. (NAB)

[9]Cf. Job 32:1. (NAB)

man; they seemed excessive to them[10] and they reproached him for them. But God was angered by this, and the holy man had to offer sacrifice to Him on their behalf to appease Him.[11] His virtue was so great and so pleasing to God that he was right in saying what he did; yet people blamed him for it. And why? Because they were like those whose eyes are sore or bleary and who cannot look at the sun's rays without being pained by them. In the same way, these two good Missionaries are attaining a higher degree of virtue than the others, who imagine that it is excessive, whereas in the sight of God it is not. They find fault with the way they act because they do not have the courage to imitate them. May God grant all of us, in Our Lord, the grace to regard as good everything that is not bad!

Thank you, Monsieur, for coming to Montpellier to replace M. Get and for what you have written me about it, which has consoled me. I am, in the love of O[ur] L[ord], Monsieur, your most humble servant.

2909. - TO EDME JOLLY, SUPERIOR, IN ROME

Paris, July 18, 1659

Monsieur,

The grace of O[ur] L[ord] be with you forever!

I received your letter of June 23. I thank God that the conditions of our vow of poverty have finally been approved through your care, vigilance, and the grace that accompanies you.[1] I ask O[ur] L[ord] to be glorified by this and to continue and increase His blessings to you.

---

[10]Cf. Job 8:2; 11:2-3; 15:12-13. (NAB)

[11]Cf. Job 42:7-9. (NAB)

Letter 2909. - Archives of the Mission, Paris, original signed letter.

[1]The Papal Brief of Alexander VII *Alias nos,* "Brief on the Vow of Poverty taken in the Congregation of the Mission," bears the date August 12, 1659 (cf. vol. XIII, no. 120).

If the faculty for the reception of Orders *ad titulum mensae communis* [2] is refused us, we will not be too upset. We should will what God wills, and nothing more. However, if it is granted us, Monsieur, it is to be desired that it be done by a separate Brief and not conjointly with the conditions of our vow of poverty. Our first Brief on the vows[3] contains two things we would have preferred separated, for certain important reasons.

I am quite convinced that your house needs a large number of workers and that they should be good ones and, if you cannot send one to Genoa in place of M. Lejuge, he will have to be replaced from somewhere else. We have fifteen or sixteen students; when they finish their studies,[4] we will select some of the best to send you so as to strengthen your family.

If the Corsican affair is going to take a long time, so much the better.[5]

There is reason to praise God for the zeal He gives you for the salvation of country folk and that your priests are always ready to go and work there, despite their past labors, which were[6] long, and the present hot weather, which is to be feared. I am deeply consoled by this, and I ask O[ur] L[ord] to continue to grant the same zeal to you and the same fidelity to them. Still, I must confess, Monsieur, that I would have been even more pleased if they had returned to Rome to rest rather than going to the Leonessa area,[7] where they are now, because they may give way after having worked so hard,

---

[2] *Under the title of common table.* Since members of the Congregation of the Mission were not diocesan clergy, their title for ordination was based on "the common table" and not on incardination in a diocese. The title for ordination is required to guarantee a permanent and proper maintenance for the ordained. Today, *Title for Common Life* is used for religious who profess simple, perpetual vows in a clerical society of Apostolic Life (Canon 266).

[3] Cf. the Brief of September 22, 1655, *Ex commissa nobis,* by which Alexander VII approved the vows taken in the Congregation of the Mission (vol. XIII, no. 113).

[4] First redaction: "many of whom have almost completed their studies." The correction is in the Saint's handwriting.

[5] The project for an establishment of Missionaries on the island.

[6] First redaction: "which are." The correction is in the Saint's handwriting.

[7] A town of central Italy, in the Province of Aquila.

and because we have a greater obligation to our Rule than to works of supererogation. Now, you know that our missions come to a halt during these three months of July, August, and September, which we set aside to catch our breath and recoup a little energy. I hope, nevertheless, that God will be the strength and virtue of those good Missionaries, will bless their present mission, and will bless your good government more and more.

Thank you for the *extra tempora* you sent us. We will try at this juncture to make use of the privilege of granting dimissorial letters.[8]

The Duchesse d'Aiguillon is greatly consoled to learn that her Mass will be said at Loreto from now on but is greatly surprised at the conduct of the person who took the sixteen hundred écus.[9]

It was with immense joy that I learned of the favor our Holy Father has granted for the canonization of the great servant of God, the Bishop of Geneva.[10] This leads us to hope that we will soon see him declared a saint.

I am, in the love of O[ur] L[ord], Monsieur, your most humble servant.

VINCENT DEPAUL,
i.s.C.M.

At the bottom of the first page: M. Jolly

---

[8]Letters giving a subject permission to be ordained by a Bishop other than his own Ordinary. Exempt religious cannot be ordained by any Bishop without dimissorial letters from their own Major Superior.

[9]Abbé Tinti.

[10]Thirteen years were still lacking for the fifty years required by the Church between the death of a servant of God and beatification. On June 21 the Pope had granted a dispensation from this requirement for the canonization of Francis de Sales.

Saint Francis de Sales, who honored Saint Vincent with his friendship, was born in Thorens, near Annecy, on August 21, 1567, and died in Lyons on December 28, 1622. "Many times I have had the honor of enjoying the close friendship of Francis de Sales," declared the Saint at the beatification process of his illustrious friend on April 17, 1628. He always spoke of the Bishop of Geneva with great admiration, considering him worthy of the honors reserved to the saints. According to Coqueret, a Doctor of the Sorbonne, Francis de Sales, on his part, used to say that "he did not know a more worthy or more saintly priest than M. Vincent." (Postulatory letter from the Bishop of Tulle, March 21, 1706.) When it came to appointing a Superior for the convent of the Visitation in Paris, he chose Vincent de Paul.

2910. - TO GASPARD STELLE, IN GENOA

Paris, July 18, 1659

Monsieur,

The grace of O[ur] L[ord] be with you forever!

I was consoled by the letter you wrote me and the request you made because they come from a heart that truly belongs to God and wants nothing to be lacking in the services you render Him. God be praised, Monsieur, for the desire He has given you to be a perfect Missionary and to join knowledge to virtue in you. You have striven after both, thank God, and are continuing to do so. You already have sufficient knowledge to begin the works to which God has called you; that was apparent to us while you were here and is still apparent to those who see you there. The desire to learn is good, provided it is moderated.

Virtue is always accompanied by two vices, and this love of learning may be imperfect either by default or excess. Yours is not of the first kind, thank God; and, so that it may not be of the second, remember the advice of Saint Paul, who recommends that we be wise unto sobriety.[1] An average amount suffices, and what a person wishes to have beyond that is rather to be feared than desired by Gospel workers because it is dangerous. It puffs up,[2] incites us to put ourselves forward, to become conceited and, in a word, to avoid humble, simple, and ordinary actions, which are, however, the most useful ones. That is why Our Lord took as His disciples men who were not capable of doing any others.[3]

Rest assured, Monsieur, that experience will soon teach you what you lack. If you are not sufficiently instructed now in the more difficult and essential subjects, such as usury, matrimony, etc., they

---

Letter 2910. - Archives of the Mission, Paris, unsigned rough draft in the secretary's handwriting.

[1]Cf. Rom 12:3. (NAB)

[2]Cf. 1 Cor 8:1. (NAB)

[3]Cf. Mt 4:18-22. (NAB)

are discussed during the mission and in conversation, when the common opinions held on the questions proposed are set forth. In addition, between the time of missions, conferences on them are held at which light is thrown on all obscure points. I will write to tell M. Pesnelle to establish this custom so that by this means you can receive a solid formation, and thereby advance securely in the service of souls.

O Monsieur, how indebted we are to God for having sent us, as He sent His eternal Son, for their salvation![4] Let us hope that, if we work at this in the Spirit of Our Lord, He will give us the light and grace to succeed. If you want to know only Jesus Christ crucified, if you want to live only His life,[5] have no doubt, Monsieur, that He Himself will be your knowledge and your action. Continue to abandon yourself entirely to Him and to put your trust in His strength and competence; this will show you that there is nothing in the world so great and so desirable as the justification of sinners, nothing so holy as to be employed at that, and nothing so well calculated to progress happily in it than the manner with which God has inspired the Company, which closely resembles the one O[ur] L[ord] adopted to enlighten the world[6] and to win it over to God.

Since, then, you love the end of our little Institute, you also love the means to attain it, which are indicated in our Rules. And if you say you have some distaste for our works, that is only a natural repugnance, which fears the embarrassment it may encounter in it if it does not surpass or equal others in practice and success. You must not leave things at that, but always delve deeper into the love of your own abjection and tend toward the lowliest positions. In this way O[ur] L[ord] will abide in you; He will be the vine[7] and you the branch that bears fruit and will bear more abundant fruit that will rejoice heaven. This is the prayer I offer Him. I am in His love, Monsieur, your most humble servant.

---

[4]Cf. Lk 4:18; Jn 6:38. (NAB)
[5]Cf. Gal 2:19-20. (NAB)
[6]Cf. Jn 8:12. (NAB)
[7]Cf. Jn 15:5. (NAB)

2911. - TO JEAN MARTIN, SUPERIOR, IN TURIN

Paris, July 18, 1659

Monsieur,

The grace of O[ur] L[ord] be with you forever!

Although I have not received your dear letters, I have learned, nevertheless, that God has singularly blessed your work during your latest missions and that, by His powerful grace, you have brought about a large number of very difficult, important reconciliations. May His Holy Name be forever blessed and glorified for this, and may He grant the people you have set on the right road the grace to walk straight on it by the practice of good works which lead to heaven! You will receive an abundant reward there for all the good works you have done, placing you in the state where an infinite number of souls will one day recognize you before God as their second redeemer!

Is not the proverb "No pain, no gain" verified in you, Monsieur, since you take such pains to reconcile these men with God and with one another? Indeed, I am afraid you are undertaking too much and are exhausting yourself, for I am told that you are quite weak and in very low spirits. In the name of God, Monsieur, get a good rest in this interval between missions, and moderate your labors in the future. You will practice greater charity by preserving yourself so as to serve your neighbor for a long time than by wearing yourself out quickly for the salvation of a few.

That is all I have to say to you now. We are all very well here, thank God; everything is going along as usual, and the same is true elsewhere in all our houses.

Speaking of houses, however, I must tell you something I have already written to a few other Superiors; namely, that the custom in all Communities, and especially in ours, is that each subject is

---

Letter 2911. - Archives of the Mission, Turin, original signed letter. The postscript is in the Saint's handwriting.

free to write to the General without showing his letters to his local Superior. There are many reasons for this, but especially so that he may pour out his heart and find some relief in the spiritual trials which many experience. I am sure you are quite content for all the members of your family to use this liberty freely.

I embrace all of them and am, with all my heart in the love of O[ur] L[ord], Monsieur, your most humble servant.

VINCENT DEPAUL,
i.s.C.M.

It would be well, Monsieur, to let the whole Community know of this practice.

Addressed: Monsieur Martin

2912. - TO AUBIN GONTIER,[1] IN TURIN

Paris, July 18, 1659

Dear Brother,

The grace of O[ur] L[ord] be with you forever!

Thank you for the good news you gave me by telling me of the good results of the missions being given there. It seems that the

---

Letter 2912. - Archives of the Mission, Paris, seventeenth-century copy.

Coste originally gave Aubin *Gautier* as the addressee for this letter, but his corrections in vol. XIII, p. 850, stated that the name should be *Gontier.* The only other place Gontier is used is in vol. V, no. 1901; Saint Vincent refers to him everywhere else simply as Brother Aubin. Aubin Gontier cannot be found in *Notices,* vol. I or vol. V (Supplement), but the information for Aubin *Gautier* is similar to that given by Coste in vol. V, no. 1901. In his *Life and Works of Saint Vincent de Paul,* trans. by Joseph Leonard, C.M. (3 vols., Westminster, MD: Newman Press, 1952), vol. 2, p. 28, Coste refers to him as Brother Gautier. The editors have adopted the spelling and clarification of the information given in *Notices.*

[1]Aubin Gautier (Gontier), born in Espaume (Chartres diocese) on October 10, 1627, entered the Congregation of the Mission in Paris as a coadjutor Brother on August 16, 1654, and took his vows in Turin, on February 9, 1657, in the presence of M. Martin.

hand of God is in them, and I would like to think that your prayers, hard work, and good example have contributed to this. May God grant you the grace, dear Brother, to continue to edify those inside and outside the family by always remaining lowly and always united to O[ur] L[ord]!

You pleased me by telling me the other things that have happened, and I will make use of this with God's help. Please keep up your care and charitable services for good M. Martin in the missions and wherever else he will have greater need of them, and continue to prepare chicken broth to nourish and sustain him in his exhaustion, whenever the Assistant thinks it advisable, no matter how others may criticize this. You know that the preservation of this good servant of God is important for the service of souls and very dear to the Company.

Have no difficulty about taking to the post letters that are for me, even though the Superior has not seen them; he is well aware that every Missionary has the right to pour out his heart to the Superior General.

I recommend myself to your prayers and to those of the Brothers with you, to whom I send heartfelt greetings.

I am, in O[ur] L[ord], dear Brother, your most affectionate brother and servant.

VINCENT DEPAUL,
i.s.C.M.

2913. - TO JEAN-JACQUES PLANCHAMP,[1] IN TURIN

Paris, July 18, 1659

Monsieur,

The grace of O[ur] L[ord] be with you forever!

I can assure you that I received as much consolation from your letter as I have experienced in a long time. God be blessed, Monsieur, for the fidelity He gives you for your vocation and the humble sentiments you have of yourself! That is the way to draw to yourself grace upon grace, since God gives it to the humble—and to the humble detached from flesh and blood.

The worries you have concerning your relatives are a sign that your heart is distanced from them and that you will have no difficulty telling them once and for all that you have given yourself to God so as not to have any further dealings with the world. If you do so, Monsieur, there is reason to hope they will allow you to serve God in peace or that God will give you the grace He gave a certain person in the Company, who was unwilling to become involved with the affairs of his family, though often urged to do so.

I will not fail to consider the proposal you make me, and I already see an opportunity of withdrawing you from the place where you are, so as to give you the means of rendering good service to God. But we must look more clearly into His plans and ask Him to make His holy Will known to you. Meanwhile, Monsieur, always remain indifferent to places and duties. This is essential if a person is to be an instrument in God's hands, as you are,

---

Letter 2913. - Archives of the Mission, Turin, original signed letter.

[1]Jean-Jacques Planchamp, born in Mionnay (Ain) on December 8, 1627, was ordained a priest in 1651. He entered the Congregation of the Mission on April 29, 1655, and took his vows in Turin on May 12, 1657, in the presence of M. Martin. Planchamp left the Company in 1659.

through His infinite goodness, to whom I ask you to recommend my soul, which cherishes yours tenderly.

I am, in the love of O[ur] L[ord], Monsieur, your most humble servant.

VINCENT DEPAUL,
i.s.C.M.

Addressed: Monsieur Planchamp, Priest of the Mission, in Turin

2914. - TO JEAN PARRE, IN SAINT-QUENTIN

Paris, July 19, 1659

Dear Brother,

The grace of O[ur] L[ord] be with you forever!

I received your letter of the fourteenth and had it shown to the Ladies, who were consoled by what you tell me and what you are doing to assure good order in the devotions at Notre-Dame-de-Fieulaine.[1] There is reason to praise God for having made use of you for this work after so many others. May His Divine Goodness be pleased to give you an ever greater share in His Spirit so that He will always be glorified by your work and your leadership! I ask

---

Letter 2914. - Archives of the Mission, Paris, original signed letter.

[1]The shrine of Notre-Dame-de-la-Paix in Fieulaine (cf. no. 2902).

Him for this with all my heart and am, in His love, dear Brother, your most humble servant.

VINCENT DEPAUL,
i.s.C.M.

Let me know if you are acquainted with the lad who sent me the enclosed, and if you think he is suitable for us and has the right intention.

At the bottom of the page: Brother Jean

2915. - TO ANNE-MARGUERITE GUÉRIN,[1] SUPERIOR OF THE SECOND VISITATION MONASTERY, IN PARIS

Saint-Lazare, July 20, 1659

Dear Sister,

The grace of O[ur] L[ord] be with you forever!

The letter you wrote me has caused me to share—and, I may say, very keenly—in the distress you are suffering. My desire to see you delivered from it has led me to ask Our Lord to be pleased to bring to a swift conclusion the business you mention, by showing you the blessed place where He wishes to be honored by your holy Institute.[2]

I do not approve of the delay any more than you do, dear Sister,

---

Letter 2915. - Archives of the Mission, Paris, unsigned rough draft in the secretary's handwriting.

[1]Anne-Marguerite Guérin entered the Visitation Order at the First Monastery in Paris (rue Saint-Antoine) but was sent to the Second Monastery (faubourg Saint-Jacques) as Assistant at the time of its foundation in 1626. Superior there from May 24, 1640, to May 21, 1643, she became the first Superior of the Third Monastery in Paris (rue Montorgueil) in 1659. She died on January 24, 1669, at seventy-seven years of age.

[2]The question of the foundation of a third Visitation Monastery in Paris was being discussed.

but have not changed my mind at all about the large house on rue Montorgueil. I cannot persuade myself that it should be purchased,[3] either in whole or in part: in whole, because, being very expensive, it could bankrupt the house where you now are; in part, because just half of the purchase price would eat up all your funds, and that is inadvisable, for something must remain to help the Sisters of the foundation support themselves. You tell me that it takes very little to feed eight nuns. I think, dear Sister, that in Paris, all things considered, it costs no less than three thousand livres; where would you get them?

You add that you are obliged by the contract to use the legacy and gift of the late Monsieur and Madame d'Amfreville[4] to purchase a house or a site, but I reply that it does not state that the entire sum should be spent only on a residence, but it should be understood that the money is to be used to the advantage of the foundation. Those who lend or give money for some acquisition usually intend that it be quite clear that their money has actually been used for that. Now, since it was the intention of the deceased to found a monastery of your Order, they certainly never meant to provide you with a splendid residence and leave you with no possibility of living in it and filling it, as would happen if you had nothing to support you.

You also say that there are some aspirants who will provide their own maintenance. I reply that their dowries would have to be used even before the Community could acquire them.

As for the lady who wants to be a benefactress, well and good, that will happen in its own good time.

I admit that we can expect something from Providence, but we should not tempt God who, having provided you with reasonable means to begin and carry on an establishment while observing the

---

[3]First redaction: "I cannot consent to its purchase."

[4]The bequest of M. Amfreville, second Chief Justice of the Rouen Parlement, increased by the liberalities of his wife, constituted a fund of 52,000 livres. The purchase of the house on rue Montorgueil amounted to 41,000 livres.

Rule of religious poverty, does not want you to make a superfluous expenditure and then to entrust yourselves to His Providence.

I must tell you at this point, dear Sister, that we are seeing a number of bankrupt Communities in Paris—not because of a lack of confidence in God, but because they have erected magnificent buildings, and this has not only exhausted their resources but put them in debt. Since the religious spirit must have as a point of reference that of Our Lord, who willed to practice radical poverty on earth, going so far as not having a stone on which to lay His head,[5] the more persons living in religion distance themselves from that poverty, the greater difficulty they will have in maintaining themselves because splendid edifices, so little in harmony with their profession, are not pleasing to God.

Nevertheless, those who have such places are not to be condemned if they have the wherewithal to keep them up and to support themselves, and I would not want to hinder you from doing likewise, if your present means allowed it. But you might succumb beneath the weight of such an expensive house, which will be very costly because it is old and will be in constant need of repairs. We know this from experience at Saint-Lazare, which is also old, and almost always in need of masons, costing us more than the interest on the money it would take for an entirely new building. Would you not have great regret, dear Sister, if your foundation should fail some day because you had undertaken this enterprise, or if your monastery should run into difficulties for not having practiced at this time the holy poverty you have vowed and which, thank God, you observe in everything else?

It seems to you, you say, that you constantly hear inwardly the late Madame d'Amfreville reproaching you because her last wishes have not been carried out. It is not she, dear Sister, who speaks to you in that way, because she is now where she wills only what God wills, and God wills only what is within your power. He wants you

---

[5]Cf. Mt 8:20. (NAB)

to be content for the present with a modest, medium-priced residence, because you have the money to pay for it, to put it in order, and to provide for other necessities. And He does not want you to go beyond that, because you do not have the means of doing so and the poverty you have embraced cannot allow it.

So, then, choose a place suitable to your plan and in line with your possibilities and situation. Can it be that such a one has not yet been found or cannot be found in such a large city, where there are so many different kinds of lodgings? I cannot imagine, dear Sister, that one cannot be found, if you have someone look for it.[6] That is what should be done, and what I very humbly ask you to do in order to accomplish the good work God has entrusted to your care. I hope He will bless it through your good governance, as He has blessed all the others that have passed through your hands, by the grace He has bestowed on you, which causes me to have such a special esteem for you and a very deep tenderness for your dear soul. With this sentiment I am, in O[ur] L[ord]. . . .

2916. - TO LOUIS RIVET, SUPERIOR, IN SAINTES

Paris, July 21, 1659

Monsieur,

The grace of O[ur] L[ord] be with you forever!

I received your letter of the thirteenth. M. Lestradie's nephew left Saint-Charles without saying good-bye. It was last Friday, when he went to transact some business he said he had in the city but did not return. I was unaware of this until today when, wishing

---

[6]The Saint's advice was not followed, perhaps because some recent donations facilitated the purchase of the house on which Sister Anne-Marguerite had set her sights. The Visitation nuns took possession of it on July 25, 1660.

Letter 2916. - Archives of the Mission, Paris, seventeenth-century copy.

to learn from your brother[1] whether they could keep him as a paying guest for 350 livres, everything included, he told me he had left. He added that, not only would they be unwilling to keep him for that sum but even for much more because that is not something with which they should get involved, no more than we should.

We will send a Visitor[2] to Richelieu in two or three days, who will go to see you in Saintes. He will also see M. Fleury,[3] whose vows he will receive, if he perseveres in wanting to take them.

Since the Greek Archbishop who was in Saintes is no longer there, it would be useless to say anything to you about him.

I think you know that I have been troubled with a sore eye for a very long time, but I am now almost cured, thank God. I recommend to Him your health and that of your family, for the services you and it render Him and also because I am, in His love, Monsieur, your most humble servant.

VINCENT DEPAUL,
i.s.C.M.

2917. - *THE DUCHESSE D'AIGUILLON TO SAINT VINCENT*

[July 1659] [1]

Enclosed is the letter you wanted from the Bishop of Poitiers [2] *for the*

---

[1]François Rivet, born in Houdan (Yvelines) on July 28, 1628, entered the Congregation of the Mission on October 12, 1647, took his vows on November 6, 1650, and was ordained a priest on April 1, 1656. Another brother, Jacques, was a coadjutor Brother in the Congregation.

[2]Saint Vincent sent Jean Dehorgny to make canonical visitations of the houses in Le Mans, Richelieu, Saint-Méen, Tréguier, Nantes, Luçon, Saintes, Agen, La Rose, and Cahors. He spent from August 1659 to September 1660 at this task.

[3]Antoine Fleury, born in Bully (Rhône) in September 1624, entered the Congregation of the Mission as a priest on August 28, 1657, and took his vows in Saintes on January 18, 1660, in the presence of M. Dehorgny.

Letter 2917. - Archives of the Mission, Turin, original autograph letter.

[1]Reference to the Huguenot Synod, held in 1659, enables us to assign this date.

[2]Gilbert de Clerambault de Palluau (1659-January 3, 1680).

Bishop of Cahors [3] *and the one written by Abbé Roquépine,*[4] *to whom I had recourse to obtain it.*

The Bishop of Cahors should leave immediately because the synod has already started.[5]

Please let me know if Brother Jean Parre has arrived, so that we can go to the meeting on Wednesday, if he is there.

The Marquise de Vigean[6] *has been very ill. That is why she did not send you any information on your affair. I recommend her to your Holy Sacrifices and entreat you also not to forget this wretched sinner during them.*

Addressed: *Monsieur Vincent, General of the Priests of the Mission*

2918. - TO EDME MENESTRIER, SUPERIOR, IN AGEN

Paris, July 23, 1659

Monsieur,

The grace of O[ur] L[ord] be with you forever!

I received your letter of the eleventh. I am too busy just now to be able to answer it. I write merely to ask you to forward the enclosed to M. Chrétien and to recommend myself to your prayers and to those of M. Admirault[1] and our Brothers, whom I embrace,

---

[3]Alain de Solminihac.

[4]Charles du Bouzet, Sieur de Roquépine, chaplain (1648-58) to Anne of Austria.

[5]In his conference of August 5, 1659, to the Missionaries, Saint Vincent speaks of this synod and of the mission organized by the Bishop of Cahors to combat the propaganda of the Huguenots (cf. vol. XII, no. 210, "On Moral Theology, Preaching, the Catechism, and the Administration of the Sacraments"). From the way he is talking, the Saint gives the impression that the mission was still in progress at that date.

[6]Anne de Neubourg, wife of François Poussart de Fors, Marquis du Vigean. The "beautiful Baroness," as the French writer Voiture, one of the models of preciosity, styled her, was closely associated with the Duchesse d'Aiguillon. Voiture also gives a description of her magnificent country house in La Barre, near Montmorency (cf. Vincent Voiture, *Oeuvres* [new ed., Paris: Firmin-Didot frères, 1858], p. 93).

Letter 2918. - Archives of the Mission, Paris, original signed letter.

[1]Claude Admirault, born in Chinon (Indre-et-Loire), entered the Congregation of the Mission on September 20, 1648, at sixteen years of age, took his vows in 1651, was ordained a priest in

prostrate in spirit at your feet. I am, in the love of O[ur] L[ord], Monsieur, your most humble servant.

VINCENT DEPAUL,
i.s.C.M.

At the bottom of the page: M. Edme

2919. - TO JEAN MONVOISIN, IN MONTMIRAIL

Paris, July 24, 1659

Monsieur,

The grace of O[ur] L[ord] be with you forever!

We are very upset by poor Brother Pinson's[1] mental instability and departure. *Mon Dieu!* Monsieur, where could he have gone? He did not come here; but, if he does come, we will receive him with joy.

Please let me know in which places you are going to give missions, where you had the honor of seeing the Bishop of Soissons,[2] who was with you, and what took place during that interview.

In the future I will be happy to know in what parishes you will be working and the results of your missions, along with anything important—spiritual as well as temporal—that occurs in your house.

You are aware that it is a Community custom to change nothing in the houses nor make any important decisions without the advice of the General or the Visitor.

December 1656, and was placed at the Agen Seminary. He was Superior of the seminaries in Montauban (1665-75, 1686-90) and Agen (1690-94).

Letter 2919. - Archives of the Mission, Paris, original signed letter.

[1]Denis Pinson, born in Villers-sous-Saint-Leu (Oise) in 1630, entered the Congregation of the Mission as a coadjutor Brother on July 17, 1654.

[2]Charles de Bourbon.

Speaking of the Visitor, I have asked M. Berthe, who is in Sedan and is about to leave there, to go to see you in passing.

Please tell M. Cornuel[3] that, since the last letter I wrote to him, nothing has happened in the Bétharram[4] affair. I am awaiting an answer from the Bishop of Lescar[5] concerning the explanation we requested of him.[6]

I embrace all of you, prostrate in spirit at your feet.

I am, in the love of O[ur] L[ord], Monsieur, your most humble servant.

VINCENT DEPAUL,
i.s.C.M.

---

[3]Guillaume Cornuel, born in Bar-sur-Aube (Aube), entered the Congregation of the Mission on November 29, 1644, at twenty-three years of age, took his vows in 1646, was ordained a priest in December of that same year, and died in the Troyes diocese in 1666. He was twice Superior in Montmirail (1649-50, and 1658-59), also at the Collège des Bons-Enfants (1652-54), and Troyes (1665-66). His first cousin, Pierre de Vienne, Seigneur de Torvilliers, mourned his death with several lyric poems in Latin, published in Troyes, to which Jacques de la Fosse, C.M., made a suitable response with several odes. (Cf. Abbé Jean-Baptiste-Joseph Boulliot, *Biographie ardennaise* [2 vols., Paris: n. p., 1830], vol. I, p. 420; Bibl. Maz., Ms. 3912.)

[4]Bétharram is situated in the commune of Lestelle (Pyrénées-Atlantiques), not far from Lourdes. In 1614, Jean de Salettes, Bishop of Lescar, had a chapel built there; under the direction of the Missionaries of Garaison (1615-21), it had rapidly become the center of a very popular pilgrimage. Léonard de Trapes, Archbishop of Auch (1600-29), once led there a pilgrimage of ten thousand persons. He erected three crosses on the top of the hill and left in the sanctuary a statue of the Blessed Virgin, which he himself had carried there. Hubert Charpentier, whom the Bishop of Lescar had put in charge of the chaplains, was a man of great virtue and integrity. In 1621 he founded in Bétharram the Congregation of the Priests of Notre-Dame-du-Calvaire, which was still serving at the shrine in 1659. The increasing renown of Notre-Dame-de-Bétharram won the favor of Popes and the aristocracy. Louis XIII, Anne of Austria, the Brienne and Montmorency families, and the leading families of Béarn and Gascony became its benefactors. The history of the shrine was written by Canon Dubarat, to whom we owe many valuable works on the Pyrénées-Atlantiques. (Cf. Victor-Pierre Dubarat, *Bétharram et le Mont-Valérien* [Paris, 1897].)

[5]Jean du Haut de Salies wanted the Congregation of the Mission to assume the direction of the shrine.

[6]The letter to the Bishop of Lescar never reached him; the Saint did not become aware of this until a year later (cf. no. 3191).

2920. - TO JACQUES PESNELLE, SUPERIOR, IN GENOA

Paris, July 25, 1659

Monsieur,

The grace of O[ur] L[ord] be with you forever!

I was very happy to receive a detailed report on the state of your family; I thank you most affectionately for it. It is compiled in such an excellent manner that I think I see things as they are. There is reason to hope that they will continue to improve under your wise leadership, which seems humble, charitable, simple, and wise. God is always present in the practice of these virtues, especially in the first two; and, to the degree that you try to put them into practice, rest assured, Monsieur, that God will work in you and through you, and everything will turn out well.

M. Caron's[1] mental and physical state demand not only that his vows be delayed but that he should not take them at all, and consequently, should not remain any longer in the Company. Therefore, please ask him to leave whenever he wishes; give him as the reason the fear that he is tubercular and unable to subject himself to a regulated life or to perform our works. Please give him a little money so he can provide for himself.

As for the young man from Chiavari who is complaining about his head and stomach, have him refrain from any mental strain, even from meditation; or, if he does make it, let it be made passively, receiving whatever God gives him, without seeking thoughts to arouse his affections. He could make an act of faith and a simple preparation at the beginning, then leave it at that because God wills it, since he is incapable of meditating and unworthy to converse with His Divine Majesty, and his only other concern should be to

---

Letter 2920. - Archives of the Mission, Paris, original signed letter.

[1]There is no entry for a M. Caron in the personnel lists available. We know from vol. VII, no. 2870 (June 13, 1659), that he was to be ordained and, from a number of letters in this volume, that he left the Company.

avoid bringing on tension headaches. He may be very distracted, but that does not matter; he is not seeking distractions and, with God's help, will not entertain any voluntarily. If the pain is very severe, he should even be dispensed from prayer for a time.

What I am saying with regard to him applies to others who might suffer from the same ailment; the seminary director[2] should be on the watch for this, often recommending and teaching the seminarians to become interior without mental strain, to immerse themselves in God by a simple consideration with no attempt to gain His presence by emotional efforts, to abandon themselves to Him without reasoning, and to strive to attain the virtues without trying to fathom them through knowledge or the imagination.

Brother Minvielle[3] can be admitted to vows at the end of his two years. We cannot prevent him from having passions, but if God so pleases, He will grant him the grace not to act on their urgings, by the attention he will pay to the opposite virtues.

Vows must be taken and renewed in the presence of the Superior or whomever he deputizes, and not before the director of the seminary as such. If this was sometimes done in the presence of the Saint-Lazare Seminary director, it was because neither I nor the person who represents me could be present for that holy act and, because of that, I asked someone else to take my place.

True, it would be a very good thing for the Superior always to stay at home, and you are right in saying that those in charge during his absence find it difficult on his return to be submissive and to give up the habit they have acquired of being in charge and giving orders. On the other hand, when the Superior does not go on mission, other inconveniences arise that are greater and more to be feared.

I am sending you the letter your brother wrote me in answer to the one he received from you. I replied to him that, since you have

---

[2]Pierre Pinon.

[3]Jean Minvielle, born in Pardies, Lescar diocese (Pyrénées-Atlantiques), entered the Congregation of the Mission in Paris on October 13, 1657, as a coadjutor Brother at twenty-seven years of age, and took his vows in Genoa on October 13, 1659, in the presence of M. Pesnelle.

already waited this long, you will still wait the length of time he requests. After mentioning some of the reasons why you feel obliged to seek your share,[4] I assured him that you have always felt this way, since it is true that you have written me along these lines from time to time. When your brother who is traveling gets back, we will see how they are disposed. I am disposed to be, in time and eternity, in the love of O[ur] L[ord], Monsieur, your most humble servant.

VINCENT DEPAUL,

i.s.C.M.

At the bottom of the first page: M. Pesnelle

2921. - TO EDME JOLLY, SUPERIOR, IN ROME

Paris, July 25, 1659

Monsieur,

The grace of O[ur] L[ord] be with you forever!

I cannot help but thank God, with my heart and voice and in writing, that our Holy Father the Pope has been pleased to approve the conditions of our poverty and to grant the Company, for ten years, the faculty to give a title to its subjects who have been driven from their country for religious beliefs, and this from the common table.[1] These are fresh benefits from God, due to the grace He has granted you, by which His Divine Goodness is pleased to bestow

---

[4]For three years Jacques Pesnelle had been contesting his brother's attempts to withhold from him his share of the inheritance from their father.

Letter 2921. - Archives of the Mission, Paris, original signed letter.

[1]This refers to the title or guaranteed basis of support needed before a man can be ordained (cf. no. 2909).

very great ones on the Company. My most humble thanks to you, Monsieur, for these latest ones and for all the trouble you have taken. Although this privilege is limited and restricted, you have still obtained a great deal as a starting point.

I am writing to ask M. Delaforcade to send you M. Abelly's books through the mail,[2] if he has not already sent them by some other means.

I ask you for another week before giving you my opinion on the approval of the Rules of the Confraternity of Charity, which M. Martin asked you to get; I want to think about it. I will say, however, that since this Confraternity is really spreading in society, I think God would bestow even greater blessings on it if the regulations were approved by His Holiness.

Please send us an *extra tempora* for *Nicolaus Arthur,*[3] *dioecesis Corkagiensis, in Hibernia.*

May God keep you, Monsieur, and bless you abundantly for the good of the little Congregation and for the particular consolation, Monsieur, of your most humble servant.

VINCENT DEPAUL,
i.s.C.M.

At the bottom of the first page: M. Jolly

---

[2]Cf. no. 2900.

[3]Nicholas Arthur (Artur) was born in Cork (Ireland) in December 1632. The only candidate to enter the Congregation of the Mission on October 23, 1654, he was officially received in Paris the following November 22, took his vows there in the presence of M. Berthe, and was ordained a priest *extra tempora* in 1659. Shortly after his ordination he was sent to Ireland, where he preached the Gospel successfully.

2922. - TO LOUIS FOUQUET, BISHOP OF AGDE [1]

Paris, July 26, 1659

Excellency,

I was taking care to find the priests you instructed me to send to Vézelay,[2] when Madame Fouquet your mother did me the honor of telling me that you, Excellency, had found some good men in that locality and that it sufficed to send you one Missionary to prepare them for your purposes. I told the above-mentioned lady that all of us are at your service, Excellency, ready to obey you everywhere and at any time, but I will venture to represent to you, as I now do, with all possible submission, that, as a rule, we suspend our work in the rural areas from July until October. We do this partly because the poor people are busy with the harvest and then with the grape gathering, and partly because our workers, who have labored hard all the rest of the year for the salvation of souls, need this time to refresh their tired bodies and minds so as to be able to return to the mission with renewed energy from All Saints' Day until about Saint John's Day.[3]

If you would agree, Excellency, to postpone your missions until October, we will send you at that time the priest you are requesting. If, however, you wish absolutely to have him with you immediately, Excellency, I will write to M. Tholard[4] telling him to be ready to leave as soon as I send him word, although he has just returned from work.

Letter 2922. - Archives of the Mission, Paris, original signed letter.

[1]Brother of Nicolas Fouquet, Attorney General and Superintendent of Finance, and François Fouquet, Archbishop of Narbonne.

[2]In the district of Avallon (Yonne). Louis Fouquet was Abbot of Vézelay.

[3]Probably June 24, feast of the Birth of Saint John the Baptist.

[4]Jacques Tholard was born in Auxerre (Yonne) on June 10, 1615, and entered the Congregation of the Mission on November 20, 1638. He was ordained a priest on December 17, 1639, and died after 1671. Throughout his life, in Annecy (1640-46), Tréguier, where he was Superior (1648-53), Troyes (1658-60), Saint-Lazare, Fontainebleau, and elsewhere, he manifested the qualities of an excellent Missionary. During the generalate of René Alméras, he was Visitor of the Provinces of France and of Lyons.

So, I will await the honor of your orders, Excellency, fully disposed to carry them out, with the help of God, on this occasion and on every other one. I am, by His grace and your permission, in His love, Excellency, your most humble and very obedient servant.

VINCENT DEPAUL,
i.s.C.M.

2923. - TO JEAN PARRE, IN SAINT-QUENTIN

Paris, July 26, 1659

Dear Brother,

The grace of O[ur] L[ord] be with you forever!

I received your letter of the twenty-first, but it was not given to me until Thursday; consequently, it was too late to be read at the meeting. They have no further instructions for you because you are busy with that holy work God is establishing, whereby you are putting a stop to superstitions and moderating the devotion of the poor people. The Ladies are very pleased with this and so am I, and I ask O[ur] L[ord] to grant you His Spirit for it.

Please let me know if there are any priests for the service of that chapel,[1] how many there are and their names, and whether the Bishop of Noyon[2] has sent one to be treasurer and responsible for the others because he instructed me some time ago to look for a

---

Letter 2923. - Archives of the Mission, Paris, original signed letter.

[1]Notre-Dame-de-la-Paix.

[2]Henri de Baradat (1626-60).

good priest suitable for that position. If he no longer needed such a person, I would not have to worry about that.

I am, in O[ur] L[ord], Monsieur, your most affectionate brother and servant.

VINCENT DEPAUL,
i.s.C.M.

Addressed: Brother Jean Parre, of the Mission, in Saint-Quentin

2924. - TO MONSIEUR DE FORGES [1]

Paris, July 27, 1659

Monsieur,

The grace of O[ur] L[ord] be with you forever!

I take the honor of writing this letter to give you news of M. Dufaur. I had assigned a priest to direct him in his retreat but was obliged to change him because I felt he agreed too much with M. Dufaur's own ideas. I gave him another one, who has just informed me that he left him determined to renounce vice and to devote himself to doing good. And because one of the obstacles to that is the way he dresses, I promised to have a cassock and a long cloak made for him and to pay the bill for it.

The problem of where to put him still remains, Monsieur. I have already told you that our rule forbids us to keep him here and give him the run of the house. We have another rule at the Collège des Bons-Enfants[2] which does not allow us to accept anyone unwilling

---

Letter 2924. - Archives of the Mission, Paris, copy of the original signed letter.

[1]Equerry for the Princesse de Conti, Anna Maria Martinozzi, Cardinal Mazarin's niece.

[2]On March 1, 1624, Jean-François de Gondi, Archbishop of Paris, turned over to Saint Vincent the direction of the Collège des Bons-Enfants so that he might have a place to lodge priests wishing to join him in giving missions in the country. Situated near the Porte Saint-Victor, on the site of the building now standing on the corner of rue des Écoles and rue Cardinal-

to subject himself to the seminary exercises—which he does not want to do, saying that he has to work on the lawsuit for which his uncle sent him here.

I do not think he can stay at Saint-Sulpice Seminary[3] either, Monsieur, nor at any other, with that stipulation of being able to come and go for a temporal affair, while skipping the instructions given there that are required for priests, for that would give bad example to the others. He suggests renting a room in a house in town with some good people.

I was anxious to give you a report of this, Monsieur, so that you might be so good as to get the instructions of the Prince[4] on this matter. While awaiting your reply, I renew the offers of my most humble service with all possible respect and affection. I am, in Our Lord, Monsieur, your most humble and most obedient servant.

VINCENT DEPAUL,
i.s.C.M.

Addressed: Monsieur de Forges, Equerry of the Princesse de Conti

---

Lemoine, this collège, nearly three hundred years old, was one of the oldest of the University of Paris. It was not a teaching center, but simply a hostel in which students were provided with shelter and sleeping quarters.

[3]Seminary founded by Jean-Jacques Olier.

[4]Armand de Bourbon, Prince de Conti, brother of the Grand Condé, was born in Paris on October 11, 1629, and became head of the Conti house, a cadet branch of the house of Bourbon-Condé. His father, who had earmarked him for the priesthood, had conferred on him a large number of abbeys, including Saint-Denis, Cluny, Lérins, and Molesme, but the military attracted him more than the Church. His passion for the Duchesse de Longueville drew him into the intrigues of the Fronde. After having him locked up in the prison of Vincennes, Cardinal Mazarin gave him his niece, Anna Maria Martinozzi, in marriage. The Prince became Governor of Guyenne (1654) and General of the armies in Catalonia, where he captured several cities. He was also Grand Master of the King's house and Governor of Languedoc (1660). Before his death on February 21, 1666, his virtuous wife was able to bring him back to God and even to instill great piety in him. Two hours of his day were devoted to prayer. A friend of Saint Vincent, he offered his services to him more than once and was present at his funeral.

2925. - TO EDME MENESTRIER, SUPERIOR, IN AGEN

Paris, July 27, 1659

Monsieur,

The grace of O[ur] L[ord] be with you forever!

God be praised that M. Admirault is recovering from the ailment he had! I pray that the Divine Goodness may cure him of it entirely.

Brother Didolet [1] always seemed to us to be a fine young man, just as you described him in your letter of the eleventh. True, he is not very strong physically, but you have to see to it that the little health he has is taken care of and be careful that mental effort does not harm his health nor bring on headaches and breathing problems. Recommend that he make his meditations in a relaxed and effortless manner, allowing his will to act, rather than his understanding, and raising his thoughts to God during the day. This should be done by simple intentions, without trying to make the presence of God perceptible.

Tell him to write to his mother to ask her [to send him a] valid title [that can be useful to him. The] attestation he [has cannot take the place] of a title because it states neither the content nor the value of his property and makes no mention of an assured estate to which the income of his title may be assigned. If his brother the Jesuit was accepted for Holy Orders on a similar attestation, perhaps it was because he was known by the Bishop who conferred them on him. If he has no safer way to write than via Paris, send me his letter; I will forward it to Chambéry and will have the answer sent. The

---

Letter 2925. - Archives of the Mission, Paris, original signed letter.

[1]Christophe Didolet, born in Aiguebelle (Savoy) on February 3, 1639, entered the Congregation of the Mission at the Paris Seminary on July 27, 1657, and took his vows on December 27, 1661, in the presence of M. Berthe.

Visitor [2] we will soon send your way, God willing, will receive him for v[ows].

I ask O[ur] L[ord] to provide for your temporal needs and to continue and increase the graces of the Spirit. I am, in His love, Monsieur, your most humble servant.

VINCENT DEPAUL,
i.s.C.M.

Addressed: Monsieur Edme

2926. - TO MARTIN BAUCHER,[1] IN SAINTES

Paris, July 27, 1659

Dear Brother,

The grace of O[ur] L[ord] be with you forever!

I was consoled by your letter and distressed by your grief. Since you know, however, that God is the cause of those accidents that deprive us of what is most dear to us in this world, so also we find in Him the remedy to our sorrows by conforming ourselves to His Will. You will have sought in this, dear Brother, the comfort of your heart, oppressed by the loss of your dear mother, and it is surely in His Will that you are finding great consolation.

I ask Our Lord to be both father and mother to you and to grant eternal rest to that good deceased lady, whom I have recommended to the prayers of the community. In addition, I had a note about her

---

[2]Jean Dehorgny was preparing to leave for canonical visitations of a number of houses, including Agen.

Letter 2926. - Archives of the Mission, Paris, seventeenth-century copy.

[1]Martin Baucher, born in Epône, in the Chartres diocese, entered the Congregation of the Mission as a coadjutor Brother in January 1653 and took his vows in Saintes on January 13, 1656, in the presence of M. Berthe. Coste refers to him as *Marin* Baucher, but in the catalogue of Coadjutor Brothers (1627-1786) he is listed as *Martin* Baucher.

placed in the sacristy and instructed the sacristan to have several Masses offered for her.

We have had your letters forwarded, and I could not refrain from writing this one to thank God, as I do, for having restored you to health. I thank Him also for granting you a special grace to serve Him faithfully in the observance of the Rules and the practice of virtue by abandoning yourself to His adorable Providence with regard to all the places and duties to which He will be pleased to call you. I see by your letter that you are disposed to do so—which I already knew from the report I received concerning you.

Dear Brother, continue to give God all the affection of your heart, the applications of your mind, and the work of your hands, and hope for great blessings from His Divine Goodness. Ask Him to have mercy on me, who am, in His love, dear Brother, your most affectionate brother and servant.

VINCENT DEPAUL,
i.s.C.M.

2927. - TO JEAN MARTIN, SUPERIOR, IN TURIN

Paris, August 1, 1659

Monsieur,

The grace of O[ur] L[ord] be with you forever!

It has been only two weeks since I wrote to you.[1] Since then I received your dear letter of July 12, which confirmed the good news given me of your health and the success of your mission. In all this, I admire the goodness of God, who brought you home safe and sound, after you had endured work capable of wearing out the

---

Letter 2927. - Archives of the Mission, Turin, original signed letter. The postscript is in the Saint's handwriting.

[1]Probably no. 2911 of July 18.

strongest men, and by means of weak instruments has obtained results beyond human power. Among these are the conversion of hardened sinners and the reconciliation of a large number of sworn enemies, who had been harboring mortal, inveterate hatred.

It is obvious, Monsieur, that Our Lord has been working along with you. May His Holy Name be forever blessed! I cannot thank Him enough for this; that is why I ask Him to be His own praise and thanks for all the graces He has granted you and, through you, to the poor people. O Monsieur, how grateful we must be that He has called us to His service in such a noble way!

We must bless God for the opposition raised in pursuit of the Sant'Antonio affair.[2] Since we desire only what is feasible, we must accept this obstacle. If it does not come from God, then His Providence will be able to remove it. We must be content that those who have undertaken the business and know the importance of the project will not be deterred, unless they see that it is hopeless.

I continue to have sentiments of reverence and gratitude for the Marquis your founder,[3] who never ceases to procure and grant you new favors. In this he imitates God who, once He has begun to do good for a creature, always continues to do so until the end.

I thank God, Monsieur, that the Nuncio is concerned with the promotion of knowledge and virtue in the priestly state and for the

---

[2]Proceedings were underway to unite Sant'Antonio Abbey in Piedmont to the Congregation of the Mission.

[3]Filippo Emmanuele Filiberto Giacinte di Simiane, Marchese di Pianezza, had distinguished himself by his bravery in the wars of Monferrato and Genoa, earning the title of Colonel-General of the Infantry. A clever diplomat, he attracted the attention of the Madame Royale, Christine of France, the Duchess-Regent, who made him Prime Minister; she had implicit trust in him, as did Charles Emmanuel II when he came of age. The sole aspiration of the Marchese, however, was to live in a religious house, far from the Court and its activities. After the death of Pope Alexander VII, who had persuaded him to defer the execution of his plan, the Prime Minister ceded all his possessions to his son, the Marchese di Livorno, and retired to San Pancrazio Monastery. Deeply grieved by this, Charles Emmanuel tried repeatedly to make him yield, but to no avail. He then suggested that the Marchese come to Turin and live in a religious house of his choice, leaving it only when called to Court to give his advice on some important affair. The Marchese accepted this proposal, choosing the house of the Priests of the Mission, which he himself had founded. He died there in July 1677, at sixty-nine years of age. Whenever Saint Vincent speaks to the men in Turin of their "founder," he is referring to the Marchese.

honor he pays our Little Company by judging it capable of contributing to that good. May it please God to grant it this grace!

The Prior of Saint-Joire must be thanked warmly for wanting to see us established in his priory and ministry in place of the twelve Canons Regular now there, whose consent he hopes to obtain by giving each one a pension. He is also offering to get the consent of the priests of the Sainte-Chapelle de Thonon, who award these stipends, and to have the union effected in Rome. In so doing, he confers on us a great honor and favor, which we have never deserved. I ask O[ur] L[ord] to be his reward for this, even if his proposal is not successful—which is to be feared, since so many persons with vested interests are involved.

Difficulties in the affair might also arise for us if we had to send there right away as many Missionaries as there are Canons, or if, after payment of the pensions, the revenues might be insufficient to maintain them there. We would have a very hard time providing such a large number of workers and could contribute nothing toward their maintenance. You tell me that the revenue is small, but you do not say how much it is. Please let me know the amount of income of the priory and the stipend allotted to each Canon, its source, the obligations entailed, and the obligations we would have; otherwise, we cannot make any decision in this affair.

The break you and the whole family are taking is all the more pleasing to God because it is a preparation for work. So please get a good rest and, in the name of God, take care of yourself at the times you will have to give unsparingly of your health. It is too useful for souls and too dear to the Company not to take the means to preserve it. As for me, I ask this of God, together with an increase of grace for you, for your leadership, and for your family, whom I embrace with all the tenderness of my heart. I am, in the love of O[ur] L[ord], Monsieur, your most humble servant.

VINCENT DEPAUL,
i.s.C.M.

The Father General of Sant'Antonio sent his Vicar-General to me to complain about the suggested union. I simply told him that I had heard about this affair and that we never seek out any establishment. I also assured him that we have adhered to this practice until now and that the Missionaries in Turin would not become involved in this business, nor would I; but neither could we do anything to dissuade those in power from doing what they consider most advantageous for the welfare of their State. I say all this for your ears only, M. Martin. He added that the King of [France][4] made a peace treaty some time ago with a Duke of Savoy, in which it is stated that His Royal Highness cannot divide the benefices of his State that depend on Saint-Antoine-de-Viennois,[5] without the consent of the King, who is its protector, and that they hope to prevent him by that means.

Addressed: Monsieur Martin

2928. - TO FIRMIN GET, IN MONTPELLIER

Paris, August 1, 1659

Monsieur,

The grace of O[ur] L[ord] be with you forever!

I received the letter you wrote me on your return from Marseilles, in which I learned what you did there. I am glad you left one of the two keys to the strongbox with M. Le Vacher[1] and the other with Brother Louis,[2] while awaiting the arrival of

---

[4]A word omitted in the original.

[5]Sant'Antonio.

Letter 2928. - Archives of the Mission, Paris, original signed letter.

[1]Philippe Le Vacher.

[2]Louis Sicquard, born in Nalliers (Vendée) on May 3, 1624, entered the Congregation of the Mission as a coadjutor Brother on October 18, 1645, and took his vows in November 1648.

M. Delespiney.[3] He left here a week ago to go to replace you, accompanied by another good priest. I would have liked you to postpone your journey until his arrival because you could have informed him of everything and acquainted him with your friends and practices. Since, however, Providence ordained otherwise, it is to be hoped that God Himself will instruct him and that M. Le Vacher will inform him of his principal duties, as I have asked him to do. Be sure to give him in writing the advice you judge necessary to get off to a good start with the Bishop of Marseilles,[4] the Aldermen, other private individuals who are good to the Company, and those with whom you have to deal for the affairs of Barbary.

The priest who is accompanying M. Delespiney is named M. Cornier;[5] he has not yet made his seminary but is a man ready to be of assistance and an almost fully trained worker.

I am worried about the fever prevalent in Montpellier. I ask you, Monsieur, and M. Parisy as well, to do your best to escape it and to take good care of your health. I am asking this of God, along with the graces of His Spirit essential to the important and holy work you have, in order to obtain the results people expect from it, especially the Bishop,[6] who has entrusted to you what is most important and precious in his diocese, namely, the formation of his priests, on which the conversion of all the rest of it depends.

I am, in O[ur] L[ord], Monsieur, your most humble servant.

VINCENT DEPAUL,
i.s.C.M.

Addressed: Monsieur Get, Priest of the Mission, at the Montpellier Seminary, in Montpellier

---

[3]Gabriel Delespiney. Born in Grandchamp (Calvados), he entered the Congregation of the Mission on August 5, 1645, and took his vows on January 25, 1656; he was Superior in Toul (1648-52) and Marseilles (1659-60).

[4]Étienne du Puget (1644-68).

[5]Charles Cornier, born in Landujan (Ille-et-Vilaine) in February 1623, entered the Congregation of the Mission in Paris on April 26, 1659, and took his vows in Marseilles in 1661, in the presence of M. Get. He was Superior in Annecy (1679-82, 1693-94) and Narbonne (1682-89, 1690-93).

[6]François de Bosquet.

2929. - TO EDME JOLLY, SUPERIOR, IN ROME

Paris, August 1, 1659

Monsieur,

The grace of O[ur] L[ord] be with you forever!

I received your letter of July 7, which I sent immediately to the Duchesse d'Aiguillon because of what you tell me about her chapel in Loreto, but she has not yet returned it to me. That is why I am not giving you any precise answer, since I cannot remember all of its contents.

You mention the dispute concerning the Carmelites; [1] please

---

Letter 2929. - Archives of the Mission, Paris, original signed letter.

[1]The Carmelite nuns of France had three Superiors: Jacques Charton, Martin Grandin, and Charles de Gamaches. Everything was peaceful until 1655, when the Superiors arrogated to themselves the right to make the canonical visitation of the monasteries of the Order. When Nicolò di Bagno, Nuncio at the time, was informed of their intention, he opposed it. After some hesitation, they decided to go ahead anyway. In April 1659, Grandin began the visitation of the Incarnation Monastery in Paris, while Gamaches went to Pontoise and Saint-Denis with the same intent. Mother Madeleine de Jésus and Mother Agnès appealed to the Sovereign Pontiff and through an apostolic notary informed the Superiors of their action. The visitations were suspended and the Superiors promised to accept with docility the decision of the Holy See. The affair, brought to the attention of the Congregation of Regulars, did not drag on for very long. On July 16 a decree declared that only Apostolic Visitors had the right to make the visitation of the Carmelite monasteries. On October 2 the Sovereign Pontiff confirmed the decree of July 16, and Abbé de Bérulle, nephew of Cardinal de Bérulle, was appointed Apostolic Visitor, as was Louis de Chandenier, Abbé de Tournus. Forty monasteries submitted; eighteen refused to accept the Brief, under the pretext that they had not been consulted. The three Superiors upheld the opposition and tried to enlist the help of Saint Vincent, who constantly recommended obedience to the Pope. The Saint died before harmony was restored. On January 13, 1661, Alexander VII had to intervene again. After the death of Charton, his two colleagues, Gamaches and Grandin, appointed a third Superior during the absence of Celio Piccolomini, Nuncio at the time. In spite of the confirmation given by one of the Vicars-General of the diocese, Alexander VII annulled the appointment on April 11, 1661, and named as Superior René Alméras, Superior General of the Priests of the Mission. Since Gamaches and Grandin continued their visitations, the Sovereign Pontiff deposed them on September 30; he also deprived René Alméras of his authority and decided that each house should choose a Superior every three years. (Cf. J.-B.A. Boucher, *Histoire de la Bienheureuse Marie de l'Incarnation* [new ed., 2 vols., Paris: Lecoffre, 1854], vol. II, pp. 460ff., which is based on the manuscript history of the foundations of the Carmelites of France by Mother Natalie and Sister Marie-Thérèse [*Histoire manuscrite de la Fondation des Carmelites en France,* 42 vols.]. This document is conserved in the archives of the former monastery on rue de Grenelle in Paris.)

continue to tell the priest who spoke to you about it that I have not given you any orders regarding that business.

I received the copy of the Brief you obtained,[2] and I read it with joy and gratitude, seeing the graces God has granted us through you. I thank you very humbly for all the trouble you took, and I ask Our Lord to draw more and more glory from your leadership and your works.

I have nothing more to say to you just now, except that I am, in the love of O[ur] L[ord], Monsieur, your most humble servant.

VINCENT DEPAUL,
i.s.C.M.

Addressed: Monsieur Jolly, Superior of the Priests of the Mission of Rome, in Rome

2930. - TO JEAN PARRE, IN SAINT-QUENTIN

Paris, August 2, 1659

Dear Brother,

The grace of O[ur] L[ord] be with you forever!

I have not yet received your letter from the last regular mail. I am hoping to find in it the answer to the request I made you to let me know whether the Bishop of Noyon[1] has sent a treasurer to his [Notre-Dame-]de-la-Paix chapel. Having previously written to ask me to find him a good one for it, he has made no further mention of it, which leads me to believe that he no longer needs one.

Both the Ladies and I are greatly consoled by the blessings God

---

[2]The Brief *Alias nos,* of which Edme Jolly had managed to procure a copy before its dispatch (cf. vol. XIII, no. 120).

Letter 2930. - Archives of the Mission, Paris, original signed letter.

[1]Henri de Baradat (1626-60). Cf. no. 2923 for Saint Vincent's previous letter to Jean Parre.

is bestowing on your works; they and I, along with our community, are praying that Our Lord will fill you more and more with the workings of His Spirit and will preserve you. Please do your part by the care you take in this.

I am, in His love, dear Brother, your most affectionate brother and servant.

VINCENT DEPAUL,
i.s.C.M.

Addressed: Brother Jean Parre, of the Mission, in Saint-Quentin

2931. - TO JACQUES THOLARD, IN TROYES

Paris, August 6, 1659

Monsieur,

The grace of O[ur] L[ord] be with you forever!

I thank God for the submission He gives you to His good pleasure, as I see from your letter of July 31 and have experienced so often. I have not yet received an answer from the Bishop of Agde, Abbot of Vézelay.[1] As soon as I do, I will let you know whether or not you should go now or at some future time. Perhaps what I told him[2] about our custom of suspending missions during this period of time will oblige him to postpone his missions until later; we shall see. If he wants to have you there, I ask M. Dupuich[3] to give you

---

Letter 2931. - Archives of the Mission, Paris, original signed letter.

[1]Louis Fouquet.

[2]Cf. no. 2922.

[3]François Dupuich was born in Arras on July 3, 1616. After his ordination to the priesthood in September 1640, he entered the Congregation of the Mission in Paris on April 19, 1641, and took his vows in Troyes in November 1643, in the presence of M. Dehorgny. He was Superior in several houses: Troyes, Marseilles, Warsaw, Metz, Saint-Charles, and twice in Richelieu. In 1679 he was sent to Poland on a very delicate mission, of which he acquitted himself with competence and success. Dupuich had the title of Visitor in both Champagne and Poland; on January 2, 1683, he was asked to substitute for Thomas Berthe as Assistant General, when the latter was detained outside Paris. Dupuich was still alive in 1697.

M. Froment[4] as a companion, for we cannot send you anyone from this house.

You are right, Monsieur, to act simply with regard to confessions, and it will be a good idea for you to continue to hear those who want to come to you, without having to go to the confessional for all sorts of people,[5] unless it is to relieve the others when there is a large number to be heard. You might first inform that good Prelate that you will not be able to devote yourself to this work.

Your good sister is at the Nom-de-Jésus[6] with M. Gorlidot's[7] aunt. About three months ago, your niece brought her here because of her infirmity. Since that time I have tried to get her into a house in Paris intended for such persons, but I could make no headway,

---

[4]Antoine Froment, born in Oeuf-en-Ternois (Pas-de-Calais), entered the Congregation of the Mission at the Paris Seminary on October 28, 1653, at twenty-six years of age. He took his vows there on November 25, 1655, and renewed them on January 25, 1656.

[5]For a long time Jacques Tholard had been assailed by scruples while hearing confessions (cf. vol. II, nos. 424, 477, 495).

[6]The Nom-de-Jésus [Name of Jesus] hospice. Its foundation was made by an anonymous rich merchant of Paris, who one day brought 100,000 livres to Saint Vincent for a good work of the latter's choice. After discussing his plan with the benefactor, the Saint decided to spend 11,000 livres for the purchase of the house called Nom-de-Jésus, which belonged to Saint-Lazare, and 20,000 livres for enlarging the living space, should it become too small. He also constituted an income of 60,000 livres, to which 20,000 were added from Saint-Lazare, which later retrieved them; he allocated 5400 livres for chapel furnishings, and 3600 livres for room and board for forty poor persons for one year. All this was on condition that the Superior General of the Priests of the Mission, together with the laymen from Paris whom he would employ, would have the spiritual and temporal direction of the hospital, and in this position would be authorized to receive and dismiss the poor. The contract was accepted on October 29, 1653, approved by the Vicars-General on March 15, 1654 (the Archbishop of Paris, Cardinal de Retz, was in exile in Rome), and ratified in the Parlement by letters patent in November. (Cf. Arch. Nat., M 53.) The work was already in operation in March 1653. Saint Vincent selected twenty male and twenty female artisans who, because of old age or infirmity, could no longer earn their living; to occupy their time, they were provided with looms and tools. Men and women were housed in separate wings; although they came together in the same chapel for Mass, they were not permitted to see or speak to one another. The Daughters of Charity served them; a Priest of the Mission, in conformity with the terms of the contract, acted as chaplain. Saint Vincent often used to come to visit and instruct them. (Cf. Abelly, *op. cit.*, bk. I, chap. XLV, pp. 211-13.) The Nom-de-Jésus later became the municipal health center (1802-16); its buildings were on the site now occupied by the offices of the Gare de l'Est.

[7]François Gorlidot, born in Charly (Aisne) on January 10, 1623, entered the Congregation of the Mission on March 3, 1647, took his vows on September 30, 1649, and was ordained a priest in 1650.

although I offered to take in exchange someone they might like to send us for the Nom-de-Jésus, where, because of this refusal, we have been obliged to place her. I did this because I felt[8] she would be better off there than anywhere else. And, in fact, Monsieur, she is fine. Do not worry about her; her state is neither better nor worse, and she does have lucid moments but they do not last long. Rest assured that we will take care of her. Meanwhile, let us honor these words of the Gospel: *Et tenuerunt eum, dicentes, quoniam in furorem versus est.*[9]

I agree to your keeping all the books that are in your bag, until Providence brings you back to Paris.

You console me greatly by your distaste of everything that is not of God or does not lead to Him, and by the physical strength you still have after such hard work. I thank His Divine Goodness for it and ask Him to continue and to increase these same graces in you.

I am, in His love, Monsieur, your most humble servant.

VINCENT DEPAUL,
i.s.C.M.

Addressed: Monsieur Tholard, Priest of the Mission, in Troyes

---

[8]First redaction: " . . . which, however, I would not have wished to have done, knowing. . . ." The correction is in the Saint's handwriting.

[9]*And they took charge of him, saying, "He is out of his mind."* This text, in the Saint's handwriting, is his loose quotation of Mk 3:21. The exact Latin text from the Vulgate is: *Exierunt tenere eum; dicebant enim: quoniam in furorem versus est.* (They went out to lay hold on him. For they said: He is become mad. [D-RB]).

2932. - TO CANON DE RUMELIN [1]

Paris, August 6, 1659

Monsieur,

The grace of O[ur] L[ord] be with you forever!

Although we are obliged to thank you unceasingly for the foundation of the Tréguier Seminary, you still give us fresh reasons to render you this duty by your renewed efforts toward the completion of this good work. So, I thank you a thousand times for this, Monsieur, with all possible humility and gratitude. These benefits concern not only our poor, wretched Company but also the pure glory of God and the service of the Church, which you procure with so much care, expense, and favorable results. Because of this, I ask Our Lord Himself to be your thanks and reward.

O Monsieur! what great consolation you will one day have for having used such efficacious means to advance the sanctification of souls—who will recognize you in heaven as their second savior—and to draw down God's special blessings on your noble, virtuous family! We shall have forever the greatest respect for you and your family, and would to God that we might be worthy of serving you! His Divine Goodness knows with what affection and joy we would do so, especially I, who renew to you my offers of

---

Letter 2932. - Archives of the Daughters of Charity, 22 rue Maupertuis, 72000 Le Mans (France), original signed letter.

[1]Maître Michel Thépault, sieur de Rumelin, Licentiate in Civil and Canon Law, Rector of Pleumeur-Bodou and Plougasnou, then Canon of the Tréguier Cathedral and Penitentiary of the diocese. Thépault was a great benefactor of the Missionaries and founded the Tréguier Seminary. He died on August 30, 1677. (Cf. Discourse of Canon Daniel in *Annales de la Congrégation de la Mission,* vol. LXIII [1908], pp. 191-201.)

obedience. I am, in His love, Monsieur, your most humble and obedient servant.

VINCENT DEPAUL,
i.s.C.M.

Addressed: Monsieur de Rumelin, Canon of Tréguier and founder of the seminary, in Tréguier

2933. - TO LOUIS DUPONT,[1] SUPERIOR, IN TRÉGUIER

Paris, August 6, 1659

Monsieur,

The grace of O[ur L[ord] be with you forever!

I received your letter of July 17. I praise God for the satisfaction you gave M. de Rumelin by beginning to carry out the obligations of his foundation ahead of time. Enclosed is a letter I took the liberty of writing him in recognition of his past and present favors. I was glad you reminded me of this and informed me of the progress of the seminary. May God be pleased to perfect it in every way!

M. Dehorgny is about to leave for visitations. He will go to see you, God willing, and will tell you our little news items. I ask O[ur] L[ord] to continue to bless your leadership and your family, according to His plan to draw glory from it.

Enclosed is a letter from M. Boussordec [2] in reply to the one you sent me to have delivered to him.

Letter 2933. - Archives of the Mission, Paris, original signed letter.

[1]Louis Dupont, born in Nemours (Seine-et-Marne), entered the Congregation of the Mission on October 23, 1641, at twenty-two years of age, and took his vows in November 1644. He was Superior in Toul (1652-53), Tréguier (1654-61), Annecy (1662-63), and at Saint-Charles (1664-71).

[2]Charles Boussordec, born in Châtelaudren (Côtes-du-Nord), was a Pastor in the Tréguier diocese before entering the Congregation of the Mission on August 21, 1654, at forty-five years of age. He took his vows in Luçon, in the presence of M. Berthe, and was Director of the Annecy

I am, in the love of O[ur] L[ord], Monsieur, your most humble servant.

VINCENT DEPAUL,
i.s.C.M.

At the bottom of the first page: M. Dupont

2934. - TO EDME JOLLY, SUPERIOR, IN ROME

Paris, August 8, 1659

Monsieur,

The grace of O[ur] L[ord] be with you forever!

I received your letter of July 14. I had someone deliver the letters you sent me for the Agent of Genoa[1] and M. Chastellain.[2] The former is with the King, who is traveling to Bordeaux to conclude the peace with Spain and to marry the Infanta.[3]

I have never seen a gentleman the age of the said Agent, who is young, better endowed than he is. He has a quick, wise mind and is clever and intelligent. I would have been greatly consoled to visit him at his home, but my infirmities have prevented me from going out for the past eight or ten months. From time to time, I have sent M. Alméras[4] in my place, and he has always returned full of

---

Seminary (1660-62). On March 31, 1665, en route to Madagascar, Boussordec got into a longboat headed for shore off the coast of Cape Verde and drowned trying to save some of the other passengers when the overloaded boat capsized. His body was recovered on April 2. (Cf. *Notices,* vol. III, pp. 341-47.)

Letter 2934. - Archives of the Mission, Paris, original signed letter.

[1]Marchese Durazzo, the nephew of Cardinal Durazzo, was Resident in France for the Republic of Genoa.

[2]Probably Father Eusèbe Chastellain, director of the Joigny hospital.

[3]Maria Teresa, daughter of Philip IV, King of Spain.

[4]René Alméras the younger, nephew of Madame Goussault, was born in Paris on February 5, 1613, and was baptized the same day in Saint-Gervais Church. By coincidence Saint Louise was married in this church that very day. A Councillor in the Great Council at the age of twenty-four, Alméras left everything--family, position, and hopes--despite the opposition of his

admiration for his good, fine mind. It is no surprise that God has granted him many gifts of grace and nature, since he has the honor of being connected with a saint of this century.

I am worried about your ailment—quite worried, in fact—although you barely mentioned it to me. I ask O[ur] L[ord] to restore you to perfect health, Monsieur, for the welfare and consolation of the Company, in which His Divine Goodness grants you so many blessings. Please make every effort on your part to stay well and, when everything is suspended, go to take the fresh air in Frascati or at your house in [Palestrina][5] and to get some rest there.

Since the fulmination of Saint-Lazare has been made, I took possession of it yesterday for the last time.[6] We are going to send

---

father (who was to follow him later) to enter the Congregation of the Mission, into which he was received on December 24, 1637. He was ordained a priest at Easter in 1639. Saint Vincent entrusted to him important positions, such as Assistant of the Motherhouse and Seminary Director. He appointed him to his council and often relied on his prudence to deal with lay persons in delicate matters; he also gave him charge of the retreatants. So much work ruined Alméras' health. The Saint, convinced by personal experience that a change of air could improve one's health, sent him in 1646 to make the visitation of several houses in France and Italy. When he reached Rome, Alméras was notified that he had been appointed Superior of the house, where he remained until 1651. On his return to France he took over the direction of Saint-Charles Seminary. In 1654 he was involved in distributing relief to the poor of Picardy and Champagne. He made visitations of some houses of the Congregation and was again named Assistant of the Motherhouse, in which position he remained until the death of Saint Vincent. He was also Visitor of the Province of Poitou. Alméras was in Richelieu when the Saint, realizing that his own death was near, begged him to return to Paris immediately. Alméras was ill and was brought back on a stretcher but had the consolation of receiving a last blessing from the Saint. Appointed Vicar-General by Saint Vincent, then elected Superior General by the Assembly of 1661, he governed wisely the Congregation of the Mission and the Company of the Daughters of Charity until his death on September 2, 1672.

[5]This word was omitted in the original.

[6]In this context *fulmination* (official proclamation) is an act by which an ecclesiastical court pronounces, without equivocation, a decree which finalizes, in perpetuity, a previously disputed judgment. On July 21, 1659, Nicolas Porcher, Officialis (ecclesiastical judge) of Paris, and Jean Roger, the apostolic notary, signed the judgment by which the Congregation of the Mission took final possession of Saint-Lazare and all its rights, revenues, and emoluments (cf. vol. XIII, no. 119).

M. Gicquel[7] to work on the one for Saint-Pourçain.[8]

We will wait patiently for God to give a successor to the late Monsignore Galtieri so we might have the Brief you are awaiting.

Please show Abbé Brisacier[9] great respect and trust. He is a fine man and is kind to us. Nevertheless, let your dealings with him always be seasoned with a grain of salt.[10]

You are right in saying that, if M. Lejuge is dissatisfied, he should not be sent to Rome. According to what M. Pesnelle writes me, he is ailing at present. We will see what course his illness takes and what his disposition will be after the mission in his birthplace, which M. Pesnelle is going to give to please him.

---

[7]Jean Gicquel, born in Miniac (Ille-et-Vilaine) on December 24, 1617, was ordained a priest during Lent of 1642, entered the Congregation of the Mission on August 5, 1647, and took his vows on May 6, 1651. He was Superior of the Le Mans Seminary (1651-54) and at Saint-Lazare (1655-60) (cf. vol. V, nos. 1908 and 1912; vol. VI, no. 2157), and was Director of the Company of the Daughters of Charity (1668-72). Gicquel wrote an interesting diary of Saint Vincent's final days (cf. vol. XIII, no. 57), which is preserved in the Archives of the Mission, Paris. He died in 1672.

[8]The Officialis of Clermont made the official proclamation of the Bull of Union on March 2, 1660; on March 6, Jean Gicquel took possession of the priory in the name of the Congregation of the Mission.

[9]Laurent de Brisacier was born in Blois on August 2, 1609. His brother Jean, a Jesuit, made a name for himself by his controversies against the Jansenists. He was also the uncle of Jacques-Charles de Brisacier, future Superior of the Foreign Missions Society. In 1632 he became Dean of Saint-Sauveur in Blois and was tutor to Louis XIV around 1649, during M. Péréfixe's absence. The Court sent him to Rome to negotiate various affairs, and he was charged by the Queen to fulfill a vow she had taken, during her son's illness, of funding a solemn Office every year on the feast of Saint Louis in the church of Our Lady of Loreto, if he were cured. Laurent de Brisacier also became State Councillor. His quarrels with the Chapter of Blois caused him many a lawsuit. He took an active part in the foundation of the Foreign Missions Seminary and died in Blois on February 15, 1690. (Cf. André Rebsomen, "Une famille blésoise, les de Brisacier," in *Mémoires de la Société des sciences et lettres de Loir-et-Cher* [June 30, 1902].)

[10]The Saint added this sentence in his own handwriting.

Once again I ask O[ur] L[ord] to strengthen and sanctify you more and more.

I am, in His love, Monsieur, your most humble servant.

VINCENT DEPAUL,
i.s.C.M.

Addressed: Monsieur Jolly, Superior of the Priests of the Mission of Rome, in Rome

2935. - TO JACQUES PESNELLE, SUPERIOR, IN GENOA

Paris, August 8, 1659

Monsieur,

The grace of Our Lord be with you forever!

I received your letters of July 15 and 22. You tell me that, on the advice of M. Jolly, you are going to give a mission in M. [Lejuge's] birthplace[1] and are taking that good priest with you. Fine! I am very glad of this, and you saw in my previous letters that I asked you to do so. I only hoped that it would not be during this period set aside for your rest, but, given the reasons you tell me for not postponing it, *in nomine Domini.* Please let us know how your work is progressing and how you are tolerating the hot weather. We will ask God to give you the strength to support it, in proportion to the need, which will be great.

We must be content with the good will of M. Rodolphe-Maria Brignole,[2] since God is satisfied with it, and be submissive to

---

Letter 2935. - Jules Gossin, *Saint Vincent de Paul peint par ses écrits* (Paris: J.J. Blaise, 1834), p. 469, after the original made known by M. Monmerqué, a member of the Institut Catholique.

[1]Diano, in the Albenga diocese. Gossin misread this as: *au pays de notre juge* (in our judge's birthplace).

[2]Son of Maria Emmanuele Brignole.

Providence in the reduction his parents have made of most of his alms to you.

I was consoled to learn of the idea with which God inspired you of proposing one-day retreats to your little community, of their fondness for making them, and of the blessing God has given this. Since God is not dependent on time, He sometimes grants more graces in one day than in eight, and we profit more by short retreats than by long ones because they are more inviting and less wearisome.

We have not included in the Rules many minor practices which are observed—and should be observed—in the Company. It has always been the custom here not to go into the garden outside the time of recreation without permission. We often recommend this, and you should do the same.

I certainly hope that M. Lejuge's fever has not lingered and that, if he was seriously ill, you did not fail to take good care of him, as we must always do for the consolation and relief of our sick men. We still have a few here in this house, but none of them is seriously ill just now.

Since M. Caron wants to leave, it is better for him to go during his [seminary][3] than after. Nevertheless, you must not pressure him.

I am, in Our Lord, Monsieur, your most humble servant.

VINCENT DEPAUL,
i.s.C.M.

This good M. Caron has not acted in an upright manner by entering the Company with the idea of leaving it. If you look only at the fact, [is it] just for him [to] leave? [4] He is asking his parents to send him money to return home. What an injustice it would be to have put the Company to so much expense, with the intention of leaving it without any plausible reason! I ask God to forgive him.

---

[3]Gossin read "semester."

[4]Gossin read "he has just left."

2936. - TO JEAN PARRE, IN SAINT-QUENTIN

Paris, August 9, 1659

Dear Brother,

The grace of O[ur] L[ord] be with you forever!

I received your letters of July 29 and the fifth of this month. I am sure you have a great deal to endure and that you are contradicted and harassed. I ask Our Lord to be your strength so that everything will redound to His honor.

I have nothing to say to you regarding the service you are rendering to God and the glorious Virgin[1] in the work entrusted to you by the Bishop of Noyon,[2] except that you may continue to do it, as long as your principal duty allows. With regard to this, I will tell you, as Mademoiselle Viole has already written you, that a small sum of money will be set aside to help a few poor persons to sow a little patch of land—I mean, the poorest, who would be unable to do so without such assistance. There is nothing for them just now, however, but an effort will be made to collect one hundred pistoles[3] for that purpose, while awaiting the season for sowing. Meanwhile, you are asked to find out in what parts of Champagne and Picardy there are very poor people who may have need of such assistance—I mean, the greatest need. You could recommend to them in passing to prepare a small plot of land, to plough and fertilize it, and to ask God to send them some seed to plant in it. In addition, without making them any promises, give them the hope that God will provide.

They would also like to enable all the other poor people who have no land—men as well as women—to earn their own living, by giving the men some tools for working and the girls and women

---

Letter 2936. - Archives of the Mission, Paris, unsigned rough draft.

[1]At Notre-Dame-de-la-Paix.

[2]Henri de Baradat.

[3]A pistole was worth about ten francs.

spinning wheels and flax or linen for spinning—but only the poorest. When peace is restored, everyone will have something to do and, since the soldiers will no longer seize their property, they will be able to put something by and gradually get back on their feet. With that in view, the assembly[4] felt that they should be helped to get started and then told that they must no longer look for any relief from Paris.

So then, dear Brother, locate those poor persons who are in the greatest need of being aided for the last time. Find out approximately how much would be required for that, as well as for putting new roofs on exposed and ruined churches, but only over the altar so that Holy Mass may be said there with some decency. I am talking about places where the inhabitants are unable to restore the churches to such a state, and where they do not depend on any chapter, abbey, or nobleman obliged to support them out of the tithes because all such persons are bound to make these repairs. If you let us know who these patrons and communities are, together with the names of the parishes in which such ruined churches are standing, and which they are bound to keep in repair, we will have them requested to do so.

All that will oblige you to travel about in order to discover where there is a real need. Then you can send us reports on it so that some little fund may be set up to remedy that state of affairs. As I told you, they have almost nothing definite so far but will make some effort as soon as you tell us approximately how much will be absolutely necessary for these three things: seeds, implements, and repairs.

When will you be able to come for your retreat? Is it incompatible with your care of the chapel[5] and the other things you have to do, which I have just mentioned? Will you drop everything there and come here to recollect yourself, or will you postpone your

---

[4]The meeting of the Ladies of Charity of the Hôtel-Dieu.
[5]Notre-Dame-de-la-Paix.

retreat until all that has been done? Please let me know your thoughts on this.

I am, in the love of O[ur] L[ord], dear Brother, your most humble servant.

At the bottom of the first page: Brother Jean

2937. - TO JEAN MONVOISIN, IN MONTMIRAIL

Paris, August 11, 1659

Monsieur,

I received your letter of the fifth, answering the questions I asked you in my previous one,[1] for which I thank you. I have nothing new to tell you.

Enclosed is a letter for M. Berthe,[2] who will soon arrive at your house, if he is not already there.

I embrace M. Cornuel with all possible cordiality. I am still awaiting the latest reply from Bétharram.

I am, in the love of Our Lord, your. . . .

Letter 2937. - Jean-Baptiste Pémartin, ed., *Lettres de Saint Vincent de Paul* (4 vols., Paris: Dumoulin, 1882), vol. IV, p. 438, L. 1914.

[1]Probably no. 2919 of July 24, 1659.

[2]Montmirail was one of the houses of which Thomas Berthe was to make a canonical visitation.

2938. - TO EDME JOLLY, SUPERIOR, IN ROME

[August 15, 1659] [1]

Monsieur,

The grace of O[ur] L[ord] be with you forever!

I thank God, Monsieur, that you are not disheartened by the extra workload being given you and are unwilling to spare yourself when there is question of the salvation and relief of poor persons who need a dispensation from Rome.

Enclosed is a memo in answer to the questions you asked me regarding the use of milk.[2]

I am worried about M. Le Gouz's[3] ailment but am still hoping that he will recover and will even relieve you in the works outside the house, despite the fact that he may seem somewhat shallow to you. In truth, he will perhaps never be other than he is now, but will still [be use]ful to you, once he [has been formed] because [basically] he is good and wants to do what is right. We have his younger brother here, and he is a very wise and promising young man.[4]

Letter 2938. - Archives of the Mission, Paris, original signed letter.

[1]This letter is from the month of June, at the earliest, because it implies that the letters from April and May had arrived in Rome and the answer returned to Paris. Saint Vincent wrote to Edme Jolly only once a week, unless there was an urgent need; none of the letters written in June, July, and August 1659 are missing, except the one of August 15. Since the present letter is from 1659 and was written in the very hot season, we can conclude that it is most likely the letter of August 15.

[2]In his letter of April 25 (cf. vol. VII, no. 2823) Saint Vincent informs Jolly that remedies recently prescribed in Paris called for a diet consisting of bread and milk. According to the Saint, it had only good effects--never bad ones. It appears that M. Jolly had further inquiries about this in a letter to the Saint.

[3]Jacques Legouz (*Legouts* in *Notices,* vol. I and vol. V [Supplement]), born in Dollon (Sarthe) on April 6, 1633, entered the Congregation of the Mission on September 2, 1654, and took his vows on September 17, 1656, in the presence of M. Berthe. In 1659 Saint Vincent refers to his recent ordination (cf. vol. VII, no. 2811).

[4]René Legouz (*Legoux* in *Notices,* vol. I and vol. V [Supplement]), born on September 17, 1643, in Saint-Michel-de-Chavaigne (Sarthe), entered the Congregation of the Mission at the Paris Seminary on October 2, 1658, and took his vows there on November 1, 1660, in the presence of M. de Beaumont. *Notices* lists him as a priest but gives no date of ordination.

I will not fail to recommend Father Hilarion[5] to God in my poor prayers and Holy Sacrifices. He honors me greatly by desiring this, and we are so indebted to him that we cannot fail to obey him in whatever he wishes.

Your cousin M. Jaillard sent us 450 livres and a letter he wrote you in reply to yours.[6] If you are designating this sum for a special purpose, we will deliver it to whomsoever you please; if not, we thank you very humbly for it and ask Our Lord to be your reward; but please feel free, Monsieur, to use it as you wish.

I hope this letter will find you in Palestrina; if not, Monsieur, please go there as soon as possible, if the time for leaving Rome according to the usual custom allows you to do so. I think someone told me that people can leave safely by night, provided they do not return until after the rains. So, I entreat you to do so, Monsieur, and I am, in the love of Our Lord, your most humble servant.

VINCENT DEPAUL,
i.s.C.M.

Addressed: Monsieur Jolly

2939. - TO JEAN MARTIN, SUPERIOR, IN TURIN

Paris, August 15, 1659

Monsieur,

The grace of O[ur] L[ord] be with you forever!

I received your letter of the second of this month; it greatly

---

[5]Abbé Hilarion, born Bartolommeo Rancati in Milan, on September 2, 1594, was the son of Baltasarre Rancati and Margherita di Bagno. He entered the Cistercians in Milan on March 10, 1608, and taught in Salamanca (1614-18), then in Milan. In May 1619 he was sent to the Convent of Santa Croce in Gerusalemme in Rome. Among the offices he held in the Curia was that of Consultor for Propaganda Fide, in which he provided many services for Religious Orders and Founders. Saint Vincent considered him a friend and protector (cf. *Annales C.M.* [1951], p. 374).

[6]Everything that follows is in the Saint's handwriting.

Letter 2939. - Archives of the Mission, Turin, original signed letter.

distressed me because of the news you gave me of the departure of M. Planchamp, and still more, of the conduct of the person who accompanied him to Fossano.[1] *Jésus!* Monsieur, what sort of behavior is that, and what can we expect in the future from that person? I see a great disadvantage in leaving him with you; I think it will be better to recall him. We will make our decision according to what you tell us. Please observe him, however, and have him make a retreat so that he may recognize his fault; meanwhile, we will have prayers said for him.

M. Planchamp was asking to be withdrawn from Turin, without giving me many reasons for this; I do not know what will become of him. We must console ourselves in the hope that nothing as bad as what happened in Our Lord's company will happen in yours.

I would really like to know, Monsieur, why the Archbishop of Turin[2] refused to give Holy Orders to M. Demortier.[3] Is it because he was unwilling to give any to anyone at that time, or is there some special reason why he refused this good gentleman?

All we can do, Monsieur, is to accept graciously the humiliation stemming from this incident and to do so for the love of God, who allows this to happen for fear lest the great blessings He bestows on your work may make you proud. Meanwhile, go your zealous way, Monsieur, and rest assured that God will be glorified in this and that it will all change for the better in every way. I ask this of His Divine Majesty and embrace you and your dear family with all

---

[1]A town in Piedmont (Italy).

[2]Giulio Cesare Bergera (1643-60).

[3]Raymond Demortier, born in Marquay (Dordogne) on November 15, 1634, entered the Congregation of the Mission on March 18, 1655, and took his vows on May 20, 1657, in the presence of M. Bertier. He was one of the witnesses at the process of inquiry with regard to the virtues of Saint Vincent.

the tenderness of my heart. Prostrate in spirit at your feet and theirs, I am, Monsieur, your most humble servant.

VINCENT DEPAUL,
i.s.C.M.

Addressed: Monsieur Martin, Superior of the Mission of Turin, in Turin

2940. - TO GUILLAUME DESDAMES,[1] SUPERIOR, IN WARSAW

Paris, August 15, 1659

Monsieur,

The grace of Our Lord be with you forever!

I received your letter of July 18, in which you tell me of the favor Our Lord granted you through the incomparable goodness of the Queen,[2] who gave you the benefice of the person who preceded you in Holy Cross parish, which Her Majesty had conferred on him. I thank God and Her Majesty for this; I ask His Divine Goodness to be the reward of the Queen and to attribute to her the merit of the services this Little Company can render God in that benefice and in all its works, in time and in eternity.

Her Majesty's idea seems to be in line with that of Our Lord: to use this benefice for the upkeep of a seminary, where those wishing

---

Letter 2940. - Archives of the Mission, Krakow, original signed letter.

[1]Guillaume Desdames, born in Rouen, entered the Congregation of the Mission on June 19, 1645, at twenty-three years of age, took his vows on March 10, 1648, and was ordained a priest on May 31, 1648. He was stationed in Toul shortly afterward, then sent to Poland where he arrived with Lambert aux Couteaux in November 1651. He worked there with praiseworthy dedication amid numerous difficulties; after the death of Charles Ozenne (August 14, 1658), he became Superior of the Mission. René Alméras recalled him to France in 1669, but he returned to Poland a few years later and assumed the direction of the house in Chelmno. He returned to France for the General Assembly of 1685 and ended his days as Superior of the foundation in Krakow on June 1, 1692. (Cf. *Notices,* vol. III, p. 166, and *Mémoires,* vol. I, pp. 24-33.)

[2]Despite her attachment to the Jansenist party, Louise-Marie de Gonzague, a former Lady of

to be ordained, or to obtain benefices, or who need a retreat to correct some vice or other and make progress in virtue could be received free of charge in proportion to the revenue. O Monsieur, how this idea seems to have the marks of an inspiration from God! I hope it will do a great deal of good in Poland, if He is pleased to bless it.

Some time ago the Bishop of Cahors[3] did me the honor of writing to tell me that his clergy had changed completely and that it was, thank God, [thanks] to his seminary, composed of about fifty or sixty clerics. All those wishing to be ordained are required to spend a year to eighteen months there to be formed for their functions and in the priestly spirit. So we must tend toward that; for that purpose, you will be sent at least two priests, whom I have already chosen, in the hope that Our Lord will bless their modest work. I will have them leave at the first opportunity you indicate to me, along with the Daughters of Charity Her Majesty is requesting.

So, you will continue to work at what will be required to effect the union of the said benefice.

If those four or five priests depend *ad nutum*[4] on the titular of that benefice, as I think you stated, those places could be filled by the first men to be formed in the above-mentioned seminary; the effect of it would be seen in a very short time.

We pray constantly for the King,[5] the Queen, and the kingdom; we have a great obligation to do so, and I can tell you that we are

---

Charity, wife of King Wladyslaw IV, then of his brother Jan Casimir, held Saint Vincent in the highest esteem. She summoned to Poland the Priests of the Mission, the Daughters of Charity, and the Visitation Nuns, gave them housing, took care that nothing was wanting to them, and never failed to protect them. She died in 1667.

[3]Alain de Solminihac.

[4]*At will.*

[5]Few Princes had as much experience of the vicissitudes of fortune as Jan Casimir, King of Poland. Born in 1609, he went to France in his youth and was thrown into prison by Richelieu. He became a Jesuit and eventually received the Cardinal's hat. On the untimely death of his brother, Wladyslaw IV, he ascended the throne of Poland. Obtaining a dispensation from his vows, he married his brother's widow, Louise-Marie, and ruled Poland under the title of Jan Casimir V. His reign was unfortunate: attacked by the Cossacks, Sweden, Brandenburg, Russia,

praying fervently that God will sanctify Their Majesties and bless their kingdom.

At present we have a program aimed at making all the priests of the Company qualified to serve equally well in the missions or in seminaries, and it seems God is blessing this effort.[6]

We are preparing to send Missionaries to Madagascar. I recommend them to your prayers, as well as M. Le Vacher[7] in Tunis, who is surrounded by the plague and in great personal danger.

I planned to write to the Queen to thank her for her inestimable goodness to her poor Missionaries, but I will not be able to do so at the moment because of some business I am just completing. Furthermore, I would be failing in the respect I owe Her Majesty, which I will better express to her by my silence than by letter. I renew here the offers of my perpetual obedience to her, and I entreat you, Monsieur, to make this known to her.

Meanwhile, I greet M. Duperroy[8] with all the tenderness of my

---

and Transylvania, and torn asunder by internal dissensions, Poland was forced to surrender a large part of its territory to its enemies. After losing his wife in 1667, he abdicated and withdrew to Flanders. From there he went to Saint-Germain-des-Prés Abbey in Paris and afterward to Saint-Martin Abbey in Nevers. He died in that city in 1672.

[6]The Saint had recently introduced at Saint-Lazare practical seminars in moral theology, administration of the Sacraments, preaching, and catechizing.

[7]Jean Le Vacher, born in Écouen (Val-d'Oise) on March 15, 1619, entered the Congregation of the Mission with his brother Philippe on October 5, 1643. He took his vows in 1646 and was ordained a priest in 1647. When Julien Guérin, a Missionary in Tunis, needed help, Saint Vincent decided to send him Jean Le Vacher. Le Vacher arrived in Tunis on November 22, 1647. Guérin's death on May 13, 1648, followed two months later by that of the Consul, Martin de Lange, placed on Le Vacher the double burden of Consul and head of the Mission. In 1650 he added Vicar Apostolic to these titles. Since the Holy See would not allow priests to be in charge of the consulate, Saint Vincent sent a layman, Martin Husson, a parlementary lawyer, who arrived in Tunis in 1653 and left in April 1657, expelled by the Dey. For two years Jean Le Vacher acted as Consul. He returned to France in 1666 and was sent to Algiers in 1668 as Vicar-General of Carthage and Vicar Apostolic of Algiers and Tunis. His life in Algiers was that of an apostle, and his death that of a martyr. On July 16, 1683, Algiers was being bombarded by Duquesne. After the Turks had used every device to make Le Vacher apostatize, they finally tied him to the mouth of a cannon, which shot his body into the sea. (Cf. Raymond Gleizes, *Jean Le Vacher, vicaire apostolique et consul de France à Tunis et à Alger (1619-83)* [Paris: Gabalda, 1914].)

[8]Nicolas Duperroy, born in Maulévrier (Seine-Maritime) on January 16, 1625, entered the Congregation of the Mission on September 13, 1651, was ordained a priest on April 4, 1654,

heart, and I embrace both of you, prostrate in spirit at your feet. I am, in the love of Our Lord, Monsieur, your most humble servant.

VINCENT DEPAUL,
i.s.C.M.

Addressed: Monsieur Desdames, Superior of the Mission of Warsaw, in Warsaw

2941. - TO FIRMIN GET, SUPERIOR, IN MONTPELLIER

Paris, August 15, 1659

Monsieur,

The grace of Our Lord be with you forever!

Although I have nothing—or very little—to tell you, I am writing, nevertheless, to give you our news and to ask for yours. Ours is that 1) our sick men are getting better, by the grace of God, and 2) we have begun a program here aimed at making all our Missionaries equally qualified for assignments in seminaries and on the missions because we have had difficulty until now finding men capable of doing both.[1] If God is pleased to bless this modest beginning, there is reason to hope that the Company will be better able to serve His Church. Would to God, Monsieur, that all were as competent as you are!

Brother Get [2] is still diligent in studying his philosophy; in fact,

---

and took his vows on December 13, 1663. After the capture of Warsaw, he was treated brutally by the Swedes and left for dead, caught the plague twice, and for a long period of time suffered from a painful physical condition. René Alméras appointed him Superior in 1670. His house sent him as delegate to the General Assembly of 1673. On his return to Poland, he continued as Superior until 1674, after which there is no further trace of him.

Letter 2941. - Archives of the Mission, Paris, original signed letter.

[1]The practicum or seminar of which the Saint spoke in the previous letter (see n. 6).

[2]Nicolas Get, Firmin's brother, was born in Chépy (Somme) in May 1635, entered the Congregation of the Mission on October 5, 1655, and took his vows on October 6, 1657, in the

they say he is first among the seventeen or eighteen philosophy students in the class. So we have reason to hope that *deficiente uno, non deficiet alter.*[3]

I embrace you and M. Parisy and offer you daily to Our Lord. I hope you are doing me the same charity, and I ask you to continue it. I am, in the love of Our Lord, Monsieur, your most humble servant.

VINCENT DEPAUL,
i.s.C.M.

Addressed: Monsieur Get, Priest of the Mission, at present in the Montpellier Seminary, in Montpellier

2942. - TO JACQUES PESNELLE, SUPERIOR, IN GENOA

Paris, August 15, 1659

Monsieur,

The grace of Our Lord be with you forever!

I praise God that you have postponed the mission in M. Lejuge's birthplace, and [I am] distressed by his illness. I am asking Our Lord to restore him to perfect health and am having the family here do likewise. I do not recommend that you take care of him; I am sure you do not fail to do so. Please greet him for me and tell him how worried I am. I hope you will soon be sending us news of his recovery.

Since the Jesuits are not teaching scholasticism,[1] and it is likely

---

presence of M. Berthe. He left for Poland in September 1660, before his ordination to the priesthood.

[3]*If one fails, the other does not fail.*

Letter 2942. - Archives of the Mission, Paris, original signed letter.

[1]The term *scholasticism* was first used in a derogatory sense by humanists and early historians

that you will have few students capable of learning it, I think that class should be deferred.

When I told you to give M. Caron one écu, I was thinking that he was an Italian and that this amount of money would suffice. I forgot that this M. Caron was one of those whom we sent you. I would have had more money given to him; but, since things turned out the way they did, well and good! [2]

That is all I can tell you for now, Monsieur, except that we have begun a program to form all of us to be equally qualified for the missions and for seminaries. If God is pleased to bless it, we hope some good will result from it. Please recommend this to Our Lord, in whose love I am, Monsieur, your most humble servant.

VINCENT DEPAUL,
i.s.C.M.

Addressed: Monsieur Pesnelle, Superior of the Mission of Genoa, in Genoa

2942a. - TO JEAN PARRE, IN SAINT-QUENTIN

Paris, August 16, 1659

Dear Brother,

The grace of Our Lord be with you forever!

I think you are right to put off your retreat until you have done what you were instructed to do by the Bishop of Noyon at Notre-Dame-de-la-Paix, regarding the distribution of seeds about which

---

of philosophy in the sixteenth century. In the historical sense, it is an intellectual movement which, from the tenth to the fifteenth century, made use of Aristotelian dialectics and the writings of the early Christian Fathers in philosophy, theology, and Canon Law. Saint Thomas Aquinas was one of its most famous proponents. After a period of decline between the sixteenth and the late nineteenth century, it was rediscovered, reevaluated, and spread throughout the Catholic world under the aegis of Pope Leo XIII, and it flourished in the twentieth century.

[2]His parents paid his way home when he left the Congregation (cf. no. 2935).

Letter 2942a. - Original signed letter. In 1934, it belonged to Madame Whitney-Hoff; a catalogue of her collection was published in Paris in that year under the title *Lettres autographes*

I wrote you. You also have to see to the distribution of alms for the sick poor and visits to the Charities of the Ladies in Reims, Rethel, and the others.

I am very consoled by what you tell me of the comfort the sick are finding at the Sainte-Chapelle of Notre-Dame-de-la Paix.

The Ladies are planning to do something for the ruined churches, but since there are very few of them, and the number of churches and the devastation is very great, I strongly doubt that they can do much.

That fine man from Saint-Quentin you sent me, who wants to become a hermit, is making his retreat to discern his vocation. I greatly fear that he is not stable enough for a state of life so subject to various anxieties.

The Archdeacon of Noyon wrote me the story of the discovery of that holy statue of Our Lady.[1]

Please let me know if the devotion of the people continues and the results of their devotion.[2]

Please offer us to God through His holy Mother; pray for our dear Brother du Corneau,[3] whom we have sent to get some fresh

---

composant la collection de Mme Whitney-Hoff. A facsimile of this letter appears on p. 110 of the catalogue. The text, with its original spelling, was published in *Annales C.M.* (1936), pp. 699-700, and reprinted, with modern spelling, in *Mission et Charité,* 19-20, no. 98, pp. 124-25. This edition uses the latter text.

[1]Cf. no. 2902, n. 6, for the story of the statue.

[2]The last three words are in the Saint's handwriting.

[3]Bertrand Ducournau, born in Amou (Landes) in 1614, entered the Congregation of the Mission as a coadjutor Brother on July 28, 1644, and took his vows on October 9, 1646. He had fine penmanship and common sense and, from the various positions he had occupied in the world, including that of professional secretary, had learned to be shrewd, frank, and reliable in business affairs. Saint Vincent, therefore, made him his secretary in 1645. By his devotion, tact, and love of work, this good Brother rendered inestimable services to Saint Vincent and his Congregation. It can be said that, through his preparation of materials and his personal notes, he contributed more than Abelly himself to the first biography of Saint Vincent. Brother Ducournau remained as secretary to the Superiors General René Alméras and Edme Jolly, and was Archivist of Saint-Lazare. He died in Paris on January 3, 1677. Brother Pierre Chollier, his assistant in the secrétariat, wrote his biography, which is found in *Notices,* vol. I, pp. 377ff.

air for an ailment he has, and pray for me, who am the most wretched sinner in the world.[4]

Your brother and servant.

VINCENT DEPAUL,
i.s.C.M.

Addressed: Brother Jean Parre, of the Congregation of the Mission, at present at Notre-Dame-de-la-Paix near Saint-Quentin, in Saint-Quentin

2943. - TO ÉTIENNE DE FLACOURT,[1] IN ROUEN

Paris, August 18, 1659

Monsieur,

The grace of Our Lord be with you forever!

My most humble thanks, Monsieur, for the honor you do me in remembering me. Your letter consoled[2] me greatly. I ask Our Lord to bless your undertaking.

Brother Étienne is preparing for ordination in order to go to

---

[4]The last three words are in the Saint's handwriting.

Letter 2943. - Archives of the Daughters of Charity, Emmitsburg, MD (USA), original autograph letter.

[1]Étienne de Flacourt, born in Orléans in 1607, had many difficulties governing the colony of Madagascar in the name of the Company of the Indies (1648-55), due especially to the colonists, who tried several times to kill him. After his return to France, he worked in the administration of the Company. Besides a history of Madagascar, he also wrote a *Dictionnaire de la langue de Madagascar, avec un petit recueil de noms et dictions propres des choses qui sont d'une mesme espèce* [Paris: G. Josse, 1658], which he dedicated to Saint Vincent.

[2]Coste has *pleased,* but the original, to which he did not have access, reads *consoled.*

exercise his ministry in Madagascar, God willing. The Maréchal's[3] intendant says that this good lord's ship will leave on October 24. I hope to have news of this soon, in the event that he might be willing to include some of our men on the voyage; if not, what shall we do? Do you think, Monsieur, that the Company[4] is going to sail also? Are they getting their ship ready? Will you be going with them? If so, when? I am running ahead—too far ahead, perhaps. All you need to tell me is what can be said without infringing on secrecy—or nothing, if you so wish.

The rumor being spread by the English seems unlikely; those who returned with them would know something about it and would say so.

Brother Étienne is sending you a note and asks you. . . .[5]

---

[3]Charles de la Porte, Duc de la Meilleraye, born in 1602, owed his rapid advancement as much to the protection of Cardinal Richelieu as to his personal valor. He was appointed Grand Master of Artillery in 1634, Maréchal of France in 1637, Superintendent of Finance in 1648, and Duke and Peer in 1663. It was he who gave Saint Vincent the idea of sending Missionaries to Madagascar. He died in Paris on February 8, 1664.

[4]The Company of the Indies.

[5]The rest of the letter is missing.

2944. - *SAINT LOUISE DE MARILLAC* [1] *TO SAINT VINCENT*

August 21 [1659] [2]

Enclosed is a letter from Madame de Bouillon, [3] *which I received this morning. I thought I should answer her promptly. I am sending it to you to see if Your Charity thinks it will be well for me to proceed in this way.*

The Sister Renée she mentions is the one figuring in the rumors being circulated by that good priest; we have already sent for her twice. She is the same Sister whom this lady wants to stay with her as long as she

---

Letter 2944. - Archives of the Motherhouse of the Daughters of Charity, 140 rue du Bac, Paris, original autograph letter.

[1]Saint Louise de Marillac, Foundress, with Saint Vincent, of the Daughters of Charity, was born in Paris on August 12, 1591. Her father was Louis de Marillac, brother of the devout Michel de Marillac, Keeper of the Seals (1616-30), and half-brother of another Louis, Maréchal de France, renowned for his misfortunes and tragic death. Louise married Antoine Le Gras, secretary of Queen Marie de Médicis, on February 5, 1613, and they had one son, Michel. Antoine Le Gras died on December 21, 1625. The devout widow had implicit confidence in her spiritual director, Vincent de Paul, who employed her in his charitable works, eventually making her his collaborator in the creation and organization of the Confraternities of Charity. The life of Saint Louise, whom the Church beatified on May 9, 1920, was written by Gobillon (1676), the Comtesse de Richemont (1883), Comte de Lambel (n.d.), Monsignor Baunard (1898), and Emmanuel de Broglie (1911). Her letters and other writings were copied and published in part in the work entitled: *Louise de Marillac, veuve de M. Le Gras. Sa vie, ses vertus, son esprit* (4 vols., Bruges, 1886). Saint Louise was canonized on March 11, 1934, and on February 10, 1960, was named the patroness of all who devote themselves to Christian social work. Therefore, in this English edition of the letters of Saint Vincent, "Saint" has been added to her name in titles of letters and in the footnotes. To the above bibliography should be added some of her more recent biographers: Alice, Lady Lovat, *Life of the Venerable Louise de Marillac (Mademoiselle Le Gras)* (New York: Longmans, Green & Co., 1917); Monsignor Jean Calvet, *Louise de Marillac, a Portrait,* translated by G. F. Pullen (1959); Joseph I. Dirvin, *Louise de Marillac* (1970); the compilation by Sister Anne Regnault, D.C., editor: *Louise de Marillac, ses écrits* (1961), of which the section containing the letters was translated by Sister Helen Marie Law, D.C.: *Letters of St. Louise de Marillac* (1972); and the revised edition of Sister Regnault's work entitled: *Sainte Louise de Marillac, Écrits spirituels* (Tours: Mame, 1983), ed. Sister Élisabeth Charpy, D.C., trans. by Sister Louise Sullivan, D.C., *Spiritual Writings of Louise de Marillac, Correspondence and Thoughts* (Brooklyn: New City Press, 1991). Hereafter this work will be cited as *Spiritual Writings* followed by the appropriate letter and number, e.g.,A. 2 or L. 350. Finally, Sister Élisabeth Charpy, D.C., ed., *La Compagnie des Filles de la Charité aux Origines. Documents* (Tours: Mame, 1989), which will be cited as *Documents.*

[2]Year added on the back of the original by Brother Ducournau.

[3]In *Écrits spirituels,* Sister Élisabeth Charpy refers to a Madame de Bouillon the younger. This is not Eléonore-Catherine Fébronie de Bergh, the deceased widow of Frédéric-Maurice de la Tour d'Auvergne, Duc de Bouillon. The letter mentioned here is no longer extant, but for Saint Louise's reply, see *Spiritual Writings,* p. 644, L. 625.

remains in the country. Will Your Charity please take all these circumstances into consideration, plus the fact that they are asking for another Sister, which may be so that she can be kept there permanently, as she wishes? I had been told more than a month ago that she never left the château and that Madame has a habit of delaying the Sisters there to engage in conversation with her, and the Sister consents to this.

We know nothing about M. Piètre, whose findings can either harm or benefit us considerably. Might we have the audacity, Most Honored Father, to entreat Your Charity to send someone to him in your name? We are supposed to meet at two o'clock today to discuss the business of the cisterns.[4] *I have been told that he might be staying near Saint-Jean.*[5] *I will send for him there and for some of our Sisters at the Hôtel de Ville.*

Will Your Charity please intercede for us with Our Lord to obtain what we need, and bless us for His holy love. Believe me, Most Honored Father, to be your most humble and obedient daughter and servant.

L. DE MARILLAC

Addressed: *Monsieur Vincent*

2945. - TO GUILLAUME DESDAMES, SUPERIOR, IN WARSAW

Paris, August 22, 1659

Monsieur,

The grace of Our Lord be with you forever!

I received your letter of the twenty-fourth of last month, giving me an ever clearer picture of the Queen's incomparable goodness to the poor Little Company and informing me that the benefice[1] she

---

[4]On August 19 the Sisters received authorization from the Aldermen to have water piped from the town to their houses (cf. Arch. Nat., Q[1] 1200). The work went on until the end of the year (cf. *Spiritual Writings*, L. 634).

[5]Saint-Jean-en-Grève, a church in Paris.

Letter 2945. - Archives of the Mission, Krakow, original signed letter. The postscript is in the Saint's handwriting.

[1]A benefice in Vitkiski which the Queen, Louise-Marie de Gonzague, bestowed on the Priests of the Mission (cf. no. 2950).

so graciously gave you has a greater revenue than what you mentioned in your last letter. I thank God for all this. I am going to take the liberty of writing to thank Her Majesty for all she does for us and for the poor Daughters of Charity.

We cannot send you M. Berthe because he has just returned from a trip to Italy and has to leave here for Rome in twelve to fifteen days. We are, however, going to send you two very wise, capable young men, whom we consider suitable for what you are asking. One of them is a priest; as for the other, although he is not yet ordained, he is still a fine, capable young man, and I hope you will be happy with him as well as with the first-mentioned. We thought we should send you young persons rather than older ones because they can learn the language faster and more easily.

Since my last letter there is nothing new here worth writing to you, except that M. Boucher[2] is seriously ill. I recommend him to your prayers and am, in the love of Our Lord, Monsieur, your most humble servant.

VINCENT DEPAUL,
i.s.C.M.

The young man about whom I am writing is pious, wise, discreet, and esteemed and loved by everyone. In addition, we have not noticed any imperfection in him. He is being asked for as a teacher by a good number of our houses. M. Duperroy may know him. His name is de Marthe,[3] and he is a native of Arras. The priest

---

[2]Léonard Boucher, born on August 29, 1610, entered the Congregation of the Mission on November 12, 1632, and was ordained a priest on September 23, 1634. He took his vows on November 6, 1642, and renewed them on October 3, 1656, in the presence of Antoine Portail. When he was stationed in La Rose, he manifested an attachment to the person and questionable ideas of his Superior, François du Coudray. Among some of these ideas was the belief that Rome, the Councils, and the Fathers of the Church had not understood Holy Scripture very well.

[3]Ignace-Joseph de Marthe.

is also from Arras and is a learned man; his name is Monvoisin.[4]

Addressed: Monsieur Desdames, Superior of the Mission of Warsaw, in Warsaw

2946. - TO JACQUES PESNELLE, SUPERIOR, IN GENOA

Paris, August 22, 1659

Monsieur,

The grace of O[ur] L[ord] be with you forever!

We must conform our will to God's Will in all things and, in particular, with regard to M. Caron's departure.

We have given ourselves to God so as not to participate in all those disputes existing today among so many holy persons and among such large groups in the Church. We have a policy of not having in this house—and not reading—the many works on these topics being printed and circulated in Paris and even in the provinces; we are satisfied with asking God to unite minds and hearts and to bring peace to His Church. Accordingly, you will most humbly entreat the Vicar to excuse us for not sending you all those pamphlets.

After M. Lejuge leaves, please tell M. Simon that I would like him to assume the duty of Assistant. Both he and M. Sappia can be your consultors, and M. Pinon will then take over the direction of the Internal Seminary.

As you desire, we will recommend you to the prayers of the Company; and, beginning right now, I am asking Our Lord to bless

[4]François Monvoisin, born in Arras (Pas-de-Calais) in December 1634, entered the Congregation of the Mission in Paris on October 15, 1654, took his vows there in 1656, in the presence of M. Berthe, and was ordained a priest in 1659. In 1671 he was a member of the Fontainebleau house.

Letter 2946. - Archives of the Mission, Paris, original signed letter.

your leadership more and more. I am, in His love, Monsieur, your most humble servant.

VINCENT DEPAUL,
i.s.C.M.

Addressed: Monsieur Pesnelle, Superior of the Priests of the Mission, in Genoa

2947. - TO EDME JOLLY, SUPERIOR, IN ROME

Paris, August 22, 1659

Monsieur,

The grace of O[ur] L[ord] be with you forever!

I praise God that you are feeling a little better, and I ask Him to restore you to perfect health. I ask you, Monsieur, to do your part in this and to use the carriage whenever you feel the need of it.

I am most grateful for the usual kindnesses of Cardinal Durazzo to the Company, and especially for his latest one in honoring the poor Missionaries of Rome by visiting them in their little house. We will always continue our poor prayers for the prosperity and health of such a holy Prelate, in accordance with the great obligations we have toward him.

I thank God for the increase in number in your little Internal Seminary; I ask Him to bless it more and more and to give the two new arrivals the spirit of true Missionaries.

You will not have to worry about receiving the seminarian about whom M. Pesnelle wrote you; he has left the Company for good.

You gave the correct answer regarding the house of the Fathers of Sant'Antonio in Piedmont, for we are contributing nothing to that affair, which has been undertaken and conducted entirely by

---

Letter 2947. - Archives of the Mission, Paris, original signed letter.

the Madame Royale. By the grace of God, we have never sought any establishment, this one included; and you can always assure the Reverend Fathers of this.

I recommend myself to your prayers and am, in the love of Our Lord, Monsieur, your most humble servant.

VINCENT DEPAUL,
i.s.C.M.

Addressed: Monsieur Jolly, Superior of the Mission, in Rome

2948. - TO FRANÇOIS FEYDIN,[1] IN RICHELIEU

Paris, August 24, 1659

Monsieur,

The grace of Our Lord be with you forever!

I received two letters from you, which touched me deeply, seeing the apostolic zeal God has given you to go to announce His Name in Madagascar. I thank His Divine Goodness for this and ask Him to be His own thanks for the part He has given you in the extension of His mission on earth.

Because Brother Ducournau is absent, I am not sure whether I have already told you the same thing. So, I repeat, Monsieur, that

---

Letter 2948. - Archives of the Mission, Paris, original. The secretary added the following words on the part of the letter left blank: "Copy of the letter written by M. Vincent to M. Feydin, Priest of the Mission, regarding the journey to Madagascar. This letter, which M. Vincent dictated to me, word for word, is in my handwriting. When M. Feydin later came to Saint-Lazare in obedience to a second letter M. Vincent had written to him in Richelieu, he told me, before leaving for Madagascar, that he treasured it dearly." This letter is no longer extant.

[1]François Feydin, born in Allanche (Cantal), Clermont diocese, on May 25, 1620, was ordained a priest in September 1645, and entered the Congregation of the Mission on September 8, 1653. On several occasions he was designated for the Madagascar mission but each time was prevented from arriving there. Feydin left the Congregation of the Mission; in 1705 he was a Pastor in the Arras diocese, at which time he testified at the process of beatification for Saint Vincent.

most willingly I adore the enlightenment and zeal God is granting you for the salvation of those poor people, and especially for those whom His Divine Goodness has planned to save through you. Go, therefore, Monsieur, *in nomine Domini.* I ask O[ur] L[ord] to take you by the hand and to defend and preserve you amid the dangers to be encountered on land and sea so that you may reach that place in perfect health. May it please Him, in His infinite goodness, to fill you with His Spirit in order to make Him known and loved among these poor people, who are so disposed to embrace our holy faith.

Brother Étienne, whom Providence is calling to the priesthood and who received the subdiaconate today, will receive the diaconate tomorrow and be ordained a priest next Sunday. He is preparing himself for this great and blessed voyage. I hope M. Boussordec, who is very zealous for the salvation of those people, will also be with you. I realize how hard it will be for the Richelieu house to lose such a good servant of God, but I hope that He who makes children of Abraham from stones[2] will send someone else in your place. I say this to M. de Beaumont[3] rather than to you, and to his family, which will undoubtedly be very distressed by your departure—which I myself feel deeply.

So, once again I say go, Monsieur, with the assurance that He who is calling you will take the same care of you as of the apple of His eye.[4] Watch out for your health, and do not jeopardize yourself by all kinds of privations and hard work, especially during the first year after your arrival. They say that, once you make it through that, you are fine. In fact, experience has shown us that those who

---

[2]Cf. Mt 3:9. (NAB)

[3]Pierre de Beaumont, born in Puiseaux (Loiret) on February 24, 1617, entered the Congregation of the Mission on February 23, 1641, took his vows on October 4, 1643, and was ordained a priest in March 1644. At one time, he was imprisoned as a result of the lawsuit over the establishment of the Saint-Méen house. De Beaumont became Director of the Internal Seminary in Richelieu, and was twice Superior of that house (1656-60, 1661-62).

[4]Cf. Deut 32:10; Ps 17:8. (NAB)

have gone to heaven most likely advanced the time of entering their new life by endangering their lives by too much hard work.

If you find good M. Bourdaise[5]—whom you resemble somewhat—still alive, listen carefully to what he tells you with regard to this and everything else. He is a person of great gentleness, strength, and wisdom, and is one of the most zealous and amiable men I know. O Monsieur! how consoled you will be to embrace him, especially when you see in him your own facial expressions, your gentleness, etc.!

So, once again, go, Monsieur; I ask O[ur] L[ord] to bless you. Please remember in your prayers an old man of seventy-nine, burdened with sins, who is your most humble servant.

VINCENT DEPAUL,
i.s.C.M.

2949. - *SAINT LOUISE TO SAINT VINCENT*

August 24 [1659] [1]

Our two Sisters who have asked your permission to take their vows, Most Honored Father, have been in the Company for five years. The one named Pétronille[2] is well aware of the matter of the vows and the esteem she should have for them. The other one is more simple, has less instruction and even intelligence, but loves God and her vocation (as does the first

---

[5]Toussaint Bourdaise, born in Blois (Loir-et-Cher) in 1618, entered the Internal Seminary of the Congregation of the Mission in Paris on October 6, 1645, and took his vows there on October 7, 1647. He was ordained a priest in 1651, even though his talent and knowledge had been questioned a number of times (cf. vol. XI, no. 177). In 1654 he was sent to Madagascar, where he died on June 25, 1657 (cf. *Notices,* vol. III, pp. 180-214).

Letter 2949. - Archives of the Motherhouse of the Daughters of Charity, original autograph letter.

[1]Date added on the back of the original by Brother Ducournau.

[2]Pétronille Gillot, who entered the Daughters of Charity in 1654, was sent to Nanteuil after her seminary (cf. *Spiritual Writings,* L. 626).

Sister), and they have never wavered in it. They have the approval of M. Portail.[3] *The second Sister is named Louise.*

My patron saint[4] *is reproaching me for my infidelity. For this reason I beg Your Charity to ask God's forgiveness for me and new graces to carry out His holy Will. Tomorrow, if I am able, I will go to Holy Mass with our Sisters so that this little group may represent the whole Company for you, in order that Your Charity may obtain for it the blessing of Our Lord and the grace of stability.*

L. DE M.

Addressed: *Monsieur Vincent*

2950. - TO LOUISE-MARIE DE GONZAGUE, QUEEN OF POLAND

August [26] [1] 1659

Madame,

In his last letter M. Desdames informs me that Your Majesty has given to his mission in Warsaw the very important benefice of Vitkiski, in accordance with your most royal kindness, and he wanted me to take the honor of thanking Your Majesty for it. I do so now with all possible humility and affection, asking Our Lord

---

[3]Antoine Portail, born in Beaucaire (Gard) on November 22, 1590, came to Paris to study at the Sorbonne. He met Saint Vincent there around 1612 and became devoted to him. From the time of his ordination (1622) until his death in 1660, he was the auxiliary of the Saint. The latter assigned him to the service of the galley convicts, received him as the first member of his new Congregation, initiated him into the ministry of the missions and the work of the ordinands, chose him as First Assistant in 1642, and entrusted to him the direction of the Daughters of Charity. In 1646 Portail left Paris to make visitations of the houses of the Congregation. He began in the west of France, then went south, crossed into Italy, and did not return to Saint-Lazare until September 1649. Except for a fairly long absence in 1655, he hardly ever left the Motherhouse again and died on February 14, 1660, after an illness of nine days. (Cf. *Notices*, vol. I, pp. 1-94.)

[4]Saint Louis, whose feast day is August 25.

Letter 2950. - Archives of the Mission, Paris, unsigned rough draft dictated by the Saint.

[1]This letter closely followed no. 2945, dated August 22. The Saint says it was written two days after a conference to the Sisters, which can only be the one given on August 24 (cf. vol. X, no. 111).

to be Himself Your Majesty's reward and thanks for the good which there is reason to hope will result from it. He tells me that the revenue accruing from this benefice will allow them to get started and make some progress toward the establishment of an ecclesiastical seminary and that we should send him two priests for this purpose. I will do so, Madame, at the first opportunity.

He also informed me that Your Majesty has purchased a large residence in which to have poor girls educated by the Daughters of Charity and that Your Majesty has already housed them there. Both Mademoiselle Le Gras and I were deeply touched, as were most of the Daughters of this Company, who were present at the conference I gave them two days ago.[2]

The gratitude of those poor Daughters was obvious to me. It was so great that I confess I have never seen them so moved as when I told them of Your Majesty's kindness and support for them, and especially when I said that Your Majesty was spinning and winding the thread needed to sew linen for the poor and for their own—something unprecedented in God's Church. We are well aware that history tells us of a Princess who each year spun the linen destined for her own shroud, but I do not recall ever having read that the devotion of any Princess led her, as it has led Your Majesty, to use the work of her hands in the service of the poor.

I think, Madame, that Our Lord is pointing this out with admiration to the angels and blessed spirits and that the Church will some day regard it in this same spirit. God be blessed, Madame, that military affairs, at which Your Majesty is working so successfully,[3] have not hindered you from applying yourself in this way to edify the Church of God!

---

[2]In the conference of August 24 (On the Perfection Required for Sisters in Parishes) Saint Vincent makes no specific mention of the Queen's work on behalf of the Daughters of Charity, but this news was doubtless given to the Sisters at that time.

[3]Poland was engaged in two wars almost simultaneously: with Sweden, which was trying to extend its possessions on the southern Baltic coast, and with Russia, which desired a port on the Baltic coast.

Mademoiselle Le Gras is preparing to send two Daughters of Charity to Your Majesty at the first opportunity. She is deeply grieved. . . .[4]

2951. - TO JEAN PARRE, IN SAINT-QUENTIN

Paris, August 27, 1659

Dear Brother,

The grace of Our Lord be with you forever!

I was very busy last Saturday, which is why, my very dear Brother, I was unable to write to tell you how consoled we were by the continued blessings God is pleased to bestow on your work. We thank His Divine Majesty for this and ask Him, in His infinite goodness, to continue to grant them to you.

Everything you have done, dear Brother, has been approved here, and you are asked to continue working to get the crops planted and to be very careful to distribute seed only to those who need it. Meanwhile, let us know all that is happening with regard to the chapel [1] and all that is being done there.

As for your retreat, given the reasons you set forth, it will be well to postpone it until the time you mention, at which time, as for all eternity, I desire to be, in the love of Our Lord, dear Brother, your most humble servant.

VINCENT DEPAUL,
i.s.C.M.

Addressed: Our dear Brother Jean Parre, at present in Saint-Quentin to assist the poor

---

[4]At the end of the draft the secretary wrote: "This letter was not finished by M. Vincent, who began another one. I do not know what the latter contained, since he wrote it himself."

Letter 2951. - Archives of the Mission, Paris, original signed letter.

[1]Notre-Dame-de-la-Paix.

2952. - TO FRANÇOIS FOUQUET, ARCHBISHOP OF NARBONNE

Paris, August 29, 1659

Excellency,

Your letter caused me to admire the incomparable zeal God gives you and the great trouble you are taking for the sanctification of your diocese. It is to be hoped, Excellency, that this ardent zeal will inflame all the souls entrusted to you and, through their example, all the people in the surrounding localities. It is a consolation for me to tell you this because I hope for this good result from your holy leadership, but I feel I should also tell you, Excellency, that I fear you are taking too much upon your sacred person and that your body will not be able to bear much longer the fatigue your spirit is imposing on it.

That is why, Excellency, I venture to implore Your Excellency most humbly to use moderation. The evil spirit, who foresees the glory God will draw from your precious preservation, asks for nothing better than to see you take on too much in the beginning so he can soon see you collapse. Even if you, Excellency, should be strong enough to continue the work begun, he would be spiteful enough to use this same work to weary your spirit, knowing well that, once he discouraged it from your holy diligence, he would cause it to consider other more agreeable and less useful work. If, on the other hand, you agree to slow down a little, you will extend far and wide the results of your apostolic functions.

I most humbly entreat Your Excellency to forgive his faithful old servant the liberty he takes in speaking to him in this way.

As for the order you have given us, Excellency, to send you some workers, I received it with respect and submission. I had already been asked for a few priests for you, but I understood that you meant priests from our Tuesday Conferences. Since, however,

---

Letter 2952. - Archives of the Mission, Paris, unsigned rough draft.

you want them from our Company, we will try to send you two, Excellency, at the time you do me the honor of indicating.

May God make us worthy of obeying you and of corresponding to your holy intentions! I desire this grace for myself in particular, and am, in His love. . . .

2953. - TO EDME JOLLY, SUPERIOR, IN ROME

Paris, August 29, 1659

Vincent de Paul informs Edme Jolly that he has received his letter and reminds him to take care of his health. He is very grateful to the Cardinal of Genoa[1] for his countless favors. This Prelate's desire to procure a house in Rome for the Priests of the Mission and the trouble he takes to find one will cause them to consider him doubly their founder and to revere him both as a father and a great saint.

". . . .We are waiting for the plan of the building Cardinal Bagni[2] wants to sell and are awaiting from God the grace to be deserving of the benefits with which he and all those other Cardinals who deign to show an interest in your establishment, honor you. I sent your letter to the Duchesse d'Aiguillon, so that she can see what you have done for her Loreto foundation."

Letter 2953. - Catalogue of M. Charavay, who described the original in the following terms: "two full pages, small in quarto, with several worm holes and words of autograph corrections; the letter is incomplete at the end."

[1]Stefano Cardinal Durazzo.

[2]Nicolò di Bagno (Saint Vincent refers to him as *Nicolas Bagni*), Archbishop of Athens, Nuncio in France from June 25, 1643 to 1657, was made a Cardinal with the titular church of Sant'Eusebio, and Bishop of Senigallia on April 9, 1657. He died in Rome on August 23, 1663, at the age of seventy-nine. Saint Vincent, with whom he had a close relationship, was very pleased with his benevolence.

2954. - TO JEAN MARTIN, SUPERIOR, IN TURIN

Paris, August 29, 1659

Monsieur,

The grace of O[ur] L[ord] be with you forever!

From your letter of the sixteenth, I learned of M. Demortier's relapse, which puts him in danger. I am really worried about this and await patiently the outcome of the illness. May it please God to cure him! I hope this visit will help him.

It looks as though those good Fathers, who are thwarting the efforts being made in Rome for a seminary, will remain in their abbey.[1] May Divine Providence be pleased to ordain for the best whatever concerns it, including the palace near you, which is at the disposal of the Pope. The Marchese is supposed to speak to the Nuncio about it, so he can explain to His Holiness how much good he will do by turning it into a seminary to receive and instruct Pastors and other local priests there!

Since that is a work of God, we must pray fervently for it and also that He may be pleased to remove from us anything that makes us unworthy of contributing to His plans. If His Divine Goodness wills to make use of us for the above-mentioned seminary, we will try to send you the men who will be needed.

I am, with the heart that God alone knows, in His love, Monsieur, your most humble servant.

VINCENT DEPAUL,
i.s.C.M.

Addressed: Monsieur Martin

Letter 2954. - Archives of the Mission, Turin, original signed letter.

[1]Sant'Antonio Abbey.

2955. - TO JACQUES PESNELLE, SUPERIOR, IN GENOA

Paris, August 29, 1659

Monsieur,

The grace of O[ur] L[ord] be with you forever!

I am replying to your letter of the twelfth. I praise God for having sent you a Jewish man to make a Christian of him—and a good Christian, I hope.

Your judges should be given the time they are requesting to deliberate on your dispute, since it is only to be able to study the affair in greater depth and to render justice to you.

The detachment God gives you from the things of this world is more valuable than all its precious assets. You will have the merit before God of having chosen the better part among your brothers, taking Him alone as your inheritance, and this will not prevent you from receiving your share of your late father's estate. We will try to persuade those good gentlemen to decide along these lines. May God bless and keep you!

I am, in His love, Monsieur, your most humble servant.

VINCENT DEPAUL,
i.s.C.M.

Addressed: Monsieur Pesnelle, Superior of the Priests of the Mission of Genoa, in Genoa

---

Letter 2955. - Archives of the Mission, Paris, original signed letter.

2956. - TO TOUSSAINT LEBAS, IN AGDE

Paris, August 29, 1659

Monsieur,

The grace of O[ur] L[ord] be with you forever!

Since Thierry is determined to leave, better that it be sooner than later, seeing that he is doing more harm than good. I have already asked M. Durand to dismiss him.[1]

If Isaac Martin, that good young man you took in as a servant, perseveres in doing well and in wanting to enter the Company, I consent to M. Durand's accepting him as a Brother[2] and for him to come to your regular common exercises, as is customary with our Brothers.

Under no circumstances should Brother Lemoyne[3] be allowed to go to confession outside of the house, because of the regrettable consequences that may result from this. Please tell M. Durand this when he returns from Narbonne so he can dissuade this Brother from that whim. If he is unable to do so, let me know; I will write to him about it.

It is quite true, Monsieur, that if we are faithful to God, we will lack nothing. If that good man who wishes to give 10,000 livres in property to your house persists in this intention, get some advice on how this gift will have to be made, in order to secure it well, for it might be contested.

Letter 2956. - Archives of the Mission, Paris, original signed letter, sent by Father John Moore, C.M., Saint John the Baptist Rectory, Brooklyn, NY (USA). The postscript is in the Saint's handwriting.

[1]The secretary had added the following words, which were subsequently crossed out: "I do not know why he has not done so."

[2]Isaac Martin is not listed in the catalogue of coadjutor Brothers.

[3]Jean Lemoyne, born in Saint-Cyr-en-Pail in 1611, entered the Congregation of the Mission in 1643 as a coadjutor Brother. He was stationed in Agde in 1655; Firmin Get sent him back there after a short sojourn in Marseilles (cf. no. 3144a). *Notices,* vol. I, does not list him at all; vol. V (Supplement) lists him as Jean *Lemoine*.

I am not writing to M. Durand at this time because I have nothing to say to him.[4] I am writing to you in reply to your letter of August 11 and to recommend myself to your prayers and to those of the whole family, whom I embrace, prostrate in spirit at their feet.

I am, in O[ur] L[ord], Monsieur, your most humble servant.

VINCENT DEPAUL,
i.s.C.M.

If that good Brother finds it difficult to go to someone else in the house, let him go to M. Durand.

At the bottom of the first page: Monsieur Lebas

2957. - TO ANTOINE DURAND, SUPERIOR, IN AGDE

Paris, August 29, 1659

Monsieur,

The grace of O[ur] L[ord] be with you forever!

You tell me in your letter of the eighteenth that M. Baillon has left; however, he has not yet arrived here. We will be happy to welcome him.

I sympathize with you in your troubles. You must not be surprised at difficulties and, still less, allow yourself to be discouraged by them; they are to be encountered everywhere, especially in a duty such as yours. Let two men live together and they will have difficulties with one another, and even if you were alone, you would be a burden to yourself and would need to practice patience, so true it is that our life is wretched and strewn with crosses. I praise

---

[4]As is evident from no. 2957, Saint Vincent changed his mind, perhaps after having received a letter from Antoine Durand that same day.

Letter 2957. - Archives of the Mission, Paris, original signed letter.

God, Monsieur, for the good use you are making of yours, as I feel sure you are doing.

I have observed too much wisdom and gentleness in you to doubt that you will lack them in these trying circumstances. Besides, you are the only one who has written to me about what is going on. I can assure you that no one has made any complaints to me about your leadership, and the person you mention seems satisfied and not discontented with it. Continue to act toward him as you wrote me you are doing.

I think you did well to ask the Bishop of Narbonne[1] to issue a statement that, when he was Bishop and Count of Agde, he was the one who had the seminary building erected in its present form, so that you may make use of it, if necessary. It will also be a good idea for you to wait until his successor [2] arrives, to discuss with the town authorities the clauses of their deliberation. He will act cautiously with them in the beginning, so you need not worry that their indignation will fall upon you.

It is very true that you need letters patent from the King to confirm your establishment and for the union of your chapels; otherwise, you have nothing. You will do well, then, to make every effort to obtain the consent of the patrons of those chapels, if there are any, and that of the members of the chapter, so that the Bishop can use them to effect the union of the above-mentioned chapels, and that, by this union we may obtain the letters patent from the King. To do this validly, the said Bishop of Agde has to agree to draw up a new act of erection of his seminary and give its perpetual direction to the Company because this perpetuity is not specified in the contract drawn up between the late M. du Chesne[3] and the Bishop of Narbonne, who was Bishop of Agde at the time. I will

---

[1]François Fouquet.

[2]Louis Fouquet.

[3]Pierre du Chesne entered the Congregation of the Mission in 1637 and became one of Saint Vincent's best Missionaries. The latter made him Superior in Crécy (1641-44), at the Bons-Enfants (1644), of the mission to Ireland and Scotland (1646-48), in Marseilles (1653-54), and in

send you a copy from one of our other establishments to serve as a model for the said Bishop, and you can consult M. Laur for the formalities to be observed for the union of the chapels.

I am, in the love of O[ur] L[ord], Monsieur, your most humble servant.

VINCENT DEPAUL,
i.s.C.M.

Addressed: Monsieur Durand

2958. - TO CHARLES BOUSSORDEC, IN LA ROSE

Paris, September 3, 1659

Vincent de Paul approves the steps taken by Charles Boussordec to put his affairs in order, and he asks him to go to Nantes as soon as possible. There, M. Boussordec will receive a longer letter and will find other Missionaries who, like him, have been assigned to the Madagascar mission—or at least they should be arriving shortly after, God willing.

". . . .You will fit yourself out in Nantes, and we will ask O[ur] L[ord] to guide you safely there and to animate you with His grace and His Spirit.

I am, in His love, etc."

Agde (1654). He also summoned him to the two General Assemblies convoked at Saint-Lazare during his lifetime. Du Chesne died in Agde on November 3, 1654.

Letter 2958. - Catalogue of M. Laverdet, a dealer in historical documents and autograph letters in Paris, January 1854, no. 1064. The original comprised two pages in quarto.

2959. - TO EDME MENESTRIER, SUPERIOR, IN AGEN

Paris, September 3, 1659

Monsieur,

The grace of O[ur] L[ord] be with you forever!

I am sending you a copy of the consent or approval you gave to the union effected between Saint-Pourçain Priory and our Company so that you may kindly draw up a new one before the same notary or some other you prefer. It should include the same terms, but not the same date, for the former was drawn up last year, and the one I am requesting of you should be dated this year.[1] Please send it to me posthaste because we need it in a hurry.

I can tell you nothing more this time, except that I am, in O[ur] L[ord], Monsieur, your most humble servant.

VINCENT DEPAUL,
i.s.C.M.

I received your letter of August 22. M. Fournier's cousin will be welcome, if he comes here.

At the bottom of the page: Monsieur Edme

2960. - TO EDME JOLLY, SUPERIOR, IN ROME

September 5, 1659

More and more, I admire God's infinite goodness in that of Cardinal Durazzo, which has no bounds as far as we are concerned;

Letter 2959. - Archives of the Mission, Paris, original signed letter.

[1]Menestrier had received Saint-Pourçain Priory *in commendam* on October 3, 1655.

Letter 2960. - Reg. 2, p. 248.

we are the object of all his acts of kindness. We should humble ourselves profoundly and abase ourselves at the sight of our eternal indebtedness to him. I admit that this is all we can do if we are not to be utterly ungrateful, and I ask Our Lord to make us less unworthy than we are of rendering God the modest services for which His Eminence honors us with the favor of his benevolence and benefits. I ask also that His Divine Majesty may, in the end, be Himself his reward.

We await the final decision to be taken on the contract for the building Cardinal Bagni is trying to sell.

2961. - TO FIRMIN GET, SUPERIOR, IN MONTPELLIER

Paris, September 5, 1659

I am sure the business puzzles you, as long as you still have no knowledge of it. All beginnings are a little strange, but be patient: the novelty will soon wear off, and you will gradually find easy those things which now seem difficult to you. In addition, Our Lord, who has given you charge of them, will give you also the knowledge required to do His Will in them. My only concern is your health; please do whatever you can to keep well.

Letter 2961. - Archives of the Mission, Paris, Marseilles manuscript.

2962. - TO JEAN MARTIN, SUPERIOR, IN TURIN

Paris, September 5, 1659

Monsieur,

The grace of O[ur] L[ord] be with you forever!

I received your letter of August 23 and will begin my reply to it where you left off, regarding the new workers you are requesting. We cannot send you any just now because we have to staff two new establishments.[1] We also have to send to Poland a few priests capable of teaching because the Queen recently donated a benefice of four or five thousand livres revenue for a seminary. This will prevent us from coming more promptly to your rescue. That is why I am asking you, Monsieur, to be patient and to do the best you can with the men you have—which I know you are doing, thank God. I am so consoled by this that I do not know how I let these words escape me. Continue to guide them according to your usual wisdom and graciousness.

There is reason to believe that M. Dem[ortier's] anxiety arises from his physical infirmity and that, as the health of his body is restored, his mind will be peaceful and content, above all in the work the missions are going to give him. If, however, the contrary occurs, you can consult M. Jolly or M. Pesnelle about an exchange with one of their priests.

I ask Our Lord to strengthen you, Monsieur, in town and in the country, in body and in spirit, since God chooses to give you cause for concern everywhere and in every way. This is how His Providence treats those whom He loves, especially those in charge of others, who bear the whole burden.

We have had several sick men here—some in danger of death—

Letter 2962. - Archives of the Mission, Turin, original signed letter.

[1]Narbonne and Notre-Dame-de-Bétharram.

but all are getting better, thank God. I am, in Him, Monsieur, your most humble servant.

VINCENT DEPAUL,
i.s.C.M.

Addressed: Monsieur Martin, Superior of the Priests of the Turin Mission, in Turin

2963. - TO JACQUES PESNELLE, SUPERIOR, IN GENOA

Paris, September 5, 1659

Monsieur,

The grace of O[ur] L[ord] be with you forever!

I received your letter of August 19. The holidays you suggest raise a very delicate point. If they are given to some—as it is sometimes right to do—others may think they have the right to ask for them; and if they are granted on one occasion, they will continue to ask for them, with the result that this will open the door to complaints instead of closing it to this custom. Still, we were obliged to do it here; in the beginning, we used to give the seminarians permission once a year for an excursion of several days. We had to reduce that, however, to one day a week, on which they went off to enjoy themselves in places one, two, or three leagues away. But the inconveniences that arose from both of these customs have forced us to do away with these outings, particularly since we have had some eighty *arpents*[1] of land enclosed, providing ample space for recreation. Nevertheless, we allowed the students to go to spend several days on one of our farms,[2] but they behaved

---

Letter 2963. - Archives of the Mission, Paris, original signed letter.

[1]An old French term for land measurement; because of regional variations, an *arpent* can be estimated only as the equivalent of one acre or a little more.

[2]Either Orsigny or Rougemont.

Orsigny was a hamlet near Saclay (Essonne), where Saint Vincent had accepted the gift of a

so badly there that I was no longer willing to allow them to go back. Even when I was pressured to do so just recently, I did not give in, by the grace of God.

I am not trying to say that what we do here, you should do there. You are in too close quarters not to send your students out a little for some suitable amusement. However, before settling this question, I ask you to let me know if the Jesuits, the Oratorian Fathers, and the Theatines in Genoa give their students holidays, and where they go. We are on a very slippery slope here. One liberty has no sooner been granted than another is requested, as you see from the fact that, when you gave your students two weeks relaxation, some of them wanted to go to Our Lady of Savona; another year they will want to go to Milan or somewhere else. They will make this a custom and go from one abuse to another, and it will end in disorder. That is where things lead.

As for your difficulty in how to help M. Simon, I think it will be a good idea for you to relieve him of the Internal Seminary and give him just one class to teach; that will be enough, along with the duty of Assistant he has to fulfill. As for the other class, ask M. Philippe to take it, and tell both of them that I asked you to tell them not to dictate any notes. I am well aware that it is good to do so occasionally and that they will find it hard not to give some notes, but the consequences are to be feared, namely, that gradually people end by dictating entire treatises, which, no matter how good

---

farm from Jacques and Élisabeth Norais (cf. contract signed on December 22, 1644, Arch. Nat., S 6687). The farm provided the Congregation of the Mission with agricultural products and served as a place of rest and relaxation. According to vol. IV, no. 1467, the farms that supplied Saint Lazare did not provide for one-sixth of the needs of the Motherhouse. As long as Jacques and Élisabeth Norais were alive, the Community possessed the farm in all tranquility; after their death, however, some cousins claimed it in a successful lawsuit (1658). It was later purchased by the Congregation of the Mission at a court-ordered auction in 1684.

The Rougemont farm, situated in the Bondy forest in the commune of Sevran (Seine-Saint-Denis), covered a vast expanse of woods and cultivated land. Adrien Le Bon donated it to Saint Vincent on February 11, 1645, "on account of the great friendship and affection" he bore the priests and Brothers of Saint-Lazare. (Cf. Arch. Nat., S 6698, pièces 1 and 2.)

they are, are never better [than what] is found[3] in books. So, it is better that they refrain from this completely.

As for the Internal Seminary, I persist in asking you to put M. Pinon in charge, if M. Simon agrees to this.[4] This duty will oblige M. Pinon to be more watchful over himself so that he can truly edify the whole house. The reasons you give me against this should not prevent an attempt being made, for we cannot send you anyone who is better suited—or who speaks Italian, which is essential.

I will let you know at the first opportunity whether you should divide the property with your brothers or be satisfied with a pension.

I am, in O[ur] L[ord], Monsieur, your most humble servant.

VINCENT DEPAUL,
i.s.C.M.

Addressed: Monsieur Pesnelle, Superior of the Priests of the Mission, in Genoa

2964. - TO THE OFFICIALIS [1] OF ARRAS

Paris, September 6, 1659

Monsieur,

I renew here the offers of my obedience and my most humble thanks for the favor you do us of thinking of us when the occasions

---

[3]First redaction: "are never as good as the ones found." The Saint added the word *better* in his own handwriting.

[4]First redaction: "if M. Simon does not find it too difficult to give it up." The correction is in the Saint's handwriting.

Letter 2964. - Archives of the Mission, Paris, unsigned rough draft.

[1]The *Officialis,* or Judicial Vicar, is appointed by the Bishop and is given the ordinary power to judge, which is distinct from that of the Vicar-General. The Officialis constitutes one tribunal

arise. The present one, Monsieur, concerns François Monvoisin and Ignace Boucher, two members of your diocese and of our Company, who are of an age and condition to receive Holy Orders. Both have done well in philosophy and theology. Monvoisin has received only tonsure so far, but he is wise and virtuous; we have not observed any faults in him since he has been with us. I very humbly entreat you to grant him a dimissorial *ad omnes,*[2] and Brother Boucher another for Holy Orders. He too is striving after virtue. He did manifest some youthful thoughtlessness but, for the past few years, has behaved in such a way that there is reason to hope that he will be a good priest,[3] and Monvoisin as well.

If it pleases you to grant them the favor I am requesting, I ask you most humbly to do so as soon as possible because an opportunity is presenting itself to put them to work for God's service and the salvation of souls.

I am writing to ask Sister Marguerite,[4] who will give you this letter, to get them from your secretary and to pay the usual fees.

If we here can be of service to you, Monsieur, in gratitude for the proofs we receive of your goodness, we will be so wholeheartedly, for I am, Monsieur. . . .

---

with the Bishop, but he cannot judge cases which the Bishop reserves to himself (cf. *Code of Canon Law,* Latin-English edition [Ann Arbor, Michigan: Braun-Brumfield, 1983], Canon 1420, p. 511). The duties of Officialis at the time of Saint Vincent did not differ markedly from what the present Code stipulates.

[2]Saint Vincent was requesting a dispensation for these two confreres *for all Orders* of the time: Minor (Orders of Porter, Lector, Exorcist, and Acolyte) and Major (Subdiaconate, Diaconate, and Priesthood).

[3]Saint Vincent had extended Boucher's novitiate by six months because of a flagrant act of disobedience toward his Director (cf. vol. VI, no. 2099).

[4]Marguerite Chétif, born in Paris, was baptized at Saint-Sulpice on September 8, 1621, and entered the Company of the Daughters of Charity on May 1, 1649. She was first sent to Chars and in May 1651 went to Serqueux. She took perpetual vows in Paris on April 4, 1655. When the Company was erected officially on August 8, 1655, she signed the Act of Establishment. In 1656 she went to Arras as Sister Servant and was there when Saint Louise died. Saint Vincent appointed Sister Marguerite Superioress General (1660-67); in 1667 she became Seminary Directress, and in 1670 Sister Servant in Angers. In 1674 she was named Treasurer General under Sister Nicole Haran; upon completion of her term of office (1677), she went as Sister Servant to the Nom-de-Jésus hospice. She died at the Motherhouse on January 9, 1694. Two

2965. - TO JEAN PARRE, IN SAINT-QUENTIN

Paris, September 6, 1659

Dear Brother,

The grace of O[ur] L[ord] be with you forever!

The Ladies have not given any new orders for you; they are waiting for you to find out which places are in the greatest need and are the best ones in which to have some seeds distributed.

M. Delahaye, the Dean of Noyon, has recommended a poor gentleman named M. Sablonnière, saying that he has been ruined by the mobile camp at Mirémont,[1] which seized his cattle and furniture and destroyed his grain crop. The Ladies would like to find out from you if this is true, if this poor gentleman has no means of getting back on his feet and maintaining himself and, if he has children, how many. Please let us know anything you can learn about this.

I am sending you a note that was written to me about a ruined chapel they want you to have restored. If you can do anything about it, fine.

I am, in O[ur] L[ord], dear Brother, your most affectionate servant.

VINCENT DEPAUL,
i.s.C.M.

Addressed: Brother Jean Parre, of the Congregation of the Mission, in Saint-Quentin

---

conferences given after her death are preserved in *Circulaires des supérieurs généraux et des soeurs supérieures aux Filles de la Charité et Remarques ou Notices sur les Soeurs défuntes de la Communauté* (Paris: Adrien Le Clère, 1845, pp. 470-78).

Letter 2965. - Archives of the Mission, Paris, copy made from the original signed letter, put up for sale by M. Charavay in 1880.

[1]Perhaps Miraumont, a small locality in the district of Péronne (Somme).

2966. - TO MADEMOISELLE DE CHANDENIER [1]

September 6, 1659

Mademoiselle de Chandenier is assured by her servant Vincent that she is sovereign and absolute in the Saint-Lazare house and that the good priest of whom she has written will be most welcome there to make an eight-day retreat. He can spend the rest of the time in the Bons-Enfants Seminary because, as a rule, we do not receive anyone here in this house for longer than those eight days.

It is also to be desired that he wait until after the ordination [retreat], which will begin next Wednesday and will keep all our beds filled and our men busy for ten or eleven days. If, however, he wants to come to the retreat exercises for the ordinands, we will receive him most willingly. Then he can make his retreat and, in that case, can stay here for eighteen days.

2967. - TO SAINT LOUISE

[September 1659] [1]

I ask Mademoiselle Le Gras to let me know on whom, in particular, she has cast her eyes for Vaux,[2] which is the Attorney

---

Letter 2966. - Archives of the Mission, Paris, unsigned rough draft.

[1]Marie de Chandenier, who never married, was the sister of the two Chandenier brothers, who figure so prominently in Saint Vincent's correspondence. She died in Paris in 1701, at the age of eighty-seven, and left her estate to Guillaume de Lamoignon, Chief Justice of the Parlement.

Letter 2967. - Archives of the Mission, Paris, copy.

[1]Reference to the Sisters' departure for Narbonne enables us to assign this date, since they went there in September 1659.

[2]Vaux-le-Vicomte, near Melun (Seine-et-Marne), where Nicolas Fouquet built a magnificent chateau. Its luxury and ostentation angered King Louis XIV and brought about the arrest of Fouquet in 1663. (Cf. *Documents,* Doc. 765.)

General's[3] house, and when they will be ready to leave. Madame Fouquet is really anxious about this.

I will find out where the King's attorney is staying in the town and will send him to Mademoiselle Le Gras; I will also send the petitions she is requesting. M. Maillard[4] is not here; I will give him the petitions tomorrow.

There is no rush for an immediate departure for Narbonne; I think it will be in a week or so.[5]

2968. - TO JEAN DE FRICOURT,[1] SEMINARIAN OF THE MISSION, IN SAINTES

Paris, September 7, 1659

Dear Brother,

The grace of O[ur] L[ord] be with you forever!

You tell me in your last letter that you are troubled, that you have no love for either the Rules or the exercises, and that you hope I will offer some remedy for this. I would like very much to do so,

---

[3]Nicolas Fouquet, born in Paris on January 27, 1615, became Attorney General of the Parlement of Paris in 1650 and Superintendent of Finances in 1653. Accused of embezzlement and arrested in Nantes on September 5, 1663, he was judged, condemned to life imprisonment, and incarcerated in the Château de Pignerol where he died in March 1680. He became reconciled with God in his last years and even composed some books of devotion. (Cf. Jules Lair, *Nicolas Fouquet, procureur général, surintendant des finances, ministre d'État de Louis XIV* [2 vols., Paris: Plon et Nourrit, 1890].)

[4]Antoine Maillard, born in Veney (Meurthe), entered the Congregation of the Mission on May 21, 1644, at twenty-six years of age. He took his vows in 1646 and renewed them on January 25, 1656. Maillard was Procurator of Saint-Lazare for a long time and Procurator General (1679-86).

[5]For several years François Fouquet, Archbishop of Narbonne, had been asking for the Daughters of Charity. The first three Sisters sent to Narbonne left Paris on September 12.

Letter 2968. - Archives of the Mission, Paris, seventeenth-century copy.

[1]Jean de Fricourt, born in Nibas (Somme) on March 7, 1635, entered the Congregation of the Mission on June 20, 1656, and took his vows in Saintes on October 20, 1658, in the presence of M. Louis Rivet. He was still there in September 1660. *Notices*, vols. I and V (Supplement), lists him as *Defricourt.*

dear Brother, and all the more so since I sympathize very deeply with your trouble because of the esteem and affection I have always had for you. In order to cure your ailment, however, we have to know what it is. As for me, I think it is a weakness of the will and a weariness of mind regarding the things God is asking of you.

This is no surprise to me because all persons are naturally in that state. And if you ask me why there is this difference between them, since some are fervent and others lax, I reply that the former surmount the repugnances of nature, and the latter do not make enough effort to overcome them. The former are at peace, since their heart is not divided because they have given it totally to God, but the latter are uneasy because, while wishing to love God, they still love other things apart from God—those bodily comforts that make the soul sluggish in the practice of virtue. This engenders and nourishes idleness, which is the vice of the clergy. It is the state of which God has the greatest horror. Yes, tepidity is a state of damnation.

O my dear Brother, what great reason you and I have to tremble, knowing as we do that cursed is he who does the work of God negligently.[2] *Mon Dieu!* what a lesson is taught us by farm workers in the fields, artisans in the cities, and soldiers who go to war! They work unceasingly and suffer greatly for things that perish with them, and we, that we may be saved, that God may be honored and served on earth, and that the Passion of J[esus] C[hrist] may be applied efficaciously to the souls He has created for heaven, are unwilling to take any trouble or master our evil inclinations!

I call *evil* all those inclinations that turn us aside from the obligations of our vocation. Yet, since this vocation binds us to follow O[ur] L[ord], it obliges us also to renounce ourselves, that is, our will, our judgment, our pleasures, property, relatives, etc., and this is done by the observance of our Rules and by our works.

---

[2]Cf. Jer 48:10. (NAB)

The fidelity we bring to this will give us the desired peace of mind and perfection, but it takes courage to work through the difficulties. So then, dear Brother, resolve, once and for all, to overcome the things that displease you, and ask God frequently for the grace to submit the inferior part to Him.

We are now in the period of retreats. I hope yours will serve to detach you completely from the pleasures of this life and animate you with zeal to attain eternity. Heaven suffers violence;[3] we must fight to bear it away and fight feelings of flesh and blood to the very end. If you do so, dear Brother, it will no longer be you who live, but J[esus] C[hrist] will live in you,[4] as I ask Him to do with all my heart.

I am, in His love, dear Brother, your most humble servant.

VINCENT DEPAUL,
i.s.C.M.

2969. - *SAINT LOUISE TO SAINT VINCENT*

Wednesday, [September 1659] [1]

Most Honored Father,

I think Sister Marie-Marthe[2] should be sent for no later than today. One of our Sisters reminded me that, except for Sister Carcireux,[3] the other

---

[3]Cf. Mt 11:12. (NAB)
[4]Cf. Gal 2:20. (NAB)

Letter 2969. - Archives of the Motherhouse of the Daughters of Charity, original autograph letter.

[1]Date added on the back of the original by Brother Ducournau.

[2]Marie-Marthe Trumeau, a native of Poissy (Yvelines), had been sent to Angers in March 1640; she returned to Paris in June 1647 after becoming seriously ill in Angers. In 1648 she served the poor in Saint-Paul parish. In 1653 she was named Sister Servant in Nantes, where she remained for two years (cf. no. 1672). She was sent to La Fère on July 31, 1656, and from there to Cahors in September 1658.

[3]Françoise Carcireux, born in Beauvais, entered the Company of the Daughters of Charity around 1640-41. Stationed first at Saint-Germain-l'Auxerrois, then with the foundlings in

Sisters named are not good workers. It is true that the others are extremely slow, and I would be afraid there would be talk if the work did not get done. Furthermore, as matters now stand in Cahors, I think we will have to send Sister Carcireux there to satisfy the Bishop.[4]

Most Honored Father, we will need one of your servants or someone else to go to Vaux on horseback and for our Sister to leave there at daybreak tomorrow. The need for this causes me to inconvenience you so I can make up for the fault I committed in thinking only of what I felt was the greater need, namely, compatible temperaments. I will have to know your decision so the horse can be readied.

Please forgive all my acts of imprudence, since I am, Most Honored Father, your most obedient and humble servant.

L. DE MARILLAC

2970. - TO LOUIS RIVET, SUPERIOR, IN SAINTES

Paris, September 9, 1659

Monsieur,

The grace of O[ur] L[ord] be with you forever!

I received your letters of August 6 and 20. They need no other reply than that given you by M. de la Noue concerning M. Martin's[1] benefice, except that I thank you for having taken possession of it and all the other trouble you have taken about it.

Bicêtre, she was sent to Richelieu in June or July 1649 but left there in September 1659 for the Narbonne hospital. From 1672 to 1675 she filled the important role of Assistant of the Company.

[4]Alain de Solminihac.

Letter 2970. - Archives of the Mission, Paris, seventeenth-century copy.

[1]This Jean Martin, born in Surgères (Charente-Maritime), entered the Congregation of the Mission as a priest on May 20, 1643, at the age of twenty-five. He is mentioned in Saint Vincent's correspondence only three times: in a letter of February 23, 1643 (vol. II, no. 646), this letter in vol. VIII, and no. 2985 later in this volume. He should not be confused with the other Jean Martin, who was Superior of the Turin house for many years.

You tell me that the physician is urging you to go to take the waters. If you have not, I beg you to do so because M. Dehorgny [2] will go to Brittany before going to your house; he is still in Le Mans and may be in Richelieu when you receive this letter. Please do all you can to keep well. God will be honored by your good health, and the Company greatly consoled.

We have a few sick men here. Messieurs Boucher[3] and Perraud[4] were at death's door, but all of them are better, thank God.

I am, in the love of O[ur] L[ord], Monsieur, your most humble servant.

VINCENT DEPAUL,
i.s.C.M.

2971. - TO DENIS LAUDIN,[1] SUPERIOR, IN LE MANS

Paris, September 10, 1659

Monsieur,

The grace of O[ur] L[ord] be with you forever!

M. d'Eu's [2] proposal, which you mention in your letter of the

---

[2]Jean Dehorgny was making a visitation of a number of houses.

[3]Léonard Boucher.

[4]Hugues Perraud, born in Arguel (Doubs) on October 3, 1615, entered the Congregation of the Mission on January 5, 1640, took his vows on March 23, 1644, and was ordained a priest in 1646. He was placed in Saintes (1646) and Richelieu (1651), and died in Paris on December 26, 1659.

Letter 2971. - Archives of the Mission, Turin, original signed letter.

[1]Denis Laudin was born in Provins (Seine-et-Marne) on January 15, 1622. He entered the Congregation of the Mission on April 21, 1647, took his vows in September 1649, and was ordained a priest on December 25, 1649. After ordination he asked and obtained permission to remake a little of his Internal Seminary. He was next sent to Montauban, then to Richelieu as Procurator (1651-57). He was Superior in Le Mans (1657-68), Troyes (1668-75), Angers (1675-79), and Fontainebleau (1679-90), and Visitor of the Champagne Province (1682-86). In 1690 he was changed to Saint-Cyr, becoming Superior there the following year. Serious illness and poor eyesight prompted his return to Saint-Lazare, where he was put in charge of the coadjutor Brothers and where he died on April 12, 1693. His brother Gabriel was also a Priest of the Mission. (Cf. *Notices,* vol. II, pp. 365-88.)

[2]Louis d'Eu, born in Fresnay-sur-Sarthe (Sarthe) on April 8, 1624, entered the Congregation

third, troubles me because I see several difficulties in carrying it out. The main ones are: (1) the inhabitants of Champfleur[3] would lose a great deal if that good servant of God were to leave them; and, since we have given ourselves to God to serve His Church, those souls should be as dear to us as any others, and we should make sure that good Pastors stay in their parishes; (2) it would be wrong to give this parish to M. Brochard, since we know he does not want to keep it; furthermore, we do not know to what kind of priest he would hand it over; (3) M. d'Eu would commit the same fault if he accepted the parish of Notre-Dame-des-Champs[4] with the intention of resigning it, especially if this were in favor of M. Pangois, since we do not know if it would be for the uncle or the nephew.

That, Monsieur, is all I can say about the matter just now. I will think it over again and, if any other ideas occur to me, I will let you know.

I gladly consent to your accepting M. Guy's offer to help you in your missions, at least temporarily, and, depending on how he conducts himself at that time, you can use him in the future, in case of need.

M. Dehorgny has written to ask me to recall Brother Taillié[5] and

---

of the Mission on May 20, 1651, left it, and reentered on March 6, 1655, taking his vows in Rome on March 7, 1657. After Saint Vincent's death, he again left the Congregation for some important business, by order of the Archbishop of Paris, but returned as soon as he was able after the Archbishop died. The Bibliothèque Nationale has acquired one of his manuscript works, *L'homme accompli* (fr. 9625).

[3]A small commune in the district of Mamers (Sarthe).

[4]Notre-Dame-des-Champs is today part of the municipality of Saint-Jean-d'Assé (Sarthe).

[5]Patrick Taylor (Patrice Taillié), born in Dublin around September 29, 1631, entered the Congregation of the Mission on July 9, 1657. As happens often enough, there are variations in the spelling of his name: *Notices*, vol. I, p. 487, has *Tallier*; vol. V (Supplement), p. 584, lists him as *Tailler*.

to send you another seminarian in his place. It will be difficult for us to find someone such as he indicates; however, we will do what we can.

Your most humble servant.

VINCENT DEPAUL,
i.s.C.M.

At the bottom of the first page: Monsieur Laudin

2972. - TO LOUIS DUPONT, SUPERIOR, IN TRÉGUIER

Paris, September 10, 1659

Monsieur,

The grace of O[ur] L[ord] be with you forever!

I received your letter of August 22. I will send M. Caset,[1] Superior of our house in Toul, the letter you wrote him, and will forward his reply to you as soon as I receive it.

Enclosed is a letter for you from Abbé Brisacier; I received it in the last regular mail from Rome, where he now is.

I think M. Dehorgny is in Richelieu right now—or at least on the point of leaving Le Mans to go there. After that he plans to go to Saint-Méen and then on to Tréguier.

I hope you will prepare the way for his visitation and that O[ur] L[ord] will bless it as, by His grace, He is blessing your leadership.

Letter 2972. - Public and University Library of Geneva, Ms. fr. 202, original signed letter.

[1]Michel Caset, born in Vautortes (Mayenne), entered the Congregation of the Mission on October 31, 1649, at twenty-four years of age, took his vows in November 1651, and was ordained a priest in 1653. He was Superior in Toul (1659-60), then in Crécy (1662-70), after having spent some time in Fontainebleau. He later became a diocesan priest and died as Pastor of Crouy-sur-Ourcq (Seine-et-Marne).

I ask Him to give you the necessary strength of mind and body to continue for a long time your good services to Him.

I am, in His love, Monsieur, your most humble servant.

VINCENT DEPAUL,
i.s.C.M.

At the bottom of the first page: Monsieur Dupont

2973. - *LOUIS AND CLAUDE CHANDENIER* [1] *TO SAINT VINCENT*

Moutiers-Saint-Jean, September 10, 1659

Monsieur and Most Honored Father,

The affection we know you have for us leads us to think that you will be consoled to know that we arrived safely in this place last Sunday, with the good, pleasant company you provided for us. Tomorrow, God willing, we will leave for Tournus and then continue our pilgrimage. This good beginning leads us to hope it will go well for us, with the help of your holy prayers, which we are very sure will not be lacking to us.

We also think, Monsieur and Most Honored Father, that you will be pleased to have news of Father de Gondi. For several reasons, we wanted

---

Letter 2973. - Archives of the Mission, Paris, original autograph letter.

[1]Louis de Rochechouart de Chandenier, Abbé de Tournus, was as remarkable for his virtue as for his noble birth. (Cf. Abelly, *op. cit.,* bk. I, chap. XLIX, p. 240.) One of the most assiduous members of the Tuesday Conferences, he took great pleasure in giving missions, especially to the poor. He declined several dioceses out of humility but accepted more modest but no less exacting functions, such as that of Visitor of the Carmelite nuns of France. To conform himself to the laws of the Church, he resigned all his benefices except Tournus. He died in Chambéry on May 6, 1660, after having been received on the previous evening into the Congregation of the Mission. Several conferences on his virtues were held at Saint-Lazare; the remarks made there are recorded in *Notices,* vol. II, pp. 511-39.

Like his brother Louis, Claude-Charles de Rochechouart de Chandenier, Abbé de Moutiers-Saint-Jean, was remarkable for his virtue, especially his humility. After the death of his uncle, François Cardinal de La Rochefoucauld (1645), he and his brother went to live at the Saint-Sulpice Seminary, which they left in 1653 to stay at Saint-Lazare. Claude-Charles died on May 17, 1710. François Watel, Superior General at the time, announced his death to his priests and recommended the deceased to their prayers. A long, beautiful epitaph placed on Claude de Chandenier's tomb is found in Collet, *op. cit.,* vol. I, pp. 584-88.

to be sure to pay our most humble respects to him, mainly because of the affection we know you have for his family and especially for him. His good health and energy are extraordinary for a man seventy-eight years old—just one year younger than you, he tells us. He did us the honor of receiving us and our dear confreres very cordially, expressing his joy at our modest tokens of respect, which it was our duty to render him, but particularly at what we told him about your health and the continuation of your usual exercises.

We implore the Divine Goodness—but with a fondness of heart we cannot put into words—to keep you well for the length of time Divine Wisdom has destined you to be of service to His Church. These are the wishes, Monsieur and Most Honored Father, of your most humble and obedient servants and sons.

L. DE CHANDENIER,
unworthy priest

CL. DE ROCHECHOUART

Addressed: *Monsieur Vincent, Superior General of the Congregation of the Mission, at Saint-Lazare, in Paris*

2974. - TO EDME JOLLY, SUPERIOR, IN ROME

Paris, September 12, 1659

Monsieur,

The grace of O[ur] L[ord] be with you forever!

I am sending you the letter the Duchesse d'Aiguillon wrote me about her foundation in Loreto, in which you will see her intention.

I received, with your letter of August 18, the Brief concerning the latest favors obtained from the Holy See.[1] God be praised, and

---

Letter 2974. - Original signed letter made available by Mademoiselle Reine Dousinelle of Caestre (Nord).

[1]Cf. vol. XIII, no. 120, *Alias nos,* the Brief of August 12, 1659, on the vow of poverty taken in the Congregation of the Mission.

may He Himself be your thanks for the trouble you have taken for it! I am taking the honor of writing to thank Cardinal Brancaccio[2] and Reverend Father Hilarion,[3] to whom, after God, we are most indebted for it.

As you suggested, I am also writing to Cardinals Durazzo and Bagni, with deep gratitude for the favors they are doing us in regard to the house.[4] We are waiting until the contract is signed before advancing the necessary sums.

We will have an apostolic notary verify copies of the Brief that deals with the conditions of the vow of poverty and will send one to each house, either by the Visitor or through the mail, together with a circular letter I will write to prepare them to receive it. If, however, you want to inform your family about it, do so; that will be better. It just occurred to me that, according to the regulations, the matter has to go before the Parlement[5] before we distribute the copies here in this house.[6]

I did not forget to write to Poitou for information regarding certain faults heretics may commit in the administration of Baptism,[7] but I did forget to send you the reply. They wrote me from Saintes and Richelieu that, after a diligent enquiry to learn the truth, they found that nothing essential is being omitted and they are baptizing validly.

---

[2]Francesco Maria Brancaccio, Bishop of Viterbo, Porto, and Capaccio, was created Cardinal in 1634 and died on January 9, 1675. He is also the author of a collection of Latin essays.

[3]Hilarion Rancati.

[4]Cardinal di Bagno's residence, Montecitorio (Rome).

[5]*Parlement* refers to the French judicial system. At the time of Saint Vincent, France had eight Parlements, each with its own legal jurisdiction, chief of which was the Parlement of Paris. They registered or gave sanction to the King's edicts, ordinances, and declarations, and supervised their implementation.

[6]The Saint did not inform his Community of the Brief until November 7.

[7]Cf. no. 2905.

I will write to Cahors what you tell me about the union of Gignac.[8] Meanwhile, I have enclosed a letter from M. Cuissot and a resignation of the parish in Chavagnac.

I am, in the love of O[ur] L[ord], Monsieur, your most humble servant.

VINCENT DEPAUL,
i.s.C.M.

2974a. - TO GABRIEL DELESPINEY, IN MARSEILLES

Paris, September 12, 1659

Monsieur,

The grace of O[ur] L[ord] be with you forever!

I am still very upset about your illness. I ask O[ur] L[ord] to relieve you of it, and I ask you to do whatever you can, through rest and remedies, for this purpose. Perhaps the cool weather of this month here will help to cure you; otherwise, we will have to see what we will do.

Both you and M. Le Vacher, in your letters of September 2, inform me that he was supposed to be leaving for Algiers four days later; that is why I am not writing to him. I am content to ask Our Lord to guide him safely to port and to bless his journey.

I am glad you have a report on the lands of Madame de Vins.[1]

---

[8]Negotiations had been taking place since November 1657 to transfer to Messieurs Cuissot and Grimal the title to a benefice in Gignac, a village in Lot (cf. vol. VI, no. 2453).

Letter 2974a. - Archives of the Mission, Paris, original signed letter. This letter was part of Coste's First Supplement of vol. VIII, no. 3315, pp. 543-45. Its date dictates its placement here. The postscript is in the Saint's handwriting, except for the last sentence.

[1]Dame Laurence Veyrac de Paulian, Baronne de Castelnau, was the widow of Melchior Dagouz de Montauban, Marquis de Vins, Maréchal of the King's troops. She died in Paris on February 20, 1659. By her will, drawn up on May 29, 1655, she left eighteen thousand livres to the Marseilles house for the maintenance of two Missionaries. There is an excerpt of this act in the Archives Nationales (S 6707).

See if you can visit M. Le Bègue,[2] who is one of those Missionary Priests of Provence and lives in their Marseilles house;[3] he is one of the executors of that lady's will—a very wise man and a good servant of God. He will clear up the doubts you have. Tell him I asked you to see him about that, and renew to him the offers of my obedience.

As for the income of that foundation, you cannot request it until one year after the death of the deceased; in addition, you have to have begun to give missions beforehand. So try to give at least one or two at the Château de Vins or elsewhere. True, you tell me that it is inadvisable for Messieurs Cornier and Beaure[4] to go there alone. That is why we will send you someone to work there as soon as possible, God willing.

God be praised, Monsieur, for the proof of benevolence you received from the Bishop of Marseilles[5] and for having several priests of the Conference[6] speak each time they come together, as

---

[2]A priest of the Congregation of the Blessed Sacrament founded by Authier de Sisgau.

[3]First redaction: "one of those missionaries people call Missionaries of Provence, who lives in Marseilles." The correction is in the Saint's handwriting.

[4]Jacques Beaure, born in Saint-Léonard-de-Noblat (Haute-Vienne) on March 22, 1627, entered the Congregation of the Mission for the second time on September 2, 1656.

[5]Étienne du Puget.

[6]This appears to be a group similar to the Tuesday Conferences in Paris.

The meetings known as the Tuesday Conferences began on June 13, 1633, as an outgrowth of the retreats for ordinands. They were to serve the clerical and spiritual development of priests selected for their proven holiness and learning. By the rules devised at the initial organizational meetings (cf. vol. XIII, no. 35), the members committed themselves to meet every Tuesday at Saint-Lazare or the Bons-Enfants "to honor the life of Christ, the Eternal Priest"; to celebrate daily Mass and confess once a week to a regular confessor; to make a spiritual retreat annually; to spend some time each day in mental prayer and the Divine Office; to read the New Testament; to make an examination of conscience; to attend the funerals of members; and to offer three Masses for the souls of the deceased.

They came together at three o'clock in the afternoon from All Saints' Day to Easter, and at three-thirty from Easter to All Saints', beginning with the *Veni Creator,* followed by discussion on the topic proposed at the previous meeting. In his letters and conferences, Saint Vincent mentions some of these topics proper to priests, such as the Beatitudes, the sanctification of Lent, modesty, humility, the spirit of poverty in the use of ecclesiastical goods, and censures. Members also gave reports on the works undertaken: confession for the sick at the Hôtel-Dieu, exhortations for prisoners, missions, etc.

The Superior of the Congregation of the Mission or his delegate directed the Conferences at Saint-Lazare, which were attended by more than 250 priests during Saint Vincent's lifetime. Of

is the custom here. You have done very well. I never knew that they did otherwise.

I do not agree to your making M. Cornier procurator while he is in the seminary. You can give him one of the keys of the strongbox in which the Barbary money is kept, but not the care of the storeroom. It will be better for you to take care of it yourself while awaiting the man we will send you.

We will reimburse the two pistoles you received from M. Bausset the Prior. I will send them to his brother at Saint-Sulpice, if he does not send someone to get them within the next two days.

We are sending to Agde two priests from our seminary: Messieurs Lemerer and Tanguy,[7] and M. des Jardins[8] is accompanying them en route to Narbonne, where he will pick up Messieurs Lebas and Dolivet in passing.

I am, in the love of O[ur] L[ord], Monsieur, your most humble servant.

VINCENT DEPAUL,
i.s.C.M.

By the same way we have sent three Sisters of Charity—one of whom is M. Cornier's niece—to the Archbishop of Narbonne,[9] who has been asking for them for a long time. Mademoiselle Le

---

these priests, twenty-two became Bishops. Similar conferences, modeled on those of Saint-Lazare, were organized in dioceses throughout France and Italy.

[7]Gilles Lemerer, born in the Tréguier diocese on September 22, 1633, entered the Congregation of the Mission on October 23, 1658, and took his vows in Agde on November 14, 1660, in the presence of M. Durand.

No information is available for M. Tanguy. *Notices*, vols. I and V (Supplement), does not list him; Coste's index (vol. XIV) provides no information other than what Saint Vincent has here.

[8]Georges des Jardins, born in Alençon (Orne) on January 6, 1625, was ordained a priest in September 1649, entered the Congregation of the Mission on August 15, 1651, and took his vows on August 17, 1653. Later, he was Superior in Toul (1655-57) and Narbonne (1659).

[9]François Fouquet.

Gras speaks very well of M. Cornier's niece; I greet him with all the tenderness of my heart.

M. Le Vacher told me he was leaving in four or five days. I am not writing to him.

I am writing to tell M. Huguier to give three livres to a man named Ballagny and thirty sous to a convict named du Rosier.

2975. - TO CARDINAL DURAZZO

Paris, September 12, 1659

Monseigneur,

When the Superior of the Rome house wrote me that Your Eminence continues to confer on us everywhere the benefits of your incomparable kindness, I let him know that I had no words convincing enough to express my gratitude for this. In fact, Monseigneur, I felt that it was better to maintain a holy silence toward Your Eminence than to thank you unworthily. I also felt that I should be satisfied to open my poor heart to God to ask that He Himself give the praise that is due to His infinite goodness for all the favors your own goodness bestows on us and, by the same token, to be Himself your reward for this.

But having learned since then, Monseigneur, of the trouble Your Eminence has taken to find a house for us, and the large contribution you have given and are obtaining for us to help us pay for it, I must happily express myself in writing, with sentiments of joy and admiration for such a benefit, and can say only: O Monseigneur, how good Your Eminence is to us, how resourceful in assisting us, how generous in showering us with blessings! Never has a Prelate made us more aware of the supreme charity of God than by your

---

Letter 2975. - Archives of the Mission, Paris, unsigned rough draft.

charity, Monseigneur, which is one of the greatest and most far-reaching that God has ever granted on this earth to our Little Company.

All we can do, Monseigneur, is to humble ourselves before God and before Your Eminence at the sight of our unworthiness and to proclaim the lavishness of your generosity and assistance. In addition we must ask O[ur] L[ord] unceasingly to preserve Your Eminence for a long time for the good of the entire Church, and to be, in the end, your infinite glory through all eternity.

With this desire and in His love, I am. . . .

2976. - TO CARDINAL DI BAGNO

Paris, September 12, 1659

Monseigneur,

I am asking Our Lord to help me to thank Your Eminence worthily for the favor you have done us by finding a place for us to stay in Rome, and in your own house,[1] and for having reduced the amount of its just worth that we should pay. For my part, I have no words to express my gratitude adequately for this, but I hope, Monseigneur, that God, for whom Your Eminence has done this act of charity, will be your great eternal reward.

Our entire Little Company will consider it a duty to pray constantly for you, as it is doing already. On its behalf and on my own, Monseigneur, I renew to Your Eminence the offers of our perpetual obedience, asking God, if He is pleased to derive some modest result from the Missionaries by the blessings they will receive in this blessed house, to attribute their merit to Your

---

Letter 2976. - Archives of the Mission, Paris, unsigned rough draft.

[1]The Priests of the Mission lived in this house, called Montecitorio, until 1913. It was situated close to the House of Representatives, of which it became an annex.

Eminence. I ask Him also to preserve you for a long time in this world for the good of the entire Church and the special consolation, Monseigneur, of your most humble and obedient servant.

2977. - TO CARDINAL BRANCACCIO

Paris, September 12, 1659

Monseigneur,

Of all the benefits God has conferred on our Little Company, I think that the one we appreciate most is to have had the honor of your benevolence, from which we receive so many outstanding favors. I thank Your Eminence a thousand times, Monseigneur, especially for the various Briefs the Holy See has granted us through the sage advice and powerful recommendation of Your Eminence, who is pleased to lavish your incomparable kindness on persons as unworthy as we are. Still, we will strive, Monseigneur, never to be ungrateful for them, although we are powerless to acknowledge the many special favors we have received from you.

May God, for whose love Your Eminence has done them for us, be pleased, Monseigneur, to be your eternal reward! We—and I in particular—will always be mindful of them, with an unfailing desire to obey you. I am, by God's grace, as much as anyone in this world can be, the most humble and most obedient servant of Your Eminence.

Letter 2977. - Archives of the Mission, Paris, unsigned rough draft.

2977a. - TO FATHER HILARION RANCATI, IN ROME

Most Reverend Father,

After learning, from letters sent to me from Rome, of the zeal and affection with which you, Most Reverend Father, had deigned to assist us in the affair of the confirmation of our Constitutions, I asked myself in my ignorance of this why you, Most Reverend Father, were so benevolent toward us, who are unworthy and incapable of rendering you service and who were, until then, absolutely unknown to you.

Since I see no reason on our part for this benevolence, I am obliged to attribute it to your charity, which had only God in view in this affair. That is why, feeling absolutely incapable of returning this favor, I fervently ask Almighty God to be Himself your abundant reward, Most Reverend Father. I have given orders to have many prayers and sacrifices offered in our Paris house; I have also written to our confreres living in other houses of our Congregation to do the same for your salvation and prosperity, Most Reverend Father. Our Congregation will always number you among its principal benefactors. Our entire Congregation, although still few in number, will proclaim publicly its joy at being always at your service.

We offer you with all due humility, Most Reverend Father, our best wishes, joined sincerely to the wishes of all good people. May you be showered with heavenly gifts and divine grace! This, Most Reverend Father, is the desire of your most humble and very obedient servant.

VINCENT DEPAUL,
Superior General of the Congregation of the Mission

Letter 2977a. - A. Fumagalli, *Vita del P.D. Ilarione Rancati . . .* , Brescia, 1762, p. 119. The Latin text, with corrections of some simple misprints, was published in *Annales C.M.* (1951), p. 375; *Mission et Charité,* 19-20, no. 142, pp. 173-74, reprinted it with a French translation. This edition uses the latter text.

The letter is undated, but, since it is addressed to the same person as no. 2978 and seems to be connected with it, it may well be from 1658 or 1659; for these reasons the editors have placed it here.

2978. - TO FATHER HILARION RANCATI, IN ROME

Paris, September 12, 1659

Reverend Father,

From most of the letters that the Superior of the Mission in Rome[1] writes to me, I learn that we have new reasons daily to be indebted to Your Reverence. These include the extraordinary favors you are constantly doing for us and the fact that the Holy See has recently granted us, through you, two important Briefs.[2] I thank Your Reverence for this, Reverend Father, with all possible respect and affection.

Since, however, I am unworthy of thanking you in proportion to so many benefits, I ask Our Lord to be Himself your reward in heaven. May He preserve Your Reverence for a long time on earth, and may the great good you are doing continue to increase for the glory of God and the edification of the whole Church, according to what you, in your incomparable zeal, desire.

We—and I in particular—will also ask God, Reverend Father, to grant us the favor of rendering you some small service. I renew

---

Letter 2978. - Biblioteca Ambrosiana, Milan (Italy), original signed letter, Ms. B 264, fol. 355; Coste, no. 2978, pp. 122-23, published the rough draft; *Annales C.M.* (1951), pp. 375-76, published the original text as it appeared in Fumagalli, *op. cit.*, p. 120. The Archives of the Mission, Paris, has the original, unsigned rough draft and a photograph of the original. It is to be noted that the Fumagalli text sometimes adheres closely to the rough draft and sometimes is different so as to conform to the original. *Mission et Charité,* 19-20, no. 99, pp. 125-26, reprinted the *Annales C.M.* text. This edition presents the text from *Mission et Charité* first, followed by the rough draft given in Coste.

[1]Edme Jolly.

[2]One of these Briefs is very probably *Alias nos,* issued on August 12, 1659 (cf. vol. XIII, no. 120). The only other extant Papal Brief of this period is *Ex commissa nobis,* issued on September 22, 1655, by which Pope Alexander VII approved the vows taken in the Congregation of the Mission (cf. vol. XIII, no. 113).

to you the offers of my obedience with all possible humility and gratitude, and am, in the love of Our Lord, Reverend Father, your most humble and very obedient servant.

VINCENT DEPAUL,
i.s.C.M.

At the bottom of the first page: Father Hilarion

ROUGH DRAFT

Paris, September 12, 1659

Very Reverend Father,

In almost every letter from M. Jolly I learn that we have new reasons daily for being indebted to Your Reverence because of the extraordinary favors you are constantly doing for us, and the fact that the Holy See has recently granted us, through you, two important Briefs. I thank you for this, Reverend Father, with all possible respect and gratitude.

Since, however, I am unworthy of thanking you in proportion to so many benefits, I ask O[ur] L[ord] to be Himself your reward in heaven. May He preserve Your Reverence for a long time on earth, and may the great good you are doing continue to increase for the glory of God and the edification of the whole Church.

We—and I in particular—will also ask God, Reverend Father, that, if He is pleased to receive some modest service from the Company because of the constant help it receives from your charity, His Divine Goodness will apply the merit to you and will grant us the favor of rendering you some small service. I renew to you the offers of my obedience with all possible humility and gratitude, and am, in the love of O[ur] L[ord], Reverend Father, your most . . . .

2979. - TO FRANÇOIS FOUQUET, ARCHBISHOP OF NARBONNE

September 12, 1659

Monseigneur,

In accordance with your orders, we are sending off today three priests and three Daughters of Charity to be of service in your holy plans. They will have the honor of accompanying your sister,[1] the Mother Superior of Sainte-Marie of Toulouse. The first of these priests, Monseigneur, named M. des Jardins, has already been Superior of one of our houses in Lorraine[2] and is proficient in all our works. The other two are not yet adequately trained in them, so I have asked M. Durand to put them to work in the seminary and in the parish in Agde and to send you in their place Messieurs Lebas and Dolivet, who are better qualified for the missions and who understand the dialect of the region.

We have done our best, Monseigneur, to try to give you complete satisfaction, as we are bound to do, regarding both the men and the Sisters; still, both will need the favor of your forbearance. We have reason to hope, however, that with your blessing, Monseigneur, they will all work effectively. I ask it for them and for myself, humbly prostrate in spirit at your feet. There is a fourth Sister, whom we are sending to Cahors.

I ask God in His infinite goodness, Monseigneur, to preserve you for a long time for His glory. I am, in His love, with the respect and gratitude I owe you, Monseigneur, your most humble and very obedient servant.

VINCENT DEPAUL,
i.s.C.M.

Letter 2979. - Archives of the Mission, Paris, copy made in 1854 from the original, in the possession of M. Laverdet.

[1]Mother Marie-Thérèse Fouquet, a professed nun of the First Monastery of Paris and the eldest of the Archbishop of Narbonne's five sisters who were in the Visitation Order.

[2]The house in Toul.

2980. - TO GUILLAUME DESDAMES, SUPERIOR, IN WARSAW

Paris, [September] [1] 12, 1659

Monsieur,

The grace of O[ur] L[ord] be with you forever!

I am writing simply to give you news of us, since I have nothing to add to my last letters, although I received one from you by the last regular mail, in which you mention the continued kindness of the King and Queen. God be praised for their great piety and their holy intentions with regard to the salvation of their subjects. We have a serious obligation to ask God for their preservation and to make us worthy of rendering to God and the people the services they expect from us.

We no longer have any patients who are dangerously ill, as we have had; they are better, thank God—I mean Messieurs Boucher,[2] Le Soudier,[3] and Perraud. We have just sent three priests and three Daughters of Charity to Narbonne, two hundred leagues from here; we need even more of them for a few new establishments that are still to be made. Some men are preparing for the voyage to Madagascar, which will take place at the end of this month. We are being asked for workers on all sides. The harvest is abundant; we must pray that God will raise up apostolic men to gather it in.[4] For this

---

Letter 2980. - Archives of the Mission, Krakow, original signed letter. The postscript is in the Saint's handwriting.

[1]The sentence, "We have just sent three priests and three Daughters of Charity to Narbonne," makes the date of August 12 at the top of the original incorrect. The Sisters left on September 12, and it was on that day that the Saint wrote this letter.

[2]Léonard Boucher.

[3]Jacques Le Soudier, born in Vire (Calvados) on October 28, 1619, entered the Congregation of the Mission on May 16, 1638, was ordained a priest in 1642, and took his vows in Richelieu on June 14, 1642. In 1646 Saint Vincent considered him for the foundation of the mission in Salé (Morocco). The project was abandoned, however, when the Saint discovered that the Order of Recollets (Franciscans) had already made a commitment to that mission. In 1651 Le Soudier was in Saint-Quentin, where he remained for two years. He became Superior in Crécy (1652-54) and in Montmirail (1655-56). A long illness interrupted his work and he died in Montauban on May 17, 1663. His brother Samson was also a member of the Congregation of the Mission.

[4]Cf. Mt 9:37-38; Lk 10:2. (NAB)

purpose, I ask you and good M. Duperroy to take care of yourselves. I greet him cordially, and I am, in the love of O[ur] L[ord], Monsieur, your most humble servant.

VINCENT DEPAUL,
i.s.C.M.

One of the Queen's gentlemen is supposed to be leaving at the end of the month to rejoin Her Majesty. He told us that Mademoiselle . . . , the wife of M. . . . ,[5] Her Majesty's physician, is not returning to Warsaw before Easter, and that a ship from Hamburg will be leaving at that time. We will have two or three young Missionaries ready to sail with him. The problem will be with the Daughters of Charity because people say that Pomerania is full of soldiers and that perhaps they will have to go to Vienna and, from there, to Krakow. This gentleman was taken prisoner by the Tartars, when the King himself led an army against the Cossacks.

At the bottom of the first page: Monsieur Desdames

2981. - TO PROPAGANDA FIDE

[September 1659] [1]

Most Eminent and Very Reverend Lords,

Vincent de Paul, Superior General of the Congregation of the Mission, has learned that, after several delays, a ship is finally supposed to leave this autumn for Saint-Laurent Island, commonly

---

[5]These names were left blank in the original.

Letter 2981. - Archives of Propaganda Fide, *Africa* 16-17, *Tunisi, Guinea,* no. 254, fol. 11, original unsigned letter, written in Italian.

[1]Below the summary on the back of the petition are the words *Die 23 septembris 1659 S.C. annuit.* [On September 23, 1659, the Sacred Congregation approved.]

known as Madagascar. He therefore presents once again to Y[our] E[minences], in addition to those subjects already presented to the Sacred Congregation, Nicolas Étienne, priest of the Congregation of the Mission, in order that Y[our] E[minences] may be pleased to appoint him as Apostolic Missionary so that he may be able to work at the cultivation of this immense vineyard, which requires many laborers. And he will regard this grace as a special favor from Y[our] E[minences].

Whom God, etc.

Addressed: To the Sacred Congregation of Propaganda Fide, for Vincent de Paul, Superior General of the Congregation of the Mission

2982. - TO EDME JOLLY, SUPERIOR, IN ROME

Paris, September 19, 1659

Monsieur,

The grace of O[ur] L[ord] be with you forever!

I received your letter of August 25 and greatly rejoiced at your fine report of the missions in Leonessa.[1] God be praised for the graces He has granted to the workers and the poor people!

I cannot thank Him enough for the fact that you have taken possession of Cardinal Bagni's house. There is reason to hope that God will bless those who will live there, through the merit of the good nobleman who has handed it over to you and of the person who procured it for you—I mean the Cardinal of Genoa,[2] whose

---

Letter 2982. - Archives of the Motherhouse of the Sisters of Charity of New York, Mount St. Vincent-on-Hudson, 6301 Riverdale Avenue, Bronx, NY (USA), original.

[1]A small town in the Province of Aquila (Italy). Only the first two, the fifth, and the sixth letters of this word remain in the original letter. Various clues and the letter of July 18, 1659, help to complete it (cf. no. 2909).

[2]Stefano Cardinal Durazzo.

goodness and confidence in the goodness of God is admirable. We must admire him for all his virtues and be ashamed at seeing ourselves so far from them and, consequently, so unworthy of his benefits. May Our Lord be pleased to crown his apostolic life with immortal glory and to be Himself the strength we need to correspond with the expectations of this holy Cardinal!

We are awaiting the final decision of Cardinal Antoine[3] regarding the completion of the foundation he accepted for Loreto, since he did not want to abide by his last opinion.

I am sending you a letter and memorandum addressed to me by M. Regnoust, a Doctor [of Theology] in charge of the priests of the General Hospital. It concerns the rehabilitation of an apostate who has returned to the Church. Please take care of it.

We have M. Le Soudier with us here; he has been ill for the past two months; M. Perraud, who was also at death's door, has been better for a few days now, but dropsy has followed on fever, so that we have reason to fear that death may snatch him from us.

I am, in the love of O[ur] L[ord], Monsieur, your most humble servant.

VINCENT DEPAUL,
i.s.C.M.

Addressed: Monsieur Jolly

---

[3]Antonio Barberini, nephew of Pope Urban VIII, was only twenty when he entered the Sacred College of Cardinals in 1627. He was placed in charge of several legations. Since the steps he took to prevent the election of Innocent X (1644-55) were unsuccessful, he went to France, was named Bishop of Poitiers in 1652, and became Archbishop of Reims in 1657. He died in Nemi, near Rome, on August 3, 1671.

2983. - TO GABRIEL DELESPINEY, SUPERIOR, IN MARSEILLES

September 19, 1659

May God, by His grace, will to guide M. Le Vacher [1] back to Algiers and free him of his worries, which have no other foundation than his own imagination!

2984. - TO JEAN PARRE, IN SAINT-QUENTIN

Paris, September 20, 1659

Dear Brother,

The grace of Our Lord be with you forever!

Thank you for the Masses you have had celebrated for our sick men and for the shirt you sent me, which I received. M. Perraud has taken it. God grant that he may make good use of it!

God be blessed for the blessings He is giving to the devotions at Notre-Dame-de-la-Paix and for the care you take in this!

Go to the area of Laon and Rethel whenever you like.

I had your letter delivered to Mlle Viole. The Ladies [1] have not authorized anything.

I am, in the love of Our Lord, dear Brother, your most affectionate servant.

VINCENT DEPAUL,
i.s.C.M.

Addressed: Brother Jean Parre, of the Mission, in Saint-Quentin

---

Letter 2983. - Archives of the Mission, Paris, Marseilles manuscript.

[1]Philippe Le Vacher.

Letter 2984. - The original signed letter is in the Vatican Library. Coste published a summary and an extract taken from an 1855 Laverdet catalogue. The original was subsequently published in *Annales C.M.* (1934), pp. 649-52, and reprinted in *Mission et Charité,* 19-20, no. 100, pp. 126-27. This edition uses the latter text.

[1]Ladies of Charity of the Hôtel-Dieu.

2985. - TO LOUIS RIVET, SUPERIOR, IN SAINTES

Paris, September 21, 1659

Monsieur,

The grace of O[ur] L[ord] be with you forever!

I received your letter of the tenth. I also received one from M. Boussordec, who has arrived in Nantes. M. de la Noue is supposed to reimburse the expenses you incurred for M. Martin,[1] so please send him the account of them.

Recently I received a letter from M. Daveroult,[2] in which his state of mind seems to be as it was described to you.

I think I told you that M. Dehorgny[3] is going to Brittany from Richelieu, where he is now, and that, consequently, you will not see him in Saintes for some time.

I thank God that your health has improved somewhat; I pray that He will restore it fully to you for the service of His glory.

We will try to give you a priest instead of a seminarian, but we cannot do so just now because we need those we have for other places—I mean that we need them badly. The harvest is abundant and the laborers are few.[4]

You will soon have a good Doctor [of Theology] there who wants to work with you on the missions. He is M. Boust,[5] a member of the Duc de Rochefoucauld's[6] household. He wanted me to ask

---

Letter 2985. - Archives of the Mission, Paris, seventeenth-century copy.

[1]Jean Martin the younger.

[2]Pierre Daveroult, born in Béthune (Pas-de-Calais) on January 20, 1614, was ordained a priest during Lent of 1638. He entered the Congregation of the Mission on April 13, 1653, and took his vows on January 13, 1656. Twice he embarked for Madagascar and twice returned to Paris without being able to set foot on the island.

[3]Jean Dehorgny was making a visitation of various houses of the Company.

[4]Cf. Mt 9:37-38; Lk 10:2. (NAB)

[5]Boust, a Doctor of the Sorbonne and Canon of Chartres, accepted a chair at the Sorbonne, where he taught brilliantly.

[6]François, Duc de la Rochefoucauld, Prince of Marsillac and Governor of Poitou, was born on December 15, 1613, and died in Paris on March 17, 1680. He was one of the most ardent of the Princes in the wars of the Fronde against the Crown. He is known especially for *Réflexions ou sentences et maximes morales* (Paris: Claude Barbin, 1665), which has often been reprinted.

you—as I do now—to let him share your company and your work for as long as his affairs will allow.

M. Le Soudier has been sick for two months, and M. Perraud as well; right now the latter is seriously ill of dropsy, which followed on his unremitting fever. The rest of this family is very well.

I embrace your family very affectionately in spirit, and I am, in the love of O[ur] L[ord], Monsieur, your most humble servant.

VINCENT DEPAUL,
i.s.C.M.

2986. - TO JEAN DEHORGNY, SUPERIOR, IN RICHELIEU

Paris, September 21, 1659

Monsieur,

The grace of O[ur] L[ord] be with you forever!

You know that it is a Rule in our Little Company, as in all well-regulated Communities in the Church, that an individual may write to the General without showing his letter to the local Superior of the place from which he writes, nor should the Superior read the letters which the General sends to the members of his house. Nevertheless, I have been informed that some Superiors—only a small number—are a little annoyed at this because they want to see and know everything. In addition, because they deprive those under them of the liberty of pouring out their hearts and placing their doubts before the person from whom alone, after God, they may expect some consolation and advice, troubles and inconveniences have arisen from such a constraint.

That is why I ask you, Monsieur, to recommend the observance of this Rule to all our families in the places where you make the visitation—even during Chapter—and to tell the subjects that they

---

Letter 2986. - Archives of the Mission, Paris, original signed letter.

may write freely to the General whenever they need to do so and to seal their letters with the Community seal. Tell each Superior that he is to give them seals, to send their letters to us without reading them, and, by the same token, to give them, unopened, the letters that bear the seal of the General. Make strict enquiries in each place to find out if this is being done, and please ask each Missionary privately if he is free to act in this way, so that you can let me know about it.

I ask God to bless you and your visitations. I am, in Him, Monsieur, your most humble servant.

VINCENT DEPAUL,
i.s.C.M.

Addressed: Monsieur Dehorgny, Superior of the Priests of the Mission of the Bons-Enfants, in Richelieu

2987. - TO DOMINIQUE LHUILLIER,[1] IN CRÉCY

Paris, September 23, 1659 [2]

Monsieur,

The grace of O[ur] L[ord] be with you forever!

I received your letter of the fourteenth. I hope God will not permit you to give grounds for discontent to any of the persons you mention, and, if they are unreasonably discontented with your proceedings, that you will profit before God from this humiliation.

Letter 2987. - Archives of the Mission, Paris, unsigned rough draft.

[1]Dominique Lhuillier, born in Barizey-au-Plain (Meurthe), entered the Congregation of the Mission as a priest in Paris on July 11, 1651, at the age of thirty-two. He took his vows there on May 5, 1659, in the presence of M. Alméras. Lhuillier was a Missionary in Crécy (1654-60) and in Toulon, where he died.

[2]The Marseilles manuscript quotes a sentence from this letter, which it dates as September 24. Could it be that the letter was written the day after the rough draft had been drawn up?

You did well to speak about it to M. de Lorthon,[3] and it will be a good idea for you to do what he told you, namely, to continue to say Mass at the hour to which you have been accustomed for the convenience of Madame de Laval,[4] in the hope he has given you that Madame de Lorthon and he will find this time acceptable. They have too much respect and deference for Madame de Laval, who is the Lady of the place, to act differently.

If, however, the misunderstanding that you fear should arise, Monsieur, you would act wisely by speaking to Madame de Laval, and once again to M. de Lorthon to try to get them to agree on the time. Since the latter is your founder, and the other person is who she is, you must obey both, and consequently act in such a way as not to displease one by giving preference to the other.

2988. - TO MONSIEUR DESBORDES [1]

Saint-Lazare, September 24, 1659

Monsieur,

The grace of O[ur] L[ord] be with you forever!

There is no command of yours that I should not obey. I know you want nothing unreasonable; therefore I venture to tell you, Monsieur, that the matter you propose raises a difficulty. The Council of Trent has forbidden Bishops and other Superiors of religious Communities to allow persons who are not members to

---

[3]Pierre de Lorthon, the King's secretary and founder of the Missionaries' house in Crécy.

[4]Marie Séguier, daughter of Chancellor Pierre Séguier, widow of the Marquis de Coislin; she later married Guy de Laval of the family of Laval-Boisdauphin.

Letter 2988. - Archives of the Mission, Paris, unsigned rough draft.

[1]Vicomte de Soudé and Auditor of the Treasury.

enter their convents, except in case of necessity.[2] Now, Madame Collin's entrance at Sainte-Marie is not of this nature.

I do violence to myself in my desire to serve her and to please you. But in this matter you see, Monsieur, that discipline is at stake as well as dangerous consequences because several ladies, on various pretexts, have often made the same request to us, and I have given them the same reply even to Princesses, including one of royal blood.[3] So, if I granted it to one I could not refuse the others. I entreat you, Monsieur, to excuse me in this and to make my excuses to Monsieur and Madame Collin, for whom I have great respect and a great desire to be of service to them. As for yourself, Monsieur, you know to what an extent I am, in the love of O[ur] L[ord]. . . .

2989. - TO EDME JOLLY, SUPERIOR, IN ROME

Paris, September 26, 1659

Monsieur,

The grace of O[ur] L[ord] be with you forever!

I received your dear letter of September 1. We owe three great acts of thanksgiving for the recent alms that were given you to help to pay for the house that has been acquired: the first is to God, the second to Cardinal Durazzo, and the third to Signor Emmanuele Brignole, to whom I will take the honor of writing for this purpose.

---

[2]Sess. XXV, chap. V, *De Regularibus: "Dare . . . tantum episcopus vel superior licentiam debet in casibus necessariis"* [But only the bishop or Superior ought to grant permission in cases of necessity].

[3]The daughter of Charles de Bourbon and wife of Thomas-François, Prince de Carignan, who became Grand Master of France (cf. vol. VI, no. 2237).

Letter 2989. - Archives of the Mission, Paris, original unsigned letter. The postscript is in the Saint's handwriting.

I am glad that you had M. Abelly's book [1] presented to the Pope and for what you tell me about it. I shared your letter with M. Abelly and we thought that, since there is no doubt in Rome regarding the opinions he has defended, and they are more interested in reading about laws and canons than about other matters—especially the material in this book—it would be of little use to have it translated into Latin. So, Monsieur, it will suffice for you to have the copies you have in our language distributed to those who understand it and whom you think most competent to approve and support the doctrine it contains. If you want more, we will send them to you.

I am, in the love of O[ur] L[ord], Monsieur, your most humble servant.

VINCENT DEPAUL,
i.s.C.M.

Please give us some news, Monsieur, concerning the health of our Holy Father, who is so precious to us and for whom we are praying constantly.

Addressed: Monsieur Jolly

2990. - TO JACQUES PESNELLE, SUPERIOR, IN GENOA

Paris, September 26, 1659

Monsieur,

The grace of O[ur] L[ord] be with you forever!

I received your letter of September 9. God be praised that the

---

[1] *Défense de la hiérarchie de l'Église et de l'authorité légitime de N.S.P. le Pape et de nos seigneurs les évesques contre la doctrine pernicieuse d'un libelle anonyme* (Paris: G. Josse, 1659). This work is a rebuttal of an anonymous author whose work was entitled: *Lettres de l'autheur des Régles très importantes au sieur de Marca, archevesque de Thoulouze.* (Cf. no. 2900.)

Letter 2990. - Archives of the Mission, Paris, rough draft.

Corsica proposal is on the way to fulfillment and that it is proceeding peacefully, without giving offense to the Company you mentioned. If you are being pressured, let me know, and, if you are not, do not push it,[1] but keep things as they are because we are having a hard time just now sending the men required for that mission, since the ones we have are involved elsewhere and are needed for two new establishments we must staff.

I say the same with regard to your request for a priest in place of M. Lejuge, who is going to Rome. Please try to manage until we are in a position to help you.

If M. Philippe, who is supposed to be the professor of your external seminarians, can also be their prefect, it would be better to entrust him with this office than to give it to Brother de Lagrange.[2]

You propose putting M. Carlo Francisco[3] in charge of the bursar's office during the missions. I find it very hard to agree to that, since he is still a seminarian, for it would be better—much better—to give that duty to someone else until he completes his two years [novitiate]. If, however, you have no one suitable for this work, do as you judge best.

Your brothers have done me the honor of coming to see me. They are writing to you almost the same things they told me and are offering to give you your share of the inheritance. Accordingly, you can tell them that it is your intention to. . . .[4]

At the bottom of the first page: Monsieur Pesnelle

---

[1]First redaction: "do not make a request. . . ." The correction is in the Saint's handwriting.

[2]Robert de Lagrange, born in Lille (Nord) on November 1, 1636, entered the Paris Seminary of the Congregation of the Mission on October 19, 1655, and took his vows on October 19, 1657, in the presence of M. Delespiney. At the time of this letter he was still a seminarian.

[3]In vol. XIV, p. 221, Coste states that he is a Priest of the Mission, but no biographical data is available. This is the only reference to him in the letters and conferences of Saint Vincent.

[4]The sentence continued on a second sheet, which is no longer extant.

At the bottom of the second page, Saint Vincent wrote in his own hand: "Reply that, since his residence in Italy and his work do not allow him to go there, he will be satisfied with such a pension."

2991. - TO JEAN PARRE, IN SAINT-QUENTIN

September 27, 1659

Vincent de Paul tells Brother Jean Parre that he has nothing to say to him.

". . . We have M. Soudier critically ill, and M. Perraud as well. I recommend both of them to your prayers."

2991a. - TO JEAN GICQUEL

Paris, September 27, 1659

Monsieur,

The grace of Our Lord be with you forever!

Our sick men are still very unwell: M. Perraud is seriously ill; M. Le Soudier, not so much; M. Berthe and M. Martin[1] have quartan fever in Turin; M. Alméras is not feeling well, nor is Brother Ducournau. Your brother is rather well, thank God. M. Étienne is in Nantes with Messieurs Daveroult, Feydin, and Brother Patte,[2]

Letter 2991. - This one-page summary of the text comes from the catalogue of M. Laverdet, who put the original up for sale.

Letter 2991a. - Archives of the Mission, Paris, photograph of the original autograph letter. The photograph seems to have been taken from an unknown facsimile. The editors of *Mission et Charité,* who reprinted it in 19-20, no. 102, pp. 128-29, state that "there is no reason to doubt the authenticity of this letter." This edition uses the *Mission et Charité* text.

[1]Jean Martin the elder.

[2]Philippe Patte, born in Vigny, Rouen diocese, in 1620, entered the Paris Seminary of the Congregation of the Mission as a coadjutor Brother on April 5, 1656, and took his vows there on April 16, 1658, in the presence of M. Delespiney. In 1659 he went to Madagascar, where he proved himself an excellent surgeon. Along with M. Nicolas Étienne, he was massacred on March 4, 1664. (Cf. *Notices,* vol. III, pp. 369-71.)

while waiting for the ship to be ready to set sail. And I, Monsieur, send [you] my most humble greetings, with all the tenderness of my heart. I am your most humble servant.

VINCENT DEPAUL,
i.s.C.M.

Addressed: Monsieur Gicquel

2992. - TO JEAN DEHORGNY, IN RICHELIEU

Paris, September 28, 1659

Monsieur,

The grace of O[ur] L[ord] be with you forever!

God be praised for your safe arrival in Richelieu, along with M. Le Blanc,[1] as I learned from your letter of the twentieth. I also praise God that His Divine Goodness has been pleased to improve the Archdeacon's health and that His Providence brought him to our house when he became ill. That gave us an opportunity to render him some little service. I hope that the house will spare nothing for his relief and consolation.

We are expecting M. Férot[2] here and he will be most welcome. M. de Beaumont should take the trouble to let me know what things

---

Letter 2992. - Archives of the Mission, Paris, original signed letter.

[1]It is difficult to determine in some letters whether "M. Le Blanc" is the Frenchman (Charles) or one of the three Irish confreres named White. After consultation of various biographical sources, the editors believe that the man in question here is Charles Le Blanc, who was born in Roye (Somme) on July 15, 1625, entered the Congregation of the Mission on November 20, 1649, took his vows on November 21, 1653, and was ordained a priest the following month. In 1658 he set sail for Madagascar but had to return to Paris, after a violent storm snapped the ship's masts and rudder and imperiled the lives of the passengers, forcing the ship to drop anchor at Lisbon. He went back to Le Mans, where he had been stationed before leaving for Madagascar.

[2]Claude Férot, born in Saint-Quentin (Aisne) on July 6, 1630, entered the Congregation of the Mission on October 3, 1647, took his vows on October 15, 1649, and was ordained a priest in Agen in March 1656. He was Superior in Montmirail (1662-66).

I should tell him. We will try to send one man to preach during the missions and another to Le Mans, where you worked with him. God be praised for it!

It seems to me that I see and touch what you have written to me about each one in particular. May God be pleased to grant all of them the grace to go from good to better, and to grant the whole Company the grace to grow in numbers and virtue! We see more clearly than ever its great need for good workers and for God's grace to correspond with His plans. Please pray and have prayers said for that intention.

I will write to M. Laudin to prepare for the ordination.

Our sick men—I mean Messieurs Le Soudier and Perraud—are seriously ill. I recommend them and myself to your prayers. I am, in the love of O[ur] L[ord], Monsieur, your most humble servant.

VINCENT DEPAUL,
i.s.C.M.

Addressed: Monsieur Dehorgny, Priest of the Mission, in Richelieu

2993. - TO A YOUNG MAN FROM DAX

September 29, 1659

To this young man, who had asked for his patronage on the grounds of relationship, Vincent de Paul declares that he will do for him what he would do for his own brother. He says he is unworthy to consider himself one of his family, seeing that he was "born of a poor farmworker" and that his "first calling was to tend his father's livestock."

Letter 2993. - Collet, *op. cit.*, vol. II, p. 195.

2994. - TO EDME JOLLY, SUPERIOR, IN ROME

[End of September-beginning of October 1659] [1]

I will send you the Rules of the Daughters of Charity with the approval that Cardinal de Retz gave them in Rome,[2] and a copy of the letters patent and their registration in the Parlement,[3] so you can see how the approval[4] should be drawn up. We just sent off four of them,[5] some for Narbonne, some for Cahors, and in a few days some will go to Poland. The only way we can direct all this is by the stamp of the authority of His Holiness.

I am awaiting the *extra tempora* for Brother Arthur.[6]

M. Étienne is preparing to go to Madagascar, [along with] Messieurs Boussordec and Feydin.

On the back: Monsieur Jolly

Letter 2994. - In 1945 the original autograph letter belonged to Abbé Auzou, a priest of the Paris diocese. The text was published with its original format and spelling in *Annales C.M.* (1945-46), p. 199, and reprinted in *Mission et Charité,* 19-20, no. 101, pp. 127-28. Coste provided only a summary taken from the Laverdet catalogue of January 1854. The editors of this edition have used the complete text of *Mission et Charité.*

[1]Coste gives the following reasons for placing in brackets what he considered the probable date of this letter: "It was written shortly after September 12, 1659, the date the Sisters left for Narbonne, and before the Saint had decided to postpone until spring the departure of the Daughters of Charity missioned to Poland; consequently before no. 2996 (October 3, 1659)."

[2]After his escape from prison in the Château de Nantes (August 8, 1654), Cardinal de Retz fled to Rome where, by order of Pope Alexander VII, he was given hospitality by the Priests of the Mission at Montecitorio. Since he was still Archbishop of Paris, it was from Rome that Saint Vincent had obtained from him the approval for the Company of the Daughters of Charity and its general Rule (January 18, 1655, cf. vol. XIII, no. 149).

[3]Cf. vol. XIII, no. 152, for the letters patent of the King, issued in November 1657, and no. 153 for their registration with the Parlement on December 16, 1657.

[4]Saint Vincent was trying to obtain the approval of the Holy See because the approval given by the Archbishop of Paris was subject to change, since a new Archbishop could abolish what his predecessor had established and approved.

[5]He is referring to the Daughters of Charity.

[6]Nicholas Arthur (cf. no. 2921, n. 3).

2995. - TO GABRIEL DELESPINEY, SUPERIOR, IN MARSEILLES

Paris, October 3, 1659

Monsieur,

The grace of O[ur] L[ord] be with you forever!

I heard that, even though you are not feeling well at all, you took the trouble of going to Grignan[1] to establish the Confraternity of Charity there. I would really be very upset if this effort had made you worse, God forbid! How have you been since that journey, and how is M. Cornier's diarrhea? I hope by the goodness of God that he is over it; otherwise, some remedy has to be considered. The distance between places and the nature of the complaint do not allow sending him back here. Furthermore, that ailment is prevalent here; M. Le Soudier is so exhausted by it that we have reason to fear he will not recover. They say that many people in the rural areas have been attacked by it. M. Durand tells me that the same is true of Agde, and that he himself has had his share of it, so we must not think of sending him there. Since it is a common complaint, I think the best remedy is patience and diet.

Nevertheless, Monsieur, see if the country air will be better for him than that of the city; send him to some neighboring parish to spend a few days there and to see if his condition of loose bowels will cease. I saw in the past that the relatives of the late M. Tratebas[2] welcomed M. Portail and some others into their home while the plague was raging in Marseilles; perhaps they will be kind enough

---

Letter 2995. - Archives of the Mission, Paris, original signed letter.

[1]Canton of La Drôme.

[2]Antoine Tratebas was born in Allauch (Bouches-du-Rhône), near Marseilles, in October 1632. He entered the Congregation of the Mission in Paris on October 7, 1651, took his vows on October 20, 1653, and died of the plague in Genoa in August 1657. His family gave hospitality to Antoine Portail and other Priests of the Mission in 1649 during the plague that was ravaging the city of Marseilles.

now to extend the same hospitality to M. Cornier, if you ask them, in consideration of the dear deceased.

The Bishop of Pamiers[3] wrote to me on behalf of a poor captive of his diocese, named Jean Castres, from Saurat,[4] twenty-five years of age, who is in Tripoli. He tells me he is detained in the castle of the Governor of Tripoli. Please arrange for some Marseilles merchant to write to the Consul there for news of him, Monsieur, and to find out exactly what must be paid to set him free. When you hear, please let me know, as well as how to forward the money to him safely.

In the name of God, Monsieur, do all in your power to keep well. I am, in the love of O[ur] L[ord], Monsieur, your most humble servant.

VINCENT DEPAUL,
i.s.C.M.

Addressed: Monsieur Delespiney, Superior of the Priests of the Mission, in Marseilles

---

[3]François-Étienne de Caulet, born in Toulouse on May 19, 1610, was endowed in 1627 with Saint-Volusien Abbey in Foix. Attracted by the spirit of Jean-Jacques Olier, he accompanied him on his missions in Auvergne, in the Chartres diocese, and in other places in the kingdom. He supported him in his parish ministry and, together with him and M. du Ferrier, founded the Vaugirard Seminary. Saint Vincent, who knew the Abbot of Saint-Volusien, thought he would make a good Bishop. Thanks to him, de Caulet was consecrated Bishop of Pamiers on March 5, 1645. In 1638 he had testified against Saint-Cyran; as Bishop, he continued for a long time to combat Jansenism, forbade in his diocese the reading of books by adherents of the movement, and made every effort to bring back those who had strayed from the truth. However, his association with Nicolas Pavillon, Bishop of Alet, won him over to Jansenism. The Bishop of Pamiers died on August 7, 1680, without having made an act of submission to the Church. (Cf. Jérôme Besoigne, *Vies des quatres évesques engagés dans la cause de Port-Royal, M. d'Alet, M. d'Angers, M. de Beauvais et M. de Pamiers* [2 vols., Cologne: n. p., 1756]; Georges Doublet, *Un prélat janséniste, F. de Caulet, réformateur des châpitres de Foix et de Pamiers* [Paris: A. Picard et fils, 1895].) M. Gazier, an authority on Jansenism, had among the rare manuscripts in his extensive library one entitled: *Histoire abrégée de la vie de M. François de Caulet, évêque de Pamiers,* by Father Gabaret.

[4]A locality in the district of Foix (Ariège).

2996. - TO NICOLAS DUPERROY, IN WARSAW

Paris, October 3, 1659

Monsieur,

The grace of O[ur] L[ord] be with you forever!

I am writing you a few lines in haste to tell you that your dear letter of August 15 arrived; it consoled me greatly because of the candor of your lovable heart, so vividly represented in the few lines it contains. I thank God, Monsieur, for the sentiments He gives you and for the benefice which the Queen has entrusted to you to enable the Company to serve the people. That will oblige us to send more Missionaries there than we had intended, but it is difficult to send them before spring, as I am writing to M. Desdames.

Please be patient in the meantime, even though you may not be doing in this public office the good you would like, and reflect that God is content with the good you do elsewhere, while awaiting something better. Remember that you have been entrusted with this benefice only to correspond with the plans His Divine Goodness has for the Company for the advancement of His glory, and that, if it had fallen into other hands, it might perhaps have served to do the contrary.

God has prepared you by too many graces for you to fear the temptation you mention. You are God's and God is yours. Oh! what happiness! He encompasses all happiness, so anything that does not tend to God is only sorrow and desolation. By His infinite grace, Our Lord will fill you with His Spirit in order to assist souls efficaciously to be detached from creatures and united to their Sovereign Good.

Oh! Monsieur, what a joy it is for me to know that you have distanced yourself from the world and from all perishable earthly things to live only by the life of Jesus Christ, who has drawn you

---

Letter 2996. - Archives of the Mission, Krakow, original signed letter.

to His service and called you to Poland for this purpose, where I hope He will make it even clearer that it is to show His divine virtues and proclaim His infinite goodness in that place! With all my heart I ask Him to do so and am, in His love, Monsieur, your most humble servant.

VINCENT DEPAUL,
i.s.C.M.

Addressed: Monsieur Duperroy, Priest of the Mission, in Warsaw

2997. - *JEAN DEHORGNY* [1] *TO SAINT VINCENT*

Monsieur,

I think Mademoiselle Le Gras would be doing a great charity for the sick of this town of Richelieu and for our two Sisters living here,[2] *if she sent two other Sisters—or at least one*[3]*—to attend to the patients as well as to the Sisters, because both of the latter have been in bed with a fever for more than six weeks. Even though Sister Perrine has been feeling a little better the last five or six days, nevertheless, for the entire fourteen months she has been in Angers, she has hardly ever been in good health. That is why, if she could improve a little, I think she should be withdrawn from here, seeing that the sick are receiving no help, except that the Ladies*

Letter 2997. - Archives of the Mission, Paris, original autograph letter. This letter is also in *Documents,* (cf. Doc. 770, p. 884), and it is from the editor's notes that we know the names of the three Sisters mentioned.

[1]Jean Dehorgny was making a visitation in Richelieu.

[2]Perrine de Bouhery and Charlotte Royer.

Perrine, also called Perrette, entered the Company of the Daughters of Charity early in 1648. At the end of the year she went to Angers; in 1658 she was sent to Richelieu.

A native of Liancourt, Charlotte Royer went to Richelieu in June or July 1649, after having served the poor in Saint-Jean parish. She was still there when Saint Louise died in 1660.

[3]Étiennette Dupuis. One of the elders in the Company, she went to Angers in 1658 as Sister Servant, remaining there for a year before going to Richelieu. In 1665 she returned to the Motherhouse and in 1667 was in Maisons as Sister Servant.

give them a little money or some raw meat—both of which are against the regulations.

I have been informed by several persons that the Sisters who come here will have to be able to persuade the Ladies to visit the sick in person, so that, when they see them, they may feel urged to contribute to the expenses, given the fact that the sick receive very little alms from the collections.

Since I started this letter, Sister Perrine has come down with a fever again.

Monsieur, your most humble and obedient servant.

DEHORGNY,
i.s.C.M.

October 3, 1659

Addressed: *Monsieur Vincent*

2998. - TO JEAN DEHORGNY, IN RICHELIEU

October 5, 1659

You sent me word that the Le Mans house needs a preacher for the missions, another priest to act as bursar, and a seminarian for the classes, and that the Richelieu house also needs a good preacher. M. Berthe, for his part, told us that we should also send two priests to Sedan; and it may be that you will find even other houses asking for new workers. Now, how are we to meet all these demands? It cannot be done. We have very few well-trained men; yet, we have a great amount of work to do, places to fill, and even a few new establishments.

I am telling you all this, Monsieur, so that you will spare us as much as you can. During visitations your main concern should be to correct those who go astray, encourage the weakhearted and despondent, and quicken the fervor of the lax and apathetic. It is

Letter 2998. - Reg. 2, p. 98.

for this purpose especially that you have been sent, since everyone should do his utmost, not only to maintain good order but also to carry out our functions in each place.

Please offer to Our Lord a little retreat I am making to prepare me for the great one, in the event that God is pleased to call me soon.

2999. - TO SAINT LOUISE

Saint-Lazare, Monday evening [October 1659] [1]

Vincent de Paul tells Louise de Marillac of the arrival in Narbonne of the first Daughters of Charity: Françoise Carcireux,[2] Anne Denoual, and Marie Chesse.[3]

Letter 2999. - Hippolyte Faure, *Documents divers sur l'histoire de Narbonne et de ses hospices* (Narbonne: F. Caillard, 1894), p. 116.

[1]We can give an approximate date for this letter because of what Saint Vincent wrote to François Fouquet, the Bishop of Narbonne, on September 12, 1659 (cf. no. 2979).

[2]Cf. no. 2969, n. 3.

[3]Anne Denoual, who became a Daughter of Charity around 1656, was sent to Narbonne in September 1659. In August 1660 she asked Saint Vincent for permission to take her vows (cf. no. 3222). In 1668 she was at the Montpellier Hospital, and in August 1672 she became Sister Servant at Saint-Jean-en-Grève in Paris.

Born in Laudujan (Ille-et-Vilaine) on October 28, 1637, Marie Chesse was received as a Daughter of Charity on September 30, 1657, and took her vows on March 25, 1662. She was first placed at Saint-Paul parish in Paris, then went in September 1659 to Narbonne, where she remained for seventeen years. Her next appointment was as Sister Servant at the Gex Hospital, followed by the same assignment at the hospice of the Nom-de-Jésus in Paris. For three years (1680-83) she served the Community as Treasurer General, after which she returned to Gex, where she died on April 19, 1699.

3000. - *SAINT LOUISE TO SAINT VINCENT*

[October 1659] [1]

Most Honored Father,

Sister Mathurine[2] *has not left yet and will not be leaving until the beginning of next week. She has expressed the desire to make a short retreat and to go to confession; it would make her very happy if you could hear her, provided that the time she takes to explain her great difficulties will not inconvenience you too much. Will Your Charity please send us your answer regarding this?*

I am forwarding to you the letter I received yesterday from the Queen of Poland, along with my reply to it, which Your Charity may retain, if you think it should not be sent.[3] *Otherwise, please return it to me so I can make a good copy.*

Enclosed also is a letter from Sister Carcireux; it will give you news of your priests who left for Narbonne.[4]

I am sending you, Most Honored Father, the document I mentioned to Your Charity concerning the spiritual means for consolidating the establishment of the Company of the Daughters of Charity. Please do not show it to anyone else for fear lest they ridicule it.

Your Charity really should have seen the weakness of my poor heart concerning a letter similar to this one which was mislaid immediately after

---

Letter 3000. - Archives of the Motherhouse of the Daughters of Charity, original autograph letter.

[1]Date added on the back of the original by Brother Ducournau.

[2]Mathurine Guérin was born in Montcontour (Brittany) on April 16, 1631. Despite the opposition of her parents, she entered the Company of the Daughters of Charity on September 12, 1648. After her formation period, she was sent to Saint-Jean-en-Grève parish and then to Liancourt. Recalled to the Motherhouse in 1652, she became Seminary Directress and Saint Louise's secretary. In 1655 she was made Treasurer but was sent to the hospital in La Fère (Aisne) in 1659 to replace Sister Marie-Marthe Trumeau as Sister Servant. In July 1660 Saint Vincent sent her and two other Sisters to serve the prisoners and to teach poor girls on Belle-Île-en-Mer (Morbihan), off the Breton coast (cf. *Documents,* Doc. 795). Since 1650 the island had belonged to Nicolas Fouquet, Minister of Finance, who had a fortress built there. She served a first six-year term as Superioress General in 1667 and again (1676-82, 1685-91, 1694-97) and died at the Motherhouse on October 18, 1704. A long sketch of her life and virtues is written in *Circulaires des supérieurs généraux,* pp. 556-68.

[3]Neither of these letters is extant.

[4]Messieurs des Jardins, Lebas, and Dolivet.

it had been written. You would see clearly the need I have, more than ever, of advice and correction, in order to be more truly called, Most Honored Father, your most humble and obedient daughter and servant.

LOUISE DE MARILLAC

Our two Sisters from Hennebont have arrived, thank God.

3001. - TO LOUIS DUPONT, SUPERIOR, IN TRÉGUIER

Paris, October 8, 1659

Monsieur,

I received two letters from you dated September 7 and 27. I praise God for the steps the Bishop[1] has taken to unite the chapels and to consolidate your establishment. These are the result of his great kindness to the Company and his admirable zeal for the perfection of his clergy. May God give you and those working with you, Monsieur, the grace to keep yourselves closely united to Our Lord so as to work with him in that holy and important undertaking, on which depends the sanctification of the whole diocese! You can do nothing in that without this adorable Savior; but, animated by His strength, you will succeed very well.

One thing to which you should pay close attention is to destroy that evil spirit of drinking, which is a source of disorder among the clergy. To do so, you must strive to make them interior, prayerful persons, who will prefer to converse with God rather than to seek out the company of others, and to carry out their duties rather than remain idle.

Because of the ill effects that may result, it is very much to be desired that the seminary not become involved in any lawsuits with

---

Letter 3001. - Pémartin, *op. cit.*, vol. IV, p. 483, L. 1957. Part of the letter was reproduced in Reg. 2, p. 193.

[1]Balthazar Grangier de Liverdi.

the members of the Chapter. The expedient proposed by the Bishop is excellent and feasible if Abbé Brisacier were here, but he is in Rome.

I have forwarded to M. Boussordec the letter you sent me. He is in Nantes now and is planning to sail for Madagascar; but, since they are not ready to embark, I have written him to go to Richelieu in the meantime. There is another ship at Dieppe which might sail on the same voyage toward the end of the month; with God's help, we will send two other priests on it, one of whom is M. Étienne.

I am really sorry about the trouble M. L. is causing you. I admit that he is a little difficult to guide; but it is also true that he is kindhearted and fundamentally good; therefore, his timidity and what he may lack in prompt and gentle submission merit our excusing him. We should look upon it as an established fact that no man is without faults—I, more than anyone else. Even if we were to send you all the priests here, one after another, there would not be a single one in whom you would not find a great deal to tolerate.

So, Monsieur, you should act in such a way as to win him over by gentleness and patience. Our Lord has strongly recommended forbearance to us,[2] knowing that, without it, union can neither come about nor subsist among men, so wretched are they—I mean fraternal union, which makes us pleasing to God and strong in attracting others to His love. By the grace of God, you have always maintained and fostered that of your little family until now, and I hope it will continue to grow in the future through your gentle spirit and wise government. I am asking Our Lord for this.

Some of our men have made their retreat and are now out giving missions; others—including me—have now entered the desert. Ask God to give us the grace to produce fruits worthy of penance that may be useful to the neighbor.

Messieurs Le Soudier and Perraud are very ill, the latter danger-

---

[2]Cf. Jn 13:35; Gal 6:2. (NAB)

ously so. M. des Jardins has gone to Narbonne and has taken Messieurs Lemerer and Tanguy,[3] who are Bretons, to Agde.

I think M. Dehorgny has now left Richelieu for Brittany, where God, in His infinite goodness, continues to bless you and all your men, whom I cordially embrace.

I will send Brother Butler's letters to Rome[4] the day after tomorrow.

I am, in Our Lord. . . .

3002. - *JEAN DEHORGNY TO SAINT VINCENT*

Richelieu, October 8, 1659

Monsieur,

Our Sisters of Charity are still sick. Sometimes Sister Perrine[1] *has periods of time that lead us to believe she is on the mend, but this does not last. As for Sister Charlotte,*[2] *six years ago at Christmas she was seriously ill; since then, her health has never been good. Perhaps a change of air might put them both back on their feet.*

I think Mlle Le Gras would be doing a great charity for this place if she made an effort to send two other Sisters here because, if she sends only one, all her time will be taken up with nursing the two Sisters, and the patients will be left alone. No one visits the Sisters and they are not very well-liked. People say that they did not take proper care of the sick and

---

[3]Gilles Lemerer (cf. no. 2974a, n. 7); no information is available for M. Tanguy.

[4]Dimissorial letters for Peter Butler (*Pierre Buthleer* in *Notices,* vol. I, p. 482, and vol. V [Supplement], p. 102). Born in Drom, Cashel diocese (Ireland) in April 1632, he entered the Congregation of the Mission in Richelieu on August 22, 1654, and took his vows there on August 15, 1656 (cf. vol. VII, no. 2694). This same letter (no. 2694) and others speak of Saint Vincent's attempt in 1658-59 to obtain dimissorial letters for his ordination. The title for ordination in the Congregation of the Mission and the authority of the Superior General were at variance with the attempts of Propaganda Fide to have all Irish seminarians ordained on the continent take an oath to return as missionaries to Ireland.

Letter 3002. - Archives of the Mission, Paris, original autograph letter.

[1]Perrine Bouhery.

[2]Charlotte Royer.

left it to the personnel of the house to make their beds. Now, sometimes the Ladies have come across a patient whose bed had not been made for a week. True, their poor health may have contributed to that. It is imperative that the ones who come know how to let blood and be very gracious with the patients because this is one of the most difficult places there is.

I ask Our Lord to assist all of us, and I am, in His love, Monsieur, your most humble and obedient servant.

DEHORGNY,
i.s.C.M.

Addressed: *Monsieur Vincent*

3003. - TO EDME JOLLY, SUPERIOR, IN ROME [1]

October 11, 1659

Monsieur,

The grace of O[ur] L[ord] be with you forever!

I strongly approve of the plan of that good Bishop who wants workers for the Indies. Would to God that we were worthy to help him! However, the few priests we have are being asked for on all sides.

Letter 3003. - Collet, *op. cit.,* vol. II, p. 67.

[1]Collet simply states that the letter is addressed to a Missionary in Italy. The contents indicate that it is Edme Jolly.

3004. - TO EDMUND BARRY,[1] SUPERIOR, IN NOTRE-DAME-DE-LORM

Paris, October 11, 1659

Monsieur,

The grace of O[ur] L[ord] be with you forever!

I am sending you the reply of the Doctors of the Sorbonne regarding the difficulty you raised about the Masses.

I forgot to tell you that we cannot receive into the Company a person who wants to leave another well-regulated Community without a legitimate reason. So, it will be a good idea for you to encourage the seminarian of the Order of Christian Doctrine,[2] about whom you wrote me, to persevere in that holy religious Order to which God has called him.

M. Dehorgny has gone to make the visitation of our houses in Brittany; if God gives him sufficient health, I hope he will go to see you.

I am, in O[ur] L[ord], Monsieur, your most humble servant.

VINCENT DEPAUL,
i.s.C.M.

Addressed: Monsieur Barry

Letter 3004. - Archives of the Mission, Turin, original signed letter.

[1]Edmund Barry, born in the Cloyne diocese (Ireland) on June 24, 1613, was ordained a priest in Cahors in 1639 and entered the Congregation of the Mission on July 21, 1641. He took his vows at Saint-Lazare a few days before his departure for Ireland in 1646, returning to France in 1652, after Limerick had been captured by Cromwell's army. He was then placed in Richelieu (1652-53) and Montauban (1653-80). While in Montauban, he directed the seminary and was Superior there (1657-64, 1675-80). Barry was also a Doctor of Theology and was still alive on May 31, 1680, as two legal documents show, but he died later that year.

[2]In 1592 César de Bus and Jean-Baptiste Romillion founded in Isle (Vaucluse) the Institute of the Priests of Christian Doctrine for the instruction of the poor, the ignorant, and the people of the rural areas. Pope Clement VIII approved it in 1597. The Institute became polarized over the question of vows, and its growth was stifled because of its trials.

3005. - TO GABRIEL DELESPINEY, SUPERIOR, IN MARSEILLES

October 17, 1659

I hope that all of you will soon be able to give a mission. Do not be afraid of announcing Christian truths to the people with the simplicity of the Gospel and of the first workers of the Church. We have heard you preach and know that you are going about it the right way in order to touch hearts. The reputation of the Company must be in Jesus Christ, and the way to maintain it there is to conform oneself to Him, and not to great preachers. You will soon have learned enough of the language[1] to hear confessions. Be very careful to learn first the words people ordinarily use to confess the most common sins, so that you will be able to understand and question the most ignorant among the people.

3006. - TO EDME JOLLY, SUPERIOR, IN ROME

October 17, 1659

People are right to congratulate you about your house, not so much for the reasons you tell me, as for the instruments God used in getting it for you. I mean two holy Cardinals [1] who, having in view the honor and service of God, wanted to place you in a position to procure the above in every way the poor Company can and should do. Two more like them would be needed to help us to thank them for all the favors they have conferred on us and for the charming way in which they take pleasure in assisting us, especially Cardinal Durazzo. This seems to be his only interest and, since God alone is the object of his actions, he can never be worthily thanked except by Him.

Letter 3005. - Archives of the Mission, Paris, Marseilles manuscript.

[1]Saint Vincent is referring to Provençal, the dialect of southeastern France (Provence).

Letter 3006. - Reg. 2, p. 248.

[1]Nicolò di Bagno and Stefano Durazzo.

3007. - TO DOMINIQUE LHUILLIER, IN CRÉCY

Paris, October 23, 1659

Monsieur,

The grace of O[ur] L[ord] be with you forever!

Brother Claude[1] is now returning. Thank you for having sent him here for such a good reason as that of bringing us one of our sick Brothers. M. Maillard will give him 135 livres, namely, 125 for the quarterly pension and 10 for his own little needs.

I am glad you received the 50 écus of your annual subsidy and that you hope to receive at the end of the year the wherewithal to establish the family and its works. I am all the more pleased that it was Madame de Lorthon[2] who told you so.

As for the foundation of the late Procurator of the King, I will write to you about that some other time; please remind me to do so. We have not yet decided to accept it. Let me know on what the income of 10 écus is assigned and if it is well secured.

I am, in O[ur] L[ord], Monsieur, your most humble servant.

VINCENT DEPAUL,
i.s.C.M.

Addressed: Monsieur Lhuillier, Priest of the Mission, in Crécy

---

Letter 3007. - Property of the Daughters of Charity of 12 rue de Limbourg, Ghent (Belgium), original signed letter.

[1]Claude Gesseaume, coadjutor Brother, born in Villers-sous-Saint-Leu (Oise) in 1615, entered Saint-Lazare on December 6, 1643.

[2]Wife of Pierre de Lorthon, the King's secretary and founder of the Missionaries' house in Crécy.

3008. - TO JACQUES PESNELLE, SUPERIOR, IN GENOA

[In 1659 or 1660] [1]

Long live justice! We have to believe that there is justice in the loss of your lawsuit. The same God who gave you the property has deprived you of it; [2] may His Holy Name be blessed!

Property is evil when it is where God does not wish it to be. The more we are like Our Lord, stripped of everything,[3] the more we will share in His Spirit. The more we seek, like Him, the Kingdom of God His Father[4] and to establish it in ourselves and in others, the more will the necessities of life be given us. Live in this trust and do not anticipate the sterile years of which you speak. If they occur, it will not be through any fault of yours, but by the order of Providence, whose ways are always adorable.[5] Let us then be guided by our Father, who is in heaven,[6] and strive to have only one will with Him on earth.

3009. - TO EDME JOLLY, SUPERIOR, IN ROME

October 24, 1659

We will not be upset about not getting a church, since it is thought inadvisable for us to have one. Thank God, we want only

---

Letter 3008. - Dom André-Joseph Ansart, *L'esprit de S. Vincent de Paul* (Paris: Nyon l'ainé, 1780), p. 134.

[1]Ansart states that this letter was written to the Superior in Genoa some time after the plague had ravaged the house. It concerned a very important lawsuit lost by the establishment, which was still pending on August 29, 1659 (cf. no. 2955).

[2]Cf. Job 1:21. (NAB)

[3]Cf. Mt 27:28. (NAB)

[4]Cf. Mt 6:33. (NAB)

[5]Cf. Rom 11:33. (NAB)

[6]Cf. Mt 23:9. (NAB)

Letter 3009. - Reg. 2, p. 248.

what He wants, and, knowing that His Will is made manifest to us by that of Our Holy Father the Pope, we will remain peacefully submissive to the intentions of His Holiness.[1]

3010. - *LOUIS AND CLAUDE CHANDENIER TO SAINT VINCENT*

Turin, October 24, 1659

Monsieur and Most Honored Father,

Because of M. Berthe's ailment, we have stayed here longer than we intended. We hope to leave tomorrow for Milan, God willing, in the company of a Genoese gentleman of the Spinola family; [1] *he is passing through there and from there is going to Rome to be the Resident for his Republic. He testified in that court that he is strongly attached to your house in Genoa, and he spoke very highly of it. We will spend the feast of Saint Charles* [2] *in Milan, while awaiting M. Berthe, who will join us after having recuperated sufficiently here to do so. We hope Our Lord will grant him this grace, and us as well.*

*I am not adding anything, Monsieur and Most Honored Father, to what I said to you in the last letter I had the honor to write you, concerning the cordial, charitable treatment we have received in this house. I will simply tell you, since I feel obliged to do so because of the real edification that was ours to take, that they live here as is done at Saint-Lazare, except for one practice, namely, that for nine months of the year, all Missionaries, both priests and Brothers, leave the key in the door to go to gather their harvest of souls. It can be said of them—indeed, here more than elsewhere—*che sono padri di camera locanda,[3] *which will always be a more honorable title than any other that people might give them.*

We considered it our duty to pay a visit to the Marchese di Pianezza, not as to the Prime Minister and Grand Chancellor of this State, but as to a gentleman of eminent piety and the temporal father of this house. He

---

[1]Alexander VII (1655-67).

Letter 3010. - Archives of the Mission, Paris, original autograph letter.

[1]Two illustrious generals had come from this family, which later gave five Cardinals to the Church.

[2]November 4.

[3]*That they are Fathers of a rented room.*

expressed to us his appreciation for that visit, before leaving for Monaco, where he has gone to bring back that Prince's daughter, whom his son is supposed to marry.

With all our heart we prostrate ourselves at your feet to receive in spirit your holy blessing, and we are, with all possible respect, Monsieur and Most Honored Father, your most humble and obedient sons and servants.

L. DE CHANDENIER,
unworthy priest

CL. DE ROCHECHOUART

I did not want to lose the opportunity of writing to you from here because I do not think we will have another chance before arriving in Rome, if God grants us that grace.

Addressed: *Monsieur Vincent, Superior General of the Priests of the Mission, in Paris*

3011. - TO PIERRE CABEL, SUPERIOR, IN SEDAN

Paris, October 29, 1659

Monsieur,

The grace of O[ur] L[ord] be with you forever!

I cannot offer to help M. Michel's [1] mother with her business affairs, since I am not in a position to do so. Moreover, M. Michel has written to me that his presence there is absolutely necessary to prevent this good mother's ruin. That is why I am sending him word to go home to put things in order for the last time and to return to

Letter 3011. - Archives of the Mission, Paris, copy verified by M. Charavay, who put the original signed letter up for sale. The postscript is in the Saint's handwriting.

[1]Guillaume Michel, born in Esteville (Seine-Maritime), left his parish in Saint-Valery to enter the Congregation of the Mission on June 19, 1646, at thirty-nine years of age. He withdrew from the Congregation of his own accord before taking vows but later returned. In 1657 he was a member of the Sedan house and was in Fontainebleau in 1666.

you as soon as possible. He tells me that you will be able to do without him in the meantime.

I am sending you a packet for M. Lambin.[2] Please have it delivered promptly to one of the persons to whom it is addressed.

I am, in O[ur] L[ord], Monsieur, your most humble servant.

VINCENT DEPAUL,
i.s.C.M.

I just received your last letter. In reply, let me say that you did well to excuse yourself from attending the banquet. I will reply to the rest.

Addressed: Monsieur Cabel

3012. - TO MARÉCHAL DE LA MEILLERAYE

October 31, 1659

My Lord,

I begin this letter by thanking God for having delivered you from the long, painful illness from which His Divine Goodness has freed and preserved you in order to continue to extend His empire among the people of Madagascar, who did not know Him. I pray that He will do so for many years, as I trust He will. Some of the Fathers have assured us that God prolongs the life of those whom His Divine Providence makes use of in extraordinary works that concern His glory.

Furthermore, My Lord, I thank Your Excellency for the favor you grant us by giving us a share in this holy work. We will send

---

[2]Banker in the Court of Rome.

Letter 3012. - Reg. 1, fol. 12, copy made from the original autograph letter.

off three Missionaries on the fourth of next month. I would have sent a fourth, My Lord, had I not promised to give two to those gentlemen,[1] who are also sending a ship to Madagascar, at the time when we were not sure whether you, My Lord, would be sending yours while you were seriously ill.

One of these priests [2] is the son of the late M. Delbène. God inspired him from his childhood to devote his life to this holy work, and he entered our insignificant Company five or six years ago with that intention. He is very zealous and, if O[ur] L[ord] preserves him, there is reason to hope that he will render Him great service in that country. The other two priests are animated with the same spirit, by God's grace. Something has come up that prevents M. Le Blanc[3] from being a member of the group. We are sending with these priests an excellent surgeon,[4] who has also been with us for the last four or five years, with the same goal in view. I hope, My Lord, that he will be useful on your ship and will contribute to the salvation of the people of Madagascar.

I ask you most humbly, My Lord, to give orders to the captain of your ship to deliver to your Missionaries in Madagascar the luggage they are taking with them.

It remains for me, My Lord, to renew the offers of my perpetual obedience and of that of this poor, insignificant Company of the Mission. I ask you most humbly, My Lord, to be pleased to allow me always to consider myself, My Lord, your most humble and very obedient servant.

VINCENT DEPAUL,
i.s.C.M.

---

[1]From the Company of the Indies.

[2]Nicolas Étienne.

[3]Charles Le Blanc.

[4]Brother Philippe Patte.

3013. - TO TOUSSAINT BOURDAISE, IN MADAGASCAR [1]

[November 1659] [2]

Let me tell you, first of all, Monsieur, of our well-grounded fear that you are no longer in this mortal life, seeing the short time that your confreres who preceded, accompanied, and followed you lived in that ungrateful land, which has devoured so many workers who were sent there to do the groundwork. Oh! If you are still alive, how great will be our joy when we are assured of this! You would have no difficulty believing that of me, Monsieur, if you knew the extent of my esteem and affection for you, for it is as great as any person can have for another.

The last little report you sent us,[3] which showed us the power of God in you and caused us to hope for extraordinary success from your labors, caused us to shed tears of gladness on your account. We also shed tears of gratitude to God, who has cared so wonderfully for you and for those people whom, by His grace, you are evangelizing with such zeal and prudence that they seem disposed to become children of God.

At the same time, however, we wept at your grief and loss in the death of Messieurs Dufour, Prévost, and de Belleville,[4] who found their rest on the site of the work they went to seek, and who added

---

Letter 3013. - Abelly, *op. cit.*, bk. II, chap. I, sect. IX, §7, p. 185.

[1]Saint Vincent was still unaware that Toussaint Bourdaise had died on June 25, 1657.

[2]The Missionaries to whom this letter was entrusted left Paris on November 4, 1659.

[3]The Saint is referring here to the two letters of February 19, 1657 (cf. vol. VI, nos. 2215 and 2216). Might this be an example of his Gascon humor? The "little report" of no. 2216 runs for thirty-nine pages in English!

[4]Claude Dufour, born in Allanche (Cantal) in 1618, entered the Congregation of the Mission on May 4, 1644, shortly after his ordination to the priesthood. He was first sent to Montmirail (1644), then put in charge of the seminary in Saintes (1646-48). He was very virtuous but of a rigid and unobliging kind of virtue. In his eyes the life of a Missionary was too soft; he persuaded himself that the life of a Carthusian was more suited to his love for prayer and mortification. Saint Vincent was of an entirely different opinion, so Dufour, always docile, abandoned his plans. To free him from temptations of this kind, the Saint put him on the list of priests to be sent to Madagascar. While awaiting the day of departure, the Saint assigned him first to Sedan, then to Paris, entrusting him with the Internal Seminary there during the absence of M. Alméras, and finally to La Rose as Superior (1654-55). Sea voyages were long in those days; Dufour left

to your sorrows when you were hoping for greater comfort from them. This abrupt separation has been since then a sword of sorrow for your soul, as the deaths of Messieurs Nacquart, Gondrée, and Mousnier[5] had previously been. When you gave us the news of their death, you expressed your feelings so well that I was as moved by your deep sorrow as I was affected by these heavy losses.

Nantes in 1655 and arrived in Madagascar in August of the following year, but died on August 18, 1656, just a few days after his arrival. (Cf. *Notices*, vol. III, pp. 14-23.)

Nicolas Prévost, born in La Roche-Guyon (Val-d'Oise), entered the Congregation of the Mission on October 20, 1646, at thirty-four years of age. He was sent to Madagascar in 1655 and died there in September 1656, leaving the reputation of being a very zealous and virtuous Missionary.

Mathurin de Belleville, born in Brix (Manche), entered the Congregation of the Mission on May 1, 1654, at twenty-seven years of age. He contracted an illness as soon as the ship left the Saint-Martin roadstead, died on January 18, 1656, and was buried at sea off the coast of Sierra Leone (cf. *Notices*, vol. III, p. 160). On September 7, 1657, Saint Vincent gave a conference to the Congregation of the Mission on his virtues (cf. vol. XI, no. 173).

[5]Charles Nacquart, born in Treslon (Marne) in 1617, entered the Congregation of the Mission on April 6, 1640. After ordination he was sent to Richelieu. Designated for the first group to be sent to Madagascar, he arrived there on December 4, 1648. He had learned the native language so well on the voyage to Madagascar that in a short time he was able to draft a brief summary of Christian doctrine, *Petit catéchisme, avec les prières du matin et du soir. . . .* (Paris: Georges Josse, 1657). Cf. also Abelly, *op. cit.*, bk. II, chap. I, sect. IX, §5 and §6. A new edition of Nacquart's work, edited by Ludwig Munthe, Élie Rajaonarison and Désiré Ranaivosoa, was published under the title of *Le catéchisme malgache de 1657* (Antananarivo: Egede Instituttet, 1987). He converted several Protestants, baptized seventy-seven Malagasy, and regularized the situation of the French who were living with native women. He evangelized not only Fort-Dauphin, but all the interior within a radius of roughly thirty miles (cf. vol. III, nos. 1179, 1183, and 1188). Exhausted by so much work, Nacquart died on May 29, 1650. In vol. IX of *Mémoires de la Congrégation de la Mission* are found his letters, diary, and testament, taken from old copies preserved in the Archives of the Mission, Paris.

Nicolas Gondrée, born in Assigny (Seine-Maritime), entered the Congregation of the Mission as a subdeacon on April 11, 1644, at twenty-four years of age. During his novitiate he was ordained a deacon and was sent to Saintes. In 1646 he returned to Paris and was ordained a priest. In 1648 he volunteered for Madagascar, where he arrived on December 4. Satisfied with his good will, God called him to Himself on May 26, 1649. Saint Vincent had a high esteem of Gondrée's virtue and considered him "one of the best subjects in the Company." (Cf. *Notices*, vol. III, pp. 43-56.)

Jean-François Mousnier, born in Saintes (Charente-Maritime), entered the Congregation of the Mission on December 19, 1643, at eighteen years of age, took his vows on January 1, 1646, and was ordained a priest in 1649. After distributing alms in Picardy, he was then sent to Madagascar, where he died in 1655. His biography was published in vol. III of *Notices*, pp. 129-46.

God seems to be treating you, Monsieur, as He treated His own Son; He sent Him into the world to establish His Church by His Passion,[6] and it seems as if He is trying to introduce the faith in Madagascar only by your sufferings. I adore His divine ways, and I pray that He will carry out His plans in you. Perhaps He has very special designs on you, since, among so many Missionaries who have died, He has kept you alive. It seems that His Will, while wanting the good they desired to do, did not wish to prevent its outcome by taking them from this life, but to have it done by you, and God has preserved your life for this purpose.

Be that as it may, Monsieur, we have deeply regretted the loss of these good servants of God, and have had great reason to admire in this last unexpected event the unfathomable reasons for His ways of acting. He knows how willingly we have kissed the hand that struck us,[7] humbly submitting to these blows, to which we were so sensitive, although we could not understand the reasons for such a swift death in men who were so promising, in the midst of a people asking for instruction, and after so many obvious signs in them of a vocation to christianize that people.

Nevertheless, this loss, like previous ones and the events that have occurred since then, has not succeeded in the least in undermining our determination to assist you, or in shaking that of the four priests and the Brother who are on their way to you. They feel drawn to your mission and have asked us over and over again to be sent there. . . .[8]

I do not know who will be more consoled by their arrival—you, who have been waiting so long for them, or they, who have such an ardent desire to join you. They will see Our Lord in you and you in Our Lord and, with this in view, they will obey you, by His grace, as they would obey us. I ask you, then, to guide them in this. I hope that God will bless both your leadership and their obedience.

---

[6]Cf. Mt 26:39; Jn 20:19-23. (NAB)

[7]Cf. Job 5:17-18. (NAB)

[8]At this point, the Saint went on to praise the Missionaries he was sending to Madagascar. We do not have this portion of the letter, which Abelly omitted.

You would not have been left so long without some relief, were it not for two unsuccessful departures. One ship was lost on the river at Nantes; two of our priests and a Brother,[9] who were on the ship, were saved by the special protection of God; but nearly a hundred persons were lost. The other ship set sail last year, was captured by the Spaniards, and four of our priests and a Brother [10] who were on board came back home.

And so God did not permit any help or consolation to reach you from here but willed that these should come to you directly from Him alone. He wanted to be the one to act in that divine, apostolic work to which He has applied you, in order to show that implanting the faith is His own affair and not the work of men. That is how He acted when He began to establish the universal Church, choosing only twelve Apostles,[11] who went their separate ways throughout the world[12] to announce the coming and the teachings of their Divine Master. But once this holy seed had begun to grow, His Providence increased the number of workers.[13] It will do the same

---

[9]Fathers Charles Boussordec and François Herbron, and Brother Christophe Delaunay.

François Herbron, born in Alençon (Orne) in November 1617, was ordained a priest on September 22, 1646, entered the Congregation of the Mission on August 20, 1653, and took his vows on January 6, 1656. When the ship on which he was to sail for Madagascar sank, he was assigned to Le Mans.

Christophe Delaunay, born in Haute-Chapelle (Orne), entered the Congregation of the Mission as a coadjutor Brother on October 4, 1653, at nineteen years of age, took his vows in Luçon on January 6, 1656, and died in 1658. In vol. VI, no. 2171, we see the courage and spirit of Faith with which he acted when the ship that was to take him to Madagascar was wrecked. Saint Vincent spoke of him with deep admiration (cf. vol. XI, no. 160).

[10]Fathers Charles Le Blanc, Marand-Ignace Arnoul, Pasquier de Fontaines, and Pierre Daveroult, and Brother Christophe Delaunay.

Marand-Ignace Arnoul, born in Cayeux-sur-Mer (Somme), entered the Congregation of the Mission on November 22, 1654, at twenty-six years of age, and took his vows on November 23, 1656, in the presence of M. Delespiney.

Pasquier de Fontaines, born in Bailleul-Sire-Berthoult (Pas-de-Calais) on September 9, 1630, entered the Congregation of the Mission on April 22, 1653, as a clerical student and took his vows on April 25, 1656, in the presence of M. Delespiney. He volunteered for Madagascar and was sent there twice, but both times conditions at sea prevented passage and he had to return to France. Vols. I and V (Supplement) of *Notices* refer to him as *Desfontaines*.

[11]Cf. Lk 6:13. (NAB)

[12]Cf. Mt 28:18-20. (NAB)

[13]Cf. Acts 6:7; 16:5. (NAB)

for your infant church which, growing little by little, will at last be provided with priests who will survive to cultivate and extend it.

O Monsieur, how happy you are to have laid the first foundations of this great plan, which is destined to send to heaven many souls who would never enter there if God did not fill them with the principle of eternal life by your instructions and the Sacraments you administer to them! With the help of His grace, may you continue this holy ministry for a long time to come and serve as a rule and an encouragement to other Missionaries! This is the prayer that the whole Company frequently offers, for it is committed in a special way to recommend you and your work to God, and I myself am strongly committed to this.

But it would be useless for us to pray for your preservation if you do not do your part in it. So, I ask you with all the tenderness of my heart to take very good care of your health and that of your confreres. You can judge from your own experience how much you need one another and how necessary this is for the entire country. Your fear that our dear deceased may have hastened their death by overwork should oblige you to moderate your own zeal. It is better to have some strength in reserve than not to have any at all. Pray for our little Congregation because it really needs men and vigor for the great, diverse harvests that we see waiting to be reaped on all sides, both among the clergy and among the people.

Please pray also to Our Lord for me because I will not last much longer, given my age, which is over eighty years,[14] and my bad legs, which are no longer willing to carry me. I would die content if I knew you were alive and the number of children and adults you have baptized; but, if I am unable to learn that in this world, I hope to see it before God, in whom I am. . . .

---

[14]In November 1659 Saint Vincent certainly did not write that his "age was over eighty years" (*mon âge, qui passe quatre-vingts ans*), as Abelly has him say in this letter. In reality, we know that his eightieth year would begin on April 24, 1660 (cf. nos. 2907 and 2948). There is an alteration in Abelly's text, and it is not the only one on this point. Would not the original have stated: *passe à quatre-vingts ans*—going on eighty?

3014. - TO JACQUES PESNELLE, IN GENOA

Paris, November 7, 1659

Monsieur,

The grace of O[ur] L[ord] be with you forever!

I have nothing to say in reply to your letter of October 22, except that I ask O[ur] L[ord] to bless your missions and to give you the means to continue them, along with the other works of the Company.

I informed your brothers in Rouen of your letters and your declaration.

Messieurs Étienne, Feydin, and Daveroult left here on Tuesday[1] for Madagascar, together with a Brother.[2] They will embark in Brittany, and two more of our priests[3] will soon be setting sail from Dieppe for the same mission. I recommend all of them to your prayers.

I am, in O[ur] L[ord], Monsieur, your most humble servant.

VINCENT DEPAUL,
i.s.C.M.

Addressed: Monsieur Pesnelle, Superior of the Priests of the Mission, in Genoa

---

Letter 3014. - Treasury of Sant'Antonio Church, Padua (Italy), original signed letter.

[1]November 4.

[2]Philippe Patte.

[3]Fathers Daveroult and de Fontaines.

3015. - TO SISTER NICOLE HARAN,[1] SISTER SERVANT, IN NANTES

Paris, November 8, 1659

Dear Sister,

The grace of O[ur] L[ord] be with you forever!

On last Tuesday, the fourth of this month, three of our priests and a Brother left here for Nantes. They will be able to visit you at the hospital, so I am sending you a letter I have written for M. Étienne, who is in charge of the others; please give it directly to him. They hope to embark at Port Louis [2] on a ship that is being fitted out there for Madagascar. They will need your prayers for this voyage, that God may be pleased to bring them safely to port and bless their Mission.

You, and all those good Daughters who are with you are in my prayers, Sister. I ask Our Lord, who has recommended union and mutual support to us,[3] to give you the grace to love and comfort one another. I pray that He Himself will be the strength of the weak, the virtue of the strong, and the prayer—both vocal and mental—of those who are unable to pray. I pray also that His Divine Goodness will be the rule of conduct for all of you in the difficulty you find in observing the little Rule regarding your spiritual exercises, while serving so many patients.

O Sisters! how good it is to do nothing else but to practice charity! In so doing, you practice all the virtues together and make yourselves one with Jesus Christ by cooperating with Him in the salvation and consolation of the poor. If you were only aware of

---

Letter 3015. - Archives of the Motherhouse of the Daughters of Charity, original signed letter.

[1]Nicole Haran, born in 1627, entered the Company of the Daughters of Charity on July 28, 1649. In October 1650 she was sent to Montmirail and in 1653 to Nantes, where she encountered many difficulties over the years. In May 1655 the Administrators of the hospital proposed her as Sister Servant; she was still in Nantes at the death of Saint Louise (1660). In 1673 she was elected Superioress General for three years, after which she served the foundlings in the faubourg Saint-Antoine in Paris, where she died on June 5, 1679.

[2]A port at Lorient, in Morbihan.

[3]Cf. Jn 13:34-35; 1 Jn 3:23. (NAB)

your happiness as it is in the sight of God, surely work, contradictions, sorrow, bitterness—even death itself—would seem sweet and desirable to you, as indeed they are to those who try to make themselves worthy of the eternal happiness of the next life.

I send greetings to our dear Sisters and recommend myself to their prayers. Mademoiselle Le Gras is not completely well; still, she has no particular illness. She is preparing some help to be sent to you in twelve to fifteen days, God willing.[4] Some of your Sisters have gone to Narbonne and Cahors, far from here.[5] They are being asked for in many places; but God is not permitting us to be able to send them everywhere—we can do so only gradually.

I am, in His love, Sister, your most affectionate servant.

VINCENT DEPAUL,
i.s.C.M.

At the bottom of the first page: Sister Nicole Haran

3016. - *SAINT LOUISE TO SAINT VINCENT*

November 12 [1659] [1]

Most Honored Father,

Sister Noelle, who has been in the Company for nine years, has done as well in it as her simplicity has allowed. She is very God-fearing and most humbly entreats Your Charity, Most Honored Father, to offer her to Our Lord and to permit her to take her vows at Holy Mass tomorrow. For a long time, she has had a very special love for little children.

---

[4]A Sister Marie was sent to Nantes; she returned to Paris in June 1660.

[5]On September 12 Sisters Françoise Carcireux, Anne Denoual, and Marie Chesse left for Narbonne; Sister Marie-Marthe Trumeau went to Cahors.

Letter 3016. - Archives of the Motherhouse of the Daughters of Charity, original autograph letter.

[1]Year added on the back by Brother Ducournau.

I think we must also decide tomorrow which Sisters to send; please let us know. With my usual confidence, I ask your holy blessing, Most Honored Father, and take the liberty of calling myself your least and most unworthy daughter and servant.

L. DE MARILLAC

Addressed: *Monsieur Vincent*

3017. - TO SISTER MARIE-AGNÈS LE ROY [1]

Saint-Lazare, Friday, [November 1659] [2]

Most willingly, my dear Mother, do I approve of your visits and those of our dear Sister Guérin,[3] along with those whom you judge suitable to accompany you together or in the absence of either one of you, in order to prepare the newly-acquired house for the use of Sainte-Marie.[4] However, I ask you, dear Mother, and our dear Sister Guérin, that these visits be only for necessary matters.

Since God does not allow me to be in a position just now to

Letter 3017. - Property of the Sisters of the Second Monastery of the Visitation, 110 rue Vaugirard, Paris, original autograph letter.

[1]Mother Marie-Agnès Le Roy, Superior of the Second Visitation Monastery of Paris (faubourg Saint-Jacques). Born in Mons (Belgium) in 1603, she was, through her mother, the niece of Philippe de Cospéan, Bishop of Lisieux. In 1624 she entered the First Monastery, which she left at the request of the Marquise de Dampierre to join the group of Sisters who were sent to the Monastery in the faubourg Saint-Jacques at the time of its foundation. She became Directress there and then Assistant. Three times the votes of the Sisters entrusted to her the office of Superior (June 11, 1634-May 24, 1640; May 27, 1646-May 13, 1652; and June 6, 1658 to 1664). She went to inaugurate the Amiens and Mons Monasteries, remaining at the latter for three months; she also founded that of Angers and the Third Monastery in Paris, and played a prominent role in the establishment of the Warsaw Monastery. Mother Le Roy died on May 18, 1669. (Cf. *Année sainte,* vol. V, p. 547.)

[2]This letter was written between July 20 (cf. no. 2915) and November 15 (cf. no. 3022), shortly before the Feast of the Presentation of the Blessed Virgin (November 21), the day the Visitation nuns renew their vows.

[3]Anne-Marguerite Guérin.

[4]The house on rue Montorgueil, which later became the Third Monastery.

preside at the two ceremonies, I am asking M. Gambart[5] to do so, and I give you permission to select whomsoever you please to be present for the renewal of the vows. Perhaps the Coadjutor of Cahors[6] will be able to do this act of charity for you, as he did last year in your house in the city, if you send someone to invite him to do so. He lives on rue Michel-le-Comte, not far from the Carmelite nuns on rue Chapon. He is supposed to come here next Sunday. I plan to mention the matter to him, if my memory does not fail me.

Very willingly, dear Mother, I will pray for our dear sick Sisters, and I will not forget dear Sister Bouvard,[7] to whom I send my warmest greetings.

We have many men here who are ill. I recommend them also to your prayers and am your most humble servant.

VINCENT DEPAUL,
i.s.C.M.

Addressed: Our dear Mother Superior of the Visitation Sainte-Marie of the faubourg Saint-Jacques

---

[5]Adrien Gambart, born in Croye, in the Noyon diocese, on September 27, 1600, was ordained a priest in 1633. Soon after ordination he made a retreat at Saint-Lazare and took Saint Vincent as his guide. He became a member of the Tuesday Conferences and participated from time to time in the Saint's missionary activities. Aware that Gambart was a prudent man, he convinced him to accept the position of confessor for the Visitation nuns of the Second Monastery of Paris. He was also the Director of the Daughters of Providence of Saint Joseph and often taught catechism in the hospitals. *Le missionaire paroissial,* published in 1668 and dedicated to Saint Vincent, is the best known of his writings. It was thought erroneously that Gambart was a member of the Congregation of the Mission. He died a holy death on December 18, 1668, after an illness of one week. His manuscripts and part of his library were willed to Saint-Lazare. His biography, *Abrégé de la vie d'Adrien Gambart, prêtre missionaire,* was published in Paris in 1670.

[6]Nicolas Sevin.

[7]Marie-Augustine Bouvard, daughter of King Louis XIII's chief physician, and Superior of the Angers Monastery (1648-54). She was also Superior of the Second Monastery of the Visitation in the faubourg Saint-Jacques, Paris, where she died on November 15, 1659, at the age of forty-eight, after twenty-eight years in religious life. (Cf. *Année sainte,* vol. XI, pp. 393-406.)

3018. - *SAINT LOUISE TO SAINT VINCENT*

[November 1659] [1]

I do not know, Most Honored Father, the name of the young lady who wrote to me. Enclosed is the reply, in case Your Charity thinks it advisable to send it. But please consider whether it might not be necessary to send one of your priests to the Vicar to find out why he refuses to hear our Sisters' confessions, as did their previous confessor, to whom they returned, despite the order that had been given them. It also appears that one of the Sisters told him about this prohibition.

I have spoken to our Sister from St-Germain-de-l'Auxerrois, and she promises to behave according to the prescribed order. For several reasons, I hope she does so.

For the love of God, I ask your blessing for my own needs and for those of everyone else, and I most humbly ask your pardon for my lack of discretion in detaining you so late, and for everything else.

Your most humble daughter and servant.

L. DE M.

Addressed: *Monsieur Vincent*

3019. - TO JEAN PARRE

[Between 1657 and 1660] [1]

Dear Brother,

The [grace of O[ur] L[ord] be with] you [forever!

This letter] is simply t[o say that] I have nothing to [tell] you.

Letter 3018. - Archives of the Motherhouse of the Daughters of Charity, original autograph letter.

[1]Date added on the back by Brother Ducournau.

Letter 3019. - Formerly the property of the Daughters of Charity, 2 rue Percheronne, Chartres, original signed letter. Its present location is unknown. The top left corner of the letter is torn.

[1]With one exception, all the letters from Saint Vincent to Jean Parre were written within these two dates, so this one probably belongs to the same period.

Live always in G[od] and take care of yourself for His service and our consolation.

I am, in His love, dear Brother, your most affectionate brother and servant.

VINCENT DEPAUL,
i.s.C.M.

At the bottom of the first page: Brother Jean Parre

3020. - TO LOUIS DE CHANDENIER, IN ROME

Paris, November 14, 1659

Monsieur,

The grace of Our Lord be with you forever!

I bow to you and to M. du Moutiers-Saint-Jean[1] in Rome, prostrate in spirit at your feet and his.

I received the letter you did me the honor of writing me when you were leaving Turin,[2] and was consoled that you arranged to be in Milan for the feast of Saint Charles.[3]

M. Berthe tells me that his fever has now become quartan.

I am sending you a copy of the letter the Nuncio[4] sent to Abbé de Bérulle.[5] That good gentleman is in Rome on behalf of the Carmelite nuns. He can share with you the Brief of which one of

Letter 3020. - Archives of the Mission, Paris, original autograph letter.

[1]Claude de Chandenier.

[2]Cf. no. 3010.

[3]November 4.

[4]Celio Piccolomini was a member of a centuries-old Sienese family that produced many Bishops of Siena and Pienza and several Cardinals and Popes, as well as political and military leaders. Celio, titular Bishop of Caesarea, was Nuncio in France (1656-63). He was made a Cardinal in 1664 and was Archbishop of Siena from 1671 until his death in 1681.

[5]Pierre de Bérulle, nephew of the famous Cardinal de Bérulle, was Abbot of Pontlevoy and Visitor of the Carmelites.

those gentlemen[6] has been served notice but has not declared whether he was appealing. It is thought that the appeal will be to Rome and not to the Parlement. Those good nuns are very upset about their dear Father.[7]

M. Girard wrote to tell me about the death of that good Prior of Jolly and to say that he thinks the title should be given to a religious, the Pastor of the parish in which the priory is situated. I ask you most humbly to let me know if M. de Saint-Jean agrees to this. I prefer that it be given to a Benedictine monk, chaplain of the Archbishop of Tours, who is going to Babylon[8] as Bishop, and it would be intended to contribute to his ministry. He knows nothing about this. That is why I will be in a position, Monsieur, to carry out your orders. M. du Plessis-Praslin,[9] seigneur of the said parish, has appointed someone to it, claiming that he has this right as founder of the Priory. This will involve legal proceedings.

I will await your orders, Monsieur, and will be, in this world and the next, eternally grateful for the great benefits which you, Monsieur, and M. de Saint-Jean have bestowed on this insignificant Company. I am, Monsieur, your most humble and obedient servant.

VINCENT DEPAUL

---

[6]One of the three Superiors of the Carmelites.

[7]Cf. no. 2929, n. 1.

[8]Placide-Louis Duchemin. He never went to his mission. The diocese was entrusted in 1675 to François Picquet, who later succeeded him as Bishop of Baghdad.

[9]César de Choiseul, Comte du Plessis-Praslin (1598-1675), who distinguished himself at the siege of La Rochelle (1627-28). Appointed Maréchal de France (1645), he commanded the Royal army before Paris during the Fronde.

3021. - TO GUILLAUME DESDAMES, IN WARSAW

Paris, November 14, 1659

Monsieur,

The grace of O[ur] L[ord] be with you forever!

All your letters console me very deeply, but your last one, dated October 10, did so in a special way because of all the good news you give me; I cannot praise God enough for this.

(1) You tell me that the King's troops are making fresh inroads on all sides.[1] Is that not very consoling news, which merits eternal gratitude to the God of armies, who takes up the cause of the Church by blessing the plans of the King and Queen of Poland?

(2) You inform me that this devout Princess is determined to do all the good in her power while God preserves her in this world. O Monsieur, what a Christian resolution! Would to God that it was in the heart of all powerful persons and that all Christians fully realized the obligation they have to grow from virtue to virtue! All things are passing, death draws near, and good works are the only things that last.

(3) You mention a good French priest there with you, who was chaplain to M. d'Avaugour,[2] and who seems to be humble and trustworthy and would like to join us. Fine, Monsieur! If he does us the honor of coming to see us with this intention on his return here, we will be delighted.

Finally, to fill the joy of my poor heart to the brim, you assure me that M. Duperroy has completely recovered from the open

---

Letter 3021. - Archives of the Mission, Krakow, original signed letter.

[1]In the First Northern War (1655-60), Charles X Gustavus, King of Sweden, declared war on Poland because King Jan Casimir refused to recognize Charles' accession to the Swedish throne and because he desired to extend the Swedish possessions on the southern coast of the Baltic Sea. By the Treaty of Oliva (May 3, 1660) Jan Casimir abandoned his claims to the Swedish throne and ceded Livonia, Poland's Baltic territories, to Sweden. During this same period Poland was experiencing incursions from the Cossacks and Muscovites.

[2]Baron d'Avaugour, French Ambassador to Sweden. He died in Lübeck in September 1657.

wound in his chest. Oh! may God be praised, Monsieur, for such a favor! I thank Him for it with as much love and tenderness as I have done in a long time for any other benefit. May His Divine Goodness be pleased to preserve both you and him in perfect health and in that close union which, by virtue of the Holy Spirit, you experience together!

God willing, when we send you some help—which will be next spring—I will pay attention to see that there is a priest capable of taking charge of the parish and the house in your absence so that you can give a mission with M. Duperroy and begin a retreat for the priests; but you must not think of resigning from the duty of Superior. I know quite well you would be glad to do so, but I also hope that God will always be pleased with your leadership, as long as you allow Him to govern, as you now do.

We have no news here. The Company is going along as usual, thank God. In His adorable Providence He has finally permitted us to have a house in Rome. Pray that this will be in order to serve Him better, and recommend to Him all our needs in general and my soul in particular. I frequently recommend yours, which is very dear to me, and that of M. Duperroy, whom I embrace most tenderly. I am, in the love of O[ur] L[ord], Monsieur, your most humble servant.

VINCENT DEPAUL,
i.s.C.M.

Addressed: Monsieur Desdames, Superior of the Priests of the Mission, in Warsaw

3022. - TO SISTER MARIE-AGNÈS LE ROY

[November 1659] [1]

I hope that the esteem and affection that the whole house[2] had for our virtuous deceased Sister will serve it as an incentive to practice her virtues: the candor she always showed, the innocence and horror of evil with which she was filled, her zeal for good, her exactness to the Rule, and her fidelity to the inspirations of the Holy Spirit.

3023. - TO A BISHOP

[After January 3, 1656] [1]

One day I brought to the late M. Molé, who was Attorney General and Chief Justice, the grievances of some Prelates who had been very badly treated by the Parlement for having tried to remedy the disorderly conduct of some priests. Seeing themselves embarrassed in this way, they had expressed, with tears in their eyes, their decision to let things take their course.

That wise magistrate told me that it was true that, when Bishops or the Officialis failed to carry out the formalities prescribed for

---

Letter 3022. - *Année sainte,* vol. XI, p. 406.

[1]Reference to the recent death of Mother Marie-Augustine Bouvard (November 15, 1659) allows us to assign the date to this letter.

[2]The Second Monastery of Paris.

Letter 3023. - Abelly, *op. cit.,* bk. II, chap. XIII, sect. VI, p. 456.

[1]Date of the death of Mathieu Molé. He was born in Paris in 1584, became Attorney General in 1614 and Chief Justice of the Parlement of Paris in 1641. Appointed Keeper of the Seals on April 3, 1651, he lost the office ten days later because of political pressure resulting from the Fronde, but was reappointed on September 9. He held the position of Chief Justice until the Queen Regent, Anne of Austria, summoned him to the Royal Court outside Paris. Molé died on January 3, 1656. (Cf. Amable-Guillaume-Prosper Brugière, Baron de Barante, *Le Parlement et la Fronde. La vie de Mathieu Molé* [Paris: Didier, 1859].)

them for the administration of ecclesiastical justice, the Court was careful to correct their errors, but when they observed the formalities properly, it took no action against their proceedings. Whereupon he gave me the following example: "We know," he told me, "that the Officialis of Paris is very competent in his office and no fault is to be found with his deliberations. So, when appeals by writ of error from his decisions are brought before us, we never admit them; and we would act in the same way toward all others, if they acted in a similar manner."

3024. - TO JEAN MONVOISIN, IN MONTMIRAIL

Paris, November 21, 1659

Monsieur,

The grace of O[ur] L[ord] be with you forever!

I ask M. Cornuel to go to Troyes as soon as he can, and you, Monsieur, to find a horse for him and to give him money for this journey. If you are in the middle of a mission and cannot conclude it without him, he may remain a few days to help you out. But, in the name of God, Monsieur, do not delay him if it is not necessary, for there is an urgent need at the Bons-Enfants Seminary, which was expecting him and is now expecting M. de la Brière,[1] whom he is going to replace in order to relieve M. Watebled,[2] who is worn out.

I am writing you this letter expressly and in such great haste that

---

Letter 3024. - Archives of the Mission, Paris, original signed letter. The postscript is in the Saint's handwriting.

[1]Nicolas de la Brière, born in Saint-Deniscourt (Oise), entered the Congregation of the Mission on May 15, 1648, at twenty-two years of age, and was ordained a priest on May 22, 1655. He took his vows on August 15, 1650, and renewed them on January 25, 1656.

[2]Jean Watebled, born in Tully (Somme) on August 19, 1630, entered the Congregation of the Mission on January 1, 1646, took his vows on January 2, 1648, and was ordained a priest in October 1654. He was Superior at the Collège des Bons-Enfants (1659-68), Saint-Charles

I cannot answer your last one; I will do so some other time. I simply ask you to let me know what the Prior of Saint-Marc did in Montmirail in the short time he was there. He is loud in his praises of you and your men and of the cordial manner in which you treated him.

I am, in the love of O[ur] L[ord], Monsieur, your most humble servant.

VINCENT DEPAUL,
i.s.C.M.

Please ask M. Cornuel for his good advice before he leaves, Monsieur.

At the bottom of the first page: Monsieur Monvoisin

3025. - TO EDME JOLLY, SUPERIOR, IN ROME

Paris, November 21, 1659

Monsieur,

The grace of O[ur] L[ord] be with you forever!

I will write to you briefly this time because it is night. I received your letter of October 27. I praise God for the retreat you gave at the collège of *Prop[aganda] Fide* and for the Bishops' considera-

Seminary (1671-73), and in Le Mans (1673-76), returning as Superior to the Bons-Enfants (1676-79). Watebled was Visitor of the Province of Champagne in 1668, and of the Province of France in 1672 or earlier, remaining in this office until April 4, 1682. His brother Pierre was also a Priest of the Mission.

Letter 3025. - Archives of the Mission, Paris, original signed letter.

tion in putting you to work for the spiritual advancement of that house.

I sent the Bishop of Pamiers [1] his *perquiratur,*[2] without telling him what it cost; if he asks you, you can let him know.

I will be happy to receive the packet you sent me by a young Parisian who is coming from Rome.

I forwarded to your brother the letter you wrote him, together with the one for M. Jaillard.[3] I willingly approve of whatever you think best to do.

The hope you give me of your having the ordinands in December consoles me. May Our Lord be pleased to grant His humility to those who will have the happiness of speaking to them and of serving them so that it will be the basis for that good work!

I thank God, Monsieur, for your abandonment to His paternal guidance. I am more certain that you are filled with holy hope than I am of the things I see and touch. I pray, Monsieur, that O[ur] L[ord]'s Spirit may be so much yours that you will never experience any impulses or inspirations but His.

I am obliged to inconvenience you once again for the affairs of others. A young man in this parish[4] named Le Roy made a young woman pregnant and married her,[5] after having taken advantage of her mother. Since he knew that this marriage was invalid, he wanted to leave his wife. He told several persons about his incest, thinking he could use it as an excuse to avoid his obligation to rectify his marriage. What is more, when his father-in-law learned of it, he presented a petition to have him make honorable amends, if this accusation were false, or to have him punished, if it were true. The

---

[1]François-Étienne Caulet.

[2]An order or commission given by the Cardinal Datary for a single examination of dates in the registries of the Datary, which takes care of certain business relating to non-consistorial benefices.

[3]M. Jolly's cousin.

[4]Saint-Laurent parish.

[5]This is the text of the original; Coste omitted part of the sentence and gave simply "who...married a young woman."

judge gave orders that the young man be summoned to answer the accusation, but that is as far as the matter went because he decided to acknowledge that young woman as his wife and to live with her, after his marriage has been rectified.

So, Monsieur, he needs a dispensation, which I am asking you to obtain from the Penitentiary [tribunal] or by whatever other way you will be advised that it can be done.[6] The young woman's name is Madeleine Férault, from Paris; when she gave herself to Le Roy, she knew from logical suspicions that he had had an affair with her mother[7] because she had often seen them together in the same bed.

Your most humble servant.

VINCENT DEPAUL,
i.s.C.M.

Addressed: Monsieur Jolly

3026. - TO MARÉCHAL DE LA MEILLERAYE

November 22, 1659

My Lord,

Immediately after receiving the letter you were pleased to do me the honor of writing me, I sent someone to ask M. Cazet [1] to come to see me, and I asked him to offer my apologies to the members of his Company for being unable to give them any of our priests because you, My Lord, do not approve of my having promised to give them some. I added that we were bound to side with you, My Lord, because you are responsible for our confrere M. Bourdaise

---

[6]The words from "by whatever other way . . . ," are in the Saint's handwriting.
[7]Coste omitted the rest of this sentence.

Letter 3026. - Reg. 1, fol. 13, copy made from the autograph rough draft.
[1]Sébastien Cazet, a member of the Company of the Indies.

and for the Christians for whose conversion God has been pleased to make use of our insignificant Company, and whom we are bound to assist. I also said that I have always claimed to be your most humble servant and want to continue to be so until death. He replied that he would talk it over with the members of his Company and that he thought their Company would see clearly that I had to act that way.

From all this, My Lord, you can see that we have no hesitation in siding with you and breaking off from those gentlemen. I give you my word once again, My Lord, that I will not give them any priests, either from our own Company or from elsewhere, and that I am writing to tell M. Étienne to have no dealings with them or with their people.[2] I most humbly entreat you, My Lord, to rest assured that matters will be carried out by us in the way I have told you. I am, in the love of O[ur] L[ord]. . . .

3027. - TO NICOLAS ÉTIENNE, IN NANTES

Paris, November 22, 1659

Monsieur,

The grace of O[ur] L[ord] be with you forever!

I received your dear letter of the thirteenth. I thank God for having brought you safely to Nantes and prepared you as well as you seem to be to meet adversities, by His mercy. You are right in saying that the world and hell are opposed to God's plan, and that it is a good sign to hope in it when it is thwarted. I was consoled to see that these are your sentiments and that you are making good

---

[2]The Saint kept his word. He refused to give his Missionaries to Cazet; Étienne de Flacourt took some Récollet Fathers (Reformed Franciscans) with him when he sailed from Dieppe on May 20, 1660.

Letter 3027. - Archives of the Mission, Paris, signed rough draft.

use of a contradiction you were not expecting. I think you acted with the wisdom and moderation demanded by the person and the event. Early trials serve as a basis for the graces God grants in other, greater ones, so I am hoping that, since you have given yourselves to Our Lord to do and to suffer all things, nothing will be able to surprise you.

When I received the last letter the Maréchal[1] did me the honor of writing me, I sent someone to ask M. Cazet to come to see me. I told him that, since we had sent priests to His Lordship for the voyage to Madagascar, we could not give any to the members of the Company[2] and I was asking him to offer my apologies to them. I also said that we were obliged to give preference to that good nobleman because he has always taken us on his ships in preference to anyone else and has one of our priests under his authority, as well as the small number of Catholics instructed and baptized by our Missionaries. He replied that he would inform the Company of these facts, and I am assuring the Maréchal, in a letter I am sending to the Duchesse d'Aiguillon to be forwarded to him, that we will not give them any priest from our Congregation or from elsewhere, binding ourselves only to God and to him, and doing no business with anyone else.

So, Monsieur, when you arrive in Madagascar—if it is His Lordship's good pleasure to take you there—I ask you and your men to have no dealings with the officers of these gentlemen but to attach yourself as zealously as possible to the interests of that good nobleman because we are bound to obey him. I am telling him you will do so, and you can confirm this with him. After this assurance, I do not think he will try to insist on an oath of allegiance either from you or from the others. But, if he does, tell him that, since you are children of obedience, it is enough for you to know the intention of those who are sending you to keep you from ever acting contrary to it, and that that is your oath.

---

[1]Maréchal de la Meilleraye.

[2]The Company of the Indies.

As for having your belongings transported to La Rochelle, where the ship is supposed to be going, fine! Go ahead, if His Lordship does you the favor of giving you passage and you have to go to La Rochelle for embarkation. In that case, let me know; I will write to you there at greater length. Meanwhile, continue to abandon yourselves to the loving care of Providence and to trust in God's paternal goodness.

As for your request to be relieved of the care of the little band, please do not even think of it, but rather of being hidden under the ashes of humility, in the Spirit of O[ur] L[ord], who will Himself be your guidance in this leadership position, your strength in your weakness, your knowledge in your doubts, and your support in your needs. For your part, Monsieur, give yourself to Him, do not be burdensome to anyone, treat every individual with gentleness and respect, always using kind words and requests and never harsh or offensive expressions. Nothing is more capable of winning hearts than this humble, gentle way of acting, nor consequently better able to help you attain your goal, which is to see that God is served and souls sanctified.

I embrace you and all the priests with you with all the tenderness of my soul.

I think M. Feydin is still trying to work up the courage to speak in public—at least to preach. That is why it will be a good idea for you not to pressure him on that point while you are on the ship. As for catechizing, see if he is willing to take the risk of doing it. I am sure he will be successful at it, if he can overcome his timidity.

I am. . . .

3028. - TO PIERRE CABEL, SUPERIOR, IN SEDAN

Paris, November 22, 1659

Monsieur,

Thanks to the infinite charity of God, the well of the alms that have been cut back has not run completely dry. I have been instructed, therefore, to ask you to get two hundred livres for the months of October and November, which have been difficult, and to draw a bill of exchange for them on Mademoiselle Viole, treasurer of the Ladies of Charity, who will pay this amount on sight. She is the sister of M. Deffita, a lawyer at the Parlement, and resides with him on rue de la Harpe. People do not want this assistance to be sent via Reims any longer; that is why you were informed that it had stopped, so you will do well to honor the silence of Our Lord in this matter. I cannot assure you that it will continue, but this is the present arrangement. One means of meriting the continuation of Our Lord's benefits is to use them as we receive them, according to His good pleasure and for the greatest benefit to the neighbor.

God willing, we will try to relieve you soon of the person you mention. First we have to find a suitable priest to send you in his place.

The young convert you saw recently in Sedan is coming for the first time with another young man, who is also a new convert and has begun to have good results in his studies. He, as well as the other, plans to serve the Church some day, if he can continue his studies. He does not have sufficient knowledge to enter the Collège des Trente-Trois; [1] nevertheless, he has to leave the house for new

---

Letter 3028. - Pémartin, *op. cit.*, vol. IV, p. 499, L. 1973.

[1]The Trente-Trois Seminary took its name from the number of seminarians (thirty-three) preparing there for the priesthood. The places were given on scholastic merit and were reserved for young men of meager means who showed sincere signs of a priestly vocation. The work originated with a poor priest named Claude Bernard, who first brought together five seminarians, in honor of the five wounds of Our Lord. When resources allowed, the number was increased

Catholics, where they gave him preferential treatment, keeping him longer than the rule allows because they saw that he was a nice young man; however, they can do so no longer. He was told that the Queen has set up a fund in Sedan to promote good works, and he wants me to ask you, as I now do, to see if he can have a share in this charity to enable him to continue for a time at the university.

I am, in the love of Our Lord, your. . . .

3029. - *SAINT LOUISE TO SAINT VINCENT*

November 23 [1659] [1]

M. Mercier, a resident priest at Saint-Barthélemy [2] *and the confessor of our Sisters of the Hôtel-Dieu, would like to join those who go to the Tuesday Conferences. He came to ask me to inform you, Most Honored Father, that I have known him for a long time. I met him at the home of M. de Villenant, whom his mother admired.*

I think you read the letter that a Lady from Saint-Cosme[3] *sent me yesterday. One of her requests is very reasonable but the others are not. I think it would be well to reply to this letter, Most Honored Father, if you think it advisable, but not by way of the Sister who brought it. I believe she is partly to blame for the very great disturbance although, in reality, it is due somewhat to my neglect and human respect. This Sister is the one who wanted to leave the Company a while ago but humbled herself and stayed. It is true that her companion, who is quite simple, was a little imprudent.*

---

to twelve, in honor of the Twelve Apostles, and then to thirty-three to honor the years that Our Lord spent on earth. In 1657 the seminary was transferred to the Hôtel d'Albiac, rue Montagne-Sainte-Geneviève.

Letter 3029. - Archives of the Motherhouse of the Daughters of Charity, original autograph letter.

[1]Year added on the back of the original by Brother Ducournau.

[2]A parish in Paris.

[3]A parish in Paris.

I myself often fail in the virtues I need in order to be able to call myself truly, Most Honored Father, your most humble daughter and obedient servant.

L. DE M.

Addressed: *Monsieur Vincent*

3030. - TO NICOLAS ÉTIENNE, IN NANTES

Paris, November 26, 1659

Monsieur,

The grace of O[ur] L[ord] be with you forever!

Last evening I received your latest letter, written from the Maréchal's [1] room, and a memorandum indicating the conditions of settlement. Immediately afterward, I sent a note to M. Cazet, in which I asked him to come here to hear Holy Mass this morning, which he did. I gave him your letter and the memorandum. He then told me that he was the Maréchal's most humble servant and would communicate to the Company [2] the conditions of settlement contained in the memorandum. He said that the Company would be meeting next Friday, but he did not think it would accept them. He immediately added that he did not see a means more just or more reasonably satisfactory to each party than the one presented in the presence of the Maréchal,[3] when the Chief Justice[4] was present, but which neither at that time nor since then was accepted by the Maréchal. The latter indicated that he was not pleased about an

---

Letter 3030. - Archives of the Mission, Turin, seventeenth-century copy made from the original letter, which was entirely in the Saint's handwriting.

[1]Maréchal de la Meilleraye.

[2]The Company of the Indies.

[3]At the beginning of 1658.

[4]Guillaume de Lamoignon (1617-77), brother of Mademoiselle de Lamoignon. On October 2, 1658, he was named Chief Justice of the Parlement of Paris.

indiscreet request made by a member of the Company, who no longer belongs to it, and that, if His Lordship chooses to reconsider these same means of settlement and to ask the Chief Justice to put an end to this affair, the Company can consent to it.

That, Monsieur, is what he told me, while I await his final reply, which the Company will give me on Friday. He added once again that he is the Maréchal's most humble servant and, as such, is bound to inform him that his Company has not decided to abandon its rights, but will, however, proceed with the respect and reverence due to the dignity of the Maréchal. What distresses me is that such an important plan for the glory of God is being thwarted by these aggravating conflicts, which can be settled easily and promptly. I am praying that Our Lord Himself will be pleased to mediate this settlement.

I renew here the offers of my cordial and perpetual obedience to the Maréchal, and I ask you please to tell him that the said Company has accepted my apologies and is looking for some priests. Please send me news of you by every opportunity that presents itself.

I send my most humble greetings to my dearest confreres, and am, in the love of Our Lord, Monsieur, your most humble servant.

VINCENT DEPAUL,
i.s.C.M.

3030a. - TO THOMAS BERTHE, IN TURIN

Paris, November 27, 1659

Monsieur,

The grace of Our Lord be with you forever!

So, you still have quartan fever, and M. Martin is troubled by

---

Letter 3030a. - Archives of the Mission, Paris, original autograph letter. Coste published it in the First Supplement of vol. VIII, no. 3316, pp. 546-47, stating that it belonged at that time to Canon Prévost of Montpellier. Its date indicates that it should be placed here.

the same ailment.[1] I think you have no doubt, Monsieur, that I am suffering with you and that we are asking God to cure both of you. I hope, Monsieur, that His Divine Goodness will hear our cries and restore both of you to perfect health. Please do all you can for this purpose, Monsieur.

There was a time when I was bothered by that for several years in succession, but one bout had hold of me for two or three months; the others lasted about a month. It finally went away, and I am still here. I hope Our Lord will shorten and lessen the suffering; we will continue to ask Him to do so.

I am going to give instructions to have some money sent to you. It is not fair for you to be a burden on the house where you now are.

Our patients here cannot seem to get their strength back. M. Perraud is in the greatest danger. M. Alméras and Brother Ducournau are not feeling well. The rest of the Company is fine.

We are working in the country and preparing for ordination. Messieurs Étienne, Daveroult, and Feydin have left for Madagascar, along with Brother Patte.

I embrace you, Monsieur, with all the tenderness of my heart, and am your most humble servant.

VINCENT DEPAUL,
i.s.C.M.

I am writing to M. Delaforcade and am asking him to see that you get one hundred écus.

Addressed: Monsieur Berthe, Priest of the Mission, in Turin

[1]Jean Martin the elder, along with Thomas Berthe, was suffering from a type of malaria in which convulsions occurred about every fourth day.

3031. - TO EDME JOLLY, SUPERIOR, IN ROME

[November or December 1659] [1]

I am grateful to God for having brought matters there to their present state regarding the ordination retreats; I thank Him most fervently for this. Providence seems to be trying to give us the opportunity to render some little service to God in such an important matter, but, since it is the work of the Holy Spirit, the Company must be animated by this Spirit, and each member should be filled with it.

We must all tend toward that and act in such a way as to live according to this Spirit and to act according to its working, if we are to merit the grace of God's blessings on our work; otherwise, we would be deceiving the world. Messieurs Portail, Alméras, and I have celebrated Holy Mass in thanksgiving for God's plan for your house and to recommend this beginning to Him. So far I have not spoken about it to the Community. I await the results, of which we have still only the promise. And because, after God, this is due to your efforts and the grace that is in you, Monsieur, I thank you for it with all the affection of my soul, as well as for all the other benefits God has granted us through you.

3032. - TO PHILIPPE PATTE, IN NANTES

[November or December 1659] [1]

I am really distressed to learn that you will have some heretics on board ship and, consequently, much to endure from them. But,

---

Letter 3031. - Archives of the Mission, Paris, *Life of Edme Jolly,* Ms, p. 26.

[1]The house in Rome began to receive ordinands around the Ember Days of December 1659. Since the work is mentioned for the first time in the letter of November 21 (cf. no. 3025), this letter should be placed around that time. It seems to have been written after no. 3025.

Letter 3032. - Abelly, *op. cit.,* bk. II, chap. I, sect. I, §4, p. 19.

[1]The Missionaries sailed to Madagascar in December.

after all, God is the Master and He has permitted this for reasons unknown to us. Perhaps it is to oblige you to be more reserved in their presence, more humble and devout toward God, and more charitable toward your neighbor so that they may see the beauty and holiness of our religion and be moved to return to it.

Be very careful to avoid every sort of dispute and contention with them, and be patient and kindly in their regard, even if they attack you or our holy faith and our customs. Virtue is so beautiful and amiable that they will be compelled to love it in you, if you practice it well. It is to be desired that, in the services you render to God on board ship,[2] you make no distinction of persons and show no apparent difference in your treatment of Catholics and Huguenots, so that the latter may know you love them in God. I hope that your good example will be helpful to both.

Please take care of your health and that of our Missionaries. . .

3033. - *EDME JOLLY, SUPERIOR IN ROME, TO SAINT VINCENT*

[November or December 1659] [1]

In our own poor way we are going to prepare ourselves to be of service to the ordinands. Our trust is in God, who is showing all the more that He is the author of this work, since we have no idea how this decision was made nor who instigated it.[2] *So I can say that* a Domino factum est istud,[3] *and thus there is reason to hope that* qui caepit ipse perficiet.[4]

---

[2]In his capacity of surgeon.

Letter 3033. - Abelly, *op. cit.*, bk. II, chap. II, sect. VI, p. 238.

[1]The information given in no. 3025 and in n. 2 below enables us to assign a date for this letter.

[2]An ordinance of November 1659 from the Cardinal-Vicar of Rome obliged anyone wishing to be ordained to make a few days retreat with the Priests of the Mission.

[3]*By the Lord has this been done.* Cf. Ps 118:23. (NAB)

[4]*He who has begun the good work in you will carry it through to completion.* Cf. Phil 1:6. (NAB)

3034. - *LOUIS DE CHANDENIER TO SAINT VINCENT*

Rome, December 1, 1659

Monsieur and Most Honored Father,

Here we are at last, safely arrived by the grace of Our Lord ad limina sanctorum apostolorum.[1] *The day after our arrival, which was Saturday, we received your letter of November 7, in which we read that your health is good, by the grace of God, and this consoled us greatly. May it please His Divine Goodness to preserve you for many long years in His service!*

We also learned with joy from M. Berthe that he no longer had a fever and was hoping to come here in a few days, if it did not recur. We were sorry, however, to hear that M. Martin[2] *had quartan fever at regular intervals. When he visited us in Milan he had already felt it coming on, but at that time both we and he thought it was nothing serious. May it please God to free him of it soon so he can go to work for His glory, as he was so well disposed to do!*

With regard to the Priory,[3] *we can only admire what you did in that situation as in everything else. I have asked M. Jolly, whose goodness toward us I cannot begin to express to you, to tell you about the discussion we had on this affair. He will do so much better than I could.*

The courier is pressuring me to finish so I greet you with all possible respect.

I am, Monsieur and Most Honored Father, your most humble and very obedient servant.

L. DE CHANDENIER,
unworthy priest

Addressed: *Monsieur Vincent, Superior General of the Mission, in Paris*

Letter 3034. - Archives of the Mission, Paris, original autograph letter.

[1]*At the thresholds of the Holy Apostles.*

[2]Jean Martin the elder.

[3]Jolly Priory; the recent death of the Prior had created the vacancy to which Louis de Chandenier is here referring (cf. no. 3020).

3035. - TO JACQUES PESNELLE, SUPERIOR, IN GENOA

Paris, December 5, 1659

Monsieur,

The grace of Our Lord be with you forever!

I send greetings to you and your little band at the summit of the highest mountains in the Genoa diocese, where you are working. Oh! How heartily I ask God to sanctify those poor people by your mission and to impute the merit of the good that is being done to the Cardinal,[1] who sent you there and who, in his incomparable goodness has provided a home for us in Rome in a good section—one of the best, in fact!

Your brothers have written me a letter that I do not fully understand; it seems to them that your business is ours. I have not been able to answer them or even to read their entire letter, but I will do so.

Our patients are in almost the same state: one giving us reason to hope and the other in a serious condition. M. Alméras and Brother Ducournau have had relapses, and I, laden with years and sins, am still full of affection for you and your dear community.

Your most humble and very obedient servant.

VINCENT DEPAUL,
i.s.C.M.

Addressed: Monsieur Pesnelle, Superior of the Priests of the Mission, in Genoa

---

Letter 3035. - Archives of the Mission, Turin, original autograph letter.

[1]Stefano Cardinal Durazzo.

3036. - TO FIRMIN GET, SUPERIOR, IN MONTPELLIER

Paris, December 5, 1659

Monsieur,

The grace of Our Lord be with you forever!

I am perplexed by what you tell me of the request being made to you for M. Parisy. All things considered, the need of Agde seems the most urgent to me; however, if the return of the Bishop of Montpellier[1] is so imminent, *in nomine Domini,* he must be retained. But if it is likely that he will remain near the King, you may, in that case, lend him to M. Durand for a while. I am writing this, overwhelmed by the illness of M. Alméras and Brother Ducournau, with the result that I have only a moment to say that I am filled with consolation by your good leadership. In the same sentiment, I also send greetings to M. Parisy, for I am, Monsieur, the most humble and obedient servant of both of you.

VINCENT DEPAUL,
i.s.C.M.

Addressed: Monsieur Get, Superior of the Priests of the Mission of Marseilles, currently at the Montpellier Seminary, in Montpellier

---

Letter 3036. - Archives of the Mission, Paris, copy made from the original autograph letter, property of M. Ferroud, a bookseller in Paris, who put it up for sale in July 1914.

[1]François de Bosquet. He had gone to Toulouse, where the Court was settled, for the second session of the Provincial Estates of Languedoc, and did not return to Montpellier until the end of January. A number of provinces maintained their own Estates to discuss provincial matters. They were structured like the Estates-General, but with more limited powers.

3037. - TO EDME JOLLY, SUPERIOR, IN ROME

December 5, 1659

For several reasons, it is inadvisable for me to get involved in the affairs of M. . . . Please tell him, Monsieur, that I have given myself to Our Lord never to petition in any lawsuit of persons outside the Company, and, still less, to induce others to do so. I have had relatives who had lawsuits in this city, but I presented no petitions for them, and if I had to do so for anyone, it would be for him, but I cannot do so for anyone without violating the resolution I made before God.

3038. - TO LOUIS DE CHANDENIER

Paris, December 5, 1659

Monsieur,

With all the tenderness of my wretched heart I tell you how deeply consoled I am at the consolation you experience in those holy places of Rome. I hope M. Jolly is so fortunate as to give you hospitality in his new residence and that from there Our Lord may let you see the power of His grace as shown in those many, many martyrs who have suffered for Him. Alas! how heartfelt is my gratitude for our extraordinary obligations to you! My heart is so struck by it that it can be relieved only by expressing it and by wishing you all sorts of benefits and consolation wherever you go.

Several houses of Carmelite nuns do not accept the Brief; there are others that have, for it has not been explained to which court they are appealing; [1] we will have to see.

Letter 3037. - Reg. 2, p. 249.

Letter 3038. - Pémartin, *op. cit.*, vol. IV, p. 503, L. 1977.

[1]The meaning of this sentence is obscure; the original was undoubtedly misread. A Papal Brief of October 2, 1659, attempted to settle a dispute among the Carmelites in France. No. 2929, n. 1, gives the history of this question.

Your dear family is well, thank God. They are very eager for your return, and they strongly desire that it may be soon.

M. Berthe tells me that he no longer has quartan fever and is leaving as soon as possible to join you. Perhaps he will have this happiness before the present letter reaches you.

God has taken to Himself Abbé de Bullion,[2] who has donated his property for pious works. Someone told me that he has thought of us. I ask Our Lord to be his reward. He gave thirty thousand livres to the clerical fund, at which I am overjoyed, and for which I thank Our Lord. In His love I send greetings to M. de Saint-Jean[3] with all the tenderness of my heart and am, in the love of Our Lord. . . .

3039. - *SAINT LOUISE TO SAINT VINCENT*

December 7, 1659

Sister Barbe Bailly,[1] *who has been in the Company of the Daughters of Charity for fourteen years, took her first vows eleven years ago tomorrow and renewed them annually until 1656 when, she says, Most Honored*

---

[2]Pierre de Bullion, son of Claude de Bullion and commendatory Abbot of Saint-Faron de Meaux. He had died on November 30.

[3]Claude de Chandenier.

Letter 3039. - Archives of the Motherhouse of the Daughters of Charity, original autograph letter.

[1]Barbe Bailly, born near Vitry-le-François (Marne) on June 1, 1628, and baptized the same day, entered the Company of the Daughters of Charity on October 8, 1645, and took her vows on December 8, 1648. Her first mission was with the foundlings, whom she helped install in Bicêtre in July 1647. During the Fronde, the constant presence of soldiers there and the difficulty of finding food caused great concern, but Sister Barbe handled these problems with great wisdom and devotedness. In 1649 she went to the Motherhouse, where she worked as infirmarian and as secretary to Saint Louise. After the latter's death, Sister Barbe was sent to Poland (September 1660). Illness necessitated her return to Paris in 1668. She served the Company as Treasurer General (1671-74) and as first Superior at the Invalides, where she helped design the infirmary wing. In 1685 she was sent to Alençon, where she reorganized the hospital. She died there on August 21, 1699.

Father, that she had permission from Your Charity to take perpetual vows, which she did. She now most humbly entreats you to offer to God the renewal she desires to make of them with your permission.

For the love of God and for the accomplishment of His holy Will regarding the Company, I also implore you, Most Honored Father, for love of the choice He made of His most holy Mother, to ask pardon of Our Lord for all the interior and exterior faults that have been committed against purity and to grant us the grace of true purity as His mercy wishes it. Since I am more at fault than anyone else, I therefore have need of greater intercession, considering myself, if you please, Most Honored Father, your unworthy daughter and servant.

L. DE M.

Addressed: *Monsieur Vincent*

3040. - TO GABRIEL DELESPINEY, IN MARSEILLES

December 12, 1659

If you see that others are giving missions, bless God for it and rejoice that God is raising up workers for the instruction and salvation of the people, while we remain useless. Provided God's work is done, it does not matter who does it.

Letter 3040. - Archives of the Mission, Paris, Marseilles manuscript.

3041. - TO JACQUES PESNELLE, SUPERIOR, IN GENOA

Paris, December 12, 1659

Monsieur,

The grace of O[ur] L[ord] be with you forever!

I received your letter of the nineteenth. I thank God for the services you are rendering the mountain people and for the blessing God is giving to your work. I greatly fear for your health in the midst of the fatigue and inconvenience you are enduring in this. I ask you to take care of yourself, and I ask Our Lord to strengthen you with His grace, together with those who are with you, whom I embrace in spirit along with you.

I also praise God that you have received two new men for the Internal Seminary.[1] I dare not tell you not to take any more because, up to the present, your house has lacked nothing. There is reason to hope that God, who has always furnished what it needed and has created all things from nothing, will provide for everything. I beg Him to do so with all my heart.

Your brother has written me that, since the pension you are requesting of him is for our Community, I should take into account the fact that he also has to pay a pension of two thousand livres to his younger brother; in addition, the property given to your sister comes to an income of eight or nine hundred livres, and, if he pays us five hundred livres for you, he will have an income of only two thousand livres for himself. So, he wants me to reduce your pension to four hundred livres and to release him from payment for the three years that have elapsed since the death of your father.

I have not yet sent him a reply, but I am going to tell him that the pension is for you and not for this house and that, if you asked

Letter 3041. - Archives of the Mission, Paris, original signed letter.

[1]Of these two seminarians who entered the Internal Seminary in Genoa in November only one appears in the personnel catalogue. Giovanni Antonio Rolando, born in Aprico, Albenga diocese (Italy), on July 26, 1643, entered the Congregation of the Mission on November 11, 1659, and took his vows in Genoa on November 13, 1661, in the presence of M. Stelle.

him to send it to us, you also wrote me to keep it for you and that it is not up to me to grant him the reduction he is requesting. Perhaps he will write to you about it. Do whatever you please about it.

I am, in O[ur] L[ord], Monsieur, your most humble servant.

VINCENT DEPAUL,
i.s.C.M.

Addressed: Monsieur Pesnelle, Superior of the Priests of the Mission, in Genoa

3042. - TO SISTER NICOLE HARAN, SISTER SERVANT, IN NANTES

Paris, December 13, 1659

I am always in a hurry when I write to you, Sister, because I am so busy. I am doing the same now, to greet you and all our Sisters and to ask you to deliver to M. Dehorgny the letter I am writing to him.[1] He is one of our senior priests, whom we have asked to go to see you. I hope he will console you and that the letter will find him in Nantes. If, by chance, he has already left, return the letter to me. I also ask you, Sister, to send the enclosed to M. Eudo[2] by the Vannes coach. Please excuse me and offer me to Our Lord, in whom I am, Sister, your most affectionate servant.

VINCENT DEPAUL,
i.s.C.M.

Letter 3042. - Archives of the Motherhouse of the Daughters of Charity, original signed letter.

[1]Jean Dehorgny was on an extended round of visitations (September 1659-March 1660). It is not known exactly when he stayed in Nantes.

[2]Louis Eudo de Kerlivio, Vicar-General of the Vannes diocese, was born in Hennebont (Morbihan) on November 14, 1621. He spent more than four years at the Collège des Bons-Enfants, where he prepared himself for the priesthood under the direction of Saint Vincent, becoming his faithful friend and imitator. He requested Daughters of Charity for the Hôtel-Dieu in Hennebont, which he had personally founded; in addition he donated generously to the construction of the Vannes Seminary. His ardent zeal hastened his death, which occurred on May 3, 1675. (Cf. Pierre Champion, *Vie des fondateurs des maisons de retraite; M. de Kerlivio, le Père Vincent Huby, Jésuite, et Mademoiselle de Francheville.* [Nantes: J. Mareschal, 1698].)

3043. - TO JEAN MONVOISIN, IN MONTMIRAIL

Paris, December 16, 1659

Monsieur,

The grace of O[ur] L[ord] be with you forever!

I received your last letter regarding the Prior of Saint-Marc. I have nothing to say about that except to thank you for it, which I now do.

I will not say anything either about M. de Mesnin except that he came to speak to M. Maillard.

Please get some advice concerning M. de Saluce's proposal and, if you are advised to make the change he wants, then go ahead. Give him the twenty *perches* [1] of meadow on the Viémoulin[2] farm that are in the middle of his own meadows, on condition that he gives you equal measure as good as your own and in a place that is convenient for you.

On Sunday, the seventh of this month, we sent you by the Châlons coach, which passes through Montmirail, M. Dumas's[3] bag and manuscripts, wrapped in a linen cloth. Twenty sous were paid in advance for transporting it, but we have been unable to inform you about this until now. If you have not received it, please have some one pick it up.

I also request you, Monsieur, to get from M. Husson[4] some Arabic books he wants to send to M. Le Vacher in Tunis, and to

---

Letter 3043. - Archives of the Mission, Paris, original signed letter.

[1]One *perche* equals about eighteen to twenty feet.

[2]By his will of May 12, 1644, Louis Toutblanc, secretary of Pierre de Gondi, Duc de Retz, had bequeathed to the Priests of the Mission the farms of Fontaine-Essart and Vieux-Moulin (cf. Arch. Nat., S 6708).

[3] Jean-Aimé Dumas, born in Annecy on March 23, 1632, entered the Congregation of the Mission on October 22, 1656, and took his vows in Montmirail in 1659, in the presence of M. Berthe.

[4]Martin Husson, born in 1623, was a lawyer in the Paris Parlement and had been Intendant in the de Gondi household since 1650. Saint Vincent had great respect for him, as is evident from the Saint's letters, especially vol. IV, nos. 1614 and 1638. Husson accepted the offer he made him of the position of French Consul in Tunis and took up residence there in July 1653.

pay him the twenty-seven livres they cost him. I am sending you unsealed the letter I have written him about this. We will soon send a priest to Marseilles, who will take those books if you get them to us.

We have no news here. M. Perraud is still in danger. M. Le Soudier is better, and the rest of the Company is quite well. M. Cornuel is working in the Troyes Seminary, and M. de Brière[5] in that of the Bons-Enfants. I think that you, too, are out giving a mission and will be there for the feast days. May God bless your work and preserve your health and that of M. Dumas, whom I greet and embrace most cordially in spirit, along with you!

We have four priests in La Rochelle, about to embark for Madagascar; namely, Messieurs Étienne, Feydin, Daveroult, and de Fontaines, together with Brother Patte, a surgeon. Pray for them and for me, Monsieur, who am, in O[ur] L[ord], your most humble servant.

VINCENT DEPAUL,
i.s.C.M.

Addressed: Monsieur Monvoisin

While in Tunis he was an invaluable help and a faithful friend to Jean Le Vacher. Ignominiously expelled by the Dey in April 1657, he returned to France and became Intendant for the Duchesse d'Aiguillon. When he died in December 1695, he left a reputation as a learned, pious, virtuous man and a celebrated author.

[5]Nicolas de la Brière.

3044. - TO MADEMOISELLE D'HAUTERIVE [1]

Paris, December 17, 1659

Mademoiselle,

I received the letter you did me the honor of writing me, with the respect that I owe you and with the desire to serve you and your whole family, which has always been good to us. I thank you most humbly, Mademoiselle, for the marks of kindness you constantly show our priests in La Rose, and which you show me in your letter. God grant that we may merit their continuation by our obedience! I will always render mine, joyfully and gratefully, to you and your children, Mademoiselle, and we will gladly deliver to the one who is coming from Flanders[2] the five hundred livres you have instructed us to give him. I am writing to ask M. Chrétien to get them from you.

I ask God in His goodness to continue to bless your dear soul and your house. I assure you, Mademoiselle, that I am, in His love, the most humble and obedient servant of both of them.

VINCENT DEPAUL,
i.s.C.M.

Addressed: Mademoiselle d'Hauterive, in Hauterive

Letter 3044. - Archives of the Mission, Curia Generalizia, Rome, original autograph letter. In 1971 John Cardinal Cody, Archbishop of Chicago, IL (USA), donated to the Congregation of the Mission the Mundelein Collection, containing nine autograph writings of Saint Vincent, including no. 3044.

[1]Antoinette de Ranse, wife of Philippe de Raffin, Seigneur d'Hauterive et Ayguesvives.

[2]One of Mademoiselle d'Hauterive's sons had just fought in the war in Flanders.

3045. - TO LOUIS DUPONT, SUPERIOR, IN TRÉGUIER

Paris, December 17, 1659

Monsieur,

The grace of O[ur] L[ord] be with you forever!

I am writing you this letter to thank God for the consolation you received from the visitation and for the results M. Dehorgny has led me to expect from the good will of the whole family and your gentle, amiable leadership. I ask Our Lord to animate all of you with His Spirit so that you may constantly do works that are pleasing to God and useful to His Church.

Enclosed is a letter from M. Laurence,[1] a priest of the Company, who is in Turin, where he is working in an edifying way in the missions and at acquiring virtue. Please deliver it to its address and send me the reply.

There is no news here worth writing to you. We have the ordinands here in this house and several workers in the rural areas. M. Perraud is gravely ill with dropsy, which came upon him after a serious illness. M. Le Soudier has not yet recovered, but he is better, and the rest of the Community is very well. True, my legs are no longer willing to support me. Please pray for me, for all the needs of the Company, and for four of our priests and a Brother, who are about to embark for Madagascar. M. Dehorgny will not see them in Nantes or Port Louis because, since the ship has gone to La Rochelle to take on its food supply, they have gone there, too.

I embrace your heart and your family with all the tenderness of

---

Letter 3045. - Archives of the Mission, Paris, original signed letter.

[1]Yves Laurence, born in La Roche-Derrien (Côtes-du-Nord) on March 1, 1632, entered the Congregation of the Mission as a deacon on June 28, 1656, and took his vows in Turin on July 25, 1658, in the presence of M. Martin. He was Superior in Marseilles (1686-92) and Vicar-Apostolic for the Regencies of Algiers and Tunis (1693-1705). Laurence died in Algiers on March 11, 1705. (Cf. *Notices,* vol. IV, pp. 38-46.)

my heart, and I am, with consolation, in the love of O[ur] L[ord], Monsieur, your most humble servant.

VINCENT DEPAUL,
i.s.C.M.

We should accept with thanksgiving and great gratitude the benefit that the Treasurer is offering the seminary, since it is the wish of the Bishop of Tréguier.[2]

At the bottom of the first page: Monsieur Dupont

3046. - TO EDME MENESTRIER, SUPERIOR, IN AGEN

Paris, December 17, 1659

Monsieur,

The grace of O[ur] L[ord] be with you forever!

The last letter I received from you was dated November 22. I sympathize with you in your trouble and hope that God will soon relieve you of it by the presence of M. Dehorgny, who is heading your way. He is returning from Brittany and, after spending a few days in Luçon and Saintes, will pass through Guyenne.

I praise God that you have seven seminarians on retreat at the seminary, in addition to your young men who are studying. May God be pleased to increase your strength and your works for the advancement of the glory of God!

It will be well for you to make your temporal wants known to His Lordship[1] so that he may be pleased to remedy them. The work

---

[2]Balthazar Grangier de Liverdi.

Letter 3046. - Archives of the Mission, Paris, original signed letter.

[1]Barthélemy d'Elbène.

is his, and you should not be afraid of importuning him, provided you go about it humbly and at the right moment and do not go often to repeat the same things, after having explained matters clearly to him. May God animate you with His Spirit and be your sole joy and eternal glory!

I am, in His love, Monsieur, your most humble servant.

VINCENT DEPAUL,
i.s.C.M.

At the bottom of the first page: Monsieur Edme

3047. - TO PIERRE CABEL, SUPERIOR, IN SEDAN

Paris, December 17, 1659

Monsieur,

The grace of O[ur] L[ord] be with you forever!

I received three or four letters from you and have accepted your bill of exchange.

I have had a little encouragement given to Régnier, but I cannot find a job for him both because of his mental state, for which I am unwilling to answer, and because I do not know to whom to turn. I no longer go out, and people object very much to being burdened with such young people who do not know how to do anything, unless they pay a pension, and we ourselves cannot be responsible for him; besides, we are overburdened.

Libauchamp is in Paris, at the same collège where he was before; he made a retreat here and was wearing a cassock.

Letter 3047. - Archives of the Mission, Paris, original signed letter.

God be praised, Monsieur, for having preserved the Maréchal[1] and his whole family from the explosion caused by the gunpowder! God's protection for this illustrious family is manifest in that accident, which did not have the usual harmful results.

I think your line of action regarding the nobleman you mention[2] is correct, and tell those who say he should be urged to do good that I approve of it. He is not one to allow himself to be persuaded. He is guided more by his own ideas than by those of others, although he makes use of good advice people give him, when it is good and offered simply by way of suggestion. Continue to give him your advice in this way. That is how the angels act with us; they inspire us to do good but do not pressure us to do it. This is a thought I learned from the late Cardinal de Bérulle,[3] and experience has shown me that we have greater influence over others by proceeding in this way than by urging them to adhere to our views and trying

---

[1]Abraham de Fabert, one of the most renowned generals of the seventeenth century, was born in Metz in 1599. His civic virtues, military talents, and administrative qualities were outstanding, and he won all his commissions on the battlefield. The famous retreat from Mainz and the siege of several fortified towns offered him the occasion of showing his bravery. He loved discipline and was the terror of looters. His fidelity to the King and his minister was rewarded with the highest dignities: Governor of Sedan (1642), Lieutenant-General (1651), Maréchal of France (1658). Fabert died in Sedan on May 17, 1662. The part of his correspondence from 1634 to 1652 has been published. His life was written by Father Joseph Barre, *Vie de M. le Marquis de Fabert, maréchal de France* (2 vols., Paris: J. T. Hérissant, 1752), and by Jules Bourelly, *Le maréchal de Fabert (1599-1662)* (2 vols., Paris: Didier, 1879-81).

[2]The Marquis de Fabert.

[3]Pierre de Bérulle was born in the Château de Cérilly (Yonne) on February 4, 1575. Ordained a priest in 1599, he was appointed chaplain to King Henry IV shortly afterward. His skill in controversy enabled him to bring several important persons back to the Church, among others the Comte de Laval, the Baron de Salignac, and a judge of the Parlement of Paris. He established the Carmelites in France in 1603 with the support of Mme Acarie and Michel de Marillac, Keeper of the Seals. In 1611 he founded the Congregation of the Oratory, of which he was the first Superior. King Louis XIII entrusted him with the honorable mission of conducting to England Henriette of France, daughter of Henry IV, who was to marry (May 11, 1625) the Prince of Wales, the future Charles I. He greatly influenced the clergy and gathered around himself the most virtuous and eminent priests of Paris. As soon as Vincent arrived in the city, he sought the assistance and advice of Bérulle. Abelly claimed that the Saint lived "about two years" under his roof (*op. cit.,* bk. I, chap. VI, p. 24), but apparently that time should be reduced to four or five months at the most. The intervention of Bérulle is evident in Vincent's acceptance of the parish of Clichy, his entrance as tutor into the de Gondi family, his withdrawal to Châtillon-les-

to get the better of them. It is the usual method of the evil spirit to act in haste, and it is characteristic of him to upset souls.[4]

I do not know what you mean by Roman propers;[5] identify them in another way, if you want them sent to you.

I thank God for the strength He is giving M. Florent[6] and for the good use he makes of it. May His Divine Goodness be pleased to strengthen him still more so as to relieve you and to edify everyone inside and outside the Company!

We have four priests in La Rochelle on the point of embarking for Madagascar on a ship belonging to Maréchal de la Meilleraye. They are Messieurs Étienne, Feydin, Daveroult, and de Fontaines, along with Brother Patte, who is a fine surgeon. Please pray for them and for good M. Perraud, who is dying. M. Le Soudier is better, and the rest of the Community is very well. As for me, my legs are so bad that they refuse to carry me any longer.

I am, in the love of O[ur] L[ord], Monsieur, your most humble servant.

VINCENT DEPAUL,
i.s.C.M.

At the bottom of the first page: Monsieur Cabel

Dombes, and his return to the General of the Galleys. We would like to be able to state that their relationship always remained the same. However, Bérulle did not approve of the nascent Congregation of the Mission and even tried to prevent its approval by Rome, as one of his letters to Pierre Bertin indicated. In 1628, referring to the new Congregation, he wrote: "The plans that you tell me belong to those who are soliciting the affair of the missions by various and, in my opinion, devious ways, should make it suspect and oblige us to put aside the reserve and simplicity with which I consider the affairs of God should be conducted." (Cf. Archives of the Mission, according to Arch. Nat., M 216, second packet, folio of Father Bertin, p. 26, in which this excerpt is no longer found.) At the time, Pierre de Bérulle had been a Cardinal for a year. He died on October 2, 1629, and his life was written by Father Cloyseault. Father Ingold published this manuscript in 1880.

[4]Cf. Eph 6:11. (NAB)

[5]The liturgical Proper of the Seasons.

[6]Jean-Baptiste Florent, born in Lille, entered the Congregation of the Mission on November 11, 1645, at twenty-three years of age.

3048. - TO DENIS LAUDIN, SUPERIOR, IN LE MANS

Paris, December 17, 1659

Monsieur,

The grace of O[ur] L[ord] be with you forever!

It will be a good idea for you to postpone the mission in Silli[1] until you have finished the ones indicated to you by the Bishop of Le Mans;[2] then you will ask his permission to give that one.

I think M. Watebled is working on having the dimissorial letter sent for Brother Descroizilles.[3]

I will get some advice regarding the question you raise, namely, whether it is lawful to have foundation Masses celebrated away from the place where they were established, without the Bishop's permission. Once that is done, I will let you know the decision.

If Brother Jean Proust[4] wants to sell the house that belongs to him in order to assist his relatives, he may do so by sending a power of attorney to this effect to the place where the house is. Leave this to his own discretion, without trying to advise or dissuade him one way or the other. I approve in advance whatever he thinks it advisable to do.

If he asks you if he may go to Poitiers, you can tell him that local Superiors do not have the authority to grant that permission.

It is a good thing for us and for you sometimes to give presents to persons of the rank of those you mentioned to me in your letter,

---

Letter 3048. - Archives of the Mission, Paris, original signed letter.

[1]Silli-en-Gouffern, in the district of Argentan (Orne).

[2]Philibert de Beaumanoir de Lavardin. Although Saint Vincent did not recommend him for the episcopacy, he took up residence in Le Mans even before receiving his Bulls. He was not a model bishop; in fact, after his death a rumor spread that, on his own admission, he never had the intention of ordaining anyone. Several priests believed this and had themselves reordained; the rumor, however, was false. (Cf. Collet, *op. cit.,* vol. I, p. 473.)

[3]Jean Descroizilles, a seminarian at this time, was born in Ault (Somme) on January 25, 1631, entered the Congregation of the Mission in Paris on August 10, 1654, and took his vows there on August 11, 1656, in the presence of M. Delespiney.

[4]Jean Proust, born in Parthenay (Deux-Sèvres) on March 12, 1620, entered the Congregation of the Mission on June 25, 1645, and took his vows on October 28, 1647.

and I ask you to remember that. Just now, however, it is advisable not to send them anything; we shall see about it in a while.

M. Brochard should not expect from us the decision he is requesting, but from M. d'Eu.

I strongly desire the settlement with the administrators, and I ask O[ur] L[ord] to make us worthy of this favor, since it is more in accord with our profession and inclination than the passion for lawsuits, which is so harmful to priests; but, at the same time, Monsieur, we have to take our time and precautions for that. We have no one in authority who can help us with it. The Governor is not there, and he is too old for us to hope that he will go; if he were going, we could ask him. It is unlikely that we will throw ourselves on the mercy of those gentlemen without some support. You tell me that M. de la Bataillère[5] is a devoted friend, and I praise God for that; but I have been told that he has no influence in the city and so, Monsieur, I do not think we should be too hasty. We will examine at leisure the articles you sent us.

I cannot advise you to retain the general lease, although it may be profitable, or to do the opposite either. There are many reasons for and against. The ones that prevent me from consenting to your turning the property to account are that you are already having a hard time providing for your domestic arrangements, and I do not see how, by increasing them through this added burden, you could meet them.

Furthermore, I feel that a *fermier général*[6] will get far more satisfaction from the tax farmers under him than you could do and, if those tax farmers are expressing the desire to do business with you rather than with him, it is because they hope you will treat them more gently, will give them a reduction, will not pressure them, and will not put them to any expense. Yet, you can get satisfaction from them only by dint of threats and seizures, and the more indulgent

---

[5]Administrator of the Le Mans Hospital.

[6]Tax farmers were contractors who collected the salt tax, *aides*, tolls, and other indirect taxes; the highest ranking among them were called *fermiers généraux*.

you are toward them, the less they will pay you; if you use harsh measures, no matter how little, they will say that you are treating them more ruthlessly than a *fermier général* and will noise it abroad that you are avaricious persons and pitiless, merciless tyrants.

That is how the spirit of the world treats priests, and especially poor people who imagine that priests should not consider their own interests. Let me know when the lease expires.

You tell me that it would be better to satisfy the Lieutenant for Criminal Affairs[7] in the matter of his claim than to embitter him further. Discuss this with M. Duval; [8] if he thinks you should pay him the claim, and it can be done without establishing a precedent, then do so.

You mention a man who is forty-five years old and who wishes to enter the Company; let me know if it is to be a Brother or to live in it as a benefactor, his situation, and what he is able to do. If he intends to be a Brother and to dispose of his property, he should sell it before being accepted so as to be able to donate the money from it; otherwise, he could not give you anything once he is accepted.

I am, in O[ur] L[ord], Monsieur, your most humble servant.

VINCENT DEPAUL,
i.s.C.M.

At the bottom of the first page: Monsieur Laudin

---

[7]A magistrate established in royal courts to deal with criminal matters.
[8]Noël Duval; no information on him is available.

3049. - TO GUILLAUME DESDAMES, SUPERIOR, IN WARSAW

Paris, December 19, 1659

Monsieur,

The grace of O[ur] L[ord] be with you forever!

Two days ago I received your letter of October 25, which I should have received three weeks ago. It has been about a month since I received any other letter from you, apart from this one, and about the same length of time since I wrote to you. That was because I had nothing to tell you, since I had already informed you several times that we were waiting until spring to send you some relief. As a matter of fact, when spring arrives we will, with God's help, send some priests, a Brother, and the Sisters for whom the Queen is asking, and I will make sure that there is someone suitable among the Missionaries, for the reasons you indicate.

God grant that the Court will return to Warsaw bringing peace or victory and, above all, that Their Majesties will be in perfect health! These are favors for which we often ask God, in a spirit of gratitude for our eternal indebtedness to them.

You console me infinitely by telling me of the endless charity the Queen constantly practices, which makes everyone realize how God, from whom all good proceeds, is kind and ready to help. Oh! may she heap up great treasures in heaven[1] for herself and teach a beautiful lesson to all the great ones of the earth by the magnitude of her alms and the consolations she procures for all the afflicted!

As for news, I can tell you that we have four priests and a Brother—whom I do not think you know—in La Rochelle, on the point of embarking for Madagascar. They are Messieurs Étienne, from Paris; Feydin, from Auvergne; Daveroult and de Fontaines, from Artois; and Brother Patte, who is a Norman and a fine surgeon. We have only one patient here: M. Perraud, who is seriously ill with

---

Letter 3049. - Archives of the Mission, Krakow, original signed letter.

[1]Cf. Mt 6:20. (NAB)

dropsy. My legs are getting worse every day and refuse to support me any longer. We have the ordinands here, who edify us greatly, and a band of Missionaries working with good results in the country. When will you, Monsieur, be able to render some service to God and to the people by these works? It will not be as soon as you would like but will be whenever God chooses to give you the means of doing so.

I am, in His love, Monsieur, your most humble servant.

VINCENT DEPAUL,
i.s.C.M.

At the bottom of the first page: Monsieur Desdames

3050. - TO JEAN MARTIN, SUPERIOR, IN TURIN

Paris, December 19, 1659

Monsieur,

The grace of O[ur] L[ord] be with you forever!

God alone can make you know the joy I experienced on hearing that you no longer had a fever. Suffice it for me to tell you that it was in proportion to the very real pain I had felt at your illness. I thank God, Monsieur, with all the sentiments of tenderness and gratitude in my power, for having placed you in a position to continue your services to Him. I ask Him to increase your strength and to give you an even greater share in His Spirit, but I ask you also, Monsieur, to take care of your health and to remember that, if it is true that several persons have been cured by the medicine you took, there are also some who have had a relapse. I strongly fear that this may happen to you.

I have received no news from M. Berthe since he left Turin. I

Letter 3050. - Archives of the Mission, Turin, original signed letter.

am glad you told him in good time about the pilgrimage the Marchese[1] is making so that someone from the Genoa house will be at Santa Maria di Savona at the same time he is there, in accord with his instructions. It would have been desirable that it be M. Pesnelle or at least M. Simon.

I was deeply edified and consoled by the details you gave me of that good nobleman's piety and his acts of kindness toward you. May God make us worthy of enjoying those favors for a long time!

You replied wisely to the Marchese di San Tommaso,[2] for it is true that, if I am not contributing to the success of the Sant'Antonio affair, to which he is devoting himself so zealously, neither will I stand in the way of its succeeding as the Prince desires. I think that good nobleman will be quite satisfied with my being content to pray, as I am doing, that God's holy Will be accomplished in this matter and that I take only a passive role in it. I continue to admire his zeal for the glory of God and the welfare of our insignificant little Company, which will be eternally indebted to him for the benefit he is procuring for it.

Four of our priests are in La Rochelle, on the point of embarking for Madagascar. They are Messieurs Étienne, Feydin, Daveroult, and de Fontaines, along with Brother Patte. I recommend them to your prayers. We have no news here, where I am always, in the love of O[ur] L[ord], Monsieur, your most humble servant.

VINCENT DEPAUL,
i.s.C.M.

I will reply to M. Demortier as soon as possible; his letters and one from M. Laurence were forwarded. I embrace both of them most cordially.

Addressed: Monsieur Martin, Superior of the Priests of the Mission of Turin, in Turin

---

[1]The Marchese di Pianezza.

[2]Savoy's First Secretary of State.

3051. - TO GABRIEL DELESPINEY, IN MARSEILLES

Paris, December 19, 1659

Monsieur,

The grace of O[ur] L[ord] be with you forever!

The last mail brought me no letters from you. I am sending you a copy of the writ of appeal addressed to M. Chrétien concerning the business about which I wrote to you last week. Let me know if any Administrators of the Hospital for Galley Convicts were in charge and at work in the year 1646, and if any mention is made in their accounts of a sum of 2,500 livres, supposedly given to the hospital at that time. You will see the reason for this; people are now trying to claim them from M. Chrétien, mistaking him for one of those Administrators.

I embrace your dear heart and your little family and am, in O[ur] L[ord], Monsieur, your most humble servant.

VINCENT DEPAUL,
i.s.C.M.

3052. - TO SISTER MATHURINE GUÉRIN, SISTER SERVANT, IN LA FÈRE

December 20, 1659

I have been deeply consoled to learn, from the letters you wrote to Mademoiselle Le Gras and from Brother Jean Parre, of the good that God is doing through you and our Sister[1] and the blessing He

---

Letter 3051. - Property of the Daughters of Charity, 12 rue de Limbourg, Ghent (Belgium), original signed letter.

Letter 3052. - Archives of the Motherhouse of the Daughters of Charity, *Recueil de pièces relatives aux Filles de la Charité,* p. 652.

[1]Julienne Allot, who entered the Company of the Daughters of Charity around 1653-54, had been at La Fère since 1658.

is bestowing on your little family and your works. I thank Him for this with all my heart; I ask His Divine Goodness to continue to sanctify your souls and to bless what you are doing for the sanctification of your neighbor. I could not refrain from expressing my joy and gratitude to you for this.

I heard the rumor that was going around about Sister Marthe.[2] I find it hard to believe what was said to me about her, and I have good reason to be convinced of the contrary. This is a calumny for her and a humiliation for you. God allows these things to happen to those who serve Him, and it is even said that those who believe in Jesus Christ and follow Him will suffer persecution.[3] That is to be expected and, instead of being surprised by it, we should consider ourselves blessed to have something to suffer. In God's eyes, it is a benefit to be treated as Our Lord was, although it may seem to be an evil according to the world. Now, the Savior was unjustly insulted, accused, and despised;[4] why then should we complain if He honors us as His followers?

So, Sister, it will be well for you not to dwell on what people say, and never to justify yourselves. Words that are not based on truth go up in smoke; souls that surrender themselves to Our Lord to do and to suffer all things will be justified by Him and will have the honor and merit of resembling Him. Trust in His infinite goodness, and you can be sure that He will strengthen you in the tests He wills to make of your patience, if you truly disdain any cause for shame that may come to you from others. I ask Him to grant this grace to you and to our dear Sister as well. I greet her and you with all the tenderness of my heart, and I am, in the love of Our Lord, Sister, after recommending myself to her prayers and yours, your most affectionate brother. . . .

---

[2]Marie-Marthe Trumeau. She had been accused of appropriating for herself money destined for the poor (cf. *Documents*, Doc. 778, p. 893).

[3]Cf. Mt 5:10-11; 24:9. (NAB)

[4]Cf. Lk 18:32; 1 Pet 2:23. (NAB)

3053. - *SAINT LOUISE TO SAINT VINCENT*

Evening of the twenty-third [December 1659] [1]

Foreseeing the disadvantages of sending the Sister back to Saint-Cosme before explaining the entire matter to Your Charity, Most Honored Father, I sent another Sister this morning to tell her to go to help our Sister serve the poor until I know how I should answer the letter sent me.[2] *I added that I had to get instructions from you about that, Most Honored Father.*

For fear of a second letter, I think we should make a decision for the present and for the future, if Your Charity judges it advisable. This can be done tomorrow at a short conference, if you like, at whatever time Your Charity tells us to come.

For a long time now, you too have been reflecting on the most effective means of caring for the little ones, Most Honored Father. I entreat Our Lord to make known His holy Will in this as in all other matters and to grant us the grace of carrying it out faithfully, since we are your poor daughters and most humble servants.

L. DE M.

Addressed: *Monsieur Vincent*

3054. - SAINT LOUISE TO SAINT VINCENT

December 24, 1659

Most Honored Father,

The coming of Our Lord has inspired three of our Sisters to empty themselves of self in order to give themselves entirely to Him by the vows, which they desire to make tomorrow, if Your Charity permits, at the time

---

Letter 3053. - Archives of the Motherhouse of the Daughters of Charity, original autograph letter.

[1]Date added on the back by Brother Ducournau.

[2]In no. 3029 of November 23, 1659, Saint Louise mentions a letter from a Lady of Charity of Saint-Cosme parish.

Letter 3054. - Archives of the Motherhouse of the Daughters of Charity, original signed letter.

you indicate to them, either while assisting at the Holy Mass you will say or at another one. The names of our dear Sisters are: Sister Jeanne Gressier [1] *from Senlis, Sister Gabrielle from Gionges,*[2] *and Sister Marie Petit*[3] *from Paris. The last-mentioned has been in the Company about five years. There is also Sister Marie Prévost,*[4] *[who] entreats Your Charity to allow her to renew her vows, as she has done several times. All four of them have the approval of M. Portail. All the senior Sisters most humbly entreat Your Charity to offer to the Infant Jesus the renewal of the gift they have made to Him for their whole lives. Sister Julienne*[5] *wanted to be mentioned to you by name.*

Most Honored Father, tomorrow is also the twenty-fifth of the month,

---

[1]Jeanne Gressier, born in Senlis (Oise), entered the Company of the Daughters of Charity around 1654. Although very young, she was named Procuratrix in 1655 and remained at the Motherhouse. She assisted Saint Louise on her deathbed (March 15, 1660) and wrote the details of her last moments. It was she to whom Saint Vincent confided the governance of the Company while awaiting the naming of a new Superioress General in August 1660.

[2]Gabrielle Cabaret, born in Gionges (Marne) in 1634, was the daughter of Bernard Cabaret, Seigneur of Gionges and of Fortel, and Anne de Launay. She entered the Daughters of Charity on October 7, 1651, although Saint Vincent showed some reluctance about her admission (cf. vol. IV, no. 1451). After a difficult adaptation she was sent successively to Saint-Nicolas-du-Chardonnet, Saint-Denis Hospital, the Nom-de-Jésus, and Arras. In 1667 Sister Gabrielle was named Treasurer of the Company for the year; she died at Saint-Germain-en-Laye on February 5, 1669.

[3]Marie Petit entered the Company of the Daughters of Charity in 1655. Her name is found near the end of the list of the Sisters who were in the Company on August 8, 1655, when the Act of Establishment of the Daughters of Charity was signed (cf. vol. XIII, no. 150).

[4]Marie Prévost, born on January 29, 1622, entered the Company of the Daughters of Charity on November 21, 1646. She was missioned to Chantilly, but left there in 1649 to serve the foundlings. Although her name is not included among those who signed the Act of Establishment, it was added to the list of those present in the Company on August 8, 1655 (cf. *Documents,* Doc. 628, p. 703, n. 13).

[5]Julienne Loret was born in Paris on October 7, 1622, and baptized the same day. Orphaned at an early age, she was raised by the parents of Jacques de la Fosse, who later became a Priest of the Mission. In a conference after her death it was said that "she had a tiny body that enclosed a great soul." (Cf. *Recueil des principales circulaires des supérieurs généraux de la Congrégation de la Mission* [3 vols., Paris: Georges Chamerot, 1877-80], vol. II, p. 524.) Julienne entered the Daughters of Charity on June 9, 1644, and took her vows on December 25, 1649. Her merit and virtue were so remarkable that, on October 30, 1647, scarcely three years after her own admission to the Community, she was entrusted with the formation of the new Sisters. At the same time, she became Saint Louise's Assistant. "It was she who directed the whole Community," Sister Mathurine Guérin would later say, "because Mademoiselle was in no state to come to any spiritual exercise." (Cf. *Recueil,* vol. II, p. 530.) Julienne also carried out the duties of Secretary and was responsible for taking down Saint Vincent's talks, to which she listened, pen in hand. In 1651, she was sent to Chars to settle a very delicate situation: the new Pastor had Jansenist ideas and was attempting to impose them on the Sisters. Returning to Paris in 1653, after two years of difficult trials, Julienne was appointed Sister Servant in Fontenay-aux-Roses

the day on which Holy Mass is to be celebrated for the needs and intentions of the entire Company; Your Charity knows what they are. Allow me to tell you, Most Honored Father, that my powerlessness to do any good prevents me from having anything pleasing to offer Our Lord other than my poor renewal, unless it is the deprivation of the only consolation His Goodness has given me for thirty-five years.[6] *I accept this for love of Him, as Providence ordains, hoping from His goodness and your charity to receive a similar assistance interiorly.*

I ask this of you for love of the union of the Son of God with our human nature; but I am still hoping to see you when this can be done without endangering the precarious state of health God is giving you. I implore you to preserve it until the complete fulfillment of His plans for your soul, for His glory and the welfare of many others, among whom I have the honor of being included. I am, Monsieur and Most Honored Father, your most humble and obedient daughter and servant.

L. DE M.

Addressed: *Monsieur Vincent*

3055. - TO GABRIEL DELESPINEY, IN MARSEILLES

December 26, 1659

You tell me that a good preacher is needed or that we should not get involved in preaching when there are so many other workers who give missions and preach excellently. We have no such men. Still, M. Boussordec speaks very effectively, and if we are concerned with instructing the poor people in order to save them—and

---

(Hauts-de-Seine), where she remained until 1655. Recalled to the Motherhouse, she was again named Assistant, remaining in office under Mother Marguerite Chétif, after the death of the Foundress, and again under Mother Nicole Haran. She died in Fontainebleau on August 9, 1699. Her manuscript life, by Antoine Durand, C.M., is in the Archives of the Motherhouse of the Daughters of Charity.

[6]It had, in fact, been thirty-five years since Saint Louise had had Saint Vincent as her Director. Because of his infirmities he could now no longer leave Saint-Lazare to see her personally, and Louise felt that God was depriving her of what she called her "only consolation."

Letter 3055. - Archives of the Mission, Paris, Marseilles manuscript.

not to put ourselves forward and make a name for ourselves—we will have sufficient talent for that. Furthermore, the more simplicity and charity we bring to it, the more grace we will receive from God to succeed in it. We must preach J[esus] C[hrist] and the virtues as the Apostles did. . . .[1]

I praise God that you had four ordinands; that is enough for a beginning. God's works are accomplished little by little. You should hope that your house will one day be used for ordination retreats and a seminary, but we must be faithful in small things in order to be placed over great ones.[2]

3056. - TO JEAN MARTIN, SUPERIOR, IN TURIN

Paris, December 26, 1659

Monsieur,

The grace of O[ur] L[ord] be with you forever!

I just now received your letter of the eleventh of this month. At first it deeply consoled me, when I saw that you were giving a mission; but subsequently my joy was dampened by reading of the return of your quartan fever, which I greatly feared. Perhaps you were in too great a hurry to go out, but perhaps also God has ordained this for the best. We must adore His ways and be submissive to them. I ask you to spare nothing for your recovery, and I ask O[ur] L[ord] to accomplish His holy Will in you. I thank God that your priests are at work, and that God is giving them the strength to carry on.

You should respect the piety of that good gentleman who is having a little church built outside the city of Turin, along with a

---

[1]Cf. 2 Cor 4:5. (NAB)
[2]Cf. Mt 25:21. (NAB)

Letter 3056. - Archives of the Mission, Turin, original signed letter.

few rooms, with the intention of housing the Company there. You should praise God for his good will and admire the Marchese's constant concern for your establishment, which God will ultimately give you as a result of his efforts and merit. Do whatever he orders regarding that good gentleman's proposal. It seems that the Will of God will be made known to us through him. Nevertheless, Monsieur, it also seems that, by living outside the city, you are putting yourself in a position whereby you will be unable to have a seminary and to devote yourself to ordination retreats. You must still keep that in view because, God willing, His Providence will make use of you sooner or later in that work, if you are in the right place.

On that point I will tell you that the Pope[1] has given orders that, in the future, retreats for the ordinands in Rome shall be given by priests of the Company, and if God blesses that we will be able to give them elsewhere. I am telling you this, Monsieur, so that you will think about everything in order not to leave out the possibility of any of our works, when opportunities arise. It is better to wait awhile than to take on commitments in a locality that is too inconvenient. However, the Marchese is the master and I am, in O[ur] L[ord], Monsieur, your most humble and affectionate servant.

VINCENT DEPAUL,
i.s.C.M.

Addressed: Monsieur Martin

---

[1]Alexander VII (1655-67).

3057. - TO THE DUCHESSE D'AIGUILLON

Paris, December 30, 1659

I most humbly thank the Duchesse d'Aiguillon for the trouble she is so willing to take by coming to Saint-Lazare to attend the meeting, but I entreat her to reserve that honor for another occasion because of a new slight infirmity that has affected my leg. I have to use some little remedies for it, and this will prevent me from having the consolation and happiness of seeing her. Other than that, by God's grace, I am quite well, as usual.

In the last letter I received from Rome, I was told that Cardinal Antoine[1] had issued his final decision, saying that he could not allow My Lady's foundation[2] to be dependent on the Sainte-Chapelle; this has led M. Jolly to approach the Pope and present him with a petition to inform His Holiness that, since the foundation has been already accepted, it is only just that it be carried out.

3058. - *NICOLAS ÉTIENNE TO SAINT VINCENT*

La Rochelle, January 1, 1660

Monsieur and Most Honored Father,

Your blessing!

Fearing that you may not have received my letter from Saint-Jean-de-Luz,[1] *explaining the reason for our delay at La Rochelle, I am going to write you another short report.*

So, I will tell you, Monsieur, that we left Nantes on the feast of

---

Letter 3057. - Pémartin, *op. cit.*, vol. IV, p. 519, L. 1991.

[1]Antonio Barberini.

[2]In Loreto.

Letter 3058. - Archives of the Mission, Paris, seventeenth-century copy.

[1]Principal town of a canton in Basses-Pyrénées.

Saint-Nicolas [2] *and went as far as Saint-Nazaire, where we stayed for six days because there was no favorable wind. Finally, God gave us one for La Rochelle and we raised anchor. As we tried to enter the river*[3] *for Bordeaux, God permitted our mast to break in two and tumble into the sea, along with the mainsail. And, what was worse, the wind was driving us on to a sandbank, which caused us to despair of our lives.*

The captain and crew came and begged me to give them absolution immediately, saying that there was no longer any hope of escaping with our lives. Everyone was crying out for mercy and was bathed in tears. So I had someone help me get up off my mattress—even though I was ill and had not eaten for four days because I had been vomiting day and night—and I gave them general absolution. Then I assured them, in the name of God, that they would not perish if they would only place their trust in God.

No sooner had I finished speaking when the Master of the winds changed the north wind to northeast, allowing us to steer clear of the sandbank and renewing our hope for living. But, since we had no mast, we were at the mercy of the wind, which cast us on to the coast of Spain. A violent storm arose and we vowed, on the octave of the feast of the Immaculate Conception,[4] *that we would go to confession and Communion, celebrate twelve Masses, and clothe twelve poor persons in honor of the Immaculate Virgin Mary. She preserved us from this storm as well as from other mishaps because the wind drove us from the coast of Spain toward Bordeaux and back again to the coast of Spain without our being able to enter any harbor because we had neither mast nor sails.*

To make matters worse, we had no food, and all thirty-four of us were on the brink of dying from starvation or of drawing straws to see who would serve as food for the others.

At this point, on the feast of Saint Thomas, Apostle of the Indies,[5] *God finally sent us an angel who, with eighteen of his men, towed us to Saint-Jean-de-Luz for the price of twenty écus, which I gave them. We then had the ship remasted. Brother Patte, M. Boutonné,*[6] *and I took the coach and rode day and night, arriving the day before our men were due to board.*

---

[2]December 6.

[3]The Gironde.

[4]December 15.

[5]December 21 (now July 3).

[6]A passenger on the *Maréchale*. In a letter dated March 1, 1661 (cf. no. 3296), Nicolas Étienne refers to him as Boutonnet and informs Saint Vincent of his desire to be a Missionary, his study of philosophy, and a retreat he has made, but he is not listed among the personnel of the Congregation of the Mission.

I cannot tell you how happy they were; the whole town—Catholics and Huguenots alike—rejoiced. The following day, the Bishop[7] *invited me to dinner and was most gracious toward me, offering me his money and everything in his power. All the Communities did likewise, and I was overwhelmed by their good will and courtesy.*

Since those priests had bought some supplies and spent M. Boutonné's two hundred livres that they had received for him, and since I had no money because of the heavy expenditures I had to make for the ship as well as for the coach, I was obliged to get five hundred livres to pay for what they bought, as well as for some other provisions, and to give M. Boutonné his two hundred livres. The Maréchal[8] *had left orders with his squire, M. Coulon, to give those priests one thousand livres, in the event that they wanted to sail on his ship. But, when he saw me arrive, he kept them, and since he knew that I was trying to draw money on a banker, he offered me some on my bill of exchange, which I did not want to accept. Finally, however, after much persuasion, I accepted and gave him a bill of exchange on you to be drawn on presentation. I informed the Maréchal of this; perhaps he may prevent M. Coulon from drawing this bill of exchange on you. Nevertheless, if he does not, kindly give the money to M. Coulon or to the person he designates; I assure you that it will be the last expenditure of this embarkation.*

Today, M. Daveroult said Mass on board ship; tomorrow morning I will board with all the others, hoping to set sail next Saturday or Sunday. Messieurs Dehorgny and Rivet [9] *spent two days with us and left today for Luçon.*

I do not think I will suffer half as much on this large ship as I did on the small boat, although this has not discouraged me; in fact, I feel more and more enthusiastic about it, and I must admit in all simplicity that, in the midst of all the dangers, I did not envisage death as something bitter, but as something very sweet, considering myself happy to die for Him who had given His life for me.

Adieu, then, dear Father, pray and have others pray for your son, and obtain for him the grace of martyrdom. I leave with this joyous expectation

---

[7]Jacques-Raoul de la Guibourgère, born in 1589, was the widower of Yvonne de Charette and father of several children when he was ordained. In 1631 he succeeded his uncle as Bishop of Saintes, then went on to Maillezais, and finally to La Rochelle when the episcopal See was transferred there. Very few other Bishops were so closely associated with Saint Vincent. He died in 1661.

[8]Maréchal de la Meilleraye.

[9]Louis Rivet.

and remain, meanwhile, in the love of O[ur] L[ord] J[esus] C[hrist] and of His most holy and Immaculate Mother, Monsieur and very dear Father, your most humble and very obedient servant and son.

NICOLAS ÉTIENNE,
i.s.C.M.

3058a. - TO GABRIEL DELESPINEY, IN MARSEILLES

Paris, January 2, 1660

Monsieur,

The grace of Our Lord be with you forever!

I pray that in this new year God will give us a renewed spirit and the love of His Spirit. Before replying to your letter of December 23, I will tell you that God has chosen to take good M. Perraud from us; he died last Friday.[1] We are going to have a time of sharing this evening on the virtues God granted him the grace of practicing. He suffered a great deal during the five months or so of his illness. There is reason to believe that he is now happy, after such a long purgatory. In addition, he lived and ended his life like Our Lord, working and dying for the salvation of souls. Please do not fail to pray and have others pray for his soul.

Before I received your letter in which you speak of having

Letter 3058a. - Copy made from *Recueil Nodet.* This collection was organized at the time of the French Revolution, at the latest, and most likely given to M. Nodet by M. Messonnier, a relative of his and the last Vincentian Superior in Marseilles. Having passed from hand to hand, it was finally lost. Before its disappearance, some very faithful copies were made, which were found in 1941. The history of this collection is related in *Annales C.M.* (1943-44), pp. 228-30. Cross-references have verified the fidelity of the copies; the originals, doubtless written by Brother Ducournau, were very legible. The copy of the present letter was published in *Annales C.M.* (1943-44), pp. 231-32, and reprinted in *Mission et Charité,* 19-20, no. 104, pp. 130-31. This edition uses the latter text.

[1]December 26.

M. de Pourrade elected Administrator,[2] the Duc de Richelieu[3] had sent me the letter he is writing to the Administrators, informing them that he has chosen Messieurs Négriau and de Saint-Jacques—at least that is what M. Desmaretz[4] wrote me. Therefore, it is no longer time to be thinking about anyone else, unless there are such major obstacles to putting the above-mentioned in office that those gentlemen may judge it advisable to name four new ones. In that case, it would be necessary to proceed according to the usual principles and to let that good nobleman know the reasons for that new election.

Do not even think about buying the house that overlooks your garden. It is too expensive and we do not have the means of paying for it. We do, however, have the means of honoring the holy poverty of Our Lord. So we will do so on this occasion, please.

M. Boussordec has returned from giving a mission. We will have him rest for a few days; the winter is so harsh here that I cannot in conscience have him make such a long journey to Marseilles during this intense cold.

You did well, Monsieur, to give some spiritual consolation to the poor men on the galleys during the Christmas season, despite the bodily misery to which they are reduced, which seems to make

---

[2]This paragraph deals with the administration of the Hospital for Galley Convicts in Marseilles.

[3]Armand-Jean du Plessis, Duc de Richelieu, was born on October 2, 1631. He succeeded his father, François de Vignerod, brother of the Duchesse d'Aiguillon, as General of the Galleys (1653-81). In virtue of that office the Hospital for Galley Convicts came under his jurisdiction. He died on May 10, 1715.

[4]Jean Desmarets, Seigneur de Saint-Sorlin, member of the French Academy and Intendant of the Duc de Richelieu, was born in Paris in 1595. He wrote some very successful tragedies and comedies before devoting himself mainly to works of piety, translations of the *Imitation of Christ* and the *Spiritual Combat, Avis du Saint-Esprit au Roi,* and some articles attacking the Jansenists, Simon Morin, Homer, Virgil, and the pagan authors. His principal work, *Les Délices de l'esprit,* a poetic apology of Christianity, was printed in 1658. He often consulted Saint Vincent and called him his "good spiritual Father"; Saint-Cyran was frequently the topic of their conversations. Despite the strong influence of the Saint, after his death Desmarets fell into strange ways, not only on the spiritual and religious level but also in the literature he wrote, leading people to think that he had more or less lost his mind. Desmarets died in Paris on October 28, 1676.

them incapable of instruction. I hope God will draw good results from it and will not fail to reward the trouble you have taken there.

I am, in Our Lord, Monsieur, your most humble servant.

VINCENT DEPAUL,
i.s.C.M.

I am writing to tell M. Huguier that we received two écus for Barriot, a convict on the *Richelieu.*

3059. - TO A SUPERIOR

[December 1659 or January 1660]

I recommend to your prayers the soul of our good M. Perraud who left us on December 26, after an illness of four or five months. Since it served him as a purgatory, this gives us reason to hope that he is now enjoying the reward of his labors, after having worked so long and so successfully in the Lord's vineyard and at the practice of virtue. Nevertheless, have your little community offer the customary prayers for him.

3060. - *SAINT LOUISE TO SAINT VINCENT*

January 4, 1660

Most Honored Father,

At the beginning of this new year, allow me to greet Your Charity most humbly and, by this means, to ask for your holy blessing to help me to be faithful to God for as long as His Goodness chooses to leave me on this earth.

Letter 3059. - Lyons manuscript.

Letter 3060. - Archives of the Motherhouse of the Daughters of Charity, original autograph letter.

I also most humbly entreat you, Most Honored Father, kindly to let me know whom you have chosen as executor of the will that the lady I mentioned[1] *wishes to make to you. I am afraid she will come before I can give her this information.*

Please pardon the liberty I have taken, Most Honored Father, in sending you this Jesus crowned with thorns. The very thought that you were suffering so much gave me the idea that nothing could be of greater comfort to you than this example. I am also sending a medal that was sent to me, along with a few rosaries, by the good lady who was sick here in this house, when she returned from Notre-Dame-de-Liesse.

For the love of God, allow me to enquire about your health. Is the swelling in your legs increasing? Do you have less pain and do you still have a fever? With the familiarity of a daughter toward her Most Honored Father, I cannot prevent myself from telling you that I feel it is absolutely necessary for you to be purged frequently, but gently, to supply for the deficiency of nature which is hindering perspiration, since it is also very dangerous to induce it by artificial means. In the evening, you should take whatever a sick person would eat, except for bread and wine; herbs, however, are useless for building good blood. Taken occasionally, Cornachin powder—eighteen to twenty-one grains only—is very good for children and the elderly. It does not upset the stomach and drains off fluids without leaving the body too dehydrated. I think my own experience with this remedy gives me the courage to suggest it, but I know you will not use it without asking someone's advice.

I am really anxious to know how you are. I think Our Lord has placed me in the disposition of bearing everything with great peace. That is how it should be, since I have the honor to be, Most Honored Father, your most humble, obedient, and grateful daughter and servant.

L. DE M.

Addressed: *Monsieur Vincent*

---

[1]Madame de Glou. (Cf. no. 3066.)

3061. - TO JEAN MARTIN, SUPERIOR, IN TURIN

Paris, January 9, 1660

Monsieur,

In this new year, I ask Our Lord to renew our hearts in His Spirit and to unite us in Himself for all eternity.

I received your letter of December 19, which revived the distress I had already experienced because of your quartan fever. We are asking Him in His goodness to free you of it for His service.[1] Please do all you can on your part for that purpose.

I thank Our Lord that the rest of the family is at work giving missions and is being successful with them. May His Divine Mercy be pleased to bless more and more both the work and the workers!

I recommend to their prayers and yours, Monsieur, the soul of our good M. Perraud, who died here on December 26, after an illness of four or five months. Since it served him as a purgatory, it gives us reason to hope that he is now enjoying the reward of his labors, for he worked long and successfully in the Lord's vineyard and at the practice of virtue.

These past few days I thought I would have to recommend to your prayers M. Étienne and Brother Patte as having died, but they have come back to life. We considered them as dead, but God has preserved their lives almost miraculously. Someone wrote to us from Nantes and La Rochelle that they had died at sea, while going from one of those towns to the other. A young Parisian, who was on the same boat, seeing death staring him in the face, jumped into a little skiff, in which he escaped. He wrote to his mother here that, after the good priest had given general absolution to thirty persons

---

Letter 3061. - Archives of the Mission, Turin, original signed letter.

[1]First redaction: "which you will have all winter long, unless God frees you of it--which does not seem likely--as we are begging Him to do through His goodness and for His service." The correction is in the Saint's handwriting.

who were on that same boat, he had seen it sink before his very eyes with all on board. So, we could no longer doubt the truth of that disaster.

The day after this young man's letter was communicated to us, however, we received two letters from M. Étienne, assuring us of the contrary. He stated that, after he had given absolution, God sent them such a favorable gust of wind that it enabled them to steer clear of a sandbank on which they were about to run aground. He added that for two full weeks they were in imminent danger, having neither masts nor sails because the storm had smashed the ones they had. Furthermore, they did not even have any provisions because they had taken enough for only three or four days, especially since this trip takes only twenty-four hours. Nevertheless, God in His goodness guided them to Saint-Jean-de-Luz in good health and with a good appetite, and finally to La Rochelle, where they are about to embark on a large ship going to Madagascar, with Messieurs Daveroult, Feydin, and de Fontaines, all priests of our Company. These men were deeply grieved because they thought they had lost their Superior, and you could not imagine how dismayed we were.

But God, who puts to death and gives life,[2] likewise consoled us by giving us back these two good servants of His whom we believed drowned, so please help us to thank Him for this, Monsieur, and to recommend fervently to Him the voyage and the mission of those five Missionaries,[3] without forgetting, in the love of O[ur] L[ord], Monsieur, your most humble servant.

VINCENT DEPAUL,
i.s.C.M.

At the bottom of the first page: Monsieur Martin

---

[2]Cf. Jn 5:21. (NAB)

[3]The Missionaries left La Rochelle on January 18 aboard the *Maréchale* which, after four months at sea, was shipwrecked off the coast of the Cape of Good Hope during a storm. They returned to France in 1661.

3062. - TO GABRIEL DELESPINEY, IN MARSEILLES

Paris, January 9, 1660

Monsieur,

In this new year I ask Our Lord to renew our hearts in His Spirit and to unite us in Him for all eternity.

Before replying to your last letter, I am going to share my joy with you, since I did not want to share my grief with you last week, even though it was great. Still, I thought I was going to have to recommend to you M. Étienne and Brother Patte as having died, but they have come back to life. We considered them as dead, but God has preserved their lives almost miraculously.

On December 6 they left Nantes to go by sea to La Rochelle. It takes only a day to get there, but more than twenty went by before we had any definite news of them. Word came from those two towns that they had been lost, and a young Parisian, who was on the same boat, seeing death staring him in the face (these are his own words), jumped into a little skiff, on which he fortunately escaped. He wrote to his mother here that, after M. Étienne had given general absolution to thirty persons who were on the same boat, he had seen it sink before his very eyes with everyone on board. So, we could no longer doubt the truth of that disaster.

The day after this distressing letter had been shared with us, however, we received two letters from that good priest, assuring us of the contrary. He said that, after he had given absolution, God sent them such a favorable gust of wind that it enabled them to steer clear of a sandbank on which they were about to run aground. He added that they had spent two weeks on the brink of death because they had neither mast nor sails because the storm had smashed the

---

Letter 3062. - Copy made from *Recueil Nodet.* The letter was published in *Annales C.M.* (1943-44), pp. 232-34, and reprinted in *Mission et Charité,* 19-20, no. 105, pp. 131-33. This edition uses the latter text, replacing the much shorter one from the Marseilles manuscript, which Coste used.

ones they had. Furthermore, they did not even have any provisions because they had taken only what was necessary for a distance of thirty leagues. Nevertheless, God in His goodness guided them to Saint-Jean-de-Luz, a French seaport on the Spanish border, in good health and with a good appetite, and finally to La Rochelle, where they are now ready to embark for Madagascar with Messieurs Daveroult, de Fontaines, and Feydin. These men, all priests of the Company, were deeply grieved, as we were, thinking they had lost their Superior. You could not imagine our sorrow and dismay.

But God, who puts to death and gives life,[1] likewise consoled us by giving us back those two servants of His, whom we believed drowned. They took the mail coach at Saint-Jean-de-Luz to go to meet their confreres. Please help me, Monsieur, to thank Our Lord for those graces and to recommend fervently to Him the voyage and mission of those five Missionaries.

To get back to your letter of December 30, thank you for your care in letting us know the dispositions of the Administrators concerning the claim they are making on M. Chrétien for a [sum of money] from the hospital. You lead me to hope that you would see if, in the book or papers of the same hospital or in the accounts of the tax officials, mention is made of the amount they are claiming. It is important to know that for the defense of M. Chrétien, so please inform me of it. I sent you the nomination made by the Duc de Richelieu of two new Administrators but, since M. de Pourrade was not presented to him in the usual time nor manner, I did not choose him, as you desired.

True, it may be inconvenient for a priest to sleep at the hospital, and it would be desirable for him not to sleep there, but this is necessary because of the large number of patients who might otherwise die during the night without assistance. Please see to that, Monsieur, while waiting until you have the means of making complete provision for it—and I hope to send you that means soon, God willing.

---

[1]Cf. Jn 5:21. (NAB)

Inform the Provost[2] that we will always obey him most willingly in whatever we can but, since it is our Rule not to work outside of our houses in episcopal cities—except for the poor convicts—you will be unable to give conferences or exhortations to the young women at the Refuge.[3] Please excuse yourself from this as politely as possible.

We received two écus for Nicolas Bonner; two for Pierre Le Gros, called La Pointe; one for Renault Lepage; and thirty sous for Jacques Mauger.[4] That makes sixteen livres ten sous in all, which I ask M. Huguier to distribute to them, and you, Monsieur, to put on his account.

I am, in the love of Our Lord, Monsieur, your most humble servant.

VINCENT DEPAUL,
i.s.C.M.

We just received another twenty-seven livres fourteen sous for François Dardane on the *Saint-Dominique* and five livres ten sous for Pierre Blondeau on the *Cologne* [*Capitaine?*].

3063. - TO GUILLAUME DESDAMES, SUPERIOR, IN WARSAW

Paris, January 9, 1660

Monsieur,

In this new year I ask Our Lord to renew our hearts in His Spirit and to unite us in Himself for all eternity.

---

[2]Pierre de Bausset, Provost of Marseilles. Coste used only this paragraph for his no. 3062.

[3]The history of the Refuge de Marseille has been written by Abbé Payan d'Augery, *Le Refuge des filles repenties; notice historique sur la maison de Marseille depuis le XIVe siècle jusqu'à nos jours* (Nimes, 1884). A second edition was printed in Marseilles in 1900.

[4]All four were prisoners in Toulon.

Letter 3063. - Archives of the Mission, Krakow, original signed letter.

This letter is to give you news of us and to ask for yours. It consoles me greatly when I receive any, and I find the time very long indeed when I am deprived of it. I think I answered your last letter, and it remains for me only to ask Our Lord, as I am doing, to keep you and good M. Duperroy in good health and to grant us the grace of seeing more and more in you how true priests are formed and what their interior and exterior dispositions should be through Jesus Christ Our Lord.

God has taken from us good M. Perraud, a man of that caliber, who died in this house on December 26, after an illness of four or five months. Since it served him as a purgatory, it gives us reason to hope that he is now enjoying the reward of his labors, for he worked long and successfully in the Lord's vineyard and at the practice of virtue.

These past few days I thought I would have to recommend to your prayers M. Étienne and Brother Patte as having died, but they have come back to life. We considered them as dead, but God has preserved their lives almost miraculously. On December 6 they left Nantes to go by sea to La Rochelle. It takes only twenty-four hours to get there, but we had no news of them until the end of the month. Letters were written to me from all sides that they had been lost. A young Parisian, who was on the same boat, seeing death staring him in the face—those were his own words—jumped into a little skiff and was fortunately saved. He wrote to his mother that, after M. Étienne had given general absolution to thirty persons who were in the boat, he had seen him go down with all of them, so we had no further doubt of the truth of this disaster.

The day after this harrowing letter had reached us, however, we received two from that good priest, assuring us of the contrary. He said that, after he had given absolution, God sent them such a favorable gust of wind that it enabled them to steer clear of a sandbank on which they were about to go aground and that they were in imminent danger for two full weeks, having neither masts nor sails because the storm had smashed them, nor even provisions, since they had taken only what was needed to go to La Rochelle.

Nevertheless, God in His goodness had guided them to Saint-Jean-de-Luz on the Spanish border, in good health and with a good appetite, and finally to La Rochelle, where they are now about to embark for Madagascar with Messieurs Daveroult, Feydin, and de Fontaines. Those men, all priests of the Company, were deeply grieved at the thought of having lost their Superior, and you could not imagine our sorrow and dismay here.

But God, who puts to death and gives life,[1] likewise consoled us by giving us back those two servants of His, whom we believed drowned. They took the mail coach to Saint-Jean-de-Luz to meet their confreres. Please help us, Monsieur, to thank O[ur] L[ord] for these favors and to recommend to Him the voyage and mission of those five Missionaries, without forgetting, in the love of Our Lord, Monsieur, your most humble servant.

VINCENT DEPAUL,
i.s.C.M.

Since writing this, I have received your letter of December 2, in which I see you have been ill. This would have worried me greatly if you had not assured me at the same time that you were better, for which I thank God. I beg you, by His Holy Name, to take care of yourself as best you can for His service.

You reiterate your request that, among the priests we will be sending you, there might be a suitable man, with broad experience, capable of being in charge. With God's help we will be attentive to that, Monsieur, but such accomplished men are needed where they now are. In addition, since they are so few, it will be difficult for us to give you entire satisfaction at first; however, the ones we designate for you will gradually become as you desire by practice and your example.

God be praised, Monsieur, that peace is being discussed,[2] and

---

[1]Cf. Jn 5:21. (NAB)
[2]The Treaty of Oliva, signed on May 3, 1660, ended the war between Sweden and Poland.

may He in His infinite goodness bring it about, for that is not under human control and is a work worthy of His power and mercy!

I praise God also for the peace of mind of the Daughters of Charity, for their work, and for the satisfaction the Queen derives from it. Do all you can to keep them united and to encourage them more and more.

Addressed: Monsieur Desdames, Superior of the Priests of the Mission of Holy Cross, in Warsaw

3064. - TO JEAN DEHORGNY, IN RICHELIEU

Paris, January 11, 1660

Monsieur,

In this new year I ask Our Lord to renew our hearts in His Spirit and to unite us in Himself for all eternity.

I received your letters of December 29 and January 1. They consoled me more than I can say, since in them I learned of your good health and how much God is pleased to bless your fine leadership. I give infinite thanks to His Divine Goodness, who uses you to establish good order wherever you go, and I pray that He will be pleased to continue.

You gave me great pleasure by going to La Rochelle to console and encourage our poor priests as they were about to embark; I am sure that this has united them more closely and that they will profit from your good advice.

I have nothing to say to you, Monsieur, about the house in Luçon, except that I await the outcome of what you did there, and we are awaiting M. Chiroye,[1] who you tell me is leaving for Paris

---

Letter 3064. - Archives of the Mission, Turin, original signed letter.

[1]Jacques Chiroye was born in Auppegard (Seine-Maritime) on March 14, 1614, and entered the Congregation of the Mission on June 25, 1638. He served as Superior in Luçon (1640-50,

at the same time that you will be leaving for Saintes. God be praised for that!

In Saintes you will find both M. Fleury and Brother Fricourt somewhat worried about their parents. I hope, however, that your presence will remedy their ill-regulated attachment to them and that you will leave them in peace in the place and situation in which they now are.

M. Chrétien is asking for a preacher for La Rose; see if they can manage without one. I think they could, if M. Chrétien would make a little effort to preach. I have been told that he allows women into their house and their garden; that should not be tolerated.

I recommend to your prayers and to those of the little family of Saintes the soul of our good M. Perraud, who died here on December 26, after an illness of four or five months. Since it served him as a purgatory, it gives us reason to hope that he is now enjoying the reward of his labors, for he worked long and successfully in the Lord's vineyard and at the practice of virtue.

The community here is quite well. True, M. Alméras was slightly ill and still is. As for myself, I can no longer go downstairs because my legs are worse than ever.

God and our Holy Father the Pope were finally pleased to send the ordinands to the poor beggars of the Mission in Rome at the last Ember Days. By God's special Providence, the Abbés de Chandenier were there, and they tried, by their modesty, piety, recollection, and the other virtues they practice, to edify this first ordination retreat. There is reason to hope for the continuation of that good work.

I just received a letter from the Officialis of Luçon,[2] who wrote to me about the parish of Chasnais[3] in the same spirit as he has

---

1654-60, 1662-66) and Crécy (1660-62). He did not take his vows until March 9, 1660. Chiroye died on May 3, 1680.

[2]Probably Canon Para, who became Rector of the seminary in 1663.

[3]A locality in the canton of Luçon.

already done. I wrote to you about this, namely, that he would like some other benefice instead of that one—an archdeaconry or a simple priory. I thanked him and told him not to give that another thought.[4]

Your most humble servant.

VINCENT DEPAUL,
i.s.C.M.

At the bottom of the first page: Monsieur Dehorgny

3065. - TO EDMUND BARRY, IN LORM

Paris, January 14, 1660

Monsieur,

In this new year I ask Our Lord to renew our hearts in His Spirit and to unite them in Him for all eternity.

Before replying to your letter, I recommend to your prayers and those of your community the soul of our dear M. Perraud who died here in this house on December 26 after an illness of four or five months. Having served him as a purgatory, it gives us reason to hope that he is now enjoying the reward of his labors, for he worked long and fruitfully in the Lord's vineyard and at the practice of virtue.

These past few days I thought I would have to recommend to your prayers M. Étienne and Brother Patte as having died, but they have come back to life. We considered them as dead, but God has preserved their lives almost miraculously. They sailed from Nantes on December 6, on a small boat which was carrying their luggage,

---

[4]This last paragraph is in the Saint's handwriting.

Letter 3065. - Archives of the Mission, Paris, original signed letter.

to go to La Rochelle, the place from which Maréchal de la Meilleraye's ship was to set sail for Madagascar; Messieurs Daveroult, Feydin, and de Fontaines had gone there by land. The journey by sea takes only twenty-four hours, but three weeks elapsed before we had any definite news of this boat. People were writing to me from all sides that it had been lost, and in the end we were forced to believe it when we read a letter from a young Parisian to his mother, in which he said that he had been on the same boat and had looked death in the face. In desperation, he and another man had jumped into a little skiff. At the same time they saw the boat go down with thirty persons who were on it; only he and his comrade were saved. In addition, he said that M. Étienne, at the request of the captain and sailors, who saw that they were lost, gave all of them general absolution a moment before the shipwreck.

When this letter was communicated to us, it filled our cup of sorrow to the brim; on the following day, however, we received letters from M. Étienne which filled us with joy. They assured us that, after he had given that absolution, such a favorable gust of wind was sent by God that they were able to steer clear of a sandbank, on which they were going aground. Moreover, after being in extreme danger for two weeks—the storm had smashed both their masts and sails—and having no provisions to sustain them, God in His goodness had brought them to Saint-Jean-de-Luz, a French seaport on the Spanish border, where they refitted their boat, restored their exhausted strength, and finally reached La Rochelle. There they revived the courage of Messieurs Daveroult, Feydin, and de Fontaines, who were despondent at the thought of having lost their Superior.

You cannot imagine our consternation here; but God, to whom alone it belongs to put to death and to give life,[1] likewise consoled us by giving us back those two servants of His, whom we believed drowned. Please help us to thank Him for this and to recommend

---

[1]Cf. Jn 5:21. (NAB)

fervently to Him the voyage and mission of those five Missionaries.

To get back to your dear letter of December 17, I praise God for the reestablishment of the Jesuit Fathers at their collège in Montauban[2] and for the other good news you send me. May the Divine Goodness be pleased to give it the good results you hope will follow!

I already told you to send to the Richelieu seminary the young Irishman who is asking to join us, and have written M. de Beaumont saying that it is our intention that he accept him. Inquire carefully into the qualities of the others who want to imitate him; when you know their age, ability, morals, and physical and mental state, let me know and we shall see.

God willing, we will pay the three hundred livres that M. Agan[3] has led you to expect, whenever he chooses and to whomsoever he indicates.

Since the Bishop[4] does not approve of your taking from your seminarians room and board amounting to more than one hundred or one hundred twenty livres, you would do well to be content with that, if you can manage; but, if you cannot do so without going into debt, point out to him humbly that it does not suffice, given the high cost of provisions and your modest income.

---

[2]As a result of the serious trouble caused by the Huguenots of Montauban, who continued to harass Catholics, especially the Jesuit collège, the King had sent M. de Saint-Luc, at the head of five or six thousand soldiers, to that city. The repression was harsh. Saint-Luc moved the Calvinist collège or academy outside the city walls, had the fortifications razed, and substituted for the two-party consulate one that was composed exclusively of Catholics.

[3]Jean d'Agan, Vicar-General of Pierre de Bertier, Bishop of Montauban.

[4]Pierre de Bertier, Doctor of the Sorbonne, former Canon and Archdeacon of Toulouse, Coadjutor of Bishop Anne de Murviel and then his successor (1652). In 1636 he was consecrated Bishop *in partibus* of Utica. He had to tolerate a great deal from the elderly Bishop of Montauban, and several times was on the point of resigning. Some time before the Prelate's death, he wrote to Mazarin: "His health is so good and his humor so bad that I cannot hope for his succession nor even his favor. Therefore, Excellency, not only am I unemployed in my ministry and deprived of sufficient revenues for my position, I am, in addition, constantly persecuted and believed guilty for no reason." (Cf. Arch. Nat., KK 1217, p. 207.) The day after Saint Vincent died, de Bertier wrote: "God granted me so much love and respect for Monsieur Vincent that I truly believe that none of his sons felt his death more than I did." De Bertier was Bishop of Montauban until 1674.

I was consoled to hear that the Jesuit Fathers are giving missions around Lorm. May God be pleased to send a large number of such workers into His Church and to grant us the grace of loving this holy work and devoting ourselves to it with all our limited strength in the Spirit of Our Lord, to whom alone the conversion of souls belongs! I am, in His love, Monsieur, with all my heart, your most humble servant.

VINCENT DEPAUL,
i.s.C.M.

Addressed: Monsieur Barry, Superior of the Priests of the Mission of Notre-Dame-de-Lorm, in Lorm

3066. - *SAINT LOUISE TO SAINT VINCENT*

January 10, 1660

Most Honored Father,

On her own initiative—or rather by an inspiration of God—Madame de Glou has entreated Your Charity to name someone suitable as the executor of her will. She has likewise sent you word this evening that she thinks the mission M. de Blampignon[1] *is supposed to give at Easter in the Chartres diocese is in Marchefroy,*[2] *provided he does not forget it.*

Sister Nicole Haran,[3] *who seemed quite discouraged, informed me that*

Letter 3066 - Archives of the Motherhouse of the Daughters of Charity, original autograph letter.

[1]Claude de Blampignon was born in Troyes in 1611. He was a Doctor of Theology, Abbot of Notre-Dame de l'Aumône, member of the Tuesday Conferences and of the Company of the Blessed Sacrament, Visitor General of the Carmelites, Director of the nuns of Saint-Thomas, and confessor of the Visitation nuns of the First Monastery in Paris. He introduced the Reform into several monasteries. Saint Vincent made use of his services in the missions at Saint-Germain (1641) and Metz (1658), and chose him several times to give the ordination retreats at Saint-Lazare. Blampignon died in 1669.

[2]Today, Saint-Ouen-Marchefroy, in the district of Dreux (Eure-et-Loir).

[3]Sister Servant at the Nantes Hospital.

they could not go on any longer without some help, and she wanted to write to Your Charity, Most Honored [Father],[4] *to ask you to give them some, reminding those gentlemen of this, since she thinks they will never give any. What does Your Charity want me to tell her, in the event that you cannot take the trouble to have someone write to her?*

I think that this continued cold weather is increasing your sufferings, which honor those of Our Lord, in whose love I am, Most Honored Father, your most humble and very obedient daughter and servant.

L. DE M.

Addressed: *Monsieur Vincent*

3067. - TO EDME JOLLY, SUPERIOR, IN ROME

January 23, 1660

[Our Missionaries who are returning from the missions] . . . give two and often three conferences daily: one on cases of conscience; the second, on Holy Scripture; and the other on matters of controversy.

3067a. - TO FIRMIN GET, IN MONTPELLIER

Paris, January 23, 1660

Monsieur,

The grace of Our Lord be with you forever!

I received your dear letter of the thirteenth, which gave me very great joy by assuring me that your eyes are really healed. I thank

---

[4]Word left out by Saint Louise.

Letter 3067. - Collet, *op. cit.*, vol. II, p. 336.

Letter 3067a. - Copy made from *Recueil Nodet.* The letter was published in *Annales C.M.* (1943-44), pp. 234-35, and reprinted in *Mission et Charité,* 19-20, no. 106, pp. 134-35. This edition uses the latter text.

God for this, asking Him, in preserving your bodily sight, to increase and perfect your spiritual vision as well, so that many persons may share your insights and be ever more enlightened by them.

I praise God for the Bishop of Montpellier's [1] return. Like you, I am afraid his seminary will remain empty because of the poverty of those who aspire to the priesthood—unless God inspires that good Prelate with some means of helping some of them pay their room and board. The dioceses certainly have great need of good priests who are capable and well formed, and the greatest service that can be rendered to God is to do one's part in providing them with some, as you are doing by His grace.

Thank you, Monsieur, for coming to the rescue of M. Durand during the Christmas season. He is greatly overburdened just now by the presence of the Bishop of Agde,[2] and I am afraid he will be crushed under the load, unless you help him again. See, Monsieur, if you can send him M. Parisy once more to relieve him during that good Prelate's short stay in his diocese. If, however, this cannot be done without your inconveniencing yourself too much, keep him with you. God will provide for everything, if He so pleases. I ask Him to draw His glory from your work, and I ask for you the greatest sanctification of your dear soul, which I embrace with all the affection of mine. I am, in the love of Our Lord, Monsieur, your most humble servant.

VINCENT DEPAUL,
i.s.C.M.

Addressed: Monsieur Get, Superior of the Priests of the Mission in Marseilles, temporarily at the Montpellier Seminary

---

[1]François de Bosquet, Bishop of Montpellier (1657-76). He was returning at the time from Toulouse, where he had been present at the provincial Estates of Languedoc.

[2]Louis Fouquet.

3067b. - TO GABRIEL DELESPINEY, SUPERIOR, IN MARSEILLES

Paris, January 23, 1660

Monsieur,

The grace of Our Lord be with you forever!

I received with your letter of January 13 the packet from Tunis, which I have not yet been able to look at.

I approve payment of his bill of exchange for one hundred piastres on what the men in Algiers owe him. Please put everything in writing so as to have a clear account for everyone. It would have been a good idea to give me the names of the ransomed captives you mentioned and whom you have welcomed. For this time, please accept this added burden; we will see if it is advisable in the future for you to take into your house those who are sent to you.

You do not tell me for whom those two lions,[1] which the Consul in Algiers [2] is sending to France, are intended. Maybe you did not

---

Letter 3067b. - Copy made from *Recueil Nodet.* The letter was published in *Annales C.M.* (1943-44), pp. 235-36, and reprinted in *Mission et Charité,* 19-20, no. 107, pp. 135-36. This edition uses the latter text.

[1]*Lions?* "Did the copyist read correctly?" asked the editor of *Mission et Charité.* We might speculate that the Consul to Algiers actually shipped two lions, and Saint Vincent is wondering if they might be an appropriate gift to the King for a royal zoo--or is he speaking of statues of the animals?

[2]Jean Barreau was born in Saint-Jean-en-Grève parish, Paris, on September 26, 1612. While still a young man, he left the position of Parlementary Lawyer to enter the Cistercian Order. He later asked Saint Vincent to receive him into his Community and began his novitiate on May 14, 1645. In 1646 Saint Vincent sent him, while still a seminarian, to Algiers as French Consul, in keeping with the wish of the Holy See not to have a priest in the office of Consul. There his dedication to the captives was boundless. The goodness of his heart moved him more than once to commit himself for sums he did not possess or which did not belong to him; for this he was ill-treated by local authorities and reproved by Saint Vincent. When his companion, Jacques Lesage, became gravely ill, Barreau took his vows before him, although he had not yet been released from the simple vow of religion he had taken as a Cistercian. This dispensation was not requested until 1652. On November 1, 1661, he was finally able to take his vows validly in the Congregation of the Mission. He was in Paris at the time, summoned by René Alméras, second Superior General, and had only Minor Orders. Barreau was ordained a priest in 1662 or 1663 and spent the remainder of his life at Saint-Lazare as Procurator. In 1672 he was associated with the Procurator General, Nicolas Talec. On May 24, 1675, during a serious illness, he made his will, to which he added a codicil on April 7, 1679. (Cf. Arch. Nat. M 213, no. 8.)

know this when you wrote to me, since you had not yet received his letters. If he is sending them to us, with no further destination, I agree that you may make a present of them to the King, when he is in Marseilles. I am writing to this effect to M. de Saint-Jean,[3] chaplain to the Queen. You may consult him to see how to present them to His Majesty in a manner suitable for persons of our social status.

I think it would have been better to put off to another time the three seminarians you have with you rather than to welcome them just now when you are so busy with the missions for Mme de Vins and do not have enough men for these two works. Nevertheless, since Providence has so ordained, we will see if we can send you some suitable men. As for M. Boussordec, he is preparing to leave as soon as possible. With God's help, he will bring you the papers and meditations the Bishop of Marseilles[4] is requesting.

I am, in the love of Our Lord, Monsieur, your most humble servant.

VINCENT DEPAUL,
i.s.C.M.

3068. - TO A SUPERIOR [1]

Works that attract notice, like that of retreats for ordinands, frequently incite rivalry. Do not be surprised if, among the many who approve it, you are opposed by some. Good works, as well as bad, are subject to criticism, and people who are opposed to us may still have good intentions. So, please let us maintain the esteem and

---

[3]Nicolas de Saint-Jean, chaplain of the Queen, Anne of Austria, was a very close friend of Saint Vincent.

[4]Étienne du Puget (1644-68).

Letter 3068. - Abelly, *op. cit.*, second ed., second part, p. 124.

[1]Probably Edme Jolly, Superior in Rome.

respect we owe them; let us consider, as they do, that we are unworthy of this work and that others would do it better than we. Let us make good use of that opinion and give ourselves to God more than ever to strive to render Him this little service faithfully.

3069. - *SAINT LOUISE TO SAINT VINCENT*

[January 1660] [1]

Most Honored Father,

From time to time, I sense strongly the pain of the state to which your charity has reduced you and the suffering of being deprived of the honor of speaking to you. I fear that my cowardice, my self-love, and the other dangers to my salvation may profit from this, since I am ever the same.

Reflecting on the present state of the Company, I worry also about being no longer able to speak to you about this, fearing that it might be difficult for you to read my letters. Nevertheless, I feel it necessary, Most Honored Father, to tell you my thoughts on it, namely, that I fear it might decline in several ways.

First, I have noticed that in several parishes the Ladies are beginning to mistrust them,[2] *although I think it is safe to say that I do not know a single one who gives any real cause for that, unless it is those who, in their zeal for the relief of the poor, accept alms from the Ladies to distribute them, without submitting to the requirement of mentioning this to the officers, who are offended by this.*

Apparently, our Sisters are not as respected or loved as they previously were, since they are treated more harshly, and there are places where people are much more wary of them because of this mistrust. In some places orders have been issued at an open meeting not to give them anything—even to the butcher who supplies the meat for the poor. Not that they had much of anything, but, little as it was, it helped them.

That has caused me to reflect, Most Honored Father, on the need for the Rules to oblige the Sisters always to lead a poor, simple, humble life.

Letter 3069. - Archives of the Motherhouse of the Daughters of Charity, original autograph letter.

[1]Date added on the back by Brother Ducournau.

[2]The Sisters.

My fear is that, if they were to settle into a lifestyle which required greater expenses and had customs tending toward ostentation and partial enclosure, this would oblige them to seek means of maintaining it. It would also cause them to turn in on themselves, become inactive, and live separated from those who go out and are poorly clothed because certain Sisters say to one another that "this person who wears a poor headdress, this Sister in name only, is not respected but causes people to despise us."

I know that, not only the Sisters, but others who are obliged to honor God's plan regarding the spiritual and corporal service of the sick poor, have a strong tendency toward this lifestyle—so dangerous to the continuation of God's work, which Your Charity, Most Honored Father, has sustained so firmly in the face of every sort of opposition.

I am really distressed to cause you this displeasure. If Your Charity sees that God may want something other than what has been done until now, in the name of Our Lord, make it known and give orders for it. I shall always be the same, putting up no argument once I have taken the liberty of presenting, as I now do, the reasons that come to my mind. Because of my infidelity, I dare not say that God is giving me these thoughts. If I am not expressing myself clearly, and Your Charity would like me to explain myself to M. Alméras or some other person whom you deem suitable, perhaps that would make me better understood.

Permit me, Most Honored Father, to ask you for news of your ailments, which I think you could relieve if you allowed yourself to be treated as Your Charity would order someone else to be treated.

I think I already mentioned the contents of this letter to you, apart from a few details. I most humbly ask you to forgive me for repeating myself, if such is the case, and I hope for this from your goodness, since I am, Most Honored Father, your most humble, most obedient, and very grateful daughter and servant.

L. DE MARILLAC

Addressed: *Monsieur Vincent*

3070. - TO GABRIEL DELESPINEY, IN MARSEILLES

Paris, January 30, 1660

Monsieur,

The grace of Our Lord be with you forever!

I received your letter of the twentieth and the account of expenditures for the administration of your [family], which are very high.

You did well to discontinue sleeping at the hospital, since the last sacraments can be administered during the day to patients who seem to be in danger.[1] Like the Administrators, I also strongly fear that it will be difficult to maintain the hospital—given the fact that the subsidy for this year is already half used—unless Providence comes through with some extraordinary aid for them. Now, I see no one from whom we can expect this, if the Cardinal,[2] who is there right now, refuses to do so. I think those gentlemen will be doing a good deed by suggesting this to him, if they have the opportunity to speak to him, or to have other persons represent to him the great need to help the sick convicts and the inability to do so because the King's alms have been cut back these past few years.

The stipends for the chaplains on the galleys are on the books

---

Letter 3070. - Copy made from *Recueil Nodet.* The letter was published in *Annales C.M.* (1943-44), pp. 236-37, and reprinted in *Mission et Charité,* 19-20, no. 108, pp. 136-37. This edition uses the latter text, replacing the much shorter one from the Marseilles manuscript used by Coste.

[1]This sentence and the passage "I thank M. Cornier . . . leaves His servants in peace" were used for Coste's version.

[2]Jules Cardinal Mazarin (Giulio Mazarini) was born in Pescina in the Abruzzi (Italy) in 1602, studied in Spain as a youth, and served in the papal army and the papal diplomatic corps. He met Richelieu in 1630 and represented the Pope in negotiating the peace of Cherasco with France in 1631. Mazarin had hardly begun preparing for the priesthood--he received tonsure in 1632, but never became a priest--when he was assigned to other important diplomatic posts: Vice-Legate of Avignon (1634), then Nuncio in France (1635-36), in which positions he demonstrated the ability and flexibility of the most subtle statesman. He became a French citizen in 1639, and Richelieu obtained a Cardinal's hat for him in 1641. Before Richelieu's death (1642), he recommended Mazarin to Louis XIII. He became the principal minister of Queen Anne of Austria during the regency of Louis XIV (1643-61) and, until his own death in 1661, was the absolute master of France.

for this year. Find out from M. Get,[3] or from someone else, to whom you should go and what you have to do to get the payment. I am well aware that, like the endowment funds of the hospital, they are allocated from the *gabelles*[4] of Provence, and that M. Amat is the *Receveur Général*[5] of them. He has his agent there; maybe he will have instructions to pay you! In my opinion, however, this will not happen very soon—you will see. If you do get something, we will see how it will be distributed among the chaplains.

I thank M. Cornier for the good news he gave me about being freed from his troubles. We could expect nothing else from the goodness of God and his own patience. Our Lord chooses to try the best souls in this way for a time so as to test them; then, all of a sudden, He calms the storm and leaves His servants in peace. I hope he will have great, continual peace and God's blessings on his work.

You received three livres for Jacques Fournier, known as La Rivière, on the *Manse;* thirty sous for Guillaume Laisné, known as La Montagne, on the *Capitaine;* and seven livres ten sous for Jacques Simon, who is also a captive.

We have no news here, where I am always, in the love of Our Lord, Monsieur, your most humble servant.

---

[3]Firmin Get.

[4]The salt tax.

[5]Official in charge of provincial taxes.

3071. - TO FIRMIN GET, IN MONTPELLIER

Paris, January 30, 1660

Monsieur,

The grace of O[ur] L[ord] be with you forever!

I am writing these few lines to find out from you if what I have been told is true, namely, that the Bishop of Montpellier[1] seems to have no intention of continuing his seminary. Please inform me, Monsieur, of what you know about this, and ask God's mercy for the greatest sinner on earth, who is, nevertheless, in the love of O[ur] L[ord], Monsieur, your most humble servant.

VINCENT DEPAUL,
i.s.C.M.

With all the tenderness of my heart I send greetings to you and M. Parisy, prostrate in spirit at your feet.

Addressed: Monsieur Get, Superior of the Mission of Marseilles, temporarily at the Montpellier Seminary, in Montpellier

3072. - TO GUILLAUME DESDAMES, SUPERIOR, IN WARSAW

Paris, January 30, 1660

Monsieur,

The grace of O[ur] L[ord] be with you forever!

I received your letter of December 19, in which I see that you are being tried by various ailments, which, however, do not last

---

Letter 3071. - Property of the Society of Saint Vincent de Paul, Marseilles, original signed letter. The postscript is in the Saint's handwriting.

[1]François de Bosquet.

Letter 3072. - Archives of the Mission, Krakow, original signed letter.

long. I am sorry about that and would be even more so if I did not know that God does all things for the best and that your suffering is worthwhile because you are suffering lovingly in Jesus Christ. Nevertheless, please do all you can to keep well because, if you have something to suffer when you are in good health, it will be from work; then your suffering will be useful to many and will be united to that of O[ur] L[ord], who consumed Himself for everyone.[1] We here are asking God to preserve and strengthen you more and more so that He may be able to manifest for a long time, through you, the effects of His charity and works.

In addition, since He loved His own even to the end[2] and did not abandon them, I ask you also to be patient in your leadership position until God chooses to relieve you of it. I am edified by your sincere request in this regard and by the insight God gives you of your own insufficiency; it is to be desired that all Superiors have the same sentiments. Still, we must not guide others by ourselves but by O[ur] L[ord], who has sufficient ability for both you and Himself.

With this in view, I ask Him to inspire you with His Spirit of humility, meekness, forbearance, patience, vigilance, prudence, and charity. You will find all these virtues in Him and, if you allow Him to act, He will exercise them in and through you. Live in this confidence, Monsieur, and be at peace; nevertheless, I will try to be attentive to your desire and send someone suitable to lighten your burden, if we cannot relieve you of your office. We sent to the Bons-Enfants Seminary three of our young priests who have done well in their philosophy and theology studies, in order that they may be even better prepared, and we plan to send them to you after Easter, God willing.

We have no news here; everyone is quite well, with the exception of our usual patients, of whom I am one; my legs have failed

---

[1]Cf. Heb 2:18. (NAB)
[2]Cf. Jn 13:1. (NAB)

me and I can no longer go downstairs nor say Holy Mass. Pray that O[ur] L[ord] may be pleased to have mercy on me and to allow me to be, in time and eternity, in His love, Monsieur, your most humble servant.

VINCENT DEPAUL,
i.s.C.M.

Addressed: Monsieur Desdames, Superior of the Priests of the Mission, in Warsaw

3073. - TO SISTER MARIE-CÉCILE THOMASSIN, [1] VISITATION NUN

Saint-Lazare, February 4, 1660

Dear Sister,

The grace of O[ur] L[ord] be with you forever!

I received your letter, and I experience in my own heart the sufferings with which God has chosen to try you. I am greatly affected by them and feel them keenly, even as I write to you. I pray that Our Lord, in His infinite goodness, will be pleased either to restore you to perfect health or to give you such a powerful grace that you may be able to make perfect use of the states in which you find yourself.

To assist you in this, I am asking Father Lallemant[2] to continue

---

Letter 3073. - This original signed letter was made known to Coste by the Daughters of Charity, 13 rue Saint-Sauveur, Saint-Malo. Its present location is unknown.

[1]Sister Marie-Cécile Thomassin was professed in the First Monastery of the Visitation on November 21, 1639, and went to live in the Le Mans Monastery (1647-53). She then returned to Paris, where she died on April 1, 1694, at seventy-one years of age.

[2]Charles Lallemant, born in Paris on November 17, 1587, entered the Society of Jesus on July 29, 1607. After teaching grammar and physics, he was sent to Canada as Superior of the mission. On his return to France, he first taught philosophy and was then put in charge of the Collège de Rouen, which he left to take over the Collège de Clermont in Paris. His writings are numerous. Lallemant died in Paris on November 18, 1674.

to do you the charity he has done you up to the present. You could not choose a person in whom religious virtues are more evident and abundant. Since, dear Sister, you are not always able to go to the parlor to receive his help, I give permission for him to enter as often as our dear Mother judges he is needed. I send her my warmest greetings once again.

I ask Our Lord to be Himself your strength and your consolation and to make known to you how much I am, dear Sister, in His love, your most humble servant.

VINCENT DEPAUL,
i.s.C.M.

Addressed: Sister Marie-Cécile Thomassin, of the Visitation Sainte-Marie in the city

3074. - TO JEAN DEHORGNY, IN CAHORS

February 4, 1660

Since M. Cuissot cannot always attend to the direction of the Daughters of Charity in Cahors because of the frequent journeys he is obliged to make and the other business matters involved in the office of Superior, he asked M. Fournier some time ago to render them, when he was unable, whatever modest services he could. However, M. Fournier pointed out to me that he was very busy with the men in the seminary and considered himself unsuitable for assisting those Sisters. I wrote him a letter to encourage him in this new little duty so he could relieve M. Cuissot. I say *relieve* and not *replace,* for I think that, as Superior of the Missionaries, he should still regard those Sisters in the same way as he does the seminarians and that those who hear their confessions, instruct,

---

Letter 3074. - Reg. 2, p. 101.

and direct them should do as he recommends and not independently of him.

From what I hear, however, as soon as M. Cuissot heard that I had written to M. Fournier about this, he wanted nothing more to do with it because he thought I was handing over their entire direction to the other man. That is not the case; I merely intended to join my request to the one M. Cuissot had made to him, asking him to give those Sisters the little assistance that he himself could not give them. Please explain my intention to both of them, Monsieur, and if, as M. Fournier informs me, he is too busy with other things, please discuss with M. Cuissot whether M. Bonichon[1] would be suitable to listen to those poor Sisters and to help them when M. Cuissot is unable to do so.

3075. - TO JEAN MARTIN,[1] SUPERIOR, IN TURIN

Paris, February 5, 1660

Monsieur,

The grace of O[ur] L[ord] be with you forever!

I received your letter of [January[2]] 14 and learned with sorrow that you have had a third attack of quartan fever. God wishes to reserve to Himself alone the glory of your good health, which I hope He will give you this spring; I ask Him to do so with all my heart. Do whatever you can on your part for this purpose.

A perfect abandonment to Providence such as yours is far more

---

[1]Nicolas Bonichon, born in Ferrières-Gâtinais (Loiret) on July 30, 1619, entered Saint-Lazare on September 24, 1641, took his vows on June 9, 1644, and was ordained a priest on September 21, 1647.

Letter 3075. - Archives of the Mission, Turin, original signed letter.

[1]Jean Martin the elder.

[2]The secretary distractedly wrote *February*. This letter, like so many written to Saint Vincent, is no longer extant.

valuable than any other establishment. I ask Our Lord to strengthen you in it so that you may honor by your poverty the state in which He found Himself on earth, when He said that the birds had nests and the foxes had holes, but He had no place in which to withdraw.[3]

I thank His Divine Goodness that your workers are toiling successfully and ardently; I implore God to continue to bless them and to give you the fullness of His Spirit in order to direct everything for His greater glory.

Please assure the good Prior of Luserna[4] of my entire obedience and perfect gratitude, and recommend me to his prayers, as I do to yours and to those of your little community, to whom I send most cordial greetings.

We have no news here, where I am, in life and in death, in O[ur] L[ord], Monsieur, your most humble servant.

VINCENT DEPAUL,
i.s.C.M.

Addressed: Monsieur Martin

3076. - TO FIRMIN GET, SUPERIOR, IN MONTPELLIER

Paris, February 6, 1660

Monsieur,

The grace of O[ur] L[ord] be with you forever!

The Archbishop of Narbonne[1] has written us a letter stating that, since the Bishop of Montpellier[2] does not wish to support his

---

[3]Cf. Mt 8:20; Lk 9:58. (NAB)

[4]Luserna San Giovanni Abbey, near Turin.

Letter 3076. - Property of the Society of Saint Vincent de Paul, Marseilles, original signed letter. The postscript is in the Saint's handwriting.

[1]François Fouquet.

[2]François de Bosquet.

seminary any longer, he has decided to send his clerics to nearby seminaries. Accordingly, he would like to have you in Narbonne for various plans he has in mind. I took the honor of replying to him that, since the Marseilles house is one of the most important in the Company, after the ones in Rome and Paris, it also requires a very capable Superior, especially right now, on account of the state of affairs and our experience that all is not going well—and cannot go on well—unless you are there. In addition, the presence of the King and the Cardinal[3] will perhaps lead to the return of the galleys to Marseilles; if so, we are bound to receive the chaplains and to open a seminary. For that and for the affairs of Barbary, as well as for other works of old or recent foundation—all of which are very important—an experienced, intelligent, vigilant man is needed, capable of handling all kinds of matters, as, by God's grace, you are.

Therefore, Monsieur, please do not take on any commitments, but consider the Marseilles house as your house and return to it as soon as possible. It may be that the length of time you resided in that place, the difficulties you encountered, and the eye trouble you suffered there have given you some dislike for it; but such a dislike should not prevail over the grace God has imparted to you for the good of that family, in which you will likely have even better opportunities than ever for promoting the glory of God. So, your presence is necessary there, even if only to train someone to manage its affairs, direct the house, and be able to keep things going, in the event that Providence should call you elsewhere.

If, however, the Bishop of Montpellier has not yet declared his intention to you, I think, Monsieur, that, since his seminary is dragging on as it is doing, you will do well to dispose him gently

---

[3]Jules Cardinal Mazarin.

and adroitly to consent to your return to Marseilles—but do not tell him that I have written to you about this.

Your most humble servant.

VINCENT DEPAUL,
i.s.C.M.

I ask you, Monsieur, to honor the silence of O[ur] L[ord] on this occasion, with regard to the present letter and to anyone whomsoever.

Addressed: Monsieur Get, Superior of the Priests of the Mission of Marseilles, temporarily at the Montpellier Seminary, in Montpellier

3076a. - TO DOMINIQUE LHUILLIER, IN CRÉCY

Saint-Lazare, February 6, 1660

Monsieur,

The grace of Our Lord be with you forever!

Brother Claude[1] arrived last evening. He is going to take care of what he has to do, and we will send him back to you in two days. Meanwhile, M. [Asseline] [2] is going off to keep you company and to profit by the good example and advice you will give him. Please welcome him.

Letter 3076a. - Copy made from *Recueil Nodet.* The letter was published in *Annales C.M.* (1943-44), pp. 237-38, and reprinted in *Mission et Charité,* 19-20, no. 109, p. 138. This edition uses the latter text.

[1]Claude Le Gentil, born in Berchères, Châlons diocese (Champagne) in 1620, entered the Congregation of the Mission in Paris as a coadjutor Brother on January 22, 1637, and took his vows on March 24, 1643. (Cf. *Notices,* vol. I, p. 494.) He had been stationed in Crécy since 1658.

[2]Jacques Asseline, born in Dieppe (Seine-Maritime) on May 10, 1633, entered the Congregation of the Mission in Richelieu on November 19, 1653, took his vows there on November 21, 1655, and was ordained a priest in 1659. He was assigned to Crécy in 1660.

I do not recommend him to you because I know that your charity needs no recommendation. I simply ask Our Lord to be the bond of your hearts. He will tell you our little items of news.

[This is] the first time I have written you since the death of our good M. Perraud, which occurred on December 26. Please offer the customary prayers for him and do not forget before God, Monsieur, your most humble servant.

VINCENT DEPAUL,
i.s.C.M.

Addressed: Monsieur Lhuillier, Priest of the Mission, in Crécy

3076b. - TO GABRIEL DELESPINEY, SUPERIOR, IN MARSEILLES

Paris, February 6, 1660

Monsieur,

The grace of Our Lord be with you forever!

I received the packet from Algiers but have not read what was in it. In your letter of January 27, you suggest going to Montpellier for the discussion between you and M. Get, but, since that is not urgent, and in the present circumstances your most important business is to stay in the house, please do not budge from it. I fear some disturbance, and I ask Our Lord that it may not occur.

M. Boussordec has not left as I told you, because of the harsh winter. Now, while waiting for the weather to improve a little, we have sent him to the Bons-Enfants so he can see the seminary, find out what is observed there, and learn something from it, if need be. He will be there for another week. After that we hope to have him leave. Perhaps he will arrive in Marseilles early enough to open the

---

Letter 3076b. - Copy made from *Recueil Nodet.* The letter was published in *Annales C.M.* (1943-44), p. 238, and reprinted in *Mission et Charité,* 19-20, no. 110, pp. 138-39. This edition uses the latter text.

mission in Vins [1] in the middle of Lent or thereabout.

Since the lions [2] have been sent to us to be given away, do it in the way I prescribed to you and M. de Saint-Jean.[3] I have nothing to add to what I told you. We received one écu for Pierre Lainé, known as Rosier, on the *Capitaine.* I am sending it to M. Huguier. M. de Saint-Jean tells me that he will see you; explain to him sincerely your urgent needs.

I am, in O[ur] L[ord], Monsieur, your most humble servant.

VINCENT DEPAUL,
i.s.C.M.

Addressed: Monsieur Delespiney, Superior of the Priests of the Mission, in Marseilles

3077. - TO JACQUES DE LA FOSSE,[1] IN TROYES

February 7, 1660

I thank God for the sentiments He has given you in regard to what I wrote to you concerning nuns. I was greatly consoled by

---

[1]Locality in the Fréjus diocese, where a mission had been funded by the Marquise de Vins.

[2]Cf. no. 3067b, n. 1.

[3]Chaplain to Queen Anne of Austria. There is no letter extant in which Saint Vincent stipulates what is to be done with the lions.

Letter 3077. - Reg. 2, p. 80.

[1]Jacques de la Fosse, born in Paris on November 25, 1621, entered the Congregation of the Mission on October 8, 1640, took his vows on April 7, 1643, and was ordained a priest in September 1648. Immediately after his ordination, Saint Vincent entrusted to him the humanities at Saint-Charles Seminary. He "often reenacted there Christian tragedies," wrote Collet (*op. cit.*, vol. I, p. 326), "whose spirit and sublimity drew the applause of connoisseurs in Paris." In 1656 he went to Marseilles, where he served in turn as missionary and seminary professor. Two years later he was sent to Troyes. He died in Sedan on April 30, 1674. De la Fosse was as generous as he was capricious, easily becoming enthusiastic and just as easily becoming discouraged. Several times he almost left the Company; only Saint Vincent's paternal encouragement kept him from doing so. His writings, all in Latin, made a name for him among the Latinists of the seventeenth century. Collet says he was "an orator, philosopher, and theologian all in one, and such a great poet that Santeuil considered him his rival and sometimes his master" (*ibid.*, vol.

them, seeing that you realized the importance the Company has attached to distancing itself from their service so as not to place any obstacle in the way of what we owe the poor people. Since you want some clarification on the reasons why we look after the Daughters of Charity—by asking me why the Company, which has a maxim not to attend to nuns, does so in regard to these Sisters—I will tell you, Monsieur:

(1) That we have nothing against assisting nuns; on the contrary, we praise those who serve them, as spouses of Our Lord who have renounced the world and its vanities in order to unite themselves to their Sovereign Good. However, not everything that is permissible to others is advisable for us.

(2) That the Daughters of Charity are not nuns, but Sisters who come and go like seculars; they are parishioners under the guidance of the Pastors in the places where they are established. If we have the direction of the house in which they are formed, it is because the guidance of God has made use of us to bring their Little Company to birth, and you know that the same things God uses to give being to things He also uses to preserve them.

(3) Our little Company has given itself to God from the beginning to serve the poor corporally and spiritually; consequently, at the same time it has worked for the salvation of the poor through missions, it has also established a means of solacing the sick through the Confraternities of Charity. The Holy See has approved this by the Bulls of our foundation. Now, as the virtue of mercy is operative in various ways, it has led the Company to use various means to assist the poor; consider, for instance, the service it renders convicts on the galleys and the captives in Barbary. See

---

I, p. 277). Dom Calmet added: "In general, there is great passion and many noble, generous thoughts in de la Fosse's poetry, but his penchant for mythology, even in his sacred verses, sometimes renders them obscure because of his unusual expressions and frequent allusions to fable." (Cf. Augustin Calmet, *Bibliothèque lorraine* [Nancy: A. Leseure, 1751], p. 376.) His works are found in the Bibliothèque Nationale (Ms. L. 10.331, 11.365), in the Bibliothèque de l'Arsenal (Ms. 1137, 1138), and in the Bibliothèque Mazarine (Ms. 3910-19, 4312, imp. 10.877). See also [Édouard Rosset, C.M.] *Notices bibliographiques sur les écrivains de la Congrégation de la Mission* (Angoulême: J.-B. Baillarger, 1878).

also what it has done for Lorraine in its great devastation, and later for the ruined border towns of Champagne and Picardy, where we still have a Brother[2] continuously engaged in the distribution of alms. You yourself, Monsieur, are a witness to the relief it has given the people in the environs of Paris, overwhelmed by famine and sickness in consequence of the armies that are camped there. You had your share in that great work and thought it would be the death of you,[3] as it was of many others who have given their lives to preserve that of the suffering members of Jesus Christ. He is now their reward for this, as He will one day be yours. The Ladies of Charity of Paris are also so many witnesses to the grace of our vocation through our collaboration with them in the many good works they do both inside and outside the city.

The Daughters of Charity have become, in the order of Providence, a means God has given us to do by their hands what we cannot do by our own in the corporal assistance of the sick poor, and to say by their lips a few words of instruction and encouragement for their salvation. Since this is the case, we are also bound to help them in their own advancement in virtue so that they can carry out well their charitable works.

So then, there is this difference between them and nuns: the latter have for their end only their own perfection, whereas these Sisters are devoted, like us, to the salvation and comfort of their neighbor. If I say *with us,* I will be saying nothing contrary to the Gospel but something very much in conformity with the practice of the primitive Church, for Our Lord took care of some women who followed Him,[4] and we see in the *Canon of the Apostles* that they adminis-

---

[2]Jean Parre.

[3]In the summer of 1652, Jacques de la Fosse had gone to Étampes to relieve the confreres who had fallen ill while ministering to the poor, suffering from the ills and deprivations caused by the Fronde. He himself was laid low with a fever (cf. vol. V, nos. 1542 and 1544).

[4]Cf. Mk 15:41. (NAB)

tered provisions to the faithful[5] and were involved in apostolic duties.[6]

If people say it is dangerous for us to speak with these Sisters, I reply that we have provided for that as far as possible by establishing a Rule in the Company never to visit them in their houses in the parishes. Furthermore, they themselves have a Rule to make their room their cloister and never to allow men, particularly Missionaries, to enter it. Consequently, if I myself were to ask to enter their rooms, they should shut the door in my face; this is strictly observed everywhere, by the grace of God.

If they come here to their house once a month to give an account of their spiritual state and to make their confession to one of our priests, you know that two or three men, whose age and virtue leave nothing to fear, are appointed to hear them. If we send others to the two hospitals[7] close by, it is not simply for those Sisters who work there, but also for the residents, whom God has entrusted to the care of the Company for their bodily and spiritual assistance.

I hope, Monsieur, that what I have just replied to your difficulty will not displease you, etc. . . .

3078. - TO GUILLAUME DESDAMES, SUPERIOR, IN WARSAW

Paris, February 13, 1660

Monsieur,

The grace of O[ur] L[ord] be with you forever!

No sooner have I received and read your dear letter of January 10 than I am answering it. I want to tell you, on the one hand, that

---

[5]Cf. Acts 39:42. (NAB)
[6]Cf. Acts 16: 13-15; 17:4, 12, 34. (NAB)
[7]The Nom-de-Jésus and the Foundlings.

Letter 3078. - Archives of the Mission, Krakow, original signed letter.

it brought me great joy because of the good health God continues to give you and the care His Divine Majesty is taking of your little family, for which I thank Him with all my heart. On the other hand, however, I am worried that you are not receiving my letters. Still, we must accept all the dispositions of Providence, which governs all things wisely.

The latest invasion of the Muscovites is a fresh source of grief, since they have recaptured Grodno[1] and spread terror among the people of Warsaw, although they have not approached it. On the contrary, the hope of peace with Sweden, which is being negotiated successfully, consoles us greatly.[2] May God be pleased to bless this treaty to the satisfaction of Poland so that she may have greater means of repulsing that other enemy who is giving her trouble! We will await assurance of this peace before sending the helpers we are preparing for you, and we will arrange the time and manner of their journey, depending on the news you send us.

Thank God that the Daughters of Charity are well and are doing some good. As for Sister Françoise,[3] she must be patient with having to stay with the Queen, since Her Majesty uses her only in the service of the poor, who are her masters, and it is difficult to have her return from there just now. Encourage her as much as you can.

Enclosed is a letter Mademoiselle Le Gras wrote to her last week.[4] Since that time, she has fallen so ill that we dare not hope she will recover, which grieves us profoundly. And what makes our sorrow more overwhelming is the fact that M. Portail is also

---

[1]Headquarters of the Polish government. Between 1654 and 1667 Russia, desiring to gain a port on the Baltic, engaged Poland in a war for the Ukraine. By the Treaty of Andrussova (January 20, 1667) Poland ceded to Russia the Eastern Ukraine, with Kiev and the Smolensk region.

[2]The Treaty of Oliva was signed with Sweden on May 3, 1660.

[3]Françoise Douelle was the youngest of the three Sisters sent to Poland in September 1652 (the others were Marguerite Moreau the Sister Servant and Madeleine Drugeon). After some difficulties, she adapted herself so well that she became known by her Polish name *Duelska* (cf. *Documents,* Doc. 556, n. 1).

[4]This letter is not extant. Perhaps it is the one to which Sister Françoise referred in her letter to Saint Louise dated February 28, 1660 (cf. *Documents,* Doc. 786, p. 903).

seriously ill. Both received Holy Viaticum on the same day.[5] I recommend them to your prayers and to those of good M. Duperroy, whom I embrace, along with you, with all the tenderness of my soul.

I am glad he is working at getting the church in Vitkiski repaired, but I am sorry that this keeps you separated and inconveniences you. May God, in His infinite goodness, be pleased to reunite and comfort you!

You did well to make your excuses to the Bishop for not using for anything else the money earmarked for these repairs. You could not do otherwise, given the need of the church. I forgot to tell M. Duperroy this in my last letter, which is a reply to the one in which he mentions that matter to me.

Take good care of yourself and of him as well.

I am, in the love of O[ur] L[ord], Monsieur, your most humble servant.

VINCENT DEPAUL,
i.s.C.M.

At the bottom of the first page: Monsieur Desdames

3079. - TO PROPAGANDA FIDE

[February 1660] [1]

Most Eminent and Most Reverend Lords,

Since Charles Nacquart, Priest of the Congregation of the Mission, whom the Sacred Congregation appointed Prefect of the

---

[5]Antoine Portail died on February 14, the day after this letter was written; Saint Louise died a month later on March 15.

Letter 3079. - Archives of Propaganda Fide, *Africa* 9-10, *Madagascar-Morocco*, no. 252, fols. 8 and 9, original unsigned letter, written in Italian.

[1]At the end of the summary given on the back of the petition are the words: *Granted on February 23, 1660.*

Mission of the Island of Saint-Laurent, commonly known as Madagascar, has passed to a better life[2] in the exercise of his ministry, the most devoted petitioner Vincent de Paul, Superior General of the same Congregation, humbly requests that Your Eminences be good enough to appoint in place of the deceased, as Prefect of the said Mission, Toussaint Bourdaise, Priest of the same Congregation of the Mission, who has been Apostolic Missionary for several years and, by order of Your Eminences, has devoted himself to the spiritual care of the people of Madagascar, where the Lord has blessed his work. And he will receive this as a special favor from Your Eminences.

Whom God, etc.

And since, by some misfortune, the above-named Toussaint Bourdaise himself may be dead,[3] may it please Your Eminences to grant the Nuncio of France the authority to appoint as Prefect of the Mission whomever Vincent de Paul will propose to him, if he seems to him to be a suitable candidate.

Addressed: The Sacred Congregation of Propaganda Fide, for Vincent de Paul, Superior General of the Congregation of the Mission

3080. - *PIERRE ANGER TO SAINT VINCENT*

Alet, February 15, 1660

Monsieur and Most Honored Father,

I entreat you most humbly to allow me to take this opportunity to renew to you the offers of my obedience and to ask you to continue to remember

---

[2]He had died on May 29, 1650.

[3]Bourdaise had died on June 25, 1657.

Letter 3080. - Archives of the Mission, Turin, original autograph letter.

me at the holy altar and in your holy prayers. I do so on this occasion when the Bishop,[1] *who greets you most cordially and respectfully, is answering M. Gavelin's letter, which you so graciously sent him.*

I think, Monsieur, that Your Charity will be pleased to know that Our Lord is blessing this little seminary, composed of eighteen or twenty seminarians, who appear to be well-intentioned and eager to attain the perfection of the Christian and priestly life and the knowledge of the duties of their profession. The men and women regents are making further progress in the care and Christian formation of the young. This is the result of the improvements you have introduced in this diocese by your prayers and by the works of the priests of your Company, who cooperated so effectively with the efforts of the Bishop in the early years of his administration.

I greet you and am, with the deepest respect, Monsieur and my Most Honored Father, your most humble, grateful, and obedient servant and son.

PIERRE ANGER,
priest

Addressed: *Monsieur Vincent, Priest, Superior General of the Mission, in Paris*

---

[1]Nicolas Pavillon was born on November 17, 1597. As a very young priest he placed himself under the direction of Saint Vincent, who had him teach catechism and work in the missions and the Charities, where his presence was deemed useful. More than once he entrusted him with the conferences and retreats for priests. Appointed to the diocese of Alet in 1637, Pavillon accepted it only upon the Saint's urging. This new office did not deter him from his apostolic works: he gave a mission in Rueil at Richelieu's invitation, then in Saint-Germain-en-Laye at the King's request. He was consecrated at Saint-Lazare on August 22, 1639, and went to his diocese accompanied by Étienne Blatiron. A zealous, intelligent Bishop, dedicated to reform, he justified the expectations placed on him. His episcopate would have been more fruitful had he been more on his guard against Jansenistic ideas. Saint Vincent begged him in vain to sign the formulary against Jansenism. Pavillon died on December 8, 1677. There are several biographies of him, notably that of Étienne Dejean, *Un prélat indépendant au XVII*e *siècle, Nicolas Pavillon, évèque d'Alet (1637-77)* (Paris: Plon-Nourrit, 1909).

3081. - ***EDME JOLLY, SUPERIOR IN ROME, TO SAINT VINCENT***

February 16, 1660

You ask me, Monsieur, to inform you how the last ordination retreat went off and if the ordinands seemed to have profited from its spiritual exercises. For what concerns the retreat and all the details of the rule observed in France, we tried, and are still trying, to have them observed in the same way as is done in Paris, regulating ourselves, day by day and hour by hour, on the reports we received from Saint-Lazare.

The ordinands declared that they were quite satisfied. Not only those of us in the house, but also various persons on the outside, recognized that a number of them have profited from these exercises, by the mercy of God. There are even some men in this second ordination retreat, which we are now directing—the first of this Lent—who are giving excellent example to the others. It seems that God, in His infinite goodness, wills to bless these retreats and by this means to communicate these graces to the priests of this country, as He has done elsewhere.

3082. - TO CANON DE RUMELIN

Paris, February 18, 1660

Monsieur,

When I recall the ordinary and extraordinary things you have done for us, the vivid impression your charity has made on me prompts me often to renew my thanks to you for them. It has led me, Monsieur, to resolve, on behalf of our little Company and myself, to fulfill by this letter that obligation which is due to you. I wish to unite it to the sentiments of gratitude which our poor Missionaries in Tréguier express to us from time to time for the favors you bestow on them. They are all the more conscious of it,

---

Letter 3081. - Abelly, *op. cit.,* bk. II, chap. II, sect. VI, p. 239.

Letter 3082. - Archives of the Mission, Paris, facsimile of original signed letter.

since you join heartfelt affection to the temporal goods they receive from you.

M. Dehorgny himself has written to me about this on several occasions with great emotion. So, Monsieur, I thank you with all possible humility; however, since I cannot do so to the extent of our indebtedness to you, I ask Our Lord to be pleased to supply for my powerlessness and to be Himself your worthy reward.

That, Monsieur, is the grace we ask of Him in heaven and on earth, and with this desire I renew the offers of the services of our insignificant Congregation and of my own obedience. I beg you to accept them and to see in what way we here can render them to you. I assure you that we will gladly do so, especially in regard to what you have entrusted to M. Dehorgny, whenever you choose to indicate to us the time and the manner. In proportion to your use of your authority over us, we will have the opportunity to acknowledge your benefits, and I will have that of meriting the happiness I have of being, Monsieur, in the love of O[ur] L[ord], your most humble and obedient servant.

VINCENT DEPAUL,
i.s.C.M.

Addressed: Monsieur de Rumelin, Canon of the Church of Tréguier, in Tréguier

3083. - TO EDME JOLLY, SUPERIOR, IN ROME

February 20, 1660

I have thought about what you told me concerning the ordination retreat, and I perceive that it is really because of our nationality that people mistrust us. It is important, then, that you ask for nothing

---

Letter 3083. - Reg. 2, p. 249.

and see that others ask only for ordinary things and that you yourself propose nothing extraordinary, either to the Pope or to any of the Cardinals. It seems that God wishes the Company to maintain in Rome the reserve it has had elsewhere and not to seek out any works nor the means to sustain them, but to humble itself before His Majesty as unworthy to render Him any service. At the same time, however, we should be prepared to entrust ourselves to His guidance and leave ourselves open to the orders of His Providence, as rough tools in the hands of a good workman.

From what people have said to you about the Missionaries obtaining in time whatever they wish, it may be inferred that this refers to the time when the family will be composed entirely of Italians, which is what is desired. For that reason, Monsieur, it is advisable to admit only carefully selected persons and to strive to know them well before granting them entrance into the seminary.

I ask you once again to make no new proposal for anything concerning us, without letting me know beforehand.

3084. - TO GABRIEL DELESPINEY, SUPERIOR, IN MARSEILLES

Paris, February 27, 1660

Monsieur,

The grace of Our Lord be with you forever!

I received your letter of the seventeenth. Since your gardener's lease has expired, women should no longer be allowed to enter your enclosure. I was unaware until now that they had this liberty in the past—at least I did not reflect on it. Find another gardener who does

---

Letter 3084. - In 1944 the original signed letter was in the office of the Propagation of the Faith, Lyons. A copy appearing in *Recueil Nodet* was published in *Annales C.M.* (1943-44), pp. 238-39, and reprinted in *Mission et Charité,* 19-20, no. 111, pp. 139-40. This edition uses the latter text, replacing the much shorter one from the Marseilles manuscript, which Coste used.

not have any. You suggest to me making a meadow out of the garden, but that is too major a change to be undertaken without giving it a great deal of thought.[1]

I hope M. Get will soon be going to see you in Marseilles; work things out with him about that. If you do not have a boat that has to leave for Algiers right away, he will help you do what is necessary for the safety of the money that has to be sent there. He will be able to stay with you awhile to give you the opportunity to preach the mission in Vins. That is why we are postponing M. Boussordec's departure.

The harsh words that the good Mercedarian Father [2] let slip give us cause for rejoicing at not having been the occasion for his calumnies and to thank God for this. Happy will we be if He finds us worthy of suffering for justice' sake and grants us the grace of loving shame and of returning good for evil to those who persecute us.[3] Happy are those servants who are treated like their Master Our Lord, in whom I am, Monsieur, your most humble servant.

VINCENT DEPAUL,
i.s.C.M.

---

[1]Except for the first sentence, this paragraph formed the material published by Coste in his no. 3084. They kept the garden, and during the year a new house was built for the exclusive use of the gardener (cf. Arch. Nat. S 6707, memo).

[2]The Order of the Redemption or of Our Lady of Mercy (Mercedarians) was founded in the thirteenth century for the redemption of slaves by Saint Peter Nolasco. Father Juan Bautista Gonzalez introduced the Reform into the Order at the end of the sixteenth century.

[3]Cf. Mt 5:10-11. (NAB)

3085. - TO FIRMIN GET, SUPERIOR, IN MONTPELLIER

Paris, February 27, 1660

Monsieur,

God has been pleased to take from us good M. Portail.[1] He died on Saturday, the fourteenth of this month. It was the ninth day of his illness, which began with a sort of lethargy that developed into a constant fever and other complications. Throughout it, his mind and speech remained quite clear.

He had always been apprehensive about death but, on seeing it approach, he faced it with peace and resignation, saying to me on several occasions when I visited him that he no longer felt any trace of his past fear. He died as he had lived, in the good use of suffering, the practice of virtue, and the desire to honor God and to end his days, like O[ur] L[ord], in the accomplishment of His Will.[2]

He was one of the first two men engaged in the missions, and he always contributed to the other works of the Company, in which he rendered important services. Consequently, were it not that God disposes all things for the best and causes us to find our good where we think we will receive harm,[3] the Company would have lost a great deal in losing him. There is reason to hope that this good servant of His will be more useful to us in heaven than he might have been on earth. Please offer the customary prayers for him, Monsieur.

At the same time he was dying, Mademoiselle Le Gras was also at death's door,[4] and we thought she would go before him; but she

---

Letter 3085. - Archives of the Mission, Paris, Sister Hains collection, original signed letter.

[1]The cold winter of 1658-59 had greatly undermined Antoine Portail's health, and he was obliged to curtail his work. "As for Monsieur Portail," wrote Saint Louise, "one would have to have the influence of a great lord to get to see him! There is a small hermitage at the back of the enclosure [of Saint-Lazare], and he never leaves it except to come here on rare occasions to hear confessions" (cf. *Spiritual Writings,* L. 650, p. 671).

[2]Cf. Lk 22:42. (NAB)

[3]Cf. Ps 34:39. (NAB)

[4]She died on March 15, 1660.

is still alive and is better, thank God, who has not willed to overwhelm us with a double affliction.

I just received your letter of the seventeenth, which greatly consoled me, not only because I see in it the perfect disposition God is giving you to follow in all things and places the orders of His good pleasure—which I never doubted—as the advisability with which God has inspired you to return to Marseilles quietly and with the consent of the Bishop of Montpellier. I therefore approve, Monsieur, of your asking his permission to go there on urgent business matters in connection with the house. Not only do I approve it, but I ask you also to take M. Parisy with you when you go, if you see that that good Prelate can do without him. Still, if this would sadden him, do not do it; leave him there awhile to continue the exercises that have begun. When you get to Marseilles, I will take the honor of writing to him to point out the difficulties of your return to Montpellier[5] and to entreat him to dispense you from doing so. If, however, your departure distresses him and he is determined to maintain his seminary, or if he has any other ideas, I will offer to send him some other priest in your place and, after that, recall M. Parisy and Brother Duchesne,[6] whom I greet affectionately.

By this regular mail I have led M. Delespiney to hope that he will see you soon. I ask O[ur] L[ord] to be your guide everywhere

---

[5]An old notebook from the Marseilles house, preserved in the Arch. Nat., S 6707, attributes the withdrawal of the Priests of the Mission to the fact that François de Bosquet, Bishop of Montpellier, had not assured the existence of the establishment by a foundation in perpetuity.

[6]René Duchesne, born in Saint-Juire-Champgillon (Vendée) in August 1607, entered the Congregation of the Mission as a coadjutor Brother in Richelieu on February 16, 1654, and took his vows on November 1, 1658.

and the eternal life and glory of your soul, which mine loves tenderly.

I am, in the love of this same Lord, Monsieur, your most humble servant.

VINCENT DEPAUL,
i.s.C.M.

Addressed: Monsieur Get, Superior of the Priests of the Mission of Marseilles, temporarily at the Montpellier Seminary

3086. - *NICOLAS ÉTIENNE TO SAINT VINCENT*

Cape Verde, February 28, 1660

Monsieur and Most Honored Father,

Your blessing!

From the Canary Islands, through a merchant from Saint-Malo, I wrote you all that happened to us since our departure from La Rochelle until our arrival at the Canary Islands. I am sure you received my letter so I am not repeating what I already told you, in addition to the fact that the occasion does not allow it. I will simply tell you that all of us arrived in excellent health at Cape Verde, where we found forty or fifty Christians, mainly Portuguese, who had been deprived of a priest for two years. M. Daveroult heard the confessions of all of them. On the feast of Saint Mathias [1] *we baptized four Portuguese with the usual ceremonies of the Church, and the following day two Muslims who were quite well instructed. We all celebrated Mass there, and every day M. Daveroult gave an exhortation—most often two—in Portuguese. I wish you might be willing to obtain authorization to have the mission established in this land; there would be good reason to hope for an abundant harvest.*

I went to pay my respects to the Governor of the locality where we had dropped anchor; he has about five or six thousand persons, all of them

Letter 3086. - Archives of the Mission, Paris, seventeenth-century copy.

[1] February 24.

black, naked, and Muslim. When he came aboard our ship for dinner the next day, I spoke to him of God. He said that he loved Him and believed in Him alone. When the question of baptism eventually arose, he said he would willingly receive it, on condition that I remain in the country. The King of the country lives only two leagues [2] away from the Governor, and he always has fifteen hundred horses around him. You can gauge all the good that could be done.

We leave the Cape tomorrow, headed for the Cape of Good Hope; all of us are in excellent health, thank God.

I have not been able to write to the Maréchal[3] this time, so I ask you to inform him that his ship is in very good condition.

I recommend myself to your prayers and to those of the whole Company, as do all my dear fellow travelers. I assure you that I am, for my whole life, in the love of O[ur] L[ord] J[esus] C[hrist] and of His most holy and Immaculate Mother, Monsieur and my dearest Father, your most humble and very obedient servant and son.

N. ÉTIENNE,
i.s.C.M.

The captains send their regards and recommend themselves to your prayers. M. Véron[4] asks if you would kindly have the enclosed letter delivered to his wife, who lives in Oléron.

---

[2]One league equals two and one-half miles or four kilometers.

[3]Maréchal de la Meilleraye.

[4]The Captain of the *Maréchale,* on which the Missionaries were sailing.

3087. - TO MOTHER ANNE-MARIE BOLLAIN [1]

February 29, 1660[2]

Dear Sister,

The grace of O[ur] L[ord] be with you forever!

It is with the greatest embarrassment imaginable that I ask your pardon for my delay in replying to you. My business affairs and infirmities are the cause of this and oblige me even now to write to you by the hand of another.

In the state of indifference in which God has placed you as to leaving or remaining in the place where you now are, the choice of doing one or the other is a matter to be settled between Him and you. After having worked so hard and so well, it is just that you return to your own monastery for a rest and, if you do, you will be doing nothing contrary to God's good pleasure.

But perhaps also, dear Sister, if you deprive yourself of this consolation for love of O[ur] L[ord], who calls you to do what is most perfect, He will be more pleased with your continued service at the Madeleine[3] than He would be elsewhere. The grace of

---

Letter 3087. - Reg. 1, fol. 37.

[1]Abelly, who quotes an excerpt from this letter (cf. bk. II, chap. VII, p. 330), identifies the recipient.

Anne-Marie Bollain was born on September 30, 1599. One time, when Saint Francis de Sales was in Paris, she presented herself to him, asking to be received into the First Monastery of the Visitation. He asked her name and she replied, "Bollain." "My daughter," the Saint said to her, using a wordplay on her name [beau lin], "the flaxseed [lin] is tiny but it multiplies extremely well; so must you in the soil of religious life, where I promise you a place." She was so mature, even in the novitiate, that Saint Jane Frances de Chantal followed her advice and moderated various articles in the Book of Customs. In 1629 she was sent as Superior to the Madeleine convent, which she left in 1633, summoned to the First Monastery by the vote of the Sisters, who wanted her as their head. Three years later she returned to the Madeleine as Superior. In 1664 she became Superior in Chaillot for a term of six years. The First Monastery asked for her again in 1673; she died there in January 1683, having served God in the cloister for sixty-three years. Saint Jane Frances stated that she was "a very fervent and virtuous soul, who would go straight to God." (Cf. *Année sainte,* vol. I, pp. 360-75.)

[2]1660 was a leap year.

[3]The Madeleine Convent in Paris.

perseverance is the greatest grace of all; it crowns all others, and a death that finds us arms in hand is the most glorious and most desirable there is.

It is only natural that a person should wish to go back home to die, surrounded by those close to her, and in the bosom of those she loves. Not everyone, however, allows herself this comfort—only those who are too tenderhearted. O[ur] L[ord] willed to die as He had lived; His life was hard and painful and His death rigorous and cruel, with the absence of all human consolation.[4] It is on this account that many have had that devotion of dying alone, abandoned by others, trusting that God alone will be there to help them.

I am sure, dear Sister, that you seek only Him and that, among the good works to be performed, you will always prefer the ones in which there is more of His glory and less of your own interest. If, then, He lets you know that, by choosing to remain at the Madeleine rather than anywhere else, you will be doing an action more pleasing to Him and more edifying to the people, I am sure you will choose the better part.

So, dear Sister, I repeat what I said to you at the beginning, that the matter is to be decided between God and yourself. The Canon Theologian did me the honor of coming here to speak to me on behalf of the house. I did not let him know that you had shared anything with me in this matter; I simply told him I was aware of your state of mind. Indeed, I ask you to let me know what inspiration God will give you, after having given yourself anew to Him so that His Will may be perfectly fulfilled in you.

I am, in His love, Sister, your. . . .

VINCENT DEPAUL,
i.s.C.M.

---

[4]Cf. Mt 20:18-19. (NAB)

3087a. - TO DOMINIQUE LHUILLIER, IN CRÉCY

[End of February, 1660] [1]

Monsieur,

God has been pleased to take from us good M. Portail. He died on Saturday, the fourteenth of this month. It was the ninth day of his illness, which began with a sort of lethargy that developed into a constant fever and other complications. Throughout it, his mind and speech remained quite clear.

He had always been apprehensive about death but, on seeing it approach, he faced it with peace and resignation, saying to me on several occasions when I visited him that he no longer felt any trace of his past fear. He died as he had lived, in the good use of suffering, the practice of virtue, and the desire to honor God and to end his days, like O[ur] L[ord], in the accomplishment of His Will.

He was one of the first two men engaged in the missions, and he always contributed to the other works of the Company, in which he rendered all kinds of important services. Consequently, were it not that God disposes all things for the best and causes us to find our good where we think we will receive harm, the Company would have lost a great deal in losing him. There is reason to hope that this good servant of His will be more useful to us in heaven than he might have been on earth. Please offer the customary prayers for him, Monsieur.

At the same time he was dying, Mademoiselle Le Gras was also at death's door, and we thought she would go before him; but she is still alive and is better, thank God, who has not willed to overwhelm us with a double affliction.

I praise God that that good boarder is so pleasant in his way of

---

Letter 3087a. - Copy made from *Recueil Nodet.* The letter was published in *Annales C.M.* (1943-44), p. 240, and reprinted in *Mission et Charité,* 19-20, no. 112, pp. 140-41. This edition uses the latter text.

[1] The first two paragraphs, announcing the death of M. Portail and the illness of Mademoiselle Le Gras, appear in several of the letters Saint Vincent wrote at the end of February and the beginning of March.

living among us. It is true that you need room for the priests who will be coming to you; still, if he wants to stay with you until then, you can keep him for five hundred livres, presuming he intends to give them to you. Then, if you have no room for him, he can leave.

I am consoled by what you tell me about that person, and I thank God for it. I will take the time to offer him a few words of congratulations so as to encourage him to keep up the good work.

M. Maillard[2] is sending you one hundred livres. I am sorry it is so little. We will send you more at another time, God willing. May God grant you the fullness of His Spirit so that all those who come to you may have a share in its workings. I am, in His love, Monsieur, your most humble servant.

VINCENT DEPAUL,
i.s.C.M.

3088. - TO GILLES BUHOT [1]

March 3, 1660

Monsieur,

I received your packet containing Brother Louvetel's[2] dimisso-

---

[2]Antoine Maillard was Procurator at Saint-Lazare at that time.

Letter 3088. - Reg. 1, fol. 52v, copy made from the unsigned rough draft.

[1]Gilles Buhot was probably the most distinguished priest in the Bayeux diocese in the seventeenth century. He was a Doctor of the Sorbonne, author of a course of philosophy (*Corpus philosophiae* [3 vols., Cadomi: J. Poisson, 1673]), and Founder and Superior of La Délivrande Seminary and the Bayeux Seminary, to which he gave a house and its annexes on March 11, 1669. Buhot died on January 5, 1674, in the seventy-second year of his age. (Cf. Abbé Jacques Laffetay, *Histoire du diocèse de Bayeux* [2 vols., Bayeux: Delarue et Grobon, 1855-77], vol. I, p. 20; Michel Béziers, *Mémoires pour servir à l'état historique et géographique du diocèse de Bayeux* [3 vols., Rouen: A. Lestringant, 1894-96], II, pp. 163-64.)

[2]Guy Louvetel, born in Monci (Orne) in February 1635, entered the Congregation of the Mission in Paris on July 22, 1657, took his vows there on August 1, 1659, in the presence of M. Langlois, and was ordained a priest in 1660. *Notices*, vol. I, p. 487, refers to him as Guy *Louwerkel;* vol. V (Supplement) lists him as *Le Louvetel.*

rial letters and such great, specific proof of the incomparable charity O[ur] L[ord] has given you for us that I cannot thank you as sufficiently as I would like to do. Nevertheless, I do thank you, Monsieur, to the full extent of my soul and affection. This, however, seems too little to me so I ask O[ur] L[ord] to be Himself your thanks and reward. Moreover, it is for love of Him that you both do and wish us good. That is a fresh motive for us, Monsieur, to give ourselves to His Divine Goodness to try to acknowledge the effects of your goodness by our most humble services. Since you have absolute authority over mine, it is for you to give me the opportunities of rendering them to you, and I very humbly entreat you to do so.

I was deeply moved with compassion by what you wrote me about poor M. Germain.[3] Alas! Monsieur, how great is human weakness, and how powerful are the goods of this world to tempt us! We must hope that God will have mercy on him and that the holy seed you have sown in his soul will not be without fruit.

I have no news of M. de Fresné other than what you tell me about him. If he does me the honor of coming to see me and proposes something to me, I will ask him to apply to you, Monsieur, for your good advice.

I had already heard about the indiscretion of those young men who had committed the excesses you mention.[4] I ask O[ur] L[ord] to draw His glory from it, to preserve you for all the good you are doing, and to make me worthy of the happiness of being, as I am, in His love, Monsieur, your. . . .

---

[3]A priest who had left the Congregation of the Mission.

[4]On February 4, 1660, five young men, followed by a crowd of curious persons, ran through the streets of Caen shouting that all the Pastors, except two whom they named, were tainted by Jansenism and were excommunicated. The police intervened and arrested them. One was sent back to his family as demented, the others were tried and fined. (Cf. D. Boulay, *Vie du Vénérable Jean Eudes* [4 vols., Paris: René Haton, 1905-08], vol. III, p. 336ff.; Raoul Allier, *La cabale des dévots, 1627-60* [Paris: A. Colin, 1902], p. 347ff.; Souriau Maurice, *La Compagnie du Saint-Sacrement de l'autel à Caen: Deux mystiques normands au XVII*[e] *siècle, M. de Renty et Jean de Bernières* [Paris, 1913].)

3089. - TO SISTER MATHURINE GUÉRIN, SISTER SERVANT, IN LA FÈRE

March 3, 1660

Dear Sister,

The grace of O[ur] L[ord] be with you forever!

I received your letter and share deeply in your grief. It is true that God has taken good M. Portail from us—he died on February 14—and that Mademoiselle Le Gras was in great danger at the time and has been so ever since. These are two harsh blows for your little Company; but, since they come from the fatherly hand of God, they must be received with submission, and we must hope from His Charity that the Daughters of Charity will profit from this visit. It is He who has called them and it is He who will maintain them. He never destroys His work; He perfects it, and, provided they are firm in their vocation and faithful to their exercises, He will always bless them and their works. I ask you, Sister, for your part, to continue to carry out your duties well and to be at peace. If you do, you will be more pleasing to God than by acting otherwise.

Mademoiselle is better, thank God. Her main problem has been a large swelling in her left arm, which required three incisions. The last was made the day before yesterday. As you can imagine, she is suffering a great deal; and, although her fever has disappeared, she is still not out of danger because of her age and her weakness. Everything is being done to preserve her health, but that is the work of God who, having preserved her for twenty years, contrary to all human appearances, will preserve her for as long as it will be expedient for His glory.

We will let you know, Sister, the outcome of this distressing illness and will also inform our other Sisters living at a distance. I ask you once again to be at peace as to whatever may happen, for

---

Letter 3089. - Archives of the Motherhouse of the Daughters of Charity, *Recueil de pièces relatives aux Filles de la Charité*, p. 18.

agitation troubles the soul and is displeasing to God, who governs all things with wisdom and love and asks of us absolute, loving resignation to His guidance. Indeed, the great secret of the spiritual life is to abandon all that we love to Him by abandoning ourselves to all that He wishes, with perfect confidence that everything will turn out for the best. That is why it has been said that all things will turn to good for those who serve God.[1] Let us serve Him then, Sister, but let us serve Him as He wishes, and let us allow Him to act. He will take the place of father and mother in your regard; He will be your consolation, your strength, and, in the end, the reward of your love. Pray to Him for me who am, in His love. . . .

3090. - TO GABRIEL DELESPINEY, SUPERIOR, IN MARSEILLES

Paris, March 5, 1660

Monsieur,

The grace of O[ur] L[ord] be with you forever!

I received your letter of February 24. The books should not be billed to our confreres in Algiers; I prefer them to be billed to the Saint-Lazare house.

If M. de Saint-Jean[1] returns to Marseilles, I do not think he will stay with anyone but you. Welcome him and treat him as graciously as you can.

We must entrust the preservation and interests of the hospital to God and hope that all will go better when man can do nothing about it. I find it hard to believe that the administration that has already

---

[1]Cf. Rom 8:28. (NAB)

Letter 3090. - Archives of the Mission, Paris, copy made from the original signed letter, property of M. Charavay, who subsequently put it on sale. The first paragraph of the postscript is in Brother Ducournau's handwriting; Saint Vincent added the second one himself.

[1]Nicolas de Saint-Jean, chaplain to the Queen Mother, Anne of Austria.

been established has been suppressed. With time, we will see if the chaplains can be assembled; for the present, I do not think that is something to be done or proposed.

As for the troubles you fear you are bound to encounter in the possession of your garden, that will be as God pleases, for both our person and our possessions belong to Him. We have to entrust ourselves absolutely to His Providence and remain at peace.

I think M. Get is with you at present. Your recent troubles caused me to wish for his return to Marseilles to give you some comfort. Furthermore, since we had to send other persons there to strengthen the family and to meet your obligations, we thought he would be better than anyone else because of his knowledge of affairs. So, it will be a good idea for you to ask him to do the things the Superior should do and have complete confidence in him, as I have in you, Monsieur, of whom I am the most humble servant.

VINCENT DEPAUL,
i.s.C.M.

We received two louis d'or[2] for Guillaume Lainé,[3] known as Lamontagne, a convict on the *Capitaine,* and seven écus for a man named Traverse. I ask M. Huguier to give each of them his due.

If M. Get raises an objection to accepting the mission[4] of Superior, please urge him to take it over once again.[5] I have always attributed that title to him because I was doubtful that the Montpellier business[6] would be successful. If M. Get remains in Marseilles—or someone else in his place—I will ask you to come back to breathe this air and to free yourself from the air there, which is so harmful to you.

---

[2]The phrase *d'or* was omitted by Coste.

[3]Coste has *Lin,* although the original is clearly *Guillaume Lainé.*

[4]Coste has *mission;* the original has *démission* (resigning).

[5]Coste has *qu'il en prenne l'exercice*; the original has *reprenne.*

[6]Bishop François de Bosquet's unsuccessful attempt to maintain a diocesan seminary.

3091. - TO GUILLAUME DESDAMES, SUPERIOR, IN WARSAW

Paris, March 5, 1660

Monsieur,

God has been pleased to take good M. Portail from us. He died on Saturday, the fourteenth of this month. It was the ninth day of his illness, which began as a sort of lethargy that developed into a constant fever and other complications. Throughout it, his mind and speech remained quite clear. He had always been apprehensive of death but, on seeing it approach, he faced it with peace and resignation, saying to me on several occasions when I visited him that he no longer felt any trace of his past fear. He died as he had lived, in the good use of suffering, the practice of virtue, and the desire to honor God and to end his days as O[ur] L[ord] did, in the accomplishment of His Will.

He was one of the first two men engaged in the missions, and he always contributed to the other works of the Company, to which he rendered important services of all sorts. Consequently, were it not that God disposes all things for the best and causes us to find our good where we think we will find harm, we would have lost much in his person. There is reason to hope that this servant of His will be more useful to us in heaven than he might have been on earth. Please say the usual prayers for him, Monsieur.

At the same time he was dying, Mademoiselle Le Gras was also at death's door, and we thought she would go before him; but she is still alive and is better, thank God, who did not wish to overwhelm us by a double affliction. At present, she is out of danger.

I have received no letters from you since the last one I wrote you, so I have nothing else to tell you.

We have no news here except the publication of the general peace,[1] at which everyone rejoices; it leads us to hope for peace for

---

Letter 3091. - Archives of the Mission, Krakow, original signed letter. The postscript is in the Saint's handwriting.

[1]The Treaty of the Pyrenees, signed on November 7, 1659, between France and Spain.

Poland, which is now being negotiated.[2] May God be pleased to hear the prayers offered Him for that and for the preservation and health of the King and Queen, so necessary to the welfare and peace of the Church!

Messieurs Alméras and Bécu,[3] who have been unwell, are better, thank God; but M. Le Soudier, instead of recovering from his prolonged attack of dysentery, is weaker and more ill from it. As for myself, I am quite well, except for my legs, which no longer allow me to say Holy Mass and oblige me to remain seated all day long. I recommend myself to your prayers and to those of M. Duperroy. Thinking of you and him brings me special consolation, and I often ask O[ur] L[ord] to be the bond of your hearts and the sanctification of your souls, your strength in your labors, and your glory in eternity.

I am, in His love, Monsieur, your most humble servant.

VINCENT DEPAUL,
i.s.C.M.

We will wait patiently for whatever you will tell us regarding the men we still owe you.

Addressed: Monsieur Desdames, Superior of the Priests of the Mission of Holy Cross, in Warsaw

---

[2]Negotiations between Poland and Sweden were concluded on May 3, 1660, with the Treaty of Oliva.

[3]Jean Bécu, born in Braches (Somme) on April 24, 1592, and ordained a priest in September 1616, came to join the first companions of Saint Vincent in September 1626. Two of his brothers, Benoît and Hubert, followed him into the Congregation, the latter as a coadjutor Brother; two of his sisters, Marie and Madeleine, became Daughters of Charity. Bécu was Superior of the house in Toul (1642-46) and spent the rest of his life in Paris. He died on January 19, 1664, having been Vice-Visitor, then Visitor, of the Province of France. (Cf. *Notices,* vol. I, pp. 125-33.)

3092. - TO EDME JOLLY, SUPERIOR, IN ROME

March 5, 1660

You suggest to me that the men who have finished their first year in the [Internal] Seminary should begin their studies so that they may be ready sooner to be put to work. For several good reasons, Monsieur, I do not think that anyone should be dispensed from his two years in the seminary; but, if you deem it advisable to send all, or some, of your French seminarians to Genoa, and if they are willing to accept this change of house, I willingly approve. They can continue and complete their seminary in Genoa, where they can pursue their studies afterward.

3093. - TO LOUIS CHANDENIER, IN ROME

Paris, March 5, 1660

Monsieur,

The grace of O[ur] L[ord] be with you forever!

I am very worried about your health which, I am told, is declining. *Mon Dieu!* Monsieur, what are we to do about that? I think the best remedy is for you to return here because the air of Rome and the poor food you eat there may be contributing to your poor health. So come, Monsieur, we await you with great eagerness and patience. We are asking Our Lord to give you sufficient strength for that long journey and to restore you to your previous state for the good services you can render Him.

Your Bresse lawsuit has not yet been settled. I had some statements of the facts taken to our Ladies of Charity and have asked

---

Letter 3092. - Reg. 2, p. 46.

Letter 3093. - Archives of the Mission, Paris, original signed letter.

them to intervene on your behalf; they have led us to hope they will do so. We are expecting M. Guérin[1] any day now to attend to this matter. We are going to send two priests to see your judges on your behalf. The court recorder seems very favorably disposed toward you. Despite all that, however, I am afraid you will lose your case; if so, you will be able to appeal.

In the name of Our Lord, Monsieur, do whatever you can to keep well; I say the same for Abbé de Moutiers-Saint-Jean.[2] I am incomparably,[3] for both of you, in the love of O[ur] L[ord], Monsieur, your most humble and obedient servant.

VINCENT DEPAUL,
i.s.C.M.

Addressed: Abbé de Chandenier, in Rome

3094. - TO FIRMIN GET, SUPERIOR, IN MARSEILLES

Paris, March 6, 1660

Monsieur,

Your last letter from Montpellier has led me to hope that this one will reach you in Marseilles, where I embrace you in spirit with all the outpouring of my heart. Please remain there and let me know what I should do with regard to the Bishop of Montpellier to get him to approve your departure and that of M. Parisy. I likewise ask M. Delespiney to relinquish the leadership of the family, and you to take it on—[assuming], however, that you would see no drawbacks in that if the Bishop of Montpellier found out and thought

---

[1]Louis de Chandenier's secretary.

[2]Claude de Chandenier.

[3]First redaction: "particularly." The correction is in the Saint's handwriting.

Letter 3094. - Pémartin, *op. cit.,* vol. IV, p. 548, L. 2016.

you had left him for that purpose and, if he does think so, that he has no fault to find in your being employed in a duty other than the direction of the seminary he confided to you, without talking it over with him.[1]

Please pay close attention to the advice I gave M. Delespiney; he will show you my letters so that you will act in conformity with it.

I ask Our Lord to give you the health and grace needed to correspond with His plans. I am, in His love. . . .

3095. - TO PIERRE CABEL, SUPERIOR, IN SEDAN

Paris, March 6, 1660

Monsieur,

May the charity of God dwell in you forever!

Mademoiselle Viole has paid the two hundred livres you drew on her for the months of December and January and wants you to draw a similar amount of two hundred livres for the months of February and March. She would like you please to mention in the bill of exchange you draw on her that it is for the Confraternity of Charity of the Ladies here for these two months.

We have ten écus here to be delivered to the mother of the late M. Lambin, banker at the Court of Rome, where he died last year; he was a native of Donchery. Please go in person to that place, Monsieur, and give those thirty livres directly to that good mother, if she is still alive; otherwise, distribute them among the closest living relatives of the deceased. The person who entrusted this money to us believed it was due to the deceased and wants to

---

[1]Some of the Montpellier seminarians were sent to Agde; the rest went to Narbonne. The diocesan seminary opened its doors again in 1665, under the direction of the Oratorian Fathers. The Priests of the Mission returned there in 1844.

Letter 3095. - Archives of the Mission, Turin, original signed letter.

unburden himself of it through us. You may, to reimburse yourself, draw it on us and add it to the bill of exchange for the first quarter you will withdraw. Meanwhile, let me know when, to whom, and how you make this restitution.

To my great regret, we are unable to send you a priest to help you during these feast days. We had settled upon a seminarian for you, but there was some problem with regard to him. We will send him, God willing, or someone else.

I am, in O[ur] L[ord], Monsieur, your most humble servant.

VINCENT DEPAUL,
i.s.C.M.

At the bottom of the first page: Monsieur Cabel

3096. - TO PIERRE DE BEAUMONT, SUPERIOR, IN RICHELIEU

Paris, March 7, 1660

Monsieur,

The grace of O[ur] L[ord] be with you forever!

I received two letters from you dated February 21 and 28. I had the letter you wrote to M. Le Bret forwarded to him and am enclosing his reply. As for M. Dehorgny's letter, we will not send it to him because he will have left Cahors, where he is now. From there he is supposed to return to Paris; with God's help, he will be here around Easter.

I praise God that all of you returned from Verteuil[1] in good health, and for the graces He gave to that mission and, through you, to its inhabitants. May God in His great mercy grant that the holy

---

Letter 3096. - British Museum, London, *Foreign Private Letters,* Egerton Collection 19, fol. 21, original signed letter.

[1]Verteuil-sur-Charente in the district of Ruffec (Charente).

seed you have scattered in the hearts of the members of the true and of the false religion may bear fruit a hundredfold for time and eternity!

We spoke once to the Duchesse de Richelieu[2] about your pavement; to go to her again and repeat the same story would be to annoy her. Furthermore, what would she do? It is unlikely that she will either take over this expense from you herself or have you released from it. All you can hope is that time will be given you to take care of it. With God's help, you can obtain that time by applying to the Seneschal[3] and the other police officials and offering to have the worst part paved at once, namely, the place that is on the street. For the section farthest from the street and closest to your garden, ask them to wait until God gives you the means of paying for it. If you do not make an attempt there to get them to give you more time, you need not count on any means of justification from the Parlement, because it has refused them, or any favor from elsewhere other than from those who are charging you.

In addition to the priest who is to come to you from Brittany for the seminary, M. Barry is supposed to send you another postulant from near Montauban,[4] whom you will please welcome. I will find out from M. Chiroye, who is making his retreat, if the deacon from Luçon, now a postulant, is to be received and, if he is, I will write to tell M. Hennin[5] to send him to you.

I will think about the coadjutor Brother you are requesting and, if there is one here suitable for you, and we can spare him, we will

---

[2]Anne Poussard, wife of Armand-Jean du Plessis, Duc de Richelieu, the grandnephew of Cardinal Richelieu.

[3]Jean Drouin (1654-68).

[4]Gabriel Fugolles, born in Fajolles, Montauban diocese (Tarn-et-Garonne), entered the Congregation of the Mission as a coadjutor Brother in Richelieu on July 18, 1660, and took his vows there on October 18, 1664, in the presence of M. Cuissot.

[5]Hugues Hennin, born in Blécourt (Nord) on August 15, 1613, was ordained a priest on June 18, 1639, entered the Congregation of the Mission on February 23, 1641, and took his vows in February 1643.

send him to you. Meanwhile, please bear with brother Servin[6] and get what you can out of him. I would be glad to relieve your house of him, if that could be done without inconveniencing another house.

We cannot leave M. Tholard with you because we need him here. Please send him to us right after the Easter holy days. Tell him it will be a great joy for us to see him again and that I embrace him in spirit with all the tenderness of my heart. I do the same for the whole family, especially your own dear soul, which I frequently offer to God.

May His Goodness be pleased to bless your ordination retreat! I am consoled that you have this opportunity to render some little service to the clergy and to the whole diocese.

I am, in the love of O[ur] L[ord], Monsieur, your most humble servant.

VINCENT DEPAUL,
i.s.C.M.

3097. - TO JEAN D'ARANTHON D'ALEX,[1] BISHOP OF GENEVA

Excellency,

Having learned of the favor God has bestowed on His Church by inspiring His Royal Highness to choose you for the See of Geneva, I thank His Divine Majesty, who has granted the desire of

---

[6]Guillaume Servin was born in Amiens (Somme) around 1610. At the end of May 1655 he entered the Congregation of the Mission in Paris as a coadjutor Brother and took his vows there on October 22, 1657, in the presence of M. Bajoue.

Letter 3097. - Innocent Le Masson, *Vie de Messire Jean d'Aranthon d'Alex* (Clermont-Ferrand: Thibaud-Landriot, 1834), p. 60.

[1]Saint Vincent's relationship with Jean d'Aranthon d'Alex dated back to the time when the latter was studying in Paris. One day, after the Saint had heard him speak at a priests' meeting, he introduced himself to d'Aranthon and asked him to come to Saint-Lazare from time to time, which he did. Shortly after ordination to the priesthood on December 17, 1644, he was appointed

so many upright persons who prayed that you would take over that important diocese and who has forearmed you with graces suitable for this holy office. Utterly wretched as I am, Excellency, since I had the happiness of seeing you, something about your dear person reminds me of Blessed Francis de Sales your predecessor, so I have scarcely ever thought of you without remembering that great saint. I ask Our Lord Jesus Christ, who is the Bishop of Bishops and their perfect model, to grant you His twofold Spirit for the sanctification of your own dear soul and the salvation of the people He has intended to be guided by you. It is a blessing for our little Company to be among them and for me, Excellency, to renew the offers of my perpetual obedience, which I now do with all the tenderness of my heart. I am, in the love of Our Lord, your most humble. . . .

VINCENT DEPAUL,
i.s.C.M.

Paris, March 12, 1660

3098. - TO GABRIEL DELESPINEY, SUPERIOR, IN MARSEILLES

Paris, March 12, 1660

Monsieur,

The grace of Our Lord be with you forever!

Last December, we sent you 189 livres by a bill of exchange

Canon of Geneva and Pastor in Ceury. The services he rendered the diocese and the Court of Savoy, his great learning, and his indefatigable zeal against heresy made him a likely candidate to succeed Charles-Auguste de Sales, who died on February 8, 1660. Some time before, Saint Vincent had foretold that he would be appointed to this position and had recently repeated his prediction to the Prelate's nephew, the Prior of La Pérouse. Jean d'Aranthon enjoyed one of the longest and more fruitful episcopates ever known to the Geneva diocese. He died on July 4, 1695, at seventy-six years of age. The Priests of the Mission, directors of the Annecy seminary, who had nothing but praise for his benevolence, inherited his library, his chapel in the country, a precious chalice, and all of his paintings.

Letter 3098. - The original signed letter was formerly on display at the headquarters of the Society of Saint Vincent de Paul in Paris, 6 rue Furstenberg, which has since moved its offices to 5 rue du Pré-aux-Clercs. The postscript is in the Saint's handwriting.

from Messieurs Simonnet on Messieurs Napollon,[1] and you informed me that you had received it and would send it to a Parisian in Algiers named Edme Guillaume.[2] Now, I have seen from the list of captives ransomed by Father Héron[3] that he is one of them; therefore, this money must not be sent to Algiers. Let me know if you still have it, because Madame Anne Guillaume, who provided it, is requesting its return and wanted me to ask you to keep it until further notice and not to give any of it to her brother, on any pretext whatsoever.

The Provincial of the Mercedarians is willing to make full satisfaction to the Consul in Algiers[4] for the avania of 800 écus which he incurred because of a priest of that Order who, in the year 1657, disguised himself in Algiers so as to effect a ransom. Consequently, he wanted me to ask you to do as follows:

(1) To stipulate that I am to receive from Father Antoine Audoire, Commander of their convent in Marseilles, acting for Father Savry, Provincial of the Mercedarians, the sum of . . . ,[5] for whatever M. Barreau, or others acting for him, can claim for the avania, which, as I have been told, was 2400 livres. Since, on March 22, 1659, M. Le Vacher received 878 livres in partial payment, 1522 livres still remain to be paid. Nevertheless, the Provincial mentions only 1300 livres, either because he does not know exactly what remains, or for some other reason Father Audoire will tell you.

---

[1]The Simonnets were bankers in Paris; the Napollons were bankers in Marseilles.

[2]A captive in Algiers.

[3]Jean Héron, a Mathurin Father, Superior of the convent in Châteaubriant (Loire-Atlantique). The Order of Mathurins goes back to the twelfth century and had as its founder Saint Jean de Matha. It took its name from the convent in Paris built on the site of an old chapel dedicated to Saint Mathurin. It is also called the Order of the Trinitarians.

[4]Jean Barreau. Between 1657 and 1659 Jean Barreau suffered greatly because of the actions of the Mercedarian Fathers and his own misguided or imprudent zeal. Besides enduring humiliating insults and calumnies at the hands of Algerian merchants, he had been imprisoned; the Dey of Algiers also extorted money from him for the ransom of Father Sérapion of the Mercedarian Fathers. During this period Saint Vincent corresponded with Gabriel Delespiney and Firmin Get concerning indemnification from the Mercedarians. Because of the mention of various denominations of money, e.g., livres, écus, piastres, sols, it is difficult to decipher the basis for the amount of the indemnification mentioned in these letters.

[5]The Saint did not indicate the amount.

Try to get whatever you can from him up to the said amount of 1522 livres. Do not, however, go to court for something so insignificant.

(2) To have struck out and canceled the act of March 22, 1659, which was recorded in Marseilles between Father Audoire and M. Le Vacher,[6] in the office of the notary Sossin, acknowledging receipt of the 878 livres received in partial payment of the said 2400 livres, due and acknowledged by the said Mercedarian Father.

(3) When you receive the balance, to inform Brother Barreau and myself that those good Mercedarians have complied with everything.

I received no letters from you nor from M. Get by the last mail; yet, I did get one from M. Huguier. I am afraid there is trouble in Marseilles, God forbid![7] If M. Get is with you, as I think he is, please share this letter with him.

I embrace both of you and the whole family with all possible affection.

Your most humble servant.

VINCENT DEPAUL,
i.s.C.M.

If there is any truth to the rumor going around that they are going to resort to trickery in Algiers to withdraw the captives,[8] please let me know so we can dispose of the money collected as alms, if such is the case and if M. Get is in Marseilles.

Addressed: Monsieur Delespiney

---

[6]Philippe Le Vacher.

[7]Following the violence committed by the people against La Gouvernelle, lieutenant of the guardsmen of the Duc de Mercoeur, the latter took severe measures to forestall further trouble and to punish the city: a blockade of the port, military occupation of the city, removal of the Consuls, disarmament of the citizens, establishment of a court of justice to investigate trouble-makers, and construction of a citadel. On March 2 the King, at the head of his army, entered Marseilles through a section of the wall that had been knocked down, as though it were a conquered city. He departed on March 8, leaving a garrison of 5,500 men. (Cf. Augustin Fabre, *Histoire de Marseille* [2 vols., Marseilles: M. Olive, 1829], vol. II, pp. 290ff.)

[8]An expedition being planned by Chevalier Paul.

3099. - *EDME JOLLY, SUPERIOR, IN ROME, TO SAINT VINCENT*

[March 1660] [1]

In the last ordination retreat, we had a Spanish gentleman from the Plasencia diocese, whose Bishop[2] *is currently Ambassador Extraordinary, in this Court, of the King of Spain. Since that good gentleman was planning to receive Holy Orders, he came with great enthusiasm to take part in the retreat. However, having listened to the conferences and understood how important it is not to enter Holy Orders unless really called by God, and having also considered the serious obligations contracted in receiving Holy Orders, he was seized with great fear and had a very hard time making up his mind whether to be ordained. Nevertheless, he finally did so with very good dispositions, and the sure sign of this was the great change that took place in him, as well as in many others, after the ordination retreat.*

When he had finished his retreat, he told all that to his Bishop, who wanted to speak with us. He sent someone to let us know, and we went to his residence this morning. There we encountered a very zealous Prelate, who has given many missions in his diocese, in almost the same way as the Company does, except that he makes them a little shorter. He preaches, hears confessions, and teaches catechism himself; but this new idea of working to form good priests enchants him. He wants to come here during the next ordination retreat and asks if, when he returns to Spain, we could give him one of our men. Meanwhile, he wants to send a report to his diocese of what we do during the ordination retreat so they can begin to put it into practice.

Letter 3099. - Abelly, *op. cit.*, bk. II, chap. II, sect. VI, p. 240.

[1]Saint Vincent answered this letter on April 2 (cf. no. 3112).

[2]Luis Crespi de Borja, an Oratorian priest, Extraordinary Ambassador to the Holy See for the King of Spain. He died on April 12, 1663.

3100. - TO SISTER CHARLOTTE ROYER, SISTER SERVANT, IN RICHELIEU [1]

Paris, March 16, 1660

Dear Sister,

It pleased God to take M. Portail to Himself about a month ago, and yesterday He took Mademoiselle Le Gras. This news will surprise you at first. I hope that, seeing in it the good pleasure of God, you will conform to it and will do as our Sisters here have done, who have given great edification by the peace and union they [have shown] [2] in these events.

Do likewise, then, dear Sister, and pray for these two deceased persons; please offer your next Communions for their intention and so that God will be pleased to be Himself the guide of your Little Company. On this occasion, renew the good resolution you made at the time you entered it, to live and die in it as true Daughters of Charity. To this end, continue your good practices.

Nothing has changed in the government of the Company; the same Sisters our deceased had chosen as Councillors will remain in office until one of them is elected to replace the deceased.[3] The latter will be buried tomorrow in Saint-Laurent Church, beside our dear departed Sisters and with only the same services that were held at the funerals of each of them.[4] Be at peace, then, until you hear

---

Letter 3100. - Archives of the Motherhouse of the Daughters of Charity, original signed letter.

[1]This same letter was sent to Jeanne Delacroix, Sister Servant in Châteaudun, and probably to the Sister Servants of the other houses.

[2]Omitted in the original.

[3]After Saint Louise's death, Saint Vincent asked Sister Jeanne Gressier to govern the Company until a new Superioress General was chosen. At the Assembly of August 27, in conformity with Saint Louise's wish that he select her successor, he appointed Sister Marguerite Chétif as Superioress General. At this same Assembly the Sisters elected Julienne Loret as Assistant, Louise-Christine Rideau as Treasurer, and Philippe Bailly as Bursar (cf. vol. X, no. 120).

[4]The body of Louise de Marillac was laid to rest in Saint-Laurent Church, under the chapel of the Visitation (today the Saint Francis de Sales chapel), from which it was removed in 1755

from us; please inform your Sister companions of this, as well as those in the surrounding areas, if there are any.

I am for all the Sisters, and especially for you, in the love of O[ur] L[ord], Sister, your most affectionate brother and servant.

VINCENT DEPAUL,
i.s.C.M.

Addressed: Sister Charlotte, Daughter of Charity, Servant of the Sick Poor of Richelieu, in Richelieu

3101. - TO CANON JEAN DE SAINT-MARTIN,[1] IN DAX

March 18, 1660

Monsieur,

I implore you by all the graces God has been pleased to grant you, to do me the favor of sending me that wretched letter which mentions Turkey—I mean the one that M. d'Agès [2] found among his father's papers. I ask you again, by the bowels of Jesus Christ Our Lord, to do me the favor I ask of you as soon as possible.[3]

---

to be placed in the chapel of the Motherhouse. From there it passed to rue des Maçons-Sorbonne during the French Revolution. Under the governments known as the Consulate (1799-1804) and the Napoleonic Empire (1804-14), it reposed in the house on rue du Vieux-Colombier; during the Bourbon Restoration (1815-30) it was enshrined in the newly-acquired Motherhouse on rue du Bac, where it remains today.

Letter 3101. - Collet, *op. cit.*, vol. I, p. 22.

[1]Canon de Saint-Martin, Doctor of Theology, had been secretary to the Bishop of Dax (1640); in 1643 he was named a Canon and in 1644 became Officialis of the diocese. He died in 1672. In writing his biography of Saint Vincent, Abelly used some material from the Canon's memoirs.

[2]M. de Saint-Martin d'Agès, son of Jean de Saint-Martin, counselor at the Presidial Court in Dax, and nephew of Canon de Saint-Martin.

[3]Collet states mistakenly that, as a consequence of this letter, Canon de Saint-Martin sent the precious document to Jean Watebled, Superior at the Bons-Enfants. The original of the letter regarding the captivity in Tunis had already been at Saint-Lazare since August 1658 (cf. Appendix 1 of this volume). For a more detailed history of this letter see vol. I, no. 1, citation.

3102. - TO THE SUPERIORS OF THE VISITATION MONASTERIES OF PARIS, CHAILLOT, AND SAINT-DENIS

March 18, 1660

Vincent de Paul informs the four nuns that his infirmities oblige him to resign as Superior of their monasteries. He hopes that his successor will remedy the numerous faults he has committed since the day Francis de Sales had him accept this office.[1]

3103. - TO GUILLAUME DESDAMES, SUPERIOR, IN WARSAW

Paris, March 19, 1660

Monsieur,

The grace of O[ur] L[ord] be with you forever!

The last letter I received from you, about two weeks ago, was dated January 30. It concerns our two Polish Brothers,[1] whom you do not think we should send there before they have taken their vows and are fully formed in our functions. I think you are right. We will observe them during their seminary, then we shall see; meanwhile, we await their baptismal certificates, which you lead us to expect.

May God be pleased to bless the arms of the King against the Muscovites and the peace treaty with the Swedes! [2] This is the prayer we all offer to Him.

Enclosed is a letter for M. Duperroy, whom I embrace most

Letter 3102. - Collet, *op. cit.,* vol. II, p. 76.

[1]The Archbishop of Paris refused to accept this resignation.

Letter 3103. - Archives of the Mission, Krakow, original signed letter.

[1]Nicolas Blotowski, born in Jardowska, Poznan diocese (Poland), on March 31, 1631, entered the Paris Seminary as a clerical student on May 14, 1659, and took his vows on May 22, 1661, in the presence of M. de Beaumont. His brother Karol, born in Iosdowa, Poznan diocese, on October 23, 1635, entered the Paris Seminary as a clerical student on November 16, 1659, and took his vows on May 21, 1661, in the presence of M. Gicquel. *Notices,* vols. I and V (Supplement), spells their name *Blotouski.*

[2]The Treaty of Oliva.

cordially, and another for Sister Marguerite,[3] which will distress those poor Daughters of Charity. God has been pleased to take Mademoiselle Le Gras to Himself. Please prepare them for this sad news and help them to bear the pain of this loss. I recommend to your prayers the soul of the deceased and mine also, which loves yours tenderly. We have no other news.

I am, in the love of O[ur] L[ord], Monsieur, your most humble servant.

VINCENT DEPAUL,
i.s.C.M.

At the bottom of the first page: Monsieur Desdames

3103a. - TO FIRMIN GET, SUPERIOR, IN MARSEILLES

Paris, March 19, 1660

Monsieur,

The grace of Our Lord be with you forever!

From your letter of the second of this month I learned of your arrival in Marseilles, where I am asking you to remain and to take over the leadership of the house and its affairs, if you have not already done so. I also ask M. Delespiney [1] to remain there for a

---

[3]Marguerite Moreau, a native of Lorraine, was born in 1623; she entered the Daughters of Charity in 1646 and was sent to Angers in 1647. A strong personality, she found it hard to get along with Cécile Angiboust, the Sister Servant. In 1651, Saint Louise was thinking of naming her Sister Servant in Angers but chose her for Poland instead, where she went on September 7, 1652, with Sisters Madeleine Drugeon and Françoise Douelle. Sister Marguerite refused to remain in Warsaw with the Queen while her two companions were going to serve the poor in Krakow. She died of typhus in Poland on September 29, 1660.

Letter 3103a. - Copy made from *Recueil Nodet.* The letter was published in *Annales C.M.* (1943-44), p. 241, and reprinted in *Mission et Charité,* 19-20, no. 113, p. 142. This edition uses the latter text.

[1]Gabriel Delespiney, the immediate predecessor of Firmin Get as Superior of the Marseilles house.

while to help with the missions you will be able to give after Easter. I am writing to him about some business in Algiers; [2] please inform yourself about it and have it carried out, along with the other instructions I gave him in my previous letters. Someone told me this morning, however, that there is a rumor circulating here, which originated with the secretary of the Duc de Vendôme,[3] that the King has fitted out some ships to go to rescue the captives in Barbary.[4] Please find out about that and, if there is any truth to it, do not send the sums of money that I indicated.

M. Delespiney tells me you are not feeling well. I am sorry about that; I ask you to let me know what is the matter—and to take care of your health.

I am, in the love of Our Lord, Monsieur, your most humble servant.

VINCENT DEPAUL,
i.s.C.M.

What you said to the Bishop of Montpellier,[5] when you were taking leave of him, seems judicious to me.

---

[2]The dealings with the Mathurins (Trinitarians) and the Fathers of Mercy (Mercedarians).

[3]César de Bourbon, Duc de Vendôme, the illegitimate son of Henry IV and Gabrielle d'Estrées, was born in the Château de Coucy. He married Françoise de Lorraine, daughter of the Duc de Mercoeur, and died in Paris on October 22, 1665. The Duke was involved in the troubles during the regency of Louis XIII and fought against the political policies of Richelieu, under whom he was jailed and exiled. He accepted the politics of Mazarin, who appointed him Minister of Navigation in 1650 and lavished many favors on him. His eldest son married Laura Mancini, the Cardinal's niece.

[4]A naval expedition was, in fact, being prepared against Algiers at the time; it would take place in July and August under the command of the renowned Chevalier Paul.

[5]François de Bosquet.

3104. - TO SISTER NICOLE HARAN, SISTER SERVANT, IN NANTES

Paris, March 20, 1660

Dear Sister,

The grace of O[ur] L[ord] be with you forever!

In the last mail I announced a sad piece of news to you, namely, the loss we have sustained in the death of Mademoiselle Le Gras. You must praise God for this and hope that He will take the place of father and mother in your regard.

I saw the last letter you wrote to the deceased, in which you ask for two Sisters.[1] It is certainly just to come to your aid and, with God's help, we will try to do so as soon as possible. True, the Fathers [2] asked for one Sister and refuse to accept two, saying that the hospital is too poor. We will try to get them to approve our sending you two of them and not give you women from the town to help you, since that is contrary to what was agreed upon, and the women are more a hindrance than a help to you.

Since our affliction, we have not had time to get our thoughts together to reflect on the needs of your Little Company. Please give us a little leisure to find a remedy for them; meanwhile, do the best you can. If you work and suffer patiently, your works will be perfect, as one of the Apostles says.[3] I ask Our Lord to give you this virtue and to strengthen you in your heavy labors.

Letter 3104. - The original signed letter was formerly the property of the Pastor of Sainte-Anne Church, Amiens. Its present location is unknown.

[1]This letter is not extant.

[2]The Administrators of the hospital.

[3]Cf. Jas 1:2-4. (NAB)

I send greetings to all our Sisters and recommend myself to their prayers and yours.

I am, in the love of Our Lord, dear Sister, your most affectionate brother and servant.

VINCENT DEPAUL,
i.s.C.M.

Addressed: Sister Nicole Haran, Daughter of Charity, servant of the sick poor of the Nantes Hospital, in Nantes

3105. - TO LOUIS DUPONT, SUPERIOR, IN TRÉGUIER

March 24, 1660

What distresses me *supra modum*[1] is that it seems that charity is being wounded in your house; still, I would like to think that this wound is not in hearts but is simply external. Please inform me of this situation, Monsieur; do all you can to bring people together again and, as it were, to be yourself the cement in this. To this end I ask the Holy Spirit, who is nothing if not love, and who is the sacred bond of the Father and the Son, to be the soul of your leadership and the gentleness of your words and actions.

Letter 3105. - Reg. 2, p. 193.

[1]*Beyond my strength* (cf. 2 Cor 1:8). (NAB)

3105a. - TO FIRMIN GET, SUPERIOR, IN MARSEILLES

Paris, March 26, 1660

Monsieur,

The grace of Our Lord be with you forever!

I am sending you a copy of the account you sent me when you left for Montpellier, regarding the sums of money you left in the strongbox for the captives. Now, in the reports M. Le Vacher sent me, he indicates that he took from Marseilles to Algiers what is mentioned on the first page, with the exception of the 500 livres for Mathurin Colin and 20 livres received by M. Guivar for Edme Guillaume,[1] which he did not mention to us at all. In addition, he took 970 piastres for the Chevalier du Brus, whom he ransomed.

From the amounts on the second page, he took 5,000 livres from the collection money and sent us an account of how it was used. He also took 1,000 of the 3,200 livres received for the ransom of three priests or religious who were captives. Included among these was Father Bonaventure de Sainte-Croix, who is now in Genoa. Apparently, he also used the 878 livres received from the Mercedarians. I do not think, however, that he wrote me anything about that.

If you still have the 20 livres for Edme Guillaume, please send them to me to be returned to that poor young man, who is here. We have already given him 189 livres, which his sister was sending to him in Algiers and which M. Delespiney received in your absence three or four months ago but did not send to Algiers. Now, since these 189 livres are still in your strongbox, please have them given to Jean Beguin, a captive in Algiers, because we have received a similar amount here from his father.

Letter 3105a. - Copy made from *Recueil Nodet.* The letter was published in *Annales C.M.* (1943-44), pp. 241-43, and reprinted in *Mission et Charité,* 19-20, no. 114, pp. 143-45. This edition uses the latter text.

[1]A Christian who had been a captive in Algiers.

I received your letter of the sixteenth. I am glad you have taken over the leadership again.[2] I thank you for this and ask Our Lord to be Himself your guide.

I will write to the Bishop of Montpellier in conformity with what you tell me, but I cannot do so today.[3]

I praise God that Messieurs Delespiney and Beaure have gone to open the mission in Vins. You make no mention of M. Cornier. I would like to think that either you or he has gone to help them out.

I have nothing against your suggestion for sending money safely to Algiers, but please do not send anything from the collections until I tell you. I did, however, send contrary instructions to M. Delespiney, but I was unaware of the news I have just learned, which comes from too reliable a source to make us believe that it is anything other than true. It is that Brother B[arreau] is at it again and has lost 2,800 écus through his own fault.

You know that, around the time you went to Montpellier, an English ship left Marseilles for Algiers. Several merchants sent various amounts of money to that poor man to ransom some captives. When the ship arrived, the captain informed the Consul of the money he had to be handed over to him. The Consul took part of it and, trusting him, left the rest with him. Now, two things happened: first, the Consul redeemed the captives he had instructions to ransom and sent them back to their own country, using for that purpose certain deposits he had, in the hope of replacing them with what the captain owed him. However, the second thing that happened is that he went bankrupt for 2,800 écus.

After that and so many other mistakes of this Brother which preceded this one, should we not be wary of his too great compliance—not to say weakness? Should we not be afraid that, if we send him money, he will misuse it again and, instead of paying off the debts, will contract new ones?

---

[2]The duty of local Superior.

[3]Good Friday.

All things considered, I think it advisable to postpone sending him the help he is requesting; give me your advice on this. I await that of the Duchesse d'Aiguillon, whom I have informed of this latest loss. The remedy would be to send a new Consul and to recall the present one. We will think about that.

We received eighteen livres for Denis Dubois, a captive on the *Capitaine;* I ask M. Huguier to give them to him.

I think it is a good idea for you personally to write to M. Le Vacher in Algiers to tell him that, since it is rumored here that he and the Consul have made the mistake I mentioned with the English captain, you are asking him to let you know what is going on because we have judged it advisable not to send any money from the collections until we learn the truth.

I am including a packet of Arabic books for M. Delespiney for Tunis; please send them there.

I am, in the love of Our Lord, Monsieur, your most humble servant.

VINCENT DEPAUL,
i.s.C.M.

3106. - *EDME JOLLY, SUPERIOR IN ROME, TO SAINT VINCENT*

[March 1660] [1]

The ordinands we had at the beginning of Lent and those we have now are so exact at all the exercises and perform them with such devotion that we are amazed. I can say that I think there is nothing more, or very little, to be desired with regard to silence and recollection. By this means, Our Lord wants to make us keenly aware that He alone is the author of all that good.

Letter 3106. - Abelly, *op. cit.*, bk. II, chap. II, sect. VI, p. 240.

[1]The ordination retreat mentioned in this letter would seem to be the second one of that Lent; the first was given on February 16.

3107. - TO MICHEL CASET, SUPERIOR, IN TOUL

Holy Saturday [1] 1660

Mademoiselle Le Gras died on the fifteenth of this month. I recommend her soul to your prayers, although perhaps she has no need of this help, for we have good reason to believe that she now enjoys the glory promised to those who serve God and the poor in the way she did.[2]

3108. - TO MADAME MARIE GIRARDIN, IN TROYES

Paris, the eve of Easter, 1660 [1]

Madame,

M. Dupuich has informed me that you have also given our poor house in Troyes a life annuity of eight hundred livres and that you are satisfied with forty livres a year annuity for yourself. I feel obliged, therefore, to thank you very humbly, Madame, for this great act of charity, which I now do with all possible humility and gratitude. Since, however, I am not worthy to acknowledge such a benefit, I ask Our Lord, for whose love you are doing this for us, to be your reward. This is a prayer we will always be obliged to offer Him, and all of us will feel obligated to serve you whenever His Divine Goodness is pleased to give us opportunities of doing so. As for myself, Madame, I will do so most devotedly all my life.

We will also pay you your income promptly during your life-

Letter 3107. - Collet, *op. cit.*, vol. II, p. 76, *note.*

[1]March 27.

[2]Cf. Mt 25:40. (NAB)

Letter 3108. - Departmental Archives of Aube, 5 G34, original signed letter. In the light of a new discovery, Coste corrected the citation from Pémartin, which he had originally given, to the present one (cf. vol. XIII, French edition, p. 851).

[1]March 27.

time, which I ask God to prolong for many years. I willingly ratify M. Dupuich's promise to you concerning this. In addition, I consent to having this letter joined to his for your assurance; furthermore, if you desire a more authentic declaration of this, Madame, I will send it to you. Such practical kindness as yours leads me to wish to please and obey you in all things. I am, in the love of Our Lord, Madame, your [2] most humble and obedient servant.

VINCENT DEPAUL,
i.s.C.M.

Addressed: Madame Marie Girardin, in Troyes

3109. - TO SISTER JEANNE DELACROIX,[1] SISTER SERVANT, IN CHÂTEAUDUN

Paris, the eve of Easter,[2] 1660

Dear Sister,

The grace of Our Lord be with you forever!

Four louis d'or have been sent to us from Le Mans for you, accruing from an annuity of four years; a copy of the settlement agreement is also enclosed. I have had them entrusted to Sister Jeanne Gressier;[3] let her know what you would like her to do with

---

[2]In vol. XIII, p. 851, Coste added from the original the end of the sentence, the signature, and the address.

Letter 3109. - Archives of the Motherhouse of the Daughters of Charity, *Recueil de pièces relatives aux Filles de la Charité,* p. 651.

[1]Jeanne Delacroix, born in Le Mans (Sarthe), entered the Daughters of Charity in 1645 or 1646. In 1649 at the latest, she was assigned to Serqueux and in 1651 became Assistant to Saint Louise. At the end of 1653 she returned to Serqueux and was still there in 1657, when she again became Assistant. At the death of Sister Barbe Angiboust in 1659, Jeanne was sent to Châteaudun to replace her. In 1664 she opened the house in Chartres; she later served the Company as Treasurer General (1668-71). Her sister, Renée, was also a Daughter of Charity.

[2]March 27.

[3]First Assistant and Procurator, she governed the Company after the death of Saint Louise, until a new Superioress General was named.

them and send me the receipt, written and signed by you, in conformity with the sample I am sending you. It will be forwarded to Brother Jean Proust[4] in Le Mans, who has given a receipt to those who gave him the money so that, when he gives them yours, he may withdraw his own.

A few days ago I wrote to tell you of the loss we have sustained in the death of Mademoiselle Le Gras. The Little Company continues to do well, thank God. The Sisters here are truly resigned to God's good pleasure in this painful separation, and are filled with confidence in Our Lord, who will hold the place of father and mother in their regard. They are faithful to their vocation, their works, and the practice of the virtues, whereby they edify everyone.

I am sure, dear Sister, that you and our dear Sisters with you do the same. There is reason to hope that the dear deceased, who is now with God, will obtain for you from His Infinite Goodness a superabundance of graces and blessings to make you more and more perfect.

I am. . . .

3110. - TO LOUIS RIVET, SUPERIOR, IN SAINTES

Easter Sunday [1] 1660

You did well to stay at home and to send M. Bréant [2] on mission; it is advisable for Missionaries, who have various ministries, to go from time to time from one to another in order to be prepared for all of them without omitting any. I praise God that, although your

---

[4]Procurator for the Le Mans house.

Letter 3110. - Reg. 2, p. 36.

[1]March 28.

[2]Louis Bréant, born in Beu, near Houdan, Chartres diocese (Eure-et-Loir), entered the Congregation of the Mission on February 12, 1654, at twenty-five years of age, and took his vows on November 13, 1656, in the presence of M. Berthe. He is listed as a priest in *Notices,* vols. I and V (Supplement), with no mention of an ordination date. Bréant was Superior in Saintes (1662-64), Tréguier (1664-70), Saint-Brieuc (1670-80), and Saint-Méen (1681-89).

personal inclination is to work in the country, you still contribute to the works of the house and to do all you can for the progress of the seminary.

3111. - TO GUILLAUME DESDAMES, SUPERIOR, IN WARSAW

Paris, April 2, 1660

Monsieur,

The grace of O[ur] L[ord] be with you forever!

I am writing simply to tell you that I received your letter of February 22, which does not require an answer, and to thank God, as I do, for your good health and that of M. Duperroy. I ask O[ur] L[ord] to continue to grant you His spiritual and temporal blessings, and that, while always keeping yourself at a certain distance from created things which you see, you may live an utterly new divine life in Jesus Christ risen from the dead. Ask Him for this grace for all of us so that we may constantly sigh for, and aspire after, the things that are above,[1] and that we may proceed in that direction through the works of our vocation so as to draw others with us to heaven.

We have no news here. Everyone is very well and things are going along as usual, thank God. I am, in Him, Monsieur, your most humble servant.

VINCENT DEPAUL,
i.s.C.M.

Addressed: Monsieur Desdames, Superior of the Priests of the Mission, at Holy Cross, in Warsaw

---

Letter 3111. - Archives of the Mission, Krakow, original signed letter.

[1]Cf. Col 3:12. (NAB)

3112. - TO EDME JOLLY, SUPERIOR, IN ROME

April 2, 1660

. . . .As for that good Prelate, the Ambassador[1] of the King of Spain, we should bless God for the sentiments He gives him regarding the work for ordinands and his zeal for the missions. But, in the name of God, Monsieur, make no move to have us sought after; and, no matter how much he expresses to you his desire to have some of our priests, do not give him any hope of this. Neither should you disregard this devotedness but accept whatever he says to you about it with respect and gratitude, without committing yourself to foster his plan. Give him the notes he has requested of you only as late as possible because, if he should make it a point of honor to have Missionaries, we will be hard put to provide him with ones who are truly suitable for that kingdom. Furthermore, we must be on our guard against pushing our own way into places and works in which we are not already engaged.

3112a. - TO FIRMIN GET, SUPERIOR, IN MARSEILLES

Paris, April 2, 1660

The grace of Our Lord be with you forever!

I received your letter of March 23. I praise God that you have received 415 livres on the one hand and 884 on the other, which make 1129 livres from the Mercedarians. This sum, along with the 885 livres that M. Le Vacher [1] received previously, from what you

---

Letter 3112. - Reg. 2, p. 249.

[1]Luis Crespi de Borja (cf. no. 3099).

Letter 3112a. - Copy made from *Recueil Nodet.* The letter was published in *Annales C.M.* (1943-44), pp. 243-45, and reprinted in *Mission et Charité,* 19-20, no. 115, pp. 145-46. This edition uses the latter text.

[1]Philippe Le Vacher.

tell me—although his receipt states only 878 livres—the 20 livres Father Sérapion[2] says he left with M. B[arreau], and the 9 livres those good Fathers have promised us come to a total of 2400 livres.[3] That is the amount of the avania suffered by B[arreau] on their account. Please hold him accountable for it.

Although you may have some safe ways of sending money to Algiers, I cannot make up my mind to entrust further sums to the Consul after the latest loss of 2800 écus he caused through his imprudence, as I have told you. My sources of information regarding this are too sure to be doubted, and since he is overstepping the repeated orders I have given him of never using the money of one captive for another and of not committing himself for anyone, putting money into his hands would be to give him the opportunity to make new mistakes because he is so inclined to use it other than he should. So, Monsieur, I think we should send someone to Algiers to ascertain what debts there are and to make the payments himself with the money he brings with him. I think M. Huguier would do that well, if you could put in his place one of the other priests you have, who would be capable of doing what he does.

We have here a Brother who had been assigned to Algiers. Please write me your advice on this as soon as possible; meanwhile, postpone sending the help those gentlemen are requesting.

I sent you word that Edme Guillaume is in this city and that he did not receive either in Algiers or in Marseilles the 189 livres[4] that his sister sent him. But we have given them to him here so that that money might be sent and handed over to Jean Bègue,[5] a captive in

---

[2]A Mercedarian who arrived in Algiers in 1655. From the outset he seemed to have difficulties with Jean Barreau, the French Consul.

[3]Some of Saint Vincent's mathematical calculations in this letter are inaccurate. As stated earlier, the mention of various denominations of money such as livres, écus, etc., makes it difficult to decipher the basis for the amounts mentioned in this letter.

[4]The copy had *1890* livres. This enormous amount doubtless came from a faulty reading; *189* livres is more likely (cf. the letter of March 20, 1660, no. 3105a).

[5]The copy has Jean *Béguin,* but it probably should read *Bègue,* which is the name of a captive mentioned several times in the correspondence.

Algiers. I am well aware that this Guillaume withdrew 500 or 600 livres which you transmitted to him three or four years ago. That is what he used for his ransom, along with about 30 piastres that the Mathurin Father gave him, but those 189 livres were sent to M. Delespiney only five or six months ago.

I would be glad to know how long ago the Franciscans were expelled from Marseilles and why. We must entrust ourselves to God for whatever He will ordain for your house and garden.

I am taking the honor of writing to the Bishop of Montpellier[6] by this regular mail, in accordance with your advice. If you have a safe way to send 20 écus to Algiers to our Brother B[arreau] or to M. Le Vacher, please do so, in order that they may be distributed to François de Lestang, a captive from Paris, a little at a time and not all at once for fear that his master may think he is better off than he actually is. Write to one or the other about this. Take these 20 écus from the collection money, which we will replace the next time we send you a bill of exchange.

I am, in the love of Our Lord, Monsieur, your most humble servant.

VINCENT DEPAUL,
i.s.C.M.

3113. - TO SISTER MATHURINE GUÉRIN, IN LA FÈRE

Paris, April 3, 1660

Dear Sister,

I received, dear Sister, a packet of letters from your area. I opened some of them to see if they contained any urgent matter.

---

[6]François de Bosquet.

Letter 3113. - Archives of the Motherhouse of the Daughters of Charity, *Recueil de pièces relatives aux Filles de la Charité,* p. 652.

Everything is peaceful here; our Sisters are giving edification and are satisfying the Ladies, thank God, by the union that is apparent among them, by their care, and by their good conduct. Continue to pray to God for them and for me. I can neither visit nor speak to them because of my bad legs, which oblige me to stay in my room; apart from that, however, I am very well.

I was consoled by your letter, seeing the good use you have made of our common loss [1] by relying on Our Lord alone, in whom you find all that He takes from you and all you can desire. God be praised, Sister, that He is the sole foundation of your hope! Furthermore, it is He who has called you to live of His life and to continue His work by the practice of charity. Therefore, Sister, have Him always in view so as to carry out your works according to His intentions, and form your entire interior life according to His example.

You can write to me about the difficulties in your work, which you say you have already presented to me but for which you have not yet received the solution. I will try to give you mine. I am, in the love of Our Lord. . . .

3114. - TO PIERRE DE BEAUMONT, SUPERIOR, IN RICHELIEU

April 4, 1660

It was a great consolation for me to hear that your ordinands departed content and deeply edified and that the Bishop of Poitiers [1] expressed his satisfaction to you about this. If he wants the ordination retreat to be held in Poitiers, and even to put the seminary there, he will please think about the means of doing so.

---

[1]The death of Saint Louise on March 15.

Letter 3114. - Reg. 2, p. 55.

[1]Gilbert de Clerambault de Palluau (1659-80).

It would have been well for you not to make any commitment about getting involved in having the Picariaux Collège because it is not fitting for us to make any such overtures. This Little Company has a maxim not to seek out any foundation nor to do anything toward that, so as not to work our own way in but to allow Providence to establish us in the places where we are; and, as a matter of fact, that is what we do.

3114a. - TO FIRMIN GET, SUPERIOR, IN MARSEILLES

Paris, April 9, 1660

Monsieur,

The grace of Our Lord be with you forever!

I received your letter of [March] 30. Since you think we should send five or six thousand livres to our confreres in Algiers on the safe boat that is being prepared, I am satisfied with that. I ask you to do so, then, in order to remedy their most urgent needs, despite the mistake of the Consul, which I mentioned to you, and our decision to send someone there to see that the money is not wasted.

I already told you that I had the honor of writing to the Bishop of Montpellier concerning your remaining in Marseilles. Since I did not offer him anyone to replace you, I await his reply to see if it is advisable to make this suggestion. I am worried about M. Parisy's illness; he has written me nothing about it. I am glad you asked M. Durand to go to see him; he will send us news of him and will perhaps let us know the Bishop's plans for his seminary and for the Company.

We received four silver écus [1] for a captive from Toulon named

---

Letter 3114a. - Copy made from *Recueil Nodet.* The letter was published in *Annales C.M.* (1943-44), p. 245, and reprinted in *Mission et Charité,* 19-20, no. 116, pp. 147-48. This edition uses the latter text.

[1]The silver écu was worth three livres at the time.

Armand Duval. I am writing to ask M. Huguier to give them to him. I am also asking him to give to a man named Richard, on the *Fiesque,* sixteen livres that have just been brought to us. A bill of exchange for six hundred livres from Messieurs Simonnet [2] is supposed to be sent today, or by the next regular mail, for two captives in Algiers named Lafortune and Champagne; it is for their small needs. If you receive them in time, please send them to Algiers on the first boat. That is what is written to you concerning the matter, and the letter is enclosed.

I am, in the love of Our Lord, Monsieur, your most humble servant.

VINCENT DEPAUL,
i.s.C.M.

I am writing to the Le Vacher brothers. Please send one hundred écus to the one in Tunis by the first opportunity; we have received them here from the Comtesse de Tonnerre[3] as reimbursement for a similar amount which he gave the Chevalier de Tonnerre. I will forward them to you when we have some other money to send you. I am informing M. Le Vacher that we are sending them to him.

---

[2]Parisian bankers, mentioned several times in Saint Vincent's correspondence.

[3]Marie Vignier (1603-79), wife of François de Clermont, Comte de Tonnerre, mother of Louis de Tonnerre, Knight of Malta, a galley Captain who was a captive in Tunis at the time.

3115. - *MADAME LE VAYER* [1] *TO SAINT VINCENT*

April 10, 1660

Live Jesus!

Monsieur,

Knowing that you like to exercise your charity, I take the liberty of giving you the opportunity to produce an important result from it by relieving the conscience of a person of rank. This person defers entirely to your opinion, which I entreat you to give with regard to a difficulty that is troubling her. In order to get an idea of it, please have the goodness and patience to listen to the summary I would like to give you in accord with my knowledge of it and the instructions given me.

It concerns, then, a lady of noble birth, highly esteemed for virtue and piety. She is thirty-nine years old and has been a widow for about ten or eleven years. She has retired from society to dedicate herself to works of charity and devotion; in this she is an example to the whole region. She has even withdrawn from the company of her male relatives, whom she sees only rarely.

For the past six or seven years her greatest consolation has come from a confessor and director, thirty-five years of age. She has grown under his guidance, and she esteems him highly for his virtue and merits because he is a man who lives apart from society, and is very spiritual, learned, and exemplary. He lives in conformity with his priestly state, as far as can be described, and is extremely conscientious, allowing not the slightest imperfection in her, guiding her always by what is most perfect. Moreover, he watches over the behavior of her children, the oldest of whom lives with him and profits greatly in the areas of learning and morals. All of this causes her to love this director tenderly and to have great confidence in him.

What distresses her is her fear that this warm friendship, which is reciprocal, may wound her conscience and become an obstacle to her perfection. She noticed too great a freedom in it this past year,[2] *when she came to see her director to thank him for the retreat he had her make in a*

Letter 3115. - Archives of the Mission, Turin, original signed letter.

[1]Renée Le Boindre, widow of René Le Vayer, Lieutenant General of Le Mans, Master of Requests for Anne of Austria.

[2]The section that follows and concludes with "but not intensely" was omitted by Coste.

convent. Because she had profited so well from it he welcomed her with such great joy that he kissed her chastely and without being forward. Still, the woman was a little surprised by this; it caused her to feel some scruple and, afterward, to be fearful of this familiarity, which she expressed to her director. Since then, he has not kissed her in that way. One day, four or five months later, however, while they were conversing, he was telling her about his vocation to the priesthood, and she felt such joy that, when they looked one another in the eye, they both experienced great sweetness and tenderness of heart, but this did not go beyond desire, although the woman was somewhat moved by it. No touching or caressing took place, just some tender words such as "my dear Father" and "my dear daughter."

A day or two later, while taking a walk together, they held hands and frequently repeated these same words. Another time, when she was saying good-bye to her director, who was going far away to a rural area, she expressed great tenderness for him and vice-versa, each kissing the other's hand. When he returned from the country, they did the same thing, embracing one another, without kissing one another or touching the face.

That caused her some scruple and she said so to her director, so they decided to refrain from such caresses for fear that God might be offended by them because their senses were aroused on these occasions. Since that time these have been moderate—expressed simply by a few tender glances or by holding hands lightly—especially because, when her director saw that she was a little ill at ease and in a state that did not allow her to lift her heart so strongly to God as formerly, he did not talk to her so constantly about God but tried to give her some consolation by the sweetness of their friendship. He did this simply, in the presence of her family, when she asked him to come and see her with her oldest son. And I think he made these visits to her out of some kind of compassion because she had no human consolation but that.

Now, Monsieur, please note that in all these acts of tenderness, neither he nor she has ever felt any harmful effects of sensual desire in the will, and their minds have always remained free, even though they may have experienced afterward some slight physical reaction that could have resulted from natural weakness, which they avoided whenever they were able to foresee it. She has acknowledged, however, that in the midst of these acts of tenderness, her senses were often aroused, but not intensely.

She is troubled about loving a person so tenderly. In addition, she has often resolved to correct herself of this weakness because her conscience reproaches her; yet, she has not been faithful in avoiding these occasions, nor in watching over the details of her conversations, although she does not experience violent passion, but only a simple desire to see and talk with him.

She mentioned this to a preacher this Eastertide. He advised her to leave her director, believing that God was asking this of her. She does not know what to do. Her director promises that he will never touch her but will direct her more firmly. She fears her own weakness, knowing that she has broken her resolutions. To reassure her, her director told her that the preacher did not see any sin in this, and that he knows her simplicity and sincerity. He told her also to have no fear for the future because he has made up his mind and has promised her that he will speak to her only in church or in the presence of others, and if not, she should leave him. He points out to her that it is to her advantage to remain under the same direction, because it would be difficult for another director to understand the state of her conscience. She is aware—or at least so it seems to her—that there are many reasons why she should not change directors, since she does not know anyone suited to her needs and she fears, with good reason, to be left on her own.

As for her director, she knows he is a very chaste man, who has never wanted to direct or hear the confession of a woman in whom he remarked an inordinate attachment to him. Furthermore, she has never noticed anything, either in the confessional or outside of it, which is not holy and tending toward what is most perfect (what is more, as far as confession is concerned, she has never experienced any emotional feelings or tenderness, having in view nothing but to make her confession to God in his person).

Nevertheless, what the preacher told her and advised her to do is giving her qualms of conscience, even though she is not so sure of his advice because he did not say the same thing nor give the same advice to her director, who earnestly begged him to tell him what he thought so that he could follow it and profit from it. She thinks he is a simple, upright man, who wants to follow what is good, really mistrusts his own weakness in this situation, and ardently desires to remedy it, for he loves and seeks God, and there is nothing wrong in this.

Please note that he knows the character of this lady; she is a little overbearing and inclined to harshness and insensitivity, and this fault is an obstacle to the good she could do. To soften this harshness, he showed some affection toward her, and did so all the more freely, being aware of her innocence and simplicity.

This is the reason, Monsieur, why I have taken the liberty of writing to you, imploring you most humbly to do this lady the charity of putting her conscience at ease by expressing your opinion. She wants to abide by it and to submit herself confidently to it because she esteems your virtue.

Should your conclusion be that she should take another person as director, I have, in that case, one more question to ask you and want to call to your attention the fact that her director is the Pastor of the parish in which she lives. He also directs several persons in this parish, in which there are some persons of rank, and even does a great deal of good in the confessional. Since she is one of the most prominent parishioners, she is fearful of harming his reputation and of dissuading others from profiting from his direction and of making some judgment that might be prejudicial to his innocence.

She asks you, then, Monsieur, whether she might sometimes go to confession to him, so as to do away with any occasion of gossip. She will patiently await your decision and most humbly implores you not to disregard her.

I ask your pardon for obliging you to read such a long letter, but I believe that this person could never be at rest if I did not tell you the details of her difficulties. Once again, I ask you to forgive me, in the name of Our Lord Jesus Christ, and to believe that I am, most respectfully, Monsieur, your most humble, obedient, and grateful servant.

R. LE BOINDRE,
widow of the late Lieutenant General of Le Mans

If you do me the honor of writing to me—which I beg you once again to do—please send your letter through the Fathers of the Mission, with the recommendation that they deliver it to me by some sure way.

Addressed: *Monsieur Vincent, Superior General of the Priests of the Mission, at Saint-Lazare, in Paris*

3116. - TO EDME JOLLY, SUPERIOR, IN ROME

April 16, 1660

We should receive the instructions of Cardinal Durazzo as orders from heaven and do, without hesitation, whatever he commands. The benevolence with which he honors the Company is a great blessing for it, by which God makes us frequently call to mind

Letter 3116. - Reg. 2, p. 253.

the effects of His adorable goodness. But what I admire most, and for which I cannot sufficiently thank Our Lord or this holy Cardinal, is that he is willing to enter into the details of our minor affairs and takes an interest in the most insignificant matters as well as the most important ones.

3116a. - TO FIRMIN GET, SUPERIOR, IN MARSEILLES

Paris, April 16, 1660

Monsieur,

The grace of Our Lord be with you forever!

I received your letter of the sixth together with the packets from Algiers and Tunis. I had thought that, if the boat that was being prepared for Algiers went there without taking anything to our Missionaries, they would be too greatly distressed and inconvenienced by this. For that reason I asked you in my last letter to send them only 5,000 or 6,000 livres until the time when we could send someone there. Now you tell me that the plan for the boat has changed because of the rumor circulating about equipping the ships. It certainly seems that, in these circumstances, it is good to suspend everything. Nevertheless, if you find a way to get some assistance to them safely, I leave that to your prudence.

I am hoping to send you by this regular mail a bill of exchange for 2,000 livres from Messieurs Simonnet on Messieurs Napollon,[1]

Letter 3116a. - Archives of the Motherhouse of the Daughters of Charity, original signed letter, published with the format and spelling of the original in *Annales C.M.* (1952), pp. 511-12. A copy of this letter forms part of *Recueil Nodet*, and was published in *Annales C.M.* (1943-44), pp. 246-47. A comparison of the two texts enables us to verify the authenticity of copies made from *Recueil Nodet*; the latter is substantially exact, differing from the original only in minor details--the evident consequence of faulty readings. This edition uses the text published in *Mission et Charité*, 19-20, no. 117, pp. 148-49.

[1]Jean and Louis Napollon, bankers in Marseilles; as with Messieurs Simonnet, their name appears often in the correspondence of Saint Vincent.

of which 1,500 livres are for the living expenses of the men in Algiers or in Tunis, received from the coaches last year.[2] If you have the opportunity to send them to Tunis rather than to Algiers, please do so. We hope to be receiving soon the other 1,500 livres and will then send them to you to be forwarded to whichever place you did not send the first payment.

As for the 500 livres remaining, here is how you will use them: first, get 300 livres, which we received here from the Comtesse de Tonnerre and which I asked you to send to M. Le Vacher in Tunis in reimbursement for a similar amount he gave to the Chevalier de Tonnerre. Second, get 60 livres, which we received here from the Parisian, François de Lestang, a captive in Algiers, and please send them to M. [J.] Le Vacher or the Consul to be distributed to him little by little. Third, get 33 livres, which I ask you to send also to Algiers to be given to the valet of the Comte d'Insiquin,[3] who is an Irish lord recently taken as a captive together with his son, and to the two young noblemen from Normandy, named Lafortune and Champagne, for whom the Marquise de Nantouillet,[4] the mother of the first named, sent you a bill of exchange for 600 livres last week. I am informing M. Le Vacher of all these sums and their destination. Lastly, take from the above-mentioned 500 livres the 107 livres to be deducted from what we owe you from the advances made to the captives.

Please send us the account of this and mention in it the 107 livres. I am writing to tell M. Huguier to give 30 sous to Jacques Fournier, known as La Rivière, a captive on the *Saint-Dominique*.

---

[2]The Congregation of the Mission had ownership and/or use of the revenues of a number of coachlines in France. The revenues helped to defray the expenses of certain houses or specific works, including those of the Missionaries working in Algiers and Tunis.

[3]Murrough O'Brien, (1614-74) sixth Baron of Inchiquin, was a notoriously anti-Catholic military leader in Ireland in the 1640s; he had previously served in the Spanish army in Italy. In 1650 he went to France and, as indicated here, fell into the hands of the Barbary pirates. On his release from captivity in Algiers, he settled in London, where he became a Catholic. He returned to Ireland toward the end of his life.

[4]Louise d'Aguesseau, second wife of Henri du Prat, Marquis de Nantouillet.

I praise God for the missions you are planning to give, and I ask Our Lord to bless them.

Take from the strongbox whatever you will need for the expenses of your family;[5] with God's help we will replace it. Keep an account of everything.

I am, in the love of Our Lord, Monsieur, your most humble servant.

VINCENT DEPAUL,
i.s.C.M.

Addressed: Monsieur Get, Superior of the Priests of the Mission, in Marseilles

3117. - *EDME JOLLY, SUPERIOR, IN ROME, TO SAINT VINCENT*

[April or May 1660] [1]

With regard to the Bishop of Plasencia the Spanish Ambassador,[2] *God has granted us the grace, as you desired, Monsieur, not to return to him since the time he asked us to go there so he could have the notes on the ordination retreat. And, in line with your orders, we will take no further steps in this matter nor in any other, with the help of God, to seek out any work or put ourselves forward. Even if we were urged to do so, we would always submit everything for your reply and decision, since we cannot do otherwise.*

---

[5]This sentence obviously refers to the confreres of the Marseilles house.

Letter 3117. - Abelly, *op. cit.,* bk. II, chap. II, sect. VI, p. 241.

[1]This letter is a response to no. 3112, dated April 2.

[2]Luis Crespi de Borja.

3118. - TO GABRIEL DELESPINEY, IN MARSEILLES

Paris, April 30, 1660

Monsieur,

The grace of Our Lord be with you forever!

I have not written you for a long time. Still, I had a great desire to do so but was prevented by my miseries. God be praised, Monsieur, for the mission you gave in Vins and the graces His Divine Goodness granted the people there through you. I can imagine how the language problem distressed you.[1] It is always hard in the beginning but gradually [2] it becomes manageable, and nothing should stop a worker of the Gospel from practicing the virtues proper to his state and from seeking to advance everywhere and in all things the glory of his Master.

I am consoled by your courage and patience, and I hope God will continue to bless your work and truly edify the family by your example. I ask Our Lord, Monsieur, to give you perfect health.

We have no news here, except for the consecration of a Bishop, which took place in our church recently. Another one will take place on the feast of the Ascension, God willing. The first was for the Bishop of Oloron[3] and the second will be for the Bishop of Chalon-sur-Saône.[4] We are expecting the Abbés de Chandenier, who are returning from Rome, and, in the absence of M. Get, we

---

Letter 3118. - Copy made from *Recueil Nodet.* The letter was published in *Annales C.M.* (1943-44), pp. 247-48, and reprinted in *Mission et Charité,* 19-20, no. 118, p. 150. This edition uses the latter text, replacing the much shorter one from the Marseilles manuscript, which Coste used.

[1]Delespiney, a native of Normandy, was doubtless unfamiliar with the Provençal dialect commonly spoken in the region where Vins was located.

[2]The Coste version of no. 3118, taken from the Marseilles manuscript, begins here, with "gradually," and goes only to the end of the paragraph.

[3]Armand-François de Maytie, Bishop of Oloron (1659-81), was consecrated on April 11, 1660.

[4]Jean de Maupeou, Bishop of Chalon-sur-Saône, was consecrated on May 9, 1660.

are expecting a little news from you about the state of public affairs, especially concerning the equipping of the ships people are talking about.

I am, in the love of Our Lord, Monsieur, your most humble servant.

VINCENT DEPAUL,
i.s.C.M.

3119. - TO SISTER MATHURINE GUÉRIN, IN LA FÈRE

May 1, 1660

Dear Sister,

The grace of O[ur] L[ord] be with you forever!

As soon as you receive this letter, please prepare to come here on the first coach; an important establishment is to be made in Brittany,[1] and we need you for it. Give the Sister who is with you[2] whatever information you think advisable so she can keep things going until we send her a companion, which will be done soon after your arrival, with the help of God.

Recommend me to her prayers, as I recommend myself to yours. I ask Our Lord to continue to grant you His protection and His grace.

I am. . . .

Letter 3119. - Archives of the Motherhouse of the Daughters of Charity, *Recueil de pièces relatives aux Filles de la Charité,* p. 499.

[1]The hospital on Belle-Île-en-Mer (cf. no. 3000, n. 2).

[2]Julienne Allot.

3120. - TO PIERRE DE BEAUMONT, SUPERIOR, IN RICHELIEU

Paris, May 2, 1660

Monsieur,

The grace of O[ur] L[ord] be with you forever!

I have received three or four letters from you, the last of which is dated April 21. I am glad you have welcomed Brother Labeille[1] and that he is disposed to do some good. May God grant him the grace for it!

As for Brother Servin, if you have the opportunity to send him to Saint-Méen, fine! do so, but tell him beforehand to correct the particular faults you have remarked in him, to ask God's grace for that, and to be attentive about them.

God be praised that you have admitted to the seminary M. Lorfebvre and the Irish cleric sent to you by M. Barry, and that both are taking so well to the seminary exercises! [2]

We have more Brothers than we need, and we cannot at present admit the young pharmacist you mention. That is why I ask you to put him off to some other time.

I have forwarded your letter to M. Le Bret. With God's help, I will pay attention to what M. Tholard told me on your part, and I hope you will see the results of it shortly.

We will follow your advice concerning the Daughters of Charity; at least we will send for two of them and will be sending you one of them soon, God willing.

We are in the same difficulty as you as far as having priests in the seminary to be formed for preaching. We have only one, but he is not suitable for that.

Letter 3120. - Archives of the Mission, Turin, original signed letter.

[1]Philippe Labeille, born in Luçon, entered the Congregation of the Mission in Paris as a coadjutor Brother on March 30, 1644, at twenty-five years of age, took his vows on May 27, 1647, and renewed them in 1656.

[2]Neither of these aspirants is listed in the personnel catalogue, vol. V (Supplement), of *Notices.*

I have forwarded to M. Serre[3] the letter you wrote him, but not the letter sent to M. Duporzo by M. de Lestang.[4] I have held it back because it was written to persuade him to enter the Company, and we have a maxim to the contrary, namely, never to urge anyone to embrace our state. It is for God alone to choose those whom He wishes to call to it, and we are sure that one Missionary given by His fatherly hand will do more good by himself than many others who would not have a true vocation. It is up to us to ask Him to send good workers into His harvest[5] and to live so well that we will give them, by our example, an attraction rather than a distaste for working with us.

I am, in the love of O[ur] L[ord], Monsieur, your most humble servant.

VINCENT DEPAUL,
i.s.C.M.

At the bottom of the first page: Monsieur de Beaumont

3121. - *THOMAS BERTHE TO SAINT VINCENT*

[Chambéry, May 4, 1660]

I informed you of the serious illness of M. de Chandenier, Abbé de Tournus; now I shall tell you, Monsieur, that God was pleased to call him

---

[3]Louis Serre, born in Épinal (Vosges), was ordained a priest in September 1643. He entered the Congregation of the Mission on March 23, 1644, at the age of twenty-six, and took his vows in July 1646. His first assignment was Crécy, where he was Superior (1646-48); from there he was sent to Saint-Méen, where he spent all his life as a missionary, including his years as Superior (1655-65, 1671-75, and 1676-81).

[4]Jean de Lestang, born in the Poitiers diocese on October 28, 1632, entered the Congregation of the Mission as a priest and took his vows on July 10, 1660, in the presence of M. Alméras. *Notices,* vols. I and V (Supplement), lists him as *Delestang.*

[5]Cf. Mt 9:37-38. (NAB)

Letter 3121. - Abelly, *op. cit.,* bk. I, chap. XLIX, p. 241.

to Himself yesterday, May 3, about five o'clock in the evening.[1] *His death was like his life—I mean very holy. I will write you the details at another time because I am too busy right now. Let me tell you simply, Monsieur, that he implored me so earnestly several times on different days to receive him among the Missionaries and to give him the consolation of dying as a member of the body of the Congregation of the Mission, which he wanted to enter, that I could not refuse him. Nor could I refuse to give him the cassock of a Missionary, which he received in the presence of his brother, Abbé de Moutiers-Saint-Jean.*[2]

3122. - TO LOUIS RIVET, SUPERIOR, IN SAINTES

May 9, 1660

You are worried about what you will have to do and say, in the event that the King visits you. I do not think you will have this honor; [1] however, you can find out from the Chaplain-in-Ordinary to the Queen Mother, M. de Saint-Jean, who is a good friend of ours, or from some of the King's almoners, who are going ahead of His Majesty and will arrive in Saintes before him, the usual method of receiving him in a private home, such as yours, where I do not think that any formal speech is made.

If, however, you are advised to make one, I am sending you a copy of the rough draft of the one I am sending to Richelieu. The Court may pass through there and go to the parish; since it is served by our priests, they will therefore be obliged to welcome Their Majesties with the proper formalities and to address them. Take from this model whatever you think suitable, and try to speak as briefly and as calmly as you can.

---

[1]Louis de Chandenier had been imprudent enough to leave Rome although he was shivering with fever. The fatigue of the journey was too much for him.

[2]Claude de Chandenier.

Letter 3122. - Reg. 2, p. 115.

[1]Saintes did not receive the visit of the King, but of his bride-to-be, Maria Teresa, the Infanta of Spain. She and the King were married on June 9, 1660, in Saint-Jean-de-Luz.

We have several Prelates here and a large number of people because the Bishop of Chalon-sur-Saône[2] was consecrated this morning in our church; the Bishop of Oloron[3] was also consecrated there recently.

3123. - TO CLAUDE LE PELLETIER [1]

[1655 or later] [2]

Monsieur,

The grace of Our Lord be with you forever!

I blush with shame, seeing that it has been two years since you ordered us to admit a poor old woman into the little hospice of the Nom-de-Jésus. I am so wretched that I forgot about it. I ask your forgiveness and do so most humbly with all the devotedness in my power.

The present vacancy has arisen from the death of a man whom Abbé de Brisacier had placed there in virtue of a foundation that one of his brothers had set up for the maintenance of six poor persons and which the Abbé had thought to make in this little hospice. However, its founder did not approve of this and instructed me to dismiss those six persons; I am responsible for informing him of this and for removing the three other poor persons who remain.

---

[2]Jean de Maupeou.

[3]Armand-François de Maytie (1659-81).

Letter 3123. - Reg. 1, fol. 7, copy made from the original autograph letter.

[1]Claude Le Pelletier, born in Paris in 1630, was to become Provost of Merchants in 1668, Councillor of State, successor to Jean-Baptiste Colbert in the ministry of finance, and Superintendent of the postal service in 1691; he died in Paris on August 10, 1711. (Cf. Jean Boivin, *Claudii Peleteri . . . vita. . . .* (Paris: F. Jouenne, 1716.) He often saw Saint Vincent at the Louvre, admired his prudence, and recognized the esteem in which he was held at the Court. He testified to all this before the tribunal in charge of the canonical enquiry for the process of beatification.

[2]The reference to the hospice of the Nom-de-Jésus, founded in March 1653, prompts us to assign this date.

Accordingly, there is no vacancy; but I beg you with all the affection of my heart not to renounce sending us this good woman. It does not matter if she is extra; a place will soon be vacant and we will gladly give it to her. So, I entreat you, Monsieur, to send her as soon as possible and to believe that I am, in the love of Our Lord and of His Holy Mother, your most humble and very obedient servant.

VINCENT DEPAUL,
i.s.C.M.

3124. - *EDME JOLLY, SUPERIOR IN ROME, TO SAINT VINCENT*

May 1660

I think I should inform you, Monsieur, of some opposition that has arisen recently with regard to continuing the ordination retreats. First, the Cardinal Vicar informed me a while ago that another Community had asked to give these retreats and that the ordinands be sent to it and not to us—which His Eminence had absolutely refused to do. Someone else had already told me of this request and also which Community it was.

Second, I have already been informed that, during the last examination held before ordination, Father . . . had stated that, since many upperclass persons were presenting themselves for ordination in Rome, it was no longer possible to continue to oblige them to make the Mission retreat and that he was going to place the matter before the Pope. Now, I have heard that it was mentioned to him and that everything possible was done to persuade him to no longer oblige the ordinands to come here. His Holiness, however, who was well aware of what was being done at the ordination retreats, took no notice of these remonstrances and remained firm in his original decision. This is the proof, Monsieur, that we have the grace of clearly depending on the protection of Our Lord and of His holy Mother.

Letter 3124. - Abelly, *op. cit.*, bk. II, chap. II, sect. VI, p. 242.

3125. - TO EDME JOLLY, SUPERIOR, IN ROME

May 14, 1660

It is a good idea not to anticipate your works. It is more in harmony with our insignificance to await rather than anticipate them, and discreet zeal is not contrary to this restraint.

3126. - TO THE SUPERIORS

1660

If your house has not already done so, please have a list compiled of all the missions that will be given in that place in the future, as well as those that have been given, indicating as clearly as possible the following particulars: 1) the number of missions given by your house since its establishment; 2) the month and year of each; 3) the place and diocese of each mission, and whether you have any that are obligatory and from a foundation; 4) the distance of the place from the town in which your house is established; 5) how many communicants there were; 6) the number of workers and the person in charge; 7) the length of time the mission lasted; 8) whether or not it was successful, and the reason why; 9) the best time to give a mission; 10) whether the Confraternity of Charity was established in the place; 11) whether there are any heretics; 12) the places in your diocese and the surrounding area that are most neglected and in greatest need of a mission; and any other important details.

This should be done mainly with the future in mind, recording exactly, on returning from each mission, all the above-mentioned details. As for the past, if you cannot compile everything, after sufficient care has been given to this for some time, you must still write it up as best you can. To get a better idea of what missions

---

Letter 3125. - Reg. 2, p. 60.

Letter 3126. - Archives of the Mission, Paris, collection of circular letters (1877-80).

have been given in the past, simply examine the ledger of house expenditures and others, and consult persons within and outside the Company who might have knowledge of them.

With a little care you can manage to do this, even if it has been entirely neglected. Before writing up past ones in a book designated for that purpose, it is advisable to keep a rough copy of them for a while, until they can be set down in the best possible order. It will even be advisable to leave a wide margin in the large register in order to insert anything of importance, if need be.

3127. - TO PIERRE DE BEAUMONT, SUPERIOR, IN RICHELIEU

May 19, 1660

I am not sending you the certified copy of the tax exemption privileges because I doubt if you could use it; in addition, I certainly do not think you should farm the land yourself because that is not our job. Instead of gaining something you would be wasting your time for want of having well-informed, vigilant, thrifty coadjutor Brothers who are used to doing the work.

We know this from experience; we are losing something by working the land here and on another farm, although we have some coadjutor Brothers who are very suited for this; and if we were not already engaged in it, we would not take it on. So you will do well to find some farmers and not burden yourself with the problems and equipment involved in farming.

Letter 3127. - Reg. 2, p. 189.

3128. - TO GABRIEL DELESPINEY, IN MARSEILLES

Paris, May 21, 1660

Monsieur,

The grace of Our Lord be with you forever!

I praise God that you have received the 2,000 livres and have an opportunity to send 1,500 to Tunis. I am glad M. Parisy is in Marseilles, and I embrace him there wholeheartedly. I would really like to leave him there, but the Archbishop of Narbonne[1] made me promise to send him to him. So, I ask him to be ready to leave as soon as we give him notice.

I cannot write either to him or to M. Cornier today, as I had planned. I have been overwhelmed with business all day long and now it is night. I cannot even write to you, Monsieur, other than briefly and in haste. I am thinking about you and your difficulties and the remedy you are considering. Please be patient a little longer, however; remember that distaste and discouragement are products of the poor nature we take with us wherever we go and that we must abandon ourselves to the Spirit of Our Lord in order to bear with ourselves and overcome our timidity, laziness, and other weaknesses. I ask this Sanctifying and Holy Spirit to animate you with His strength and to shower His blessings upon you.

I am, in His love, Monsieur, your most humble servant.

VINCENT DEPAUL,
i.s.C.M.

Letter 3128. - Copy made from *Recueil Nodet.* The letter was published in *Annales C.M.* (1943-44), p. 248, and reprinted in *Mission et Charité,* 19-20, no. 119, p. 151. This edition uses the latter text. The text from "remember that distaste" to the end of the paragraph, taken from the Marseilles manuscript, is what Coste used for no. 3128.

[1]François Fouquet.

3129. - TO N.

May 21, 1660

Referring to the grief of Claude de Chandenier, whose brother had just died, Vincent de Paul writes:

". . . He is inconsolable at the loss he has sustained, and all of us are overwhelmed by it. God's Will, however, is above our grief and the sorrowful sentiments he is experiencing."

3130. - *EDME JOLLY, SUPERIOR, IN ROME, TO SAINT VINCENT*

[1660] [1]

Some of the Cardinals and other Prelates came to listen to the conferences. Among the ordinands were various persons of rank and merit. They included Cardinal Mancini's nephew, a Canon of Saint John Lateran, and another from Saint Peter's, named Count Marescotti, as well as other notables, since the Pope remains firm in being unwilling to excuse anyone from attending these exercises.

3131. - TO SISTER MATHURINE GUÉRIN, SISTER SERVANT, IN LA FÈRE

Paris, May 22, 1660

Dear Sister,

I have not answered your letters because I was hoping that you would be coming here, and I have not pressured you to leave

---

Letter 3129. - Collet, *op. cit.*, vol. II, p. 79.

Letter 3130. - Abelly, *op. cit.*, bk. II, chap. II, sect. VI, p. 240.

[1]Reference in the letter to Cardinal Mancini allows us to assign this date. Francesco Maria Mancini was appointed Cardinal on April 5, 1660, and died in Rome on June 18, 1672. His elder brother had married one of Mazarin's sisters.

Letter 3131. - Archives of the Motherhouse of the Daughters of Charity, *Recueil de pièces relatives aux Filles de la Charité*, p. 499.

because I did not know whether you could tolerate the journey. God be praised for your telling me in your last letter that you can! I am consoled by your present condition; so, come, Sister, by the first favorable opportunity.

Please tell the Sister who is with you[1] to keep things going as best she can, while awaiting another Sister whom we will send her soon, God willing. We will try to select one such as you describe. There is no need for you to stop at Saint-Quentin; come directly here. I ask Our Lord to bring you safely here and to be the object of your thoughts and the rule of your actions.

I recommend myself. . . .

3132. - TO SISTER MARGUERITE CHÉTIF, SISTER SERVANT, IN ARRAS

May 24, 1660

Dear Sister,

My ailments and my usual business affairs are my excuse for not answering your letter sooner. Reply to that good young woman[1] who wants to be assured she can stay for life before entering your Company, that this cannot be done, that no one among you has yet been given this assurance, and that it will not be given to any women who enter, for fear that, slackening in their duties, they may become a source of scandal and make themselves unworthy of the grace of their vocation. If this misfortune should befall some

---

[1]Julienne Allot.

Letter 3132. - *Conférences spirituelles tenues pour les Filles de la Charité par saint Vincent de Paul,* ed. Jean Grappin (Paris: Adrien Le Clère, 1845), vol. I, p. 639, letter 10.

[1]Jeanne de Buire, born in Arras on February 28, 1636, entered the Daughters of Charity on June 16, 1660. After several years at the Hennebont Hospital, she was named Sister Servant in Bléré, where she died on August 8, 1686, having given the example of the most beautiful virtues. (Cf. *Circulaires des supérieurs généraux et des soeurs supérieures,* vol. II, p. 388; see also, *Documents,* Doc. 797, p. 913.)

misguided person, is it not reasonable to amputate the gangrenous member so that it does not infect the others?

Still, Sister, you know that very rarely do we dismiss anyone and then only for serious faults—never for ordinary shortcomings, nor even extraordinary ones, unless they are frequent and conspicuous. Furthermore, we do it only as a last resort, after having borne with these failings for a long time and having tried in vain to apply remedies to correct the person. This charity is practiced especially toward those who are not exactly newcomers and still more with regard to older members. Therefore, if many leave, they do so on their own volition, or from want of reflection, or because, they are remiss and tepid in God's service, so God Himself vomits and rejects them[2] before Superiors even think of dismissing them.

By the grace of God, those who are faithful to God and submissive to holy obedience do not leave the Company, and this can be said of those who are in good health as well as those who are ailing. The utmost is done to keep everyone, and all possible care is taken of both until they die.

If, then, that good young woman from Arras is willing to be determined to enter your Company and to remain in it until death, she will likewise be treated with great kindness; but please tell her that it is up to her to assure her vocation by good works, according to the advice of the Apostle Saint Peter,[3] and that, in order to do so, she must rely on God alone and expect from Him the grace of perseverance. If she is looking for this assurance from human beings, she is probably seeking something other than God. In that case you must let her be and not worry about her any longer.

I am sure, dear Sister, that you were deeply affected by the loss of your dear mother.[4] But, God be blessed! You have told Him that He did well in taking her from you and that you would not want it any other way. As yet, you do not have another Superioress.[5]

---

[2]Cf. Rev 3:16. (NAB)

[3]Cf. 2 Pt 1:10. (NAB)

[4]The death of Saint Louise on March 15, 1660.

[5]Cf. no. 3100, n. 3.

We have appointed M. Dehorgny as Director in the place of the late M. Portail; he is the eldest of our priests, and one of the gentlest, wisest, and most strongly attached to your little Institute.

Sister Jeanne Gressier, who assisted our dear deceased, continues in her duty of house Assistant and is responsible for the other houses. I think everyone is satisfied and everything is going along smoothly in the city and in the rural areas, thank God. Yet, you thought all was lost; but, since His Divine Goodness has begun and given growth to the Charity,[6] you must hope that He will sustain and perfect it. Your prayers and good example will contribute to this, with the help of God. Yes, Sister, I hope that, by acting as true Daughters of Charity, as you have done up to the present, you will invite Our Lord effectively to bless and multiply the work of His hands[7] for the relief and salvation of His poor members, who are our masters.

I say the same to Sister Radegonde,[8] to whom I send greetings, and I hope for the same from all the Sisters who have good will.

---

[6]To prevent the early Daughters of Charity from being considered nuns and therefore bound to a cloistered life, Saint Vincent and Saint Louise organized them as a Confraternity.

[7]Cf. Ps 90:17. (NAB)

[8]Radegonde Lenfantin was sent to Arras on August 30, 1656. Born around 1637, she entered the Company of the Daughters of Charity in 1653. In September 1660, after the departure of Sister Marguerite Chétif, who had been named Superioress General, she went through a period of discouragement and left Arras. She returned, however, and died as a Daughter of Charity (cf. no. 3288, n. 1). In 1705 and 1713, she testified at the beatification process of Saint Vincent (cf. *Documents,* Doc. 663, n. 2).

3133. - TO GUILLAUME DESDAMES, SUPERIOR, IN WARSAW

Paris, May 28, 1660

Monsieur,

The grace of O[ur] L[ord] be with you forever!

I received your letter of April 31,[1] which consoled me all the more because it is rather long. I was pleased to see the state of your temporal affairs and the remedies you have applied to the bodily and spiritual needs of your village. You did well to change its treasurer and to have the old parish buildings repaired, since this had to be done and you foresaw that it was beneficial. Continue to let us know from time to time how things are going; they can only go from good to better if God is pleased to confirm the peace which you tell me has been concluded there. God be praised for this, Monsieur! I feel inexpressible joy about this and about the health and return of the King and Queen. May His Divine Goodness be pleased to give them and all their Estates a complete and lasting peace!

It is to be desired, Monsieur, that the union of the Vitkiski benefice be effected as soon as possible, while God is pleased to preserve Their Majesties for us. As for how to do it, here is the procedure followed in France for unions: the titular of the benefice resigns it to the Bishop or to the Pope, to be united to the Company; after this resignation, the consent of the patron and other interested parties—if there be any—is obtained, particularly that of the Bishop when the union is effected in Rome. When it is effected by the Bishop himself, it is confirmed by the Holy See; next, letters patent are obtained from the King who consents to and authorizes this union; then these letters are registered in the Parlement. The motive for the union may be the establishment of a seminary whose

---

Letter 3133. - Archives of the Mission, Krakow, original signed letter.

[1]This is the date given in the original; therefore, since April has only thirty days, it is either an error of Brother Ducournau the secretary or is the date M. Desdames mistakenly wrote in his letter to Saint Vincent. Perhaps it should read April 30 or 21.

perpetual direction is granted to the Company, but the union is made to the Company itself. Let me know if the custom there is similar to or different from that of France, and in what respect it differs.

We will try to keep ready the persons you are expecting and will have them leave as near as possible to the time you indicate on behalf of the Queen, whose orders you wish to take.

I greet good M. Duperroy most cordially and recommend to his prayers and yours the soul of the late Abbé de Chandenier,[2] who died in Savoy on his way back from Rome. He was a person of rank and a nephew of the late Cardinal de la Rochefoucauld. A man of outstanding piety, he had retired here about five or six years ago, along with his brother, Abbé de Moutiers-Saint-Jean,[3] who traveled from Rome with him and returned here a few days ago with M. Berthe and another priest of the Company who accompanied them.

The dear deceased was very detached from creatures, very humble and mortified, very deeply recollected and interior, very cheerful, discerning, and exemplary, totally given to God, and most zealous for the advancement of the priesthood; in short, we see no one else like him. He is a great loss to the Church and a very great loss to this house, which he edified marvelously. This evening we are supposed to discuss his admirable virtues,[4] which are rather the virtues of Our Lord, practiced by Him in this servant of His.

This will cause you to ask if he was a Missionary. I will reply that he was one in affection for a very long time, but, since we were most unworthy to have such a Prelate as a confrere, we did not receive him into the Company until a day or two before his death. At that time he requested this so earnestly that we had to give him

---

[2]Louis de Chandenier.

[3]Claude de Chandenier.

[4]The conference of May 28 did not suffice; it was followed by three others on June 4, 18, and 25, none of which is extant, although the summary of remarks on the Abbé's virtues has been preserved for us. (Cf. *Notices,* vol. II, pp. 515-39; also, André Dodin, ed., *Entretiens spirituels de Saint Vincent de Paul à ses missionaires* [Paris: Éditions du Seuil, 1960], p. 1086).

that consolation. His body was taken to our little chapel in Annecy. All that God does is well done; without this faith, we would be inconsolable at such a loss.

I am, in the love of O[ur] L[ord], Monsieur, your most humble servant.

VINCENT DEPAUL,
i.s.C.M.

At the bottom of the first page: Monsieur Desdames

3134. - TO JEAN MARTIN, SUPERIOR, IN TURIN

Paris, May 28, 1660

Monsieur,

The grace of O[ur] L[ord] be with you forever!

Your letter of the seventh found us mourning the death of Abbé de Chandenier, which occurred in Chambéry, as you may have heard. This is a great loss for the Church and a very great one for us. He lived like a saint and died a Missionary, for he begged to be received into the Company in accord with the affection he had long conceived for it. That is why this house, which was edified by him for such a long time, is to hold a conference on his virtues this evening in order to revive his memory and example. His brother has arrived here with Messieurs Berthe and Théroude[1] and is very much grieved, as you can imagine.

I am deeply consoled to learn from you that you have shaken off the fever again and are with our dear confreres in Bene.[2] With all

---

Letter 3134. - Archives of the Mission, Turin, original signed letter.

[1]Toussaint Théroude, born in Guilmécourt (Seine-Maritime) on January 9, 1633, entered the Paris Seminary on October 27, 1657, and took his vows in Rome on December 10, 1659, in the presence of M. Jolly. He was Superior in Amiens (1670-75).

[2]Bene Vagienna, a town in Piedmont.

the tenderness of my heart, I thank God for this, Monsieur, and for the blessings He has bestowed on their work, and I ask Him to give all of you strength of body and the grace of the Spirit to procure His glory in whatever way He asks of the Company. To do so, please take good care of yourself, Monsieur, and recommend the same thing on my part to those priests who are working so zealously with you.

We have no news here. Everyone is very well. True, I am suffering somewhat from my bad legs, which no longer allow me to move from any place except with great difficulty.

I am, in the love of O[ur] L[ord], Monsieur, your most humble servant.

VINCENT DEPAUL,
i.s.C.M.

Addressed: Monsieur Martin, Superior of the Priests of the Mission of Turin, in Turin

3134a. - TO FIRMIN GET, SUPERIOR, IN MARSEILLES

Paris, May 28, 1660

Monsieur,

The grace of Our Lord be with you forever!

I am writing to you, even though I have not received any letters from you, because M. Delespiney tells me that you should be back in Marseilles after the Pentecost feast days. I am forwarding to you a bill of exchange for 1,903 livres on Messieurs Napollon; send 1,500 livres of this to Algiers for the living expenses of our

---

Letter 3134a. - Copy made from *Recueil Nodet.* The letter was published in *Annales C.M.* (1943-44), pp. 248-49, and reprinted in *Mission et Charité,* 19-20, no. 120, pp. 151-52. This edition uses the latter text.

confreres, and please keep the other 403 livres for the needs of your house.

A few weeks ago, I asked you to send either to Tunis or to Algiers another 1,500 livres of the 2,000 that I entrusted to you about two months ago. Now, since you have not yet done so, please send those first 1,500 livres to M. Le Vacher in Tunis. I am really sorry that you lost the opportunity of a boat that left recently for there.

We have to think seriously about helping the men in Algiers as soon as possible in some way or another—I do not mean only for living expenses but also to pay their debts. Let me know if any boat is being prepared and what is being said about fitting it out.

I have nothing else to say either to you, Monsieur, or to M. Delespiney, except that I am waiting to hear the results of your missions.

I am, in the love of Our Lord, Monsieur, your most humble servant.

VINCENT DEPAUL,
i.s.C.M.

When I tell you to send money to Algiers, I mean on condition that the wisest and most experienced persons will judge that there is no risk involved and will be prepared to receive some insults on the head of it.[1]

Enclosed is a letter for Algiers; it must not be sent as it is but in an envelope to the Consul.

[1]This part of the postscript, in Saint Vincent's handwriting, is less easy to read than the body of the letter written by the secretary. The copyist, to show his uncertainty about it, added the words "Is this what it says?"

3135. - ***EDME JOLLY, SUPERIOR, IN ROME, TO SAINT VINCENT***

[1660] [1]

By the mercy of God, the good results of past ordination retreats are apparent. Several of those priests who made their retreat here come to see us now and again to tell us that they are still keeping the good resolutions they took away with them. One of them, a nobleman who participated in three ordination retreats, came here yesterday to celebrate his first Mass, having made another few days of retreat beforehand to prepare himself better for it.

3136. - TO A PRIEST OF THE MISSION IN BARBARY [1]

[May or June 1660]

About six or seven years ago the Abbés de Chandenier retired to Saint-Lazare. That was a great blessing for the Company, which they have edified marvelously. Now, a month ago, God was pleased to call to himself Abbé de Tournus,[2] the elder of the two, who was as filled with the Spirit of God as any man I have ever known.

He lived like a saint and died a Missionary. He had gone to Rome with his brother and two of our priests but died in Chambéry on his way back home. He earnestly entreated one of our priests who was with him to admit him into the Company, which he did. Several times he had begged me personally to do so but, because his birth and his virtues were so far above us, I was unwilling to grant his request. We were unworthy of such an honor. And indeed it is only our house in heaven that merited the grace of having him as a

---

Letter 3135. - Abelly, *op. cit.,* bk. I, chap. II, sect. VI, p. 240.

[1]This letter was obviously written after no. 3081, dated February 16, 1660.

Letter 3136. - Abelly, *op. cit.,* bk. I, chap. XLIX, p. 241.

[1]Jean or Philippe Le Vacher.

[2]Louis de Chandenier.

Missionary; the ones on earth have merely inherited the examples of his holy life, which are as much to be admired as imitated.

I do not know what he saw in our insignificant Company that gave him this devotion of desiring to appear before God clothed in our rags, under the name and habit of Priest of the Congregation of the Mission. It is under this title that I recommend him to your Holy Sacrifices.

3137. - TO EDME JOLLY, SUPERIOR, IN ROME

June 4, 1660

I do not know a gratitude worthy enough to acknowledge the immense goodness of Cardinal Durazzo, who deigns to cast his eyes and his heart on our Little Company and to extend his care to all our present and future needs. May it please Our Lord, who has poured into his beautiful soul His own divine inclinations for the exercise of His mercy, to glorify it eternally for the favors he bestows on us!

3137a. - TO FIRMIN GET, SUPERIOR, IN MARSEILLES

Paris, June 4, 1660

Monsieur,

The grace of Our Lord be with you forever!

My joy would have been complete at knowing that you had returned from the missions satisfied with their outcome, if your

---

Letter 3137. - Reg. 2, p. 253.

Letter 3137a. - Copy made from *Recueil Nodet.* The letter was published in *Annales C.M.* (1943-44), pp. 249-50, and reprinted in *Mission et Charité,* 19-20, no. 121, pp. 152-54. This edition uses the latter text.

eyes were not bothering you. I thank God for everything and ask Him to be pleased to heal them. I really hope He will do so, since that ailment stemmed from an unusual source not found in Marseilles, where you now are.

I praise God also, Monsieur, that the bill of exchange for 1,200 livres from the Pastor in Le Havre[1] was accepted, and payment promised within three days.

Since that time, I sent you another bill of exchange for 1,903 livres, that is, 1,500 livres for the living expenses of our confreres in Barbary and the rest for those of your own house.

I think the reasons M. Delespiney pointed out to me for sending M. Cornier—and not M. Parisy—to Languedoc are good. However, since the Archbishop of Narbonne[2] had asked me for the latter, I am committed to sending him. Since that time, I have been told that this good Prelate is returning to Paris; in which case, he will put pressure on us to keep our word.

We received two écus for André de Paris on the galley *La Reine;* I am notifying M. Huguier of this.

I wrote to M. Delespiney about the death of Abbé de Chandenier, but I did not tell him that he wanted to appear before God with the name and habit of Missionary. During his illness, he earnestly requested them of M. Berthe,[3] who received him into the Company a few days before his death.

He had made the same request of M. Jolly,[4] and even of me, several times during the past few years, but I was unwilling to listen and tried to change the subject because I felt that the poor Mission was unworthy of someone of his rank and virtue. I have never

---

[1]Michel Bourdon, Doctor of the Sorbonne in 1654, Pastor in Le Havre (1655-68), was close to Saint Vincent, under whose direction he had made several retreats at Saint-Lazare.

[2]François Fouquet.

[3]Thomas Berthe, who was returning from Turin, where he had been making a visitation, wrote to Saint Vincent from Chambéry that Louis de Chandenier had just died (cf. no. 3121). He probably met the Chandenier brothers there, as they were making their way from Rome to France.

[4]Superior in Rome during Louis de Chandenier's last stay there.

known anyone closer to God, more detached from the world and from creatures, more attached to the interior life, and more disposed to help the neighbor.

O Monsieur! what a great loss for the Church and what a very great one for us! Only our house in heaven has merited having him as a Missionary. He merely left the one on earth the examples of a holy life to be admired as well as imitated. We have had one conference on them and will have another this evening, God willing. I do not know what he saw in this insignificant Company that made him want to clothe himself with its rags to present himself before the majesty of God. I hope he will obtain new blessings there for those who are clothed with them on earth, so that they may work ever more courageously in the Lord's vineyard. The men in Rome[5] have been put to work in it by the Pope himself, who sent eight of them to accompany four Bishops to visit the suffragan dioceses of Rome. Since the ordination retreat of last September, His Holiness has also been sending the ordinands to them during the Ember Days. God is also pleased to bless the members of the Company and its works everywhere. Please thank Him for this and ask Him for good workers.

I am, in His love, Monsieur, your most humble servant.

VINCENT DEPAUL,
i.s.C.M.

We just received twenty-one livres for a convict named Traverse, and three livres for Jacques Fournier, called Larivière, on the *Saint-Dominique*.

---

[5]The Missionaries of the Rome house.

3138. - TO A NIECE OF ANTOINE PORTAIL [1]

June 4, 1660

Vincent de Paul writes about Antoine Portail, who had died on February 14, 1660.

3139. - TO SISTER JEANNE DELACROIX, SISTER SERVANT, IN CHÂTEAUDUN

June 5, 1660

Dear Sister,

The grace of O[ur] L[ord] be with you forever!

Circumstances have arisen that require your presence here; please come at the first opportunity, Sister, and bring with you Sister Claude, who is in Varize.[1] I am writing to her as well, asking that she come. Try, Sister, to leave things in such good order that the Sisters who remain can carry on in your absence in such a way that the poor will not suffer from it. Tell your good Sisters that they will be alone for just a short time; inform the Administrators also so they will not be anxious about your return.

I ask Our Lord to bless you and your journey. Please recommend me to the prayers of our Sisters. I often offer them to God, and you also, Sister, for whom I am in His love, your most affectionate brother.

VINCENT DEPAUL,
i.s.C.M.

Letter 3138. - Collet, *op. cit.*, vol. II, p. 75, *note.*

[1]An Ursuline nun in Beaucaire.

Letter 3139. - Archives of the Motherhouse of the Daughters of Charity, *Recueil de pièces relatives aux Filles de la Charité,* p. 499.

[1]The Daughters of Charity had been in Varize (Eure-et-Loire) since 1652 or 1653. They nursed the sick and taught poor girls there.

3140. - TO DOMINIQUE LHUILLIER, IN CRÉCY

Paris, June 8, 1660

Monsieur,

The grace of O[ur] L[ord] be with you forever!

I have not written you for a long time, although I have received two letters from you. It is certainly right that we send you men to do the work, since we received some money a month or six weeks ago; but we encountered some objection on the part of M. de Lorthon,[1] who sent me word that he could not consent to that if Madame de Laval[2] does not give us the house the King has provided for us.

I will send him a priest as soon as possible to learn his final decision and to act in such a way that it will not delay us but will allow us to resume the missions on All Saints' Day at the latest; for we will soon be in harvest time and the very hot summer weather. Moreover, we already have four priests working in the diocese; they are accompanying the Bishop of Meaux [3] on his visitations.[4]

You must have heard of our great, incomparable loss of Abbé de Chandenier, so I will say no more to you about that except that, after having lived as a saint, he wanted to die a Missionary and to appear before God under the name and habit of a poor Priest of the Mission. Under this title, I recommend him to your prayers and Holy Sacrifices.

I had the honor of seeing the Dean of Saint-Fargeau,[5] but we did

---

Letter 3140. - The original signed letter was formerly the property of Abbé Ney of the Marseilles diocese; its present location is unknown.

[1]Pierre de Lorthon, Secretary of the King and founder of the Missionaries' house in Crécy.

[2]Marie Séguier, Marquise de Laval-Boisdauphin, a benefactress of the Missionaries in Crécy.

[3]Dominique de Ligny.

[4]The secretary had added here: "I send greetings to M. Asseline, and recommend myself to his prayers and yours." These words were then crossed out.

[5]Today Saint-Fargeau is the principal town of a canton in Yonne.

not settle anything, and I told him we would see about taking our decision regarding the legacy in question.

Please let me know how M. Asseline is behaving.

I am, in the love of O[ur] L[ord], your most humble servant.

VINCENT DEPAUL,
i.s.C.M.

Addressed: Monsieur Lhuillier, Priest of the Mission, in Crécy

3141. - TO FATHER EUSÈBE CHASTELLAIN

Paris, June 8, 1660

Reverend Father,

I ask your pardon for not having replied to you sooner. Perhaps you have been anxious about that good child you sent us. We welcomed him and I warmly recommended him to the Daughters of Charity who are looking after him. He is well, and there is reason to hope that the good seed you have sown in this innocent soul will bear fruit in due time, since it is being carefully cultivated.

I thank God, Reverend Father, for all the good being done in your hospital through the good order you have established there and your governance. I ask His Divine Goodness to continue to bless them both and to preserve you for a long time for the solace and salvation of the poor. The consolation Father de Gondi[1] receives from it consoles me greatly, and I admire his continual devotion to works of mercy. By them he sanctifies his soul more

---

Letter 3141. - The original signed letter is in the Treasury of the Sens Cathedral. It was donated by Jean-Claude Chastellain, delegate of the Department of Yonne to the National Convention at the time of the French Revolution.

[1]Philippe-Emmanuel de Gondi of the Oratory.

and more, meriting that God may pour forth new blessings on his afflicted family, to which your prayers can greatly contribute.

I very humbly thank you, Reverend Father, for the blessings you bestow on me and our Little Company. We would doubtless experience their effects, if I did not hinder them by my very great wretchedness. Please continue to do this charity for us. I offer you my most humble service in thanksgiving for it, and it will be a great joy to me if God is pleased to give me the opportunity to render some service to you. I am, in His love, Reverend Father, your most humble and obedient servant.

VINCENT DEPAUL,
i.s.C.M.

Addressed: Reverend Father Chastellain, Religious and Director of the Joigny Hospital, in Joigny

3142. - TO GEORGES [1] DES JARDINS, SUPERIOR, IN NARBONNE

June 11, 1660

We must always point out to the Bishops and the Vicars-General that our Rule forbids us to hear the confessions of nuns, to visit them, or to preach to them; and we should never disregard this prohibition, unless they formally command us to do so.

Letter 3142. - Reg. 2, p. 78.

[1]Coste mistakenly addressed this letter to *Gabriel* des Jardins; the editors have inserted the more certain name of *Georges*.

3143. - TO EDME JOLLY, SUPERIOR, IN ROME

June 18, 1660

Father Eudes,[1] together with some priests he brought with him from Normandy, came to give a mission in Paris, which caused quite a stir and produced excellent results.[2] The crowd was so great that the courtyard of the Quinze-Vingts[3] was too small to accommodate the congregation.

At the same time, several good priests—most of whom are members of our Tuesday Conferences—left Paris to go to other towns to give missions as well. Some went to Châteaudun and others to Dreux, where God was pleased to bestow similar great blessings. We have no part in these good works because our lot consists of the poor country people. We simply have the consolation of seeing that our modest works have spurred on a number of good workers, who are devoting themselves to doing them—not only in the missions, but also in seminaries, which are multiplying quickly in France. Even retreats for ordinands are being given in several dioceses. Let us ask God to sanctify His Church more and more.

Letter 3143. - Reg. 2, p. 254.

[1]Saint John Eudes, born in Pierrefitte, near Argentan (Orne), on November 14, 1601, entered the Oratory on April 7, 1623. He left it to found the Congregation of Jesus and Mary (Eudists) for the direction of seminaries and the work of the missions. Despite the similarity of the work of the Eudists and the Congregation of the Mission, Saint Vincent upheld him against the attacks of which he was the object and obtained for him the favor of the Queen. Saint John Eudes also established the feminine Congregation of Our Lady of Charity. He wrote devotional books, promoted devotion to the Sacred Hearts of Jesus and Mary, and gave many missions that had great influence. He died on August 19, 1680, and was canonized in 1925. (Cf. D. Boulay, *op. cit.*)

[2]This mission began on May 1 and closed on June 20. The crowd was so large that Father Eudes had to preach in the open air (*ibid.*, vol. III, p. 361).

[3]A hospice founded by Saint Louis, King of France (1226-70), for three hundred (*quinze-vingts*) poor blind people. The institution, situated near the Louvre, between the Place du Carrousel and the Place du Palais-Royal, was suppressed during the French Revolution and reestablished in another location in 1814.

3144. - TO GUILLAUME DESDAMES, SUPERIOR, IN WARSAW

Paris, June 18, 1660

Monsieur,

The grace of O[ur] L[ord] be with you forever!

I think it has been three weeks since I had any letters from you; I am anxious for some to arrive. God grant that the news will be better than the rumors that are circulating here! As for me, I have no news to tell you. Everything in the Company is going on as usual, and I think its members are striving everywhere to acquire virtue and to work in the Lord's vineyard in the way He asks of the Company and, by His mercy, with the success we can desire.

On all sides we are being asked for men, but we have none to give. *O Dieu!* what a great treasure is a good Missionary and how few people in this world are willing to serve God and His Church in purity of faith, detachment from creatures, and self-abnegation! Nevertheless, that is how our holy religion was established and spread, that is how it will be maintained, and that is how we must strive to repair the breaches caused by the laxity of evangelical workers. Let us ask Our Lord unceasingly, Monsieur, to send good ones and to animate the priesthood with His own Spirit.

Some priests from Normandy, led by Father Eudes, of whom I think you have heard, came to Paris to give a mission, and it was blessed in a wonderful way. The courtyard of the Quinze-Vingts is very large, but it was too small to hold the crowds who came to hear the sermons. At the same time, a large number of priests left Paris to go and work in other towns—some to Châteaudun and others to Dreux—and all had extraordinary success.

We have no part in all that because the poor country folk are our lot. We have only the consolation of seeing that our modest works have appeared so beautiful and useful to others that they have been inspired to devote themselves to them as we have done, and with

---

Letter 3144. - Archives of the Mission, Krakow, original signed letter.

greater blessing from God—not only in missionary work, but also in seminaries, which are rapidly multiplying in France. It even happened that, when a certain Company [1] in Rome saw that the Pope was sending candidates for ordination to the poor Priests of the Mission, as is done in Paris, they asked that those men be sent to them and offered to conduct the retreats—which they would doubtless have done successfully, if His Holiness had judged it fitting. There is reason to praise God for the zeal He is stirring up in many persons for the advancement of His glory and the salvation of souls.

Enclosed are some letters from Marseilles; please have the one addressed to Patto delivered, if you can.

I am, in the love of O[ur] L[ord], Monsieur, your most humble servant.

VINCENT DEPAUL,
i.s.C.M.

At the bottom of the first page: Monsieur Desdames

3144a. - TO FIRMIN GET, SUPERIOR, IN MARSEILLES

Paris, June 18, 1660

The grace of Our Lord be with you forever!

I received your letter of the eighth; it frightened me at first, when I saw that it was written in someone else's handwriting, but it really consoled me toward the end, when I read that your eyes have healed, thank God.

---

[1]The Society of Jesus (cf. vol. XIII, no. 57). This is the only place where the Jesuits are specifically mentioned as opposing the work of the Congregation of the Mission in Rome.

Letter 3144a. - Copy made from *Recueil Nodet.* The letter was published in *Annales C.M.* (1943-44), p. 251, and reprinted in *Mission et Charité,* 19-20, no. 122, pp. 154-55. This edition uses the latter text.

We must adapt ourselves to the orders of Providence after all, which increases the means you have of helping our confreres in Algiers and of waiting patiently until God gives you the opportunity of doing so, which I hope you will not lose. Knowing that the poor French captives in Tunis are closer to freedom and to going home, because of the peace treaty that has been concluded and will be put into effect, is cause for great consolation. Perhaps Algiers, like that city, will demand the same terms and will be forced to return the men it has captured and not seize any more of them. *O Dieu!* what a grace it will be if God is pleased to answer our poor prayers and the hopes of the entire Church!

Since Brother Le Moyne is ailing in Marseilles but was not ailing in Agde,[1] I consent to his returning there, and I am writing to tell M. Durand[2] to welcome him.

I am sending M. Truillard's[3] letters to Poland this very day.

As I informed M. Huguier, we received one [écu] [4] for Guillaume Laisné, called La Montagne, a convict on the *Saint-Dominique.*

I am, in the love of Our Lord, Monsieur, your most humble servant.

VINCENT DEPAUL,
i.s.C.M.

Since you have started the cesspool wall, it is advisable not to complain—nor even to discuss it.[5]

---

[1]The Agde Seminary was entrusted to the care of the Congregation of the Mission in 1654; repeated difficulties caused the Missionaries to leave there in 1671.

[2]Antoine Durand had been Superior of the Agde Seminary since 1656.

[3]A French officer on duty in Poland, whose father lived in the Marseilles area. The letter in which Saint Vincent encloses the elder M. Truillard's letters for his son is addressed to Guillaume Desdames, Superior in Warsaw, and bears the same date as this letter (cf. no. 3144). In 1656 M. Truillard had previously sent at least one letter to his son through Saint Vincent (cf. vol. VI, no. 2149).

[4]The copyist put an ellipsis here because he could not read the word; the original probably has *escu.*

[5]The postscript is in the Saint's handwriting, but the copyist could not decipher it correctly, so what he has written makes no sense.

3145. - TO MONSIEUR TRISTAN

Paris, June 22, 1660

Monsieur,

The grace of O[ur] L[ord] be with you forever!

Since the good girl you were kind enough to send us returned home three or four days ago with some of her relations who had come to see her, I could not then take the honor of writing to you—as I now do—to tell you, Monsieur, that in accordance with your good and wise advice, we took the opportunity of testing her in one of the works she found difficult. When, however, she realized that her repugnance was increasing instead of diminishing, she decided to leave. She did so after getting our consent, which we granted, presuming on yours, Monsieur, which you could not have refused when you saw that there was no hope of her overcoming her aversion.

She is too sincere to fail to tell you about this and is close enough to God to serve Him well in whatever state of life she may be, with the help of His grace, for He has given her good will and granted her that of behaving so well here that she has left us this hope, although she did not receive here all the good example or satisfaction that was to be desired.

I ask O[ur] L[ord] to preserve you, Monsieur, and to give me some good opportunity to obey you, Monsieur, for I am, in His love, your. . . .

VINCENT DEPAUL,
i.s.C.M.

Letter 3145. - Reg. 1, fol. 30.

3146. - TO DENIS LAUDIN, SUPERIOR, IN LE MANS

Paris, June 23, 1660

Monsieur,

The grace of O[ur] L[ord] be with you forever!

When I asked M. de Beaumont to come to Paris, he told me he would leave Richelieu on the twenty-second and stop by Le Mans, where he would arrive on the twenty-fifth or twenty-sixth of this month. Please welcome him with the cordiality due to a good servant of God like him.

I already recommended to you the soul of the late Abbé de Chandenier,[1] but I did not tell you that he died as a member of the Company and that, as such, it is fitting to render him the assistance we usually give our deceased. I do not know, Monsieur, what this holy man saw in the poor Congregation of the Mission that could have inspired him with the great ardor he had to assume its name and to cover himself with its rags to present himself before God. On several occasions he had spoken to us of his intention, but I was unwilling to listen to him, since I saw that he was too far above us by his birth and virtue. Indeed, Monsieur, it is only our house in heaven that has deserved the grace of having him as a Missionary. Our houses on earth have merely inherited the examples of his holy life. This Friday, God willing, we will hold the fourth conference on them.

Messieurs Alméras and Cruoly [2] left here yesterday for Richelieu by the Tours coach.

Letter 3146. - Archives of the Mission, Turin, original signed letter.

[1]Louis de Chandenier.

[2]Donat Crowley (Saint Vincent spells his name *Cruoly*), born in Cork (Ireland) on July 24, 1623, entered the Congregation of the Mission on May 9, 1643, took his vows in November 1645, and was ordained a priest in 1650. He was among the group of Missionaries sent to Picardy in 1651 for the relief of the people reduced to destitution by the war. Later, he was named Director of Students and theology professor at Saint-Lazare (1653-54) and was sent after that to Le Mans as Superior, returning to Saint-Lazare in 1657 to teach moral theology. Crowley was also Superior in Richelieu (1660-61), at Saint-Charles (1662-64), Montauban (1664-65), Agen

I send most affectionate greetings to your little company, and I am likewise, in the love of O[ur] L[ord], Monsieur, your most humble servant.

VINCENT DEPAUL,
i.s.C.M.

At the bottom of the first page: Monsieur Laudin

3146a. - TO FIRMIN GET, SUPERIOR, IN MARSEILLES

Paris, June 25, 1660

Monsieur,

The grace of Our Lord be with you forever!

I received your letter and was overjoyed to hear that God is pleased to bless the mission M. Delespiney is giving. You did well not to go to it because of your sore eyes. I would have been very annoyed at that, and I ask you to do whatever you can to be healed—to say nothing of doing anything that might aggravate your ailment. Your health is too precious to the Company and too necessary to your duty for you not to take very good care of it.

We will welcome M. Bayn[1] as graciously as we can, if he takes the trouble to come here, and will express to him the greatest

(1665-66), and Saint-Brieuc (1667-70). Sent to Le Mans again in 1676, he was Superior there (1687-90), after which there is no trace of him.

Letter 3146a. - Copy made from *Recueil Nodet.* The letter was published in *Annales C.M.* (1943-44), pp. 251-52, and reprinted in *Mission et Charité,* 19-20, no. 123, pp. 155-56. This edition uses the latter text.

[1]Joseph Bayn, who, together with his brother Thomas, plays a small part in the Saint's correspondence at this time. Little is known of the brothers except their connection with Firmin Get and the house in Marseilles. When Joseph became ill while visiting Paris, Saint Vincent saw that he was taken care of, although he could not stay at Saint-Lazare because the infirmary was full. (cf. no. 3215).

possible gratitude for his goodness to your family and for the help and support we have received from him.

We cannot get out of sending M. Parisy to Narbonne; for, we are now being asked for him because I led the Archbishop[2] to hope for this. Still, do not be in any hurry to send him off.

Enclosed is a small bill of exchange for fifty écus which I ask you to withdraw. They are for Nicolas Chocquart,[3] a convict on the *Montolieu,* who asked his mother for them. He said he had found a way to obtain his freedom for that amount, but that was when he was on another galley; now he writes that he is going to sea for three months and is requesting only twenty livres for his living expenses. His mother, however, had that money ready and wanted it to be given to you in case it is all that is needed to extricate her son from his wretched situation. Still, she asks you not to give him that money, unless it is for his release, but to keep it as long as you see some uncertainty about it—with the exception of the twenty livres he is requesting for his own needs, which you will please give him.

We received six écus for another convict in Toulon, named Denis Dubois, on the galley *Princesse.* I am writing to tell M. Huguier to give them to him.

Someone has written here that an Ambassador from Algiers has arrived in Marseilles. Please let me know what the story is.

I am, Monsieur, in the love of Our Lord, your most humble servant.

VINCENT DEPAUL,
i.s.C.M.

---

[2]François Fouquet.
[3]Nicolas Chocart.

3147. - TO A VISITATION NUN

June 27, 1660

Dear Sister,

The grace of O[ur] L[ord] be with you forever!

I ask your pardon for having delayed so long in giving you a reply. It was due to the pressures of business and my infirmities, which cause me to miss many things I would really like to do, if I were not prevented from doing so.

I will tell you now, dear Sister, that I sympathize deeply with you in your difficulties, which are prolonged and diverse. This is a big cross, which encompasses your mind and body, but it also raises you above earth, and that is what consoles me.

You should also be greatly consoled at seeing yourself treated as O[ur] L[ord] was treated, and honored by the same marks of love by which He has loved us. His sufferings were both interior and exterior, and the former were continual and incomparably greater than the latter.[1] Why do you think He tries you in this way, dear Sister? It is for the same purpose that He suffered, namely, to purge you of sins and to adorn you with His virtues in order that His Father's name may be sanctified in you and His Kingdom may come to you.

In the name of God, dear Sister, remain at peace and have perfect confidence in His goodness. I know of no soul in the world who has greater reason to do so than you. Do not dwell on any thoughts to the contrary, mistrust your own sentiments, and believe rather in what I tell you and in the knowledge I have of you than in anything you might think or say. You have a thousand reasons to rejoice in God and to hope for everything from Him through O[ur] L[ord] who dwells in you. Furthermore, after the recommendation He

---

Letter 3147. - Reg. 1, fol. 37v.

[1]Cf. Mk 26:39. (NAB)

gives you to renounce yourself,[2] I see nothing that can give you any reason to be fearful—not even sin, which is the only evil we must fear—because you have done penance for the past and hate it too much for the future.

So, like David, say to God: "Restore unto me, Lord, the joy of your salvation, and strengthen me with a perfect spirit."[3] Stir up this joy in yourself by considering the evil you have avoided in leaving the world and the graces He gives you in religion, as well as the blessing you enjoy of being numbered among the children of God[4] and the spouses of His Son, which is the grace of graces, embraces all good things, and puts you, even in this world, in possession of eternal glory. Be very grateful to God for this, thank Him often, and ask Him for mercy for me, who fear my ingratitude and am, in the love of Jesus Christ our Liberator, dear Sister, your. . . .

VINCENT DEPAUL,
i.s.C.M.

3148. - TO THE SUPERIORS

June [28] [1] 1660

Vincent de Paul eulogizes Louis de Chandenier who, as a benefactor and a Missionary, has a right to the prayers of the members of the Congregation. He adds that four conferences on his virtues [2] have been held at Saint-Lazare, where his body will be taken.

---

[2]Cf. Lk 14:33. (NAB)
[3]Cf. Ps 50:14. (DR-B).
[4]Cf. Gal 3:26; 1 Jn 3:1. (NAB)

Letter 3148. - Collet, *op. cit.,* vol. II, p. 79.

[1]Collet has *18,* but this date is contradicted by no. 3146. Saint Vincent probably wrote his circular on June 28.

[2]These conferences were given on May 28, June 4, 18, and 25 (cf. vol. XII, Appendix 2, which lists the dates and gives a brief synopsis of each).

3148a. - TO FIRMIN GET, SUPERIOR, IN MARSEILLES

Paris, July 2, 1660

Monsieur,

The grace of Our Lord be with you forever!

I received your letter of June 22. I praise God that your eyes are improving and for the foresight you had for our confreres in Algiers when you asked M. Le Vacher in Tunis to help them, if he has the opportunity to do so.

I praise God also for the success of M. Delespiney's mission, especially for the reconciliation of the inhabitants and the settlement of that important lawsuit. May it please His Goodness to strengthen and multiply all the good things that have been done there.

God willing, I will have a copy of the last will and testament of the late Mme de Vins drawn up in proper form to be sent to you. We have already drawn one up, but it is inadvisable for us to part with it.

I will have your account of the sums of money advanced to the convicts checked against our records. It would have been better to send a detailed account rather than a general one.

It is certain that the foundation for the hospital[1] and the salaries for the chaplains have been put in this year's statement. Payment must be sought there from the *receveurs*[2] or the clerk of the salt tax collectors. As for next year, however, I do not know if the statement has already been drawn up; I will find out.

We received thirty sous for Jacques Gabat, a convict on the *Saint-Louis,* and three livres for Claude Lefebvre, called Lanal; the

---

Letter 3148a. - Copy made from *Recueil Nodet.* The letter was published in *Annales C.M.* (1943-44), pp. 252-54, and reprinted in *Mission et Charité,* 19-20, no. 124, pp. 157-58. This edition uses the latter text.

[1]The Hospital for Galley Convicts in Marseilles.

[2]Officers responsible for the initial receipt of the tax before transmitting it into the hands of those in charge.

latter is in Marseilles; the other is in Toulon. Please see that each is given his money; I am saying a word to M. Huguier about that for the first man.

We are very worried about a captive named Vital Bernusset, detained in Napolly de Romani[3] or Scio;[4] I think the Abbés de Chandenier sent twelve hundred livres to Marseilles for him through M. Le Vacher,[5] who asked Mme de Valbelle[6] to entrust the ransom of that poor man to a merchant she knew—at least the money was sent to him. He acknowledges receipt of 354 piastres, as I saw in the statement of account in one of his letters; neither his name nor his address is noted in it, nor even the date. He says that the Father Guardian, a Capuchin, has taken the trouble to write to his priests in Scio about it in order to negotiate it at the best possible price, thinking it quite right that the ransom be handled by the Superior of his convent. Nevertheless, in conformity with his order, this merchant says that he will not part with the money until Vital is here.

Please find out exactly from Mme de Valbelle, Monsieur, who this merchant is. Where is he? Has he written anything more about that captive? What do we have to do to ransom him? For what purpose has the rest of the money been used? In a word, try to get complete information on the present state of this affair, and see what remains to be done to implement matters and to move it forward as much as you can. In addition to what you will do for this poor captive so he can procure his freedom as soon as possible, you will give great pleasure to Abbé de Moutiers-Saint-Jean,[7] the brother of the late Abbé de Chandenier.[8] He is concerned about this

---

[3]Napoli di Romagna, in the Peloponnesus; today it is referred to in English as Navplion.
[4]Chios, an island in the Aegean Sea, near Asia Minor.
[5]Philippe Le Vacher.
[6]A relative of the Lieutenant of the Admiralty of Marseilles.
[7]Claude de Chandenier.
[8]Louis de Chandenier.

affair because this captive is the brother of one of his good priests, and we have every duty imaginable to obey him.

While awaiting this from your usual vigilance, I am, in the love of Our Lord, Monsieur, your most humble servant.

VINCENT DEPAUL,
i.s.C.M.

3149. - *CHARLES DE LATRE TO SAINT VINCENT*

Monsieur and Reverend Father,

As Deputy of the clergy of Artois, M. Lepruvost of our Chapter is going to Paris to pay His Majesty the homage and respects due to him. I have asked him to greet you for me in order to assure you of my modest services and to tell you that not a day passes that I do not think of Your Reverence because I am, Monsieur, your most humble and grateful servant.

CHARLES DE LATRE

From our house in Béthune,[1] *July 7, 1660*

Addressed: *Monsieur Vincent, Priest and General of the Community of the Mission, at Saint-Lazare, in the faubourg Saint-Denis, Paris*

Letter 3149. - Archives of the Mission, Turin, original signed letter.

[1]Principal town of Pas-de-Calais.

3150. - TO SISTER FRANÇOISE CARCIREUX, SISTER SERVANT, IN NARBONNE

Paris, July 9, 1660

Dear Sister,

The grace of O[ur] L[ord] be with you forever!

Because of my business affairs, I have delayed longer than I wished in replying to your letter. I thank God for all the things you told me, which deeply consoled me. It seems that God is with you and that He guided you while you were at work in the Alet diocese, since, on the one hand, He preserved you from the dangers that threatened you and, on the other, He has been glorified by your works.[1]

All that demands deep humility and gratitude from you. Acknowledge before God that you have done only evil, which always arises from imperfections in good works, even were it only to prevent the good that God does from being greater and purer, through a lack of faith and fidelity in the instruments He uses. It would be even worse to attribute to oneself the honor due to His Divine Goodness.

I know, Sister, that you have committed no such fault, thank God. Continue to prefer embarrassment to praise, to mistrust yourself always, and to surrender yourself to God so that He may make use of you according to His good pleasure and not according to your own ideas. Be steadfast in the little practices of the Company, as far as your work will permit. Treat your Sisters with love and cordiality, and sympathize with their little weaknesses. I praise God for the satisfaction you have in this and for the edification your neighbor receives from it.

If the Bishop comes to Paris, we will try to arrange everything with him so that you may be free to live and act according to the

---

Letter 3150. - Reg. 1, fol. 22.

[1]François Fouquet, Archbishop of Narbonne, had sent Sister Françoise Carcireux to an institution in the Alet diocese to be prepared there to teach young people.

spirit and customs of your Company, which is getting on quite well everywhere, thank God. There is nothing new here except that we are preparing to elect a Sister as our Superior; [2] pray for that and for all the other needs. I recommend myself to your prayers and to those of our Sisters, whom I greet. . . .

VINCENT DEPAUL,
i.s.C.M.

3151. - TO SISTER ANNE DENOUAL, IN NARBONNE

Paris, July 9, 1660

Dear Sister,

The grace of O[ur] L[ord] be with you forever!

I was pleased to have news of you, and still more to hear of the graces God is giving you. I thank Him for them with my whole heart and ask Him to grant you the grace of being very faithful to Him. He allowed you to experience the aversion that caused you so much pain to let you see that, of yourself, you are incapable of anything else, and in the end He changed this antipathy into affection, to establish in you union and charity. These are so necessary that you should earnestly implore them of His Divine Goodness for yourself and your Company and do all in your power to acquire and preserve them.

Always humble yourself; consider yourself as the most imperfect; look at what is good in your Sisters and what is bad in yourself and, no matter what feeling to the contrary may arise, try to turn your thoughts from it and raise your heart to God so as to dispose yourself then to love what He loves in the way He wants you to love it.

---

[2]Cf. no. 3100, n. 3.

Letter 3151. - Archives of the Motherhouse of the Daughters of Charity, original signed letter.

Bear separation with patience because it proceeds from Providence and not from your own choice. You and your Sisters have done your best to be reunited but have been unable to obtain this consolation from the Bishop.[1] So then, you must submit to God's Will and remain at peace in the hope that all will go well; for, as a rule, where we do not find our own satisfaction, God finds it to His advantage.

Let Him act, Sister; rely strongly on His assistance; be exact at your morning prayer and in recommending yourself frequently to God during the rest of the day. In all your works, make your intention to honor and please Him; have as little contact as possible with persons on the outside; follow the advice of M. des Jardins and Sister Françoise,[2] and you will see that Our Lord will bless your soul and your spiritual exercises. But even if you do not see this, Our Lord will still consider them pleasing to Himself, and will sanctify you imperceptibly, as long as you are faithful to Him. I implore Our Lord that this may be so always and in all things.

I am, in His love, Sister, your most affectionate brother and servant.

VINCENT DEPAUL,
i.s.C.M.

Addressed: Sister Anne Denoual, Daughter of Charity, in Narbonne

[1]François Fouquet.
[2]Françoise Carcireux.

3152. - TO JEAN PARRE, IN REIMS

Paris, July 10, 1660

Dear Brother,

The grace of O[ur] L[ord] be with you forever!

I was very worried about you when I received your letter of June 29, since I had not received one for two weeks.

God be praised that you are coming and going to do His work! That is a sign that your health is somewhat restored and that the charity of Jesus Christ still urges you on.[1]

A week ago I wrote to you at Saint-Quentin,[2] since I had not then received your letter telling me that you had gone to Reims. I told you that we had some church linens and vestments for the poor churches of Champagne and Picardy and would send them by the first passenger coach or mail coach leaving for Saint-Quentin; however, we have not done so because we were informed that perhaps you would prefer to have them sent to you elsewhere.

Please let me know where you are supposed to distribute them. They will be sent to you in Amiens, Reims, or Saint-Quentin. The parcel is all ready. I sent you the list of its contents. True, we did remove a small candlestick and a silver cup to be made into a little chalice or converted into something that will be used for the altar, in accordance with the intention of the donor. The Ladies will give orders about that and about some cash we have for the same purpose; that will be for their next meeting.

I do not think the mail will find you still in Reims, so I am sending a duplicate letter to you in Saint-Quentin.

Letter 3152. - Archives of the Mission, Paris, copy made from the original at the home of a Florentine lady. The present location of the original is unknown.

[1]Cf. 2 Cor 5:14. (NAB)

[2]Principal town of the district of Aisne.

I ask Our Lord to continue to grant you His protection and His strength.

I am, in the love of O[ur] L[ord], your most affectionate brother and servant.

VINCENT DEPAUL,
i.s.C.M.

3153. - TO FRANÇOIS FOUQUET, ARCHBISHOP OF NARBONNE [1]

[1660] [2]

I blush with shame, Monseigneur, every time I read the last letter you did me the honor of writing me, and even every time I think of it, seeing to what an extent you, Excellency, have humbled yourself before a poor swineherd by birth and a wretched old man full of sins. At the same time, I feel deeply troubled at having given you cause to do so. When I ventured to point out to Your Excellency that we were not in a position to give you the men you requested, you can be very sure that it was not due to any lack of respect or submission regarding whatever you desire, but to our sheer powerlessness to obey you on this occasion.

I ask you most humbly to grant us a six-month extension. We would be greatly consoled to give you this satisfaction sooner, but God has not chosen to enable us to do so.

In the name of God, Monseigneur, kindly excuse our poverty, and please put off your journey to Paris for a more important

---

Letter 3153. - Abelly, *op. cit.*, bk. III, chap. XI, sect. VI, p. 143.

[1]Abelly merely states that the letter is addressed to an Archbishop. Now, with the exception of Paris, Saint Vincent established his Congregation in only two archdioceses in France: Reims and Narbonne. The tone of the letter makes it clear that he is writing to François Fouquet.

[2]In August 1659 François Fouquet wrote to Saint Vincent requesting some priests for his archdiocese (cf. no. 2952). Shortly after obtaining three of them for his seminary (cf. no. 2979, dated September 12), he wrote again asking for others. The present reply can refer only to the second request. The Prelate insisted, and this resulted in no. 3281, dated September 17, 1660.

occasion. It would be a blessing of God for me to receive Your Excellency's blessing once again, but you cannot imagine how much I would regret your fatiguing yourself by coming here for a matter that would be advanced no further by it. You are well aware, Monseigneur, that there is no one on this earth more disposed to receive your commands than we are, and I in particular, over whom God has given you sovereign power.

3154. - TO CARDINAL DURAZZO

1660

Vincent de Paul begs the Cardinal to take care of his health, so necessary for the welfare of the Church.

3155. - TO JEAN PARRE, IN REIMS [1]

Paris, July 14, 1660

My very dear Brother,

The grace of Our Lord be with you forever!

I already wrote to you on Saturday both in Reims and in Saint-Quentin to find out where you want us to send you a parcel of cloth, vestments, and altar linens, of which I sent you a list; we will await your reply regarding this. Now I am writing to let you know that we have received 848 livres to restore some ruined churches in Champagne and Picardy. Withdraw this sum whenever you wish and put it on my account, etc.

Letter 3154. - Collet, *op. cit.,* vol. II, p. 68.

Letter 3155. - This letter is known to us through its Italian translation, inserted into one of the documents of the collection for the process of beatification, *Summarium Responsivum,* p. 54.

[1]Cf. no. 3152.

3156. - TO JEAN MARTIN, SUPERIOR, IN TURIN

Paris, July 16, 1660

Monsieur,

The grace of O[ur] L[ord] be with you forever!

I just received your letter of the third, which consoled me all the more since it is the only one I have had for about six weeks. I thank God, Monsieur, that the family has returned to Turin in good health and for the blessings His Goodness was pleased to shower upon it and upon the peoples it evangelized. You could not give me more pleasing news nor any that inspires me with a more lively sense of gratitude to Our Lord for the graces He bestows on you. I thank Him for this with all my heart.

So, take a rest, Monsieur, and see that those priests who have worked so hard get some rest also. It is certainly right in this season to restore the strength that has been lost and to be renewed in Our Lord, the source of life and virtue of priests. This can be done by the practice of prayer and the grace of recollection, so as to continue subsequently the conquest of souls with new arms. Being taken from the arsenal of Holy Scripture, these arms will always be victorious, if they are used in the spirit of O[ur] L[ord].

With the full extent of my affection I embrace your little community, together with your own dear heart.

The Company here is in the same state as ever, and I think God continues to bless it everywhere. We have no one sick at present. True, I am suffering a little from my poor legs, which give me no rest at night nor allow me to walk by day nor even to stand upright; apart from that, I am very well. M. Alméras went to Richelieu

---

Letter 3156. - Archives of the Mission, Turin, original signed letter.

because the King and the new Queen were passing through.[1] He is now on his way back.

I recommend myself to your prayers and am, in the love of O[ur] L[ord], Monsieur, your most humble servant.

VINCENT DEPAUL,
i.s.C.M.

Addressed: Monsieur Martin, Superior of the Priests of the Mission, in Turin

3156a. - TO FIRMIN GET, SUPERIOR, IN MARSEILLES

Paris, July 16, 1660

Monsieur,

The grace of Our Lord be with you forever!

We have had the consolation of seeing M. Bayn,[1] who did us the honor of coming here twice. I sent your brother [2] and someone else to see him. We showed him all the respect and gratitude we owe him and his kindness and, if the opportunity presents itself to be of service to him, we will do so wholeheartedly. He certainly deserves it; for, in the short time I spoke with him, he seemed very honorable and virtuous to me.

I deeply sympathize with you in your trials and in the inconveniences with which God is pleased to try your little family. May His

---

[1]Louis XIV, his young bride Maria Teresa of Spain, and their retinue stopped in Richelieu on July 7. On that day René Alméras performed in their presence the ceremonies of the solemn baptism of Louis de Gallard de Béarn, a six-year-old child for whom the King and Queen were godparents.

Letter 3156a. - Copy made from *Recueil Nodet.* The letter was published in *Annales C.M.* (1943-44), p. 254, and reprinted in *Mission et Charité,* 19-20, no. 125, pp. 158-59. This edition uses the latter text.

[1]Cf. nos. 3146a, 3214a, 3215, and 3230.

[2]Nicolas Get.

Infinite Goodness be pleased to draw His glory and your sanctification from them! As for the rest, please do whatever is to be desired for you and for the others to keep well, and do not be in any hurry to send M. Parisy to Narbonne. Write to M. des Jardins[3] and tell him I have asked you to wait until further notice, which I am postponing giving you because of the uncertainty of the Archbishop of Narbonne's journey to Paris; if he were to come, things might change.

Since the Annecy house is satisfied with the Brothers it has, it is not advisable to send Brother Le Moyne there. I will write to the houses in Lorm[4] and La Rose[5] to find out if one or the other could use him, and I will let you know.

I asked Mme Fouquet to find out what you want to know about the hospital and the chaplains, and I am awaiting her reply. I received the packet from Algiers and am pleased about that; however, I have not yet been able to look at it.

I am writing to tell M. Huguier to give four livres ten sous to a captive named Jean Fanson and six livres to François Fremin.

I hope to send you by the first opportunity some money for the Comte d'Insiquin,[6] who is in Algiers, and to reimburse you for the money you have lent to the captives.

I am, in the love of Our Lord, Monsieur, your most humble servant.

VINCENT DEPAUL,
i.s.C.M.

---

[3]Georges des Jardins.

[4]Notre-Dame-de-Lorm, in the Montauban diocese, where the Missionaries were established since 1652.

[5]Notre-Dame-de-la-Rose, Agen diocese, where the Missionaries were established in 1639.

[6]Cf. no. 3116a, n. 3.

3157. - *MONSIEUR DESNOYERS TO SAINT VINCENT*

The peace of O[ur] L[ord]!

Monsieur,

I offered our humble services to that respectable lady, the sister of one of the older men at Saint-Lazare, whom you did me the honor of recommending to me. I am sorry that she did not accept anything. I would have been happy to witness to you on that occasion the esteem I have for anything that comes from you. Please continue your patronage and the assistance of your good prayers for the completion of our poor hospital.

I am, with all possible respect, Monsieur, your most humble, grateful, and obedient servant.

DESNOYERS

Sainte-Reine[1] *Hospital, July 17, 1660*

That respectable lady was in a hurry to leave; I was not informed of this in time to send you an answer by her.

Addressed: *Monsieur Vincent, Superior General of the Mission of Saint-Lazare, in Paris*

Letter 3157. - Archives of the Mission, Turin, original autograph letter.

[1]A small commune in the district of Gray (Haute-Saône). M. des Noyers was the administrator of its hospital, which was greatly indebted to the generosity of the Ladies of Charity.

3158. - TO JEAN PARRE, IN REIMS [1]

Paris, July 17, 1660

Dear Brother,

The grace of O[ur] L[ord] be with you forever!

I just received your letter of the twelfth. It has been a week since I wrote to you in Reims, and since then I wrote to you also in Laon and Saint-Quentin because I was not sure if you were still in Champagne. As far as I can see, however, this letter will find you there still. I am sending it to you in Reims and am sending a duplicate to Rethel[2] so that, wherever you are, you will receive news from us quickly.

I sent word to you in Laon that the assembly has earmarked 848 livres[3] for you to restore a few of the most ruined and neglected churches in Champagne and Picardy. They are not for extensive repairs—for one alone would suffice to use up this sum—but to make the most needed repairs in several churches so that Holy Mass can be celebrated in them with some decency, and the altars sheltered from wind and rain. In addition, this does not apply to those churches for which the tithe-collecting[4] *seigneurs* and the inhabitants can shoulder the expense because, if they can, they should do so and should be urged to do so. We have the 848 livres here; you can obtain and draw them on me whenever you wish, as also the 500 livres set aside to buy seed to be given to the poor people to sow next winter, as I wrote you previously. This is not a new alms; I mention it simply as a reminder.

Letter 3158. - The original signed letter is the property of the Daughters of Charity, Grosseto, Italy.

Uncertain of the whereabouts of Jean Parre, Saint Vincent wrote to him both in Reims and in Rethel. Coste published the Reims letter as no. 3158; the one sent to Rethel was published in *Mission et Charité,* 19-20, no. 126, pp. 159-61. This edition published the latter as no. 3158a.

[1]Cf. no. 3152.

[2]Cf. no. 3158a.

[3]This sum, allotted at the meeting of the Ladies of Charity, is mentioned in no. 3155.

[4]Some local landowners collected the tithes that should normally have been given to the clergy serving there.

I am waiting for you to let me know where to send you a small bundle of vestments and church linens.[5] I had written you that we would send them to you in Saint-Quentin, but this has not been done because we thought it better to await your reply.

We cannot tell you yet when you will be leaving Champagne.

I will inform the Ladies of what you tell me and will find out if they can do anything for those two girls who would like to enter some Community. I strongly doubt that they will want to get involved in that. As for the third one, who wants to be a Daughter of Charity, given her good qualities she may be accepted with time, if she perseveres, but it is advisable to delay her in order to test her. Meanwhile, you can observe her.

I repeat to you that you may take the 900 and as many livres as we have here whenever you wish. I mentioned them to you about two months ago; they are intended for the poor of Champagne and Picardy.

I am, in the love of O[ur] L[ord], dear Brother, your very affectionate brother and servant.

VINCENT DEPAUL,
i.s.C.M.

[5]These were mentioned in both nos. 3152 and 3155.

3158a. - TO JEAN PARRE, IN RETHEL

Paris, July 17, 1660

Dear Brother,

The grace of Our Lord be with you forever!

I wrote to you a week ago in Reims; since then I also wrote to you in Laon and Saint-Quentin because I was not sure if you were still in Champagne. I am writing this letter to you in Rethel so that, wherever you are, you will receive news from us.

As I have already told you, the last assembly earmarked 848 livres for you to use to restore a few of the most ruined and neglected churches you will find in Champagne and Picardy. They are not to be used for extensive repairs—one alone would be enough to use up all the money—but to do what is most necessary in several of them so that Holy Mass can be celebrated in them with some decency, and the altar sheltered from rain and wind.

This does not include those churches for which the tithe-collecting *seigneurs* and the inhabitants can shoulder this expense; for, if they can, they should do so, and we have to be satisfied with urging them to this. We have the 848 livres here; you can obtain and draw them on me whenever you wish, as also the 500 livres set aside to buy seed to be given to the poor people to sow next winter, as I wrote you previously, for this is not a new alms. I mention it to you simply as a reminder.

I am waiting for you to let me know where you want us to send a small bundle of church linens and vestments. I had written you that we would send them to you in Saint-Quentin, but this was not done because we thought it better to await your reply.

We cannot tell you yet whether you will be leaving Champagne.

Letter 3158a. - Property of the Congregation of the Mission, Florence (Italy), original signed letter. This is one of three letters (cf. vol. II, no. 804a, and vol. VII, no. 2490a) discovered in 1947 when the confreres moved from a house devastated by the war to a new house in Florence (cf. *Annales C.M.* [1947-48], pp. 307-08). The text was published in *Annales C.M.* (1947-48), p. 311, and reprinted in *Mission et Charité,* 19-20, no. 126, pp. 159-61. This edition uses the latter text. The similarity in both subject matter and style between no. 3158 and this letter is

I am, in Our Lord, dear Brother. . . . [1]

I just received your letter of the twelfth. I will inform the Ladies of what you tell me. I strongly doubt that they will want to get involved with those two young women who want to enter some Community. As for the third one, who wants to become a Daughter of Charity, given her good qualities she could be accepted with time, if she perseveres, but it is advisable to delay her in order to test her. Meanwhile, you can observe her.

I am, in the love of Our Lord, dear Brother, your most humble servant.

VINCENT DEPAUL,
i.s.C.M.

3159. - TO PIERRE PINGRÉ, BISHOP OF TOULON

1660

Vincent de Paul urges the Prelate to take care of his health for the good of the Church.

---

apparent, although certain variants can be detected. It is for this reason that the editors have published both letters.

[1]The editor of *Mission et Charité* states that the "bottom of the letter was cut off here," but gives no explanation about the paragraph which follows. Could it be that Saint Vincent wrote this letter before he wrote no. 3158, that he received Parre's letter of July 12 before he finished the former, and that he then added what followed? That might explain why no. 3158 begins with reference to the letter of July 12.

Letter 3159. - Collet, *op. cit.*, vol. II, p. 68.

3160. - TO A PRIEST OF THE MISSION

[July 1660] [1]

God has chosen to take from us one of our best Brothers,[2] namely, Brother Sirven, who was the living Rule of the Company in Sedan. A wise, intelligent man, he did good to everyone and devoted himself willingly to the care of the sick and the consolation of the afflicted. The whole town looked upon and loved him as a saint and has expressed great regret at losing him—even heretics, who were edified by his unassuming behavior.

We have good reason to believe that God has crowned his soul in heaven, giving him the crown He has prepared for His beloved who practice works of mercy [3] on earth, as did this servant of His.[4] Still, we must not fail to pray for him, since we are not sure of God's judgments. I recommend to your prayers this sinner who is writing to you.

Letter 3160. - Lyons manuscript.

[1]This letter must have been written shortly after the death of Pierre Sirven on July 12.

[2]Pierre Sirven, coadjutor Brother, born in Verdun-sur-Garonne (Tarn-et-Garonne), entered the Congregation of the Mission on March 12, 1640, took his vows on January 1, 1643, and died in Sedan on July 12, 1660. His outstanding qualities had earned the confidence of the Bishop of Montauban. Saint Vincent's high esteem for him is expressed in this letter, as also in nos. 3161, 3162, 3169, and 3181.

[3]Cf. Mt 7:9. (NAB)

[4]The secretary added the following note at the bottom of the Saint's rough copy: "An older priest, who lived for a long time in Sedan with this dear deceased Brother, told me that, along with his other talents, he was very skilled in pharmacy and brought about some marvelous cures. He also stated that he had done his studies and that M. Vincent had accepted him to become a priest, but he had preferred to remain a poor Brother."

3161. - TO GUILLAUME DESDAMES, SUPERIOR, IN WARSAW

Paris, July 23, 1660

Monsieur,

The grace of O[ur] L[ord] be with you forever!

I received your dear letter of the twelfth, in which I see that it is now time to send you the promised help. I really want you to receive it for your encouragement, Monsieur, for God knows how much I have at heart your health and satisfaction. So, we are going to get three—or at least two—priests ready for you, along with a student Brother who teaches philosophy here.

Our difficulty is with the Daughters of Charity who are supposed to be sent at the same time; for, since Mademoiselle Le Gras has left us, and the others do not know the Sisters, we have had to take the ones the deceased had intended for Poland and to send them elsewhere; now we are in somewhat of a quandary regarding the choice that has to be made. We will, nevertheless, do the best we can. God, who sees the greatness of our obligation and our very earnest desire to satisfy the Queen, will help us if He so pleases.

We will most willingly pray, as we have already done, for the confirmation of the peace,[1] as well as for the success of Their Majesties' projects and the affairs of the kingdom.

God has chosen to take from us one of our good—one of our best—Brothers; namely, Sirven, who was the living Rule of the Company in Sedan. A wise, intelligent man, he did good to everyone and devoted himself willingly to the care and relief of the sick poor and the consolation of the afflicted. The whole town loved him dearly; its inhabitants, from the most prominent to the lowliest—even heretics, who were edified by his unassuming behavior and charity—came to his funeral, expressing great regret at losing him.

Letter 3161. - Archives of the Mission, Krakow, original signed letter.

[1]The Treaty of Oliva, which was signed on May 3, 1660.

We have good reason to believe that God has crowned his soul in heaven, giving him the kingdom He has prepared for His beloved who practice works of mercy [2] on earth, as did this servant of His. Nevertheless, Monsieur, we must still pray for him, since we are not sure of God's judgments; this prompts the entire Church to pray for the faithful departed.

We have three or four men here who are seriously ill with a constant fever. It seems that God wants to try us. May His Holy Name be blessed and His Will be done always!

I am in a special way, in His love, Monsieur, your most humble servant, and that of M. Duperroy as well, whom I embrace with all my affection.

VINCENT DEPAUL,
i.s.C.M.

Addressed: Monsieur Desdames, Superior of the Priests of the Mission of Holy Cross, in Warsaw

3162. - *MADAME DU BOULET-BRULAR TO SAINT VINCENT*

Madame du Boulet-Brular asks M. Vincent not to sign anything for the aides[1] *of Melun because the agreement mentioned to him, and which is ready for him, took them by surprise, to the prejudice of many other offers more advantageous to the owners.*

July 23, 1660

Addressed: *Monsieur Vincent, at the Mission*

---

[2]Cf. Mt 7:9. (NAB)

Letter 3162. - Archives of the Mission, Turin, original autograph letter.

[1]Indirect taxes on consumer goods such as meat, fish, wood, and especially wine.

3162a. - TO FIRMIN GET, SUPERIOR, IN MARSEILLES

Paris, July 23, 1660

Monsieur,

The grace of Our Lord be with you forever!

I have had someone mention your income due from the heirs of the late Marquise de Vins. Before proceeding further, it is advisable for you to send us a list of the names of the estates where missions have been given, how long they lasted, and how successful they were. You should even join to this the attestations you received from the Pastors so you can show them to those who administer the inheritance.

God has chosen to take from us one of our good—one of our best—Brothers, namely, Sirven, who was the living Rule of the Sedan house. A wise, intelligent man, he did good to everyone and devoted himself willingly to the care and relief of the sick poor and to the consolation of the afflicted. The whole town loved him and came to his funeral, from the most prominent to the lowliest—even heretics, who were edified by his unassuming behavior and charity—and they expressed great regret at losing him.

We have good reason to believe that God has already rewarded his soul in heaven for the good services he rendered Him on earth. Nevertheless, Monsieur, we should still pray for his soul because we are not sure of God's judgments, and should conform ourselves to the custom of the Church and the practice of the Company.

I simply remind you to help our confreres in Algiers as soon as you can do so safely.

Abbé de Chandenier thanks you, as do I, for what you wrote me

---

Letter 3162a. - Copy made from *Recueil Nodet.* The letter was published in *Annales C.M.* (1943-44), pp. 255-56, and reprinted in *Mission et Charité,* 19-20, no. 127, pp. 161-62. This edition uses the latter text.

about Vital Bernusset; [1] we ask you to change the first order given to the Consul in Smyrna and to request of him once again that he transmit the money he has for the ransom of this slave, when that will be necessary, and even to furnish what will be needed, in the event that the 354 piastres do not suffice. You can stand surety for his reimbursement, which we will send you as soon as we receive notice. M. Le Vacher [2] has not sent us the one he had someone give to the Consul.

I am still concerned about your gout, and we are asking Our Lord to be pleased to rid you of it.

We have three or four men here who are seriously ill with a constant fever. It seems as if God wants to try us. May His Holy Name be blessed and His Will be done always!

I am writing to ask M. Huguier to give three livres to Laisné, called La Montagne. We received 384 livres for the Comte d'Insiquin,[3] a captive in Algiers. We will send them at the first opportunity. Meanwhile, if you have an occasion to transmit them to our confreres to be given to him, please do so.

I am, in the love of Our Lord, Monsieur, your most humble servant.

VINCENT DEPAUL,
i.s.C.M.

---

[1]A captive in Návplion, in whom the Abbés de Chandenier had taken an interest. Since Louis de Chandenier had died on May 6, 1660, Saint Vincent must be referring here to his brother Claude.

[2]Philippe Le Vacher (cf. no. 3148a).

[3]Cf. no. 3116a, n. 3.

3163. - TO JEAN PARRE, IN REIMS

Paris, July 24, 1660

My very dear Brother,

The grace of Our Lord be with you forever!

I received your letter of the nineteenth and shared your preceding ones with the assembly, which does not think it advisable for you to leave just now because you have to work at restoring and repairing some of the ruined churches.

Let us know when you have spent the 848 livres I sent you, and we will do what we can to send you something else, etc.

3164. - *MONSIEUR DUFRESNER [1] TO SAINT VINCENT*

Monsieur,

We will send you that good girl. We hope you will find in her at least part of what is necessary for the fulfillment of her wishes and that you in your goodness will supply what is lacking. I entreat you also to include me in your prayers, as a person upon whom you can count perfectly, Monsieur, to be your most humble and obedient servant.

DUFRESNER

Nantes, July 25, 1660

Addressed: *Reverend Father Vincent, General of the Fathers of the Mission, at Saint-Lazare, in Paris*

Letter 3163. - This letter is known to us through its Italian translation, inserted into one of the documents of the collection for the process of beatification, *Summarium Responsivum,* p. 54.

Letter 3164. - Archives of the Mission, Turin, original autograph letter.

[1]Apparently M. Dufresner was one of the Fathers of the Poor, the title given to the Administrators of the Nantes Hospital (cf. no. 3165).

3165. - *SISTER NICOLE HARAN, SISTER SERVANT, IN NANTES, TO SAINT VINCENT*

Nantes, July 25, 1660

My very dear and honored Father,

Your blessing, please!

I am taking the liberty of bothering you with this little note to entreat you to kindly send us some precious news of you, for which we are at a loss and troubled at being deprived of this consolation. We desire this so ardently that our dear Sisters and I ask it of you for the love of God.

That good girl, about whom the Fathers of the Poor wrote to you again and whom you have accepted, is due to leave tomorrow morning to come to enter our Company. I think she will be a good Sister. Since we had her with us to help us, we ask you, now that we are alone, to send us our Sister as soon as possible to relieve us; for we have a large number of patients and all of us are really unwell and tired out. Our Administrators are very dissatisfied because she is so long in coming.

We send our most respectful greetings to all our good Fathers at the house. We recommend ourselves to their prayers, especially I, who am and always will be, my very dear Father, your most obedient daughter.

SISTER NICOLE HARAN,
Unworthy Daughter of Charity

Addressed: *Monsieur Vincent, Superior General of the Priests of the Mission, at Saint-Lazare, in Paris*

Letter 3165. - Archives of the Mission, Turin, original autograph letter.

3166. - TO MADEMOISELLE D'AUBRAI [1]

July 26, 1660

Vincent de Paul gives some wise advice to Mademoiselle d'Aubrai, who had consulted him on her vocation,[2] adding that "*he has asked God for some great graces through the intercession of M. Olier.*"

3167. - TO JACQUES PESNELLE, SUPERIOR, IN GENOA

July 30, 1660

You should never expect to see your house without some failings; provided, however, that there are no grounds for complaint or nothing scandalous occurs, make up your mind to bear with others and, at the same time, do whatever you can to lessen them, both in quality and quantity.

After the conversion of sinners, however complete it may be, some imperfections always remain in order to test them. This is

---

Letter 3166. - Collet, *op. cit.,* vol. II, p. 144.

[1]Niece of Jean-Jacques Olier, the celebrated founder of Saint-Sulpice Seminary. The latter was born in Paris on September 20, 1608. After a few hesitations, which Saint Vincent succeeded in dissipating, Olier decided to become a priest and was ordained on May 21, 1633. The first years of his priestly career were dedicated to the work of missions. He participated in the works of the priests of Saint-Lazare, whom he edified by his zeal and humility. Saint Vincent calls him "a man given over to the grace of God and completely apostolic." In 1635, for reasons still unexplained, Olier changed from the direction of Saint Vincent, his confessor for three years, to that of Father de Condren. This was not a desertion--far from it. In 1649 he wrote, "For extraordinary affairs, we do not fail to see Monsieur Vincent, and for ordinary matters, all our brothers assembled." He did not open the Vaugirard Seminary or accept the pastorate of Saint-Sulpice until he had consulted the Saint. "Monsieur Vincent is our father," he often used to say to his seminarians. Olier died on April 2, 1657, assisted by his holy friend. The latter consoled the priests of Saint-Sulpice in their sorrow; we still have an excerpt from the address to them on this occasion, which has been attributed to Saint Vincent (cf. vol. XIII, no. 51).

[2]In August, she entered the Congregation of the Daughters of the Blessed Virgin, also known as the Daughters of the Inner Life of Mary, which her uncle Jean-Jacques Olier had planned to found, but which did not materialize until after his death (cf. no. 3224).

Letter 3167. - Reg. 2, p. 214.

apparent in the Apostles, who followed Jesus Christ and who nevertheless discussed among themselves several blameworthy topics.[1] I see no other remedy for the general failings—which, by God's grace, are not great—than public and private admonitions, joined to prayer and patience.

3168. - TO FIRMIN GET, SUPERIOR, IN MARSEILLES

Paris, July 30, 1660

Monsieur,

The grace of Our Lord be with you forever!

I have not received any letters from you by this regular mail. I am sending you a copy of the will of the late Marquise de Vins and its final codicil, to be kept in your house. I await the report I requested of you on the missions you have given, so that we can seek payment of your benefits.

I am sending you the bill of exchange for which I led you to hope; it is for 984 livres, namely, 600 livres for money you have advanced—and will advance—for the poor convicts, and 384 livres to be sent to the Comte d'Insiquin[1] in Algiers. Please forward them at the first opportunity. If Providence sets him and his son free before this alms arrives, it can be used for other captives.

The Marquise de Nantouillet[2] is anxious to know whether you forwarded the sum she sent you for her son, whether communication is open between Marseilles and Algiers, and what she should do to secure the liberty of that young nobleman. Please write her a

---

[1]Cf. Mt 9:33-34. (NAB)

Letter 3168. - Archives of the Mission, Paris, copy made from the original in the Hains Family collection.

[1]Cf. no. 3116a, n. 3.

[2]Louise d'Aguesseau, second wife of Henri du Prat, Marquis de Nantouillet and Commander of the cavalry regiment of Queen Anne of Austria.

few words by some hand other than your own, and let me know the state of your health. I am very worried about it; I pray and am having others pray that it will be restored to you.

I am writing to M. Huguier to give 6 livres, which we have received here, to Denis Beauvais, a convict on the *Capitaine,* and 30 sous to Jacques Fournier, known as Larivière, on the *Saint-Dominique.*

Since I began writing this I received M. Delespiney's letter of the twentieth, in which I see that, by God's grace, you are better. I thank Him infinitely for this and ask Him to complete your cure. It is in His love that I am, Monsieur, your most humble servant.

VINCENT DEPAUL,
i.s.C.M.

3169. - TO JEAN MARTIN, SUPERIOR, IN TURIN

Paris, July 30, 1660

Monsieur,

The grace of O[ur] L[ord] be with you forever!

I received your dear letter of the seventeenth. I praise God for the rest the members of your family are taking and for the good health they are enjoying after such hard work. It seems to me that you include yourself among them, since you say nothing of your quartan fever, which greatly increases my joy. I ask O[ur] L[ord] to be pleased to renew all of you in His Spirit so that all your operations may be His and the good results proceeding from them may be fruits of eternal life.

God has chosen to take from us one of our best Brothers, namely, Sirven, who was the living Rule of the Company in Sedan. A wise,

---

Letter 3169. - Archives of the Mission, Turin, original signed letter.

intelligent man, he did good to everyone and willingly devoted himself to the relief of the sick poor and the consolation of the afflicted. The whole town, which loved him dearly, expressed great regret at losing him—even heretics, who were edified by his unassuming behavior and charity.

We have good reason to believe that God has crowned his soul in heaven, giving him the kingdom He has prepared for His beloved who practice works of mercy [1] on earth, as did this servant of His. Nevertheless, Monsieur, we must still pray for him, since we are not sure of God's judgments, and this prompts the whole Church to pray for the faithful departed.

You must not think of receiving Vaugin,[2] who has left the Company, but you can give him up to fifty écus if you have them and he wants to get them there. We will repay them here, on your bill of exchange, to whomever you indicate to me. Meanwhile, I am, Monsieur, in the love of O[ur] L[ord], your most humble servant.

VINCENT DEPAUL,
i.s.C.M.

Addressed: Monsieur Martin, Superior of the Priests of the Mission, in Turin

---

[1]Cf. Mt 7:9. (NAB)

[2]Jean Vaugin, born in Puzieux (Vosges), entered the Congregation of the Mission as a coadjutor Brother in November 1644, at nineteen years of age.

3170. - *J. DE BREVEDENT TO SAINT VINCENT*

Rouen, July 30, 1660

Monsieur,

Very humble greetings in O[ur] L[ord] J[esus] C[hrist]!

Despite my infidelities, lack of confidence, and other hindrances, God in His Infinite Goodness has had mercy on me and calmed most of my interior turmoil. You prayed for this, for which I thank you as much as possible, begging you once again to thank Him with all your heart for this inestimable benefit conferred on my unworthy and wretched person. I ask you also to have your friends do the same and to continue to pray that He will grant me the grace to do His most holy Will in the way He wishes.

It has been judged advisable for me, such as I am, to write down some of the sentiments and lights God has been pleased to give me concerning the heresy of the Jansenists. This amounts to describing their present situation, the way to recognize them, the deceptions they use to corrupt the faithful, and, lastly, what Catholics must do to remain Catholics and to defend their Mother the Church in these circumstances.

On this point, mention should be made of a detail relating to St-Cyran,[1] *which became known through you. It is something I heard you say one day in church at Saint-Lazare during repetition of prayer, and you also said it to Father François Sevin, a Capuchin, who (I think) was Guardian of St-Jacques Convent in Paris at the time. He repeated it to me about twelve days or two weeks ago in this town. You said that you were a friend of St-Cyran, and, while you were praying together one day, he told you at its conclusion that he had made a very good meditation but was having great*

Letter 3170. - Archives of the Mission, Turin, original autograph letter.

[1]Jean du Verger de Hauranne, Abbé de Saint-Cyran, was born in Bayonne in 1581. He had met Saint Vincent in Paris around 1622 and soon struck up a friendship with him. According to his nephew, Martin de Barcos (cf. *Défense de feu M. Vincent de Paul),* he had supposedly rendered important services to the Saint, and the Congregation of the Mission was in some measure indebted to him for the possession of the Collège des Bons-Enfants and for Saint-Lazare, as well as for the Bull of approbation obtained from the Roman Court. What is certain is that their meetings, rather frequent while Saint Vincent was living at the Bons-Enfants, became more rare after 1632 and almost ceased after 1634. In 1638 Saint-Cyran was arrested on the authority of Cardinal Richelieu and imprisoned in the Château de Vincennes. Shortly after the Cardinal died in 1642, Louis XIII allowed the prisoner to communicate with people outside. This measure of clemency was soon followed by a second: on February 16, 1643, Saint-Cyran was set free. He did not enjoy the royal favor for long, dying of a cerebral hemorrhage on October 11, 1643.

scruples about sharing it with you. After you had strongly urged him to do so (which was what he wanted), he told you he had made it on the words Tempus destruendi, tempus aedificandi; tempus evellendi, tempus dissipandi[2] *and that God had made him see clearly that, until now, God had wanted to make use of the Roman Church, but the time had come when He wanted to destroy it, and a few other details. On another occasion, stamping his foot, he said "Oh! what a coward Calvin was for not knowing how to defend himself!" And you replied that he was defending heretics; but he did not listen to you or yield in any way.*

So, I am asking you now, Monsieur, whether you think it is a good idea for me to use that and to make these truths known to those who are still ignorant of them, which I think can be useful to Catholics. I ask this because the members of that party are trying to get others to think highly of their authors.

I also know other important details concerning Jansenius. In this regard it is said that the Abbot of St-Germain,[3] who was with the late Queen Mother,[4] was very close to him for twelve or fifteen years and that he was an out-and-out Calvinist. It is also said that he knows many important things about this, which he has even written down and is ready to have printed but is awaiting the Queen's[5] instructions in that regard. I think that this is because he expressed his opinion of Cardinal Richelieu[6] too freely one day and was forbidden to speak any more. I think also that you will be rendering an important service to God and to the Church if you oblige him to do this and get permission for him to do so.

Persons who are staunch Catholics and zealous in defending the Church in the present circumstances feel that one of the most important

---

[2]*A time to destroy, a time to build; a time to tear out, a time to scatter*--thoughts from the third chapter of Ecclesiastes: "There is an appointed time for everything,. . . ." Eccl 3:1ff. (NAB)

[3]Henri de Bourbon, Bishop of Metz, Abbot of Saint-Germain since 1623.

[4]Marie de Médicis (1573-1642), mother of Louis XIII.

[5]Anne of Austria, wife of Louis XIII and Regent for their son, Louis XIV.

[6]Armand du Plessis, Cardinal Richelieu, was born in Paris on September 9, 1585, the youngest of five children of François du Plessis and Suzanne de la Porte. As Bishop of Luçon he acted as a spokesman for the clergy at the Estates-General of 1614. Raised to the Cardinalate in 1622, he entered the Council of the King (1624) and quickly became its head. His guidance of foreign affairs helped to raise France to the highest echelon among European powers. In the administration of French internal affairs Richelieu imposed useful reforms in finances, the army, and legislation (Code Michau). He was the author of royal absolutism: he destroyed the privileges of the Huguenots and of the Provinces and reestablished the authority of the intendants throughout France. He died on December 4, 1642, attended by--among others--his niece, the Duchesse d'Aiguillon, and King Louis XIII, who followed the Cardinal's deathbed advice in appointing Mazarin as Chief Minister.

affairs in the Church of God right now is that of the Carmelites, especially since it is one of the holiest and most perfect Orders. They consider it the one that has best preserved the spirit of its Institute, and they think that those from the big convent are wrong.

(1) There is the influence of the holiest persons in the Order—among others, Sister Marguerite du Saint-Sacrement who has just died, and Mother Jeanne who is in Pontoise. They are on the other side. They have refused their requests and have thought and said that this will be the ruin of their Order. Now, you know how influential is the opinion of persons on intimate terms with God and who have His ear.

(2) There is no danger in maintaining this primitive discipline and line of conduct established by the Pope, since the Sisters felt that none among them had been led astray from the perfection of their Order and Institute and the spirit of Saint Teresa while being guided in this way. In addition, it can be reasonably presumed and hoped that the same will hold true for the future, since there is nothing clearer to the contrary, and they do not have the same assurance concerning the new style of direction because they have no experience with it.

By the same token, however, there appears to be some danger in that, and it is great; for, since the leadership is in the hands of those two Abbots who have the authority to perpetuate it by naming others of their own choice, I suppose that one of the two who remains will be Catholic (of which, however, not everyone is convinced, and several doubt it) but may unwittingly appoint someone who is a Jansenist, especially since he will not know him (because I am sure you are aware that such a person today does not appear to be one and, imo,[7] *strongly opposed, whereas he is so in reality; consequently, he is all the more dangerous). Even if he were not, there are those who will come after him. And if Jansenism enters that house, what a loss it will be for the Church and what an advantage for that heretical sect!*

Now, we do not foresee this danger from the other side, for they are all Doctors of the Sorbonne, who belong to the sound Catholic party and are strongly opposed to that heresy. It is not only probable but certain that they will never appoint any men whom they have excluded from their membership because of their unworthiness and corruption and whom they consider open enemies of the Church and of themselves, unless those persons give such irrefutable proof of repentance and conversion that it

---

[7]*But rather.*

is judged that there will no longer be any danger. This must be the case not only for the present but for the future.

Another difficulty we see is that the Bishops will step into this dispute to take over the leadership and end the dissension. It is said that they have the right to do so and that the Sisters in the big convent seem to be willing to accept this—at least this is what is feared. Now, should this happen, just imagine the danger for this Order, given the state of several Bishops, such as those in Sens,[8] *Beauvais,*[9] *and many others.*

Another reason is that people see no problem with the small convent in this matter, no indication or cause for doubt, nor even a suspicion. The same cannot be said for the big convent, not to mention the others, for here in Rouen in the house of that Order, which sides with the big convent, we have a Superior who is upsetting the good Catholics in this place, and with good reason. There is much scheming with Madame de Longueville,[10] *the great defender of the Jansenists in our province and perhaps in the whole of France. The same holds for the Fathers of the Oratory and the appointment of someone about whom people were suspicious and had warned her about the danger—and with good reason. Recently, she had a sermon preached on the feast of Mount Carmel by a person who is suspect, and when efforts were made to alert her to those things, she went in hiding, refused to listen to the warnings, and lied about it, saying that the Rector of the Jesuits had ordered her to act as she did, which was false.*

What is proving a stumbling block to respectable people in this affair, Monsieur, is the rumor that you are siding with the big convent. I would like to think that you have no idea of these difficulties or that you have noted even greater ones on the other side and some good things that we do not see. Nevertheless, having been informed of these things by upright persons, staunch Catholics to whom I think God has given the zeal and knowledge or the enlightenment to defend the affairs and interests of His

---

[8]Louis-Henri de Pardaillan de Gondrin (1646- September 19, 1674).

[9]Nicolas Choart de Buzenval.

[10]Anne-Geneviève de Bourbon, second wife of Henri II, Duc de Longueville, was a beautiful, learned, and witty woman with a passion for intrigue, who took an active part in the second Fronde. She was the sister of the Grand Condé and, like him, a resolute enemy of Mazarin. She had a profound veneration for Saint Vincent. After her husband's death (1663), she went to live close to the Carmelite nuns on rue Saint-Jacques, spent the rest of her days carrying out the penitential exercises and austerities practiced at Port-Royal, and died a Jansenist on April 15, 1679. Her life has been written by Joseph-François Bourgoin de Villefore, *La véritable vie d'Anne-Geneviève de Bourbon, duchesse de Longueville* (2 vols., 2e ed., Amsterdam: J.F. Jolly, 1739) and by Victor Cousin, *Madame de Longueville. Nouvelles études sur les femmes illustres et la société du XVIIe siècle* (Paris: Didier, 1853).

house the Church, and having followed their advice in this, trusting in the goodness and virtue with which I have remarked God has endowed you, I have taken the liberty, in all possible humility, respect, and simplicity, of placing these scatterbrained arguments before you, just as they are, so that you may examine them and see if they are in any way reasonable.

If you deem it appropriate, please ask God where the truth lies in this. In any case, you might share with us the enlightenment God has given you regarding this affair and which led you to support them with your approval (if this is indeed the case, for I am not sure of this and say it only to you, repeating what these persons have said and on their advice) so I can give some satisfaction to those persons.

People think that the death of Abbé de Chandenier [11] *occurred by divine permission so that you might see for yourself the danger in which that Order was under that sort of leadership, as I have already explained previously with two arguments.*

Assuming that those arguments are considered reasonable, supported by a few even better ones that God will give to those who are willing to ask Him for enlightenment on this matter, the persons to whom God has given those insights feel that the remedy would be to present them to His Holiness and entreat him to study them and, if he thinks it appropriate, to command that things remain as they were originally ordained by his predecessors. They also think it advisable to send to him one or several persons capable of carrying out this business well; for, as I have already stated, this is considered one of the most important affairs in the Church of God today.

Another solution would be to place the leadership in the hands of the monks of the same Order, the Discalced Carmelites, rather than allow it to fall to the Bishops.

Finally, Monsieur, it suffices for me to bring these matters to your attention for the Order I have mentioned. Examine whether these modest opinions come from God; in which case (if you think it appropriate), speak to Him yourself and see what He has to say to you about it.

It is said that poets are allowed special poetic license. I hope that you in your goodness will grant me, whom you know, an even greater one, allowing me to send you my impertinences, just as they stand, so disorganized and in disarray, with their crossing out, mistakes, etc., without my writing them over.

---

[11]Louis de Chandenier, Abbé de Tournus.

If you deem it appropriate to send me a note of reply, especially on the second point regarding St-Cyran, please address it to the Pastor of St-Nicolas in this town. I will be here only until next Friday; but, if you are unable to write so soon, he will forward my letters to me, wherever I am.

I am, with all my heart and with all due respect, in the love of O[ur] L[ord] J[esus] C[hrist], Monsieur, your most humble and obedient servant.

J. DE BREVEDENT,
unworthy priest

Some upright persons have asked me to recommend to your prayers an affair they consider important, concerning the peace of a family and, consequently, the glory of God. Would you please be so kind as to do this?

3171. - TO JEAN PARRE, IN REIMS

Paris, July 31, 1660

Dear Brother,

The grace of Our Lord be with you forever!

I received your letter of the twenty-sixth of this month. On the order of M. Séraucourt, your bill of exchange for 848 livres, intended for the restoration of ruined churches, has been paid. I hope that at the first meeting they will say that something else should be sent for this purpose. I will have your letter presented at it, which will provide an additional reason to mention the missions to be given. Whenever you like, draw also on our account the sums about which you wrote us in a separate note, namely, 984 livres 10 sous on the one hand, and 85 livres on the other, as well as another 500 livres. This comes to a total of 1570 livres and not 1603 livres,

Letter 3171. - This letter is known to us through its Italian translation, inserted into one of the documents of the collection for the process of beatification, *Summarium Responsivum,* p. 54.

as you wrote me. Please remember that the 984 livres 10 sous are to assist and relieve the poorest and neediest people in Champagne and Picardy. As for the 500, I will let you know for what they are intended. The 85 livres 10 sous are for poor priests. I mentioned to you only 76 livres 10 sous, but now I am adding to that 9 livres which I received since then.

Today or tomorrow we will have a bundle of church vestments taken to the Saint-Quentin coach or mail coach; the other bundle is not ready yet; that will be for another time.

I remain, in Our Lord, dear Brother, your most affectionate brother and servant.

VINCENT DEPAUL,
i.s.C.M.

3172. - *MONSIEUR BOURDET TO SAINT VINCENT*

Melun, this last day of July, 1660

Monsieur and Venerable Father,

The honor Your Reverence paid me last Friday, in explaining your intention to me, has led me to believe that Your Reverence will allow me to inform you by the present letter that I have fulfilled my obligations toward good Mother de Maupeou[1] *and the two other ladies accompanying*

Letter 3172. - Archives of the Mission, Turin, original autograph letter.

[1]Madeleine-Élisabeth de Maupeou, Assistant in the First Monastery of the Visitation in Paris, had gone to Melun (Seine-et-Marne), accompanied by Sister Élisabeth-Angélique Fouquet, at the request of Henri de Pardaillan de Gondrin, Archbishop of Sens, to reestablish order and union among the Ursulines there.

The daughter of Gilles de Maupeou, Intendant and Comptroller General of Finances under Henry IV, she entered the First Monastery of the Visitation in Paris in January 1628, at thirty-two years of age. On May 24, 1635, the nuns of the Caen convent elected her as their Superior and reelected her on May 20, 1638. In 1641 she went to Bayonne to found a monastery of her Order, at the request of her nephew, François Fouquet the Local Ordinary. Mother de Maupeou remained in Bayonne and was again elected Superior there on June 2, 1650. On her return to Paris, she became Superior of the First Monastery (1655-58), where she died on July 3, 1674, at the age of seventy-eight. (Cf. *Année sainte,* vol. VII, pp. 249-54.) Her niece Sister Élisabeth-Angélique was the sister of Bishop Fouquet.

her, with regard to the courteous attentions you instructed me to show them. They received them with joy and with great respect from me, seeing that I will have no hope in the future of rendering any service in this house, due to the suspicion in which I am held. Those good Sisters have been at variance for so long that some of them think I have espoused the cause of the Bishop of Sens too passionately, although throughout my entire proceedings I have taken no side but that of our good Jesus.

This obliges me to entreat Your Reverence to kindly do me the charity of giving me some small duty since they no longer want my services, although I have served them very faithfully. You have been able to remark this in the letters I showed Your Reverence, addressed to me by the Nuncio.[2]

I hope for some help from Your Charity, considering the very great difficulties I am experiencing during this disunion of persecution with regard to my benefice, caused by M. Daisne[3]*, who is forcibly stealing my benefice from me, to put it bluntly. I hope from your goodness, for the love of our good Jesus, that you will assist me in my dire need and allow me to dare to consider myself respectfully, for the rest of my days, venerable Father, your most humble and obedient servant.*

BOURDET,
unworthy confessor of the Ursulines of Melun

3173. - *JEAN LARMURYE TO SAINT VINCENT*

Saint-Léonard,[1] *August 2, 1660*

Monsieur,

My confidence in Your Charity leads me to hope that you will listen to the most humble request I am addressing to you with regard to a good man

---

[2]Celio Piccolomini.

[3]Chrétien Daisne, born in Sedan, entered the Congregation of the Mission on September 21, 1644, at twenty years of age, took his vows in 1646, and was ordained a priest in March 1651. He left the Congregation twice; in April 1659 he wanted to work with the Pastor of Saint-Jean-en-Grève, but Saint Vincent wrote to Pierre Loisel that he did not know Daisne well enough to give him a letter of recommendation (cf. vol. VII, no. 2822). M. Bourdet's benefice and the direction of the Ursulines seem to have attracted M. Daisne.

Letter 3173. - Archives of the Mission, Turin, original autograph letter.

[1]Principal town of a canton in Haute-Vienne.

of the poorer class, the only cousin of the late M. Constantin, Canon of Luçon. On hearing a vague rumor that his cousin had died, he went to Luçon to learn that what he feared was true and was informed by the Missionaries that M. Chiroye,[2] *who is away, had inherited the estate of the poor deceased man but that he was not one to try to take advantage of this; when he had taken care of certain expenses, he would hand over to him what remained, when he gave proof of his relationship.*

Monsieur, you are upright and charitable; I entreat you to kindly take the trouble to tell those priests that it is your wish that they be pleased to relieve his great need because he is responsible for his family. Those priests must have known that, since they let him stay in their house in Luçon, while awaiting M. Chiroye's return from the country. However, when he realized that he had no proof of his relationship with the deceased Canon and that these priests might not believe what he might tell them, he left. When he was leaving, they told him to have someone write to you about this matter and to ask you, as I am doing most earnestly for him, to be willing to continue your holy charities in his regard. I assure you, on my word of honor as a priest, that they are being put to good use and that I have no greater glory than to declare myself, Monsieur, your most humble and obedient servant.

JEAN LARMURYE,
priest

If you honor me with a reply, please address it to M. Philippe Michel, merchant in Limoges.

Addressed: *Monsieur Vincent, General of the Missionaries, living in the faubourg Saint-Denis, at the Lazare, in Paris*

[2]Jacques Chiroye.

3174. - TO RENÉ ALMÉRAS, IN TOURS

August 4, 1660

I was deeply affected by the first news of your illness, fearing that the fever had followed your great weakness, but, as I see in your second letter that, instead of this, your weakness has greatly lessened, my concern is less as well. God be praised for that, Monsieur! It belongs to Him alone to put to death and to raise to life.[1]

I am greatly consoled to know that you are at the Oratory, where you find charity, as it were, on its royal throne, causing you to experience what it really is, through the kindness and help you receive from those good Fathers. I ask Our Lord to be their reward for this. You already had your life restored in their house in Bourbon,[2] where they thought you were going to die, and I hope you will now receive good health in the house in Tours, where you have already found some relief.

At the first opportunity, I will take the honor of thanking Reverend Father Séguenot[3] for this in a letter written expressly for that purpose. Meanwhile, do not be in any hurry to return; wait until you are strong enough for the journey. Get whatever money you will need. I will be more consoled by your return than I could be by anything else that might happen to me. I ask God that it may be as soon as possible and that you come back in perfect health. In the name of God, take care of your health in the meantime; spare nothing; hire a litter. I thought I was doing well when I sent you to

---

Letter 3174. - Reg. 2, p. 268.

[1]Cf. Jn 5:21. (NAB)

[2]Bourbon-l'Archambault (Allier), where René Alméras had gone for its mineral baths.

[3]Claude Séguenot, born in Avallon (Yonne) on May 6, 1596, left the law courts to enter the Oratory in 1624. He soon struck up a friendship with Abbé de Saint-Cyran. His translation into French of Saint Augustine's book on virginity earned him about four years' imprisonment in the Bastille (1638-43) and the censure of the Sorbonne. He was Superior in Nancy, Dijon, Rouen, Saumur, and Tours, and was appointed Assistant to the General in 1661, 1666, and 1669. He governed the Oratory of Paris (1667-73) and died in that city on March 7, 1676. Several of his works are still in manuscript form.

Richelieu,[4] but I will never do so again, even if you and I should live for fifteen or twenty years in the same state.

3175. - TO MELCHIOR GAUDOIN,[1] IN LE MANS

Paris, August 4, 1660

Dear Brother,

I received your letter with joy, and it revived the warm feelings I have always had for you. I thank God for the offering you want to make Him by the vows that are customary in the Company, and I ask His Holy Spirit, who has inspired you to take them, to fulfill this desire in you. I am asking M. Laudin to admit you to this holy act, which is the one that will be most pleasing to God in your whole life, if you do it in a spirit of sacrifice through Our Lord Jesus Christ. Happy will you be, dear Brother, to be crucified with Him[2] for the glory of His Father and the salvation of the people, for you will also reign with Him for all eternity! Amen.

I am sending you the receipt you requested for the sum of money you left with M. Maillard.

I recommend myself to your prayers. I am, in the love of Our Lord, your. . . .

---

[4]René Alméras had been sent by Saint Vincent to Richelieu on the occasion of the King's passing there en route to Paris with his young bride Maria Teresa.

Letter 3175. - Pémartin, *op. cit.*, vol. IV, p. 584, L. 2058, from the original placed on sale by Laverdet in January 1854. The latter wrote: "The Saint tried to write five short lines as a postscript but crossed them out because they were illegible. His signature seems to have been written with the greatest difficulty."

[1]Melchior Gaudoin, coadjutor Brother, was born in Surcamps (Somme) on March 6, 1620. He entered the Congregation of the Mission in Paris on June 5, 1658, and took his vows on December 8, 1660, in the presence of M. Laudin.

[2]Cf. Phil 2:8-11. (NAB)

3176. - *JEAN DE FRICOURT TO SAINT VINCENT*

Saintes, August 4, 1660

Monsieur and Most Honored Father,

Your holy blessing!

When M. Fleury told me he was taking the honor of writing to you, it made me wonder at the same time if it was appropriate for me to take the same liberty. At first I felt it was contrary to the respect I owe you; but, having reflected on the warm welcome and love you show to all sorts of persons, I thought that, being your son, I should have as much and even more confidence in your goodness than anyone else.

I must confess, Most Honored Father, that if I had sufficient mastery over myself always to consider my lowliness and nothingness, I would not have the temerity to take it into my head to write to such an exalted, holy person. But I would willingly pass for someone rash, provided I obtain what I am seeking, namely, the assistance of your prayers, an elevation of your heart toward God on my behalf, and a little remembrance of one of the most wretched children you have conceived in J[esus] C[hrist] and received into your Company. In it I hope to be all my life, by the grace of God, Monsieur and Most Honored Father, your most humble and obedient servant.

J. DE FRICOURT,
Seminarian of the Mission

Addressed: *Monsieur Vincent, Superior General of the Congregation of the Mission, at the Bons-Enfants*

Letter 3176. - Archives of the Mission, Turin, original autograph letter.

3177. - *SISTER JOLLY TO SAINT VINCENT*

Paris, August 5, 1660

Monsieur,

Most humble and respectful greetings in Our Lord!

Since my father told me your opinion and sentiments concerning our departure, I thought you would want to hear my account of it. I can assure you, Monsieur, that we left without any intention of selling our house; that would have been pointless because my father has been responsible for it for more than a year. Our only grounds were the incessant humiliations we endured from the nuns because we were a burden to the house and, although my sister was well disposed toward her vocation, she was suffering more than I.

Since the Community did not want to keep her any longer, Monsieur, how could she not be allowed to leave in her religious dress, since she had no other? Even if she might have had one, she had no pension and nothing to live on. I felt that nature and charity obliged me, rather than someone else, to accompany her and to trust in Providence, which I found first, through the Duchesse de Noirmoutiers,[1] *without hoping for it, and then, through you, Monsieur, without deserving it, and this has overwhelmed me.*

Right now we are with our father, who will look out for her. If, however, after we have made known to you our upright intentions, you decide that I should return to my religious house, I will not fail to do so, determined to endure as much as I can. I will leave my sister behind in her religious habit, glad not to fail in my vocation and to follow your wise instructions.

Letter 3177. - Archives of the Mission, Turin, original autograph letter.

[1]Renée-Julie Aubéry, wife of Louis de la Trémouille, Duc de Noirmoutiers; she died on March 20, 1679.

That is why, Monsieur, I await your orders in all humility, and am respectfully, Monsieur, your most humble and obedient servant.

Sister C. N. du Saint-Sacrement JOLLY,
U[nworthy] B[enedictine] N[un]

I am sending you our obedience,[2] *since my papa told us to return it to you.*

Addressed: *Monsieur Vincent, General of the Priests of the Mission, at Saint-Lazare*

3178. - *CANON LE MARESCHAL TO SAINT VINCENT*

[August 1660] [1]

Very Reverend Father,

The benefit gained by those you receive into your house to be instructed for the priesthood has seemed so great to us, when they have presented themselves for ordination, that it leads me to ask you to kindly assist this good young man by your wise instructions. He is anxious to make a few days' retreat before coming here for the Order of Subdiaconate.

Out of consideration for us, do him the kindness of accepting his direction. Although I do not have the honor of being well known by you, I am convinced that you will receive this petition favorably, since I am writing to ask it for reasons of charity, on behalf of the bearer. We are placing a great deal of hope in him because of his natural goodness.

In a short time I hope to join M. de Beausse, a Canon in this church in Évreux, to make a retreat. That will be a good opportunity for me to get

---

[2]A document authorizing monks or nuns to travel outside their monastery.

Letter 3178. - Archives of the Mission, Turin, original autograph letter.

[1]Date added on the back of the original by Brother Ducournau.

to know you and to assure you in person, as I do now, that I am, Very Reverend Father, your most humble and obedient servant.

LE MARESCHAL,
Priest, Canon, and Promoter [2] of Évreux

Addressed: *Monsieur Vincent, Superior General of the Mission, at Saint-Lazare, at the end of the faubourg St-Denis, in Paris*

3179. - *MADAME DE FLACOURT [1] TO SAINT VINCENT*

[August 1660]

Monsieur,

Please be so kind as to write to the Duchesse d'Aiguillon to ask her if she would be willing to lend me a room in her home, the ugliest and smallest in her house, provided it is over the garden. The reason is that I cannot sleep in the house we have rented. At present I am at Madame de Brinvilliers' home, but her sister-in-law has recently arrived so I have to leave. I ask Madame d'Aiguillon for a room for only three weeks or a month.

If you do me the kindness of making this request of the Duchess, you will be performing the greatest act of charity in the world because I have not slept for the past six months. I will be at Madame d'Aiguillon's house only during the night and will not inconvenience her because I will stay at the rented house during the day. The carriage will come for me. I will do this for only one month because we are looking everywhere for something either for sale or for rent.

[2]The Promoter of Justice, an official in the diocesan Curia, dealt with contentious cases in which the public good was at stake (cf. *Code of Canon Law* [1983], canons 1430-1437).

Letter 3179. - Archives of the Mission, Turin, original autograph letter.

[1]Marie Sublet, wife of Julien le Bret, Seigneur de Flacourt, Counselor at the Parlement of Paris; she died on July 29, 1686.

Please request this of her, and you will be doing a favor for me, who am, Monsieur, your most humble and obedient servant.

M. DE FLACOURT,
daughter of Madame de Romilly

I also recommend myself to your good prayers for our business affairs, which are not going very well.

Please let me know the reply as soon as possible because I am in a hurry.

3180. - *CLAUDE DE POUILLY TO SAINT VINCENT*

[August 1660] [1]

The high esteem in which you are held, Monsieur, prompts the Marquis de Pransac [2] *and me to hope you will do us the favor of accepting into your house our eldest son, who is twenty years of age. While my husband and I were in the city, he acted on some bad advice and climbed up a ladder to our apartment, carrying off all the gold and silver he could find. At the same time, he also took all the silver plate in the pantry and left our house. Since his departure, several persons have warned us about his behavior and told us that he is completely dissipated, attracted to brothels and dissolute living, uses foul language, and is a renegade. In a word, he is in utter disgrace and has abandoned our gentle Savior and His august Mother, to whom I had offered and dedicated him for their greater glory and service, as I did with all our other children.*

Please take into consideration, Monsieur, the representation I am making to you here of the state of the soul and conscience of this wretched young man and the danger he is in of being lost and damned for all eternity. Then, too, I most humbly entreat you to have compassion on us, who see him in this danger. We are trying to have him apprehended.

I entreat you to do me the honor of letting me know whether you will grant us and him the favor of taking him and, in which case, to let us know

---

Letter 3180. - Archives of the Mission, Turin, original autograph letter.

[1]Date added on the back of the original by Brother Ducournau.

[2]Alexandre de Redon, Marquis de Pransac. His wife, Claude de Pouilly, also had the title of Marquise d'Esne.

the conditions; namely, how much we should give you for his room and board and everything else, and whether we should pay in advance, quarterly, or otherwise.

If you are pleased to honor me with a reply, Monsieur, please seal it. I am hoping from your perfect charity that you will undertake the conversion of this sinner.

I am, with profound respect, Monsieur, your most humble and obedient servant.

De Pouilly d'Esne

Addressed: *Monsieur Vincent, at Saint-Lazare*

3180a. - TO FIRMIN GET, SUPERIOR, IN MARSEILLES

Paris, August 6, 1660

Monsieur,

The grace of Our Lord be with you forever!

I received your letter of July 27. I just forwarded to M. Desdames in Poland the one from M. Truillard. [1] I have not yet been able to look at the ones from Tunis.

Last week [2] I sent you a bill of exchange for 984 livres from Messieurs Simonnet on Messieurs Napollon. Six are to reimburse you for the money you advanced to the captives and the rest is for the Comte d'Insiquin,[3] a captive in Algiers.

When you send me the attestations of the missions you have given, we will seek payment from the foundation of Madame de Vins.

Letter 3180a. - Copy made from *Recueil Nodet.* The letter was published in *Annales C.M.* (1943-44), p. 256, and reprinted in *Mission et Charité,* 19-20, no. 128, pp. 162-63. This edition uses the latter text.

[1]Captain of the Cavalry for the Prince of Maldonia.

[2]Cf. no. 3168.

[3]Cf. no. 3116a, n. 3.

The Attorney General told his mother[4] that not only is the foundation of the hospital[5] on the books of the State, but it is to be paid; consequently, so are the stipends for the chaplains of the galleys. In which case, it will be a good idea for you to give each of them his share.

Thank God you are in better health and your little family is well. We had a few sick men here, but they are better, thank God, with the exception of Brother Le Gouz,[6] who is in danger of death. It will be a great loss if he dies, for he is one of the best men in the seminary, in every sense.

M. Alméras had to stay in Tours on his way back from Richelieu because he became quite weak. This made us very apprehensive, but in his last letter—which he was unable to write in his own hand—he told me that he was gradually improving.

I embrace the priests who are with you, and especially your own dear heart. I am, in the love of Our Lord, Monsieur, your most humble servant.

VINCENT DEPAUL,
i.s.C.M.

3181. - TO DENIS LAUDIN, SUPERIOR, IN LE MANS

Paris, August 7, 1660

Monsieur,

The grace of O[ur] L[ord] be with you forever!

I received two letters from you, the last of which is dated the

---

[4]Madame Fouquet, the mother of Nicolas Fouquet, Attorney General and Superintendent of Finances.

[5]The Hospital for Galley Convicts in Marseilles.

[6]René Legouz.

Letter 3181. - Archives of the Mission, Paris, original signed letter.

first of this month. In view of Brother de la Pesse's [1] infirmities, which prevent him from devoting himself to study and teaching, I approve of your proposal to give him a duty in the procurator's office, but for M. Turpin[2] to retain the title of Procurator for the time being, so he can sign the necessary documents.

I would like to consult M. Dehorgny about what decision to take regarding the keys of your treasury, which Brother Jean Proust has to use frequently. I have not yet been able to do so. I will send you the reply about this some other time, or I will have him do so.

I am writing to Brothers de la Pesse and Gaudoin about the vows which one has taken and the other is asking to take.

Please let me know how the nephew of M. François, who is a painter in Paris, is keeping and acting; whether he is well behaved, does well in his studies, and shows promise.

God has chosen to take from us one of our best Brothers, namely, Sirven, who was the living Rule of the Company in Sedan. A wise, intelligent man, he did good to everyone and devoted himself willingly to the relief of the sick poor and the consolation of the afflicted. The whole town and the environs deeply regret his passing—even the heretics, who were edified by his unassuming behavior and assisted by his charity.

We have good reason to believe that God has crowned his soul in heaven, after having given him the grace to practice the works of mercy[3] on earth the way he did. Nevertheless, Monsieur, we must not neglect to pray for him, since we are not sure of God's judgments; this prompts the whole Church to pray for the departed, even for the just.

---

[1]Jean-Antoine Delapesse, born in Annecy on February 9, 1638, entered the Paris Seminary on September 19, 1656, and took his vows on September 22, 1658, in the presence of M. Delespiney. The date of his ordination is not indicated (cf. *Notices,* vol. V [Supplement], p. 176).

[2]Pierre Turpin, born in Roye (Somme) on April 9, 1629, entered the Congregation of the Mission on September 16, 1655, and took his vows in Le Mans on October 6, 1658. He had left the seminary for health reasons but was readmitted.

[3]Cf. Mt 7:9. (NAB)

We have had several sick men, but they are better, thank God, with the exception of young Brother Le Gouz, who is in danger of death. It will be a great loss if he dies, because he is one of the best men in the seminary, in every sense.

M. Alméras had to stay in Tours on his way back from Richelieu because he became quite weak. This made us very apprehensive, but in his last letter he told me that he was gradually improving, thank God, in whom I am, Monsieur, your most humble servant.

VINCENT DEPAUL,
i.s.C.M.

If I delay in answering you about the keys, remind me as soon as possible.

Addressed: Monsieur Laudin, Superior of the Priests of the Mission, in Le Mans

3182. - *MOTHER DE MONLUC TO SAINT VINCENT*

August 7 [1660] [1]

Reverend Father,

Your very great goodness, with which I am well acquainted, easily convinces me that you will not take amiss my boldness in requesting a favor of you for this holy priest. He asks your blessing and the honor of your patronage regarding his pious intention to go to Rome, where he will greatly need your powerful recommendations. When you get to know him, you will not regret having granted him your assistance there.

He has never been to Paris and is totally unfamiliar with it. He is a person of high social rank, although his humility causes him to make himself appear the lowliest, keep the fact quiet, and lead a very poor, apostolic life. He has preached and heard confessions in this town with good results. He will be very much indebted to your charity if you deign

---

Letter 3182. - Archives of the Mission, Turin, original autograph letter.

[1]Year added on the back of the original by Brother Ducournau.

to assist him and to procure help for him in that city from those men and women who esteem the faithful servants of God, among whom he is included.

If I was not aware that you respect [those] who bear my name, I would not approach you with this very humble recommendation. It will not displease you because you are so zealous in the service of God, which you so worthily procure.

These reflections lead me to hope that you will hear and answer my plea and also that I have a prerogative which is quite precious to me, Reverend Father; namely, that of being your most humble and very obedient servant.

M. DE MONLUC,
Abbess of St-Jacques

3183. - *MONSIEUR MONTIGNY-SERUYENT TO SAINT VINCENT*

Monday evening, [around August 1660] [1]

Very Reverend Father,

This evening I saw Reverend Father Eudes. He asked me to tell you that, because of the great distance, he would urge you to have M. Desbordes come to visit you tomorrow afternoon, Tuesday, since you are a friend of his, to try to dissuade him from thwarting the establishment at the Quinze-Vingts.[2] *He is vehemently opposing Father Eudes. I do not know what is causing him to act that way. It seems to me he could proceed differently.*

We are hoping for this through your intervention. It will have to be done tomorrow afternoon because all those gentlemen will be meeting Wednesday to deliberate on this matter.

Letter 3183. - Archives of the Mission, Turin, original autograph letter.

[1]The context of the letter and the information about the mission at the Quinze-Vingts prompted Coste to assign this date.

[2]Following the mission given at the Quinze-Vingts by Father Eudes during May and June, the Administrator of the hospital had made up his mind to entrust the spiritual direction of the establishment to the followers of the renowned missionary. The plan did not materialize (cf. Boulay, *op. cit.*, vol. III, p. 375).

I am, with all my heart, Very Reverend Father, your most humble and very obedient servant.

MONTIGNY-SERUYENT

M. Desbordes is one of the Administrators of the Quinze-Vingts Hospital. I will have your letter to M. Desbordes delivered early.

Addressed: *Monsieur Vincent, at Saint-Lazare*

3184. - *THE SISTERS OF THE FIRST VISITATION MONASTERY OF PARIS TO SAINT VINCENT*

Live Jesus!

Most Honored and Very Dear Father,

When we heard that our most worthy Abbé de Blampignon had received a Brief from His Holiness appointing him Visitor of the Reverend Carmelite Mothers of France, we were deeply affected—not that we are upset that he is contributing to God's greater glory by this good work, but we fear that such an important responsibility will prevent him from continuing his charitable assistance to us. This would be one of the greatest misfortunes that could befall our Community.

Prostrate at your feet, Most Honored Father, we come to implore you most humbly, and with all possible respectful affection, to grant us the favor of your paternal patronage so that someone who is so extremely helpful to us and so necessary for the good of this house and the salvation of our souls may be retained for us. We will be infinitely indebted to you, Most Honored Father, if you procure this happiness for us. Joined to all the others for which we will be eternally grateful to you, it will keep us in profound respect and most humble submission until our last sigh, Most Honored and very dear Father.

Letter 3184. - Archives of the Mission, Turin, original autograph letter.

Your most humble, most obedient and very grateful daughters and servants in Our Lord.

THE SISTERS OF THE COMMUNITY
OF THE VISITATION SAINTE-MARIE

B[lessed] b[e] G[od]!

From our monastery in Paris, rue St-Antoine, August 8, 1660

Addressed: *Monsieur Vincent de Paul, Superior General of the Reverend Fathers of the Mission, at Saint-Lazare*

3185. - *LOUISE-EUGÉNIE DE FONTAINE* [1] *TO SAINT VINCENT*

Live Jesus!

My One and Only Father,

We are deeply distressed because of our justifiable apprehension that the additional duties assigned to Abbé de Blampignon will deprive us of the grace that he in his goodness has so paternally bestowed upon us until now. This causes us to prostrate ourselves in all humility at your feet, my One and Only Father, there to implore your help and to entreat you most humbly, with all possible affection, to have pity on us and to arrange

---

Letter 3185. - Archives of the Mission, Turin, original autograph letter.

[1]Louise-Eugénie de Fontaine (Fonteines), born in Paris of Huguenot parents on March 13, 1608, entered the Visitation Monastery (rue Saint-Antoine) in 1630, seven years after her abjuration of heresy. She soon became Mistress of Novices; after her election as Superior in 1641, she was reelected so often that the convent had her at its head for thirty-three years. In 1644 she went to La Perrine Abbey near Le Mans to establish the renewal. On her return, the Archbishop of Paris asked her to work on the Rule of Port-Royal Abbey. Saint Vincent, who observed her behavior in certain difficult situations, stated that "an angel could not have comported herself with more virtue." (Cf. *Sainte Jeanne-Françoise Frémyot de Chantal. Sa vie et ses oeuvres.* [8 vols., Paris: Plon, 1874-80], vol. VIII, p. 446, *note.*) She died September 29, 1694, at the age of eighty-six, leaving the reputation of a holy religious. "God always blessed her leadership and her undertakings," states the *Book of Professions* (Arch. Nat. LL 1718). Her biography has been written by Jacqueline-Marie du Plessis Bonneau, *Vie de la vénérable Mère Louise-Eugénie de Fontaine, religieuse et quatrième supérieure du premier monastère de la Visitation Sainte-Marie de Paris.* (Paris: F. Muguet, 1696).

matters in such a way that the appointment of our truly good Abbé de Blampignon as Visitor General of the dear Carmelites will not require him to make visitations outside of this city. That would be more prejudicial to our Community than we could express because we have greater need than ever of the charitable ministrations of that Most Honored Father.

For this reason, in the name of God, my One and Only Father, use your paternal patronage on our behalf in this important matter. I implore it of you with all my heart, and I thank you with the same gratitude as for the great charity that you in your goodness bestowed on us in the affair of our dear Sister Marie-Euphrosine Renault, who is in Bayonne, for which, Most Honored Father, we could never be grateful enough.

I beg Our Lord to be Himself your reward and to preserve for us the only Most Honored Father He has granted us the grace of giving us. Bestow your holy blessing, my Only Father, to your most humble and very obedient daughter and servant in Our Lord.

LOUISE-EUGÉNIE DE FONTAINE,
of the V[isitation] Sainte-M[arie]

B[lessed] b[e] G[od]!

August 8 [1660] [2]

Addressed: *Monsieur Vincent de Paul, General of the Missions of France*

---

[2]Since this letter deals with the same matter as no. 3184, it is assumed that it was written in the same year.

3186. - *EDME PICARDAT [1] TO SAINT VINCENT*

Angers, August 8, 1660

Monsieur and Dear Father,

Your blessing!

I entreat you to forward the enclosed letter to the Superior of Troyes,[2] and I also entreat your paternal goodness, in the name of O[ur] L[ord] J[esus] C[hrist] and of the Blessed Virgin, to grant me the grace of reentering the Company. I am ready to receive your orders at any time. Meanwhile, our whole group, especially our poor little ones, about ninety in number, continue to pray every day for your health and for the dear Company of which I am, and will be all my life, in the love of O[ur] L[ord], my very dear and Most Honored Father, your most humble and very obedient servant and little son.

EDME

I beg M. Dehorgny to take the trouble to answer the last letter I wrote him. We are praying for him and we kiss his hands.

3187. - *MADAME POTIER DE LAMOIGNON [1] TO SAINT VINCENT*

Monsieur Vincent is most humbly requested by the wife of the Chief

Letter 3186. - Archives of the Mission, Turin, original autograph letter.

[1]Edme Picardat, born in Rumilly-lès-Vaudes (Aube) on April 23, 1613, entered the Congregation of the Mission as a coadjutor Brother on October 5, 1639, and took his vows on January 1, 1643. As indicated in this letter, he left the Company--perhaps sometime after April 1656, since Coste mentions him in a footnote in vol. V, no. 2030, and again in no. 2053, regarding an incident of disobedience when he was asked to move from Le Mans to Troyes. So serious was it that Saint Vincent believed that there were grounds for withholding absolution.

[2]François Dupuich.

Letter 3187. - Archives of the Mission, Turin, original autograph letter.

[1]Madeleine Potier, daughter of Nicolas Potier, Seigneur d'Ocquerre and Secretary of State; niece of Augustin Potier, the former Bishop of Beauvais; wife of Guillaume de Lamoignon, Chief Justice of the Paris Parlement. A Lady of Charity of unusual liberality, foundress of a charitable assistance work for prisoners, the bashful poor, and the sick (cf. Bibl. Maz., Ms. 10694, documents 91 and 94), she died on October 17, 1705, at the age of eighty-two.

Justice to let her know whether she can hope for two Daughters of Charity to serve in the Charity of Auteuil. These Sisters must be able to teach young people to pray well, to learn their catechism and the truths of their faith, how to read, and other things, if possible, because many young people in Auteuil are wasting their time for lack of instruction. This work is worthy of the piety of M. Vincent, and the above-mentioned wife of the Chief Justice, who sends him greetings and recommends herself to his prayers, will be greatly indebted to him.

Monday morning, August 9, 1660

Addressed: *Monsieur Vincent at Saint-Lazare*

3188. - *PIERRE BAUSSET, PROVOST OF MARSEILLES, TO SAINT VINCENT*

Marseilles, August 10, 1660

Monsieur,

In extreme need one must have recourse to his best and most powerful friends, among whom I count you, Monsieur. You may have been informed that, because of the unrest in Marseilles,[1] *the King sent my brother* [2] *and my nephew the lieutenant*[3] *to Issoudun in Berry. They have been there for six months, after having previously been under house arrest in Marseilles for two months. Public opinion has it that, on the occasion of the King's marriage, all those in disgrace will receive clemency.*

I beg you, Monsieur, for the love of J[esus] C[hrist], to be willing to help us in this situation by speaking to the Queen and to the Cardinal[4] *for their return. I can assure you that their absence is greatly inconveniencing our family, which is not very wealthy. It also inconveniences the town*

Letter 3188. - Archives of the Mission, Turin, original autograph letter.

[1]Cf. no. 3098, n. 7.

[2]Philippe Bausset, Canon of the Cathedral Church of Marseilles.

[3]Antoine Bausset, Assistant Seneschal in Marseilles.

[4]Jules Cardinal Mazarin.

because of the absence of the chief officer of justice, against whom no complaint has been lodged and who has not committed the crime for which the state is punishing him.

DE BAUSSET,
Provost

Monsieur, since I do not know the address of the Bishop of Grand-Caire, to whom I am writing for the same reason, please have the enclosed letter delivered to him.

3189. - *LOUISE-EUGÉNIE DE FONTAINE TO SAINT VINCENT*

August 10 [1660] [1]

Live Jesus!

My One and Only Father,

We could never sufficiently thank Your Goodness for the very paternal charity you have bestowed on us. It has filled our hearts with joy, along with our very humble and filial gratitude. I hope God will reward you abundantly, Most Honored Father, and will grant us the grace to profit more than ever from the favor Your Goodness has procured for us in our truly good Abbé de Blampignon.

Yesterday we had the honor of a visit from Abbé de Benjamin, who told us that he was no longer going to beg for mercy, since he was convinced that justice had to be done. He showed us a letter from our Most Honored Sister Assistant,[2] *in which she told him that, since she had to return at the end of the month for the affairs of our Institute, if they did not hurry up with the election of a Superior in the community where she is,*[3] *she would leave them before it took place—or at least, immediately after the election—because the affairs of this dear community might suffer from that.*

Letter 3189. - Archives of the Mission, Turin, original autograph letter.

[1]Year added on the back of the original by Brother Ducournau.

[2]Madeleine-Élisabeth de Maupeou.

[3]The Ursuline Sisters in Melun.

Thereupon, M. de Benjamin assured us that he would leave today, together with our very dear Sister Assistant, to see what was needed to have that election held as soon as possible and to return that dear, honored Sister to us by the end of the month. He suggested that we leave our two Sisters there—or at least one—a little longer, but when we explained to him why we felt that this should not be done, he accepted our reasons. So, we hope to have the joy of having these three dear Sisters return by the end of the month, if it be the Will of the One whom I entreat to preserve for us your worthy and sacred person, for His greater glory. I entreat this also for the happiness of her who is prostrate in spirit at your feet, requesting there your holy blessing for this little community, which is so grateful to you, as is also, my One and Only Father, your most humble and very obedient daughter and servant in Our Lord.

LOUISE-EUGÉNIE DE FONTAINE,
of the Visitation Sainte-Marie

B[lessed] b[e] G[od]!

Addressed: *Monsieur Vincent de Paul, General of the Missions of France*

3190. - *ANNE-MARGUERITE GUÉRIN TO SAINT VINCENT*

Live Jesus!

From our Third Monastery, August 10 [1660] [1]

My Only Most Honored Father,

This is just a note to inform Your Goodness that Sister Louise-Madeleine Gimat arrived here late last evening from Flanders. Since her route brought her right by our door, she knew you would not take it amiss, nor would our dear Mother in the faubourg,[2] *if she stopped to see us. So we*

Letter 3190. - Archives of the Mission, Turin, original autograph letter.

[1]This date has been assigned because of the content of this letter and that of no. 3192.

[2]Marie-Agnès Le Roy.

took your permission for granted and asked our dear Mother to allow us to keep her with us until after the feast of Our Lady to help us chant our office on that day. She and our entire little band, together with me, offer Your Goodness our most humble regards and obedience. All of us, prostrate at your feet, ask for your holy blessing.

Abbess Dupart is supposed to ask your permission to enter this house, as she did for our two other monasteries. I think you know that she is the daughter of Madame Fouquet, who is also planning to make you a certain proposal. These are persons of such outstanding virtue and example that whatever you grant them will always be received with the respect and submission due to you by her who is, with incomparable affection and great respect, my Only Most Honored Father, your most humble, very obedient, and unworthy daughter and servant in O[ur] L[ord].

SISTER ANNE-MARGUERITE GUÉRIN,
of the Visitation Sainte-Marie

Blessed be God!

Addressed: *Monsieur Vincent, Superior General of the Priests of the Mission of Saint-Lazare*

3191. - TO JEAN DU HAUT DE SALIES, BISHOP OF LESCAR

August 11, 1660

I had heard that Your Excellency did not receive the letter I had the honor of writing to you last year,[1] in reply to the orders you gave me to send four of our priests to you for Bétharram, but it was only a few days ago that I learned it for a fact, when I was assured of it by the Chief Justice of Pau.[2] There was a letter for him in the same packet, which he did not receive either.

I am very sorry, Monseigneur, for the trouble caused you by the

---

Letter 3191. - Reg. 2, p. 89.

[1]This letter is not extant.

[2]Thibaut de la Vie.

loss of this packet and for the reason you have had for doubting my obedience. I should certainly be ungrateful if I failed to express it to you on this occasion, when you in your kindness are doing us the favor of calling us, not only to your diocese, but to one of the most advantageous positions in the kingdom, to render some service to God in that place. We are, Monseigneur, infinitely indebted to Your Excellency for this.

It is true that you mentioned it to me in veiled terms which, if taken literally, would put us in no position to avail of your good will because, Monseigneur, after telling me you had obtained the consent of those priests in Bétharram, you added that our priests would be received among them as members of their body. That obliged me—and still obliges me—to represent most humbly to Your Excellency that the proposal to become members of that group is incompatible with what we are, a body of Missionaries, because the men we might send could not be at one and the same time members of the Mission and members of the Bétharram Community. They would have to leave one to join the other because they are two different bodies—unless one body be formed of the two, and the body of the Mission be united to the Bétharram Community, or the Bétharram group be united to the Company of the Mission.

If it could, Monseigneur, the latter would willingly unite with the former and give up the title of Congregation of the Mission to assume that of the Bétharram Community. However, as our little Institute has been approved under the title of The Mission by the Popes, the Kings of France, the Parlement of Paris, and by other sovereign courts, we cannot give up that name to take another, without the consent of all those authorities and of our benefactors who have had dealings with those of us who compose the body of the Mission. I also think that it is not your intention, Monseigneur, that this be done. Furthermore, we could not do so without the consent of the houses that make up our Company, and even of their members, which is very difficult.

To say now that only those four priests will detach themselves from the Mission to be incorporated in the Bétharram Community is not possible. They cannot do so, Monseigneur, because they have given themselves to God to live and die as Missionaries in the same Congregation of the Mission.

To say also that the Bétharram Community—so worthy of consideration because of its institution, its approval by the Bishops of Lescar, the holiness of the place, and the grace of the miracles that occur there—will unite itself to our Congregation and adopt its name, Rules, and manner of acting is something those priests would find hard to do and Your Excellency to approve—and with good reason, given our insignificance.

The following, Monseigneur, is the procedure adopted for the union that was effected between the house of Saint-Lazare-lez-Paris and our Congregation: the Canons Regular of Saint-Augustin were there, and the Prior, with their consent, came to the Collège des Bons-Enfants, where we were living, to offer me their house. We accepted the offer and made arrangements with them, subject to the good pleasure of the Archbishop, who was the collator of the benefice. He himself effected the union and put us in possession of that house and all its dependencies, on condition of paying the Prior and each of the religious the pension we agreed on, of carrying out the divine service, and of fulfilling all the obligations. It was also agreed that it would be lawful for them to reside with us or to withdraw, as they saw fit. Although this union was opposed from the beginning by a monastery of the same Order,[3] it was nevertheless confirmed by letters patent of the King, two decrees of the Parlement, and then by our Holy Father the Pope.[4]

It seems then, Monseigneur, that the same procedure could be used for this union of Bétharram, if it is desired to establish us there on a sound basis.

Perhaps it will be said that, with the union of Bétharram to the

[3]Saint-Victor Abbey.

[4]Cf. vol. XIII, nos. 77-84.

Mission, the devotional exercises will no longer be carried out as they are at present and that, in future, no other practices will be seen there except those of the other houses of the Mission. But we reply that the Priests of the Mission will commit themselves to carry out in Bétharram all the usual duties of piety: to recite the Divine Office, to maintain the chant, to welcome pilgrims, to fulfill the obligations of foundations, and to maintain the buildings; in short, to satisfy all the obligations, especially that of paying those priests whom we will replace whatever pension you, Monseigneur, ordain. In view of that, it would be advisable to let us see the accounts of the entire fixed revenue and perquisites and all the old and new obligations they will want to impose upon us.

It may also be objected that, once this union is effected, the Bétharram priests who do not want to become Missionaries will be forced to leave. That, however, will not be the case, for, if they want to remain in the house and work there with the same conditions and responsibilities they have had until now, they will be free to do so.

Lastly, it may be objected that the Bishop will no longer have the same authority over the chapel as he has had. To that I reply, Monseigneur, that you will always have the same power you have had in regard to the divine service and the administration of the holy Sacraments, and will have much more over the Priests of the Mission than you have over those Bétharram priests, or any others in your diocese, because the Missionaries have given themselves to God and to the Prelates to obey them as the servants in the Gospel obey their master.[5] Therefore, when they are told: "Go and preach, catechize, and carry out the other functions of the Mission in such a place," they are bound to go; when they are recalled, they are bound to return; and when they are told: "Do that," they must do it, in accordance with our Institute.

However, for the internal governance of the families and persons of our Congregation, wherever they may be, that rests with

[5]Cf. Mt 8:9. (NAB)

their Superior General. It is up to him to change them, to send and to recall them from one house to another, to appoint local Superiors and other officers, and to send Visitors from time to time to each locality on his behalf in order to maintain charity and the observance of Rule and to examine the accounts of expenditure and receipts, etc.

That, then, was what my first letter contained, Monseigneur. I am ashamed to send you such a long, wearisome repetition. Our desire to have everything clarified and to obviate any difficulties that might arise from not doing so has obliged me to give such lengthy explanations. I very humbly ask Your Excellency not to be displeased at this and to believe that, however you choose to receive what is said above, I will always be. . . .[6]

3192. - *MARIE-AGNÈS LE ROY TO SAINT VINCENT*

Live Jesus!

Our monastery of the faubourg Saint-Jacques, August 11, 1660

Very Dear and Most Honored Father,

I received your letter for which I thank you most humbly. I was greatly consoled to see your heart softened in my regard. Furthermore, Most Honored Father, Sister Louise-Madeleine Gimat, who was in Mons, arrived Monday evening and went of her own accord to stay with our Sisters of rue Montorgueil,[1] *where she is now. I must admit that I was somewhat surprised that she took this liberty since, as you know, that is not in order.*

The Superior is asking to keep her until after the feast of the Blessed Virgin so that she can help them chant the office; for, I must say that,

---

[6]The proposed establishment in Bétharram never materialized.

Letter 3192. - Archives of the Mission, Turin, original autograph letter.

[1]The Third Visitation Monastery in Paris, of which the Sisters took possession on July 25, 1660.

among all the Sisters they have chosen, only one can sing. If they wanted to keep that dear Sister permanently, would you have any objections? Our number is sufficient to enable us to manage easily without this extra person, and they perhaps would find it very advantageous. I think she would deserve this, since she acted as she did; the Community here is somewhat surprised at it.

I am writing only to apprise you of all this; I have nothing to ask of you, since I left it up to the Superior to make her own request. The idea I propose to you of leaving her there, since she went there to visit, is entirely my own because it seems to me she would deserve it—if not permanently, at least for a time.

I most humbly beg you, Most Honored Father, to keep these little thoughts to yourself. You can certainly see the importance of that. Be so good also as to burn this letter, to which I am not expecting any answer. My only intention was to tell you my humble thoughts; they would be better expressed in person, but God does not allow that.

I am, in His love, Most Honored Father, your most humble and very obedient daughter and servant in Our Lord.

SISTER MARIE-AGNÈS LE ROY

Blessed be God!

Addressed: *Monsieur Vincent, Superior General of the Congregation of the Mission*

3193. - *MARIE-CATHERINE LE GAY TO SAINT VINCENT*

Live Jesus!

Monsieur and Most Honored Father,

May it please our gentle, divine Savior to grant you a long life for the good and consolation of many and, above all, of our own hearts, who hope for this in the most holy and adorable Will of God! From what I have been told, the kind of illness you have leaves me no hope of seeing you again in

Letter 3193. - Archives of the Mission, Turin, original autograph letter.

this world. This has emboldened me to write you this little note to implore you most humbly to give me your holy blessing and a small share in your holy prayers to obtain mercy for me from our good Savior. My very great and longstanding indebtedness to you in your goodness lead me to hope for this grace, so that the short time remaining for me in this life may be put to better use than in the past. I beg this of you, Monsieur and Most Honored Father, and I thank you most humbly for all your support and kindness to me. May God in His infinite goodness be your reward for it!

Please continue to remember me before the Divine Majesty of Our Lord and His most august Mother, and allow me, Monsieur and Most Honored Father, to declare myself with all possible humility and respect, your most humble, most grateful and very obedient daughter and servant in Our Lord.

SISTER MARIE-CATHERINE LE GAY,
novice of the Visitation Sainte-Marie

Our First Monastery of Paris, August 12, 1660

Blessed be God!

Addressed: *Monsieur Vincent de Paul, at Saint-Lazare*

3194. - *FATHER CLAUDE SÉGUENOT TO SAINT VINCENT*

Tours, August 12 [1660] [1]

Monsieur,

I would consider myself happy to have rendered some service to one of your sons, especially to such a deserving and important person as M. d'Alméras. What we did for him on the occasion that presented itself, however, is so insignificant that I am no less ashamed than surprised that you should even mention it. It is not an expression of gratitude due to us but a mark and the effect of your affection for those under your guidance

---

Letter 3194. - Archives of the Mission, Turin, original autograph letter.

[1]Since both nos. 3194 and 3195 deal with the stay of M. Alméras in Tours, they have been placed near each other, and the year 1660 assigned to no. 3194.

and of how you share in whatever concerns them. If he is pleased in any way by our simplicity, we are even more so by the edification we have received from his conversations and virtue. We are infinitely more indebted to him for the honor he so kindly bestowed on us than he can be to us for the very modest assistance he received from us.

You will see from the letter he is writing you that he has decided to return to Richelieu, while waiting until he is strong enough to go on to Paris. I will send him your letter; he will receive it on Saturday.

If there is anything else we can do here as a service to you or to him, you could not give orders to anyone over whom you have more authority than you have over me. I am, with all possible respect and sincerity, Monsieur, your most humble and obedient servant.

SÉGUENOT,
priest of the Oratory

Addressed: *Monsieur Vincent, Superior General of the Congregation of the Mission, in Paris*

3195. - *MONSIEUR PINON TO SAINT VINCENT*

Tours, August 12, 1660

Monsieur,

When God's Providence permitted that M. d'Alméras should remain in this town when he became ill on returning from Richelieu, it gave me an excellent opportunity to become acquainted with a person of such lofty virtue and holiness, established on the foundation of the greatest saints, which is deep humility. I have tried to express to him, by my most humble marks of respect, the very deep gratitude I owe him and you, Monsieur. I could never repay you, since my indebtedness continues to increase infinitely and because of the favor you grant me in allowing my son[1] *to belong to your holy Company. I ask Our Lord with all my heart to continue to shower His blessings on it and its members, who are so necessary to His Church and do so much for the advancement of His glory.*

Letter 3195. - Archives of the Mission, Turin, original autograph letter.

[1]Pierre Pinon.

Still, the pleasure I experienced at the honor of meeting him was tempered by seeing him so ill and being unable to do anything for his relief—as I made a point of trying to do—because he never did me the honor of staying in my home. If God grants him the favor of coming back to Richelieu, I hope he will not deny me this honor, as he has promised.

He informed you that he has changed his plans and, instead of returning to Paris, has decided to go back to Richelieu because of his frequent attacks of weakness. He left today on a litter, and I hope, by the grace of God, that he has arrived there by now.

I had shared with him a plan I had for my son, your follower. It is as follows: if you deem it advisable, Monsieur, I would be glad to make some arrangement with you to assure him a lifetime revenue, so that after my death—which may be very near because I am in the critical year that puts many people in their graves—there would be no reason, because he would be so far away, to have an official seal affixed and to commission someone to divide up the property, which might cause strife within the family.

As long as Our Lord gives him the grace of remaining in your holy Company, I would like to assign to him from my entire estate the sum of two hundred livres, and three hundred livres in the event that he should withdraw because of illness or for some other reason. This is what I am able to do out of my slender means; if you think it feasible, Monsieur, please be so good as to have someone write to him about it to obtain his consent, as I am doing, with your permission. M. d'Alméras assured me that I could write to you about this and that he thought you would understand.

I will close this letter by paying my most humble respects to you, Monsieur, which I entreat you most humbly to accept, along with my very humble service, which is assured you from my whole family. With your permission, Monsieur, I implore you to give me a share in your most Holy Sacrifices. I recommend myself to them with all my heart and am, Monsieur, your most humble and very obedient servant.

PINON

Addressed: *Monsieur Vincent, General of the Priests of the Mission, at Saint-Lazare*

3196. - *JOSEPH BAYN TO SAINT VINCENT*

Monsieur,

Yesterday I paid a visit to the Duchesse d'Aiguillon to satisfy my curiosity about certain unusual things that I was told were in her house. I also went so that, when she would hear someone mention my name, it would remind her of the letter she had promised me. But, as luck would have it, she was busy with some people who were visiting her. That is why no one dared to ask for the keys, nor to mention me, so I have decided to go there next week to take my leave of her. This will help her to remember it, if she has not already taken care of it.

Meanwhile, allow me to tell you that in my latest letter from Marseilles my brother instructed me to send you his humble greetings and regards. I take the liberty of adding my own to them, Monsieur, as your most humble and very grateful servant.

JOSEPH BAYN

Paris, August 12, 1660

Addressed: *Monsieur Vincent de Paul, General of the Priests of the Mission, in Paris*

3197. - TO EDME JOLLY, SUPERIOR, IN ROME

August 13, 1660

I praise God that the plan formed in Rome to establish a seminary there for foreign missions has included you. If God wills it to be carried out, it looks as though He will make use of your family to work at it and will give it His blessing for that purpose. Humanly speaking, however, it will be difficult to find suitable men who are determined to devote themselves to this apostolic life.

Letter 3196. - Archives of the Mission, Turin, original autograph letter.

Letter 3197. - Reg. 2, p. 254.

True, some may willingly present themselves to enter this seminary, but few will be found with the necessary detachment and zeal to actually undertake to go to those distant missions.

3198. - TO JACQUES PESNELLE, SUPERIOR, IN GENOA

August 13, 1660

Our Rule prescribing one hour of mental prayer daily makes no exception for days of rest. Therefore, Monsieur, it should be made for an entire hour on those days, just as if they were not days of rest. It is not right that resting should supersede the most important action of the day. We still have to take care of necessary business affairs. Sometimes we have business matters that cannot be put off or do not fit in with the hour for prayer. Well and good, we respect such difficulties, after however having reflected on them before God and found them reasonable; for God does not ask anything unreasonable of us.

Since, however, this does not happen all the time, nor to everyone, it is advisable, generally speaking, to keep the Rule—and not just in what concerns prayer, for it is also expedient to consult the same Rule in whatever doubt or difficulty that may arise, so that we may conform ourselves to it as far as possible.

The Prince de Conti will one day be our judge—at least he will be mine. He is admirable in his fidelity to mental prayer, which he makes daily for two hours, one in the morning and the other in the evening. No matter how busy he is or what important people may be with him, he never fails to do so. Granted, he is not so attached to certain times that he does not advance or postpone them according to the demands of business. May God be pleased to give us this inclination to unite ourselves to Our Lord, in whom I am. . . .

Letter 3198. - Reg. 2, p. 215.

3199. - *ANNE-MARGUERITE GUÉRIN TO SAINT VINCENT*

Live Jesus!

From our Third Monastery in Paris, August 13 [1660] [1]

My Only Most Honored Father,

We had the honor of writing to you to inform Your Goodness of the arrival of dear Sister Louise-Madeleine Gimat. We asked you, Monsieur, if she might remain with us until after the feast of Our Lady to help us chant our office for the feast of the Assumption. Because there are so few of us, her voice will be a big help to us.

Now we most humbly entreat Your Goodness, Most Honored Father, to grant our dear Mother Dufaux permission to spend a day with us, along with two or three companions whom she would choose to accompany her on her trip. Her visit to this house is not only helpful to us but necessary, so that she can get a look at the buildings that are finished, for which she did the negotiating. We are having difficulties because the mason did not do as he promised her, and we would be glad if Her Charity would see these things with her own eyes.

We hope that you in your goodness will not refuse us this favor, Most Honored Father, as well as another which is an absolute necessity, namely, that of having one of our lay Sisters here for a time. When we came, we thought we could manage without one, but we find it quite impossible because we are unable to train others for the kitchen; we know neither the preparations nor the orders observed in religious Orders. Not one of us knows enough to teach them, and that is so necessary for us that, if our Sisters in the faubourg were unable to help us, we would ask your permission to turn to our dear Sisters in the city to see if they could lend us someone for a short time. If our dear Mother in the faubourg [2] *can give us one, she could send her to us right away or bring her with her when she comes to take Sister Louise-Madeleine Gimat home.*

We will await the honor of a reply to all these little needs, but especially regarding a lay Sister. If Your Goodness sees our dire need of this, I think you in your very great goodness will have no objection to granting it. This

---

Letter 3199. - Archives of the Mission, Turin, original autograph letter.

[1]Since this letter deals with the same material as nos. 3190 and 3192, the year 1660 has been assigned to it.

[2]Marie-Agnès Le Roy.

is the very humble petition we present to you from our little community, which joins me in asking for your holy blessing. I am, with all possible respect, Most Honored Father, your most humble, most obedient, and unworthy daughter and servant in Our Lord.

SISTER ANNE-MARGUERITE GUÉRIN,
of the Visitation Sainte-Marie

Blessed be God!

Addressed: *Monsieur Vincent, Superior General of the Priests of the Mission of Saint-Lazare*

3199a. - TO FIRMIN GET, SUPERIOR, IN MARSEILLES

Paris, August 13, 1660

Monsieur,

The grace of Our Lord be with you forever!

I received your letter of the third along with the attestations for the four missions you gave on the estates of the late Marquise de Vins. We will use them to seek payment of her annuity.

Since Abbé de Chandenier[1] sees that there is talk of 1,000 piastres for the ransom of Vital Bernusset, he is unwilling to stand surety for such a large sum of money but will do so only for up to 500.[2] I mean that, in the event that he can be freed for 500 piastres, he is asking that someone supply what is needed to complete the amount that was sent, and he will reimburse what is over and above, all expenses included. Please guarantee this amount, but no more.

We are being strongly pressured by the mother of La Rue, a captive in Algiers living in the Consul's house, for 600 livres she

Letter 3199a. - Copy made from *Recueil Nodet.* The letter was published in *Annales C.M.* (1943-44), p. 257, and reprinted in *Mission et Charité,* 19-20, no. 129, pp. 163-64. This edition uses the latter text.

[1]Claude de Chandenier.

[2]The copy has *1500*; this is doubtless a misreading because the context calls for *500.*

sent him and which you or M. Delespiney received eight or nine months ago. If you have forwarded this aid to him, let me know, or remember to send it by the first opportunity.

Please hold on to the 130 livres you still have for a convict who is at sea, until his mother lets you know what to do with the money, since it is not enough to ransom her son. We do not know where she lives so we might notify her of this; we have to wait until she comes or sends someone here.

I praise God that you are getting better and better. Our sick men are also out of danger now, by the grace of God.

I am telling M. Huguier to give 30 livres to Pierre Laisné.

I am, in the love of Our Lord, Monsieur, your most humble servant.

VINCENT DEPAUL,
i.s.C.M.

3200. - TO JEAN PARRE, IN SAINT-QUENTIN

Paris, August 14, 1660

Dear Brother,

Today, please God, we will have someone pack up whatever vestments and altar linens we have so we can send them to you by the first mail coach or by passenger coach; I will also send you a list of them. There are six chasubles, two albs, six silver ciboria, three or four altar cloths, and some veils, corporals, and purificators, of which I do not yet know the number. There are also a few used cassocks for poor priests, etc. . . .

Letter 3200. - This letter is known to us through its Italian translation, inserted into one of the documents of the collection for the process of beatification, *Summarium Responsivum,* p. 55.

3201. - *JEAN HUDICOURT TO SAINT VINCENT*

Monsieur Vincent, I recommend myself to your kind favor and humbly kiss your hand. I am not recommending my son[1] *to you because I would like to think that, after God, you are his father; I do, however, recommend my two other sons, who ardently desire to come and cast themselves at your feet. If God is calling all three of them to His service, my every wish will be fulfilled.*

When I was in Paris and realized from my son's conversation how content and consoled he was, I was quite satisfied. I have clearly seen that he has found the road to heaven. May it [please] God that his two brothers, by the grace of God and of Superiors . . . [2] *and it is well [for] us to be able to do the same for them.*

Please give my regards to M. Rose,[3] *his sister, and all your good friends.*

Written by me,

JEAN HUDICOURT,
mason, in Hamelincourt

August 14, 1660

Addressed: *To be given to P . . . the Paris house, at Saint-Lazare, for Monsieur Vincent*

Letter 3201. - Archives of the Mission, Turin, original autograph letter.

[1]Charles-François Hudicourt, born in Bapaume (Pas-de-Calais) on July 14, 1637, entered the Congregation of the Mission in Paris on October 19, 1655, and took his vows on October 21, 1657, in the presence of M. Delespiney. He was ordained a priest, but no date of ordination is given. The personnel catalogue of *Notices,* vol. V (Supplement), contains no other listing for a Hudicourt.

[2]Word illegible in the original.

[3]Nicolas Roze, born in Transloy (Pas-de-Calais) in 1616, entered the Congregation of the Mission as a priest on December 7, 1641. He was Superior in Troyes (1653-57).

3202. - *PIERRE DE BERTIER, BISHOP OF MONTAUBAN, TO SAINT VINCENT*

Montauban, August 15 [1660]

Monsieur,

My ailment has prevented me this week from doing what remains for me to do for the seminary business. I hope God will grant me the strength to work in two or three days and to put the finishing touch to what I wish to do on this occasion.

I am sending you the letter and remain always, with all my heart, Monsieur, your most humble and very affectionate servant.

PIERRE,
Bishop of Montauban

Addressed: *Monsieur Vincent Depaul, General of the Mission*

3203. - *MARTIN HUSSON TO SAINT VINCENT*

Montmirail, August 15, 1660

Monsieur,

Since I was unable to say good-bye to you, I entreat you at least to accept the excuses I offer you in this letter and to allow me to pay my respects to you in spirit at the feet of O[ur] L[ord], since I could not receive in person the consolation of being embraced by you before my departure.

As for the income of Saint-Lazare, the Duc de Noirmoutiers [1] *sent it to this town to M. de Soufliers, his attorney for fiscal matters; before my*

Letter 3202. - Archives of the Mission, Turin, original autograph letter.

Letter 3203. - Archives of the Mission, Turin, original autograph letter.

[1]Louis de Trémouille, Duc de Noirmoutiers, was born on December 25, 1612, and died on October 12, 1666. The Duc de Retz had sold him the Montmirail estate in 1655.

arrival the latter gave the aldermen the note good Brother Robineau[2] *had shown me. They found the difficulty with it that I mentioned to Brother Robineau concerning the account being requested of them of the good use of the profits; besides, your declaration states very clearly how your men used them, and having accepted your document at face value without the slightest objection, they have recognized satisfactorily that you have spent the revenue in good faith and used the profits effectively. They say the same for the expenses, which do not even amount to thirty sous and for which they could never ask anything of you, since there are no claims against the mission. It is harvest time, and since there are two aldermen and a court appointed receiver holding office, it has been impossible until now to bring the three together.*

A member of the Duc de Noirmoutiers' household asked me to find out about something important that has occurred in Lyons, and since you were so good, Monsieur, as to direct me to M. Delaforcade, I would like to know if he is still residing in Lyons and if, through your favor, I could get a letter to him and receive the reply to it.

This is a liberty I dare to take, after the many favors you have showered upon me, and which have made me, in the love of O[ur] L[ord], Monsieur, your most humble and very affectionate servant.

HUSSON

Addressed: *Monsieur Vincent, General of the Priests of the Mission, at Saint-Lazare, in Paris*

[2]Louis Robineau, coadjutor Brother, born in Neuvy-en-Dunois (Eure-et-Loir), entered the Congregation of the Mission on November 8, 1642, at twenty-one years of age, and took his vows on November 1, 1650. He was Saint Vincent's secretary for thirteen years; the notes he wrote for the Saint's biographer are still in the Archives. (Cf. André Dodin, ed., *Monsieur Vincent raconté par son secrétaire* [Paris: O.E.I.L., 1991].)

3204. - *JACQUES-BÉNIGNE BOSSUET [1] TO SAINT VINCENT*

[August 15, 1660] [2]

Monsieur,

My father writes me that we will receive word by the next ordinary mail that everything is in the same state to be sold as last year, and all we will have to do is to hold our own for the price. [3] *He also writes me that perhaps he will address the letters to you.*

Letter 3204. - Archives of the Mission, Turin, original autograph letter.

[1]Jacques-Bénigne Bossuet, Bishop, preacher, and author, was born in Dijon on September 27, 1627, into a family whose ancestors on both sides had occupied judicial posts in France for over half a century. He pursued a classical education at the Collège de Navarre, where he came under the influence of Vincent de Paul, whose guidance prepared him for the priesthood, which he received on March 18, 1652. He was a Canon of the Cathedral Chapter of Metz and for seven years was engaged in preaching, discussions with the Protestants, and study of the Bible and the Fathers of the Church. In 1659 he went to Paris on Chapter business and was induced by Saint Vincent and the Queen Mother, Anne of Austria, to remain there as a preacher. In 1670 he was consecrated Bishop of Condom but had to resign later that year when he was named tutor and guardian for the Dauphin. He wrote a number of works for the latter, of which he considered the most important his "philosophy of history": *Discours sur l'histoire universelle.* After the Dauphin's marriage in 1681, Bossuet was named Bishop of Meaux but continued to have great influence at Court, especially on Louis XIV's religio-political policy with regard to the Protestants (revocation of the Edict of Nantes in 1685). It was he who inspired the promulgation of the Gallican Principles in 1682, which he also wrote at the behest of the Assembly of the Clergy of France. He was involved in the disputes both with the Jansenists and the Quietists of Fénelon. Bossuet died on April 12, 1704.

[2]Proceedings for the establishment of a house for the Congregation of the Mission in Metz, which is the context of this letter, began in 1660.

[3]The idea of founding an establishment of the Priests of the Mission in Metz for the instruction of the clergy and the evangelization of poor peasants came from Queen Anne of Austria, who had given Saint Vincent sixty thousand livres, half of which were to be used for buying a house and half for the purchase of a piece of land. Jacques-Bénigne Bossuet's father was a Counselor in the Parlement of Metz, and he personally researched the matter.

I leave this evening for the country, where I will be staying for three or four days. As soon as I return, I will come to find out from you how matters stand so I can give an account of them to the Queen, who often asks me for news of them. If the letters are addressed to me, I will leave orders for them to be delivered to you.

I am, Monsieur, your most humble and very obedient servant.

BOSSUET

Feast of the Assumption

Addressed: *Monsieur Vincent, Superior General of the Mission*

3205. - *FRANÇOISE-MARIE SIBOUR TO SAINT VINCENT*

Live Jesus!

Our monastery in Compiègne, August 17, 1660

Most Honored and Very Dear Father,

Being what I am, that is, so insignificant, I have reason to believe that I no longer have any place in your worthy thoughts. Therefore, dear Father, please allow me to come to you as one of your daughters, taking advantage of the timely occasion of the return of M. Bertost, to repeat to you the assurance of my humble obedience as well as that of all our dear Sisters your daughters, who, along with us, have a very humble favor to ask of you. It is, dear Father, that, with your consent, they might put Sister Marie-Agnès Chevallier on their list of those whom our dear Sisters of rue Saint-Antoine could give us.

Letter 3205. - Archives of the Mission, Turin, original autograph letter.

From what we have written, especially to the dear Mother, those Sisters are well aware that, although this community is a good one, it has no one to fill the office of Superior and can receive help only from you in your goodness, through those good Sisters and Mothers in Paris. In our needs, then, we have recourse, with all confidence, to you and to the charity of the Mother who is there, asking that she provide for us what is within her power and with her usual kindness.

Most Honored Father, I had shared with her our thinking regarding our dear Sister G. M. de La Haye; namely, that, because of the virtue she has shown during her stay here, acting with very remarkable humility and submission and giving us every reason for satisfaction and edification to this community, she might have the consolation of knowing that you are pleased with her conduct and that, consequently, you were kind enough to dispense her from all special penances, since I think that being so far from the dear house in Paris for as long as you choose is a penance sufficiently great to cover all other penances.

I make this suggestion, Most Honored Father, with the submission which I know I owe your paternal goodness, and I respectfully request your blessing and the grace of being acknowledged by you, Most Honored and very dear Father, as your most obedient daughter and servant in Our Lord.

SISTER FRANÇOISE-MARIE SIBOUR,
of the Visitation Sainte-Marie

Blessed be God!

I feel obliged to add, dear Father, that our dear Sister G. M. de La Haye knows nothing about the request I address to Your Goodness and has never mentioned to us anything on this subject.

Addressed: *Monsieur Vincent de Paul, Superior General of the Mission, in Paris*

3206. - TO RENÉ ALMÉRAS, IN RICHELIEU

August 18, 1660

Your letters have not only deprived me of the consolation I felt at the prospect of your immediate arrival but have also profoundly grieved me by giving me the news of your latest bouts of weakness, which have kept you at a distance from us when we were hoping that you were quite near. God be praised, Monsieur, for all His dispositions in our regard! I would certainly find it hard to bear them if I considered them apart from the divine pleasure, which ordains all things for the best.

You did very well to return to Richelieu, where I ask you, Monsieur, to get all the rest and relief you can. This entire community feels your illness deeply; it is intensifying its earnest prayers to the Divine Goodness for your preservation, and I cannot tell you the share I take in them. However, praised be the Will of God!

As for myself, I am still tried by my infirmities, and our good God, who leaves me weakened, still sustains me in the wretched state in which I am living.

The Company is suffering from the loss of your presence.[1]

Letter 3206. - Reg. 2, p. 269.

[1]The author of the manuscript life of René Alméras quotes the second part of this letter. His version, which is rather different from the one in Register 2, inserts into this letter sentences that are found in the letter of August 4.

3207. - TO JEAN PARRE, IN SAINT-QUENTIN

Paris, August 18, 1660

Dear Brother,

By the Saint-Quentin mail coach, which left Paris last Monday, I had someone send you the bundle of church vestments, the main items of which I listed for you. You have not written to tell me whether you received the other bundle, which was sent to you by coach about three or four weeks ago. Let me know when both of them have arrived.

3208. - *MONSIEUR PESNELLE TO SAINT VINCENT*

Monsieur,

You will readily excuse me for having put off so long writing to you about the latest letters of my eldest brother,[1] *when I tell you what happened to me. The affair was so important that I was obliged to call my younger brother to help me and had him advance his return from Paris so that together we could see what legal action we might take to make amends for the insult done to us.*

Our younger sister, who was living with us, allowed herself to become involved in an imprudent attachment. Fearing she would not be able to pit her passion against our will, she finally decided to get married secretly. With the complicity of those who took it upon themselves to encourage her in her folly, she acted with such absolute secrecy that I heard about her elopement and so-called marriage at the same time. This event has left me almost no time to think about anything else, with the result that, although I feel strongly obligated both to the kindness of my brother for having responded to my request and to your generosity for having urged him to do us this service, I have still put off for five days the acknowledgment of the gratitude I owe to both of you.

Letter 3207. - This letter is known to us through its Italian translation, inserted into one of the documents of the collection for the process of beatification, *Summarium Responsivum,* p. 55.

Letter 3208. - Archives of the Mission, Turin, original autograph letter.

[1]Jacques Pesnelle, Superior in Genoa.

Now that I have calmed down a little, I could not refrain any longer from telling you that I will be very grateful to you all my life for your efforts on my behalf to persuade my brother to grant us what we asked of him. Carrying it out will maintain union and order in our family. It is to you principally that I want to acknowledge this great indebtedness and to beg you to support him even more in the willingness he is showing us in his letters. I am not answering them by this mail because we have been unable to give adequate consideration to the format of the document he intends to draw up in our favor, but I will delay only a week.

Meanwhile, I am anxious to send you the eight hundred livres he told me to send you; I am asking that, if you find some occasion to have someone collect them here, you will not neglect to do so. I assure you that I will pay the bill on sight, and my son, who is ready to return to Paris, will get from you the receipt that you can give us.

I am, as ever, Monsieur, your most humble and very obedient servant.

PESNELLE

Rouen, August 19, 1660

Addressed: *Monsieur Vincent, Superior General of the Mission, at Saint-Lazare, faubourg Saint-Denis, in Paris*

3209. - *JACQUES-BÉNIGNE BOSSUET TO SAINT VINCENT*

[August 19, 1660] [1]

Monsieur,

My father writes me that he has sent you a detailed report on the state of affairs, and he is referring me to you for it. If you could arrange for Abbé de Chandenier [2] *to send his carriage in the morning, I will go to your house to make my prayer and say Holy Mass; after which I will have the*

Letter 3209. - Archives of the Mission, Turin, original autograph letter.

[1]This letter seems to be from the Thursday following the one written on Sunday, August 15.

[2]Claude de Chandenier, Abbé de Moutiers-Saint-Jean.

honor of discussing with you how to work out what I have to tell the Queen, who often asks me how the matter stands.

I am, respectfully, Monsieur, your most humble and very obedient servant.

BOSSUET

Thursday morning

Addressed: *Monsieur Vincent, Superior General of the Mission*

3210. - *JACQUES-BÉNIGNE BOSSUET TO SAINT VINCENT*

[August 19, 1660] [1]

When M. Vincent's man came, I sent that note to ask him if tomorrow I might have Abbé de Chandenier's carriage to go to Saint-Lazare in the morning. This is still my plan, and I ask him to procure this favor for me so that I may have the honor of speaking with him.

I remain, wholeheartedly, his most obedient servant.

BOSSUET

Thursday, at two o'clock

Addressed: *Monsieur Vincent, Superior General of the Mission*

Letter 3210. - Archives of the Mission, Turin, original autograph letter.

[1]This note is a follow-up to the preceding one, written that morning.

3211. - *BALTHAZAR GRANGIER DE LIVERDI, BISHOP OF TRÉGUIER, TO SAINT VINCENT*

Monsieur,

The entreaties M. Dissez [1] *is making to me to beg you to take him back into your Congregation, and his assurance that you will never be discontented with him, have obliged me to write you this note. He recognizes that he was at fault in the past, but the knowledge and detestation of his error convince him that he will not make the same mistake in future, if he has the honor of being readmitted into your Company. For my part, because of the good dispositions I see in him, I am sure you will be satisfied with him. Therefore, this compels me to join my prayers to his and to request for him the favor he is asking of you.*

That is the whole reason for this letter, except to assure you that I am, Monsieur, your most humble and very grateful servant.

BALTHAZAR,
Bishop of Tréguier

August 19 [1660]

Addressed: *Monsieur Vincent de Paul, Superior General of the Mission, at Saint-Lazare*

Letter 3211. - Archives of the Mission, Turin, original autograph letter.

[1]Could this be the M. Dizes who made a retreat at Saint-Lazare in preparation for his entrance into the Congregation of the Mission (cf. vol. VI, no. 2458)? If Saint Vincent accepted him a second time, he did not persevere, since he is not listed in the personnel catalogue.

3212. - *MONSIEUR D'ABANCOUR* [1] *TO SAINT VINCENT*

[August 1660] [2]

Monsieur,

In reply to the letter you did me the honor of writing me on August 7, I will tell you that the heretics[3] *have obtained another court decision, giving them liberty to continue their preaching in the environs of the place they had started to build, but it does not, in fact, give them permission to continue their building. Furthermore, they have obtained a plea against the Lieutenant for Criminal Affairs*[4] *of Saint-Quentin to keep him from learning any more about M. Ameline's business. The order states that claims made against the heretics will be sent immediately to the Court to be satisfied there, so now it is up to the Parlement to take action against those venomous tongues.*

But M. Ameline, who is the opposing party, has been unable to get to Paris to apply to the judge about the affair. Unless the Ladies of Charity do it for him, I fear that the mischief will continue and the heretics will behave as they always did during the war in similar circumstances, since they have not yet found any adversaries powerful enough to push them against the wall in court cases. They often win them with money, which, in these unfortunate times, is often the arbitrator between life and death and determines part of the lawsuit when it is joined to the favor of powerful friends. This often makes me say that, if religion, the discipline of the Church, and law and order were restored in France, we would have everything to hope for from the goodness of God during this period of peace.[5]

Today, Brother Jean Parre is going to visit Father Ameline at Notre-Dame-de-la-Paix and, if he is still of the same mind, we will do our utmost to help him in his mission. We would have liked to have had your opinion on this situation sooner, Monsieur, because harvest time is approaching.

Letter 3212. - Archives of the Mission, Turin, original autograph letter.

[1]Chancellor in Saint-Quentin, a village in Aisne.

[2]Date added on the back by Brother Ducournau.

[3]The Huguenots.

[4]A magistrate created within the royal headquarters to deal with all criminal matters.

[5]It might be of interest to note here that sentiments like these against the Huguenots eventually found expression in the revocation on October 18, 1685, of the Edict of Nantes (April 5, 1598), which in large measure had granted the Huguenots religious and political freedom within France.

I ask Our Lord to preserve your health, Monsieur, which is so necessary to us for the glory of Our Lord and the advancement of His service in the Church.

I am, very cordially and truthfully, with the respect that I owe you, Monsieur, your most humble and very obedient servant.

D'ABANCOUR

Addressed: *Monsieur Vincent, Superior General of the Congregation of the Priests of the Mission, at Saint-Lazare, in Paris*

3213. - TO JACQUES PESNELLE, SUPERIOR, IN GENOA

August 20, 1660

You point out to me the reasons you had for allowing M. Simon to dictate notes, and you question whether you have done the wrong thing. Yes, Monsieur, you have done the wrong thing, not in what concerns M. Simon, for, by God's grace, he is capable enough for that, but because that method of teaching is not the surest nor the most useful and has been judged unsuitable to the Company, and several of the most expert doctors [of theology], past and present, have judged it subject to various drawbacks.

This obliges me to tell you that it would be better not to teach philosophy at all than to present it in that way. However it may be done, I approve of your having it studied just this once by the two seminarians who are nearing the end of their seminary.

Letter 3213. - Extract quoted in the circular letter sent by Jean Bonnet, Superior General, on December 10, 1727, to the members of the Congregation of the Mission. Collet (*op. cit.*, vol. II, p. 80) states that, in a letter dated August 20, 1660, Saint Vincent speaks of René Alméras' illness; this may be the present letter, of which we have only a fragment.

3214. - *MATHURINE GUÉRIN TO SAINT VINCENT*

Monsieur and Most Honored Father,

Your blessing, please!

If I thought you had received the letter I had the boldness to write you when we arrived here, I would not dare to bother you with this one. Since, however, we have received no reply to it nor to the one we sent to M. Dehorgny, we do not know what the cause of this may be, except perhaps that we sent our first letters by way of the seigneur, *and he may have held on to them, especially since I named the place from which we were writing, which is not done here.*

This has upset us, since we have had no news of you, although I asked M. Dehorgny very earnestly for news and for his advice on a personal matter. Perhaps I am unreasonable to complain, Monsieur, and my questions do not deserve a reply. The fact still stands, however, that we are obliged for lack of advice to be uncertain about what we are doing and are perhaps not interpreting correctly your intention, which I would, nevertheless, like to be able to follow in everything.

Enclosed is a letter for Madame Fouquet, the President's wife, concerning the affairs of her poor people of this place.

We have not written to anyone since we have been here, although the seigneur *has often recommended to the man who brought us here to take care of all our needs.*

It will be difficult, Monsieur, for you to be able to read all the letters we need to send since, quite the contrary, those we address to you are in danger of being read before being given to you.

We have in this place the tax collector's wife, who is a close friend of the seigneur's *intendant. She absolutely insists that we take her son, about seven years of age, into our school. I asked her to excuse us, giving her the reasons that prevent us from acceding to her wishes, but she is not satisfied. She got the Superintendent, the child's godfather, to use his influence, and he asked us to do this only on condition that it were possible. She is still not satisfied and says she will continue to send him to us, which she did three times in one day, boasting that she could obtain what the intendant was unable to do. I told her we could not do this, and to show her that it was not through disrespect, as she says, I said I would write to*

Letter 3214. - Archives of the Mission, Turin, original autograph letter.

you about it. If we take that boy, there are others who have already requested this for their children. So, Monsieur, please let us know what you want us to do. I am not asking permission in order to prove a point to them, but I simply want a word to let them see that this cannot be done.

You gave us no instructions, Most Honored Father, about the confessor we should have. Since coming here we have been going to a good, elderly priest with the title of Promoter. I think you are aware, Monsieur, that this place is not under any Bishop but under the Holy Father. The trouble is that the preceding seigneurs *took such care to retain their temporal power that they neglected spiritual matters, for the older priests could not produce their titles, with the result that the young priests have had great difficulty being admitted to Holy Orders, even if they had a dimissorial letter from their Officialis.*

I have been told that two of these priests—one of whom hears the confessions of our patients—have never received permission from any Bishop to hear confessions. It was a priest who informed me of this, apparently as a charity, saying that our patients are not secure in his hands. I mentioned that to a few of these priests, without saying who had told me, and it turned out that those good priests could not prove that they had this legitimate authority. That is why, Monsieur, most people here are assailed by scruples. As for ourselves, if we knew how to manage without going to confession rather than go to persons suspected of not having the power to give us absolution, we would await your advice on the subject.

This has upset me somewhat with regard to our poor, especially since I do not want to cause offense to the person administering the sacraments to them. I feel obliged, therefore, to remain silent, in addition to the fact that very few here do not give cause for gossip.

I did not listen to these things just for the sake of being informed, but you know, Monsieur, how quickly bad rumors spread. There is only one priest on the island who has a good reputation, and he lives two leagues from here.

Our two Sisters and I take the liberty to send you our most humble greetings and to recommend ourselves to your holy prayers. I entreat you to allow me to say respectfully that I am, in the love of Jesus crucified,

Monsieur and Most Honored Father, your most humble and very obedient daughter and servant.

SISTER MATHURINE GUÉRIN

B[elle]-Île, August 20, 1660

Addressed: *Monsieur Vincent, General of the Priests of the Mission, at Saint-Lazare, in Paris*

3214a. - TO FIRMIN GET, SUPERIOR, IN MARSEILLES

Paris, August 20, 1660

Monsieur,

The grace of Our Lord be with you forever!

Here is a piece of news that will sadden you: good M. Bayn[1] has been ill with stomach pains for four or five days now. I am very sorry about this, although there is nothing to fear in it, thank God.

What increases my sorrow is that we have not been able to lodge him here in this house, as he would like. This may disedify him because he could think that we lack gratitude and charity. Yet, Monsieur, I wanted to give him this satisfaction more than I ever wanted to do for anyone, not only because you recommended him to us, but also because of the great goodness I have seen in him. I even tried two or three times to have him taken into our house, and I made arrangements for this with Brother Alexandre[2] and others,

---

Letter 3214a. - Copy made from *Recueil Nodet.* The letter was published in *Annales C.M.* (1943-44), pp. 257-58, and reprinted in *Mission et Charité,* 19-20, no. 130, pp. 164-65. This edition uses the latter text.

[1]Joseph Bayn.

[2]Alexandre Véronne, coadjutor Brother, born in Avignon on May 15, 1610, entered the Congregation of the Mission on July 22, 1630. He was infirmarian at Saint-Lazare and was so dedicated and capable that he won the esteem of all, especially Saint Vincent. His death on November 18, 1686, was announced to the whole Company in a circular from Edme Jolly, Superior General (1673-97). Brother Chollier wrote his life, which was published in *Miroir du frère coadjuteur de la Congrégation de la Mission* (Paris, 1875), pp. 145ff. This work also served as the basis for his biography in *Notices,* vol. III, pp. 528-48.

but it has been impossible for us to find a suitable place anywhere in the house because our infirmaries are occupied by our own patients. We have only four rooms with fireplaces; one is being used by the Bishop of Oloron,[3] another by Abbé de Chandenier,[4] and the third by our benefactor M. Pignay,[5] Doctor of the Sorbonne; all of them are staying here. The fourth has been promised to a person of rank who is supposed to come to make his retreat; the room will then be occupied by one of the preachers for the next ordination retreat, who is a priest from the outside. As for our little rooms, you know that they are absolutely unsuitable for the sick and that, instead of pleasing M. Bayn by giving him one of them, we would be offending him by lodging him so poorly. Moreover, most of our own priests do not have one, and, what is more, we usually have fifteen or twenty retreatants whom we are obliged to put up in the large halls because there are no more rooms.

So, only sheer helplessness has prevented us from lodging that good gentleman. Furthermore, we have offered to do anything we can for him, and have given him a Brother to look after him during his illness, in the place where he is staying.

I will discuss with the Duchesse d'Aiguillon whether the new tax farmers[6] will be willing to see that the wages of the chaplains who are on the books of the state for this year are paid. I am really afraid that they will object to that.

We have been led to hope that an order regarding the collector of the property taxes for the estates of Mme de Vins will be in the next regular mail; it is needed to receive from him the revenue for the first year.

I am writing to tell M. Huguier to give the convict Jean de Bréquigny thirty sous, and I am asking God to complete your cure

---

[3]Armand-François de Maytie.

[4]Claude de Chandenier.

[5]Nicolas Pignay, priest of the Rouen diocese and Doctor of the Sorbonne. In his will, dated August 10, 1671 (Arch. Nat., M 213, n. 8), he is mentioned as "Headmaster of the Collège de Justice . . . , living at the Bons-Enfants."

[6]Collectors of the *gabelles,* or salt tax.

and to sanctify you through Our Lord Jesus Christ, in whom I am, Monsieur, your most humble servant.

VINCENT DEPAUL,
i.s.C.M.

3215. - *THOMAS BAYN TO SAINT VINCENT*

[August 1660] [1]

Monsieur,

I am deeply grateful for your charity in having my brother cared for during the few days he was ill in Paris by sending one of your men to look after him. Now it is my ardent desire to be so happy as to find some opportunity to be able to be of service to you.

Meanwhile, Monsieur, I ask O[ur] L[ord] to be your reward and to give me the means of being able to let you know that I am, unconditionally, Monsieur, your most humble and very obedient servant.

THOMAS BAYN

Addressed: *Monsieur Vincent, General of the Priests of the Mission, at Saint-Lazare, in Paris*

3216. - TO RENÉ ALMÉRAS, IN RICHELIEU

August 22, 1660

Your letter and the one from Brother Gautier,[1] who wrote to me

---

Letter 3215. - Archives of the Mission, Turin, original autograph letter.

[1]Date added on the back by Brother Ducournau.

Letter 3216. - Reg. 2, p. 269.

[1]Christophe Gautier, born in Sablonnières (Seine-et-Marne), entered the Paris Seminary on April 16, 1655, at twenty years of age, and took his vows there in the presence of M. Berthe on June 29, 1657. He died in Sedan on October 11, 1671. Gautier was a very virtuous Brother, and the Superior General, René Alméras, praised him highly in his circular letter of October 23 (cf. *Notices,* vol. III, pp. 349-50).

about the state of your illness, have dispelled my great anxiety by the hope they have given me that you will soon be restored to health. This is based on several reasons, for which I thank God. When, then, will we have the perfect consolation of knowing that you have completely recovered? Oh, how I desire this! Oh, may God give us that great grace! I often ask Him for it, not only for my personal interest—which is not small, since, being filled with esteem and tenderness for you, I am the first to suffer from your illness and absence—but also for the welfare of the Company which, having been greatly edified by you, by the grace of God, still needs your help and example.

I tell you this, Monsieur, with sentiments of gratitude to God and to you, and I will say no more about it because that suffices for the purpose I have in view, which is to let you see that you will be making a sacrifice to God by preserving yourself and by recovering. I very humbly entreat you to do so.

You may say, however, "Does that depend on me? " Yes, Monsieur, I think it does, in so far as it depends on rest and remedies, which are in your power. Above all, it depends on the good pleasure of God, who will not refuse you the strength of body and mind necessary to His plans for you in the Company, if you ask Him for them through His Son Our Lord. Having established the same Company for His service, He has also called you to it in such an efficacious manner by His grace.

Spare nothing, then, that can contribute to your good health and your speedy return, for which we are longing. Do not, however, set out on your journey without the consent of the doctors, especially during the hot weather. We will be patient.

3217. - *MADAME POTIER DE LAMOIGNON TO SAINT VINCENT*

Monsieur,

Last evening I received a note from the Pastor of Saint-Nicolas-du-Chardonnet,[1] *who wrote me that you had had the kindness to grant me two Sisters of Charity for Auteuil, for which I am most grateful to you. If women were allowed to go to see you, I would have the honor of visiting you to thank you for this. The Pastor of Auteuil will have the honor of going to see you for this purpose and to get your instructions regarding what is necessary for those poor Sisters.*

I am really distressed at not being able to get them settled myself, due to my trip to Bourbon,[2] *where I am going for a few ailments I have, but I will entrust them to some good Ladies, who will look after them, and to a certain Madame Guerrier, whom those Sisters know. She is in charge of the Charity of St-Barthélemy and of the prisoners. The Fathers of Sainte-Geneviève,*[3] seigneurs *of Autueil, have a share in this good work. Madame Chahu will visit them sometimes, and I will ask Madame Traversay*[4] *to take them there.*

I recommend my journey to your good prayers, and I ask you to do me the honor of believing that I am, Monsieur, your most humble servant.

M. POTIER

Paris, August 22, 1660

Addressed: *Monsieur Vincent, General of the Missionaries, at Saint-Laurent*

Letter 3217. - Archives of the Mission, Turin, original autograph letter.

[1]Hippolyte Féret, born in Pontoise (Val-d'Oise), was a Doctor of Theology and later became Pastor of Saint-Nicolas-du-Chardonnet, Vicar-General of Alet, and then of Paris. Saint Vincent thought so highly of Féret that he proposed him as Coadjutor Bishop of Babylon.

[2]Probably Bourbon-l'Archambault, a city in Allier still noted for its thermal baths. She may also have gone to the curative waters of Bourbon-Lancy nearby.

[3]Canons Regular of Sainte-Geneviève.

[4]Anne Petau was the widow of René Regnault, Seigneur de Traversay and Counselor in the Paris Parlement. She was also the sister of President Méliand, and was one of the Ladies of Charity most devoted to Saint Vincent and his works. Madame de Traversay founded the Monastery of the Conception, rue Saint-Honoré, and was responsible for the Daughters of the Cross after the death of their foundress, Madame de Villeneuve.

3218. - *THE MARQUIS DE LIONNE* [1] *TO SAINT VINCENT*

Berny,[2] *August 22, 1660*

I entreat M. Vincent to grant me the favor of sending me a short letter, in which he orders the Mother Superior of the Visitation of the faubourg St-Jacques[3] *to allow my daughters*[4] *to leave when I send someone to call for them in my name, so that they may see the ceremony of the entrance of the Queen.*[5] *I will be very grateful to him for this.*

Your most humble servant.

DE LIONNE

3219. - *NICOLAS SEVIN, BISHOP OF CAHORS, TO SAINT VINCENT*

Mercuès,[1] *August 22 [1660]* [2]

Monsieur,

It really worries me not to hear a word about you; that is why I am writing this letter to ask how you are. I also want to remind you of the promise you made not to forget me before God, either on earth or in heaven.

Letter 3218. - Archives of the Mission, Turin, original autograph letter.

[1]Hugues de Lionne, a confidant of Mazarin, whom he had met in Rome. After serving as Secretary of the Orders of the Queen Regent, he became Grand Master of Ceremonies and Commandant of the King's Orders. He was sent to Italy (1654-56), where he contributed to the election of Pope Alexander VII (1655-67), and to Germany (1658) as extraordinary Ambassador; he negotiated the preliminaries for the Treaty of the Pyrenees for peace between France and Spain (1659) and was appointed Minister of State. He continued to hold this position after Mazarin's death and died in Paris on September 1, 1671, at sixty years of age.

[2]A locality incorporated today into the commune of Fresne (Seine).

[3]Marie-Agnès Le Roy.

[4]Élisabeth, who later became a Visitation nun, and Madeleine, who, on February 10, 1670, married François-Annibal d'Estrées, Marquis de Coeuvres, later a Duke and Peer of France.

[5]Paris was preparing with great pomp to welcome, on August 26, Louis XIV and the new Queen, Maria Teresa, the Infanta of Spain. They had been married in Saint-Jean-de-Luz (Pyrénées-Atlantiques) on June 9.

Letter 3219. - Archives of the Mission, Turin, original autograph letter.

[1]A small locality in the district of Cahors.

[2]First year of the episcopate of Nicolas Sevin in Cahors.

With God's help, I soon hope to make the rounds of my whole diocese to see all the priests in their deanery meetings. I thought that, having only about six more weeks of this year during which I could make visitations, if I started now, I could only visit a small area. This would not give me a very good idea of my diocese, and the rest of it would remain unknown to me. Instead, by going everywhere, as I can do during these six weeks, I will have at least a vague idea of it and, seeing all the priests who are to animate the rest of the diocese, the whole diocese will profit from it. You see how much I need prayers on this occasion. I entreat you, therefore, not to spare yours, nor those of all your good priests.

I am sending you two hundred little pills, and I hope God will bless them so that they will contribute to your health as much as I hope they will.

Thank you very much for having spared my purse, as you did in the case of M. Insiguin.[3] *You may use it for whatever occasions you judge appropriate, on the part of one who is totally, in Our Lord, Monsieur, your most humble servant.*

NICOLAS,
B[ishop] of Cahors

I am sending the pills to M. Cuissot to be delivered to you by the mail coach.

Addressed: *Monsieur Vincent, Superior General of the Mission, in Paris*

3220. - TO THE SUPERIORS

1660

Monsieur,

In the future, please keep the letters written to you and to the members of your house, no matter from whom they may come,

---

[3]A captive in Algiers (cf. no. 3116a, n. 3).

Letter 3220. - Archives of the Mission, Paris, *Collection of Circular Letters, 1877-80.*

whenever they contain any noteworthy details that may be important or may be instructive for the future.

(1) Simply make different files of them, according to subject matter or the year in which you receive them. When they have been arranged in these bundles, keep them in a place set apart for this purpose, where those who come after you can have recourse to them in their need. If there are any such letters in the house from the past, please sort them according to the aforesaid order.

(2) Make note throughout the year of the most important spiritual and temporal affairs that occur in your house and during the missions and other spiritual exercises that take place outside the house. Summarize them in a letter after the feast of Saint John the Baptist,[1] at which time the missions are usually concluded, and send us the letter so we can make a circular letter of it, if it is judged advisable.

(3) If you have a priest, seminarian, or Brother who has not finished his second year of probation or seminary, let us know, two or three months before the end of the said year, the state or dispositions of the person, so we can tell you whether you may allow him to take his vows after he has completed the two years. When he has taken them, send us immediately his name, surname, etc., in the following manner:

François, born on the . . . day of the month of . . . , in the city, town, or village of . . . , in the diocese of . . . , entered the Congregation of the Mission in (Paris) on the . . . day of the month of . . . , in the year . . . , and took his vows in (Paris) in the presence of M. . . . , on the . . . day of the month of . . . in the year. . . .

If he has any Holy Order, it is advisable to specify when he received it. If anyone does not know the day, for instance, of his birth, have him give the month; if he does not know either one, have him give the time and season of the year when he was born; and so on for the others.

---

[1]June 24.

(4) When you inform us of the death of any of our men, please state at the same time—or as soon as possible—the most important things that have been observed during the life and illness of the person. I ask you to inform us from now on of the men who have died in your house, with the day and year of their death, etc., and hereafter to keep a register of them, in which any information sent to the Superior General will also be recorded.

3221. - TO FRANÇOIS PÉAN [1]

August 23, 1660

I am very annoyed that we did not take advantage of the favor you offered us. The reason is that the Company has been devoting itself to its usual exercises. Furthermore, everyone flatters himself that he knows the method of controversy. I hope, however, by the grace of God, that one day we will avail ourselves of the special lights you have and which you share with everyone through your writings. Meanwhile, I am returning to you your apologia and the order of the conferences, and I renew to you the offers. . . .

Letter 3221. - Reg. 2, p. 83.

[1]François Péan is the author of several works on controversy, among others: *Le parfait controversiste ou manière invincible pour convaincre toutes les sortes d'hérétiques* (Paris, 1650); *Méthode facile pour convaincre les hérétiques, ensemble les nullités de la religion prétendue reformée* (Paris, 1659). He had written to Saint Vincent to ask permission to give a series of lectures at Saint-Lazare on the subject of controversy.

3222. - *FRANÇOISE CARCIREUX TO SAINT VINCENT*

Very Dear and Honored Father,

Your blessing!

Monsieur, the absolute trust, love, and awe I have with regard to M. des Jardins have kept me silent for a long time, with the result that I have neglected to take the honor of writing to you because His Charity thought it fit for us to make our communication to him once a month, which I do unreservedly, thank God. His Charity instructed me to take this honor. I acquiesce with all my heart and will tell you that we are finding it very hard to preserve some slight image of our Institute. We seem to be suffering the worst agonies. We have shocks to absorb, and they are not small ones. It seems to me that all this turbulence comes from those fine demoiselles with whom Sister Anne[1] *and I are associated.*

Our only supporter and defender, after God, is M. des Jardins; we are deeply indebted for this grace, and we will acknowledge it. He told us that you want us to show an interest in the young women whom God will honor with the grace of our vocation. We gladly accept this in the hope that, through us, God will instill in them the spirit of our Company and that you in your goodness will not allow what is contrary to that to subsist. This is the petition we address to you so that, in the love of Jesus and of you, assuring you always of our very humble respect and obedience, we may all be, my very dear Father, your most humble and obedient servants and unworthy daughters in O[ur] L[ord].

FRANÇOISE CARCIREUX,
Daughter of Charity

Narbonne, August 23, 1660

Our Sisters are doing their duties fairly well, and God is honoring us with His blessing by the union existing among ourselves.

Sister Anne wishes to take her vows; she has spoken to us several times about this.

Most Honored Father, I almost forgot to thank you for having honored us several times with news of your dear self. It is an apt topic for

---

Letter 3222. - Archives of the Mission, Turin, original autograph letter.

[1]Anne Denoual.

conversation and meditation, of which all three of us make use, as we do of your dear letters. And since M. des Jardins in his charity often gives you news of us, he makes up perfectly for my faults. That is why I also have nothing to say.

The above-mentioned demoiselles have managed—for what they believe are good reasons—to deprive us of at least a large part of the good reputation God had given us with His Excellency [2] *and those near him.*

Lastly, there are two cliques here, and it would appear that they are trying adroitly to strengthen their position. It seems, Most Honored Father, that M. des Jardins has had the gift of prophecy, at least in this respect.

God be blessed!

Addressed: *Monsieur Vincent, Superior General of the Mission, in the faubourg Saint-Denis, at Saint-Lazare, in Paris*

3223. - *MARIE-AGNÈS LE ROY TO SAINT VINCENT*

August 23, 1660

Live Jesus!

Very Dear and Most Honored Father,

I raised no objections with M. de Lionne about giving him his dear daughters, since there was no opportunity to do so and no one had said anything to us on his part. If someone had mentioned it to us, I would have represented that we had refused permission to Madame de Sévigné[1] *for her daughter,*[2] *and for that reason I held firm regarding everyone else,*

---

[2]François Fouquet.

Letter 3223. - Archives of the Mission, Turin, original autograph letter.

[1]Marie de Rabutin (1629-96), granddaughter of Saint Jane Frances de Chantal, was the widow of the Marquis de Sévigné and a woman gifted with incomparable literary talent. Her letters have immortalized her name. (Cf. M. Monmerqué, *Les grands écrivains de France. Lettres de Madame de Sévigné, de sa famille et de ses amis* (new ed., 14 vols., Paris: Hachette, 1862-66). She died in Grignan.

[2]Françoise-Marguerite de Sévigné. There is no reason to doubt, as does Monmerqué, that Madame de Sévigné's daughter, the future Comtesse de Grignan, was a boarder at the Second Monastery of the Visitation.

such as the two daughters of the Chief Justice,[3] *President Amelot's daughter,*[4] *and others. In the case of Madame de Sévigné, I had even told her that, because of the consequences for each, I would do nothing whatsoever to obtain that permission because everyone says that there are no other consequences in this situation, and they even tried to bring in M. Joly to convince us on that point.*

So it will be whatever you choose for the little Lionne girls but, if they go, then I think it will be a good idea for you to give the same permission to all the others, and to Madame de Sévigné for her daughter—in a word, to those eight who are wearing the little habit. They could wear caps and take off their little veils. The other two lay boarders who are with us, and the little Bouillon girl,[5] *should also be included, if this is requested.*

Consider, Most Honored Father, whether you want to give us a word of reply to this, or whether you prefer to wait until the parents come to you to request this permission. Tell us your wishes on this and I will wait for your instructions.

I am, Most Honored Father, your most humble and very obedient daughter and servant in Our Lord.

SISTER MARIE-AGNÈS LE ROY

Blessed be God!

Addressed: *Monsieur Vincent, Superior General of the Congregation of the Mission*

---

[3]At that time Guillaume de Lamoignon had four daughters, aged respectively fifteen, eleven, ten, and six: Marie married the Maréchal de Broglie; Madeleine became the wife of Achille de Harlay, Chief Justice of the Parlement; and the two younger girls, Marie-Élisabeth and Anne-Élisabeth, became Visitation nuns. All four were boarders at the Second Monastery. This letter apparently refers to the two older girls.

[4]Charles Amelot, Seigneur de Gournay, Presiding Judge of the Great Council, died in Paris on February 12, 1680. His daughter Catherine married Louis-Claude d'Haussonville de Nettancourt.

[5]Mauricette-Fébronie de la Tour d'Auvergne, daughter of Frédéric-Maurice de la Tour, Duc de Bouillon. On April 24, 1668, she married Maximilien, Duke of Bavaria, brother of the Elector; she died childless on June 20, 1706.

3224. - *ANNE DE SAUJON* [1] *TO SAINT VINCENT*

Luxembourg,[2] *August 24, 1660*

Monsieur,

Although I do not have the honor of being known very well by you, I still think you will be good enough to grant the humble petition I am presenting to you, which is to let me know through the bearer of this letter, whether the Daughters of Sainte-Marie[3] *present their Superiors to the Bishops. If this is the case, I would be even more grateful if you would lend me their letter for a day or two. You probably realize, Monsieur, that I am asking this favor for the second work of the late Abbé Olier, which is about to blossom, with the help of God.*[4]

Some time ago, M. de Bretonvilliers[5] *and I went to see you to discuss this with you, but your illness, Monsieur, prevented me from having this honor. M. de Bretonvilliers, who discussed the matter with you, told me*

Letter 3224. - Archives of the Mission, Turin, original autograph letter.

[1]Anne-Campet de Saujon, lady-in-waiting and lady of the bedchamber of the Duchesse d'Orléans. She was thought to wield considerable influence over Gaston, Duc d'Orléans. In 1649 she entered Carmel, from which she was withdrawn against her will and brought back to the Court. Although her director, Jean-Jacques Olier, to whom she often manifested her desire for the cloister, told her constantly to be patient and to await God's time, he felt she could be useful for a work he had in mind: the foundation of a Community dedicated to the interior life of Mary, which would welcome well-to-do ladies who wanted to make a retreat. He shared his plan with Madame Tronson and Madame de Saujon and even advised them to give themselves to God for this purpose on January 19, 1654, in the church of Notre-Dame. At the time of the Founder's death (April 2, 1657), the Rules of the new Institute had been drawn up. M. de Bretonvilliers, Olier's successor, with whom he had discussed it, did not let the project drop. In a house he had built for them on rue Garancière, he brought together as a Community Madame Tronson, Madame de Saujon, Mademoiselle d'Aubrai, and other persons of distinction. Madame Tronson became the first Superior; when she died, the office was given to Madame de Saujon, who held it for nine years. When the Archbishop removed her from that position because of complaints--which unfortunately were only too well-founded--she got her revenge by obtaining from the Court the suppression of the little Community. Jean-Jacques Olier had recommended that she never be given the highest office; only too late did people realize that they should have listened to him. (Cf. Étienne-Michel Faillon, *Vie de M. Olier, fondateur du séminaire de Saint-Sulpice* [3 vols., Paris: Poussielgue, 1873], vol. II, pp. 567-70.)

[2]The Luxembourg Palace in Paris.

[3]The Visitation Order.

[4]The Community of the Daughters of the Blessed Virgin, also called the Daughters of the Inner Life of Mary.

[5]Alexandre Le Ragois de Bretonvilliers, born on January 22, 1621, became Pastor of Saint-Sulpice in 1652 and Superior General in 1657. Until his death in Paris on June 13, 1676 he presided over the expansion of the Company of Saint-Sulpice.

that you approve wholeheartedly of this holy work, and this gave me great joy. I am sure that, since then, you have spoken to O[ur] L[ord] about its realization. We have the letters and permissions of His Majesty, drawn up in the correct form, and we are going to get those of the Bishop of Metz,[6] *who has promised them to us.*

I take the liberty of asking for a share in your holy prayers and of assuring you that I am, very respectfully, Monsieur, your most humble and very obedient servant.

ANNE DE SAUJON

Addressed: *Monsieur Vincent, Superior of Saint-Lazare, at Saint-Lazare*

3225. - *JACQUES CHARTON*[1] *TO SAINT VINCENT*

Poissy, August 24, 1660

Monsieur,

Peace and love in J[esus] C[hrist]!

I cannot believe what was told me from Paris—I mean that very often you blame Gamaches,[2] *Grandin,*[3] *and me for the affair of the Carmelites, which is creating such a stir, and for a decision emanating from His Holiness, without having sent for or listened to the persons involved.*[4] *Perhaps this is because no one told you our defenses, Monsieur, which*

---

[6]Henri de Bourbon, Duc de Verneuil and Abbot of Saint-Germain. Without his permission no Community could be established in the district of Saint-Germain-des-Prés. By letters dated August 30 he granted authorization for this to the Daughters of the Inner Life of Mary.

Letter 3225. - Archives of the Mission, Turin, original autograph letter.

[1]Jacques Charton, Doctor of Theology, member of the Council of Conscience and Director of the Trente-Trois Seminary.

[2]Charles de Gamaches, Doctor of the Sorbonne and Canon of Notre-Dame de Paris; he died on January 27, 1670.

[3]Martin Grandin, Doctor of the Sorbonne, Professor in the faculty of theology, and author of a six-volume treatise on theology. Born in Saint-Quentin (Aisne) on November 11, 1604, he died in November 1691.

[4]Cf. no. 2929, n. 1, which explains the problem to which Charton here alludes.

persons of great integrity and ability have approved and continue to approve. I am too well acquainted with your inclination, which is rather to sympathize with those who are oppressed.

There is one thing in this affair that astonishes me above all the others, namely, that some upright persons have become the counselors and advocates of those religious women, in opposition to their Superiors and, because of a minor squabble, have sown discord in an Order that was rendering glory to God. For love of Him I hope you will always keep a place for me in your heart and, when occasions such as the present one arise, you will continue to extend to me the friendship you have always shown me, for which I am obliged to be all my life, Monsieur, your most humble servant.

J. CHARTON

Addressed: *Monsieur Vincent, Superior General of the Mission, at Saint-Lazare, in Paris*

3226. - *MONSIEUR DELAFORCADE TO SAINT VINCENT*

Lyons, August 24, 1660

Monsieur,

I have just received the letter, dated August 20, with which you were pleased to honor me. Enclosed with it was a bill of exchange for one thousand livres on M. Jacques Ceré to be delivered to M. Boussordec,[1] *who is supposed to arrive soon in this town on his way to Annecy. I will not fail to follow your orders either to give him the amount or to have him paid it in Chambéry or somewhere else that I will find more convenient for him and . . .* [2] *of which I will be notified.*

I will also serve him wholeheartedly in every way possible. This will be a great honor for me because he is coming on your behalf and because I

Letter 3226. - Archives of the Mission, Turin, original autograph letter.

[1]Saint Vincent had just named Charles Boussordec Superior of the Annecy house.

[2]Apparently Coste found this word *sieur* difficult to read in the original and omitted it. The gentleman in question is M. Boussordec.

am, Monsieur, your most humble, affectionate, grateful, and obedient servant.

DELAFORCADE

Addressed: *Monsieur Vincent, Superior General of the Mission, at Saint-Lazare, in Paris*

3227. - TO MADAME ANNE DE SAUJON

August 25, 1660

Madame,

I received your orders with a great desire to obey you. Pardon me for not having replied to you yesterday; I had too many business affairs.

It is true, Madame, that some of the Visitation houses present to the Bishops the priests they would like to have as their Superiors, but not all the Bishops are willing to accept them, claiming that it is up to them to choose and appoint them. I am going to write to the Mother Superior of rue Saint-Antoine[1] to ask her to let me know the reasons why the Sisters think they have that right, how they have used it, and, if they have any document on the matter, to send it to me.

I am very embarrassed, Madame, by the honor you did me in coming here with M. de Bretonvilliers and that I was deprived of the consolation of seeing you on account of my wretchedness and ailments. I am even more so because of the confidence with which you honor me, since I am so unworthy of it, especially regarding such an important work as the one you do me the favor of mentioning. I esteem, respect, and praise it as God's inspiration to that holy man[2] who is its author, and I ask His Divine Goodness to be pleased

---

Letter 3227. - Reg. 1, fol. 51v, copy made from the unsigned rough draft.

[1]Louise-Eugénie de Fontaine. For her answer see no. 3236.

[2]Jean-Jacques Olier.

to bless it in view of the many good souls who participate in it.

I would consider myself fortunate, Madame, if I could do anything to please you. Rest assured that no occasion will ever arise in which I will not strive to do so with all the humility and affection due you, in the love of O[ur] L[ord], Madame, by your. . . .

3228. - *MONSIEUR ROBINEAU TO SAINT VINCENT*

Monsieur,

Although it hardly seems necessary to add anything to what dear M. Paul has said, I am writing to you, nevertheless, Monsieur, to send you most humble greetings and to testify to you, by my feeble recommendation, that the person for whom he is requesting the favor of making a short retreat at your house is considered one of the holiest men we know. He wants to ask Our Lord for the grace to be a true priest and, to tell the truth, Monsieur, God has already granted him a lively disposition for this. I leave it up to M. Paul, who is better able to make a judgment on this, to tell you what he thinks of it, but I will ask you, as usual, for a small share in your holy prayers and for your continued blessing.

I am, Monsieur, your most humble and obedient servant.

ROBINEAU

Feast of Saint Louis [1] *1660*

Addressed: *Monsieur Vincent, Superior General of the Missions*

Letter 3228. - Archives of the Mission, Turin, original autograph letter.

[1]August 25.

3229. - *FRANÇOIS FOUQUET, ARCHBISHOP OF NARBONNE, TO SAINT VINCENT*

Cannes, August 26, 1660

Monsieur,

I await with extreme impatience the fulfillment of your promises regarding the two Missionaries and the Brother you promised me for the month of September. On this assurance, I have scheduled my missions and visitations for the beginning of October. I can do neither without this assistance because I have allowed some Doctrinaires,[1] *who worked for me there last winter, to be engaged in other dioceses. I did so for several good reasons, so you can well imagine, Monsieur, the confusion and disorder that would result if you failed to keep your word to me. I will see that travel expenses are reimbursed.*

I say nothing to you regarding M. Parisy because he has given us his word that he will be here at the end of the summer.

Please allow me, Monsieur, to express my surprise—or, to put it more accurately, my chagrin—at the length of time you are taking and your objections in consenting to the union I am making to the seminary of the little parish of Maiour, after all my objections to your relieving your men of that parish, although it has only two or three hundred communicants. Several times I have repeated to you that all the members of my council, as well as your own priests, are convinced that the seminary, as I have formed it, composed only of experienced priests, is entirely useless to me, if your men who are directing it have no authority in a parish to have those priests, who are already Pastors or destined to become so, carry out its functions. You know better than I that theory without practice is useless.

Meanwhile, never dreaming that you would raise any objections in this area, since you did not do so for Agde, where there was greater reason for it, I purchased a large house and went to great expense to furnish it, so as to establish them there, as well as in the rectory of Maiour. All that is to no avail if we do not set up something permanent that can endure after me. I repeat that this will be impossible if they do not have charge of the parish.

I thought I had shown you sufficient evidence of the affection I have for your Institute and my knowledge of it to assure you that I would do nothing

---

Letter 3229. - Archives of the Mission, Turin, original autograph letter.

[1]The name given to the Priests of Christian Doctrine, a Congregation founded in 1592 by César de Bus (cf. no. 3004).

that might be prejudicial and that, if you did not accept my judgment, you should accept that of many capable persons whom you know and who work with me. We have had countless discussions on this topic and on your fears and have agreed unanimously that the latter were unfounded; otherwise, all the money I had spent was wasted.

I am still determined to purchase for them, as soon as possible, a very pretty house by the water, with a very lovely garden. It is about a quarter of a league from town, and both teachers and seminarians can go there for retreats and recreation.

In the name of God, Monsieur, let this be the last letter I am obliged to write to you on this matter and free me of the greatest trouble and chagrin I have in my diocese at present and which is such a headache for me. If not, resign yourself to receive every week letters longer than this one, on which the success or the failure of all my plans depends. In the latter case, I might as well go to Paris and just give up.

I know that you have in your house right now a large number of excellent workers, whom you have recalled from various places, and that you have only to make a slight effort on my behalf. You have already done me so many favors and have shown me such great friendship! This occasion will confirm that or cause me to forget everything.

Were it not for the six-week journey I made in Auvergne, I would not have left you in peace for such a long time. I was sure that, on my return from there, I would find your consent to what I requested of you and what I now ask you with such urgency.

I am, Monsieur, your most humble and very obedient servant.

FRANÇOIS,
Arch[bishop] of Narbonne

In the name of God, send our priests some good servant who knows how to do the buying; the ones they have here lack either loyalty or intelligence. They pay much more for things than what they are worth, besides the fact that their house is so dirty and disorderly that it turns one's stomach to set foot in it. Treat us as you have treated your men in Cahors, which I just left.

Addressed: *Monsieur Vincent, Superior General of the Priests of the Mission, at Saint-Lazare, in Paris*

3230. - *JOSEPH BAYN TO SAINT VINCENT*

Monsieur,

Even if I were capable of expressing myself, I could never find words corresponding to my desires to thank you for your service and charity to me through Brother Christophe's[1] *care of me during my illness. However, although he nursed me with great care, I am convinced that my recovery is due to your prayers because I flatter myself with having your affection and love. That is why I implore you in the name of God, Monsieur, to continue and to believe that I will consider myself all my life, Monsieur, your most humble and very grateful servant.*

JOSEPH BAYN

Paris, August 26, 1660

Addressed: *Monsieur Vincent de Paul, General of the Priests of the Mission, at Saint-Lazare house, in Paris*

3231. - *MONSIEUR PESNELLE TO SAINT VINCENT*

Monsieur,

I was prepared to pay you the sum of eight hundred livres, as my elder brother[1] *had instructed me to do in his letters of July 13, but, since you have not been in a position to answer the letters I had written you on this subject, I hope you will allow me to defer this payment until my return from the country, where I have business to transact until the end of September. If, however, you want this money or have an urgent need for it, I will drop everything else and come to do whatever you wish. Tomorrow I will write to tell my younger brother to go to see you to find out your decision so he can inform me at the place where I will be.*

Letter 3230. - Archives of the Mission, Turin, original autograph letter.

[1]Several coadjutor Brothers bore this name. In this case it is most likely Christophe Gautier.

Letter 3231. - Archives of the Mission, Turin, original autograph letter.

[1]Jacques Pesnelle, Superior in Genoa.

Meanwhile, I am writing to my elder brother about his latest letters, asking him to send me, as soon as possible, your documents, drawn up correctly for the resignation he wants to make in my favor. Because he asked me which format would be best, I am sending him a model, on which I would really like him to pattern his document.

Since you were so good as to serve as mediator in an affair of this consequence to secure an agreement between two brothers, I entreat you, Monsieur, to be willing to contribute to its conclusion and accomplishment. It is very important for me to know your decision before the feast of Saint Martin.[2] *That is why I entreat you to add your request to the one I am making to my elder brother so that he will answer me promptly. I solemnly declared to you in my most recent letters that I am very anxious to acknowledge this obligation to your generosity.*

These will always be my sentiments, together with that of being, Monsieur, your most humble and very obedient servant.

PESNELLE

Rouen, August 26, 1660

Addressed: *Monsieur Vincent, Superior of the Mission of Saint-Lazare, in the faubourg Saint-Denis, in Paris*

3232. - *MAURICE DE LA TOUR D'AUVERGNE*[1] *TO SAINT VINCENT*

[August 1660][2]

Monsieur,

Having left the Daughters of Sainte-Marie[3] *to witness the entrance of the King, I entreat you to allow me not to return there until my sister from*

---

[2]November 11.

Letter 3232. - Archives of the Mission, Turin, original autograph letter.

[1]Since the writer of this letter is obviously a woman, it can only be surmised that the title and signature are erroneous or that (Frédéric) Maurice de la Tour d'Auvergne, Duc de Bouillon, signed what his daughter Mauricette-Fébronie had written.

[2]This letter was written a few days after no. 3223; no. 3256 refers to the same request.

[3]The Second Monastery of the Visitation, where she was a boarder.

Château-Thierry[4] *receives the habit, which will take place on the feast of Our Lady.*[5] *Because so very little time remains, I feel sure you will not refuse me this favor, since it is only right for me to be present at that ceremony.*

I entreat you then, Monsieur, to have this kindness and to believe that I am, Monsieur, your most humble and very affectionate servant.

MAURICE DE LA TOUR D'AUVERGNE

Addressed: *Monsieur Vincent*

3233. - TO JEAN MARTIN, SUPERIOR, IN TURIN

Paris, August 27, 1660

Monsieur,

The grace of O[ur] L[ord] be with you forever!

I received your letters of July 28 and August 14. You must be patient about the delay in procuring a house. God will give you one in due time and when you have sufficiently honored the poverty of O[ur] L[ord], who had no house nor even a stone on which to lay His head.[1] Our family in Rome lived in a rented house for eighteen or twenty years. Provided that yours is faithful to its employments and to its rule to firmly establish the kingdom of God in itself and in others, it will lack nothing.[2] However, it is essential, first of all, that you work at this—as you are doing, by God's grace—and, trusting in His Providence for the rest, that you are at peace.

In addition to this reason, you have another for not worrying about a residence; namely, that the Marchese[3] is thinking enough

---

[4]Émilie-Léonore, born in Maastricht in 1640, had entered the Carmelite Order.

[5]September 8.

Letter 3233. - Archives of the Mission, Turin, original signed letter.

[1]Cf. Mt 8:20; Lk 9:58. (NAB)

[2]Cf. Mt 6:33. (NAB)

[3]Filippo di Simiane, Marchese di Pianezza.

about it for you. From what you tell me, he is giving the same idea to others and is even willing to yield the title of founder to anyone who would like to give you more than he does. I admire his great goodness, and I ask Our Lord to make us less unworthy than we are to receive its effects and to acknowledge them.

Do not be afraid of the fever; most likely it has gone and will not recur, and God does not intend to afflict us any more in that respect. The chills you experience whenever the weather is a little cold are not indications of the return of this fever; they do not proceed from an intrinsic cause but from something exterior to which you are more susceptible as a result of the past fever, which has weakened you. I ask Our Lord to restore your former strength to you so that you may continue to serve Him with as much vigor and as many good results as ever. I have high hopes that He will, if you do everything that is to be desired to preserve your health.

We have no news. Our patients are better, thank God, and so is M. Alméras. When he left Richelieu to return here, he was forced to go back there from Tours because he felt so weak.

I am, in the love of O[ur] L[ord], Monsieur, your most humble servant.

VINCENT DEPAUL,
i.s.C.M.

Addressed: Monsieur Martin, Superior of the Priests of the Mission, in Turin

3234. - *ANNE-MARGUERITE GUÉRIN TO SAINT VINCENT*

Live Jesus!

Our Third Monastery in Paris, August [1660] [1]

Most Honored Father,

We just heard that the boarders—that is, all of our little Sisters, the young ladies, and Madame de Melun[2]*—have left our monastery in the faubourg for the entrance of the Queen and are supposed to be coming to see us. That is why, Most Honored Father, we ask you most humbly to kindly allow them to enter here one time before returning to their enclosure. Madame Canos also asks us to grant her this favor before she becomes cloistered forever in our above-mentioned monastery. If, however, you have any objections to this latter request, I ask you to give us permission for all the rest, if possible.*

They sent word that they will be coming today or tomorrow. That is why we most humbly entreat you in your goodness to give us an immediate reply and your holy blessing, and we ask God to preserve you in perfect health, Most Honored Father.

Your most humble and very obedient and unworthy daughter and servant in Our Lord.

SISTER ANNE-MARGUERITE GUÉRIN,
of the Visitation Sainte-Marie

Blessed be God!

Addressed: *Monsieur Vincent, Superior General of the Priests of the Mission of Saint-Lazare*

Letter 3234. - Archives of the Mission, Turin, original autograph letter.

[1]This letter refers to the same question as is treated in no. 3223. Since the date of the latter is certain, it enables us to assign the year 1660 to no. 3234 as well.

[2]Ernestine de Ligne-Aremberg, widow of Guillaume de Melun, Prince d'Épinoy, High Constable and Seneschal of Flanders.

3234a. - TO FIRMIN GET, SUPERIOR, IN MARSEILLES

Paris, August 27, 1660

Monsieur,

The grace of Our Lord be with you forever!

I received your letter of the seventeenth. The Duchesse d'Aiguillon had someone contact the tax farmers of the *gabelles* of Provence to ask them to instruct their agents to pay the chaplains' salaries, but I did not hear what reply they gave.

M. Grimancourt,[1] the honorary executor of the last will and testament of the late Marquise de Vins,[2] promised us that he would give orders to the collector of the property taxes on her estates to pay you the income of the first year of her foundation. I sent someone to his office to collect it. If I get it before the regular mail leaves, you will receive it along with this letter; if not, it will go with the next one.

It suffices that you are thinking about the great, pressing needs of our confreres in Algiers; I am sure you will do whatever you can to help them as soon as possible. M. Bayn has recovered, thank God. I am writing to tell M. Huguier[3] to give 6 livres 15 sous to M. Ebran, a convict.

I am, in the love of Our Lord, Monsieur, your most humble servant.

VINCENT DEPAUL,
i.s.C.M.

Letter 3234a. - Copy made from *Recueil Nodet.* The letter was published in *Annales C.M.* (1943-44), pp. 258-59, and reprinted in *Mission et Charité,* 19-20, no. 131, p. 166. This edition uses the latter text.

[1]Jean de La Roche-Lambert, Seigneur de Grimancourt, the King's steward, who was living in Paris.

[2]This will, with its two codicils, was published in *Annales C.M.* (1943-44), pp. 264-73.

[3]The copyist wrote *Gagnaire*, an obvious error in reading.

3234b. - TO DOMINIQUE LHUILLIER, IN CRÉCY

Paris, August 27, 1660

Monsieur,

The grace of Our Lord be with you forever!

Here is good Brother Servin,[1] who is heading for Saint-Fiacre[2] with the intention of passing through Crécy on his way back. Please welcome him as cordially as possible, as one of the good servants of God in the Company.

The Bishop of Meaux[3] sent word to me through M. Brin[4] that he wanted to make use of you on his visitations. I replied to him that you have not yet had enough experience to be able to preach every day. His Excellency is satisfied with whatever you are able to do. That being the case, I am asking you to render him whatever services you can in this holy occupation.

I sent word to M. Brin to release you from that painful, unbearable burden which Providence has imposed on you. It causes you to practice the virtue of patience so constantly that there is good reason to bless God for the strength He has given you to put up with

---

Letter 3234b. - Copy made from *Recueil Nodet.* The letter was published in *Annales C.M.* (1943-44), p. 259, and reprinted in *Mission et Charité,* 19-20, no. 132, pp. 166-67. This edition uses the latter text.

[1]The copy has *Souvin,* but the confrere in question is most probably Guillaume Servin.

[2]A locality near Crécy.

[3]Dominique de Ligny (1659-81).

[4]Gerard Brin, born near Cashel (Ireland), entered the Congregation of the Mission on October 14, 1639, at the age of twenty-one. He took his vows on November 2, 1642, and was ordained a priest in 1644. Of all the Irishmen whom Saint Vincent received into his Congregation, Brin was perhaps the most accomplished. He was sent from Le Mans in 1646 to the mission in Ireland, which was financed by the Duchesse d'Aiguillon; there, with several other confreres and compatriots, he did boundless good (cf. Abelly, *op. cit.,* bk. II, chap. 1, pp. 154-55). Driven back to France by persecution, Brin went as a missionary to Saint Vincent's native region. Some time later he was named Superior in La Rose (1652-54), and subsequently held the same position in Troyes (1657-58), Meaux (1658-60), and Toul (1660-62). He returned to Ireland in 1662 or 1663, resuming his apostolic work with a zeal that age had not slackened. Neither illness, which brought him twice to the brink of the grave, nor a month in prison could stop this heroic Missionary. Brin died in Thurles (Ireland) sometime between October 9, 1683, the date of his will, and February 25, 1684, the date of its admission to probate.

such an annoying, unreasonable man for so long.[5] I hope that is as good as done now. I am planning to send a priest to Crécy to stay there while you are on the visitations. Please let me know when he should set out.

I am, in Our Lord, Monsieur, your most humble servant.

VINCENT DEPAUL,
i.s.C.M.

3235. - *THE PRIOR OF LA PÉROUSE [1] TO SAINT VINCENT*

Live Jesus in Mary!

Monsieur,

I thought I would have the honor of going to see you, but God has not given me time for that. With the usual trust that I have in your charity, I ask you to continue to pray for Commander Alex. As soon as I have the honor of seeing you, I will explain the persecution he has suffered—and is still suffering—because of the attacks on his promotion to the office of Bishop of Geneva.[2] I entreat you to commend him earnestly to Our Lord and to ask the prayers of your holy Community for this intention. You would not believe how far the anger and calumny of those persecuting him have gone. I have been informed, however, that the news from Rome leads us to hope that his appointment will be confirmed at the next consistory.

---

[5]Pierre de Lorthon, secretary of the King and founder of the house in Crécy. Because of his demands and unstable disposition, he was a constant source of difficulties to the Missionaries there.

Letter 3235. - Archives of the Mission, Turin, original autograph letter.

[1]The Prior of La Pérouse, nephew of Jean d'Aranthon d'Alex, came to Paris in 1658 to prepare for the priesthood under the direction of the Priests of Saint-Sulpice. He later became a Doctor of the Sorbonne and Dean of the Sainte-Chapelle in Chambéry.

[2]The appointment of Jean d'Aranthon d'Alex as Bishop of Geneva had provoked an opposition that took a long time to subside. The most infamous accusations were leveled against him, and his enemies took them to the Court of Savoy, the Nuncio, and even Rome. Tired of having to defend himself incessantly against calumny, the Commander handed in his resignation, but the Prince refused to accept it. The storm finally abated, and the Prelate was consecrated on October 9, 1661. (Cf. Le Masson, *op. cit.*, pp. 61-79.)

I have twelve pistoles to be delivered to Canon de Montfort in Annecy. I very humbly request you to let me know by the bearer if you would have the kindness to do me the charity of accepting the money here. It is for the same affair for which you have already done me the favor of often sending me some. I ask you please to give me the answer in writing, for fear lest the secret be revealed; I have heard that there are already strong suspicions concerning it.

The bearer of this note is a young man from a very good family in Chambéry; there is thought of placing him in the Albiac Seminary. He would like to make a retreat before entering and has been asking me for a long time to ask you to allow him to make it at Saint-Lazare. I think he is very well disposed. So, I take the liberty of joining my request to his to ask you this favor, along with all the others. If you add to it that of welcoming him before the ordination, you will be doing a double act of charity because you will be giving him the opportunity to assure his entrance into that seminary that much sooner.

I never write to you or see you without asking "What would you do about such and such?" You have really attracted a bothersome person to you. I assure you that he acts this way with great respect and confidence because those matters pertain to the glory of our good Master.

I very humbly ask you to remember me before Him, Monsieur, and I am your most humble and very obedient servant.

LA PÉROUSE

Saint-Sulpice, August 28, 1660

Addressed: *Monsieur Vincent, Priest and Superior General of the Mission, at Saint-Lazare*

3236. - *LOUISE-EUGÉNIE DE FONTAINE TO SAINT VINCENT*

Live Jesus!

Most Honored Father,

Enclosed is what is written in our Constitutions and custom book concerning the choice of a spiritual Father; we are sending it to you, Most Honored Father. I most humbly ask your pardon for not having done so sooner, but all the coming and going of people who were at our house for the entrance of the Queen, added to what happened to poor Sister Marguerite-Dorothée, prevented us from doing so.

We felt so sorry for that dear Sister, who had such a swollen arm and severe pain after her bloodletting. M. Rufin and our regular surgeon are hoping that it is nothing serious, but, because of her other ailments, I am not so sure.

We entreat you, Most Honored Father, to recommend her to the prayers of your holy community and to give her a share in yours as well. I ask this favor with the same affection and respect with which I am, Most Honored Father, your most humble and very obedient daughter and servant in Our Lord.

LOUISE-EUGÉNIE DE FONTAINE

B[lessed] b[e] G[od]!

August 28 [1660] [1]

3237. - *FATHER FULGENCE DAUDIGNIER TO SAINT VINCENT*

Monsieur,

When one of our venerable Fathers heard that I had the honor of being included among your servants, he asked me to recommend to you the

---

Letter 3236. - Archives of the Mission, Turin, original autograph letter.

[1]The year Louis XIV married Maria Teresa of Spain. Her entrance into Paris is also mentioned in several other letters.

Letter 3237. - Archives of the Mission, Turin, original autograph letter.

bearer of this letter, which I am happy to do now with all my heart. He told me that the latter is a recent convert to the Catholic religion and has been disowned by all his heretical relatives. That is why, in his urgent need of body and soul, he has decided to serve in any capacity in some religious house where he will be able to receive further instruction in all that a good Catholic must know, while waiting to be reconciled with his relatives and strengthened in the truths of our religion. Since he heard that your holy house was the right place for this, I venture to join my request to his, Monsieur, as your most humble and very obedient servant.

F. FULGENCE DAUDIGNIER,
unworthy Carthusian

From our cell at Saint-Ambroise, August 28, 1660

Thank you for our postulant, who made a retreat at your house two months ago, directed by M. Gicquel.[1] *I hope he will soon be a Carthusian in this house.*

Addressed: *Monsieur Vincent, Superior General of the Order of the Missionaries, at Saint-Lazare*

3238. - *THE PRIOR OF LA PÉROUSE TO SAINT VINCENT*

Live Jesus in Mary!

Monsieur,

I was very grateful to receive the note with which you were pleased to honor me, and I will do my best to have the honor of bringing you the twelve pistoles for Annecy tomorrow. Meanwhile, I take the liberty of writing you this note by order of President de Chamosset. He is the Assistant Chief Justice of our Senate, whom you mentioned to me previously, and he told me that he has great respect for you. He is now in Paris and has said that he would like to see you. Meanwhile, he begs you

---

[1]Jean Gicquel.

Letter 3238. - Archives of the Mission, Turin, original autograph letter.

to recommend earnestly to O[ur] L[ord] an important affair that concerns him very closely. He has great confidence in your prayers and has instructed me to ask you for them.

I am, with all due respect, Monsieur, your most humble and very obedient servant.

LA PÉROUSE

Today I received some letters from Savoy, in which there is no good news about the business of Commander Alex. In fact, I think we need the influence of all our friends so that, by a just judgment, God will not deprive us of the graces this entire poor diocese expects from his promotion.

M. du Bazzione entreats and petitions Your Charity anew for the workers for which you have led them to hope; they need them more than you could imagine.

Your most humble and very obedient servant.

LA PÉROUSE

Saint-Sulpice, August 29, 1660

Addressed: *Monsieur Vincent, Priest and Superior General of the Mission, at Saint-Lazare*

3239. - *PRÉSIDENT FREMYN TO SAINT VINCENT*

Soméricourt,[1] *August 30 [1660]*[2]

Monsieur,

The letter you did me the honor of writing me on the fourteenth of this month was not delivered to me until Friday the twenty-seventh. That is why I was unable to thank you sooner and to assure you that I defer to your

---

Letter 3239. - Archives of the Mission, Turin, original autograph letter.

[1]A locality in the district of Chaumont (Haute-Marne).

[2]The mention of Michel Caset and Nicolas Demonchy indicates that this letter was written toward the end of Saint Vincent's life. The words *Friday the twenty-seventh* permit no other choice than 1660.

wish that I entrust the parish of Pompierre[3] *to M. Descroizilles, which is the very least I would like to do for you. For this to be done, however, you know, Monsieur, that it must be vacant, and I can see that M. Le Bret is not ready to give it up. He told me he had taken the honor of replying to the letter he received from you and had so many cogent reasons of honor and conscience for not resigning this benefice that he is certain you will consent to them, when he has the opportunity to explain them to you in person. So, Monsieur, you see that my good will is ineffective, and I think God is allowing this because that position is not equal to the merits of M. Descroizilles.*

I think you have been informed of some minor dissatisfaction Mademoiselle Maillet received from M. Caset, and I must confess that it upset me considerably. M. Caset thought he could justify himself by denying it, but I know that this lady is too wise to imagine that she was offended in her honor when she was not. The only satisfaction my wife and I have in this instance, is that you, Monsieur, and M. Demonchy are aware of this woman's virtue, and in the twenty years that she has been in my wife's service, I can honestly say that we have never found any fault with her behavior. God be praised for everything!

I ask you, Monsieur, to please continue your holy prayers for me and to believe that I am, with the utmost humility, in the love of Our Lord, Monsieur, your most humble and very obedient servant.

PR[ÉSIDENT] FREMYN

3240. - *THE PRIOR OF LA PÉROUSE TO SAINT VINCENT*

Live Jesus in Mary!

Monsieur,

Divine Providence arranged that I should meet the good Brother Treasurer in the street. Certain business made me doubt that I would have the honor of being able to see you today. I took advantage of this meeting to entrust fifty écus to him.

---

[3]A locality in the district of Neufchâteau (Vosges).

Letter 3240. - Archives of the Mission, Turin, original autograph letter.

Please excuse the liberty I have taken and rest assured that I remain, with all possible respect, Monsieur, your most humble and very obedient servant.

LA PÉROUSE

Saint-Sulpice, August 30, 1660

3241. - *SISTER AVOIE VIGNERON* [1] *TO SAINT VINCENT*

Live Jesus, Mary, and Joseph!

Ussel, August 30, 1660

Most Honored Father,

The grace of Our Lord be always with you!

Truly, it was with a great deal of sorrow that I learned from your letter about the return of Sister Anne.[2] *It would be impossible for me to tell you how distressed I am about this because, now that she has become accustomed to things and was not thinking of going back—at least not as much as usual—she has to return, after having suffered so much in so many ways. We tried everything to persuade her to stay until we had asked Your Charity to be willing to leave her with us, at least until we had seen what*

Letter 3241. - Archives of the Mission, Turin, original autograph letter.

[1]Avoie Vigneron entered the Daughters of Charity around 1646-47. She was in Paris in August 1655 and was sent to Ussel in May 1658. There she encountered many difficulties but made her sufferings known to Saint Vincent, as this letter shows, and to Saint Louise (cf. vol. VII, no. 2767). In 1672 she was Sister Servant in Corbeil. Her two sisters, Geneviève and Marie, were also Daughters of Charity.

[2]We get to know Sister Anne Hardemont from the many letters she preserved. In 1640 she was missioned to Saint-Paul parish; in 1647 she was chosen to establish the house in Montreuil-sur-Mer, and in 1650 the one in Hennebont (Morbihan). In 1651 she was stationed in Nantes, and the following year in Châlons-sur-Marne. Because of illness she returned to Nantes, where she remained until 1653, at which time she went to Sainte-Menehould, then to Sedan in 1654, and La Roche-Guyon in 1655. She was present in Paris on August 8, 1655, and signed the Act of Establishment of the Company of the Daughters of Charity (cf. vol. XIII, no. 150). In 1656 she was at the Petites-Maisons in Paris, and in Ussel in 1658. Because of her leadership ability, she was named Sister Servant in all these places, despite what Saint Vincent wrote to Saint Louise (cf. no. 1405) that she was "somewhat to be feared"--undoubtedly the cause of her many changes. (Cf. vol. IV, no. 1342, and *Spiritual Writings,* L. 110, pp. 120, 121.)

the Duchess[3] *would like to do for the poor; for, if she were to establish the hospital, there is no place where Sister Anne might be more useful or do more good, since she is at peace. It is also true, however, that there is no other place where she might be more wretched, if Madame does not do more than she has done until now.*

Please give a little thought to the satisfaction that the Sister who will be coming might hope for—and I as well. It is not that we do not have plenty to do and then some, but I repeat that we have been subject to all the grumbling and calumnies we have had to bear until now on the part of persons from whom we should have expected some help, but who were unwilling to contribute one sou from their purse to feed the poor under our care. While Sister Anne was here, she made them understand clearly what was reasonable and what was not. But now they will be able to act according to their whim. I have neither the ability nor the strength to hold them at bay. Not that I want to abandon everything into their hands—no, God forbid! I will try my best to make them see things clearly; moreover, it will be as Our Lord wills.

If Madame does not put things in order and say how she wants us to proceed for the service of the poor, both in the hospital and with transients, I do not think we can hope for any less trouble in the future than we have had in the past. Blessed be God, who will not burden us with more trials than we can bear! If we must resign ourselves to suffer, well and good, provided we do so patiently and constantly!

Everything would be well with us if only Sister had returned with Madame or had seen her before leaving Paris. She would have made her understand what would be for the best; but it so happens that they will be traveling at the same time. If you and Madame were willing for me to go to see her in Bourbonnais, I would explain to her some of our greatest

---

[3]The Duchesse de Ventadour, née Marie de la Guiche de Saint-Gérand. On February 8, 1645, she married Charles de Levis, Duc de Ventadour, widower of Suzanne de Thémines de Montluc, who had bequeathed forty thousand livres to Saint Vincent for the foundation of a mission in Cauna (Landes). After her husband died (May 19, 1649), she sought consolation in works of charity, becoming one of Saint Louise's principal auxiliaries and best friends. On the eve of Saint Louise's death, the Duchess came to be with her, caring for her with all the devotedness of a Daughter of Charity. She spent part of the night with her and, after a short rest, stayed by her bedside until the end, holding the blessed candle herself. (Cf. Abbé Nicolas Gobillon, *La vie de Mademoiselle Le Gras, fondatrice et première supérieure de la Compagnie des Filles de la Charité* [Paris: A. Pralard, 1676], pp. 178, 181.) In 1683 the Duchess was elected President of the Ladies of Charity. She died at the age of seventy-eight, at her château of Sainte-Marie-du-Mont (Normandy), during the night of July 22-23, 1701. Thanks to her generosity, this locality had an establishment of Daughters of Charity as early as 1655.

needs because writing to her is not very effective. We have done it so often with so little satisfaction that I feel it is useless.

God grant that this time it will be different and that His Goodness may give Sister Anne Sisters and duties that are more satisfying to her than I have been! They will be more condescending toward her, but I do not think they will offer her greater friendship or desire to help her in her trials. I ask Our Lord to guide her safely and surely.

It would be a very special consolation to me to know that she was at ease and at peace, but I do not think that, either in Paris or in Ussel, we can be exempt from crosses—although, in truth, they are more painful in Ussel than in Paris.

I hope Sister will remember to tell you that we need a Sister who is somewhat stronger than I and who understands the sick better, for Sister is well aware that I do not know much about that. Even though this may not seem very necessary, it truly is; then, too, it is better to know too much than not enough. It is not as though we were living only two leagues away from Paris.

Your Charity had given us permission to make a retreat, but I was unable to do so before Sister went away. I would, however, be very consoled to make it for All Saints' and, if you approve, the renewal of the vows as well. I had asked the same permission last year, but either the answer got lost or it was never sent, for I never heard a word about it. I had requested it of Mademoiselle[4] *and did so in the required manner.*

I also entreat you to kindly write a note to the Pastor—our Director in this region, according to the order given us by M. Dehorgny—so he might take greater care of us in order that the Sister who is coming, and I as well, may remain subject to his counsels, and do nothing according to our own whim. M. Dehorgny knows his worth and knows that he is not a person to let us do anything that is not strictly in line with our vocation and the orders of our Superiors.

I recommend myself to your holy prayers and ask you to believe that I am, with all the affection of my heart, Monsieur and Most Honored Father, your most humble and very obedient daughter and servant.

S. AVOIE VIGNERON

Addressed: *Monsieur Vincent*

---

[4]Saint Louise.

3242. - *JACQUES COIGNET TO SAINT VINCENT*

Monsieur,

Please be so good as to accept this gentleman to make a retreat at your house as soon as possible. He is one of my brothers and has not yet made up his mind which profession to follow, now that he has completed his studies. He would like to make a retreat at your house in order to know God's Will and to follow it, under the guidance of a director you will kindly assign to him.

I will be greatly indebted to you for this, and am, Monsieur, your most humble and obedient servant.

COIGNET,
Pastor of Saint-Roch

Saint-Roch, August 30, 1660

3243. - *M. LEPRESTRE TO SAINT VINCENT*

Monsieur,

After having greeted you and paid my respects, let me tell you that I sent my letter to M. Charton, as you instructed me to do. He is ill right now and had the enclosed note written to you, which M. Moussardière gave me this morning to deliver to you. Through M. Grandin he replied to me that consciences should not be troubled, that we are being obedient to His Holiness,[1] *and that if, after we have been heard, he insists on the Brief, it will be received with total submission. I also saw M. Abelly once; he used to come as extraordinary confessor to the Carmelites. He assured me that I should have no objection to hearing the nuns' confessions as before and that he believes that they are all acting in good conscience.*

I will try to visit you so you can kindly reassure me and direct my conduct in all this, for it is from you alone, Monsieur—the person from whom I believe God wants this—that I seek direction.

Letter 3242. - Archives of the Mission, Turin, original autograph letter.

Letter 3243. - Archives of the Mission, Turin, original autograph letter.

[1]Regarding the affair of the Carmelites (cf. no. 2929, n. 1).

If it should please Our Lord to inspire you to write down some means of settling this affair, you would be doing a great service to this entire holy Order. I think there is a certain middle course which would alleviate everything, as has happened in all the emotionally-charged controversies until now—neither too much nor too little to the Superiors; neither too much nor too little to the Visitors.

The Superiors seem so well meaning to me, and have been legitimately authorized since the establishment of the Order in France, and their administration so holy and dedicated that it is sad to see them upset for not having been heard.

Excuse me, Monsieur, for voicing my opinion so freely; offer me totally to God that He may dispose me always to be, Monsieur, your most humble, most obedient, and very grateful servant.

D. LEPRESTRE

August 31, 1660

Addressed: *Monsieur Vincent, Priest and Superior General of the Mission, at Saint-Lazare*

3244. - *JACQUES CHARTON TO SAINT VINCENT*

[August 31, 1660] [1]

The senior Penitentiary[2] *requests that the letter he wrote to M. Vincent a week ago*[3] *be for him alone; he will be very grateful if he sees fit to burn it after having read it.*

Addressed: *Monsieur Vincent, Superior of the Mission, at Saint-Lazare, in Paris*

Letter 3244. - Archives of the Mission, Turin, original autograph letter.

[1]This note is probably the one indicated in no. 3243.

[2]Jacques Charton himself.

[3]Cf. no. 3225.

3245. - *M. AUBERT* [1] *TO SAINT VINCENT*

Tuesday morning, August 31, 1660

Monsieur,

Since Her Highness Madame de Longueville would like her children[2] *to receive your blessing, and since they are most anxious to see you, I hope to bring them to you after dinner and to assure you that I am, Monsieur, with all possible respect, your most humble and very obedient servant.*

AUBERT

Addressed: *Monsieur Vincent, Superior General of the Mission, at Saint-Lazare, faubourg Saint-Denis, in Paris*

3246. - *ANNE-MARGUERITE GUÉRIN TO SAINT VINCENT*

Live Jesus!

Our Third Monastery in Paris, August 31, 1660

My Most Honored Father,

We are sending someone to ask for news of your health and for permission to withdraw about six thousand livres in income—or less, if we can manage it. We need them to finish paying our workmen because we had to incur a rather large expense to house ourselves, although very modestly and in line with religious simplicity and poverty. However, on the orders of our Mother Superior in the faubourg,[1] *who did the contracting, we had to build a brand-new chapel or small church, a choir, and other small rooms, and then renovate some bowling galleries to make all*

Letter 3245. - Archives of the Mission, Turin, original autograph letter.

[1]Chaplain to Anne-Geneviève de Bourbon, Madame de Longueville.

[2]Charles d'Orléans, Comte de Dunois, then aged fourteen; and Charles de Paris, Comte de Saint-Paul, aged eleven.

Letter 3246. - Archives of the Mission, Turin, original autograph letter.

[1]Marie-Agnès Le Roy.

the regular offices and dormitories. Although it is only a jerry-built house, as they say, it still cost us plenty, including other smaller items, doors, and windows, as if they were for a much larger building because the main part of the house faces the street and outside courtyard, which obliges us to rent it to persons outside, who pay us six hundred livres. That is why we had to go to such expense.

If someone redeems our Rouen income for us, as Messieurs Delahaie, Aubert, and the heirs lead us to hope, since they are ready to sell a piece of land, then we will be able to pay our bills. Although that revenue began to accrue only since our purchase, they still paid us half a year's income, which they forwarded to us here in Paris. There is an additional one, from which we are expecting the same thing as the other two. We are telling Your Goodness this to inform you of the whole situation.

I trust in God that, since this work is entirely His, He will guide its progress, as His Divine Providence guided its beginning. Our dear Sisters who have come here are so zealous in our holy observances that I hope in the Divine Mercy that, if we strive to seek the kingdom of God and His justice, we will lack nothing that we need.

We also most humbly entreat Your Goodness to grant us permission to dismiss a lay Sister who has no vocation and who, furthermore, lacks the qualifications to fulfill her duties. [At the same time, allow us] [2] *to accept another in her place, who we feel will have what the former lacks—at least as far as we can judge.*

We are really sorry to annoy you with such a long letter, Most Honored Father, for fear lest it overburden you in your continuous sufferings. We pray that God will increase your strength and patience. These are the prayers this little community offers to God.

Prostrate at your feet, all of us ask for your holy blessing, especially for the last and the least of all, who is, with incomparable affection and filled with genuine respect, Most Honored Father, your most humble, most obedient, and very unworthy daughter and servant in O[ur] L[ord].

SISTER ANNE-MARGUERITE GUÉRIN,
of the Visitation Sainte-Marie

Blessed be God!

Addressed: *Monsieur Vincent, Superior General of the Priests of the Mission of Saint-Lazare*

---

[2]Text of the original: *and which, at the same time, will allow us.*

3247. - *THE BARONESS DE RENTY* [1] *TO SAINT VINCENT*

September 1 [1660] [2]

Monsieur,

The meeting I am having with that priest who is uncertain about what he should do in the work God is placing before him for the salvation of souls has given me the idea of presenting him to you, knowing the enlightenment God gives you to guide those who seek your counsel and the great charity you have for this. I told him he can be sure of the advice you will give him.

I entreat you most humbly to do this because I think his intentions are good. He is a gentleman who comes from a good place. This is what has made me fearful for him when he returns to his own locality. I will be at peace when he follows your advice and will have high hopes if you continue to remember me in your prayer before God.

I stand more in need of it than ever and am, Monsieur, your most humble and very obedient servant.

L. DE BALZAC DE RENTY

It will be necessary for you please to decide immediately what the bearer should do, and one of these days to see how to settle the affairs of the late M. de Chaudebonne.

Addressed: *Monsieur Vincent, at Saint-Lazare*

Letter 3247. - Archives of the Mission, Turin, original autograph letter.

[1]Élisabeth de Balzac, an active Lady of Charity. The daughter of M. de Dunes, Comte de Graville, she married, on February 21, 1634, Baron Gaston de Renty, who died on April 24, 1648.

[2]Year added on the back of the original by Brother Ducournau.

3248. - *MADAME POTIER DE LAMOIGNON TO SAINT VINCENT*

Monsieur,

I had found it hard to believe that you raised no objections to giving us Daughters of Charity for Auteuil, seeing that the Pastor [1] *does not agree entirely with your opinions, but the Pastor of Saint-Nicolas-du-Chardonnet* [2] *had assured me of it and also of the fact that you had no problem with it. This had obliged me to see that the Pastor of Autueil talk to you so you might get to know him because I found it difficult to believe that you were not raising any objections. This would still be a great charity, especially with regard to the instruction of the children because it is very dangerous for them to be taught only by the Pastor.*

I had thought that, for confession, those Sisters could go to Chaillot, which is nearby and has some good Minim Fathers[3] *there. Were I not in such a hurry to leave for Bourbon to take the waters, I would have had the honor of going to see you and to explain matters in greater detail. But, I have to leave today. Meanwhile, I hope God will inspire you with what is best for His glory in this matter and for the welfare of those poor people who are, moreover, very good.*

I recommend my journey to your holy prayers and to those of your community, please, asking you to do me the honor of believing me to be, Monsieur, your most humble and obedient servant.

M. POTIER

September 1 [1660] [4]

3249. - *MONSIEUR PETIT, PASTOR OF SAINT-FARGEAU, TO SAINT VINCENT*

M. Vincent is most humbly requested to give his final decision on whether he wishes to accept the legacy of thirty livres income a year, left

---

Letter 3248. - Archives of the Mission, Turin, original autograph letter.

[1]Saint Vincent believed that the Pastor espoused Jansenism.

[2]Hippolyte Féret.

[3]Franciscan Community founded by Saint Francis of Paola.

[4]Because the same matter treated in no. 3187 (August 9, 1660) and no. 3217 (August 22, 1660), whose dates are certain, is mentioned in this letter, the year 1660 has been assigned.

Letter 3249. - Archives of the Mission, Turin, original autograph letter.

by my late uncle, for the benefit of the Priests of the Mission established in Crécy. I am ready to deliver it, should it be accepted. And even should the establishment of Crécy be transferred to Meaux or elsewhere, I would willingly consent, in my capacity as executor of the will and as sole legatee, that the legacy be transferred to whatever place it will be desired.

He is likewise most humbly entreated to allow Sister Jeanne Lepeintre[1] *to travel to Paris on business for the Saint-Fargeau Hospital, and he would greatly oblige the one who is his most humble and very obedient servant.*

PETIT

Saint-Lazare, September 1, 1660

Rue des Maçons, at the Nom-de-Jésus, near the Sorbonne, Saint-Séverin parish

3250. - *ANNE-GABRIELLE DOREAU TO SAINT VINCENT*

Live Jesus!

My Very Dear Father,

The affection you have for our Order and the all-embracing charity you show for all persons in distress cause me to believe that you will kindly

---

[1]Jeanne Lepeintre had been sent to the Daughters of Charity by her mistress, Madame Goussault. Saint Vincent says elsewhere that she was "a very fine, wise, and gentle girl." Both he and Saint Louise had great confidence in her because of her intelligence and organizational skills. She was first sent to the school of the Charity in Saint-Germain-en-Laye (1642). In the spring of 1646, after installing the Sisters in the Le Mans hospital, she returned to Paris, where she was put in charge of the Motherhouse while Saint Louise was establishing the house in Nantes. Jeanne then became Sister Servant in Nantes (1646), where great difficulties were being encountered. In 1654 she made the foundation in Châteaudun and, in 1657, at the Salpêtrière (cf. *Spiritual Writings*, L. 64, p. 77, n. 1). In *Recueil de pièces relatives aux Filles de la Charité*, Ms, p. 24, preserved in the Archives of the Motherhouse of the Daughters of Charity, we read: "During the lifetime of Mademoiselle Le Gras, she seemed to be a hypochondriac. Moreover, she could not be made to do anything she did not like, nor would she accept opinions other than her own." She was reprimanded for this fault more than once by Saint Vincent. Her last years were sad ones spent at the Nom-de-Jésus hospice, where she had to be committed because of mental illness.

Letter 3250. - Archives of the Mission, Turin, original autograph letter.

allow me to very humbly implore you to use your influence for the deliverance of a poor young man of this town named Guillaume Bauvoy. He is a painter, the brother of one of our dear Sisters, and was captured by barbarians from Algiers two leagues from Cabo da Roca at the mouth of the Tagus, on Holy Innocents' Day[1] *last year. He was on his way to Lisbon with Comte de Seguin, Sieur Laudoy, on a thirty-gun ship called the* Saint-Étienne. *After their capture, they were taken to Algiers, where Guillaume Bauvoy has borne his misfortune as best he could. He is staying in Barbary with the French Consul*[2] *in Algiers, where he spends his time painting in a new house the Consul is having built.*

Your Reverence and my very dear Father, from what I have written you can consider what means will have to be taken to liberate this young man. When you write to him and are trying to procure his release, treat him like a poor slave, for fear lest they demand a very high ransom. He must be freed for as little money as possible because, although God caused him to be born into a very good, fairly well-off family, he lost his father several years ago, and his mother became involved in a number of complicated business affairs, costing her a great deal of money, so she is in no position to be able to furnish a large sum.

I depend on your prudence and charity, my very dear Father, to handle this release so carefully that his widowed mother will not be overburdened by it. That is the very humble request I make of you, together with his dear sister and several relatives of his, who are nuns in this house. All of them will be greatly indebted to you. This monastery is especially grateful to the prisoner's family because it is very good to us and helps us most kindly on occasion. This obliges us to very special gratitude.

Dear Father, I very humbly ask for the assistance of your holy prayers for this community, which offers you its respectful and filial obedience and, together with me, wishes you perseverance in the sacred love in which I call myself, with your permission, my very dear Father, your most humble and obedient daughter and unworthy servant in Our Lord.

SISTER ANNE-GABRIELLE DOREAU,
of the Visitation Sainte-Marie

From our Monastery in Nevers, September 1, 1660
Blessed be God!

---

[1]December 28.
[2]Jean Barreau.

My very dear Father, the bearer of this letter, M. de Saulieu, will provide what is necessary to ransom the above-mentioned captive. I think that, if two hundred livres—or three hundred, at the most—are offered, that will suffice for a man of such modest condition.

Addressed: *Monsieur Vincent de Paul, Superior of Saint-Lazare Seminary, in Paris*

3251. - *LOUISE-EUGÉNIE DE FONTAINE TO SAINT VINCENT*

Live Jesus!

My Only Father,

Our dear Sister Councillors, and we along with them, have learned of Mademoiselle Marin's desire to become a nun and to enter here in this house. We consider it favorable to the glory of God to support her pious desire, if you kindly agree to grant us permission to allow her to enter here. We also ask if we may take in Father Castillon[1] *and, if possible, another person who will stay with him. This is the favor requested by her who is, with deepest gratitude, my only Father, your most humble and very obedient daughter and servant in Our Lord.*

LOUISE-EUGÉNIE DE FONTAINE,
of the Visitation Sainte-Marie

B[lessed] b[e] G[od]!

September 2 [1660] [2]

Letter 3251. - Archives of the Mission, Turin, original autograph letter.

[1]André Castillon, born in Caen on March 12, 1599, entered the Society of Jesus on March 20, 1614, and died on March 25, 1671. He had been Rector of the houses in Rennes, Arras, and Paris, and Provincial of France.

[2]The reference to Sister Marguerite-Dorothée in nos. 3236 and 3272, whose dates are certain, allows us to assign this date for the present letter because of the mention of her health made in the postscript.

Our very dear Sister Marguerite-Dorothée is much better, thank God, and completely out of danger.

Addressed: *Monsieur Vincent de Paul, General of the Missions of France*

3252. - *SISTER MADELEINE MAUPEOU TO SAINT VINCENT*

September 2, 1660

Most Honored Father,

We have recourse to your prayers and to those of your holy Community for the election of a Superior for this house,[1] *which is to take place on Saturday. You are aware, Most Honored Father, how important this is to maintain the peace God has established here and which He maintains by His holy grace. That is what urges us to recommend it most earnestly to your charitable prayers.*

Once it has taken place, we will still need to stay here a short time for the consolation of the dear Mother because every one of the Sisters eligible here is very apprehensive of it. This leads me to hope that God will bless the election.

Sister Fouquet[2] *has highly recommended to us a good priest whom she considers suitable for hearing the confessions of those good nuns. I am asking her, in the event that he has not left yet, to send him to Your Reverence for your holy instructions, which I ask you to give him as you did for M. de Monboisin, whom you in your goodness sent us in Caen.*

In all humility, I ask your holy blessing for our two dear companions,

---

Letter 3252. - Archives of the Mission, Turin, original autograph letter.

[1]The Ursuline Monastery in Melun.

[2]Élisabeth-Angélique Fouquet, one of several of Madame Fouquet's daughters who became Visitation nuns.

who declare themselves to be your most obedient servants, and for myself as well. I am, very respectfully, Most Reverend Father, your most humble and very obedient daughter and servant in Our Lord.

MADELEINE MAUPEOU,
of the Visitation Sainte-Marie

B[lessed] b[e] G[od]!

Addressed: *Monsieur Vincent de Paul, Superior General of the Mission of France*

3253. - *SISTER MARTHE DE JÉSUS* [1] *TO SAINT VINCENT*

Most Honored Father,

Very humble greetings in Jesus Christ!

The interest your very ardent charity causes you to take in the affairs of our Order obliges us to let you know that Our Lord seems to want to help us; for, one of the convents which had protested against the Brief is reconsidering. M. Giraud had the honor of telling you something about this, but we have had definite proof of it since yesterday. I am talking about the convent in Reims.

The Prioress (who is not a professed nun of our convent but of the one in Angers) has written to our Mother Marie-Madeleine de Jésus [2] *that her conscience is very troubled and upset because of her disobedience to the Holy Father's Brief, that she is absolutely determined to do something to negate the opposition she made to it, and that she has a great deal to say on this subject. The foundress of the said convent, named Madame de*

Letter 3253. - Archives of the Mission, Turin, original autograph letter.

[1]Marthe du Vigean, daughter of the Marquis du Vigean, was Subprioress of the Carmelite Monastery on rue Saint-Jacques. She died on April 25, 1665, at forty-four years of age and sixteen of profession. At a time when everything seemed to engage her in the world, Saint Vincent had predicted her entrance into religious life. (Cf. Collet, *op. cit.*, vol. II, p. 516; also, Cousin, *op. cit.*, p. 466.)

[2]Lancry de Bains, Prioress of the Carmelite Monastery on rue Saint-Jacques; she died in Paris in 1679, in the sixtieth year of her profession.

Bouvant, has written the same thing, and both of them have spoken to the Bishop of Le Puy,[3] *who is entirely on our side.*

That good Prelate asked for an appointment with Mother Marie-Madeleine de Jésus to come here to discuss this. We have informed Messieurs de Blampignon and de Prières and the Pastor of Saint-Nicolas-du-Chardonnet.[4] *They sent us word that they were blessed with the opportunity of going to see you tomorrow. We will be quite satisfied with whatever you order in this affair, as we were with your decision on good Madame de Breauté.*[5]

Everything that comes to us from you, Most Honored Father, is received by our Mothers and by us, unworthy though we be, with such great respect, deference, and submission that it seems that God has spoken to us through your mouth. Therefore, Most Honored Father, have no fear to tell us whatever you judge reasonable for us to do, and we will be extremely happy to put it into effect without any hint of trouble, since I am, more than words could express, Most Honored Father, your most humble and very obedient daughter and servant.

SISTER MARTHE DE JÉSUS,
unworthy C[armelite] Nun

Sunday morning, September 2, 1660

The Pastor of La Madeleine[6] *is much better, thank God. He no longer has a fever, and he recommends himself strongly to your good prayers. He says that he envied M. Giraud for having had the blessing of seeing you—which he himself did not have.*

---

[3]Henri Cauchon de Maupas du Tour, a member of the Tuesday Conferences. He was Bishop of Le Puy (1641-61), and of Évreux from 1661 to August 12, 1680, the day of his death. A renowned orator, he preached the funeral panegyrics for Saint Jane Frances de Chantal and Saint Vincent. He also wrote biographies of Saints Francis de Sales and Jane Frances, and was one of the two Bishops who approved Abelly's life of Saint Vincent.

[4]Hippolyte Féret.

[5]Probably Marie de Fiesque, lady-in-waiting of Queen Anne of Austria; she was the widow of Pierre, Marquis de Bréauté.

[6]Nicolas Autin, Pastor of the Church of the Madeleine in Paris.

3254. - TO GUILLAUME DESDAMES, SUPERIOR, IN WARSAW

Paris, September 3, 1660

Monsieur,

The grace of O[ur] L[ord] be with you forever!

I received your dear letter of July 25. It is true that our priests and the Daughters of Charity will soon be ready to leave; they await only the departure of a ship that might be going to Danzig.[1]

Since you think it will be advantageous to sell the garden and the building behind your house for 5,500 livres, which it cost the Queen, I gladly approve of your selling it and [investing] [2] that sum in some other more useful fund or using it to build. This is so that you may be more comfortably and solidly housed than you are now—provided, however, that Her Majesty gives her consent and that M. Duperroy and your close friends advise it. Please be careful, however, not to attract by this sale any bad neighbor who, in the course of time, might cause you trouble; it may be that you would want to have that place then and will not be able to get it.

I give you the same permission, and on the same conditions, for the house in the suburbs, for which you are being offered 2,500 livres.

May God, by His grace, bless the King's armies and Their Majesties' journey so that, willingly or by constraint, the Cossacks may be reduced to obedience to them. We have no news here. I recommend myself and the entire Little Company to your prayers

---

Letter 3254. - Archives of the Mission, Krakow, original signed letter.

[1]Today the port city of Gdańsk (Poland).

[2]The original has "replacing."

that O[ur] L[ord] may accomplish in it and through it His most holy Will, which has made me, in His love, Monsieur, your most humble servant.

VINCENT DEPAUL,
i.s.C.M.

Addressed: Monsieur Desdames, Superior of the Priests of the Mission at Holy Cross, in Warsaw

3255. - *LÉONARD DANIEL* [1] *TO SAINT VINCENT*

Monsieur,

I could not lose an opportunity to write to you and, if I have received no replies to my preceding letters, I attribute this to my unworthiness and do not feel rebuffed by it. In this letter I am asking you for a clarification on a matter that upsets me considerably. I am sure you will be good enough not to refuse to give it to me.

Since, by the grace of God, I am determined to work out my salvation and am striving in my weakness to put into practice the saintly lessons you gave me, I am apprehensive about something that is troubling me deeply, namely, whether the vows I took when I had the honor of being one of your members still bind me outside of your house, since I was never dispensed from them either by you or by anyone else. If I am bound by them, I am ready to observe them for the rest of my life and, with all possible submission, I ask for the occasion to do so, with the assurance I give you that I will try to repair my past disobedience by my future service.

Please believe, Monsieur, that my words are very sincere and that in my present state I seek only God and the means of pleasing Him. I know of nothing obliging me to speak to you by way of complaint and, although my soul is very lowly, it is still above such cowardly self-interest, which I will not seek even in that cowardly way. Nothing is obliging me to leave

---

Letter 3255. - Archives of the Mission, Turin, original autograph letter.

[1]Born in Saint-Léonard (Haute-Vienne), Léonard Daniel entered the Congregation of the Mission on November 27, 1644, at the age of twenty-three, and took his vows on November 27, 1646; he left shortly thereafter.

the world, except the glory of God and my salvation; and, no matter how blameworthy I may be, neither a public sin nor poverty obliges me to leave it.

Even if they do not oblige me, I for my part assure you that the vow of obedience I made before you will endure as long as I do. I will add something further: I would really wish that it did oblige me so I might find some pressing occasion of obeying you. I have many reasons compelling me to do so; for, in addition to justice and right, the unfortunate end to which those who have left the Mission before or after me have come gives me reason to fear their punishment, since I am as guilty as they are—or more guilty. Lastly, whether awake or asleep, I belong more to the Mission than to myself.

Please enlighten me on this subject, Monsieur, and give some direction for the remainder of my life. I am ready to leave for Bordeaux, where I am to see M. de Fonteneil,[2] *a very virtuous man, filled with zeal for the priestly state. He has established a seminary in that city to prepare priests to help him to give missions in Gascony until Advent, since he has finished the ones in Limousin, and I am going to work in them.*

If you deign to do me the favor of writing to me, as I hope from your goodness, my nephew, the bearer of this letter, will deliver your answer to

---

[2]Jean de Fonteneil, born in Bordeaux around 1605, was a friend and admirer of Saint Vincent. His outstanding qualities earned him the highest positions in the diocese. Appointed Canon of Saint-Seurin in July 1623, he became special archiepiscopal Vicar-General on November 1, 1639, Vicar in perpetuity of the parish church of Sainte-Colombe, then of Saint-Siméon in Bordeaux, Grand Archdeacon, Chancellor of the University of Bordeaux in 1650, and Vicar-General of the diocese on September 10, 1655. Like his friend Saint Vincent, he was convinced of the great good that could result from seminaries, missions, retreats, and weekly meetings of priests to discuss questions of theology, discipline, or piety. For that purpose, he founded the Congregation of the Missionaries of the Clergy, who directed the seminary for ordinands in Bordeaux and the seminaries in Aire and Sarlat. They were given the chapels of Notre-Dame-de-Montuzet and the parishes of Saint-Louis-du-Marais and Saint-Simon-Cardonnat (Gironde). This Congregation was short-lived, surviving its founder by only three years. He died in Bordeaux on March 2, 1679. In 1682 the *Prêtres du Clergé* (the title under which they were then known) transferred their works to the Priests of the Mission of Saint-Lazare. (Cf. Louis Bertrand, *Histoire des Séminaires de Bordeaux et de Bazas* [3 vols., Bordeaux: Féret, 1894], vol. I, pp. 207ff.)

me without fail. Meanwhile, please believe that I will remain, all my life, Monsieur, your most humble, most submissive, and very obedient servant.

DANIEL,
Prior of La Chapelle

Limoges, September 3, 1660

Addressed: *Monsieur Vincent, Superior General of the Missionaries, living at Saint-Lazare, in Paris*

3256. - *MARIE-AGNÈS LE ROY TO SAINT VINCENT*

Live Jesus!

From our Monastery in the faubourg Saint-Jacques, September 3, 1660

My very dear Most Honored Father,

I received the letter which you in your kindness wrote to Mademoiselle d'Auvergne[1] *concerning her desire that her younger sister* [2] *remain outside until her sister's* [3] *habit-taking at the Carmelites. I have nothing to say about that, Most Honored Father, except that we will do whatever you wish.*

An aspirant has presented herself who seems to have a very solid vocation. She is giving fifteen thousand livres, on condition that we promise to give her parents, who are quite elderly, three hundred livres a year. We found this devotedness so praiseworthy that we did not want to raise any objections and, if you are pleased to agree to that, Most Honored Father, we will accept her. Abbé Gedoyn[4] *is the one who introduced her to us.*

Letter 3256. - Archives of the Mission, Turin, original autograph letter.

[1]Louise de la Tour d'Auvergne; she died on May 16, 1683.

[2]Mauricette-Fébronie de la Tour d'Auvergne.

[3]Émilie-Léonore de la Tour d'Auvergne.

[4]Nicolas Gedoyn, Abbé de Saint-Mesmin, became Chaplain of the Duc d'Orléans and Superior of the Ursulines in Saint-Cloud. The missions he gave in Paris and in the provinces were very effective. Toward the end of his life he retired to the General Hospital of Paris, where he died on June 10, 1692, at sixty-four years of age.

One of our young ones has fallen ill since she returned; she is one of the little Lamoignon girls.[5] *If by chance the illness should develop into either smallpox or a high fever, I ask your permission to hire one or two nurses because our Sisters have their hands full with taking care of our sick Sisters, of which we still have a very large number, thank God. His goodness does not leave us without that.*

I am, very respectfully, Most Honored Father, your most humble and very obedient daughter and servant in Our Lord.

SISTER MARIE-AGNÈS LE ROY

Blessed be God!

Addressed: *Monsieur Vincent, Superior General of the Congregation of the Mission*

3257. - *JACQUES COIGNET TO SAINT VINCENT*

Monsieur,

Please have the kindness to receive M. Gonesté into your house to make his retreat during this month of September. He is a priest who is residing in my parish for a short time after the ordinations because in October he is going to study philosophy.

I will be very grateful for this, and am, in Our Lord, Monsieur, your most humble and affectionate servant.

COIGNET,
Pastor of Saint-Roch[1]

Saint-Roch, September 3, 1660

---

[5]Cf. no. 3223, n. 3.

Letter 3257. - Archives of the Mission, Turin, original autograph letter.

[1]A parish in Paris.

3257a. - TO FIRMIN GET, SUPERIOR, IN MARSEILLES

Paris, September 3, 1660

Monsieur,

The grace of Our Lord be with you forever!

We still have not been able to obtain from M. de Grimancourt the order for which he led us to hope, for the receipt for your revenue from the estate of the Marquis de Vins. He is dragging things out to gain time, but I will put pressure on him, with God's help.

We received twelve livres for Denis Beauvais, three livres for a man named Urbain Hanis, and three livres for Jean Lavergne, all convicts in Toulon. I am writing to M. Huguier to give each his part, plus three livres to Desloriers.

We still have no reply from the tax farmers of the *gabelles* [1] regarding the chaplains' salaries.

Abbé de Chandenier [2] does not intend to be responsible in any way for M. Bernusset the captive, unless he can be ransomed and sent back to France for five hundred écus. In that case, he will vouch for payment of what is over and above the four hundred écus he has already sent, namely, the one hundred écus, on the one hand, and the expenses incurred or to be incurred for the exit tax and other fees included in the five hundred écus. They should be given in cash to Bernusset, presupposing that no further reductions can be obtained from his master and, as I said, that the latter is at least willing to release him for that amount.

I received the letters from Tunis. We will reflect on what we will have to do to preserve that consulate.

Letter 3257a. - Copy made from *Recueil Nodet.* The letter was published in *Annales C.M.* (1943-44), p. 260, and reprinted in *Mission et Charité,* 19-20, no. 133, pp. 167-68. This edition uses the latter text.

[1]Collectors of the salt tax. They were supposed to pay the salaries of the chaplains at the hospital for convicts.

[2]Claude de Chandenier.

Please take one thousand livres from the funds collected to assist M. Le Vacher[3] in Tunis; out of those one thousand livres send him the clothing and other provisions he is requesting and, at the same time, have him given whatever money is left. We will see later whether those collections are to extricate M. Le Vacher in Tunis and the Consul in Algiers[4] as well, which is the wish of the Duchesse d'Aiguillon.[5] In which case, we will have gained that much; in the opposite case, those one thousand francs from the first sum of money we will send to Tunis will have to be replaced. Please keep this in mind.

It is absolutely necessary to relieve our confreres in Algiers, but you really have to keep a very close watch so as not to risk anything in the present trouble. Get information beforehand about the success of the army, and take the trouble to inform us of it; then we shall see.

I have not yet been able to read the report concerning the Franciscan Fathers; tell the Superior of the Observantines[6] that I am asking him for another week to think over what he is proposing and to seek advice on it.

I am, in our Lord, Monsieur, your most humble servant.

VINCENT DEPAUL,
i.s.C.M.

3258. - TO N.

As far as possible, I have concealed my state of health from you, and I did not want you to know about my ailments, for fear of

---

[3]Jean Le Vacher.

[4]Jean Barreau.

[5]The well-known benefactress of the missions in Algiers and in Tunis.

[6]The Franciscan Conventuals were split by the Franciscan Spirituals (Zelanti) in the fourteenth century; in the fifteenth century the Friars Minor of the Observance (Observantines) separated themselves from the Conventuals.

Letter 3258. - Abelly, *op. cit.*, bk. III, chap. XXIII, p. 327.

saddening you; but, *O bon Dieu!* how long will we be so tender-hearted as not to dare to declare the happiness we have of being visited by God? May Our Lord be pleased to make us stronger and to find our good pleasure in His!

3259. - *CARDINAL LUDOVISIO*[1] *TO SAINT VINCENT*

Very Reverend Father,

My awareness of your age, your fatigue, and the merits of Your Reverence is sufficient motive for me to write to you and to urge you to allow yourself to be directed by your good religious. They know what should be done and what you need in your present state. I think that placing yourself in their hands is therefore an action that corresponds well with your religious sentiments, so I trust that you will do it willingly, as I desire. In conclusion, I recommend myself affectionately to your Holy Sacrifices.

I repeat to Your Reverence my very special affection for you and for the holy Institute in which Our Lord has willed you to have such a large part. I am forever your most affectionate servant.

CARDINAL LUDOVISIO

Rome, September 4, 1660

Please remember me always in your holy prayers and Sacrifices.

Letter 3259. - Departmental Archives of Vaucluse, D 274, register, copy, written in Italian.

[1]Nicolò Albergati-Ludovisio, who became Cardinal-Archbishop of Bologna in 1645. From 1649 to 1687, the year of his death, he served as Grand Penitentiary in Rome.

3260. - TO A PRIEST OF THE MISSION

September 5, 1660

Do not be surprised at the temptations you are undergoing. This is a trial God sends you to humble you and make you fearful, but trust in Him. His grace is sufficient for you,[1] provided you flee the occasions, declare your fidelity to Him, and acknowledge your poverty and your need of help. Accustom yourself to placing your heart in the sacred wounds of Jesus Christ whenever you are assailed by those impure thoughts; it is a refuge inaccessible to the enemy.

3261. - *MADELEINE MAUPEOU TO SAINT VINCENT*

Live Jesus!

September 5, 1660

Most Honored Father,

I think Your Goodness will be glad to hear of the canonical and unanimous election that took place here yesterday. It was so peaceful and satisfactory for M. Benjamin, who presided over it, and for the whole community[1] *that nothing more could be added. When I write, Most Honored Father, that out of thirty votes she received twenty-four, this most surely speaks for itself. She is a good Sister, the most senior of those who stood by the Archbishop of Sens.*[2] *After her, the other officers were elected in the same peaceful manner. The five Councillors elected by the community are also among those who supported the Bishop.*

Letter 3260. - Collet, *op. cit.*, vol. II, p. 269.

[1]Cf. 2 Cor 12:9. (NAB)

Letter 3261. - Archives of the Mission, Turin, original autograph letter.

[1]Of the Ursulines in Melun.

[2]Louis-Henri de Pardaillan de Gondrin. Several Bishops, among them the Archbishop of Sens, were involved in a dispute with the Carmelite nuns (cf. no. 3170).

You can see clearly from this, Most Honored Father, that there is no longer any question of past resentment; the number of Sisters in the latter group is much smaller than the other and, if any resentment remained, they would not have made this choice.

It is an ineffable consolation for me to see the mercies of God, which are indeed admirable with regard to this house. I implore you, Most Honored Father, to thank Him for the gratitude they deserve and to ask Him to continue to grant them.

What is now to be desired is a good confessor. The one they had[3] *so intimidated the one Sister Fouquet*[4] *had sent us that he left almost as soon as he arrived. Nevertheless, very little remains to be done right now, and the situation is good. He is being given room and board, the sacristan serves him, and he has a pension of two hundred livres.*

Do us the favor, Most Honored Father, of seeing if you can make inquiries about someone and to let us know whether we should refuse the Attorney General,[5] *who wants us to go to Vaux, just one league from here. Sister Fouquet, who is supposed to come for us, would receive us there. It is on the way to Paris. He has been very good to us since we have been here and has provided us with money to give to those good nuns, who need his protection. My only wish, Most Honored Father, is to follow the orders you will give us.*

I am writing to the Dean to obtain his obedience,[6] *since he put into the one he gave us to come that we should remain here as long as he sees fit. That is the only thing I am going to mention to him, and I do not know how we can leave here. The greatest difficulty arises when we speak about leaving; everyone becomes unbelievably upset. Nevertheless, this has to happen because everything is peaceful and our dear Mother wishes it; otherwise, we would have had them make their retreat, which they begin*

---

[3]M. Bourdet.

[4]Élisabeth-Angélique Fouquet.

[5]Nicolas Fouquet.

[6]A document that nuns needed when traveling from one convent to another.

with their renewal of vows, which they make on the feast of the Presentation.[7]

I am, Most Reverend Father, your most unworthy daughter and servant in Our Lord.

SISTER MADELEINE MAUPEOU,
of the Visitation Sainte-Marie

B[lessed] b[e] G[od]!

Addressed: *Monsieur Vincent de Paul*

3262. - *MONSIEUR FOURNIER*[1] *TO SAINT VINCENT*

Monsieur,

My gratitude to you in particular and my eagerness to be at your service and that of your entire renowned Society has given me the courage to inform you of the recent death of the Bishop of Noyon,[2] *in Picardy, and Abbot of Clermont,*[3] *about two leagues from this town.*[4] *We heard it in this town from the Bernardine nuns of that abbey and from other persons returning from Paris. The late Bishop, Count and Peer of France, had obtained this benefice from King Louis XIII, when his brother M. de Baradat*[5] *was in favor with His Majesty our late monarch. I thought that if you judged it advisable to open in this town a seminary staffed by your men, by the favor of the Queen Mother,*[6] *who loves you, this abbey, worth about ten thousand livres income or more, could be very useful to you for the maintenance of the seminary. That virtuous Queen could confer it on you, if it has not already been presented.*

---

[7]February 2.

Letter 3262. - Archives of the Mission, Turin, original autograph letter.

[1]M. Fournier-Dupont, a lawyer in Laval and father of François Fournier, a Priest of the Mission in the Cahors house.

[2]Henri de Baradat, who had died on August 25, 1660.

[3]Today Clermont is a part of the commune of Olivet; remains of the old Cistercian Abbey can still be seen.

[4]Laval.

[5]François de Baradat, Seigneur de Damery, died in 1683.

[6]Anne of Austria.

Henry the Great [7] *began the foundation of the Collège de La Flèche by the donation of the abbey of that branch of the same Order. Since then, they have always possessed it in common and in peace, and merely set aside and separated the section for the coadjutor Brothers. The smallest seminary*[8] *would be sufficient for your men to come and go to your other houses in Brittany, besides the fact that your priests would do a lot of good in this town, in the country, and in the parishes surrounding the abbey. Moreover, the Bishop of Le Mans*[9] *twice sent some of your men from Le Mans to give a mission in that place. My son the lawyer and I visited there and used to deliver their letters. In addition, the goodness of the Bishop entrusted them with visiting La Gravelle,*[10] *about one and a half leagues from the abbey, to administer the sacraments to the prisoners—ten . . .* [11] *whom the officers were detaining there—because it had been so long since they had heard Mass, received Holy Communion, and made their confession.*

Consequently, may it please you to decide on this information to do what your usual prudence will dictate to you for the good of your illustrious Community; I have always eagerly desired to see it increased and to have the opportunity to serve you. Please, therefore, accept my good will and consider me always, Monsieur, your most humble and very obedient servant.

FOURNIER THE ELDER

Laval, September 5, 1660

Monsieur, please always look favorably on my son the Missionary.

---

[7]Henry IV, who was assassinated in 1610. La Flèche was a Jesuit collège.

[8]Coste found this word illegible and omitted it.

[9]Philippe-Emmanuel de Beaumanoir de Lavardin.

[10]A place near Laval.

[11]This word is illegible in the text.

3263. - *MONSIEUR FOURNIER TO SAINT VINCENT*

[September 5, 1660] [1]

Monsieur,

Please excuse the freedom of my zeal for your service and the fact that I may be too liberal with the advice I have included in this letter—advice which is perhaps too late or useless. However, since I did not hear that news sooner, I would not know how else to remedy the situation, which is harmful to no one. I express to you my good will; please take it for the result if the remedy is not successful, and consider me always your most humble and obedient servant.

FOURNIER THE ELDER

3264. - *MONSIEUR MARIN TO SAINT VINCENT*

Paris, September 6, 1660

Monsieur,

I have a fifteen-year-old daughter, who is leaving Montmartre, but she tells me she wants to become a nun at Sainte-Marie with her sister Duplessis.[1] *Since, however, this cannot be done without your permission, please grant it to me and believe that I am unreservedly, Monsieur, your most humble and very obedient servant.*

MARIN

Addressed: *Monsieur Vincent, General and Superior of the Mission*

Letter 3263. - Archives of the Mission, Turin, original autograph letter.

[1]This letter was enclosed with the preceding one.

Letter 3264. - Archives of the Mission, Turin, original autograph letter.

[1]At the First Monastery of the Visitation.

3265. - *SISTER FRANÇOISE CARCIREUX TO SAINT VINCENT*

My Very Dear Honored Father,

Your blessing!

I feel obliged to write you this letter, Monsieur, seeing how abundant is the harvest in this region and, that among such a large number of laborers, so few are working as they should in the Lord's vineyard. In addition, the Bishop of Narbonne[1] *is looking everywhere for good workers.*

My brother the Pastor[2] *wanted to be a member of the Mission and left only to satisfy the divine law, as I have always been told. He has, in fact, been very faithful to that, thank God, by the modest annuity he has given my father, at great inconvenience to himself, because of an illness he had. I can assure you, my very dear Father, that I think he would not have been able to subsist without that pension. Would you in your goodness grant him that grace which is granted only very rarely; namely, to readmit him into the Company?*

I had—and still have—strong but gentle interior feelings about this, and not just because I would like to be near him. I thought it would be a consolation to you and an edification to the neighbor, given the good indications he has shown since childhood toward this work. Your Charity could place my father at the Nom-de-Jésus *or at the* Renfermés[3] *because only concern for him prevents him from following his inclination, as my father explained to me some time ago.*

I am writing to tell my brother to take the honor of sharing all that with you to see if he might be able to have the great benefit of being included among the small number of good workers in this region through your paternal goodness.

My very dear Father, I have to tell you this for your consolation. It seems that God wants us to help one another in this to bring us to His holy service because, if you recall, it was through him that His Goodness honored me with the grace of my vocation.[4]

Letter 3265. - Archives of the Mission, Turin, original autograph letter.

[1]François Fouquet.

[2]Paul Carcireux, born in Beauvais, entered the Congregation of the Mission on July 27, 1640, at the age of twenty, took his vows on March 20, 1644, and was ordained a priest in 1645. He left the Congregation to assist his father in his financial difficulties (cf. vol. II, no. 781).

[3]The General Hospital.

[4]Saint Vincent was not sufficiently satisfied with Paul Carcireux's past conduct to condescend to his sister's entreaties to take him back. In one instance, Carcireux had even instituted a lawsuit against the Congregation (cf. vol. III, no. 1068).

With your permission, we here send our most humble greetings to all your holy Community, especially M. de Beaumont, with all possible humility and respect, to ask its prayers for our concerns. Do not forget us, for the love of Jesus, in whom we are and should [be], if you please, Most Honored Father, your most obedient servant and unworthy daughter in O[ur] L[ord].

FRANÇOISE CARCIREUX,
unworthy Daughter of Charity

Narbonne, September 6, 1660

M. des Jardins assures you of his very humble regards.

Addressed: *Monsieur Vincent, Superior General of the Mission, in Paris*

3266. - *NICOLAS DEMOUSOL TO SAINT VINCENT*

Jesus, Mary, Joseph!

Reverend Father,

May the blessing of the Holy Sacrament of the altar be always with you and with all those in the monastery!

Perhaps you may remember a man who came from Germany to make an eight-day retreat in your house around the feast of Corpus Christi and who made a general confession. The priest who heard my confession was very fair-haired, but I do not know his name; the Brother who gave me instructions was dark-skinned, but I do not know his name either.

Reverend Father, the reason I am writing to you in this way is that, poor sinner that I am, I have a great desire, if it is God's Will and the will of the Church, to live in solitude for the rest of my days to serve God and to withdraw from the world. Although I am bound by the bonds of marriage and am responsible for children, this will not be an obstacle, because everything is possible with the consent of the Church.

Letter 3266. - Archives of the Mission, Turin, original autograph letter.

I also know a very devout man who is also living in chastity with his wife. He, too, has a strong desire to enter a convent. He is a thread spinner by trade, and I am a braid trimmer. As far as he is concerned, he may still become a priest; but I, who am the greatest sinner in the world, ask only to be the least of all the domestic servants or the attendant of the man who locks the door of the house. That is why, Reverend Father, for the honor of God and the Holy Virgin, I ask you to let me know by letter whether we can be accepted into your holy Rule, O Reverend Father Superior, and to be obedient to everyone in the house.

The man I mentioned is a very devout German and does fine work as a thread spinner in the making of church vestments. I also speak good German, so perhaps we could render service with the German language.

Reverend Father, by the five mortal wounds of Jesus Christ I ask you to assist us, if this can be done. Take pity on these two poor friends, especially on me, who am the greatest sinner in the world. The priest who heard my confession and the Brother who instructed me can tell you why I have withdrawn from the world; for, I told them, outside of the confessional, about my bad life.

Reverend Father, if this can be done, we will be willing to accept any duty in whatever place you choose to have us do it.

While awaiting a favorable reply, I remain until death your most humble servant.

NICOLAS DEMOUSOL,
braid trimmer in Fulda, Germany

Fulda, September 6, 1660

My most humble regards to the priest who heard my confession, the Brother who instructed me, and to everyone in that holy place.[1]

Addressed: *Reverend Father Superior of the Monastery of the Fathers of the Mission, at Saint-Lazare, in the faubourg Saint-Laurent, in Paris*

---

[1]Nicolas Demousel's desire never materialized.

3267. - *MONSIEUR SANGUINET TO SAINT VINCENT*

Monsieur,

May that same grace of O[ur] L[ord] that you wished me in your letter of August 25 be continued for you forever!

I was glad that the decree of authorization I had obtained for the Prior of Bussière[1] *reached him with the modification.*

Thank you, Monsieur, for the eighteen livres of my reimbursement. I am satisfied with that. If the Prior intends to tax the expenses, the specific modification will have to be sent back to me, together with the decree. Furthermore, I explained to M. Masson how good you were to my nephew, for which we thank you very humbly. He is a boy who would need to be disciplined for his vanity. Please God he has profited from your spiritual exercises!

If I could increase your interior consolations[2] *by my prayers, or by my services augment them with respect to myself, you would sense at least through them, Monsieur, how earnestly I wish to remain in the honor of your good graces and in your common prayers, which I request constantly. I remain cordially and for always, Monsieur, your most humble and obedient servant of long standing.*

SANGUINET

With your permission, I send greetings to M. de Veyris. I did not dare jeopardize his lawsuit by doing anything to hasten repayment of that loan.[3]

Bordeaux, September 6, 1660

Addressed: *Monsieur Vincent, Priest, Superior of the Fathers of the Mission, at the Saint-Lazare Hospice, in Paris*

Letter 3267. - Archives of the Mission, Turin, original autograph letter.

[1]In 1656, Claude de Blampignon had resigned the Priory of Bussière-Badil (Dordogne) in favor of Gilbert Cuissot, who, in his turn, resigned it in favor of Denis Laudin, the Superior in Le Mans. The Bulls substituting Denis Laudin for Gilbert Cuissot were signed in Rome on June 4, 1658 (cf. Arch. Nat., S 6703; vol. VII, no. 2634). In October of that year, Saint Vincent asked Laudin, as Prior of Bussière-Badil, to send him a power of attorney, with the name left blank, so that the priory's farmland and crops could be rented out to whomever the Saint designated (cf. vol. VII, no. 2674).

[2]The original has "your interior satisfactions."

[3]Although the meaning of this postscript is unclear, Coste has faithfully reproduced the text of the original. Perhaps it refers to some business matter known to Saint Vincent but not to the reader.

3268. - ***JACQUES-BÉNIGNE BOSSUET TO SAINT VINCENT***

[September 1660] [1]

From the enclosed letter from my father, M. Vincent will see that he has not yet reached a settlement and that the owner of the house we had decided upon is making matters difficult in order to try to obtain a higher price. I am sure he will yield in the end and, despite all the reasons my father advances, I cannot decide in favor of the hôtel de Montgommery, although it certainly is more spacious, because it would require too much construction, and that would delay the establishment too long. [2]

Nevertheless, if M. Vincent thinks we should change our opinion, he will please notify me so we can send the final decision to my father in the regular Wednesday mail. I will not be able to go to Saint-Lazare before then because I am extremely busy; but, if someone could come here[3] *on his behalf, we could discuss all this. I will wait for M. Vincent to set the day and time.*

I ask the assistance of his prayers and am, in O[ur] L[ord], his most humble servant.

BOSSUET

Letter 3268. - Archives of the Mission, Turin, original autograph letter.

[1]Probably about two weeks passed between the letter of August 19 (cf. no. 3210) and this one.

[2]The hôtel de Montgommery, belonging to the Carmelite nuns of Verdun, who were looking for a buyer. The property extended the entire length of rue Saint-Symphorien, between rue Neufbourg and rue des Huilliers; its five buildings, courtyards, and gardens, surrounded by walls, were valued at twenty-five or twenty-six thousand Metz livres. The purchase was concluded in 1661 and the hôtel de Montgommery became Sainte-Anne Seminary. (Cf. M. Hamant, "Histoire du Séminaire Sainte-Anne," in *La Revue ecclésiastique de Metz* (February, 1907.)

[3]At the Deanery of Saint-Thomas du Louvre (cf. *Revue Bossuet* [April, 1903], p. 110).

3269. - *MONSIEUR PILLÉ* [1] *TO SAINT VINCENT*

Monsieur and Very Reverend Father,

The grace of the Infant Jesus be with you forever!

The bearer of this letter is a very virtuous priest whom the Providence of God has given me as Vicar. He has been in Ferrières [2] *for more than four years. He has to take a trip to his home town because of a letter he received from his mother, telling him about the misfortune that has befallen them, namely, that they no longer have control of their property. This has come about because her deceased husband (the Vicar's father) had stood surety for his brother, who became quite insolvent and then died. Now the surety is being called in and the estate has to go for that. So, his dear mother is reduced to destitution.*

That good Vicar is not at all upset by this misfortune; on the contrary, he blesses God for it. I believe He is permitting this for the salvation of his mother and for his sisters, who live with her. He would very much like her to become a Servant of the Poor under the direction of Mademoiselle Le Gras, for he feels she is quite suited to that kind of life. That is why he asked me to write you these lines to see if you would kindly grant him this grace for his mother and sisters. He will persuade them—or do his best to persuade them—to go along with this, if you give him a word of hope that they will be received. If this is not possible, I am in danger of losing that good Vicar, who is so outstanding that there is very little hope of finding another like him; he is a hidden treasure whom God revealed to us.

The greatest pleasure you could give me is to persuade him to come back to Ferrières, where he is considered a man totally given to God and very zealous for the salvation of souls. If his mother can be settled somewhere with his sisters, we would have great hope of seeing him again. I ask you most humbly to take the trouble of listening to him in this matter and to contribute as far as you can to the piety of his intentions. In so doing

---

Letter 3269. - Archives of the Mission, Turin, original autograph letter.

[1]The brother of Jean Pillé, (cf. vol. II, no. 622) a member of the Congregation of the Mission, who had died in Paris on October 7, 1642.

[2]Ferrières-Gâtinais (Loiret).

you will oblige to no end, Monsieur and very Reverend Father, your most humble and very obedient servant.

E. PILLÉ,
unworthy Pastor of Ferrières

Ferrières, September 7, 1660

I am writing to my nephew Nicolas Bonichon, a priest residing in Cahors. His mother, who lives in our residence, greets you very humbly and recommends her other son, Barthélemy, to you. My sister and I send greetings to good M. Dehorgny and ask for a share in his prayers.

Addressed: *Monsieur Vincent, Superior General of the Mission, living at Saint-Lazare, in Paris*

3270. - TO FIRMIN GET, SUPERIOR, IN MARSEILLES

Paris, September 9, 1660

Monsieur,

The grace of O[ur] L[ord] be with you forever!

A slight indisposition will require me to make this letter brief. I received your letter of August 31, which mentioned only the complaints that His Lordship of Mercoeur [1] has lodged against M. Le Vacher of Tunis, condemning him without a hearing, even though he is not guilty. In the present circumstances, however, it will be difficult to prevent that good nobleman from sending another Consul there, and for us to do it before he does. We must await the outcome of M. Paul's [2] undertaking; then we shall see.

Letter 3270. - The original was formerly the property of the Daughters of Charity, 20 rue Mage, Toulouse; its present location is unknown.

[1]The Duc de Mercoeur, Governor of Provence.

[2]When returning from the Ionian Isles, where he had gone to lead the troops to bring reinforcements to the Venetians at war against the Turks, Commander Paul had taken the Algiers route. He was planning to force the Dey to give back the French slaves he was detaining in his galleys, in violation of the treaties. After remaining five days outside the city, which violent winds prevented him from approaching, he sailed away with no other result except the liberation of forty slaves, who had escaped by swimming when they saw his ships.

We have not yet been able to obtain the mandate for the tax collector of the estates of the Marquis de Vins.[3] This has not been from want of petitioning for it.

We received twelve livres for Remi Droue, alias Vitry, six livres for Claude d'Hirbec, and thirty sous for Pierre Laisné, alias de Rosier, all of them convicts in Toulon. I ask M. Huguier to give each of them his due, plus six livres to Pierre Blondeau. As for the affair of the Franciscans, we have not yet discussed it, for lack of time. Besides, I do not think it is urgent.[4]

I will take the honor of writing to M. Thomas Bayn, who did me the honor of writing to me. His brother [5] is well, thank God.

Someone just brought us six more livres, namely three livres for Guillaume Laisné, alias Lamontagne, and the other three for Jacques Fournier, alias Larivière.

I do not know what advice to give our good confreres in Barbary in their present danger, nor even how to communicate it to them. I ask Our Lord to inspire them with what they should do and to deliver them from harm.

I did not tell you that we are sending your good brother[6] to Poland with M. de la Brière and Brother de Marthe, who taught philosophy here, because he himself is writing to you about it.

I am, in O[ur] L[ord], Monsieur, your most humble servant.

VINCENT DEPAUL,
i.s.C.M.

---

[3]Melchior Dagouz de Montauban, Seigneur de Vins and Brigadier General of the King's armies.

[4]For reasons unknown to Saint Vincent, the Franciscans had been expelled from Marseilles (cf. nos. 3112a and 3257a).

[5]Joseph Bayn.

[6]Nicolas Get. Both he and Ignace-Joseph de Marthe were preparing for ordination to priesthood.

3271. - *LOUISE-EUGÉNIE DE FONTAINE TO SAINT VINCENT*

Live Jesus!

Most Honored Father,

Enclosed is a letter for Your Goodness from our Most Honored Sister Assistant.[1] *I am sure she tells you in it of the blessings God continues to shed more and more on His work, and how the election of the Superior and the officers took place last Saturday*[2] *with such peace and unity that we can scarcely believe it. This Most Honored Sister is also asking us to send her obedience to her so she can return, to let her know how much time she may give to our dear Sisters in Melun, and whether she may go to Sainte-Madeleine*[3] *and to our Sisters in Paris—I think she means our dear Sisters in the faubourg and at rue Montorgueil.*

Do us the charity, Most Honored Father, of giving us your instructions for all that, and do us the favor of sending us the obedience for the return of our three dear Sisters. Since time is scarce, I think she will have to be satisfied with giving one day to our dear Sisters in Melun, if you agree. As for Sainte-Madeleine and our monasteries in this city, we will do whatever you in your goodness think best, Most Honored Father, desiring nothing in that except to carry out your holy, paternal will. I am, respectfully, your most humble and very obedient daughter and servant in Our Lord.

LOUISE-EUGÉNIE DE FONTAINE,
of the Visitation Sainte-Marie

B[lessed] b[e] G[od]!

September 9 [1660][4]

Addressed: *Monsieur Vincent de Paul, General of the Missions of France*

Letter 3271. - Archives of the Mission, Turin, original autograph letter.

[1]Sister Madeleine Maupeou.

[2]At the Ursulines of Melun.

[3]Before returning to the First Monastery of the Visitation in Paris, Sister Madeleine visited Port-Royal and the Madeleine Convent, where urgent business required her presence.

[4]This letter accompanied no. 3261.

3272. - *FRANÇOISE-MARIE SIBOUR TO SAINT VINCENT*

Live Jesus!

From our Monastery in Paris, September 10, 1660

Very Dear and Honored Father,

I would be remiss in my principal duty if I did not pay my most humble respects to you immediately after our arrival and ask your holy, paternal blessing, which I will receive prostrate in spirit at your feet. This is the favor awaited from your goodness by the person who is and calls herself, with your permission and with all possible respect, very dear and Honored Father, your most humble and obedient daughter and servant in Our Lord.

SISTER FRANÇOISE-MARIE SIBOUR,
of the Visitation Sainte-Marie

I do not know if a letter we had the honor of writing you a month ago was ever delivered to you.

Would you please allow us to have dear Sister Marie-Catherine Tounère, a professed nun of our dear Sisters in Compiègne, enter our house? If you approve this, we would be happy to give her this consolation, very dear Father. She could even help us nurse our dear patient,[1] *whom we fear is going to lose an eye; nothing can be done about it. We entreat you, Most Honored Father, to ask your Community to pray for that dear patient and to bless your most humble and very obedient daughter and servant in Our Lord.*

LOUISE-EUGÉNIE

Blessed be God!

Addressed: *Monsieur Vincent de Paul, in Paris*

Letter 3272. - Archives of the Mission, Turin, original autograph letter. The postscript is written by Mother Louise-Eugénie de Fontaine, Sister Françoise-Marie Sibour's Superior.

[1]Sister Marguerite-Dorothée.

3273. - *PRINCE DE CONTI TO SAINT VINCENT*

[September 1660] [1]

I ask M. Vincent kindly to continue to give the Missionaries two or three of his workers for the missions to be given this winter in my territory,[2] *and I will be very grateful to him for this.*

J. A. DE BOURBON

3274. - *MARTIN HUSSON TO SAINT VINCENT*

Live Jesus!

Montmirail, September 12, 1660

Monsieur,

I wish His Lordship[1] *had been here so I could have asked him to give you through our people what he promised you. But the entrance of the Queen has detained him in Paris until now. As soon as he gets here, I will ask him to give you satisfaction.*

Enclosed is a note for good M. Le Vacher [2] *and another for M. Delaforcade, since you are so good as to see that it is forwarded to him. It will suffice to send it when you write to him. Please recommend that he reply to it.*

I am, in the love of O[ur] L[ord], Monsieur, your most humble and very obedient servant.

HUSSON

Letter 3273. - Archives of the Mission, Turin, original autograph letter.

[1]Date added on the back by Brother Ducournau.

[2]He had just been appointed Governor of Languedoc.

Letter 3274. - Archives of the Mission, Turin, original autograph letter.

[1]The Duc de Noirmoutiers.

[2]Jean Le Vacher.

3275. - *MONSIEUR ROY TO SAINT VINCENT*

Monsieur and Venerable Father,

A good widow asked me to work on the redemption of a poor captive in Algiers, named Étienne Gaultier, who is about fifteen years old, a native of this town, and at present in the power of Mustapha Agibirabi, on rue Agnisexin, in Algiers. I thought, therefore, that I could do nothing better than to appeal to Your Reverence about this. Then, in two or three months, when I hope to be with you, all I will have to do is to collect the money needed for this boy and others as well, through the means being offered me, which I will have the honor of explaining to Your Reverence.

The enclosed note will help him more easily to return and to remain steadfast in our religion. It comes from the above-mentioned widow, who believes he esteems, loves, and respects her, and will even be of service so people can get to know him better.

I am, Monsieur and Venerable Father, your most humble and very devoted servant.

ROY

Lyons, September 14, 1660

Addressed: *Monsieur Vincent, Superior General of the Priests of the Mission, at Saint-Lazare-lez-Paris, in Paris*

3276. - *JEAN FOUQUET TO SAINT VINCENT*

Maule, September 16, 1660

Monsieur,

We ask you to do us the favor of letting us know whether or not M. Senant is coming back, especially since his sister is more agitated than ever. She is sometimes in Paris and sometimes here. She has no one to console her; all her hopes are pinned on her brother's return. None of her husband's relations have dared to take her in. Even a good priest, one of those relatives of her husband, has done everything he could, taking the

---

Letter 3275. - Archives of the Mission, Turin, original autograph letter.

Letter 3276. - Archives of the Mission, Turin, original autograph letter.

trouble to write to M. Senant, hoping that you will do us the favor of sending a reply by the bearer of this letter. This is what we are asking of you and await this act of charity from you.

We will always remain, Monsieur, your most obedient servant.

JEAN FOUQUET

Addressed: *Monsieur Vincent, Superior at Saint-Lazare*

3277. - *LOUISE-EUGÉNIE DE FONTAINE TO SAINT VINCENT*

Live Jesus!

My Most Honored and Very Dear Father,

The number of our young ladies has diminished by one recently, with the entrance of one of them, our dear Sister Hacedette, into the novitiate. President Miron wants to do us the honor of giving us in her place one of his dear little nieces, whose sister we already have. Please grant us permission, Most Honored Father, to accept her into our house and to keep her among the little Sisters. This latest obligation will make me, more and more, with all the most humble respect possible, Most Honored and very dear Father, your most humble and very obedient daughter and servant in Our Lord.

LOUISE-EUGÉNIE DE FONTAINE,
of the Visitation Sainte-Marie

B[lessed] b[e] G[od]!

From our Monastery in Paris, rue Saint-Antoine, September 16, 1660

Addressed: *Monsieur Vincent de Paul, General of the Reverend Fathers of the Mission, at Saint-Lazare*

Letter 3277. - Archives of the Mission, Turin, original autograph letter.

3278. - *NICOLAS GEDOYN TO SAINT VINCENT*

Monsieur,

My firm belief in your goodness prompts me to take the liberty of writing to you, believing that you will not object to this, especially since, being in the country, I am unable to have the honor of going to discuss with you an affair that requires your decision. It concerns, Monsieur, the mission in Épinay,[1] *near Saint-Denis, which we are prepared to open this October 1 or 2.*

Certain young women of known piety would like to come and work there along with the priests—although in a separate house—and to gather some girls and women together to instruct and catechize them in a house they want to rent for this purpose. This would be done at hours different from the ones we will take for our regular exercises in similar meetings—I mean our sermons, catechism, and discussions.

They go there in a body, as do the priests, and even use the place where the mission of two or three weeks is to be given to prepare the girls and women for confession. During the time of that mission they do in their own house what the priests are doing in public in the church.

We have heard that it is not customary among you to have women working in the missions, and we do not wish to act contrary to your course of action because we have the honor of being united to you through the Company.[2] *We were unwilling, then, to decide anything until we had heard your opinion, since that must be our guideline.*

So, in the name of all the priests who are to work at this mission, I ask you, Monsieur, to let us know as soon as possible what you think we should do because, if those young ladies are coming, they need to look for a place to live. I assure you that we will never deviate from whatever you tell us,

---

Letter 3278. - Archives of the Mission, Turin, original autograph letter.

[1]Épinay-sur-Seine (Seine-Saint-Denis).

[2]The group of priests who took part in the Tuesday Conferences.

especially I, who for many years have had the honor of being, Monsieur, your most humble and very obedient servant.

GEDOYN,
unworthy Priest

Créteil,[3] September 16 [1660]

Addressed: *Monsieur Vincent, General and Superior of the Priests of the Mission, in Paris*

3279. - TO JEAN MARTIN, SUPERIOR, IN TURIN

Paris, September 17, 1660 [1]

Monsieur,

The grace of O[ur] L[ord] be with you forever!

From your letter of August 21 I learned of M. Demortier's illness, and, in the one you have written to M. Berthe since then, we were assured that he was improving. God be praised for this, and may He be willing by His grace to give all of you the strength of body and mind required for the work you have to do!

We received Vaugin's receipt; we will pay the fifty écus to whomever you indicate to us. M. de la Brière, Brothers de Marthe and Get,[2] a coadjutor Brother, and three Daughters of Charity have just left for Poland, and will sail from Rouen.

---

[3]A locality in Val-de-Marne.

Letter 3279. - Archives of the Mission, Turin, original signed letter. Because the letter is torn at the top and at the bottom, it is missing both the signature and the date. As a result, the meaning of about five lines of the contents is not clear.

[1]Date written in the secretary's handwriting on the back of the letter.

[2]Nicolas Get.

Because M. Alméras is unable to recover in Richelieu from his [great] weakness, [he is returning here on a li]tter.[3]

[Our community is going to beg]in its retreats. [Recommend] to O[ur] L[ord] the individuals and [their needs], especially mine, as I often recommend to Him your dear soul and your little family, which I most cordially embrace. I am, for both, in the love of O[ur] L[ord], Monsieur, [your most humble servant.

VINCENT DEPAUL,
i.s.C.M.]

Addressed: Monsieur Martin, Superior of the Priests of the Mission of Turin, in Turin

3280. - TO FIRMIN GET, SUPERIOR, IN MARSEILLES

Paris, September 17, 1660

Monsieur,

I received your letter dated the seventh. Enclosed is the order for M. de Grimancourt for the one thousand livres due you, payable on three dates, which have already passed. A note is attached to give you the address and to enable you to find the counterfoil, along with a copy of the power of attorney for the proof of his act. He did not wish to have it notarized, saying that this was unnecessary, since he had already sent another one that is certified. At your leisure, you can see those gentlemen mentioned in the note in order to ascertain their dispositions and to bring them around in the right

[3]To reconstruct this sentence, we followed an old notation written on the back of the letter. René Alméras arrived in Paris on September 24, 1660, just three days before the death of the Saint, whom he was to succeed.

Letter 3280. - Pémartin, *op. cit.*, vol. IV, p. 598, l. 2073.

way to paying this order. If they raise any difficulty, you will have to send it back to us.

Enclosed also is the dispensation from Rome for the vow made by M. Cornier. M. Jolly has written me that the Director of the seminary, in accordance with the wishes of the petitioner, may open the Brief and put it into effect in his regard. He did so because he thinks he is still in the seminary. I think he would have said the same for you, if he had known that he was in Marseilles.

Like you I feel keenly what is happening to our poor confreres in Algiers. What anguish! What violence in the present circumstances! May God be pleased to protect them!

I recommend to your prayers the journeys of M. de la Brière, Brothers Get and de Marthe, a coadjutor Brother, and three Daughters of Charity, who left today to sail from Rouen for Poland. Your brother left quite satisfied and very determined, thank God. He gave instructions that the letter from the good young man from Picardy, which he wrote for home, should be sent to his parents. We will also see that M. Cornier's packet is delivered.

Enclosed are two letters for Tunis to be forwarded to M. Le Vacher; the opportunity presented itself before I had time to write to him.

The Archbishop of Narbonne[1] has urged me to complete the number of six priests he would like to have, but our shortage of men like Messieurs Delespiney and Parisy obliges us to have recourse to them for the new establishment. I am asking them, then, to go there as soon as possible, and you to give them what they need. I embrace them in spirit with heartfelt emotion. We still have to make some little arrangement with the good Prelate, but that should not interfere with the departure of these Missionaries, who will be joyfully received and usefully employed. I ask Our Lord to bless and preserve them.

Kindly tell M. Delespiney that his friend, good M. Dubouchart, has died.

---

[1]François Fouquet.

I cannot refrain from saying a few words to you about your good brother. We selected him and Brother de Marthe from among all our students as the ones most ready to be ordained priests and as the most capable and exemplary. They gave great edification in the house. M. de la Brière is also an excellent Missionary; he taught scholastic philosophy and moral theology. All of us hope that the choice of these three workers will be a good one.

I am worried about something that makes me inexpressibly anxious. Rumor has it here that Commander Paul has besieged Algiers,[2] but we do not know the outcome; and you tell me that people are beginning to leave for Algiers, but you make no mention of our poor confreres. In the name of God, tell us what is going on.

Please recommend to M. Huguier M. Dubignon, whom M. Grimancourt recommends in this note.

I am, in the love of Our Lord, your. . . .

3281. - TO FRANÇOIS FOUQUET, ARCHBISHOP OF NARBONNE

September 17, 1660

I admire Your Excellency's forbearance toward me—who am fit only to try your patience—and your habitual fatherly tenderness toward our little Company, despite our delays and difficulties in carrying out your orders. I very humbly ask your pardon for our boorishness and I thank you for your steadfast constancy in doing and wishing us well.

We are, Monseigneur, about to make one of the greatest efforts we have yet made to send you the Missionaries you request, but I implore Your Excellency to allow me to tell you quite simply that, on rereading again today the plan for the union of your seminary to our Company, we have noted several things in it that are contrary to our customs.

---

[2]The rumor was false.

Letter 3281. - Reg. 2, p. 62.

It seems that Your Excellency wants to oblige us to give an account of our finances. This is something no Prelate has required us to do in our establishments inside or outside the kingdom. We were even unwilling to accept Saint-Lazare on those terms, although the place offered many advantages to our Congregation. And when the Archbishop of Paris [1] urged us to accept it on that condition, we told him we would rather leave than be subject to that obligation, and he had the kindness to release us from it in order to retain us; otherwise we would have withdrawn.

As for the authority to dismiss from your seminary any members of our Company whom Your Excellency will no longer wish to employ, please allow me to tell you, Monseigneur, that, in all the places where we are established, the Prelates have deemed it fitting to leave the direction of persons in the Congregation to the Superior of the same Congregation. He, then, is the one who recalls them and send others in their place. This is what we have done until now.

We will be deeply indebted to Your Excellency if you draw up the act of union in the way the other Prelates of France and Italy have done. The hope you give us of not wanting our little Institute to suffer any infringement in your diocese has given me the confidence, Monseigneur, to point out to you the things that might be injurious to it so that, in line with your customary prudence and charity, you may be pleased to avoid them.

3282. - *MONSIEUR AMELINE TO SAINT VINCENT*

Notre-Dame-de-Paix, September 17, 1660

Monsieur and Reverend Father,

I heard that you had received the letter I took the liberty of writing with

---

[1]Jean-François de Gondi.

Letter 3282. - Archives of the Mission, Turin, original autograph letter.

regard to the lawsuit we have initiated against the heretics in Saint-Quentin and that you, together with all those good Ladies of Charity, had the goodness to be willing to do what you could to assist us.[1] *I am so busy now, and will be for the next few days, with the new pilgrimage that has begun here with many blessings that I have been unable to devote all the time needed to that affair, which everyone considers extremely important.*

We are working to get the results of the preliminary investigation and the other documents against them, but one of the King's attorneys and a clerk are here, and we can get no help from them. We have asked M. Bourdin[2] *to send us a warrant to force the clerk to hand over to us the preliminary investigation so that it can be sent to Paris. What we need now is the reply to a petition I sent to the court, which is in the hands of M. Emery the attorney so we can continue the investigation already begun, especially since the Minister has obtained a decree of interdiction for the local judges to take cognizance of it, in order to avoid going to court as usual.*

If, Monsieur, we could have some trustworthy man in Paris to appeal this case, that would be the real means of succeeding. He would be able to see you and the persons who might act ruthlessly; then he could justify the state of affairs. If, Monsieur, through Madame Fouquet or some Ladies of Charity whom you consider apt for this business, you can obtain for us the reply to the petition that is in the hands of M. Emery, it would advance matters considerably.

I hope to spend a few days in Saint-Quentin to lend some support to our Brothers and to work on the most urgent needs.

You heard, Monsieur, that the Minister recently obtained an adjudication from the Parlementary Court to hinder the execution of the decree of the Privy Council, which forbids the civil judge to take cognizance of their business but allows them to continue with their plans—which the Privy Council had prohibited.

Please excuse me; it is simply that I am aware of your zeal for the advancement of religion, and I fear that M. Bourdin is so busy with other affairs that he may not be able to work as much as he would like on this lawsuit, which is very important for the glory of God. I am praying

---

[1]M. Ameline's previous letter is not extant, but no. 3212 (M. d'Abancour's letter of August 1660 to Saint Vincent) mentions his lawsuit and the help he had received.

[2]Vicar-General of Noyon.

wholeheartedly that God will preserve your health for the good of His Church, Monsieur and Reverend Father.

Your most humble and obedient servant.

AMELINE,
priest

If you favor me by giving me some news of yourself, M. Abancour[3] *the chancellor will have it brought for me to the house where Brother Jean*[4] *is staying.*

Addressed: *Monsieur Vincent, Superior General of the Priests of the Mission, rue Saint-Denis, at the Saint-Lazare house, in Paris*

3283. - *MONSIEUR GARBUZAT*[1] *TO SAINT VINCENT*

Monsieur,

I would be an ingrate if, after all the favors I have received from your kindness, I did not diligently seek out occasions to express my gratitude to you. This is what has prompted me to take the honor of assuring you of this, immediately after my arrival in this city in perfect health, thank God. I also want to thank you most humbly for the favor you were pleased to grant me on behalf of my brother. I did not find him here because he has gone to Belley to receive final authorization for the Mass, which he hopes to celebrate immediately after his return.

At the same time, I will prepare him for his journey to Paris to anticipate the honor of going to pay his respects to you and to express the gratitude we both have for your goodness, assuring you, Monsieur, that I could never adequately repay you for it. Nevertheless, I still entreat you to honor me

---

[3]The Chancellor of Saint-Quentin.

[4]Jean Parre.

Letter 3283. - Archives of the Mission, Turin, original autograph letter.

[1]A merchant in Lyons.

with your orders and to assure you that I will consider it a great honor to be, all my life, Monsieur, your most humble and very obedient servant.

GARBUZAT

Lyons, September 17, 1660

3284. - *ANNE-MARGUERITE GUÉRIN TO SAINT VINCENT*

Live Jesus!

From our Third Monastery in Paris, September 18 [1660] [1]

Most Honored Father,

We are sending someone for news of your health, which we are asking God to make as good as we wish it to be. We very humbly request that you, Most Honored Father, allow Abbess Dupart, Madame Fouquet's daughter, to enter this house with two of her nuns, as you in your kindness have permitted for our two other Mothers of the faubourg and of rue Saint-Antoine. In this, we are considering her religious state more than anything else. We feel that you in your goodness will have no objection, according to the opinion expressed by our blessed Mother [2] *in her* Replies, *namely, that, with the permission of Superiors, we may open our monasteries to nuns who would open theirs to us.*

Most Honored Father, I did not think I could refuse asking your permission for that virtuous Abbess, since two of her Sisters are here in this house. This has always been granted to others among our Sisters

---

Letter 3284. - Archives of the Mission, Turin, original autograph letter.

[1]This letter belongs near no. 3295.

[2]Saint Jane Frances Frémiot was born in Dijon on January 23, 1572. She and her husband Baron de Chantal had four children. Widowed at a very young age, she placed herself under the guidance of Saint Francis de Sales and with him established the Order of the Visitation. The foundation of the First Monastery in Paris drew her to that city where she remained from 1619 to 1622. There she became acquainted with Saint Vincent, whom she requested of Jean-François de Gondi, Archbishop of Paris, as Superior of her daughters. Until her death in Moulins on December 13, 1641, as she was returning from a trip to Paris, she kept in close contact with Monsieur Vincent, whom she consulted for spiritual direction and the business affairs of her Community. (Cf. Henri de Maupas du Tour, *La Vie de la Vénérable Mère Jeanne-Françoise Frémiot, fondatrice, première Mère et Religieuse de l'Ordre de la Visitation de Sainte-Marie* [new ed., Paris: Siméon Piget, 1653].)

toward whom we were not so obligated. Nevertheless, Most Honored Father, you are the one to decide this as you do everything else, and our duty is to submit and obey. Madame Fouquet intended to ask you but did not have the opportunity to do so.

Yesterday our dear Superior came to spend a few hours here, leaving to go to our Sisters in the faubourg. We did not have time to notify you of this. She said she would give us the six thousand livres as the settlement we respectfully requested. We await the contract for this and will send it to you since you in your kindness are willing to take the trouble to sign it. She has to leave soon and would like to take care of this business before her departure.

Please excuse this mistake. I did not intend to continue the page I had started.

Someone has just brought the document, Most Honored Father, and we are sending it for your signature. She has to go back on Monday; that is why the matter is somewhat urgent. We are praying for your health, Most Honored Father; one of our greatest consolations would be to be able to have the honor of seeing you, to assure you in person of our humble submission, and to receive your holy blessing. I am, Most Honored Father, your most humble and very unworthy servant in Our Lord.

SISTER ANNE-MARGUERITE GUÉRIN,
of the Visitation Sainte-Marie

Blessed be God!

Addressed: *Monsieur Vincent, Superior General of the Priests of the Mission of Saint-Lazare*

3285. - *CARDINAL PAUL-NICOLAS BAGNI TO SAINT VINCENT*

Very Reverend Monsieur,

I have heard from several quarters that Your Reverence is not enjoying the good health I would like and which you would need for the benefit of everyone. I say this because of the cordial affection I have for you and which I know you have for me. You can imagine how distressed I am; I

Letter 3285. - Departmental Archives of Vaucluse, D 274, register, copy; original in Italian.

think of you every day, and I ask you to avoid tiring occupations, which can be prejudicial to your need for sleep and peace of mind. The benefits of the latter will enable you to devote yourself more efficaciously to the care of souls and to your more important duties.

I have heard and I rejoice that Our Holy Father has dispensed you from reciting the Divine Office, allowing you to substitute for it other, less fatiguing prayers. I implore you, with all the affection I have for you, to use this dispensation as others have done for lesser indispositions and who are less involved than you are in the salvation of souls.

I ask you to make use of me in all confidence in whatever I can do to be of service to you.

The most affectionate servant of Your Reverence.

PAOLO,
Cardinal di Gardi-Bagni

Rome, September 19, 1660

3286. - *CARDINAL DURAZZO TO SAINT VINCENT*

Very Reverend Monsieur,

I am ever more aware of how useful to the neighbor are the works of the Priests of the Mission inspired by the teachings and example of their Superior General. All well-meaning persons, therefore, should ask God to give him a long life and good health in order to make the source of so much good more lasting. So, since I am deeply interested in the happy progress of this holy Institute and have a tender affection for Your Reverence, I feel obliged to ask you, as I am now doing, to be docile in listening to your confessor with regard to the care of yourself and your health and to refrain from any occupation that might be prejudicial to maintaining your life for a longer time. Your confessor has sufficient authority to dispense you from the obligation priesthood imposes on you of reciting the Divine Office. I hope Your Reverence is willing to obey him and to be convinced that his recommendations on this point will be the greater service of God.

I am in Rome and often visit M. Edme.[1] *I do not know, however, if God*

Letter 3286. - Departmental Archives of Vaucluse, D 274, register, copy; original in Italian.

[1]Edme Jolly.

will want me to end my days here or to return to my own diocese. I ask the assistance of the prayers of Your Reverence for this intention. Meanwhile, I am striving to be indifferent in order to carry out with equal promptness whichever of the two decisions His Holiness will make, and I conclude by asking God's choicest blessings on Your Reverence.

The most affectionate servant of Your Reverence.

CARDINAL DURAZZO [2]

Rome, September 20, 1660

3287. - *JACQUES LAMBERT TO SAINT VINCENT*

My very dear Reverend Father,

I am making a nuisance of myself, but you are a person filled with love and charity who is putting your goodness into action on behalf of a poor captive who hopes to obtain his freedom through you; and if I were so unfortunate as to be deprived of your charity, I would be detained eternally in irons for the rest of my life.

Please accept this note concerning a letter from Toulon, which I am told I received but, because [those] letters from Toulon must have been lost, I am in trouble, as is evident from the letter I am asking you to read. I have also been told that the person cannot send any others—only a passport certificate.

The Masters of Requests and the King's chaplains are supposed to come to visit us at La Tournelle.[1] *If the extract from the letter I am sending you were signed by your hand and in the proper form to be presented later as a petition, mentioning how my letters were delivered to me, as your extract signed by you would also attest, I would surely obtain my freedom. This would allow me to end my days in some convent. If I cannot succeed in this way, all I can do is to end my days wretchedly.*

---

[2]Abelly gives what purports to be a translation of the original letter (cf. bk. I, chap. LI, p. 253), but Coste states that the translation is incomplete and inexact. An examination and comparison with the Italian and Coste's French translation point up several discrepancies.

Letter 3287. - Archives of the Mission, Turin, original autograph letter.

[1]A prison in Paris near the Porte Saint-Bernard, where men waiting to be shipped out on the galleys were detained.

Hoping for this favor from you, and continuing my prayers for your health and prosperity, I will remain, with your permission, your most humble and obedient servant.

JACQUES LAMBERT

La Tournelle, September 20, 1660

The letter addressed to the father is not here.

Addressed: *Reverend Father Vincent, at Saint-Lazare*

3288. - *MADAME POIRIER TO SAINT VINCENT*

Arras, September 21, 1660

Monsieur,

Please forgive me for taking the liberty of sending you this note to inform you of the departure of one of your Daughters of Charity, who was in Arras. Her name is Sister Radegonde,[1] *and she went off last Monday without saying a word to anyone. This is causing us a great deal of trouble because of the confusion it has brought to the Charity you were pleased to establish in Arras, and it will cause great turmoil in matters relative to the service of God. That is why I entreat you, Monsieur, not to abandon us in all these circumstances, and to let us know what is to be done. She left just when the operation of the Charity was beginning to go better than ever.*

While awaiting the honor of your orders, I conclude with all respect, Monsieur.

Your most humble and very obedient servant.

C. POIRIER

Addressed: *Reverend Father Vincent, General of the Mission, in Paris*

Letter 3288. - Archives of the Mission, Turin, original autograph letter.

[1]Radegonde Lenfantin. She would die as a Daughter of Charity.

3289. - TO NICOLAS SEVIN, BISHOP OF CAHORS

September 22, 1660

Vincent de Paul promises Nicolas Sevin that he will not forget him before God.

3290. - *MADAME FIESQUE* [1] *TO SAINT VINCENT*

The Carmelites, Wednesday morning, September 22 [1660] [2]

Monsieur,

I am really very perplexed about my retreat here. Since I cannot have the honor of seeing you, I have disclosed my concerns in detail to the Pastor of Saint-Nicolas-du-Chardonneret[3] *so he can share them with you and together decide what I should do. He is supposed to be at your house at two o'clock tomorrow afternoon. Please see him because the matter cannot be postponed; we need a prompt solution to the question, as he will explain to you.*

Entrusting myself, therefore, to him for everything, all that remains for me is to ask you and your entire good Company most earnestly for prayers for this between now and that time, especially tomorrow during the Holy Sacrifice of all the Masses.

Your most humble servant.

FIESQUE

Addressed: *Monsieur Vincent, at Saint-Lazare*

Letter 3289. - In a letter of October 10, 1660, to René Alméras, Nicolas Sevin mentioned a letter he had received from Saint Vincent, written five days before the Saint's death. A copy of the Bishop's letter to Alméras, from the Archives of the Diocese of Cahors, Alain de Solminihac collection, file 22, no. 45, is given in Appendix 3. The Saint's letter to Bishop Sevin is no longer extant.

Letter 3290. - Archives of the Mission, Turin, original autograph letter.

[1]Marie de Fiesque, Marquise de Bréauté.

[2]The letters in the file to which this belongs are almost all dated 1660; furthermore, September 22 fell on a Wednesday in 1660.

[3]Saint-Nicolas du Chardonnet, of which Hippolyte Féret was the Pastor.

3291. - *MONSIEUR BARBIER TO SAINT VINCENT*

Monsieur,

I have to tell you that M. Senant's sister—that poor woman—is the most afflicted person on earth. Her husband's ill-treatment and bad temper is driving her to despair, and he is unwilling to hear anything of reconciliation. I myself presented your letter to him, to which I joined all the remonstrances I could think of but was unable to have any influence over him. I admit that the poor woman may be somewhat flighty, but her husband is more malicious than a demon.

I had already written to M. Senant that he needed to come to Maule to bring peace to this disunion or to separate them entirely. I would be surprised if you gave credence to the letters of that imposter without any proof or the testimony of persons who can bear witness to you of the truth.

Awaiting the happiness of seeing you, Monsieur, I remain your most humble servant.

C. BARBIER,
Pastor in Maule

September 22, 1660

Addressed: *Monsieur Vincent, Superior of the Mission of Saint-Lazare, in Paris*

3292. - TO EDME JOLLY, SUPERIOR, IN ROME

September 24, 1660

You caused me to admire the unparalleled kindness of Cardinal Durazzo when you told me he held a meeting to discuss the reply to be made to Genoa regarding the proposal for Corsica. You said that, finding the form in which it had been drafted disadvantageous

---

Letter 3291. - Archives of the Mission, Turin, original autograph letter.

Letter 3292. - Reg. 2, p. 254.

to the Company, His Eminence stated that the plan, as it was proposed, was not feasible and could become so only by granting a permanent establishment of Missionaries in that kingdom, with no obligation for them to travel through other dioceses, and by assigning them a separate fund for their maintenance. This would not make them objectionable to the Bishops, as would be the case if the proposal were adopted.

O Dieu! what charity in this holy Cardinal! Oh! how indebted we are to him for having extricated us so discreetly and skillfully from that business! For I hope they will no longer think of us, at least with any thought of committing us to it in the first form, and that, if we are mentioned in connection with it, it will be in line with His Eminence's thinking, which fits in so well with what we can and should desire.

I am writing to M. Simon, in the absence of M. Pesnelle, to tell him that he must remain firm in this, and I ask God in His infinite goodness to help us to express our gratitude in proportion to the infinite obligations we are under to Monseigneur.

3293. - *NICOLAS CABART TO SAINT VINCENT*

Paris, September 24, 1660

Monsieur,

I am writing this note simply to ask you most humbly to accept the offers that the bearer of this letter, my nephew, will make of his very humble service and to grant him the favor of being able to make a retreat of eight to ten days in your house. M. de Saint-Aignan[1] *gave him this good advice*

Letter 3293. - Archives of the Mission, Turin, original autograph letter.

[1]Paul Chevalier, who had been Canon of Saint-Aignan at Notre-Dame de Paris since 1638 and later became Vicar-General for Cardinal de Retz. In 1642 he offered Saint Vincent a number of priories, with the hope that their income would help defray the expenses of the retreats for the ordinands (cf. vol. II, no. 582). The Saint was reluctant to join these foundations to the Congregation of the Mission (cf. vol. II, no. 594). Saint-Aignan died in 1674.

of making a retreat before beginning his law studies, for which he has come to Paris. He wrote to M. Alméras to further this plan.

I will join this obligation to so many others I already have to you, Monsieur, asking God to thank you for it better than I could ever do.

I cannot sufficiently declare to you that I am and will be all my life, Monsieur, your most humble, very grateful, and very obedient servant.

NICOLAS CABART,
unworthy Doctor

Addressed: *Monsieur Vincent, Superior General of the Mission, at Saint-Lazare*

3294. - TO JEAN DE MAUPEOU, BISHOP OF CHALON-SUR-SAÔNE, IN PARIS

September 25, 1660

The simplicity that the Bishop of Chalon wants his servants to profess leads me to make an avowal to His Excellency that, having studied his proposal and taken the advice of our senior members, we have decided to abide by the resolution already taken not to admit to our Company anyone presented to us by his relatives or friends. Our experience has been that few succeed who do not apply on their own and do not come to us out of devotion and a desire to give themselves to God. This is also observed by other well-regulated Communities. I do violence to myself in saying this to Monseigneur, good as he is, because I have a very sincere desire to obey him, but he is too good to wish us to waive this procedure.

Letter 3294. - Reg. 2, p. 39.

3295. - *ANNE-MARGUERITE GUÉRIN TO SAINT VINCENT*

Live Jesus!

From Our Third Monastery, September 25 [1660] [1]

My Most Honored Father,

Madame Fouquet informed us that you had the kindness to permit her to enter this house, provided we put that in writing for you. I do so most willingly and would have already done so had we known you would allow it. We also very humbly ask you to let us know if it is permanent—that is, for whenever she chooses; we are sure she will not abuse it.

As for Abbess Dupart her daughter, we have interpreted your permission to mean for as long as she is in town.

We will be very consoled to see our Most Honored Sister, the former Superior of the monastery in the city,[2] *when she returns from her journey to Melun. Madame Fouquet is supposed to bring her to us.*

We pray that God in His divine goodness will be pleased to restore you completely to perfect health. This is also the wish of her who is, with all possible respect and submission, after having prostrated ourselves in spirit to receive your holy blessing, Most Honored Father, your most humble and very obedient daughter and servant in O[ur] L[ord].

SISTER ANNE-MARGUERITE GUÉRIN,
of the Visitation Sainte-Marie

Blessed be God!

Addressed: *Monsieur Vincent, Superior General of the Priests of the Mission of Saint-Lazare*

Letter 3295. - Archives of the Mission, Turin, original autograph letter.

[1]This letter should be placed near no. 3284.

[2]Madeleine-Élisabeth de Maupeou.

3296. - *NICOLAS ÉTIENNE TO SAINT VINCENT*

From the Cape of Good Hope, March 1, 1661 [1]

My very dear and Honored Father,

I cannot but exclaim with the great Apostle of the Gentiles: "Oh! How deep are the riches and the wisdom and the knowledge of God! How inscrutable His judgments, how unsearchable His ways!" [2] *since for several years we have been trying to get to Saint-Laurent Island, also called* Madagascar, *to work in the Lord's vineyard but, having used every care and precaution imaginable, we have not yet been able to accomplish anything effective and assured there to support the new converts and extricate all the other inhabitants from the tyranny and slavery of Satan. For what more can be hoped for this land from your charity, O Monsieur, than what you have done! Your Company is small; yet, no opportunity to go there has presented itself without your providing a good number of workers to cultivate that vineyard. This is evident in the glorious deaths of your dear sons Messieurs Nacquart and Gondrée,* [3] *the first to do the groundwork on this land.*

The latter lasted only three months there; the other, after visiting several villages and bringing a good number of persons to the knowledge of the true faith, died after two years, in the odor of sanctity. This is apparent in what his successors wrote about him and the esteem in which he was held by the French and the indigenous inhabitants alike, and which they still have for him.

M. Mousnier, driven by zeal to be the first to announce the Gospel of Jesus Christ Our Lord in places where His sacred name was unknown, went off, as soon as he arrived, to a place twenty-five days distant from where he was living. Disregarding hunger and thirst, he would go two or three days without finding water, bearing the fatigue of the journey because of the great heat of that country. He reproached himself tacitly that, if so many young men were so courageous in going there, spurred on perhaps by the sole motivation of profit or honor, he had an even greater

---

Letter 3296. - Archives of the Mission, Paris, Madagascar file, copy. Not until his return to Holland early in July 1661 did Nicolas Étienne learn of the death of Saint Vincent on September 27 of the previous year.

[1]Étienne continued his letter after March 1, 1661.

[2]Rom 11:33. (NAB)

[3]The biographical sketches for Fathers Nacquart, Gondrée, and many of the other Missionaries who had been sent to Madagascar are in no. 3013.

motive to go, since it was for the glory of God and the salvation of souls. It was a journey on which he lost his life. But why do I say that he lost it because, as the Son of God says, he found it—not a feeble, ailing life, subject to earthly accidents here below, but a glorious, immortal one, free from every misery!

And what shall we say about Messieurs Dufour, Prévost, and de Belleville? The first has always been considered a bright star in our Company, not only because of his exhortations and his frequent, fervent sermons, but much more because of the practice of all the virtues he displayed, especially zeal for souls. He was so caught up by it that storms, shoals, shipwrecks—in a nutshell, all the inconveniences attached to a few worm-eaten planks, floating on a stormy, swollen sea, and those that are encountered in a foreign land—could not deter him, for the space of ten or twelve years, from begging Superiors to grant him the grace of dying beyond the seas among unbelievers.

In 1655 he finally obtained this with great joy and an intense desire to obtain, as far as possible, the glory of God and the conversion of souls. This was obvious on the ships, where he preached, catechized, instructed the ignorant, and admonished offenders—great or small—with no concern for human respect; so much so that, on one occasion, when the ship was in danger of being lost because no land was in sight and it was taking on a great deal of water, he had everyone assembled and, addressing the officers, who were despairing of their voyage, told them to raise their hands and promise God to do whatever he proposed to them. He assured them, in the name of God, that if they did, they would sight land within two weeks. They did so, and all promised to make a good general confession and Communion—except for two men, who died without the Sacraments.

The day finally arrived but, seeing no land, they went after this holy, apostolic man, telling him that they were sure their lives were over. Quite undisturbed, and placing his trust in God, he told them that the sun had not yet set and that they should come to Vespers, which he was going to chant. They did so, and behold—Oh! the wonders of God, who never abandons those who hope in Him—in the middle of all that, a sailor shouted "Land ho! Land ho!" This gladdened and consoled everyone, all the more so since it was the long-desired land of Madagascar. It turned out that those who had hated and persecuted him the most really changed their minds and, from then on, considered him a saint, as they themselves told me.

In the end, after his arrival on that island for which he had been yearning, he was able to remain there only one week, but not to be refreshed and to rest, since he accomplished a great deal there in that short time by his talks to the French, his acts of charity to the sick, and his many conversations with M. Bourdaise concerning ways to further the affairs of Jesus Christ in that land and to destroy those of Satan. He took to sea once again and went on to Sainte-Marie, an island about two hundred leagues from the fort. Immediately after his arrival there, after embracing his dear companion M. Prévost, he visited the sick, who were quite numerous, taking with him a young native to serve as interpreter and to carry twelve crosses that he had made to plant on the twelve mountains of that island. But, since he was able to plant only eleven, he planted the twelfth one in his own heart; for he became ill and died, after suffering unbearable bouts of fatigue.

He was, in addition, one of the most mortified men we four priests have ever known—all of us had the honor of being under his guidance at the same time in the seminary. May God grant that, as we were his sons and followers on his journeys, we may likewise be his imitators in the practice of virtue!

After having led a life like his companion M. Dufour, M. Prévost also died on Sainte-Marie Island, taking care of a good two hundred sick persons, who died there almost immediately afterward.

As for M. de Belleville, he died during the voyage.

The loss of so many great, fine workers does not deter you, Monsieur, from sending others to that land, which seems to be only a cemetery for your dear children. So, we can say of it what the Israelites said of the Promised Land: Illa terra devorat habitatores suos.[4]

In 1658 you sent still others, Messieurs Boussordec and Herbron, but the ship was wrecked on a sandbank, preventing them from coming to the aid of M. Bourdaise. Finally, in 1659 you sent four other priests, who were similarly prevented because they were captured by the Spanish.

Mais quoi! *All this has not sufficed to make you stop or to abandon your dear son, alone for seven or eight years, so you are sending four more priests—Messieurs Daveroult, de Fontaines, Feydin, and me—plus a seminarian, a Brother,*[5] *and a servant, to try this time to relieve him and to help him to bear the sweet yoke of the Son of God in the conquest of souls. But God, whose judgments are to be adored, has still not willed it this time, either because those people have proved themselves unworthy or to test our perseverance. I am more inclined to believe, however, that it is because of my enormous, innumerable sins, which I had committed before entering the Company, and even since I have been a member of it,*

---

[4]*That land consumes its inhabitants.* Cf. Nm 13:32. (NAB)
[5]Philippe Patte.

as well as the scandal and bad example I have given to both the confreres and the lay persons during our voyage. May God forgive me and grant me the grace of doing penance for this for the rest of my days!

This is the grace I entreat you to ask earnestly of God for me so that I may no longer be the cause of M. Bourdaise and these poor neophytes being deprived of the assistance your charity is trying to provide for them. Nor may I myself be prevented from going to help and serve them for the rest of my days; for I must confess in all simplicity, dearest Father, that my most heartfelt desire is to die for Our Lord Jesus Christ in a foreign land. I ask this very often of Him every day and will never stop asking until He grants it.

I hope that you in your goodness will make the same prayer for me and that I will no sooner be home than you will send me back again—but not to be in charge of others because no one in the Company is as unworthy of that as I, since I am young, ignorant, proud, and sinful. An experienced man is needed, one who is knowledgeable and proficient in temporal affairs, because there are many serious difficulties. Above all, he should be a man of solid virtue—not a beginner, but one seasoned by the years, who has gained many victories over himself—for experience shows only too clearly that, without solid virtue, which has been tried and tested for a long time, he will fall flat on his face, to the great detriment of the Christian religion. In addition, the one to whom you give this responsibility must be as strong and healthy as he is zealous and holy because, from my limited experience, working in foreign lands makes all that a necessity.

May our good God be pleased, then, to grant you the grace of choosing another Saint Francis Xavier for such a holy undertaking, and God grant that I may have the happiness of being under his guidance! I will consider myself blessed and will be most grateful to you for this.

CHAPTER I - OUR DEPARTURE FROM PARIS TO NANTES

After Messieurs Daveroult, de Fontaines, Feydin, Brother Patte, and I had received so much good advice from Your Charity, along with your blessing, and had embraced you as though for the last time, we left Saint-Lazare on November 4 to go to meet the Duc de la Meilleraye in Nantes. We arrived there the day he had appointed for us in his letter, namely, the twelfth of that month.

Along the way, in keeping with the custom of our Congregation, we taught Christian doctrine in front of inns, and elsewhere when the occasion arose. We even had the lay persons with us make the particular examination of conscience before dinner and supper, as well as the general one, pray the Itinerarium,[6] *the litany of the Holy Name of Jesus in the morning, and some hymns to the Most Holy and Immaculate Virgin Mary in the afternoon, with a short reading from the life of the Apostle Saint Paul by Godeau.*[7]

We applied ourselves particularly to the observance of our Rules, well aware that they are the channels by which favors and heavenly blessings flow into our souls. That is why we tried to spend the day in nearly the same way we do in our own houses. On Friday, we did what is usually done in the morning, and in the evening we had a conference; we always observed this. But all the glory of this must be attributed to God, and the good to the kindness and cooperation of the persons in our group; whereas, all the scandal and evil that slipped into it is entirely my fault—I who am the stumbling block and disgrace of your children.

While we were riding at full speed through Étampes, God allowed the braces of our carriage to become detached and its body to overturn. The door near which I was sitting was shattered, and my foot went through it, with the result that the wheel passed over it two or three times. I really thought my foot was broken in several places and my journey at an end, but God just wanted to give me a scare, and in five or six days' time I was perfectly healed.

When we arrived in Nantes we went to pay our respects to the Duke. To tell the truth, he surprised us at first by the way he spoke to us. That, however, did not frighten us, since we were completely resigned to whatever God might allow to happen to us. But the Divine Goodness, which had made use of you, Monsieur, to remove all obstacles and hindrances in the way of the execution of our plan, changed everything, and that good Duke subsequently showed us a great deal of affection. He often invited us to his table, and I spent several hours alone with him, speaking of pious subjects. We discussed in particular his plans for Madagascar and how he wanted to do his utmost to establish the Catholic religion by erecting several forts on the land and placing our priests there. I hope that, if God preserves his life, he will be instrumental in the growth of the faith in that country and the progress of our Company. He esteems you very highly and feels the same love for your sons. He manifested this when we said good-bye, weeping openly as he embraced me.

---

[6]Special prayers said at the beginning of a journey by those who were traveling, especially clerics.

[7]Antoine Godeau, *La vie de l'apôtre saint Paul* (Paris: Vve J. Camusat, 1647). A new edition appeared in 1651 and was translated into English in 1653.

The whole time we were in Nantes, we observed exactly what is done in our houses, including reading at table, even though other people were sometimes present. We nearly always stayed at home; after finishing our duties, we prepared materials for the mission we were supposed to give aboard ship.

When we were ready to leave for La Rochelle, we decided to go by sea. But the senior members of the crew and M. Beaulieu, to whom we are greatly indebted for their gestures of friendship and courtesy, did their best to dissuade us, as did many other persons. Nevertheless, considering that, in the boat where our baggage was stored, there were thirty-eight persons who were to be our flock, I could not bring myself to abandon them, preferring to perish with them rather than to see them die without their priest and shepherd. That would have been one of the worst things that could have happened to us, and I am sure God would have demanded an account of it from me.

So, having made this decision, I asked those men to kindly go by coach and to allow Brother Patte, Messieurs Boutonnet and Cordelet,[8] *and me to go by sea. They did their best to change my mind, but I persisted in my decision, trusting that God would grant me the grace of guiding me safely into port, since my only aim in that was His glory.*

CHAPTER II - FROM NANTES TO LA ROCHELLE

After spending twenty-four days in Nantes, we finally set sail from La Fosse between 11 a.m. and noon on December 6, the feast of Saint Nicolas, patron of ferrymen and my own patron, whom I am asking and have asked during Holy Mass to be our pilot and guide. God permitted our boat, however, to be stranded for ten hours on a sandbank opposite the port of La Vigne. We dropped anchor and around six in the morning went ashore in a longboat. It was Sunday, December 7; Brother Patte and I heard Mass and received Communion at Saint-Pierre de Bouguenais, where we were very edified. After the priest had said: Domine non sum dignus, *another priest arrived, who gathered all the children and young people around him and recited before the people the* Pater, Ave, Credo, Confiteor, Benedicite, *the Commandments, the thanksgiving prayers, the Sacraments, and a few other prayers, all in Latin and French. Then he went on to recite the substance of the mysteries of our faith. This takes place every Sunday and*

---

[8]Boutonnet and Cordelet were laymen who sailed on the ship that was to take Nicolas Étienne and his confreres to Madagascar.

holy day. O mon Dieu! *how I wish that holy practice might be observed in all the churches in the world!*

The following day, December 8, consecrated to the Immaculate Conception of the Blessed Virgin Mary Mother of God, we dropped anchor in the harbor of Paimboeuf. After celebrating Holy Mass there, we went on to the port of Saint-Nazaire, where we remained for five days, leaving on Saturday the thirteenth with the wind behind us. This led us to hope that we would reach La Rochelle in less than twenty-four hours, but God, who does all things for the best, had other plans: we were trying to round the dunes of Bordeaux because our skipper had taken us about ten leagues off course; however, the Lord of the winds allowed a northwest wind to come up, which snapped our main mast in two and toppled it into the sea, along with the mainsail. But what was much worse is that it was driving us on to a sandbank called Soulac, causing everyone to fear for his life.

I was very seasick at the time, vomiting night and day, unable to keep anything on my stomach, when M. Guelton,[9] *Brother Patte, the skipper, and the pilot, weeping copiously, came to me and said that there was no chance of saving their lives and that I should hurry to give them absolution. So I had myself hoisted immediately on top of our mattress and gave general absolution, as best as I could. Then I asked them to carry me to the hatchway—not so much to observe the fury of that tempestuous sea as to try to console the men, who were letting out pitiful, lamentable cries. No sooner was I there than I seemed to take on new strength and an assurance of life. This prompted me to assure them that they would not perish but should put their trust in God's goodness and mercy.*

Then something both amazing and admirable happened! I had no sooner exhorted them to hope in God, when, at the same instant, the northwest wind shifted to the north! This caused us to avoid the Soulac sandbank, which, without God's special protection, would have become the burial place of all of us. The wind was so wild that our ship, called the Maréchale, *having left Port-Louis on December 14 for La Rochelle to take on victuals for the voyage to Madagascar, lost its longboat there, and the great* écouet [10] *snapped at the same time our mast did, so they told us. Its mainsail was ripped to pieces, and a sailor, who was on the tip of the main yard, fell to the deck and died. It was decided to drop a heavy anchor and ride out the storm until the good weather, but no sooner was it in the deeps than it broke away.*

---

[9]Governor of Fort-Dauphin (Madagascar), who was returning to that post.

[10]Rope whose thickness gradually diminishes from one end to the other.

Finally, after avoiding the sandbank, we were borne by our foremast and its useless sail—although we thought they were still good—toward the Spanish coast, when suddenly the wind drove us back toward the mouth of the river of Bordeaux. We drifted for two or three days at the mercy of the waves; no one dared to appear on the deck because the waves, seven to eight muids [11] high, were sweeping over it. If our boat had not been so solid and well joined, and had it taken on water, it would have been the end of us.

In this peril and danger, I suggested to the entire group, soldiers and sailors alike, that they take a vow in honor of the Immaculate Virgin Mary around midnight of this octave of the feast of her Conception, and all of them willingly accepted. The vow consisted in celebrating twelve Masses in her honor, which I have done, by the grace of God; in all of us going to confession and communion, which we have also done; and lastly, in clothing twelve poor persons, which I have written to ask you to have someone do, since there are no poor here who need clothes, because it is a hot country. Besides, the majority of those who had taken the vow went their way and are poor workmen. Just one gave me a pistole and the others promised money. But, given the uncertainty of the poor and of the very risky future, I implore and entreat you once again to kindly give instructions to have twelve poor persons clothed in a garment of plain homespun fabric.

In addition to the prayers we said morning and evening, we recited the Office of the Immaculate Conception. Despite this, God still willed to visit us with another gust of wind, which drove us back onto the Spanish coast, and, for want of mast and sails, we were unable to enter any harbor. This added to our distress because there were thirty-six of us without bread, meat, or water, crying out with hunger and thirst. In this dire situation, we did our best to run the ship aground for four or five days, preferring our lives to our supplies and merchandise; but it was impossible to do this, causing everyone to despair of his life. I am ashamed to say that a man as wicked as I, the worst of all sinners, having committed so many crimes, abominations, and sins in my past life, deserving no less temporal than eternal fire, and who still daily offends the Divine Majesty because of my lack of reverence and devotion and my frequent scandals, received such abundant consolation and grace that I was quite unafraid in the midst of such clear danger, while everyone else was sobbing and frightened to death.

---

[11] A muid is a measure of capacity that varied from province to province.

And, although the words of Jesus Christ: "He who finds his life shall lose it; and he that loses his life for me, shall find it,"[12] *are very easy to listen to simply in a theoretical context, they are not so easy when they have to be put into practice. For, when you reach a point of no return, and life must be lost in order to find it in God; when death is hanging over your head and you see clearly that, if you obey God, you must die; then fear grips the basest part of the soul and throws the spirit into such black darkness that the precept that previously seemed so clear is hidden from the eyes of reason and is suddenly enveloped in an unbelievably obscure night, to the point that not even those to whom education and human prudence have given greater insight can conceive this excellent truth properly. Only those to whom God, by a special favor, deigns to communicate a few rays of His divine light can understand the strength and the meaning of those words. In this our poor nature clearly shows its weakness and wretchedness.*

Finally, in this extremity, God was pleased to visit and console us on December 21, the solemnity of the feast of Saint Thomas,[13] *the glorious Apostle of the Indies, after we had spent two weeks of distress and anguish on this vast, terrifying ocean.*

Near San Sebastián He sent us an angel who, with eighteen of his companions, towed us to Saint-Jean-de-Luz. This angel was a true pilot and a very upright man, who was going fishing in his longboat with his friends. When one of our men on watch saw it, he notified M. Guelton, who had them hailed in Spanish, telling them they should come aboard because we had neither mast nor sail. He said that we were Frenchmen on our way from Nantes to La Rochelle, who had been driven by the wind to this place, and that we would give them anything they wanted if they would take us to Saint-Jean-de-Luz.

We agreed with the pilot, then, for sixty livres and a few bottles of brandy for his men. So, they hitched their longboat to our boat and, by dint of rowing, guided it there at daybreak.

When we arrived, we disembarked; but, partly because of illness, partly because of the little I had eaten during all that time, or because of the motion and agitation of the rough seas, I could barely stand up straight. We heard Mass that day, then started to furnish our boat with necessary items such as masts, sails, ropes, and victuals. The following day, the twenty-third, having given thirteen golden louis as our share and leaving

---

[12]Cf. Mt 10:39. (D-RB)

[13]Now July 3.

Cordelet to return in the boat to mind our baggage, I left Saint-Jean-de-Luz by mail coach. To make better time, M. Boutonnet, Brother Patte, and I traveled night and day to try to stop the Maréchale *if it had not already left, reaching the boat, which was there ahead of me. It took us six and a half days to get to La Rochelle because the weather was very cold and riding was very difficult because of the icy roads. We were always afraid of falling, but God took care of us as well as He had done on the boat.*

We finally reached La Rochelle on December 29, between six and seven in the evening, to the astonishment of most of the townspeople, who thought we had drowned, and especially of our confreres, who were no longer expecting us and were ready to depart the following day. I leave you to imagine what a joyful reunion we had.

The next day I went to pay my respects to the Bishop,[14] *who embraced me warmly, as did the religious and the communities, who had already celebrated Requiem Masses for my soul. For my part, I confess that I was quite surprised at the joy expressed at my arrival by everyone, even the Huguenots. I received some visits that I tried to repay, especially to the religious Orders, the Jesuits, and the Oratorian Fathers. During the short time we remained in that town, M. Dehorgny, who was making a visitation in Luçon, honored us with his presence; this gave us great consolation.*

CHAPTER III - WHAT MESSIEURS DAVEROULT, DE FONTAINES, AND FEYDIN DID IN LA ROCHELLE

They left Nantes on December 3, arriving in La Rochelle on the fifth and going to pay their respects to the Bishop, who welcomed them very affectionately and cordially. They offered to do whatever he wished of them during the time they would have the happiness of residing in his town. He asked them, through one of his chaplains, to render some services in Saint-Jean parish, one of the poor, destitute parishes in the town, which had been abandoned by its Pastor; he himself did so at a later date. So, they obeyed his voice as if it were the voice of God because they saw how much help that church needed. Moreover, although they had offered in the beginning to go and stay on the ship, the owners did not think that advisable yet.

One of them used to celebrate daily Mass there; another did so at the Hospitallers.[15] *They heard confessions there throughout Christmastide*

[14]Jacques-Raoul de la Guibourgère.

[15]Hospital Sisters of Charity of Notre-Dame.

and all during Midnight Mass. M. de Fontaines, who had arrived in the town on the eighteenth, taught catechism there, as well as at the prison, as did all the others, to prepare the detainees to spend that season well. They also offered to help the Brothers of Charity with the care of the sick. All the religious Orders and communities gave them a very warm welcome, telling them how much they shared their sorrow and affliction because everyone had given us up for dead.

CHAPTER IV - OUR ARRIVAL ON BOARD SHIP

M. Daveroult left La Rochelle on the last day of the year with Brother Patte and all our baggage so he could board ship in order to begin well the work of 1660. He did so by hearing a few confessions, celebrating Mass, and giving a sermon, followed by Vespers, which he chanted. We remained in town another two or three days after him to put all our little affairs in order; then we left, fortified by the Bishop's blessing. He sent his chaplain to bring us corporals, purificators, palls, and three large flasks of holy oils, which we accepted. He stayed with us for three or four hours until we were afloat, saying that Monseigneur had instructed him to do so, and that, were it not for his infirmity, that good Prelate would have come in person because he has such great esteem for you and your entire Company. He insisted that I write to him from Saint-Laurent.

On January 3 Messieurs de Fontaines and Feydin my companions and I, along with Messieurs Boutonnet and Cordelet, arrived at the ship called the Maréchale. *The officers gave us a warm welcome. The gunners' room, called Sainte-Barbe, which seemed to be the most convenient place for us, was assigned us as living quarters. They also offered us the use of the poop area and the captain's large salon, but we refused it for fear of inconveniencing them, as we ourselves also might have been. So they rigged up five beds of planks and cords for us and a hammock for our servant, the only gunner who had to sleep in our room.*

We remained on board for two weeks before raising anchor, during which time we looked at what we would have to do and had a few conferences on this topic.

On the first Sunday of the year, M. de Fontaines went to say Mass on the island of Aix, where there are no priests. The Oratorians are its seigneurs, but they come there only on the four principal feasts of the year. It is about three or four leagues from La Rochelle. Only eight to ten families live in the place; I visited them on the Epiphany, after celebrating Holy Mass there. They are fairly well instructed in the mysteries of our faith. Their church is totally in ruins; all that is left is a little underground chapel.

While I was on the island, news was brought to me that a man had died on board. I sent for the body and, meanwhile, had a grave dug on the seashore. Since it was already late and it was getting harder to see, I gave orders to notify me at the place where I was staying with M. Coulon, squire to the Duc de la Meilleraye; unfortunately, however, the sailors buried him themselves without informing me.

The following day, Brother Patte arrived, bringing me a packet of letters from you. In them I learned of your sorrow and resignation to God's Will regarding our death, about which you had been notified. I also learned that good M. Perraud had died, for whom each of us has said three Masses, and that His Holiness has granted the ordination retreat to our house in Rome. This makes us very happy in the hope that God wanted to make use of the Little Company to reform the clergy of Italy as it had done for that of France. He also informed me that the dead man I had asked to be brought to me for burial was Brother Ambroise.[16] *I had visited him on board when he was sick and encouraged him to go to confession but had not recognized him, even though he had our manner of acting. That surprised me.*

A brief reflection might be made here on the misfortune of those who leave the Company; for this poor boy left the sheltering wings of his good mother without her permission. Even though he died fortified by all the sacraments, God allowed him to be the plaything and laughing stock of most of the crew. He was quite naked, shoeless, and abandoned like some forlorn person for whom no one wished to care. After his death they found that he had a cross, a rosary, and four silver écus, which the captain gave to Brother Patte to be given to us. We accepted them only on condition that the money be used to buy some little refreshments for the sick. That is why we asked Brother Patte to go to La Rochelle on this errand and to see if we had any letters from you. Each of us has said three Masses for the poor deceased.

While the ship was riding at anchor in the harbor, four or five men died. This was due more to the severe cold than to anything else because I do not think we have had such biting weather for a long time nor has it lasted so long.

I also visited the château on Oléron Island to try to get an architect to come with us. M. Véron our captain led me to hope for this, provided I go

---

[16]Ambroise Tumy, born in Argenteuil (Val-d'Oise), entered the Congregation of the Mission as a coadjutor Brother on August 10, 1644, at twenty years of age, and took his vows in December 1652.

there in person. But that good man did not dare to commit himself to such a long voyage. He would have been a man that we really needed, and if you were to have the kindness of sending us one on one of the next ships to come—along with some bricklayers, carpenters, joiners, locksmiths, and lumbermen—you would be doing a tremendous favor for our little establishment.

I wrote you several letters from Saint-Jean-de-Luz, Bordeaux, Saintes, La Rochelle, and aboard ship, Monsieur, but *I never received any from you to let me know that you received mine.*[17] *To be frank, this made me a little sad, knowing how keenly you felt the accident that everyone thought had befallen us—all the more so, because we were about to raise anchor and set sail and, consequently, would have no hope of receiving any letters for two or three years.* Adieu, *then, our very dear and Most Honored Father. My companions and I ask for your blessing because we have no further hope of seeing you again, except in heaven, and with your blessing we will sail better on this vast and terrifying element.*

CHAPTER V - THE MOST NOTEWORTHY EVENTS OF OUR VOYAGE

On Sunday, January 18, 1660, feast of the Chair of Saint Peter in Rome, we got under way for the voyage to Madagascar, after celebrating most holy Mass. God gave us very fine weather, which brought us safely to the Canary Islands on Thursday, February 5.

We dropped anchor in the harbor of Santa Cruz, near the island of Tenerife. Several Spaniards paid us a visit and expressed their great joy at the peace made between the two crowns.[18] *A few days before, when the captains had opened the orders of the Duc de la Meilleraye as to what they should do both during the journey and on the island of Madagascar, they read that His Lordship wanted them to undertake nothing of importance without communicating it to me. So, they informed me of his wishes and had me read everything contained in the orders. That is why they thought it advisable for me to go to greet the Governor and to assure him of the peace between the two Kings. He received us most cordially and, while I was with him, the Governor General of all the islands sent him a written note with a servant to notify him of our arrival, telling him to give us whatever we needed for our ship and that he would soon come to the fort.*

---

[17]Only two other letters (nos. 3058 and 3086) from Nicolas Étienne are extant.

[18]The result of the marriage of Louis XIV to the Spanish Infanta Maria Teresa.

I had no sooner left than he arrived, which obliged me to go pay my respects to him. He welcomed M. Daveroult and me with great cordiality. He is a venerable old lord of great piety. We remained one-half to three-quarters of an hour with him, speaking partly in French and partly in Spanish. He was so overjoyed about the union between the two monarchs that at that very hour he ordered a longboat to be readied for him to go to board our ship and to express this to the captains.

I entreated him most humbly to defer his visit until the next day because of his age and ailments and because he had just alighted from horseback. In addition, night was falling and all that could have been prejudicial to his health; everyone around him told him the same thing. Although his age prompted me to speak in that way, I was doing it even more so in order that the captains might be forewarned and have time to receive him according to his rank.

Early the next morning he came aboard, and the first thing he requested was the Mass. He was very cordial with the officers. He did not wish to stay for dinner, excusing himself because of his ailments and accepting only a drop of brandy. His visit to our ship surprised all the Spaniards and every other foreign ship anchored in the same harbor because he had not yet done this honor to any ship other than ours.

I wrote to you from that island, Monsieur, through a merchant from Saint-Malo; I also wrote to the Duke, who had asked me to do so.

There is a very high mountain on that island; they say it is one of the highest mountains in the world and that, from one side it can be seen from a distance of thirty leagues. Personally, I was able to see it from only fifteen or sixteen leagues away.

On Saturday, February 7, after having offered the most august Sacrifice of the Mass that the Eternal Father might be pleased to give us favorable weather, we raised anchor at five o'clock in the morning and got under way from the Santa Cruz harbor, setting our course toward the islands of Cape Verde. En route, since the weather was calm for three or four days, we fished at fifty-eight fathoms for parquet, *a very tasty fish.*

On Wednesday, February 18, we rounded Cape Verde at about four o'clock in the afternoon. We dropped anchor in twenty-two fathoms of water in the great bay inside the Cape, just above a little island inhabited by the Flemish.

That same evening, we saw four Dutch ships anchored near the island; around nine o'clock the next morning, they came to reconnoiter (there were two fleets). One of them had a flag flying from the main mast and carried about eighteen guns; another, twelve; and the other two, from six to eight guns. They were equipped as frigates and were approaching our ship. They arrived under the north wind and ordered us to bring our commission aboard their ship. This they were refused and were ordered to come aboard our ship themselves, which they were unwilling to do. So, we separated in order to try to reach the harbor of Rufisque[19] *to take on our water supply.*

The following morning, Friday, the twentieth of the month, our long-boat, with M. Guelton on board, was sent to the island where the Flemish are living to find out from the Governor the reason for the four ships. He replied that he had acted only as a measure of security since, under cover of the French flag, M. Duquesne[20] *had pillaged them. The Governor was very polite to M. Guelton. The two forts saluted us with eight or ten salvos. The four ships and ours returned the salute. That same day, at about four o'clock in the afternoon, we dropped anchor in the harbor of Rufisque in eight fathoms of water, where the bottom is sandy.*

CHAPTER VI - CAPE VERDE AND ITS INHABITANTS

Rufisque is a place on dry land about two leagues from the Cape. The site is very pleasant. It is flat country, covered extensively with evergreens. About six or seven thousand persons live there. Their houses are huts covered with rushes. The people are very black and completely naked and are, for the most part, Muslims. They work at making cotton cloth, going fishing in small dugout canoes, and hunting with arrows and darts. The water there is very salty; sweet water is found only one or two leagues inland. Fowl, wild game, goats, cattle, and horses are quite plentiful. Millet and rice, from which they make their bread, are less common. They drink palm wine, which has a very pleasant taste when it is fresh.

There is a King in the area, living a few leagues from the Cape, who is very powerful and always keeps about three or four thousand horses. He likes white persons very much—I mean foreigners—and will not allow them to be harmed or wronged in any way.

Men from Dieppe often come here and are good friends of theirs. In fact, a boat arrived while we were there, which gave me the chance to write to you through them.

In years past, the Portuguese traded extensively in the area, but now the Dutch and the Flemish occupy most of their forts. So much so that, in Rufisque, where they used to be numerous, they are now down to ten or

---

[19]A city on the west coast of Africa, in what is today known as Senegal.

[20]Abraham Duquesne (1610-88), a noted French admiral.

twelve and have been without a priest for two years. They had someone ask us to come to celebrate Holy Mass for them.

So, the following day we dropped anchor, and M. Feydin and I went there to say Mass. The sea was rough and drove our longboat onto a rock, which should have been our tomb if God had not sent a wave that flung us off it, and in this way we were saved. When we set foot on land, I knelt down to beg God in His goodness to have pity on those poor souls and not allow them to be lost.

Next, we went with our captain to pay our respects to the local Governor. After that, we went to the place where the Portuguese were living, celebrated the Most Holy Sacrifice of the Mass, and blessed a pail of holy water. They told us of their trials and asked us, while we would be in the harbor, to come to celebrate daily Mass in their chapel—which was very clean but had no priestly vestments—and to hear their confessions. When we hesitated, they countered with so many good reasons and expressed such great desire that we would have felt guilty and would have had to answer to God had we not complied with their holy request. We all dined with them.

After that, my companion and I went into the woods to converse with one another and say our Office. When a group of children gathered around us, I showed them our crucifix and a picture of the Most Holy and Immaculate Virgin Mary Mother of God, which they all admired and kissed. I even drew a cross on their chest with a red pencil and they were delighted. They believe in one God, paradise, and hell, and highly esteem Jesus Christ, whom they consider a great prophet; but they make no mention of His Virgin Mother. They would have been quite happy to follow us, provided we had been in France. Most of them speak French fairly well because of the men from Dieppe who often come there.

When we returned to our ship that evening, we discussed what we would have to do during our stay in that place and thought it fitting that M. Daveroult, who understood Portuguese, should go every day with one of us to celebrate Mass and give an instruction morning and evening in Portuguese. He also heard confessions, which went on for five or six days from morning to evening, since he heard about thirty-nine or forty persons. For, although I said that there are only ten or twelve in that locality, there are others living four or five leagues away. Then, too, there are some tenant farms where converted slaves are working.

On the feast of Saint Mathias,[21] *M. Daveroult, assisted by M. Feydin,*

[21]February 24 (now May 14).

solemnly baptized two children, and the following day he baptized four more without the ceremonies because he had not been notified ahead of time, and we were not going to return ashore. It certainly was a great joy to your sons, Monsieur and very dear Father, to have begotten children to Our Lord Jesus Christ in a heathen country and to have reconciled those who had separated themselves from Him by sin.

Only one thing upset us, and that was to leave them without help and assistance. Oh! would to God that Your Charity might be willing to obtain from His Holiness a mission for this country! The workers would reap a fine harvest because of the number of persons living there and the King's love and affection for the French! Then, too, this would be an excellent port of call for Missionaries going to Madagascar. Ah! As I write this letter, I cannot help but cry out with the great Apostle of our own time, Saint Francis Xavier, against those Doctors who are more capable than charitable; more knowledgeable than conscientious, and who, through their own fault, allow so many souls to be lost daily, who would be saved if they were to come to their assistance.

On Sunday, February 28, after saying Mass, we raised anchor to head for the equator.

On the feast of Saint Joseph,[22] *one of our sailors fell overboard but, either through the intercession of this great saint or because he had made his peace with God just a few days previously, God rescued him and saved him from the waves of that ocean.*

At noon on March 22, we crossed the equator and sang the Te Deum *in thanksgiving. The heat is not as intense as I would have thought from the way experienced persons describe it. It did not inconvenience us at all, although we were in Lent; and I must admit that, even with the sun directly overhead, I found it more bearable than the heat of August in France.*

On April 3, M. Feydin, one of our dear confreres, became ill with a constant fever and diarrhea, putting him in danger of death. He was quite sick for five or six weeks but is very well now, by the grace of God, except that he sometimes suffers from stomach ache.

On the seventh of the same month, God granted us the grace of passing the place they call Ouvre logues *("Open your eyes"), which are very dangerous rocks*[23] *off the coast of Brazil, extending for more than forty leagues into the sea. When they cannot be rounded, there is nothing else*

---

[22]March 19.

[23]"Reefs," from which the city of Recife takes its name.

to do but turn around and go back home or spend the winter in Brazil. This obliged us to sing the Te Deum *once again in thanksgiving.*

At daybreak on Friday, May 7, we encountered two Dutch ships coming from the Cape of Good Hope. We were only about thirty leagues southeast and northwest from there, and that same day, about seven in the morning, we sighted land eight or ten leagues to the north of the Bay of Saldanha. When night overtook us, we could not locate Saldanha and had to take to sea again, veering west toward the Cape. Around seven or eight o'clock in the evening, however, the wind blew west and west-southwest, bringing very bad weather; since we were only three or four leagues from land, we were in danger of hitting the coast and of being lost, but God preserved us that time.

Throughout that night we were busy hearing confessions and encouraging our people to trust in the mercy of God, since they were expecting to die at any moment. I was convinced, however, that God would protect us, and felt no fear within me. I considered myself fortunate to die like a good soldier, sword in hand—I mean while hearing the confessions of our flock. And I would never have believed that once again a soul in the jaws of death, burdened with crimes like mine, could have enjoyed so much peace and tranquility and have such trust in God. Only those who have experienced this can believe it and be convinced that it is so. That is why the servants of God should not fear crossing the seas to go to help their brothers, regardless of any dangers and tribulations there may be.

On Saturday, May 8, we were only four or five leagues from land and unable to move off, so we had to sail into Table Bay at seven or eight in the evening. Since we could not keep from drifting onto the coast, we dropped anchor in ten or twelve fathoms of water, very close to land.

The weather was very bad on Sunday and continued on Monday; so, to avoid the coast, we had to let out one of our cables to its full length and anchor near the Dutch port.

On Pentecost Monday, the Governor received us splendidly in his fort.

On Tuesday the weather worsened considerably and, to make matters worse, our cable was severed while we were dropping a second anchor. We think this was due to another one left in the anchorage. We replaced it immediately, but when the wind increased instead of dying down, our main anchor broke and the other cable snapped. This brought us to the coast around eight o'clock Thursday morning, May 19. All through the night we heard the confessions of our men, who fully expected to die. However, when daylight came, we saw that we had been saved by the Providence of God from the rocks that were not very far from us. The sea was so rough that only four or five men were able to swim to safety that day. Our ship had lost its longboat, and the Governor sent us one on a wagon, but it could not be launched because of the violence and fury of the sea. So, Captain Véron and I embarked—but not without danger because our longboat was swamped by a wave. The captain was afraid it would break into pieces because it was already leaking, but God preserved us again that time and, thanks to Him, we escaped with nothing worse than a fright and a dousing.

CHAPTER VII - HOW WE SPENT OUR TIME ON BOARD SHIP

Before I launch into a description of our activities at the Cape of Good Hope, Monsieur, I am sure you would like to know about our conduct and occupations aboard ship for the four entire months we spent on it. That is why I will give you a simple account of it here.

From the time we embarked until we reached the Cape of Good Hope, we celebrated Mass on all Sundays and feast days—except three or four times when the weather did not allow it—as well as once or twice during the week. We used the captain's quarters for this and, although he was a Huguenot, he never raised any objections nor prevented us from making our devotions, leaving the room at our disposal. Only one of us said the Mass; the others donned surplices and stoles and received Holy Communion; we each took turns at this.

Every Sunday we replenished the holy water. At two o'clock we preached on mission themes; after that, we put on our stoles and birettas and sang Vespers and Compline in plainchant, as in Richelieu. We did this throughout our voyage and did the same on all the feast days. Morning and evening we recited prayers publicly, as our Congregation does during our missions.

We had the blessing of candles on the feast of the Purification of the Blessed Virgin Mary [24] *and distributed them to all the chief officers.*

On Ash Wednesday, we had the usual ceremony and distributed ashes to all the Catholics. The previous evening we had given them a brief instruction to prepare them for the proper reception of the ashes and to spend this holy season of Lent well. By the grace of God, we ourselves observed it as we do in our houses, regardless of the fact that meat is served on Sunday, Monday, Tuesday, and Thursday because of the heat, illness, and other inconveniences of sea voyages. For that reason, we gave permission to eat it, except on Wednesdays, Fridays, and Saturdays.

---

[24] February 2. This feast is now known as "The Presentation of the Lord."

On Palm Sunday, we distributed palms to all those of our faith; we had made provision for this at Cape Verde and distributed them in the way it is done at Saint-Lazare. In the afternoon we preached on the General Judgment, since the preceding evening we had spoken to them about the obligation everyone had of going to confession and Communion during those two weeks, and how to do it properly.

On Holy Thursday, we sang High Mass on the poop deck, which was well decorated, for a ship. We had set up a small altar of repose in the captain's quarters, on which to place Our Lord until the following day, and at the end of the Mass we took Him there in the accustomed way. Then we stripped the altars and had the washing of the feet. After dinner we sang Tenebrae,[25] *which almost everyone attended. We did the same on Wednesday and Friday and, wearing surplices, we, and one of our Catholics, took turns every two hours before the Blessed Sacrament.*

On Good Friday I preached a sermon on the Passion from six to seven-thirty in the morning, then we began the customary service, with M. Feydin chanting the Passion. After everyone had venerated the Cross, we went to bring Our Lord back and terminated the service because of bad weather.

On Easter Sunday each of us celebrated Mass with the utmost solemnity possible, and most of our flock received Holy Communion at High Mass. Before distributing Our Lord, we gave the exhortation on Communion as is done during our missions. God blessed this, and the men responded more with their eyes than with their voices to the questions I addressed to them—even the officers and others of whom I would not have expected it. After dinner I spoke about the mystery; then we chanted Vespers.

During Lent, Messieurs de Fontaines and Feydin alternated teaching catechism three times a week, and all of us took our turn giving the exhortations.

Every day M. de Fontaines gathered the young people together, reciting the rosary with them one day and the Seven Psalms[26] *the next. In the evening he often discussed with them what they had been taught at catechism and other instructions.*

Our whole flock, composed of about one hundred eight or one hundred ten Catholics, made their Easter duty, with the exception of three or four

---

[25]The term given to the hours of Matins and Lauds in the Divine Office for Holy Thursday, Good Friday, and Holy Saturday, as they were observed before the 1955 reform of the Holy Week liturgy by Pope Pius XII.

[26]Recitation of the Seven Penitential Psalms (Psalms 6, 31, 37, 50, 101, 129, and 142) was a popular devotion in the past.

persons. The rest—thirty-six to forty—were Huguenots. Some came to divine services and our little instructions, but none of them was converted by them.

Our daily schedule was more or less the same as the one in our houses, except that we had to adapt ourselves to the weather, places, and persons.

After mental prayer and the Divine Office, we recited the Itinerarium *so that God might be pleased to give us a safe journey. Then each read his New Testament privately and applied himself to study what he needed most. Between one and two in the afternoon we read together the letters of Saint Francis Xavier to try to pattern ourselves on him, since you had given him to us as patron and model. On Fridays, we did not omit what is practiced in the morning in all our houses,*[27] *enclosing ourselves for this purpose in the little room belonging to M. Karkadiou, one of the captains. Immediately after this act, we began our conference, sometimes on the five virtues that make up the spirit of the Mission, sometimes on our Rules and on our needs and those of the ship, in order to remedy them.*

We did not have repetition[28] *very often because the location did not lend itself to it.*

We took turns caring for the sick; each one had his week, visiting them twice a day and bringing them holy water.

We had extra conferences on the sacraments and, with regard to visiting the sick, we decided that none of us priests would take food to the patients any longer, nor advise them to be bled, nor take their pulse, but leave all this (to follow our manual on this point) to Brother Patte, who would also visit them twice a day and notify us of those who might be ill. He had instructions to tell them that, if they wanted some relief in their suffering, they should go to confession before he applied his remedies so that God might bless them. Most of them did so. That good Brother fulfilled his task so well that everyone loved him, important persons as well as ordinary

---

[27]The chapter of faults: "So that we in our weakness can to some extent imitate Christ's self-humiliation and his willingness to be ranked with sinners, each one every Friday, in the presence of others, is to acknowledge his failings to the Superior or someone replacing him." (Cf. *Common Rules of the Congregation of the Mission* X, §13.) With the revision of the Constitutions and Statutes after Vatican Council II, this practice is no longer in force.

[28]Repetition of prayer, another pious practice in the Congregation of the Mission. According to the *Regulae seminarii interni Congregationis Missionis* (Paris, 1888), a novice/seminarian, at the request of the Superior or Novice Master/Director of the Internal Seminary, would stand and give an account of his morning meditation, a reflection, judgments, inspirations, and the resolutions resulting from pondering the topic assigned for meditation. Until the 1983 revision of the Constitutions and Statutes of the Congregation of the Mission, this practice perdured not just in the seminary but in all the local communities.

ones, Huguenots as well as Catholics. I am sure that God sent him to this ship for the welfare and relief of everyone, since the only other medical person was a young apprentice, and for a long period of time he was very ill.

So, Monsieur, you can judge from that what a heavy workload he had, both in caring for us and in being occupied almost the entire time of our voyage with nursing about twenty to twenty-five sick men, not one of whom died. I am convinced that this favor—truly extraordinary for such long voyages—as well as the excellent, perfect health he always enjoyed, was granted him by God as a reward for the great care and charity he had for them.

This voyage, as far as the Cape of Good Hope, can be considered one of the most fortunate ever made, except for the death of one man. We had no bad weather or unfortunate encounters; there was also no dissension but, rather, great union and regular order, as you have been able to see from what I have written. It seemed, Monsieur, that after all the graces and favors God bestowed on us during the course of our voyage we had to come safely to port and land happily on that favored Saint-Laurent Island. God, however, did not will that it be at that time. May His Holy Name be blessed and glorified forever for it!

CHAPTER VIII - WHAT WE DID DURING THE TIME WE SPENT IN TABLE BAY AT THE CAPE OF GOOD HOPE

Having briefly described what we did on the ship called the Maréchale, *I thought it my duty also to give you a report of the ten to twelve months we spent at the Cape of Good Hope. So, let me tell you, Monsieur, that we landed—M. Daveroult and I a little wet—on Thursday, May 20. M. Daveroult remained on the shore to look after the men who had reached land by swimming; two or three of them died because they had drunk brandy. Accompanied by Messieurs Véron and Guelton, I went immediately to see the Governor to try to get him to agree to help us in our misfortune and advise us what to do. We dined there and he treated us with the greatest courtesy. He always continued to act this way with us, even though he belonged to a different religion. I would not say he acted as one friend to another, but as a brother toward his brothers and even as a father toward his children.*

His wife was especially kind, as you will be able to see further on. Except for her religion, she is one of the wisest women I have ever met; in fact, everyone loves her. I never noticed in her the slightest indication of passion, although I visited her often. No matter what she was involved in, she had such excellent self-control that she never seemed to react, even in a few debates I had with her, considering that she is the daughter of a Rotterdam minister and well versed in Holy Scripture. She is not at all opinionated, which is rather rare, and I do not think it would be difficult to convert her, if she were a widow. I am ashamed to write this about a Huguenot, when I myself am so filled with passions. Even though I am a priest and doing the work of an Apostle, instead of enlightening and serving others, I am a stumbling block and a source of scandal to them.

After dinner Messieurs de Fontaines and Feydin came ashore, and we found a place to stay near the fort. We remained there only two weeks, partly because our landlady was rather difficult and partly because we had to find 220 livres every month, not counting other small, unforeseen expenses, although we were poorly fed and even more poorly housed. Imagine my worry at having seven persons on my hands and no money, and being in an unknown place at the other end of the world, living among pagans and heretics. This would assuredly have been a very great worry if God had not come to our rescue, which I earnestly hoped. You can add to that my work during that first month, which was:

(1) To satisfy our little family, when there is so much to be done in such circumstances;

(2) To console the captains and their crew of 140 men and to keep the peace among them because it is very difficult in such situations to prevent divisions among the officers as well as among the crew;

(3) To deal with the Governor, to whom I had to go almost every day because he would treat matters with the captains only in my presence, and the captains would make no decision without telling me because that was the written order they had received from the Duc de la Meilleraye.

Brother Patte, whom we had left on board to watch our supplies until we could send a boat to bring them ashore, arrived on May 24 with all our bundles. So, when I saw that our men and our possessions were safe, I started hunting for a place to live, where we could set up our little household and live as we do in our own houses. God favored our plans in a wonderful way; all the kitchen utensils we had brought from Nantes, along with the small plates, soup bowls, mugs, and other essentials we had provided for our little community in Madagascar, turned out to be very useful to us. I found two rooms, a kitchen, and a loft on a farm, where some Roman Catholics were living, situated a good league from the fort. With our wood supply and a plate of fish on the days when there was fishing, it would come to twenty livres a month. So, I offered this to the confreres, and they were very satisfied with it.

Since, however, we had to have the Governor's permission, I presented a very humble request to him. At first he seemed to be opposed to it for fear lest we might work up some conspiracy with all the officers and soldiers on the ship, who were camped halfway up the road, and also because he was afraid that those soldiers, almost half of whom were Catholics, might come to Mass. Their Company is very sensitive about this and had expressly forbidden them to do so for fear lest they stir up a revolt against him. But I continued to insist on this point, even telling him that our landlady had evicted us and that we would be obliged to sleep in the open. I added that we were giving him our word not to do anything that might be prejudicial to his interests in the eyes of the Company. On hearing this, he granted my request, on condition that we pray behind closed doors and not open them either to his soldiers or to ours, and that I give him my word on this point. I did not want to do that, stating that I was the Pastor of everyone on the Maréchale; *therefore, anyone who came would be most welcome, and I would be offending God by acting otherwise. And not only would they themselves be welcome, but his men also, whether they came to hear Mass or to have the sacraments administered to them.*

He made it clear that he was not satisfied with my answer, so M. Guelton, the interpreter, asked me to accede to his request, which he felt was reasonable enough, since we were dealing with a Company that abhorred priests, and if I acted otherwise, I would put everyone in danger of being badly treated along with us. "No matter," I said. "Tell the Governor I could not grant what he desires of me in this situation, that I would answer for it before God, that I am happy to die for the salvation of souls, and that I will consider it a very great glory to imitate the Son of God, who deemed it an honor to shed the last drop of His blood for them. Tell him also that this is what made me leave my country, my relatives, and the few possessions God had given me. In a word, tell him that, if he does not want us to live on his land, even though we are his allies, we will leave under the guidance and protection of God." I said this not just once, but three or four times, interiorly disposed to accept whatever God might have in store for us.

When he saw my determination, he began to relent and finally let me have the house I was asking of him, without demanding of me anything that might prevent me from administering the sacraments to those who would wish them, stating only that he would prevent Catholics from coming to see us. And in fact, for six or seven months he sent a guard to the house every Sunday to prevent the Catholic soldiers from coming; he even reprimanded two of them for having heard Mass. This, however, did not stop us from hearing confessions and distributing Holy Communion to some of them; the guard allowed this, and he himself was very knowledgeable about our religion. The Governor even stated several times, and in the presence of many persons, that we had better watch our step because the revenue officer would be making a careful visit and, if he caught us celebrating Mass, he would confiscate everything we had, and if he asked him for help, he could not refuse him. But we heard later that this was only sheer politics, and the Governor was simply doing it so that his ministers might have nothing with which to reproach him.

He admitted this himself, having often told me that there should be freedom of religion. In fact, whenever he honored us with a visit, besides the time he chose—after our Masses were celebrated—he always sent a messenger to find out if it was convenient for us. Furthermore, we received him in the room where we said Mass, having no other more suitable one. In it was a huge crucifix, about six or seven feet high, a gift from the Duchesse d'Aiguillon, which the Governor's wife found very devotional and well made. I was told that she informed her husband that she had never seen any more beautiful and touching work of art, with—among others—Mary Magdalen at the foot of the Cross.

On June 4, we moved from the house near the fort to our farm, where we began to live a little more peacefully and in the way we did in our houses in France. I have to admit that this did not apply to me, for I had to be in our officers' tent at the fort almost every day—nearly the whole month of June—for the Maréchal's affairs. Every day new written suggestions came in from here and there concerning the ship, its fittings, its victuals, its arms, and the 140 men camping on the seashore; all these matters had to be taken care of. And while we were involved in defending the Maréchal's rights, two large ships from Holland arrived around June 8, which gave me hope that we would soon be free of so much trouble and business.

The Governor and his wife, at whose house I had dined three times a week for a month because of our business with the captains, said they would like to come to visit us in our new home. Knowing how much they wanted us to have them dine in the French style, I invited them to a simple meal, which they accepted. We welcomed them in a barn, with all their retinue, serving them venison and fowl from the countryside according to the French custom. They enjoyed this immensely and have been much more friendly ever since.

Among the reasons for this reception, helping me to overcome the repugnance I had for it because it is not a custom of the Mission nor of persons professing an apostolic life as we do, was the fact that no greater honor can be paid them than to invite them to a meal and to eat with them in their home. Since we were going to be living in their territory for a long time, we needed to win their friendship so they would not keep us from our duties, would supply our basic needs upon payment and, with regard to the loss of My Lord's ship, would do what they could for its officers and crew.

The main reason was, however, that he might allow us to continue our voyage to Madagascar on one of his Company's ships or on the one being sent to him to be used wherever he wished. I promised to pay him what he felt proper, and I have to tell you frankly that, short of offending God, there is nothing I would not have done and would still not do to go to the assistance of my very dear brother and Superior M. Bourdaise, especially since Saint Francis Xavier, the great apostle of our time, has left me an example of this, based on the words of Saint Paul, who became all to all so as to win them all for Our Lord Jesus Christ.[29] *When he could not obtain an audience with a Japanese King because he was poorly clothed and had no retinue, he dressed himself in the most beautiful clothes of the country and had himself followed by some Portuguese. By this means he spoke to the King, converted him—if I am not mistaken—and got what he wanted from him.*

The captains of the Dutch ships, who had accompanied the Governor, invited us on board to see and sign the provisions that had been agreed upon with the officers of the Maréchale *and the Governor and to visit the* Maréchale *with skilled carpenters to see, before dismissing the whole crew, whether there was any way the ship could be saved. They also wanted to show us all they could do to be of service to us.*

As for the first point, concerning the articles the Governor and the officers were urging me to sign, I refused, despite their insistence—not that they contained anything damaging to the Maréchal, but simply because it was stated that we could not function in any way as priests in that country.

On the second point, the ship was found to be so damaged that they said it was impossible to save it. The keel was broken and some of the ribs were missing, with the result that it leaned to port and was, moreover, deeply embedded in the sand.

Regarding the third point, we were received with all possible courtesy, the artillery doing its share, for they gave us a one-hundred-fifty-round salute from their guns, to say nothing of wanting to entertain us with several instruments and fanfares because the captain of the ship and many of his crew were Roman Catholics, even though they were Dutch.

After twelve or thirteen days at anchor they left for Batavia,[30] *taking with them one hundred twenty-five of our men. I took the opportunity at that time to write to the Commander-in-Chief of the town of Batavia, which*

---

[29]1 Cor 9:22. (NAB)

[30]Former name of Djakarta (Indonesia).

is sixteen hundred leagues from the Cape of Good Hope, asking him very humbly to give us passage to Madagascar, if possible—or at least to Holland—for which we would pay our passage. People say he is a very wise man and had been a Jesuit priest, although he is now married. The whole time they were in port, the Governor often invited us to visit him and to dine with them, sending his carriage and horsemen for us and sending us back home the same way, despite my requests and entreaties to keep him from doing so. Sometimes he would come to take us for a ride, and whenever he met us he took us into his carriage. All winter long, whenever we went to visit him or he sent for us, he always had us accompanied by soldiers.

He left orders for his gardeners to supply us with herbs and vegetables. Whenever there was something new in his garden, he sent us some—melons, artichokes, asparagus, peas, beans—and even sent us mutton, veal, and fish. I can say only that we were always shown the utmost courtesy and kindness; had we been related to them, they could not have done more.

That proves clearly, my very dear Father, what Our Lord has said, that anyone who has left a home, sisters, father, mother, wife, children, fields, or some other possession or inheritance for love of Him, will receive a hundred times as much and will inherit eternal life afterward.[31] *By this He means that the person will receive a hundredfold or one hundred times as much in this life, and then eternal life in the next, as this same Jesus Christ expressed it in Saint Mark: "Not only will you receive an eternal reward in the next life because you became poor for the sake of Jesus Christ, but in this life you will receive a hundredfold."*[32]

And we actually see this fulfilled to the letter, not only in the kingdoms and provinces in which we are established, where, for one house we have left, we find we have several, which God has given us for the one we left behind; for the father and mother we have left, God gives us many others in their place, who love us more than those we left behind, and who take greater care of us and watch out more for our well-being.

As for brothers and sisters, we find so many of them; they love us in a way different from those of flesh and blood because they cherish us disinterestedly for God and in God, while those of flesh and blood love us out of self-interest and profit and only as long as they need us—which really means loving at the expense of another.

Now, what can I say about the contentment enjoyed in a Community

---

[31]Mt 19:29. (NAB)
[32]Mk 10:30. (NAB)

established for the service of God? We receive from it a hundred times more than we might have received in the world, even from those who are the best paid and are at the top of the wheel of fortune. People will see the dangers into which they are ready to fall at every step, the dissatisfaction that racks them at every moment, and the constant fears and apprehensions that give them neither peace nor respite.

If it is a question of honor, do we not receive a hundred times more than if we were in the world? For, if we had remained in the world, Prelates, Princes, and great lords would perhaps never have glanced our way; whereas, seeing us now, dressed in old clothing and patched cassocks, they show us great honor and respect. We can bear witness to this, even though we are living among heretics in a strange, distant, pagan land. For have we lacked anything necessary, or have we not rather enjoyed an abundance of everything, and more than we would have had in our houses in Europe, as can be verified by what follows in this report? As for what concerns honors, I have to say frankly that, had I been a lay person, I would never have received so many as I have received from the French seigneurs and especially from the Governors, captains, and officers from Holland.

As for my interior peace of soul, although I experience and am surrounded by a great number of difficulties, which are not slight, I nevertheless enjoy a peace greater than any I have ever had in my life.

Excuse your son, Monsieur, for writing to you in this vein, but the gratitude I feel toward Our Lord Jesus Christ and the Most Holy and Immaculate Virgin Mary His mother, and toward you, dear Father, for having admitted me into your Company and sent me to pagan lands, causes me to speak this way. I thank you infinitely, assuring you that I never forget this great favor, for which I will be grateful all my life. And, if it had to be done all over again, even if I had a whole world I would most willingly renounce it so to live in my present situation. O happy state—happier even than I could ever express!

Who, then, would be afraid to cross the seas to gain souls for God since, in the midst of storms, we encounter only peace of mind and calm; in shipwrecks, only help and extraordinary assistance. In a word, amid great difficulties and even when all appears to be lost, it is then that God reveals His Providence, as we ourselves have experienced, and this can be verified in what has been said and what will be said later in this report. It is at times like this, I repeat, that God consoles a soul and showers such joys and spiritual delights on it that only persons who have lived through it can describe it—so much so, that even death which, according to the philosopher, is the most terrible of terrible things, is sweet, agreeable, and viewed favorably by all those who are totally given to God to serve Him among unbelievers.

So, once the ships had left with the Maréchal's entire crew, except for twelve or thirteen persons who remained on land with the captains, I began to enjoy some rest. In order to savor it better and to find out what God was asking of us during the time we would be living in this country, I suggested to the Company that we make our retreat, which they approved heartily. So we began it one Sunday evening, June 19, and had such satisfaction for the eight entire days of it that I do not think I ever had one like it. God showered so many graces on my confreres that He seemed to be tangibly with us in our repetitions, our humiliations, the spiritual communications each one made and has continued to make from time to time, and, lastly, in the renewal of the practice of our Rules, which we have tried to observe very exactly, by the goodness and mercy of God. We used Philagie[33] *for our meditations and followed the same schedule we are accustomed to observe in our houses in France. Brother Patte likewise made his retreat for the same number of days.*

M. Boutonnet, the young man we brought with us from Paris, did likewise, but with such blessings from heaven that, shortly after the closing on July 17, the feast of Saint Alexis, he donned the cassock of a clerical student. He was so impassioned with the love of God and afire with devotion that he needed not the spur but the bridle to restrain him, for had I listened to him, there would not have been enough penitential instruments nor mortifications to suit him. That caused him to spend his time at recreation making tin belts with points, with pins for the chain so he could use them either to gird his loins or to take the discipline.

He really wanted me to admit him into the Internal Seminary for the Company and urged me strongly to do so; but, to satisfy him somewhat, I told him it would be better for him to study philosophy, with M. Daveroult as his tutor, and that as soon as we arrived in Paris he could be admitted into the Company and would be better satisfied and more deeply imbued with its spirit. He agreed to this, and his reply was so beautiful that I would like to have it engraved on my heart (and on those of members of Communities and religious Orders): "Fine, Monsieur, I will do whatever you wish. I place myself entirely in your hands to do with me exactly what the potter does with clay and the candlemaker with soft wax. Mold and turn me as you see fit; moreover, I ask you to remind me of all my faults

---

[33]Paul de Barry, *Solitude de Philagie* (Lyon: C. Rigaud and P. Borde, n.d.).

and to tell me how you wish me to act by giving me a rule for this." I did so most willingly, and I am sure you realize the joy with which God filled my soul. There is none similar to that of seeing God loved and honored beyond measure.

His rule was as follows: Daily rising at 4:00 a.m., except on Fridays when he rested until the Angelus. *At 4:30 a.m. meditation until 5:30 a.m. and reading of the New Testament until 6:00 a.m. At 6:00 a.m. he prepared the priest's vestments for Mass and then studied philosophy until 8:00 a.m. At 8:00 a.m. he served Mass, then went over his lesson with his tutor until about 10:30 a.m., after which he would go set the table. He always read Holy Scripture at meals.*

He often spent his recreation alone, working on something or sewing and mending his clothes, etc., except for the day we took off each week, when we brought him with us, and a few other hours of recreation during the week.

After he had done his assigned tasks, M. Feydin taught him plainchant; this was followed by half an hour of spiritual reading and then study until 4 o'clock. From 4:00 p.m. to 5:00 p.m. he conversed with his tutor, then studied until it was time for him to set the table.

He received Holy Communion on Sundays and feast days and spent almost the entire day in prayer, even reciting the Office with us. He made a monthly retreat and received Communion. After the general examination of conscience, he would sometimes come and ask for a penance for some slight fault he had committed.

That, then, was the life of this young man, Monsieur; and if that is how it was exteriorly, you can imagine what it was interiorly. If he progressed so rapidly alone, guided by a blind man and among pagans, just think what he would have done in the Saint-Lazare Seminary! I never cease to be amazed that a young man of twenty-one remained so devout and faithful to the practice of his rule, despite so many occasions that might have deterred him from this.

Cordelet also made four days of retreat.

Once our little family was renewed and fortified by enlightenment from on high, we began to live like Carthusians, occupying ourselves in prayer and the practice of all the Rules and customs observed in our Company. In order to succeed better in this we made a monthly retreat and spiritual communication.

Each one applied himself to studying according to his need; as for myself, I spent seven or eight hours a day at it. In the morning I read

Bonacina;[34] *after dinner I composed and learned talks for the missions, so I had no time to be bored. The time passed so quickly that I felt that morning had hardly begun when evening was upon me.*

On July 15, more Dutch ships arrived on their way to Batavia. Since we no longer had any hope of ships coming from the Bishops and merchants of France, I suggested to the Company that it might be advisable for us to go to Batavia to obtain from the General permission to go to Madagascar. I did so because the Governor and his officers led us to hope that it would be easy for us to book passage on the ships of free people, if the General allowed this. Moreover, we would have greater assurance and be in a better position for our return to Holland, and I was very worried about how we were going to live without money. No one could buy our supplies, but we could easily sell them in Batavia, where there were quite a number of Catholics of all nationalities, to whom we could be of very great service.

When the pros and cons were placed before the confreres, they found the matter so important that they felt it advisable to offer special prayers to recommend it to God so that He might reveal His Will to us; meanwhile, the Governor and the captains should be consulted to find out their sentiments and how we should proceed—or whether the voyage should be undertaken at all.

That is why, on the same day the ships arrived, I went to see the Governor, who urged me to go ahead, saying that he would go aboard the following day to prepare lodgings for us. On my return home to inform the others—who were all anxious to go, with the exception of one who, however, did not want to remain behind, but to follow us everywhere—I found M. Daveroult in bed with a fever, caused by an infected cyst, which was really very painful. Thinking that it would amount to nothing, I was hoping we could leave in two weeks' time, but things turned out otherwise, for he became more seriously ill and the cyst began to fester. That made the Brother think that it was going to be a long, drawn out affair and that he might have to lance it, which he did three weeks or a month later. This obliged us to change our plans, adoring the Providence of God, who by

---

[34]Martino Bonacina, one of the princes of moral theology, was born in Milan around 1585. For three years he taught Canon and Civil Law at the seminary in his native city before being appointed Rector of the Swiss College. In recognition of his merits, Ferdinand II named him Palatine Count and Knight of the Golden Fleece. Consecrated Bishop of Utica, he died while on his way to the Court of Vienna, where Urban VIII was sending him as Nuncio (1631). He composed a manual of moral theology, which went through eighteen editions by 1754, and many tracts on law, dogma, and moral theology.

this incident manifested His Will, and to go to thank the Governor for all his courtesy. We likewise said farewell to M. Véron, captain of the Maréchale, *who was going to Batavia on the sixth.*

Poor M. Daveroult was in bed for ten weeks. He was in extreme pain and showed admirable patience, greatly edifying the whole company. Thus, God, for whom he had acquired this cyst on Mount Lebanon, was pleased to relieve him of it at the Cape of Good Hope, as a reward for the patience it had caused him to practice. To see his knee now, you would never know he ever had a cyst.

When M. Daveroult first fell ill, M. de Boissy, who was previously in command of the Duc de la Meilleraye's fleet of ships, and who was captain of the soldiers and passengers aboard the Maréchale, *was suffering a great deal from gout and was confined to bed for the entire voyage. Seeing that M. Véron had left for Batavia, and finding himself so ill that we had to give him the sacraments of Penance, Holy Eucharist, and Extreme Unction, even staying with him during the night, he earnestly entreated me to let him come and stay with us. In charity I could not refuse him, and also because he was our benefactor, leaving us in his will about eleven hundred livres to have Masses said for him.*

Divine Providence's care of us was clearly manifest in giving us and providing in this way the means of feeding and maintaining ourselves in this distant land, just at the time when we needed it so much. After that, who would lose courage and confidence—or rather, who would not rely on God in the most urgent need! Oh! how good it is to serve such a Master, who always takes care of His own and never abandons them, wherever they may be!

So we brought him to live with us on July 26, but it was not for long because God took him to Himself three days later, on July 29, between 8:00 and 9:00 in the morning, just as the Mass for the dying was coming to an end. We buried him that night behind the wall of the altar where we celebrated Mass, after we had performed the burial rites over the body.

He was a mirror of patience; for although he was very quick-tempered, and his members were all ulcerated (causing him very great pain), the only words he was heard to utter were: "My God, have pity on me, have mercy on me, forgive my sins, receive me into your glory." I believe he is enjoying that glory because for six or seven months he suffered excruciating pain with unalterable patience. In fact, God willed to reward him for it in this life by granting him the grace of being fortified by all the sacraments, of dying in our house in the care of priests, and of having four Masses for him daily for eight months. These are tremendous graces that are not granted to everyone, especially when you consider that we were living in a far distant country, among pagans and heretics. Oh! would to God that

I might die in this way, if He does not grant me the grace of martyrdom, that I desire more than the deer which, although chased by hunters and hotly pursued by dogs, yearns for the fountain of living waters!

M. Daveroult made such a complete recovery—thanks to the care and diligence of Brother Patte—that he was able to give M. Boutonnet two philosophy classes a day. Brother Patte is very skilled in his profession—so much so that the Dutch surgeons send for him whenever someone in the region has a serious illness. The Governor and his wife do the same, and they have greater confidence in him than they do in their own people.

M. de Fontaines taught Binsfeld[35] *to M. Karkadiou, second captain of the* Maréchale, *who is planning to leave the service of his earthly King to enroll in that of the King of heaven. He is a devout gentleman and has always given excellent example; he received the sacraments often and came to Vespers and the sermons every Sunday and feast day. In addition, although he lived almost half a league away, he came to Mass every day, even when it was raining.*

Once or twice a month we preached to the Company; all the French came and sometimes some of the Dutch, a few of whom went to confession. We celebrated Mass every day after prayer and the Little Hours,[36] *and followed step by step the schedule observed in our houses.*

Since we could afford only one sheep a week for our food—and this with great difficulty—we had to send Brother Patte out hunting twice a week. He went with M. de la Cloche, Lieutenant of the Maréchale *and nephew of M. Karkadiou, and they shared the game equally. God blessed their efforts so well that they brought home more than we could consume—sometimes deer or roebuck; sometimes rhinoceros, which are animals the size of three bulls; sea cows, stags, flamingos, ostriches, which are birds as large as a man; hares, partridges, cranes, pheasants, peacocks, ducks, geese, plovers, sea gulls, sea magpies, and other kinds of birds that are not found in France. So, we lived very well and had to spend money only for our rent, firewood, and household needs, amounting to forty livres a month at the most for eight persons, which was our usual number.*

That good Brother did the cooking once a week and took care of the laundry and the kitchen, except for the two days he went hunting. And I must confess that, were it not for him, we would have found it difficult to manage; such a Brother is priceless in foreign countries.

---

[35]Pierre Binsfeld, *Enchiridion theologiae pastoralis* Trier: H. Bock, 1594 (new ed., Paris: M. and J. Henault, 1646).

[36]According to the arrangement of the Roman Breviary at that time, the Little Hours consisted of the daytime prayers of Prime, Terce, Sext, and None.

That is how he fulfilled his office of Martha, joining to it that of Mary Magdalene by observing his Rules, making a little retreat one day a month, along with his communication, often asking to be reminded of his faults on Fridays, humbling himself and requesting a penance for his failings at almost every repetition of prayer. In a word, all I can say of him is that he is a good Brother of the Mission.

Since M. Feydin was nearing the end of his seminary, he asked me to allow him to live like the novices and to follow their exercises. So he began on Our Lady's birthday and continued until All Saints' Day[37] *to prepare himself as well as possible for that great sacrifice,*[38] *which he made in my presence on November 4, feast of the great Saint Charles Borromeo, the model of good priests. He did almost everything that is done in our seminaries, such as manual work, looking after the lamps and chamber-pots, and washing the dishes. In addition, he came to ask for a penance after prayer at 4:00 p.m., requesting that I reprimand him sharply before the others and give him difficult penances.*

I did so in order to satisfy his humility, and by these holy exercises he greatly edified the Community so that those priests found nothing in him to prevent him from being admitted into the body of the Congregation of the Mission; on the contrary, they found that, by his example, he would be able to do a great deal of good. He always had the role of admonitor—the duty you had told me to assign to him—as well as sacristan and director of plainchant; he also taught reading. That is how he spent his time, outside of his studies and spiritual exercises.

We celebrated the Birth of Our Lord Jesus Christ with great solemnity, decorating our chapel as best we could with pictures, flowers, and a crib filled with hay, in which there was a marvelous waxen Infant Jesus, which Madame Traversay had given us.

All our Frenchmen came not only to Matins sung in plain chant and to High Mass, during which M. Karkadiou, captain of the Maréchale, *offered the blessed bread, but also to Lauds, the Masses of the day, the sermons preached by M. Daveroult on the mystery, and Vespers. Several Catholic Dutchmen also came so that the whole chapel was full. Almost everyone, they as well as the French, received their Savior.*

---

[37]From September 8 to November 1.

[38]The holy vows. François Feydin was ordained in 1645 and entered the Congregation of the Mission as a priest in 1653. Although there is no indication in Saint Vincent's letters, Feydin apparently wanted to follow for a time the lifestyle of a major seminarian and seems to have used this voyage to make his Internal Seminary as a preparation for taking his vows. Eventually, he left the Congregation.

That same day, December 25, a small English ship dropped anchor in the harbor. This prompted me to go to see the Governor on Saint Stephen's Day[39] *to find out where the ship was going and to see if it could give us passage either to Madagascar, if it were heading for the Indies, or to Europe. He informed me that it was going to Leghorn in Italy, that he had requested passage for us, and that this was possible. On his part, he offered to give us whatever we might need and invited me to dine with him on Holy Innocents' Day,*[40] *when the English captain was supposed to be there. He also said that he would lend me his longboat so I could board his ship to see if the quarters were convenient for us and our baggage.*

On that day, then, M. Daveroult and I boarded the little English ship with the captain and Marchand, deciding on the Sainte-Barbe room for our lodging. Although it was quite small for seven persons, and still more inconvenient because the only light came from a candle, nevertheless we wanted to stay together and to gain three months, which we had to wait for the fleet, and to take only two months—or ten weeks at the most—for our voyage. In this way we could come sooner to the aid of poor M. Bourdaise and the good neophytes of Saint-Laurent Island. All that made us decide, after discussing it with the Company, which agreed to it unanimously, to put up with that inconvenience. It was not the only one; there were also a few others, such as running the risk of being captured by the Turks, when they visited the ship, doing our own cooking, and having to furnish everything we needed—even wood and water—and these are not just minor inconveniences nor small expenses.

We had, however, gone beyond that; all that remained was the question of the price of our passage, but it was so costly that we could not consent to it. They were asking eleven hundred écus, without supplying us with so much as a glass of water. Both the Governor and our captain found it exorbitant and asked us to wait for the Dutch ships, where we would be much better off, with no fear of the Turks or worry about anything, in addition to the hope of a free passage.

So we let it sail away on the first day of 1661, without writing to you; I humbly ask your pardon for this because it was entirely my fault. I feel sure, however, that the Duc de la Meilleraye must have given you news of us because the Governor wrote a detailed letter to his Company about the wreck and ourselves, asking them to inform the Duc de la Meilleraye.

---

[39]December 26.

[40]December 28.

On January 16, 1661, I baptized with the name of Christine the little daughter of a black Catholic slave, who was captured in the war of the Dutch against the Portuguese; he is a God-fearing man, well instructed in our religion. On February 6, he brought another little girl, whom I baptized Marie. In the ten months we stayed in such a large country, those were the two Christian souls we were able to win over for Our Lord because we had no freedom and no idea of the language of the country nor of the Dutch language either.

On January 30, we began our retreat to prepare ourselves better for our return to France. M. de Fontaines and M. Feydin could make only five days because they were not feeling well, but M. Daveroult and I finished the remainder. We used Busée[41] *and concentrated on the meditations on the virtues required by Saint Paul for priests. These are very useful subjects for meditation, and excellent fruits may be gathered from them.*

M. Boutonnet also made an eight-day retreat at the same time we did. I visited him after attending to the Company. Brother Patte made four days as did Cordelet, who for two months at the Cape was tormented by a spirit, which sometimes pulled at his mattress, sometimes his feet, and sometimes his head. It kept him from sleeping and troubled him considerably with the racket it made, waking everyone up. This obliged M. de Fontaines and myself to spend one night in stole and surplice to exorcise it when it came between midnight and one o'clock. I began to exorcise it in the name of God, asking who it was and what it wanted. When I exorcised it in one place it went to another, but, by pursuing and pressuring it in three or four different places for half an hour, it stopped for that time. Still, it came back every night to the room where Cordelet was sleeping with some of our men, and it continued to do so the entire time we were at the Cape.

On February 24, feast day of the glorious Apostle Saint Mathias, the Dutch fleet arrived, composed of seven large ships. Wearing lay clothes, as the Governor had requested us to do, we all went in a body to greet the Admiral. The Jesuit Father Martin Martinion had dressed like that when traveling on their ships from China to Holland. The Jesuits living in Amsterdam wear a black suit and jerkin, which is how we are dressed.

On the twenty-sixth, accompanied by M. de Fontaines, I went to visit the Admiral to find out our orders. He received us very courteously, promised to do whatever he could to satisfy us, and said he would let us

[41]Jean Busée [Johannes Busaeus], *Enchiridion piarum meditationum in omnes dominicas, sanctorum festa, Christi passionem et caetera* (Douai: G. Patté, 1624).

know within two or three days what we would have to do, after he had discussed the matter with the Governor.

On March 3, he sent me four tickets for four ships. M. Daveroult and M. Cordelet are berthed on the Vice-Amiral, *which has a minister on it and is going to Zealand; M. de Fontaines is on the* Naclebon; *M. Boutonnet on the* Lambrafort; *and M. Feydin, Brother Patte, and I are on the* Malague. *All of us are eating in the captain's mess and each has a private room. This shows clearly the care God takes of His servants and the obligation they have to abandon themselves entirely into His hands.*

Having accepted this arrangement as coming from Divine Providence, we began to prepare our little affairs and to provide ourselves with what we needed for the voyage. This was not as easy as if we were going to be all together or even in two groups, but Our Lord, who has always assisted us on this voyage, did not fail us on this occasion either because the Governor and his wife, to whom we are deeply indebted, supplied our modest provisions. In this way, each man had what he needed: wine, brandy, biscuits, fish, and butter so that we could observe Lent with greater facility among persons who eat meat every day. This did not make it awkward to eat at their table.

On March 6, the first Sunday of Lent, all our Frenchmen made their Easter duty, and not only they but a number of Portuguese, Spaniards, Irish, and Dutch, who had arrived with the fleet and wanted to be included. After dinner, I preached on perseverance as a final recommendation to everyone, both our men and the others, and to entrust them to Our Lord Jesus Christ and His Holy and Immaculate Mother so that, by the merits of the former and the prayers and intercession of the latter, they might remain as pure and orthodox among heretics as the rays of the sun that shine on mud without being contaminated.[42]

On Thursday the tenth, after all of us had celebrated Mass for our voyage and said good-bye to one another, we boarded our respective ships, but not to practice with our neighbor what we did on the Maréchale—*at least not on our ship, where there was only one French Catholic out of a crew of almost two hundred men. God permitted it to be so; may His Holy Name be blessed!*

So, dear Father, that is how your sons spent their time at the Cape of Good Hope—which would have been very different had they been guided by a good leader and not by a wicked, ignorant man like me.

I almost forgot to tell you that M. Guelton, who was made very welcome

---

[42]An allusion to the Common Rules, chap. 9, §2.

in Batavia by the Commandant, told me that he had spoken to some sailors recently returned from Madagascar, and they declared to him that the French had abandoned the fort and settled on an island where the arsenal was, which served in the past as a fortress for the Portuguese, to make war on the natives. It is not even known whether there is any dissension among them. Rumor has it that M. Chamargou, a Lieutenant and ally of the Duke, is dead. He was a very devout gentleman, highly thought of by the late M. Dufour and very much attached to the Company, to the point that people were saying that he wanted to become one of us. You can imagine what a loss this is for the poor neophytes and for M. Bourdaise, who they say is still alive. They also say that he was so well loved by all the French that they deeply regretted his loss and, if I am not mistaken, that war did not break out until after his death. We did hear something to this effect at the Cape from the Governor.

M. Guelton arranged for a merchant to charter from the Dutch Company a little two-hundred tonner, loaded with merchandise needed for the country. On the sly, he also slipped onto it arms and gunpowder belonging to the Duke and a man to whom he gave verbal orders for M. de Rivaux, the Governor, as well as wine, flour, and a few other luxuries for him. In addition, he wrote a letter to M. Bourdaise concerning our shipwreck and told me that, if I had been in Batavia, I could have had passage there and that it was even discussed in Council whether the merchant could pick us up at the Cape. They feared, however, that, if the ship did not round the Cape, it would be in danger. That is why they would not agree to this—or rather, God did not will it that way because He was reserving a better one for us.

CHAPTER IX - THE CAPE OF GOOD HOPE AND ITS INHABITANTS

The Cape of Good Hope is a very mountainous land, with many very good, clear streams, whose waters irrigate the valleys and plains, making the land remarkably rich and productive. It yields wheat, rye, barley, oats, wine, and many watermelons and French melons, as well as all kinds of vegetables. Fruit has a hard time ripening there because of the strong winds that blow almost continually. In the ten months I was there, I saw hardly a day that was not windy. This makes the country very healthful; consequently, no sick people are seen there. And when the Dutch ships arrive, which always have people on board who are ill, the sick are cured after spending a week or so on land.

The country, like Portugal, lies on the thirty-fourth parallel, but it is not nearly so hot because of the winds. The Dutch have been established there for about ten years. They built a fort with four bastions and a surrounding moat and have begun to bring in water. Inside the fort is the Governor's house, which is quite large, comfortable and clean; the officers' quarters; and housing for the soldiers and slaves. It is surrounded on all sides by mountains, except for the harbor side, and the guns on the ships could cause it trouble. A nearby canal that brings the water in makes it very convenient for taking on a water supply—ships can fill their tanks in a day or two. Because of the tides there is a long wooden jetty from which barrels and casks can be rolled and unloaded onto the ships. There are scarcely three hundred men there, soldiers and natives included. About a dozen houses are close by the fort; the others are scattered one, two, three, and four leagues away.

They have all kinds of workers and lack nothing because of the ships coming from Holland and the Indies, which come alongside the quay and bring everything they need. From the newsletters people send them, they even know all that is going on in Europe.

They plough the land with oxen, which are plentiful in the country, as are sheep. With a little tobacco or copper they barter for them with the natives. These sheep have an enormous, frightful tail, but it is just fat.

They have a good thirty horses, imported from Batavia, which have been very useful in preventing the natives from making raids on them. They have eight or ten watchtowers around the bay and further inland. About three leagues from the fort there are thick woods with fully-grown trees, abounding in game and all sorts of wild animals, such as lions, elephants, rhinoceros, antelope, buffalo, tigers, and beautifully marked horses that no one can get near. In addition, there is a large number of ostriches, and just one of their eggs is enough to feed eight persons. Fish is also plentiful, but it is almost all of the same kind. They also fish for many ray there.

Very few natives—maybe thirty or forty—live near the fort because all of them have left. They do nothing all day but walk about or play. Those who do not own cattle live on shellfish, which they pick up on the shore, and on a kind of nut that they find on the ground. The men eat together as do the women. They are easily the ugliest natives the earth has ever borne. They smell very bad because of the grease they smear on themselves. They are stark-naked except for a cowhide they wear over their shoulders—and when it is very hot they do not wear even that.

There are some Kings among them, and these Kings have officers in each district. Their wealth is in their cattle. They look no better than their subjects and are dressed no differently from them. They war among themselves over their cattle, using arrows, darts, short spears, and assegais.[43] *They are intelligent, as the Governor pointed out to me and as I myself have been able to observe.*

They come to the fort with their cattle from as far as forty or fifty leagues away to trade them for tobacco, which they enjoy very much. So do the Dutch, who have set the example for them because, before their arrival, they did not know it existed. They also trade for copper, which they put around their arms, and for red rassade that they hang from their ears.

One of the most powerful Kings of the country arrived with his daughter-in-law, riding on oxen—for these animals serve as mounts for these lords—with about 150 armed followers. They remained a day's distance from the fort because they are not allowed to enter it when they are armed. I went to see them at the home of the Governor, who received in his chamber this petty King and his daughter-in-law, along with two or three of his favorites. The latter preceded him, carrying a beautiful mat that they spread on the floor, on which they sat down. I gave each an imitation ruby and emerald ring, which they put on their fingers without thanking me; for they do not know what "thank you" means. I spoke a few words about God, but they did not understand me.

Another time, I went with the King of Saldanha. His sister-in-law works for the Governor; she speaks Portuguese and Dutch like a native and is interpreter for the Governor. It is said that this King has twenty thousand men under him. As I said, I went to dine on the Dutch ships but was unable to communicate with the King in any way. I did speak several times to a few men on the side, showing them a crucifix and some pictures, at which they looked in amazement. But, since they could not understand me and nobody dared interpret for me, I was unable to do anything with them; yet, I do not think that would be difficult, especially if we went inland, where they are not tainted nor imbued with the religion of those gentlemen. If I were not afraid that you would disapprove, and if I did not have such a large family on my hands, I would willingly have gone to visit them and announce the Gospel to them. This was indeed my intention if the Dutch had been unwilling to give us passage; I also wanted to go as far as the kingdom of Monopotapa, where the Governor sent a dozen soldiers, but they returned before getting that far because they lost their way.

While we were at the Cape, he sent them back a second time to a town called Vigiti Magni, about sixty leagues from the Cape; but they were not able to reach it because it was the wrong season and was rainy. I learned from those soldiers that they had come across many of those people who,

---

[43]An assegai is a kind of javelin or throwing spear, often with an iron tip, used by some African tribes.

in some districts, were as big as giants and in others were as small as dwarfs. They told me that they were very friendly and had treated them very well.

O mon Dieu! *must so many souls be lost because they have no one to instruct them? That is why it would be most fitting to obtain from the Holy See a general authorization for all those pagan lands where we might be, since there is no Bishop or Vicar-General from whom we could get permission to work there and carry out all the duties of a good Missionary. Could you not make your will known to the one responsible for the mission band in such circumstances, which might often arise if the Company continues to send its members to foreign countries?*

They believe in one God, the creator of heaven and earth, in the devil, in paradise for the good and hell for the wicked—which for them consists in making those sent there walk and run hither and yon, with never any rest or satisfaction. They do not offer any sacrifices, at least from what I have heard, except that, when there is a full moon—and I myself have witnessed this—they all clap their hands and do nothing but shout and jump about all night long.

They know something about the first man, but not according to what is in Scripture. That is what I was able to learn partly from them and from the Dutch.

As for their language, it is unique and very difficult because it is guttural. All the men you assign to the Indies would really have to know Portuguese because it can be used everywhere, and there are hardly any black people, especially in the Indies, who do not speak it. That is what everyone has told me, and I have noticed it myself, and it is even what the great Francis Xavier strongly recommended in his letters to those coming to assist him in the Lord's vineyard.

CHAPTER X - OUR DEPARTURE FROM THE CAPE OF GOOD HOPE

Monday, March 14, we raised anchor and left the harbor of Table Bay, arriving at Saint Helena Island on Wednesday, March 29. There we found our Admiral, whom we had lost the day after our departure from the Cape. We stayed there for three days, during which M. Feydin and I visited our men, except for M. Daveroult, whom we were not able to see, and they were happy for the opportunity to go to confession.

We left the island on April 1 and headed toward the equator, which we crossed two hours after midnight on Easter Monday, April 18. From the time we left the Cape, we always had fine weather and, by the grace of God, everyone remained in good health.

On May 29, four ships came to join us: two English ones coming from the Indies and two Dutch ones coming from America. Only one English ship remained with our fleet; the other three continued on their way.

On June 15, seven warships from Amsterdam appeared before us with two small galleons; the next day, feast of the Most Blessed Sacrament of the Altar, three or four others from Zealand arrived, and they gave some refreshments to our ships. All told, then, we were eighteen or twenty ships. They were a little afraid that the English might attack their fleet. That is why M. de Ruyter a Dutch Admiral had ten large warships stationed near Vlieland, the port where we are supposed to drop anchor, eighteen leagues from Amsterdam.

On the twenty-third of the same month, our Vice-Admiral, who was on the same ship as M. Daveroult, left with six other ships headed for Zealand.

Our Admiral, whom I had visited on Saint Helena, had urged me to have M. Daveroult transferred to our ship when we neared Holland so that all of us could land together. I would have done so had I not had a disagreement with our captain over a Spaniard, who we thought was going to die soon. This obliged M. Feydin and myself to go and give the man absolution, without anyone noticing. The patient expressed great contrition, even shedding many tears.

When the captain heard that we had visited the patient, he sent for me the next day and asked me in anger who had given me permission to go to see him. Until this time we had been very good friends, and he had been very courteous to us, but he has not been the same since, especially for two weeks when he gave us a cool reception. This prevented us from having M. Daveroult with us; because his ship was becalmed for almost two weeks he could make no headway on his journey, since his ship was obliged to remain with the fleet.

On June 26, M. de Ruyter the Dutch Admiral appeared before us with eight large warships about fifty leagues out of Amsterdam. This alarmed our own warships, and they went to reconnoiter, fearing that it was the English. The Dutch Admiral did likewise because thirty English ships had passed through the channel to get to Portugal. This forced him to come and join us, because he feared they might attack the fleet, which is very rich, since it is valued at more than . . . million in precious stones, gold, silver, and in merchandise such as gold and silver brocade, silk and taffeta from China, cotton cloth, jade, sugar, pepper, cloves, and nutmeg.

Those gentlemen are very well organized among themselves, and would to God that they were as concerned about their souls and their salvation as they are about acquiring and preserving the perishable riches and goods of this world!

Besides the three pilots assigned to each of our ships, we were each given two others called coastal pilots, who are familiar with the bottom of the sea and its depths, even to one foot, so as not to give proof of the proverb: in portu naufragium,[44] *as happened to us, and to one hundred fifty ships in the harbor of Texel, fourteen leagues from Amsterdam, which perished in a sudden blast of wind last winter, including the one being sent to China by some Bishops.*

On the last day of June we reached Vlieland, where God preserved us from death because the Amiral *and our ship almost collided. From Vlieland we took a boat that brought us to Amsterdam on July 1.*

Our occupations on those ships were just about the same as in our houses, except that we were deprived of offering the Holy Sacrifice of the Mass.

CHAPTER XI - OUR ARRIVAL IN HOLLAND AND OUR DEPARTURE FOR PARIS

On the feast of the Visitation[45] we went to hear High Mass at the Béguines. They are nuns who go out into the city but each has her own house, like the Carthusian monks; their Order is quite extensive in Flanders. We celebrated Mass to thank God for our voyage. The city of Amsterdam is one of the most beautiful in Europe; half of its citizens are members of the Catholic, Apostolic, Roman Church. There are a good one hundred churches and great freedom of religion, but it is not publicized. Even members of the so-called religion put ushers at the church doors on Sunday to keep the children from making fun of the Catholics. There is a Bishop, various religious, and several secular priests; they do not wear clerical attire but, for the most part, are dressed in grey. On Sundays they preach in their churches, which are very well attended.

That same day, we went to pay our respects to the members of the Company of the Indies, and they were most courteous toward us. They would not accept any money from us, nor did they open our boxes and bundles, although they opened everyone else's luggage. Many people were surprised at that.[46]

It was in this city that I learned of the death of the person dearest to me

---

[44]*Shipwrecked in the harbor.*

[45]July 2 (now May 31).

[46]Although what follows does not, strictly speaking, form part of the letter to Saint Vincent, still, because Nicolas Étienne's report forms a single entity, we give it in its entirety.

in this world after God: my very dear and Most Honored Father M. Vincent de Paul. I was so upset that were it not for the conformity to God's Will that we must always have, I would have feared becoming ill because of it. I learned it from M. de Chameson, a great servant of God, who is going to China with the Bishops. We were almost always together in the churches, and in our visits to assist the poor spiritually and corporally.

M. de Sweerts also went with us; he is one of the greatest—if not the greatest—artists in the world, not only because of his excellent paintings, for he never charges less than one hundred pistoles for a portrait, but even more because of his holy life. He eats no meat, fasts almost every day, sleeps on a board, distributes his goods to the poor, is very devoted to prayer, and receives Communion three or four times a week. He recently placed himself under the authority of the Bishop of Heliopolis[47] *to do whatever he sees fit for him. He knows seven languages and has traveled extensively. His conversion and his life are quite extraordinary and miraculous. He also has many beautiful secrets that he said were communicated to him from God only through the Cross, and he never undertakes anything except through the Cross.*

While making these visits, I learned how much those poor people needed catechetical instruction. They would really like to have Missionaries for this purpose and to hear their general confessions. A great number of them would have made one, if we had had permission to hear them. It would also be good to assist them with a certain amount of money so as to prevent a misfortune that occurs almost daily: many of these poor people, driven by necessity, become Huguenots because the members of the so-called religion give them what they need to feed and clothe their families. Among the members, persons called deacons visit all the homes of those poor people to persuade them to change their religion, assuring them that they will lack nothing. Consequently, for want of a sum of money, a large number are shipwrecked, to the great detriment and scandal of the Church. O mon Dieu! *how many persons will have to answer on Judgment Day for*

---

[47]François Pallu, born in Tours in 1626, was a Canon of Saint-Martin and one of the founders of the Foreign Missions Society [Société des Missions-Étrangères]. In 1655 he went on a pilgrimage to Rome with some friends, but a letter from the Duchesse d'Aiguillon prompted him to approach Pope Alexander VII and Cardinal di Bagno for the erection of Vicariates Apostolic in the Far East. The Pope received the suggestion favorably and appointed a commission of four Cardinals to study it. On May 13, 1658, Propaganda Fide approved the report presented to it; on August 14 François Pallu was appointed Titular Bishop of Heliopolis and Vicar Apostolic of Tonkin, Laos, and southwest China. He died in Moyang, China, on October 29, 1684. (Cf. manuscript life of François Pallu, Archives of the Missions-Étrangères, vol. 106.)

the loss of these souls because of the millions and treasures hidden away in their strongboxes! And yet, thirty thousand livres a year would prevent this disaster and would even bring back into the bosom of the Church many who have fallen away. What a shame, what a humiliation for Catholics to see heretics more zealous and better distributors of alms than they are!

We left Amsterdam on July 8 and passed through Haarlem, which used to be the residence of the Bishops and the Count of Holland. The church there is considered the largest in the country.

From Haarlem we went through Leiden, where there is a large university, and from Leiden we continued to The Hague, arriving that same day. This is the residence of the Prince of Orange, the state officials, and all the Ambassadors. Although it is only a town, there are always at least four hundred carriages, and because of its houses, streets, air, and fine paths, people consider it as beautiful as Amsterdam.

The following day, after celebrating Holy Mass at the church of Father Bernard, a discalced Carmelite, M. de Fontaines and I went to pay our respects to M. de Thou, the French Ambassador, who received us very well, although he was still in bed. He pressed us to dine with him and would have liked to keep us for two days, but we begged him to allow us to leave. He did so reluctantly, after issuing us a passport for ourselves and our baggage, which is in Amsterdam at the home of M. Vignon, a merchant. He is supposed to send it to his brother M. Le Roux in Nantes, who will deliver it to the Daughters of Charity.

That good Ambassador could not do enough for us. He is very much in favor of establishing the faith in foreign countries and, when we told him how well the Dutch had treated us, he promised to go to thank them for it.

On Sunday, July 10, one of us celebrated Mass and the others received Holy Communion. Then we went to spend the night in Rotterdam, which is another large and very beautiful city.

The following day we left there, after celebrating Mass at the Béguines, who have a very beautiful church, and heard a Requiem High Mass that was sung there. We embarked and passed by Dordrecht and Tholen but were obliged to go ashore in Bergen because we were becalmed. There we took two coaches, bringing us as far as Antwerp on the twelfth, where we took off the lay clothes we were wearing and put on our cassocks.

Antwerp is one of the large, beautiful cities of Flanders. The Jesuit church, with its paintings and marble, is magnificent. The harbor, the parade ground and the ramparts, surrounded by avenues of trees, add to its beauty.

From Antwerp we went to Malines, which is called "the lovely town," and from there to Brussels, where we hired a carriage that brought us to Saint-Lazare. All along the way we carried out all the exercises that

Missionaries are accustomed to practice; namely, besides our Rules, the Itinerarium, *or the litany of the Holy Name of Jesus in a kind of chant and, after dinner, the litany of the Blessed Virgin and catechism for children, for the poor, and for the maids and male servants. We concluded the exercises of our journey with a* Te Deum laudamus *near La Villette to thank God for having brought all of us back safe and sound, and with a hymn the late M. Dufour often used to sing, starting with the words:* Unus es, Deus, super omnia.[48]

From Brussels we went to Notre-Dame de Halle, which is a favorite spot for pilgrims to visit and where miracles take place. From there we went to Soignies, then to Mons in Hainaut, where there is a very beautiful church for the Canonesses of Sainte-Vautrude. These must all be single women of nobility, going back eight generations on both parents' sides. They chant the Office very well. When they go to choir they all wear white, but in their house they dress like the other townswomen. They all have carriages, and the most prominent lords choose them as wives, except for the four leaders, who are not allowed to marry. They answer only to the King of Spain, and the Archbishop has no right to make the visitation of their house.

From Mons we went to Valenciennes, then on to Cambrai, Péronne, Roye, Senlis, and finally Paris, where we reached Saint-Lazare on July 20, all in perfect health, by the grace of God. There we received a very cordial welcome from M. Alméras—now our General and Most Honored Father—and from all his sons, our very dear confreres, to whom, after God, we are very deeply indebted for having preserved us by their prayers from so many dangers, in which death seemed inevitable. That is why, Monsieur, all of us prostrate ourselves at your feet and before the Company to thank you for this and to assure you that we will never forget such great benefits.

---

[48] *You are one, O God, above all things.*

APPENDIX

1. - BROTHER DUCOURNAU TO CANON DE SAINT-MARTIN [1]

August 1658

Monsieur,

M. Portail, M. Dehorgny, and M. Alméras, with whom you are acquainted, have asked me to write to you, until the time they can do so themselves, to thank you most humbly for the letters you sent them. Nothing in this world could be more precious to them than those letters because their contents will one day add luster to the holy life of the person who wrote them.

Certainly, none of us ever knew that he had been in Barbary and still less that he had converted his master. For my part, Monsieur, I admire the conversion of that apostate, the humility of his slave, the assurance he felt within himself of being free, and the grace he had of making himself loved by the Turks, who are inhuman, especially by the doctor who taught him so many fine secrets. I assure you, however, that I admire still more his constraint in never

---

Appendix 1. - This document, taken from *Notices* (vol. I, pp. 423-26), is an excerpt from the life of Brother Bertrand Ducournau, compiled by Brother Pierre Chollier, his assistant and successor in the secretariat of Saint-Lazare (*ibid.*, pp. 377-451).

[1]Canon de Saint-Martin was a close friend of Saint Vincent and was related by marriage to M. de Comet in Dax. When Saint-Martin d'Agès, the son of Jean de Saint-Martin and Catherine de Comet, was going through the family papers in 1658, he found the letters mentioned here (cf. vol. I, nos. 1 and 2). Pleased with his discovery, he took them to Canon de Saint-Martin his uncle. Thinking that Monsieur Vincent would be very pleased to read these pages, the good Canon immediately had a copy made for his illustrious friend. The copies did not remain long in the hands of Monsieur Vincent, who burned them as soon as he had read them. His letter of thanks, which is no longer extant, was also one of supplication, in which he begged M. de Saint-Martin to send him the originals. As seen here, Saint Vincent's secretary, at the urging of the Saint's advisors, wrote a separate letter to Canon de Saint-Martin about these letters.

breathing a word of all these things to anyone in the Company, although he has had hundreds of occasions to do so when speaking of the assistance to captives that he undertook twelve to fifteen years ago.

He told us quite often that he was the son of a plowman, that he herded his father's swine, and other humiliating details, but he kept silence about anything that could bring him honor, such as having been a slave, so he would not have to tell the good ensuing from it. Finally, Monsieur, I admire the wisdom of God who, wishing to make use of this servant of His to assist poor Christians groaning under the cruelty of the Muslims, permitted him to fall into the hands of those barbarians himself so that he would know firsthand what the captives suffer, the dangers they run of being lost, and the obligation we have to assist them.

Perhaps you do not know, Monsieur, that among the important works this man of God has done—amazing in number and results to those who consider them—he found the means of establishing Missionaries in Tunis and Algiers, where they assist the poor captives spiritually and corporally.

So, the captivity of this charitable man gained for him the knowledge of alchemy, but he made better use of it than those who try to change the nature of metals; for he has converted evil into good, the sinner into a just man, slavery into freedom, hell into paradise through the many works undertaken by his Company and by the ingenuity of which a zealous man is capable. He has discovered the philosopher's stone because his charity, inflamed by a divine fire, has changed everything into pure gold, like that of which the Holy City is built, according to the description of Saint John.[2]

Monsieur, in sending us those letters you have revealed to us a hidden treasure, and you will greatly console those priests if you

---

[2]Cf. Rev 21:1-27. (NAB)

can send them any others, even though they contain nothing extraordinary. They would very much like to know how he parted company with the Legate from Avignon who took him to Rome, what he did at that Court, where he went upon leaving Italy, when he came to Paris and why, in what year and where he became a priest. In addition, Monsieur, if you know other details about his youth, we will be most grateful if you inform us of them. He never talks to us about himself except to humble himself, and never to reveal the graces God has given him nor those granted to others through him.

Had those two letters fallen into his hands no one would ever have seen them, so those priests have judged it advisable to hold on to them without mentioning them to him. And so that he will have no idea that we have them, they have even destroyed your letter, thinking that you will not be offended by that, as they most humbly entreat you. If he should ask you again for them,[3] you could write him that you sent them to him and are very chagrined that he did not receive them. We ourselves are really sorry to deprive him of the consolation he would have in reading his past history and, in his old age, to see himself as a young man, but we had either to make that decision or lose the original letters—which would have been far worse.

I thank God, Monsieur, for this opportunity to offer you my obedience, which I now do with all due respect. Since you do not know me, I would not take this liberty if I did not have the honor of belonging to the Mission and, consequently, am obliged to honor and serve you perfectly, after the example of our Most Honored Father, your perfect friend. I am most willing to do so, thank God, but, since I am only a poor Brother, useless to everyone, I fear I will never be able to prove to you by deeds to what point I am, in the love of Our Lord, your. . . .

---

[3]Cf. no. 3101.

2. - CANON CRUCHETTE TO BROTHER BERTRAND DUCOURNAU

My very dear Brother,

It is always a great consolation for me to receive all your letters. Thank you for the honor you do me and for your goodness in satisfying my desire to learn of the establishment of your priests in Bétharram and to be able to promote its execution.[1] I hope we will soon have this happiness and that Our Lord will complete His work.

M. Peyresse, one of the head chaplains of Bétharram, was in this town last week and did me the honor of coming to see me. He asked if I had received any news from Paris concerning this affair. By way of distraction, he stated that he was distressed at M. Vincent's silence and assured me that the Bishop of Lescar [2] had written to him again. He also showed me a letter that the tutor of the children of the Chief Justice of Pau, who is very interested in this establishment, had written him on his orders to get him to see that it would be carried out. In speaking with him I learned that he strongly desired this. I did not show him your letters because you had sworn me to secrecy. I was content simply to justify M. Vincent's manner of acting—as was my duty—and to give him my own motives for facilitating the execution of the contract and the advantages accruing to the chaplains by a union with the Priests of the Mission or by remaining in Bétharram with a pension that could be established for life. Furthermore, in the event that any of them may not wish to bind himself to the Mission either by union or by a pension, there is no Prelate in the area nor in the suffragan See of Auch who will not give the Chief Justice some benefice to remunerate the chaplains, which is the last and sovereign remedy.

Since everything has been prepared in this way, I can only imagine that the affair will soon be settled without difficulty. I

Appendix 2. - Archives of the Mission, Turin, original autograph letter.

[1]The deliberations concerning the shrine in Bétharram were mentioned in no. 2919.

[2]Jean du Haut Salies.

desire this with all my heart for the glory of Our Lord, the sanctification of that house and of those entering it, the general good of the surrounding dioceses, and my personal interest.

While awaiting news that the agreement has been concluded, I ask you, as a favor and out of compassion, to offer me to Our Lord and to believe that I am entirely yours in Him.

CRUCHETTE

Tarbes, August 5, 1660

3. - NICOLAS SEVIN TO RENÉ ALMÉRAS

Mercuès, October 10, 1660

Monsieur,

In losing Monsieur Vincent you have lost your good father and Founder, and I have lost one of the best friends I believe I ever had. I am convinced that he had a certain affection for me, so we are both greatly to be pitied. I have, however, this consolation: in the last letter he did me the honor of writing me five days before his death, he promised that he would never forget me before God. This makes me think that, in the place where he is now, he continues to practice his same acts of charity toward me and will not stop praying for me there until he has won from God the favor of making me a Bishop according to His own heart.

For my part, Monsieur, it would be impossible for me ever to forget him and, as long as I live, I will honor his memory as something very precious in my heart. I would really like to be able

---

Appendix 3. - Archives of the Diocese of Cahors, Alain de Solminihac Collection, file 22, no. 45, copy. This letter refers to no. 3289, a summary of the letter Saint Vincent wrote to Nicolas Sevin, Bishop of Cahors.

to express this to him in what he has left behind, and I would cherish any opportunity that should present itself for me to be of service to you and his Congregation. This is a fresh motive joined to the special devotion I have always had of being, all my life, Monsieur, your most humble and very affectionate servant.

NICOLAS,
Bishop of Cahors

4. - LIST OF ESTABLISHMENTS AND SUPERIORS (1625-1660) [1]

1. COLLÈGE DES BONS-ENFANTS, PARIS (1625)

Superiors: Vincent de Paul (1625); Jean Dehorgny (1632); Jean Pillé (1635); Jean Dehorgny (1638); Antoine Dufour (1643); Pierre du Chesne (1644); Gilbert Cuissot (1644); Lambert aux Couteaux (1646); Thomas Berthe (1649); François Lièbe (1650); Pierre du Chesne (1651); Guillaume Cornuel (1652); Jean Dehorgny (1654); Jean Watebled (1659).

On June 8, 1627, Archbishop Jean-François de Gondi put at the disposal of the nascent Congregation of the Mission the Collège des Bons-Enfants, whose principal and chaplain since 1625 had been M. Vincent de Paul. The Priests of the Mission were to fulfill the clauses of the foundation established by Jean Pluyette in 1476 (cf. vol. I, no. 39a). Letters patent of

---

Appendix 4. - This list of the houses of the Congregation of the Mission founded between 1625 and 1660, with the name of each Superior, is based on a manuscript in the Archives of the Mission, Paris, entitled: *Catalogue des maisons et des supérieurs.* Using information in the letters of Saint Vincent and other sources, Coste made additions and corrections to it. *Notices,* vol. I, pp. 510-35, provides a similar listing, along with a brief history of many of the houses. In the 1960-70 period, the noted Vincentian historian, Father Félix Contassot, delved into the history of the various establishments in Saint Vincent's time and attempted a reconciliation of the discrepancies among the various records. The editors have made use of these three sources to draw up the present list.

[1]During this period other establishments were opened but were often connected to one of those listed here and therefore not considered as independent houses. Still others did not perdure long enough to be listed. Finally, some were opened but did not take on an official status until a later date. For these reasons some discrepancies exist in the dates assigned.

the King, dated September 15, 1627, provided governmental approval of the transfer, with the added proviso that the Collège maintain its relationship with the University of Paris.[2] Besides being the residence for new members of the Congregation of the Mission until Saint Vincent took possession of Saint-Lazare, the Collège provided housing for students of the University of Paris, accommodated retreatants preparing for ordination, hosted the meetings of the members of the Tuesday Conferences, and in 1636 became a minor seminary for the Congregation of the Mission. In addition to the initial endowment of Madame de Gondi, scholarships funded by Cardinal Richelieu and payments by boarders and retreatants helped sustain this establishment.

2. SAINT-LAZARE (1632)

Superior: Vincent de Paul (1632-60).

Since the Priory of Saint-Lazare was no longer fulfilling the mission for which it had been entrusted to the Canons Regular of Saint Augustine in 1518, the Prior Adrien Le Bon resolved to turn it over to the Congregation of the Mission, if the Archbishop of Paris Jean-François de Gondi gave his approval (cf. vol. I, no. 91), which he did on January 8, 1632, and again on December 31 of the same year. Vol. XIII, nos. 77-80, 82-84, 112, 114, 119, and 124, documents the ecclesiastical and civil approval of this transfer. As the Motherhouse of the Little Company, it housed confreres in various stages of formation, Priests and Brothers of the Mission returning to Paris after mission tours, men preparing by retreats for ordination as diocesan priests, and others desirous of making retreats; from time to time it served as a house of correction.

3. TOUL (1635)

Superiors: Lambert aux Couteaux (1635); Antoine Colée (1637); François du Coudray (1638); Étienne Bourdet (1641); Jean Bécu (1642); Charles Aulent (1646); Augustin Lefebvre (1647);

[2]Cf. vol. XIII, nos. 62-65, for documents relative to the Bons-Enfants.

Gabriel Delespiney (1648); Louis Dupont (1652); Nicolas Demonchy (1653); Georges des Jardins (1656); Nicolas Demonchy (1657); Michel Caset (1659); Gerard Brin (1660).

In 1238 the Aldermen of Toul entrusted the care of a newly constructed hospital for orphans and the infirm to the Military Order of the Holy Spirit. In 1635, lack of personnel forced the Order to turn over their house to Charles-Chrétien de Gournay, Titular Bishop of Scythia and Administrator of the Toul diocese. At his request the Congregation of the Mission moved into the house. The King authorized this union by letters patent, which Parlement subsequently ratified. There the Community carried out its functions of missions, conferences to ecclesiastics, and retreats; until 1637, it also continued the work of the Order of the Holy Spirit at the hospital.

4. NOTRE-DAME-DE-LA-ROSE (1637)

Superiors: François du Coudray (1637); Benoît Bécu (1639); Gilbert Cuissot (1640); François Soufliers (1642); François du Coudray (1644); Guillaume Delattre (1646); Bernard Codoing (1648); Emerand Bajoue (1649); Gerard Brin (1652); Claude Dufour (1654); Jean Chrétien (1655).

By a contract between the Duchesse d'Aiguillon and Saint Vincent, signed on August 18, 1637, the Saint established the house for four priests in La Rose, a place of pilgrimage in the Duchy of Aiguillon. The Duchess gave to the house 22,000 livres. In 1640 Barthélemy d'Elbène, the Bishop of Agen, united to the Congregation of the Mission in perpetuity the chapel of Notre-Dame-de-la-Rose. The contract stipulated that the Missionaries would preach missions in the towns and villages of the Duchy, offer daily Mass for the Duchess and her relatives, conduct retreats for ordinands, and that two priests would serve the chapel of Notre-Dame-de-la-Rose. A subsequent contract with the Duchess, signed on July 4, 1642, stipulated that an additional three priests be stationed there so that the works of the Missionaries could be extended to her lands in Agen and Condom; she also gave another 13,500 livres to the house.

5. RICHELIEU (1638)

Superiors: Lambert aux Couteaux (1638); Denis Gautier (1645); Bernard Codoing (1649); Lambert aux Couteaux (1650); Jean-Baptiste Le Gros (1651); Pierre de Beaumont (1656).

Cardinal Richelieu established the Congregation of the Mission in the town of Richelieu (Indre-et-Loir) by a contract entered into with Saint Vincent on January 4, 1638. Four of the priests to be stationed there were to conduct retreats for ordinands, give retreats to priests in the Poitiers diocese, and preach missions there; within two years, three other priests were to staff a parish which the Cardinal planned to establish. He committed himself to having a house built for the Missionaries, which would also accommodate the ordinands and retreatants who were extended hospitality. The Missionaries were provided an income of 1455 livres from the revenues of the Records Office, plus the revenue from certain farms.

6. LUÇON (1638)

Superiors: Gilbert Cuissot (1638); Jacques Chiroye (1640); Jacques Lucas (1650); Jacques Chiroye (1654).

Cardinal Richelieu established a house in Luçon to support three priests dedicated to preaching missions four times a year in his Luçon diocese. At first the Missionaries were content with a rented house, until a gift of 24,000 livres from the Cardinal facilitated the purchase, on December 7, 1641, of a mansion called Pont-de-Vie. Over the years this house assumed the responsibility of offering for the intentions of the various donors to this foundation the Masses to be said in perpetuity on stipulated days, and sometimes at specific hours. One of these, called the *Bishop's Mass,* was said daily at 8 o'clock, as mandated and funded by Bishop Pierre Nivelle.

7. TROYES (1638)

Superiors: François du Coudray (1638); François Dufestel (1638); Jean Bourdet (1642); Charles Ozenne (1644); Nicolas Roze (1653); Gerard Brin (1657); François Dupuich (1658).

In March 1638 René de Breslay, Bishop of Troyes, with an initial sum of 1200 livres for rent and a one-time donation of 6000 livres, financed a house in Paris and later in Sancey, a suburb of Troyes, so that the Congregation of the Mission could preach missions in the Troyes diocese, be available to conduct retreats for Pastors sent to them by the Bishop, and conduct a ten-day retreat each year for the ordinands. In 1640 a house in Troyes was provided by the Commander de Sillery, and another priest was added to the number of confreres. During Saint Vincent's lifetime, other bequests provided for an increase in the number of confreres and their obligations. After the death of Saint Vincent, François Bouithillier, Bishop of Troyes, established in the house of the Missionaries a seminary for the Troyes diocese (1662).

8. ALET (1639-42)

Superior: Étienne Blatiron (1639).

On August 22, 1639, Nicolas Pavillon, of whom Saint Vincent had been spiritual director and mentor, was consecrated Bishop of Alet at Saint-Lazare. He went to his diocese accompanied by Étienne Blatiron. Saint Vincent wrote to Louis Lebreton in Rome on October 12, 1639 (cf. vol. I, no. 404), that he was going to send four priests to begin a foundation in Alet; missions were to be their apostolate. In October 1642 the Saint found it necessary to close this foundation. In a letter of October 8, 1642 (cf. vol. I, no. 622), he directed Étienne Blatiron and Jean Brunet to proceed to Rome; he had no one to replace them. In subsequent years vain attempts were made to establish the Community in the diocese until 1678 when a house was opened and lasted until the French Revolution.

9. ANNECY (1640)

Superiors: Bernard Codoing (1640); François Dufestel (1642); Jean Guérin (1642); Achille Le Vazeux (1653); Mark Cogley (1658); Charles Boussordec (1660).

By a contract dated June 3, 1639, Noël Brulart de Sillery, priest of the Order of Saint-Jean-de-Jérusalem and Commander of its Temple in Troyes, funded, with 40,000 livres to be taken from the taxes of Melun, two priests and a Brother to give missions in the Geneva diocese; an additional 5000 livres were to be used for the purchase of rosaries and pamphlets. The Missionaries were to work gratuitously for eight months each year in the parishes designated by the Bishop; beginning in 1641, they were to give missions every five years in Brie-Comte-Robert. In the beginning, they accepted lodging from Saint Jane Frances de Chantal because the Commander had not provided the house he had promised, but in January 1640 he gave them an additional 2000 livres with which to purchase a house. A further donation, on February 26, 1640, enabled Saint Vincent to add two priests and one Brother to the Annecy local community. The Congregation of the Mission eventually took on the work of the seminary in the diocese.

10. Crécy (1641)

Superiors: Pierre du Chesne (1641); Guillaume Delville (1644); Guillaume Gallais (1644); François Grimal (1645); Guillaume Delville (1646); Louis Serre (1648); Jean-Baptiste Gilles (1651); Jacques Le Soudier (1652); Dominique Lhuillier (1654);[3] Jacques Chiroye (1660).

King Louis XIII established the Priests of the Mission in Crécy-en-Brie (Seine-et-Marne). In 1641 he gave them the château and 4000 livres from the sale of the salt of Lagny-sur-Marne to support eight priests and four Brothers. The confreres of this house were to give missions in the Meaux diocese, provide alms for the needy, conduct free of charge one annual retreat for ordinands from the Meaux diocese, and offer two Masses a day: one for the King and Royal Family, the other for the seigneurs of Crécy. Bishop Dominique Séguier of Meaux approved this foundation on April 12, 1641, and Saint Vincent put his signature to the approbation.

11. Rome (1642)

Superiors: Louis Lebreton (1639); Bernard Codoing (1642); Jean Dehorgny (1644); René Alméras (1647); Jean Dehorgny (1651); Thomas Berthe (1653); Edme Jolly (1655).

---

[3]Dominique Lhuillier administered the house without having the title of Superior; a coadjutor Brother was his only companion.

Louis Lebreton first went to Rome in 1639; in 1642 a house was canonically established. At Saint Vincent's request, it was called "house of the Mission;" its chapel had the Most Holy Trinity as its title. Cardinal Richelieu died (1642) before he fulfilled his promise of a permanent house in Rome. In 1659, through the good offices of Cardinals di Bagno and Durazzo, the confreres moved into the permanent residence at Monte Citorio. The Priests of the Mission gave missions in the countryside, fulfilled the Pope's mandate to conduct retreats for the ordinands of the diocese, and provided spiritual direction for the Collège of Propaganda Fide. Much of the financial support of the house came from the Duchesse d'Aiguillon, who contributed 5000 livres from the revenues of the Rouen coach lines.

12. Marseilles (1643)

Superiors: François Dufestel (1644); Jean Chrétien (1645); Pierre du Chesne (1653); Firmin Get (1654); Gabriel Delespiney (1659); Firmin Get (1660).

A contract between the Duchesse d'Aiguillon and Saint Vincent, dated July 25, 1643 (cf. vol. XIII, no. 90), established four Missionaries in Marseilles and set up a fund of 14,000 livres to support their works. The contract stipulated that they were to oversee the chaplains and teachers for the galley convicts, give a mission every five years on each of the galleys of Marseilles and other ports of the kingdom "to console poor Christian captives" in Barbary, when appropriate, and "instruct them in their faith and in the love and fear of God," take care of the hospital for the poor convicts of the city, and offer two Masses daily, one for the repose of the soul of Cardinal Richelieu, the other for the Duchess herself. In a decree dated January 16, 1644, the Queen Regent, Anne of Austria, granted the Superior General the lifetime title of Royal Chaplain to the Galleys and conferred on him the faculty of delegating his authority and rights (cf. vol. XIII, no. 91).

13. Cahors (1643)

Superiors: François Dufestel (1643); Guillaume Delattre (1644); Charles Testacy (1646); Gilbert Cuissot (1647).

Bishop Alain de Solminihac brought three priests and two Brothers to Cahors to give missions, instruct the clerics of the diocese, maintain free of charge three seminarians chosen by the Bishop, and conduct ordination retreats. To support the works, he placed at their disposal the income from the two priories of Vaurette and Balaguier. The act of establishment was signed in Paris on January 4, 1643, by Saint Vincent and Bishop Solminihac, confirmed by letters patent the same month, and registered by the Parlement of Toulouse. A fourth priest was to be given, at which time the Bishop would immediately add 800 livres income, and the number of clerics admitted free to the seminary would be increased from three to six.

14. SEDAN (1643)

Superiors: Guillaume Gallais (1643); François Grimal (1644); Charles Bayart (1646); Mark Cogley (1649); Jean Martin (1654); Mark Cogley (1655); Pierre Cabel (1657).

On September 8, 1643, René-Louis de Fiquelmont, Abbot of Mouzon and collator [the person who admitted to or instituted a cleric in a benefice] for the parish in Sedan, signed over the parish to the Congregation of the Mission. He stipulated that: 1) the Abbots of Mouzon would remain the primal Pastors of Sedan and would retain the right of chanting High Mass in the church twice a year; 2) should the Priests of the Mission withdraw, the Abbots of Mouzon would resume their rights as collators (cf. vol. II, no. 681). The contract of establishment provided for seven priests and two Brothers. Four priests were to give missions in the environs of Sedan and Balan and later in other places designated by Léonor d'Estampes de Valençay, Archbishop of Reims; the other three priests were entrusted with the care of the parish. Louis XIII bequeathed 24,000 livres for the missions in Sedan. Another 40,000 would help to provide for the needs of the poor and missions throughout the Archdiocese (cf. vol. II, no. 660). The Archbishop sanctioned this union on October 23, 1643, and on September 24, 1644, signed a more formal agreement with the Congregation of the Mission (cf. vol. II, no. 723).

15. MONTMIRAIL (1644)

Superiors: Guillaume Delville (1644); François Grimal (1646); Guillaume Cornuel (1649); Guillaume Delville (1650); Charles Bayart (1651); René Champion (1652); François Grimal (1654); Jacques Le Soudier (1655); Nicolas Guillot (1656); Guillaume Cornuel (1658); Jean Monvoisin (1659); François d'Hauteville (1660).

On September 29, 1643, Pierre de Gondi, Duc de Retz and Baron de Montmirail, asked François Malier, Bishop of Troyes, to unite La Chaussée Priory to the Congregation of the Mission. The Bishop issued a decree of union on June 20, 1644. The two priests and a Brother sent there were to be engaged in the work of the missions in that area or wherever the Bishop would designate. The King signed the necessary letters patent in December 1645, and the Parlement registered them on February 23, 1646. Because of the devastation of the final stages of the Thirty Years' War, the house was moved to Fontaine-Essart, a farm which was bequeathed, along with that of Vieux-Moulins, to the Congregation of the Mission by Louis Toutblanc, Secretary of the Duc de Retz.

16. SAINTES (1644)

Superiors: Louis Thibault (1644); Claude Dufour (1646); Louis Rivet (1648); Pierre Watebled (1650); Philippe Vageot (1651); Louis Rivet (1656).

On November 22, 1644, Saint Vincent accepted the Saintes Seminary from Bishop Jacques-Raoul de la Guibourgère on condition that three priests and two Brothers were to be stationed there and two clerics educated free of charge. The diocesan clergy would contribute 1200 livres for their support. Moreover, revenue was to be derived from Saint-Preuil parish, which was united to the seminary. When the number of priests increased, at least two were committed to preaching missions.

17. Le Mans (1645)

Superiors: Guillaume Gallais (1645); Antoine Lucas (1647); Jean Gicquel (1651); Donat Cruoly (1654); Denis Laudin (1657).

On January 26, 1645, Martin Lucas, Commendatory Abbot of Saint-Hilaire, entered into a contract with Saint Vincent by which the Congregation of the Mission would assume the obligation of M. Lucas, principal Administrator of the Hôtel-Dieu in Le Mans and Provost of the collegial church of Notre-Dame de Coëffort. M. Lucas and his confreres were to receive the revenues of the benefice during his lifetime: some 24,000 livres; the Congregation of the Mission agreed to station sufficient men there to celebrate the Divine Office, offer the Masses stipulated by the original foundation, and act as chaplains at the Hôtel-Dieu. Guillaume Gallais took possession of the Priory on June 30, 1645. Emmeric-Marc de la Ferté, Bishop of Le Mans, sanctioned this contract on November 18, 1645, and added the obligation that the Congregation of the Mission accept seminarians into its house and preach missions in the diocese. The King signed the letters patent in August 1645, which the Parlement registered on January 15, 1650.

18. Saint-Méen (1645)

Superiors: Jean Bourdet (1645); Bernard Codoing (1646); Louis Thibault (1648); Louis Serre (1655).

On July 14, 1645, Achille de Harlay de Sancey, Bishop of Saint-Malo, established a seminary in Saint-Méen Abbey and entrusted its perpetual direction to the Congregation of the Mission. Two of the five priests to be stationed there were assigned to preach missions in the diocese. The three priests designated for the seminary were to educate twelve clerics for two or three years free of charge; they were also to see to the care of the monks remaining in the abbey. The Bishop provided an annuity of 500 livres to support the house. The troublesome early years were bedeviled by lawsuits brought by the Benedictines of Saint-Maur (cf. vol. III, no. 832, n. 8). In 1658, Pope Alexander VII issued a Bull by which the Abbey was canonically united to the seminary; letters patent, issued in July 1661, gave civil sanction to this union.

19. SAINT-CHARLES SEMINARY (1645)

Superiors: Bernard Codoing (1645); N. (1646); François Hurtel [Heurtel] (1650);[4] Lambert aux Couteaux (1650); Jean-Baptiste Le Gros (1651); René Alméras (1651); Thomas Goblet (1653); Nicolas Talec (1654).

In 1645 Saint Vincent felt it necessary to withdraw from the Collège des Bons-Enfants the young boys who were studying the humanities there; he transferred them to a building situated at the end of the enclosure of Saint-Lazare. This became Saint-Charles Seminary, also known as the Petit Saint-Lazare. Not all the students there necessarily aspired to Holy Orders.

20. GENOA (1645)

Superiors: Étienne Blatiron (1645); Jacques Pesnelle (1657).

The Genoa house was established through the munificence of Stefano Cardinal Durazzo, Archbishop of Genoa, a pious Prelate who was always admirably gracious and devoted to Saint Vincent and his priests. This house devoted itself primarily to missions, although an Internal Seminary was opened there in 1651, and other works, such as the Tuesday Conferences and retreats for ordinands, were provided.

---

[4]The biographical data on Bernard Codoing states that François Hurtel [Heurtel], who died in 1650, followed him at Saint-Charles. Coste apparently had some information to verify that Hurtel was Superior for a short time before his death.

21. TUNIS (1645) and ALGIERS (1646)

Superiors: Tunis: Julien Guérin (1645); Jean Le Vacher (1648). **Algiers:** Boniface Nouelly (1646); Jacques Le Sage (1648); Jean Dieppe (1649); Philippe Le Vacher (1650).

In 1645 the Duchesse d'Aiguillon gave the Congregation of the Mission 40,500 francs, income from various coach lines which she controlled, to enable Saint Vincent to purchase the consulates in Tunis and Algiers. The King immediately sanctioned the transaction. This measure had the great advantage of avoiding all fear of conflict or even disagreement between the representatives of France and the Missionaries and gave a prestige to the latter that could only be advantageous to religion. Consul and Superior were distinct offices filled by different men. The Consuls looked to the temporal welfare of the Europeans dealing with the Turks; the Missionaries cared for their spiritual needs as well as those of the Christian captives in Tunis, Algiers, and other places in Barbary (North Africa). They instructed them and endeavored to preserve them in the faith. In 1655 Saint Vincent received another 30,000 francs, the income from this investment to be used to defray expenses in Tunis and Algiers and to assist in the ransom of captives.

22. IRELAND and SCOTLAND (1646)

Superior: Pierre du Chesne (1646).[5]

On February 25, 1645, Antonio Cardinal Barberini, Prefect of Propaganda Fide, requested Saint Vincent "to send some workers to Ireland to teach the clergy there the correct use of sacred ceremonies and rites" (cf. vol. II, no. 740). In October 1646 the Saint sent eight confreres to Ireland, who preached in the dioceses of Limerick and Cashel (1646-52) despite the English persecutions. In the same period Missionaries were sent to Scotland and the Hebrides. During the lifetime of Saint Vincent, especially after 1652, a few Missionaries ministered in this mission, but they worked alone, isolated from one another.

---

[5]Du Chesne returned to France in 1648. We do not know whether the title of Superior was passed to someone else.

23. Madagascar (1648)

Superiors: Charles Nacquart (1648); Jean-François Mousnier (1650); Toussaint Bourdaise (1655).

In 1648, on the authority of Propaganda Fide, Nicolò di Bagno, Nuncio in France, requested Saint Vincent to send men to Saint-Laurent Island, known as Madagascar. Charles Nacquart and Nicolas Gondrée were the first of many Missionaries who were sent there during the Saint's lifetime. The confreres had to endure the dangers of a long sea voyage; many of those who survived succumbed to fatal climatic conditions and the treachery of the inhabitants. Despite this, and the long time it took to receive news from this mission, Saint Vincent persevered in sending Missionaries there, even though some of the confreres in France became discouraged over the situation.

24. Tréguier (1648)

Superiors: Jacques Tholard (1648); Denis Pennier (1653); Louis Dupont (1654).

Michel Thépault de Rumelin, Canon of the Cathedral Church and Penitentiary of the Tréguier diocese, established a seminary in that diocese and entrusted its perpetual direction to the Congregation of the Mission. He provided a sum of 7700 livres, along with revenues from various houses and from a chapel in which he served. A contract was eventually signed by Saint Vincent on July 25, 1654. Bishop Balthazar Grangier de Liverdi gave his approval at the same time and contributed an annual pension of 1000 livres, as long as three priests and a Brother were stationed there and missions were given in his diocese.

25. Agen (1650)

Superiors: Guillaume Delattre (1648); François Grimal (1650); Edme Menestrier (1651).

As early as 1643, Saint Vincent mentions a proposal for a seminary in Agen (cf. vol. II, no. 678), and in 1644 the Agen diocese had what could be called a minor seminary (*ibid.,* no. 709). In October 1648 the Saint wrote of "two [seminaries] we are going to open in Agen." What appears to have been a major seminary opened a few days later, but it was not founded canonically until 1650 (cf. vol. III, no. 1068). On March 1, 1650, Bishop Barthélemy d'Elbène officially entrusted the perpetual direction of the diocesan seminary of Agen to the Congregation of the Mission, and Saint Vincent accepted the establishment on March 15. The revenue from the seminary and 900 livres from the clergy were to support three priests and a Brother.

26. Périgueux (1650-51)

Superior: Charles Bayart (1650).

The establishment in Périgueux was short-lived. On September 4, 1649, Saint Vincent wrote to M. des Vergnes, the Officialis of Cahors, who at the time was staying with Philibert de Brandon, Bishop of Périgueux, stating that, if the Bishop wished to open a seminary, he would send him some of his best men, but he needed at least two months to make the necessary preparations (cf. vol. III, no. 1133). Although the Bishop needed only two priests for the seminary, the Saint wanted to send two others to preach missions also. Two priests took up their seminary duties in December 1650. By April 1, 1651, the Saint had recalled them, informing the Bishop that he was doing so because of opposition from priests in Périgueux and some of the Bishop's councillors (cf. vol. IV, no. 1135).

27. Warsaw (1651)

Superiors: Lambert aux Couteaux (1651); Charles Ozenne (1653); Guillaume Desdames (1658).

Louise-Marie de Gonzague, Queen of Poland, requested the Priests of the Mission, the Daughters of Charity and the Visitation nuns. When the Missionaries arrived in November 1651, she gave them housing and saw that they lacked nothing. The confreres first opened a seminary in Vilnius (Lithuania). The Queen purchased a house for them in Warsaw and assigned a substantial revenue for its maintenance. Plague, civil unrest, and invasions from neighboring countries affected their ministries and temporarily drove some of them back to France.

28. Notre-Dame-de-Lorm and Montauban (1652)

Superiors: Emerand Bajoue (1652); François Liébe (1654); Edmund Barry (1657).

Pierre de Bertier, Coadjutor Bishop of Montauban, entrusted the sanctuary of Notre-Dame-de-Lorm to the Congregation of the Mission by an act of union signed on September 5, 1652. Subsequently, the Congregation of the Mission assumed direction of the diocesan seminary in Montech, later transferred to Notre-Dame-de-Lorm (1656) and then to Montauban (1657). The Bishop supported it with 2000 livres. In addition to the seminary, the Bishop authorized the preaching of missions anywhere in the diocese.

29. Agde (1654)

Superiors: Pierre du Chesne (1654); Jean-Jacques Mugnier (1654); Antoine Durand (1656).

François Fouquet, Bishop of Agde, brought the Congregation of the Mission to Agde for a new foundation. Saint Vincent had high expectations for this house. Pierre du Chesne proposed to open two seminaries: one for the diocese and one for the Congregation. The Bishop prepared a contract for this establishment, but Saint Vincent refused to sign it because he considered it too onerous. No contract was ever ratified; the house closed in 1671.

30. Turin (1655)

Superior: Jean Martin (1655).

In 1654 Filippo di Simiane, Marchese di Pianezza, Prime Minister of Christine de France, Regent for Savoy (the *Madame Royale*), proposed to bring the Congregation of the Mission to Turin. The following year, Saint Vincent sent four priests to preach missions and to work with the members of the Tuesday Conferences. The confreres lived in a succession of houses because suitable lodging was difficult to find. The Marchese di Pianezza finally retired to the confreres' house and died there in 1677. Jean Martin has left us many descriptive letters on the work of the missions in Piedmont.

31. Meaux (1658)

Superior: Gerard Brin (1658).

In 1657 Gerard Brin seems to have investigated the feasibility of the Congregation of the Mission accepting the seminary which Dominique Séguier, Bishop of Meaux, wanted to establish in his diocese. The Community became involved in this project in 1658, but the establishment lasted only three years. The Superior of the seminary was also the principal of a collège and administrator of a hospital.

32. Montpellier (1659)

Superior: Firmin Get (1659).

François Bosquet, Bishop of Montpellier, requested that Saint Vincent establish a seminary in his diocese; the Saint readily agreed because the foundations of this work were so important, especially since heresy was rooted in the region. Nevertheless, Saint Vincent became disenchanted with the Bishop's treatment of the confreres. The Bishop finally decided to close this seminary and to send his candidates to seminaries in neighboring dioceses. The Congregation of the Mission withdrew in 1660.

33. Narbonne (1659)

Superior: Georges des Jardins (1659).

François Fouquet, the newly installed Archbishop of Narbonne (1659), urged Saint Vincent to send him some workers. The Saint received the request with respect and submission and designated three priests for a seminary and a parish attached to it. The Archbishop asked for two more priests and a Brother, but Saint Vincent had to inform him that insufficient personnel made that impossible at the time. After a second foundation in 1671, this house perdured until the time of the French Revolution (1791).

INDEX

This index proposes to facilitate reference to the biographical data used in this volume and to the explanation of terms and places which recur frequently in the text and have been explained when first used. Names of persons are in **bold** print, alternate spellings are given in brackets, those of terms or places in *italics*. The accompanying numbers indicate the letters to which the reader should refer for the desired information.

G

H

I

J

L

S

T

V

W